Lecture Notes in Artificial Intelligence 11740

Subseries of Lecture Notes in Computer Science

More information about this series at http://www.springer.com/series/1244

Haibin Yu · Jinguo Liu ·
Lianqing Liu · Zhaojie Ju ·
Yuwang Liu · Dalin Zhou (Eds.)

Intelligent Robotics and Applications

12th International Conference, ICIRA 2019
Shenyang, China, August 8–11, 2019
Proceedings, Part I

 Springer

Editors
Haibin Yu
Shenyang Institute of Automation
Shenyang, China

Jinguo Liu
Shenyang Institute of Automation
Shenyang, China

Lianqing Liu
Shenyang Institute of Automation
Shenyang, China

Zhaojie Ju
University of Portsmouth
Portsmouth, UK

Yuwang Liu
Shenyang Institute of Automation
Shenyang, China

Dalin Zhou
University of Portsmouth
Portsmouth, UK

ISSN 0302-9743   ISSN 1611-3349   (electronic)
Lecture Notes in Artificial Intelligence
ISBN 978-3-030-27525-9   ISBN 978-3-030-27526-6   (eBook)
https://doi.org/10.1007/978-3-030-27526-6

LNCS Sublibrary: SL7 – Artificial Intelligence

This Springer imprint is published by the registered company Springer Nature Switzerland AG
The registered company address is: Gewerbestrasse 11, 6330 Cham, Switzerland

Preface

On behalf of the Organizing Committee, we welcome you to the proceedings of the 12th International Conference on Intelligent Robotics and Applications (ICIRA 2019), organized by Shenyang Institute of Automation, Chinese Academy of Sciences, co-organized by Huazhong University of Science and Technology, Shanghai Jiao Tong University, and the University of Portsmouth, technically co-sponsored by the National Natural Science Foundation of China and Springer, and financially sponsored by Shenyang Association for Science and Technology. ICIRA 2019 with the theme of "Robot Era" offered a unique and constructive platform for scientists and engineers throughout the world to present and share their recent research and innovative ideas in the areas of robotics, automation, mechatronics, and applications.

ICIRA 2019 was most successful this year in attracting more than 500 submissions regarding the state-of-the-art development in robotics, automation, and mechatronics. The Program Committee undertook a rigorous review process for selecting the most deserving research for publication. Despite the high quality of most of the submissions, a total of 378 papers were selected for publication in six volumes of Springer's *Lecture Notes in Artificial Intelligence* a subseries of *Lecture Notes in Computer Science*. We sincerely hope that the published papers of ICIRA 2019 will prove to be technically beneficial and constructive to both the academic and industrial community in robotics, automation, and mechatronics. We would like to express our sincere appreciation to all the authors, participants, and the distinguished plenary and keynote speakers.

The success of the conference is also attributed to the Program Committee members and invited peer reviewers for their thorough review of all the submissions, as well as to the Organizing Committee and volunteers for their diligent work. Special thanks are extended to Alfred Hofmann, Anna Kramer, and Volha Shaparava from Springer for their consistent support.

August 2019

Haibin Yu
Jinguo Liu
Lianqing Liu
Zhaojie Ju
Yuwang Liu
Dalin Zhou

Organization

Honorary Chairs

Youlun Xiong	Huazhong University of Science and Technology, China
Nanning Zheng	Xi'an Jiaotong University, China

General Chair

Haibin Yu	Shenyang Institute of Automation, Chinese Academy of Sciences, China

General Co-chairs

Kok-Meng Lee	Georgia Institute of Technology, USA
Zhouping Yin	Huazhong University of Science and Technology, China
Xiangyang Zhu	Shanghai Jiao Tong University, China

Program Chair

Jinguo Liu	Shenyang Institute of Automation, Chinese Academy of Sciences, China

Program Co-chairs

Zhaojie Ju	The University of Portsmouth, UK
Lianqing Liu	Shenyang Institute of Automation, Chinese Academy of Sciences, China
Bram Vanderborght	Vrije Universiteit Brussel, Belgium

Advisory Committee

Jorge Angeles	McGill University, Canada
Tamio Arai	University of Tokyo, Japan
Hegao Cai	Harbin Institute of Technology, China
Tianyou Chai	Northeastern University, China
Jie Chen	Tongji University, China
Jiansheng Dai	King's College London, UK
Zongquan Deng	Harbin Institute of Technology, China
Han Ding	Huazhong University of Science and Technology, China

Xilun Ding	Beihang University, China
Baoyan Duan	Xidian University, China
Xisheng Feng	Shenyang Institute of Automation, Chinese Academy of Sciences, China
Toshio Fukuda	Nagoya University, Japan
Jianda Han	Shenyang Institute of Automation, Chinese Academy of Sciences, China
Qiang Huang	Beijing Institute of Technology, China
Oussama Khatib	Stanford University, USA
Yinan Lai	National Natural Science Foundation of China, China
Jangmyung Lee	Pusan National University, South Korea
Zhongqin Lin	Shanghai Jiao Tong University, China
Hong Liu	Harbin Institute of Technology, China
Honghai Liu	The University of Portsmouth, UK
Shugen Ma	Ritsumeikan University, Japan
Daokui Qu	SIASUN, China
Min Tan	Institute of Automation, Chinese Academy of Sciences, China
Kevin Warwick	Coventry University, UK
Guobiao Wang	National Natural Science Foundation of China, China
Tianmiao Wang	Beihang University, China
Tianran Wang	Shenyang Institute of Automation, Chinese Academy of Sciences, China
Yuechao Wang	Shenyang Institute of Automation, Chinese Academy of Sciences, China
Bogdan M. Wilamowski	Auburn University, USA
Ming Xie	Nanyang Technological University, Singapore
Yangsheng Xu	The Chinese University of Hong Kong, SAR China
Huayong Yang	Zhejiang University, China
Jie Zhao	Harbin Institute of Technology, China
Nanning Zheng	Xi'an Jiaotong University, China
Weijia Zhou	Shenyang Institute of Automation, Chinese Academy of Sciences, China
Xiangyang Zhu	Shanghai Jiao Tong University, China

Publicity Chairs

Shuo Li	Shenyang Institute of Automation, Chinese Academy of Sciences, China
Minghui Wang	Shenyang Institute of Automation, Chinese Academy of Sciences, China
Chuan Zhou	Shenyang Institute of Automation, Chinese Academy of Sciences, China

Publication Chairs

Yuwang Liu   Shenyang Institute of Automation, Chinese Academy
                             of Sciences, China
Dalin Zhou   The University of Portsmouth, UK

Award Chairs

Kaspar Althoefer   Queen Mary University of London, UK
Naoyuki Kubota   Tokyo Metropolitan University, Japan
Xingang Zhao   Shenyang Institute of Automation, Chinese Academy
                             of Sciences, China

Special Session Chairs

Guimin Chen   Xi'an Jiaotong University, China
Hak Keung Lam   King's College London, UK

Organized Session Co-chairs

Guangbo Hao   University College Cork, Ireland
Yongan Huang   Huazhong University of Science and Technology,
                             China
Qiang Li   Bielefeld University, Germany
Yuichiro Toda   Okayama University, Japan
Fei Zhao   Xi'an Jiaotong University, China

International Organizing Committee Chairs

Zhiyong Chen   The University of Newcastle, Australia
Yutaka Hata   University of Hyogo, Japan
Sabina Jesehke   RWTH Aachen University, Germany
Xuesong Mei   Xi'an Jiaotong University, China
Robert Riener   ETH Zurich, Switzerland
Chunyi Su   Concordia University, Canada
Shengquan Xie   The University of Auckland, New Zealand
Chenguang Yang   UWE Bristol, UK
Tom Ziemke   University of Skövde, Sweden
Yahya Zweiri   Kingston University, UK

Local Arrangements Chairs

Hualiang Zhang   Shenyang Institute of Automation, Chinese Academy
                             of Sciences, China
Xin Zhang   Shenyang Institute of Automation, Chinese Academy
                             of Sciences, China

Contents – Part I

Compliant Mechanisms

Human Centered Robotics

Development of High-Performance Joint Drive for Robots

Modular Robots and Other Mechatronic Systems

**Compliant Manipulation Learning and Control
for Lightweight Robot**

Collective and Social Robots

Promoting Constructive Interaction and Moral Behaviors Using Adaptive Empathetic Learning

Jize Chen[1], Yanning Zuo[2], Dali Zhang[1], Zhenshen Qu[1], and Changhong Wang[1(✉)]

[1] Space Science and Inertial Technology Research Center,
Harbin Institute of Technology, Harbin 150001, People's Republic of China
cwang@hit.edu.cn
[2] Department of Biological Chemistry and Department of Neurobiology,
University of California, Los Angeles, CA 90095, USA

Abstract. Moral system assists people with constructive interaction by maximizing the inner stimulus transfered from outer feelings. For this reason, building an intrinsic sense of morality is one potential way of regulating agents' behaviors. Incorporating ideas found in social neuroscience, we hardwired a theoretical model of empathy in rational reinforcement learning-based agents to enable affective state sharing between agents. Our learning algorithm accounts for the impact of social comparison and companion impression, which play an important role on the update of empathy and make it possible for agents to change between cooperation and competition adaptively. Empathetic learners' behavioral dynamics were tested and analyzed in multiple game settings. In iterated prisoner dilemma, empathetic agents showed increased cooperation in most cases except exhibiting self-protection awareness vigilantly when their partners were in the antagonistic state. Empathetic agents also showed a strong sense of fairness in the ultimatum game which resulted in an evenhanded allocation scheme on resources.

Keywords: Empathy · Constructive interaction ·
Multi-agent system · Reinforcement learning

1 Introduction

In recent years, the development of artificial intelligence (AI) has enabled agents to master different skills. Yet while this field is rapidly blooming, wide concerns arise about machine ethics [5,9]. In order to forbid unethical doing and allow autonomous agents to self-regulate their own behaviors in multi-agent interaction or human-agent interaction, building an intrinsic sense of morality is one potential way. From evolutionary aspect, morality can be defined as "a

---

Y. Zuo—This author's contribution is the same as Jize Chen's.

© Springer Nature Switzerland AG 2019
H. Yu et al. (Eds.): ICIRA 2019, LNAI 11740, pp. 3–14, 2019.
https://doi.org/10.1007/978-3-030-27526-6_1

suite of interrelated other-regarding behaviors that cultivate and regulate complex interactions within social groups", such as wolves, chimpanzees, elephants, and humans [2]. Large differences exist between human morality and the analog of other species, while there are some shared components including reciprocity, cooperation, altruism, a sense of fairness and justice [2]. Similarly, AIs may develop their own ethics which, with a large chance, differ from human-being's and hard to predict. That's not what the academia as well as the public anticipates, and thus finding a mechanism to regulate AI moral behaviors is imperative.

There are two ways of regulating moral behaviors in agents: extrinsically and intrinsically. Rules and laws can act as extrinsic drives [9]. Extrinsic regulation can also be achieved by establishing a reputation system, where other agents in the environment can rate each other based on performance [15]. The rate is visible to each agent and acts as a negative feedback from the environment. In contrary, intrinsic regulation is usually achieved by hard-wiring certain strategies, or modeling psychological internal properties such as emotions, which is an internal drive, feedback and self-discipline. While external factors such as law and reputation contribute tremendously in regulating moral behaviors in human society, we focus on creating intrinsic sense of morality in AI by modeling internal mechanism. In this case, AI behaviors may become more "human-like" and thus closer to general intelligence. Previous studies have focused on modeling emotions or affective functions such as guilt and forgiveness, or by modeling social fairness to achieve prosocial behaviors [11,14,16,21]. While these studies have successfully enhanced cooperation in certain games, there are no result of eliciting other facets of morality such as sympathy, altruism and a sense of fairness. These moral behaviors also act profoundly in human society.

According to neuropsychology, empathy may act as a general and fundamental internal property to guarantee intrinsic regulation of moral behaviors in agents in different situations. Affective functions such as guilt relies on this evolutionary basic process. Empathy is a spontaneous mind state sharing process between individuals, an evolutionary ancient mechanism underlying altruism and plays an important role in moral learning [6,7,10]. According to the Russian-doll model of empathy, empathetic expressions has evolved into three levels, including emotional contagion, sympathetic concern, targeted helping and perspective taking. Emotion contagion is the most basic manifestation of empathy, producing similar affective state between individuals and causing shared happiness or distress in other individuals. Sympathetic concern, or empathetic concern, is concern about other's misfortune and often provokes consolation and/or altruistic helping. The empathetic manifestations of the highest level are perspective taking and targeted helping, which is the ability of taking other's goals and situations, and giving correspondent help [7,19].

Very few papers exploited empathy to promote collaboration in game settings. Ventura's work showed that empathy could promote cooperation in iterated prisoner dilemma using a simple utility and empathy implementation [18]. However, this model took empathy as a whole, but only elicited basic level of empathy-emotion contagion. Higher level of empathy such as sympathetic concern, perspective taking and moral behaviors other than cooperation were not discussed. There are also several papers concerning empathy, theory of mind (which refers to the ability to interpret other's mind), or emotion contagion, but these models were used for value learning, state sharing or proofing psychological theory, but not being tested in a game setting [3,12,17].

In our study, we follow a basic assumption that empathetic learners are rational enough to maximize its long-term discount utility and empathy plays an essential role in the forming of utility evaluation function. We introduced two major factors which had effect on the degree of empathy – companion impression and social comparison. Companion impression can identify the characteristics of companions' behaviors and social comparison may cause the psychology of winning and losing relatively. A good companion impression can induce empathy while comparison with large profit will be suppression of empathy. Based on this, Adaptive Empathetic Learner (AEL), a learning algorithm using extended reinforcement learning structure was designed. Finally, we test the algorithms in several classic environments. Empathetic learner showed increased cooperation in the iterated prisoners' dilemma and vigilantly protected the safe payoff if the partner was in antagonistic state. Moral behaviors, especially absolute fairness was also detected when agents were transferred into the ultimatum game.

2   Learning with Adaptive Empathy

In this section, we will present the mechanism of empathetic learning. First, we'll give the method of building value model with empathy and the original intention of this design. Next, we'll show how agents use this model to learn in multi-agent environment.

2.1   Building Value Model

According to social psychology, the utility evaluation of a rational agent on its own behavior is mainly affected by two factors. One is the mentality of comparing the difference between individual payoff, mainly referring to the positive or negative emotion generated by the wealth gap. The other is impression of one's companion, by which agents can identify the characteristics of companions' behaviors.

In this respect, we assume that the empathetic agent's utility evaluation consists of social comparison and companion impression. In order to introduce these two factors more clearly, we defined several concepts of payoff.

Real Payoff: The average payoff of an agent under specific state and action. For agent i, with memory window m, the average static payoff is defined by

$$\bar{r}_i(t,m) = \sum_{k=1}^{m} \frac{r_i(s_i(t), a_i(t), k)}{m} \tag{1}$$

Referential Opponent Payoff: The average payoff of opponents under observer's specific state and action. For agent i in a group of n, with memory window m, the opponent static payoff is defined by

$$\bar{\bar{r}}_i(t, m) = \sum_{k=1}^{m} \sum_{\substack{j=1 \\ j \neq i}}^{n} \frac{r_j(s_i(t), a_i(t), k)}{m(n-1)} \tag{2}$$

Referential Safe Payoff: The average payoff of an agent under specific state and action if other agents act stochastically with the actions which are observed and recorded by the observer in the process of interaction. For agent i, if observed others' actions in memory have p kinds of joint form, the stochastic static payoff can be defined by

$$\hat{r}_i(t) = \sum_{k=1}^{p} \frac{r_i(s_i(t), a_i(t), k)}{p} \tag{3}$$

We can see that if comparing real payoff with the referential opponent payoff, agents can estimate the payoff gap between its partner and itself. On the other hand, by comparing real payoff and referential safe payoff, agents can perceive degree of environmental friendliness. In more detail, we'll give the definitions of these two factors below.

Social Comparison Factor: Gap of payoff between the observer and other agents. For agent i, with memory window m, the social comparison is defined by

$$C_i(t, m) = \bar{r}_i(t, m) - \bar{\bar{r}}_i(t, m) \tag{4}$$

Companion Impression Factor: Goodwill measured by the average static payoff and stochastic static payoff. For agent i, with memory window m, the companion impression is defined by

$$I_i(t, m) = \bar{r}_i(t, m) - \hat{r}_i(t) \tag{5}$$

From observer's prospective, equality of (1) and (3) infers the opponents are unintentional and acts stochastically. Similarly, if the real payoff is bigger, we believe that the opponents act in good faith. Otherwise, opponents are deemed to be malevolent.

Based on the social comparison and companion impression, we can build a model describing the relationship between empathy and empathetic utility.

Empathetic Utility: Part of utility aroused by empathy. For agent i, with memory window m, the empathetic utility is defined by

$$E_i(t, m) = (1 - \lambda_i(t)) \cdot \bar{r}_i(t, m) + \lambda_i(t) \cdot \bar{\bar{r}}_i(t, m) \tag{6}$$

Note that the empathetic parameter λ, standing for the degree of empathy, changing from 0 to 1, which imply total selfishness and total altruism respectively. The update rule of empathetic parameter λ_i follows

$$\Delta\lambda_i(t) = \begin{cases} +\delta_p, & I_i(t,10) > 0 \ and \ C_i(t,10) > 0 \\ -\delta_n, & I_i(t,10) < 0 \ or \ C_i(t,10) < 0 \\ 0, & else \end{cases} \tag{7}$$

where δ_p stands for the update step in positive mode, while δ_n is for negative mode. Generally, δ_p is bigger than δ_n, with the implication that empathetic agent is always well-intentioned. Agent's empathy increases only if its opponents show goodwill and its own profits is above the safe value. Although this condition seems stricter than the one to decrease, bigger δ_p make agents more sensitive to increase empathy.

Finally, the integrated utility could be defined as below.

Integrated Utility: The utility considering both empathy and discrepancy. For agent i, the integrated utility is defined by

$$U_i(t) = \frac{\exp(E_i(t,1))}{\exp(|C_i(t,1)|)} \tag{8}$$

2.2 Extended Structure of Reinforcement Learning

In the conventional reinforcement learning structure, the value orientation is reflected in the maximization of expected return (basic value), and the formation of the complete values require complex guide in the physical environment. Traditional return in reinforcement learning is mapping from state and action to material reward based on the game rule. In this setting, driven by the basic value we mentioned, agents will make a decision that most benefit to their own long-term material reward and hardly regard others. What we expect is to endow the feedback of environment more psychological guidance.

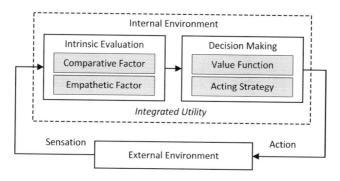

Fig. 1. Schematic representation of dynamic interaction between external environment and internal environment based on [13].

In this work, we won't change this conventional structure a lot except introducing the value model as a kind of weak guidance for agents from external environment. We divide the feedback into two stages, first of which is the state transition based on the game rule (or physical law) while the next is mapping the current state to the psychological reward according to the value model (shown in Fig. 1). The psychological reward, output of the value model, stands for the guide information we want agents to learn. Then the definition of integrated utility is corresponding with the intrinsic evaluation depicted in Fig. 1. Agents receive the sensation of external environment and output the intrinsic stimulus, here called integrated utility based on the psychology of comparison and empathy.

Considering training agents with adaptive empathy in the extended RL structure, we modified the simple reward using integrated utility.

$$Q_i\left(s_i\left(t\right),a_i\left(t\right)\right) \leftarrow (1-\alpha)\,Q_i\left(s_i\left(t\right),a_i\left(t\right)\right) \\ + \alpha\big[U_i\left(t\right)+\gamma\max_a Q_i\left(s_i\left(t+1\right),a\right)\big] \tag{9}$$

where $s \in S$ and $a \in A$ denote the state and action of an agent, $s' \in S$ denotes the state resulting from action a in state s, $r' : S \times A \times S \to \mathbb{R}$ denotes the reward functions, γ denotes the discount-rate parameter of payoff and α denotes a constant learning rate. Then we used the softmax policy to choose a from s, which is following Boltzmann distribution and defined as

$$\pi_i\left(s,a\right) = \begin{cases} 1/\left|A_i\left(s\right)\right|, & \zeta_i \leq \epsilon_i \\ \dfrac{\exp\left(\frac{Q_i(s,a)}{\theta}\right)}{\sum_{a' \in A_i(s)}\exp\left(\frac{Q_i\left(s,a'\right)}{\theta}\right)}, & else \end{cases} \tag{10}$$

where $\zeta_i \in [0,1]$ is a random number, ϵ_i is a decayed parameter with initial value $\epsilon_0 \in [0,1]$, $A_i\left(s\right)$ denotes the set that contains all possible actions for agent i under state s, θ is the temperature parameter. With these above, the algorithm called Adaptive Empathetic Learner (AEL) for agent i can be formalized as below.

Algorithm 1. Adaptive Empathy Learner for agent i

Input: initialize agents number n, m, α, γ, θ, Q_i, s_i, λ_i, δ_p and δ_n
Output: output π_i

1 **while** *not end of training* **do**
2   **while** *not at end of each episode* **do**
3   Choose action a_i with the probability in (10) and observe other agents' actions a_j;
4   Get next state s_i' and observe other agents' rewards r_j;
5   Calculate C_i with (4) and I_i with (5);
6   Adjust λ_i with (7);
7   Calculate integrated utility U_i with (8);
8   Update Q_i with (9);
9   **end**
10 **end**

3   Experimental Results

We simulated our algorithm in two classic games, Prisoner's Dilemma (PD) and Ultimatum Game (UG). The parameter setting of each simulation is consistent ($m = 10$, $\alpha = 0.9$, $\gamma = 0.02$, $\theta = 0.1$, $\lambda(0) = 0.0$, $\delta_p = 0.005$, $\delta_n = 0.001$). All the results were collected after 50 times of 10000 iterations training.

3.1   Iterated Prisoner's Dilemma

The Iterated Prisoner Dilemma (IPD) game is the iterated version of Prisoner Dilemma [1]. In this game, two suspects are arrested by the police. If both choose to remain silent (*cooperate*), both have their sentences reduced by 3 months. If one of them testifies (*defect*), the betrayer's sentence is reduced by 5 months and the silent one cannot be reduced. If each betrays the other, both have their sentences reduced by 1 month.

Generally, it's impossible to trust the partner or concern the partner's emotion for rational agents. Therefore, agents tend to testify to pursue the maximization of their own interests, rather than keep silent jointly to maximize the mutual benefit. Our aim of this experiment is to test the trend of agents' behaviors after empathy is introduced in the prisoner's dilemma environment, and discuss the influence on agents' decision when the partner using different strategies (shown in Table 1).

Table 1. Strategies considered in prisoner's dilemma

Strategy	Characteristics
AEL/AEL1/AEL2	Choose action to maximize (8)
WOLFPHC	Choose action to maximize (1)
Deteriorated (Re1)	Reverse action from *coop* to *defect*
Ameliorated (Re2)	Reverse action from *defect* to *coop*
Probabilistic	Choose action in fixed probability

Figure 2 recorded the simulation between two agents with AEL and the contrast test between agents with AEL and WOLFPHC (Win or Learn Fast Policy Hill-climbing). According to the results, a stable cooperative relationship could be established quickly between two AELs, which means the algorithm is effective for solving dilemma problems. By contrast, if the partner of AEL was changed with a rational agent WOLFPHC, we can see that AEL adjusted its action strategy to competition after fully expressing goodwill without receiving response from the other party. This shows that AEL does not blindly cooperate, but can adjust the strategy in a timely manner, which is also beneficial to elicit constructive interaction among agents in a dynamic environment.

To further test the dynamic performance of the algorithm, we paired the AEL with agents using switching strategy. As shown in Fig. 3. When faced with Re1

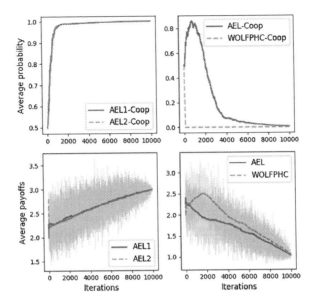

Fig. 2. The average probability of *coop* action and the average payoff of participants in IPD when AEL played with AEL and WOLFPHC. AEL showed increased cooperation when facing with AEL, while tending to defeat when facing with rational agent using WOLFPHC strategy.

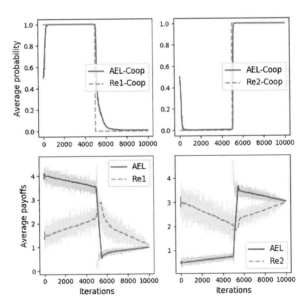

Fig. 3. The average probability of *coop* action and the average payoff of participants in IPD when AEL played with deteriorated agent (Re1)) and ameliorated agent (Re2). AEL can dynamically adjust strategy if opponents change their strategies in progress of interaction.

who reverse action from always *coop* to always *defect*, AEL responded adaptively to its opponent's switching behavior. A consistent result could also be achieved when AEL faced with Re2, a agent reverse action from always *defect* to always *coop*. It's worth noting that, comparing with the time AEL paid for coping with the conversion of Re2, AEL took more time to adjust its behavior when Re1 changed to be *defect*, which fully embodies the characteristics of agents to suppress hostile behavior.

In addition, the situations that opponents had different probability on choosing action *coop* were tested contrastively and the results were recorded in Fig. 4. We observed that AEL showed increased cooperation as opponent's action got well-intentioned progressively. Note that AEL won't converge to a pure strategy of *coop* until the opponent choose to cooperate with probability of 1. This is how AEL protected itself with the most benevolent intentions.

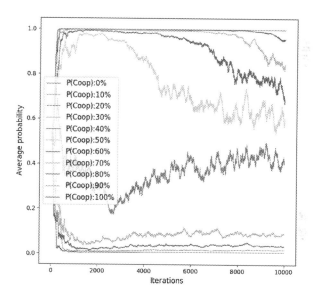

Fig. 4. The average probability of *coop* action of AEL when AEL played with different probabilistic agents which choose *coop* in fixed probability varying from 0 to 1. AEL showed increased cooperation as opponent's action got more well-intentioned.

3.2 Ultimatum Game

The Ultimatum Game is a classic non-zero game with two participants [4,8]. The classic description of this game is "A proponent and a respondent bargain for the distribution of a certain amount of income. The proponent bids a portion of the income to the respondent and the rest is left to himself. If the respondent accepts, the respondent gets the corresponding part and the proponent gets the rest. If the respondent refuses, neither party can get anything."

The rational strategy suggested by classical game theory is for the proponent to offer the smallest possible positive share and for the respondent to accept in turn [20]. So it is a appropriate experiment to test our focus on the sense of fairness.

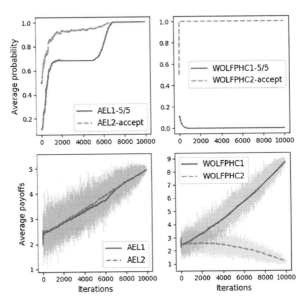

Fig. 5. The average probability of equal distribution proponent offered and action *accept* respondent selected when the participants interact with AEL (top-left) and WOLFPHC (top-right). The corresponding average payoff is depicted in the two subgraphs below.

The total resource we set in this experiment is 10 and the tick size (minimum proposal change) is 1. We first trained both agents with AEL strategies and then we modified both with WOLFPHC strategies as a control. The results were depicted in Fig. 5. We only recorded the average probability of equal distribution, here referring to $(5 - 5)$, and the corresponding average payoff in order to highlight the main feature – fairness which is expected to achieve.

It's obvious that an equal distribution $(5 - 5)$ was reached between agents with AEL strategies. By contrast, agents with rational strategies converged to the Nash equilibrium $(9 - 1)$. According to this, proponent with AEL can relinquish the vast majority of resources and adaptively choose a proposal more fair to the respondent. We consider such behavior as an intrinsic moral improvement because the two sides in UG are competitive on resources in particular with the condition that respondent is in a weaker position. This also proves that the realization of fair behavior is also influenced by the constructive interaction triggered by dynamic empathy to some extent.

4   Conclusions

In this stage, our work is to design an empathetic learning method for agents to make them interact constructively and generate the sense of morality in social interaction. To achieve this, we followed a natural setting that agents in the interactive environment are mainly affected by two factors – social comparison and companion impression, which is determined by agents' evaluation on the dynamic payoff of themselves and their partners. A conservative empathy model with update rules was built by associating the payoff between different agents and a learning method AEL is present to guarantee orderly interaction of multi-agent system. Our algorithm illustrates that empathy can act as a fundamental affective drive underlying constructive interaction and moral behaviors.

Our research focuses on introducing psychology, especially empathy into the learning procedure of agents. This provides novel methods and insights in regulating AI behaviors in multi-agent systems, as well as artificial subjects in psychology and behavioral economics experiments. In summary, AEL is a principled adaptive algorithm, with which agents can learn in the model free environment and release positive signals proactively on the premise that the security benefits are guaranteed. Meanwhile, the constructive interaction between cooperation and competition can further elicit intrinsic moral improvement, especially the sense of absolute fairness, even if the state has no Pareto improvement or Kaldor - Hicks improvement, such as the situation in Ultimatum Game.

Perspective taking is the highest level of empathetic behavioral manifestation, which is mastered almost exclusively by humans. To achieve perspective taking, there should be a set of shared beliefs and knowledge between agents. We leave this possible key to task-oriented autonomous agent specialization and cooperation for future work.

References

1. Axelrod, R., et al.: The evolution of strategies in the iterated prisoner's dilemma. In: The Dynamics of Norms, pp. 1–16 (1987)
2. Bekoff, M.: The moral lives of animals. Libr. J. **136**(5), 129 (2012)
3. Bosse, T., Duell, R., Memon, Z.A., Treur, J., Wal, C.N.V.D.: Agent-based modeling of emotion contagion in groups. Cogn. Comput. **7**(1), 111–136 (2015)
4. Brosnan, S.F., de Waal, F.B.: Evolution of responses to (un)fairness. Science **346**(6207), 1251776 (2014)
5. Conitzer, V., Sinnottarmstrong, W., Borg, J.S., Deng, Y., Kramer, M.: Moral decision making frameworks for artificial intelligence (2017)
6. Cushman, F., Kumar, V., Railton, P.: Moral learning: current and future directions. Cognition (2017)
7. De Waal, F.B.M.: Putting the altruism back into altruism: the evolution of empathy. Ann. Rev. Psychol. **59**(1), 279 (2008)
8. Debove, S., Baumard, N., Andre, J.B.: Models of the evolution of fairness in the ultimatum game: a review and classification. Evol. Hum. Behav. **37**(3), 245–254 (2016)

9. Goldsmith, J., Burton, E.: Why teaching ethics to AI practitioners is important. In: AAAI, pp. 4836–4840 (2017)
10. Jong, S.D., Verbeeck, K., Verbeeck, K.: Artificial agents learning human fairness. In: International Joint Conference on Autonomous Agents and Multiagent Systems, pp. 863–870 (2008)
11. Martinezvaquero, L.A., Han, T.A., Pereira, L.M., Lenaerts, T.: Apology and forgiveness evolve to resolve failures in cooperative agreements. In: Benelux Conference on Artificial Intelligence, p. 10639 (2015)
12. Mei, S., Marsella, S.C., Pynadath, D.V.: Modeling appraisal in theory of mind reasoning. Auton. Agents Multi-Agent Syst. **20**(1), 14–31 (2010)
13. Moerland, T.M., Broekens, J., Jonker, C.M.: Emotion in reinforcement learning agents and robots: a survey. Mach. Learn. **5**, 1–38 (2017)
14. Moniz Pereira, L., Lenaerts, T., Martinez-Vaquero, L.A., et al.: Social manifestation of guilt leads to stable cooperation in multi-agent systems. In: Proceedings of the 16th Conference on Autonomous Agents and MultiAgent Systems, pp. 1422–1430. International Foundation for Autonomous Agents and Multiagent Systems (2017)
15. Parkes, D.C., Wellman, M.P.: Economic reasoning and artificial intelligence. Science **349**(6245), 267 (2015)
16. Pereira, L.M., Santos, F.C., Lenaerts, T., et al.: Why is it so hard to say sorry? Evolution of apology with commitments in the iterated prisoner's dilemma. In: Proceedings of the Twenty-Third International Joint Conference on Artificial Intelligence, pp. 177–183. AAAI Press (2013)
17. Potapov, A., Rodionov, S.: Universal empathy and ethical bias for artificial general intelligence. J. Exp. Theor. Artif. Intell. **26**(3), 405–416 (2013)
18. Ventura, R.: Emotions and empathy: a bridge between nature and society? Int. J. Mach. Conscious. **2**(02), 343–361 (2010)
19. de Waal, F.B., Preston, S.D.: Mammalian empathy: behavioural manifestations and neural basis. Nat. Rev. Neurosci. **18**(8), 498–509 (2017)
20. Van't Wout, M., Kahn, R.S., Sanfey, A.G., Aleman, A.: Affective state and decision-making in the ultimatum game. Exp. Brain Res. **169**(4), 564–568 (2006)
21. Yu, C., Zhang, M., Ren, F.: Emotional multiagent reinforcement learning in social dilemmas. IEEE Trans. Neural Netw. Learn. Syst. **26**(12), 3083–3096 (2015)

A Fast Visual Feature Matching Algorithm in Multi-robot Visual SLAM

Nian Liu, Mingzhu Wei[(✉)], Xiaomei Xie, Mechali Omar, Xin Chen,
Weihuai Wu, Peng Yan, and Limei Xu

University of Electronic Science and Technology of China (UESTC),
Chengdu 611731, China
mingzhu.wei@uestc.edu.cn

Abstract. To reduce the feature matching time in visual based multi-robot Simultaneous Localization and Mapping (SLAM), a feature matching algorithm based on map environment is proposed in this paper. The key idea of our algorithm is to establish feature libraries by classifying the collected features into two categories during the mobile process of every sub-robot. Then all features are matched based on the categories so that the invalid feature matching time will be reduced. At last, experiment is conducted to verify the performance of proposed algorithm. In comparison with traditional BoW method, its feature matching time is reduced by 20% at no expense of accuracy.

Keywords: Multi-robot · Feature matching · Visual SLAM

1 Introduction

In the past decades, research on Simultaneous Localization and Mapping (SLAM) for single robot has been discussed in depth way. However, problems will be encountered when dealing with the multi-robot system SLAM, such as information association between two robots, multi-robot pose calculation, time synchronization, global map optimization, etc. Among them, the information association between robots is the most important step to achieve map fusion of multiple sub-robots [1]. It contains two steps. One is to match the information between the local maps, and the other is to obtain the transformation matrix by aligned information [2]. At present, four methods are applied to study the multi-robot map fusion. They are: (1) SLAM with given initial poses, it's an efficient method but may not be applied in unknown field; (2) Map fusion based on robots' convergence [3], it requires the meeting of sub-robots, but this is not the case in most situation [3, 4]; (3) SLAM with extra sensors, it's helpful but those sensors may not be applied in certain circumstance, for example GPS cannot be applied in indoor [5, 6]; (4) SLAM with searching repeated region between sub-maps [7], it overcomes the problems existed in the previous methods, and its effectiveness has been validated.

For repeated region searching, the feature matching time will increase with the system's running. This is mainly contributed by increasing feature points and adopting algorithm of traversing features without priority. The increased feature matching time will restrict the performance of the multi-robot visual SLAM greatly. This problem has not been well solved.

© Springer Nature Switzerland AG 2019
H. Yu et al. (Eds.): ICIRA 2019, LNAI 11740, pp. 15–24, 2019.
https://doi.org/10.1007/978-3-030-27526-6_2

Gálvez-López used binary words' bag of Features From Accelerated Segment Test (FAST) to reduce the time consuming effectively for feature extraction and matching [8]. Mur-Artal et al. not only combined the BRIEF descriptors with FAST feature, but also proposed a fitting strategy to filter the unstable features in the map [9]. This method effectively reduced the feature matching time in closing loop, especially for large scale SLAM. However, additional computational time is needed because scoring every map point is required during the fitting strategy. In paper [10], to improve the efficiency, the visual information fusion process of the drone and the ground robot is completed by using the landmarks which have been put in the field in advance. But for an unknown field, this method cannot work well. Rublee et al. proposed a method to avoid the generation of invalid key frames and it was proved to be feasible [11].

For the multi-robot visual-based SLAM, we find the visual information association between robots mostly appears at the intersection of the global map or corners. In this context, a method is proposed to classify the obtained visual information to make feature matching more efficient.

This paper is organized as follows. In Sect. 2, the traditional Bag of Words feature matching method is described. Section 3 states the fast feature matching algorithm we propose. In Sect. 4, experiments are implemented to test the performance of our algorithm.

2 Traditional Bag of Words Feature Matching Algorithm

The main idea of the traditional Bag of Words (BoW) feature matching algorithm in loop closure is to match all the key frames one by one in the feature library established by each robot [8]. The algorithm is as follows.

$$
\begin{aligned}
Z^1 &= \left\{ z_1^1, z_2^1, z_3^1, \cdots, z_m^1 \right\} \\
Z^2 &= \left\{ z_1^2, z_2^2, z_3^2, \cdots, z_m^2 \right\} \\
&\cdots \\
Z^n &= \left\{ z_1^n, z_2^n, z_3^n, \cdots, z_m^n \right\}
\end{aligned}
\tag{1}
$$

where Z^i represents the visual feature libraries of robot i in the multi-robot system and Z_j^i represents the set of feature points detected from key frames j.

In BoW multi-robot visual feature matching method, after the establishment of each robot's visual feature library, the new key frames will be matched one by one with other robots' features in the process of system operation. BoW method as shown in Fig. 1 is to cross-match all the collected visual features Z^i indiscriminately. The accuracy can be guaranteed, but time consumption will increase drastically and slow down the system efficiency. Figure 1 and Table 1 give the process and pseudo code of traditional BoW method.

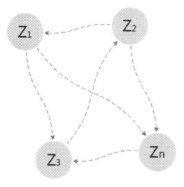

Fig. 1. Traditional BoW method

Table 1. Steps of BoW

Traditional Bag of Words algorithm	
1:	Input new frame **F**
2:	put **F** into **Z**
3:	**while** $F \not\subset Z^i$
4:	**for** j=0 **to** size of Z^i
5:	match **F** and Z^i_j
6:	**if** match is good **then**
7:	**database merge**
8:	**else end** for, **end** while
9:	**back to 1**

3 Fast Multi-robot Vision Matching Association Algorithm

In order to reduce the time-consuming, we propose a fast visual information matching algorithm based on environmental character which can reduce the invalid feature matching during multi-robot visual information association. In the process of SLAM based on multi-robot vision, the feature information of maps can be potentially divided into two categories: (1) the intersection or corner of maps, (2) the non-intersectional parts. It is found that data association can occur with high probability at intersections and corners during robots' rendezvous. In this context, the visual features is divided into two categories, CORNER-type and non- CORNER-type via the information obtained from visual Odometry or IMU.

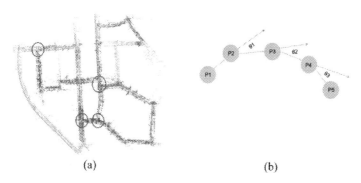

(a)   (b)

Fig. 2. Multi-robot SLAM. (a) CORNER and map fusion [11], (b) corner angle in single SLAM (Color figure online)

From Fig. 2(a), we can see that the common area of multiple robots appears mostly at the corner of the map labelled by red circle. The so-called corner information acquisition is represented in Fig. 2(b), where P_i represents the pose of the camera, and θ_i represents the Euler angle between two adjacent key frames in the camera motion. In the ground-based robot visual SLAM, the difference of angle is derived from the yaw angle.

If the transformation matrix **T** between two key frames is

$$\mathbf{T} = \begin{bmatrix} r_{11} & r_{12} & r_{13} & t_1 \\ r_{21} & r_{22} & r_{23} & t_2 \\ r_{31} & r_{32} & r_{33} & t_3 \\ 0 & 0 & 0 & 1 \end{bmatrix} \tag{2}$$

Based on the relationship between **T** and Euler angle [12], the yaw angle between two considered key frames will be

$$\theta_y = \arctan 2(-r_{31}, \sqrt{r_{32}^2 + r_{33}^2}) \tag{3}$$

Based on the obtained yaw angle between two considered key frames θ_y, we may identify whether the considered key frame is CORNER or not by comparing θ_y with the threshold θ_{th} we prescribes. If the key frame is CORNER, we add the CORNER information feature library to visual feature database collected by each robot based on formula (4):

$$Z_{N-c}^1 = \{z_1^1, z_2^1, z_3^1, \cdots, z_s^1\}; \ Z_c^1 = \{z_0^1, z_1^1, z_2^1, \cdots, z_m^1\}$$
$$Z_{N-c}^2 = \{z_1^2, z_2^2, z_3^2, \cdots, z_s^2\}; \ Z_c^2 = \{z_0^2, z_1^2, z_2^2, \cdots, z_m^2\}$$
$$\cdots$$
$$Z_{N-c}^n = \{z_1^n, z_2^n, z_3^n, \cdots, z_s^n\}; \ Z_c^n = \{z_0^n, z_1^n, z_2^n, \cdots, z_m^n\} \tag{4}$$

where Z_c^i represents the CORNER-type feature library of robot i and Z_{N-c}^i represents the non-CORNER-type feature library of robot i. Up to now, each key frame has been identified as CORNER-type and non-CORNER-type.

Table 2 is the pseudo code of the proposed fast visual feature matching algorithm. Firstly, the category of key frames in matching process is identified. Then the matching is conducted. If the key frame belongs to CORNER-type, it will be matched with the established CORNER-type features of other robots, and non-CORNER-type features of other robot will not be matched. Otherwise, the key frame is matched with the established non-CORNER-type features of other robots, and CORNER-type features of other robot will not be matched. This will reduce the invalid matching number and improve the efficiency of feature matching.

Table 2. Fast visual feature matching algorithm

Fast matching algorithm			
1:	Input new frame **F**	**13:**	if match is good **then**
2:	**if F $\not\subset$ CORNER-type**	**14:**	database merge, back to 1
3:	put **F** into $\mathbf{Z_{N\text{-}c}}$	**15:**	**else end** for, **end** while
4:	match $Z(\mathbf{F}, \mathbf{Z_{N\text{-}c}})$	**16:**	end **Function** match $Z(\mathbf{F}, \mathbf{Zc})$
5:	**else**	**17:**	**Function** match $Z(\mathbf{F}, \mathbf{Z_{N\text{-}c}})$
6:	put **F** into $\mathbf{Z_c}$	**18:**	**while F** $\not\subset \mathbf{Z^i_{N\text{-}c}}$
7:	match $Z(\mathbf{F}, \mathbf{Z_c})$	**19:**	**for** j=0 **to** size of $\mathbf{Z^i_{N\text{-}c}}$
8:	**back to 1**	**20:**	match **F** and $\mathbf{Z^i_{N\text{-}c}}$(j)
9:	**Function** match $Z(\mathbf{F}, \mathbf{Z_c})$	**21:**	if match is good **then**
10:	**while F** $\not\subset \mathbf{Z^i_c}$	**22:**	database merge, back to 1.
11:	**for** j=0 **to** size of $\mathbf{Z^i}$	**23:**	**else end** for, **end** while
12:	match **F** and $\mathbf{Z^i_c}$(j)	**24:**	end **Function** match $Z(\mathbf{F}, \mathbf{Z_{N\text{-}c}})$

After feature matching, PNP method [13] is applied to judge if the matching is accurate and calculate the accuracy rate of the feature matching result as shown in Fig. 3. It contains four parts including feature detection, feature classification, feature matching and error judgement. The abbreviation 'KPs' represents the key point extracted from key-frames.

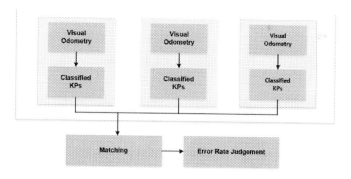

Fig. 3. Multi-robot feature detecting and matching process

To make our algorithm be seen clearly, we also give the steps of the algorithm process and an error rate judgment in Fig. 4.

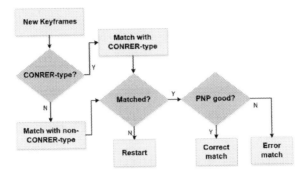

Fig. 4. Steps of fast visual feature matching algorithm.

In Fig. 4, where correct matches and error matches will be accounted, so as to calculate the matching error rate.

4 Experiments

4.1 Experiment Setup and Data Collection

To evaluate the fast visual feature matching algorithm, experiments are performed via Turtlebot2 equipped with two Baumer VCXU-23c industrial cameras which are build a stereo camera system. By manual control robot moving, we collect the vision data. The processing is executed on Asus GL 552 VW laptop with Intel Core i7-6700HQ@2.60 GHz and Nvidia GeForce GTX 960M (4 GB) and the operating system used is 64-bit Ubuntu16.04. Robot Operation System (ROS) is used to control the mobile robot movement. The resolution of collected picture is 1920 × 1200 pixels as shown in Fig. 5(b).

(a)   (b)

Fig. 5. Equipment and data. (a) Turtlebot2 and stereo camera system, (b) Collected image from the camera.

4.2   Parameter Selection

In terms of key frames' selection, we apply the existing single robot-based SLAM algorithm to construct visual odometry based on acquired data. And solvePnPransac [13] method is used to calculate the transformation matrix between frames. Furthermore, several tests are conducted to select the suitable value of inlier from the collected data. Figures 6(a) and (b) show the experimental field (Institute Building Atrium of UESTC) and robot trajectory, respectively.

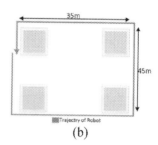

(a)   (b)

Fig. 6. Data collection field. (a) Experiment field, (b) Robot trajectory.

During experiment, 325 source pics are obtained. The visual odometry is executed to select the keyframes. Table 3 lists the number of keyframes in terms of different values of inliers. It is easy to see that the number of keyframes deceases as the value of inlier increases.

Table 3. Keyframes number with different inlier

Inlier	Keyframes	Inlier	Keyframes
1	247	2	187
3	120	4	98
5	76	6	61
7	52	8	39

For the proposed method, whether the keyframe is CONRER-type or non-CONRER-type depends on the threshold value θ_{th}. Hence, another test is conducted to calculate the number of CONRER-type keyframe with different inlier and θ_{th}. The numerical results are summarized in Table 4.

Table 4. CONRER-type number with different inliers and θ_{th}

Inlier	θ_{th}			
	6°	8°	10°	12°
1	21	6	0	0
2	32	30	2	0
3	55	25	27	0
4	50	31	31	32
5	41	**40**	**33**	**29**
6	35	**42**	**35**	**30**
7	40	34	27	25
8	35	21	21	20

In Table 4, the number of CONRER-type keyframe is calculated based on different inliers and θ_{th}. As shown in Fig. 6(b), the entire trajectory is a square. If the starting point coincides with the ending point, the sum of offset angles should be approximately equal to 360°. Then, the suitable values of CONRER-type number and θ_{th} should meet the following relation:

$$CN \times \theta_{th} \approx 360° \tag{5}$$

where CN represents the number of CONRER-type keyframes.

Based on the data in Table 4 and Eq. (5), the suitable value of inlier is between 5 and 6, and the threshold value θ_{th} is between 8° to 12°.

4.3 Performance Analysis

To analyze the performance of the proposed algorithm, we time and calculate the accurate rate of the experiment process including feature point extraction, descriptor generation, feature classification and matching. The results obtained by the proposed algorithm and traditional BoW algorithm are compared.

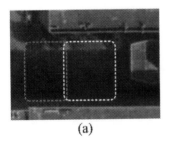

(a)

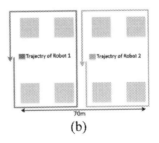

(b)

Fig. 7. Multi-robot field. (a) Experiment field, (b) Robots' trajectory.

Fig. 8. Feature detection and matching

The experiment field is shown in Fig. 7(a). The trajectories of two robots shown in Fig. 7(b) are square and converge in the middle. There are CORNERS and non-CORNERS at their common trajectory. Figure 8 is the feature detection and matching during the robots traveling the trajectory.

Based on the value of inlier and the threshold θ_{th} selected in Sect. 4.2, matching time consuming and matching error rate are compared between the two algorithms. All the results are listed in Table 5 for matching time consuming and Table 6 for matching error rate. Table 5 shows that the processing time of proposed method is reduced by nearly 20% in comparison with BoW approach. The matching error rate is close to each other as shown in Table 6. The results indicate that our proposed algorithm is more feasible with short computing time.

Table 5. Matching time consuming and improvement (ms)

Inlier		8°	10°	12°
5	Traditional BoW	52674	45005	42257
	Fast algorithm	41612	35103	33383
Improvement		21.0%	22.0%	21.0%
6	Traditional BoW	40231	38994	36994
	Fast algorithm	32989	30025	29965
Improvement		18.0%	23.0%	19.0%

Table 6. Comparison of matching error rate (%)

Inlier		8°	10°	12°
5	BoW algorithm	28.14	26.88	25.12
	Fast algorithm	27.97	24.23	22.23
Difference		0.17	2.65	2.89
6	BoW algorithm	23.12	23.10	23.99
	Fast algorithm	25.23	22.87	21.59
Difference		2.11	0.23	2.40

5 Conclusion

In multi-robot visual SLAM, the process of multi-robot visual information fusion is time-consuming. In this paper, an algorithm to make fast visual feature matching is proposed. Before the process of matching, the obtained key frames are classified as CORNER-type and non-CORNER-type via comparing the yaw angle. Then only the key frames with same characteristics are matched each other. The experimental results indicate that the proposed algorithm can reduce the visual feature matching time and keep the matching error rate in the same level by comparing with BoW algorithm. It should be mentioned that the experiment is based on an ideal model and needed to test on a real multi-robot visual SLAM. Also, the environment involving T-junction-type corner or big-Corner type (for example RING-type) is not considered in this paper. Further work should be done to verify the effectiveness for the rigorous conditions.

Acknowledgments. The author would like to acknowledge the support from the Advanced Research Project of Manned Space under Grant No. 0603(17700630), the National Natural Science Foundation of China under Grant No. 61803075, the Fundamental Research Funds for the Central Universities under Grant No. ZYGX2018KYQD211.

References

1. Saeedi, S., Paull, L., Trentini, M., et al.: Group mapping: a topological approach to map merging for multiple robots. IEEE Robot. Autom. Mag. **21**(2), 60–72 (2014)
2. Zhou, X.S., Roumeliotis, S.I.: Multi-robot SLAM with unknown initial correspondence: the robot rendezvous case. In: IEEE/RSJ International Conference on Intelligent Robots and Systems, pp. 1785–1792. IEEE, New York (2006)
3. Ahmad, A., Lawless, G., Lima, P.: An online scalable approach to unified multirobot cooperative localization and object tracking. IEEE Trans. Robot. **19**(7), 1–16 (2017)
4. Wu, P., Liu, Y., Ye, M., et al.: Geometry guided multi-scale depth map fusion via graph optimization. IEEE Trans. Image Process. **26**(3), 1315–1329 (2017)
5. Lei, J., Wu, M., Zhang, C., et al.: Depth-preserving stereo image retargeting based on pixel fusion. IEEE Trans. Multimed. **19**(7), 1442–1453 (2017)
6. Howard, A., Parker, L.E., Sukhatme, G.S.: Experiments with a large heterogeneous mobile robot team: exploration, mapping, deployment and detection. Int. J. Robot. Res. **25**(5), 431–447 (2005)
7. Grisetti, G., Stachniss, C., Burgard, W.: Improved techniques for grid mapping with rao-blackwellized particle filters. IEEE Trans. Robot. **23**(1), 34–46 (2007)
8. Gálvez-López, D., Tardos, J.D.: Bags of binary words for fast place recognition in image sequences. IEEE Trans. Robot. **28**(5), 1188–1197 (2012)
9. Mur-Artal, R., Montiel, J.M.M., Tardos, J.D.: ORB-SLAM: a versatile and accurate monocular SLAM system. IEEE Trans. Robot. **31**(5), 1147–1163 (2015)
10. Potena, C., Khanna, R., Nieto, J., et al.: AgriColMap: aerial-ground collaborative 3D mapping for precision farming. IEEE Robot. Autom. Lett. **4**(2), 1085–1092 (2019)
11. Rublee, E., Rabaud, V., Konolige, K., et al.: ORB: an efficient alternative to SIFT or SURF. In: ICCV 2011, vol. 11, no. 1, p. 2 (2011)
12. https://blog.csdn.net/shenxiaolu1984/article/details/50639298. Accessed 12 Apr 2019
13. http://www.opencv.org.cn. Accessed 16 Mar 2019

Mechanical Design and Kinematic Control of a Humanoid Robot Face

Yu Qiu, Chongming Xu, Manjia Su, Hongkai Chen, Yisheng Guan,
and Haifei Zhu[✉]

School of Electromechanical Engineering,
Guangdong University of Technology, Guangzhou 510006, China
hfzhu@gdut.edu.cn

Abstract. Faces are very important for human social activities. However, most of the current humanoid robots only have a stiff face. This paper aims at developing a humanoid robot face system can express facial expressions. Bio-inspired by the anatomy of a human head, mechanical structures, including eyebrows, eyes, and mouth, are designed. The mechanisms are actuated by cables or linkages. Moreover, the cables which lay inside the rigid mechanism can pull a soft facial skin for fulfilling micro facial expressions. Kinematics of eyebrows, eyes, and mouth are built up for motion control. Vivid and intuitive experimental instances of these three parts are presented, with quantitative kinematic controlling. The results show the reliability and friendly feeling of this robot face system.

Keywords: Humanoid robot face · Mechanical design · Kinematics · Control framework

1 Introduction

Humanoid robot is a kind of robot that imitates human's special structure or functions, which interact with people friendly. Among these structures or functions, the head organs' motion and facial expression are some of the important and intuitive parts for human-robot interaction. A lot of research on this have been done in recent few decades. For instances, Yang and Ke designed and implemented the SHFR-III expression robot with a relatively simple structure of 11 degrees of freedom [1]. Although it can express certain expressions, its structure is not compact enough. The overall space utilization is too small, and its design is lacking in soft elastic skin. Qingmei and Weiguo from Harbin Institute of Technology designed the H-F robot-II, which can express eight kinds of basic expressions [2]. This robot can express various mouth shapes, but the movements that can be expressed with the mouth has not been considered. Waseda University developed the WE series robots in Japan [3]. The robots have the most

© Springer Nature Switzerland AG 2019
H. Yu et al. (Eds.): ICIRA 2019, LNAI 11740, pp. 25–38, 2019.
https://doi.org/10.1007/978-3-030-27526-6_3

complete sense organs including vision, hearing, touch, smell, etc. ASIMO, the robot developed by Honda in Japan, can recognize and respond to 50 different greetings and questions [4], but it cannot generate expressions at all when getting along with humans. iCub, the robot with the ability of learning which was developed by the University of Genoa in Italy [5], has a high degree of joint flexibility and can highly reproduce human's movement. However, it is easy to make confusion and lacks stability when different applications are executed. Sofia, developed by Hanson Robotics of the United States, expresses itself through 62 muscles in the face and neck and uses artificial intelligence to recognize faces and maintain dialog [6]. However, the face has certain limitations. It cannot be torn down and fit on the skin installation quickly, and it is unable to meet the demands of rapid 'changing face'. Sofia's mouth system still has some shortcomings that the mouth and voice are less consistent when talking like the mouth' motion is little later than the voice. Furthermore, a variety of actuating structural schemes of humanoid robots have been investigated [7–10].

However, there are some outstanding problems in the research of 'robot face' for humanoid:

- complex structure,
- less friendly expression interaction, and
- high cost.

Aiming at improving these disadvantages, we developed a high bionic humanoid robot face system in this paper. For distinct facial motion, the mechanical structure of eyebrows, eyes and mouth are designed using cables or rods for actuation, which makes the structure compact like muscles. Cable-driven provides high driving force and enough control precision. Also, the outer structure is completely the same as a real human skull. Numbers of high power density-to-size servo motor are adapted to cable-driven, which are well controlled in an interface friendly software system. The system integrates easy facial control user interface, with lower motion control functions packed. Geometrical kinematics of eyebrows, eyes and mouth are established, for motion analysis and accurate control. Demonstrative experiments are taken to verify the motion and control of this prototype.

The remainder of this paper is organized as follows. We brief the design philosophy in Sect. 2. We then present the mechanical design and control framework of the robot in detail in Sect. 3. We move on to the kinematics of the robot in Sect. 4. In Sect. 5, we conduct experiments to verify our proposed design and analysis. Finally, we conclude our work in Sect. 6.

2   Design Philosophy

To design a highly biomimetic humanoid head, a study of the arrangement and movement of the facial muscles would be instrumental and necessary. The muscles of the face can be divided into two groups: mimetic muscles and muscles of mastication [11]. The mimetic muscles play an important role in the expression of feelings and thoughts by elevating or depressing the eyebrows and lips. As shown in Fig. 1(a), the facial muscle mainly includes frontalis, zygomatic major, procerus, depressor anguli oris, buccinator and so on. The frontal muscles mainly cause the eyebrows up and down and the depressor glabellus cause the frown movement, as shown in Fig. 1(b). The orbicularis oris is a circular muscle performs various movements such as closing, compressing, puckering, and protruding the mouth. Other muscles move the lips or the corners of the mouth, helping us produce the range of movements that is necessary for speech. Based on the philosophy and the facial movement requirements, we design a humanoid robot face including eyebrow mechanism, eye mechanism design and mouth mechanism in this paper.

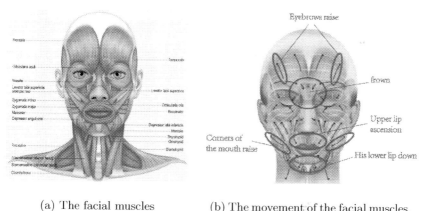

(a) The facial muscles   (b) The movement of the facial muscles.

Fig. 1. The facial muscles and their movements

3   Design of the Robot

3.1   Eyebrow Mechanism Design

As shown in Fig. 2, there are two control points on the inside and outside of each eyebrow. To simulate the movement of eyebrows, the outer control points are driven up and down by linkage, which cause raised eyebrows. Moreover, the inside control points are driven by linkage to move up and down synchronously, and the movements of left and right are the same, which cause frown.

Fig. 2. Eyebrows mechanism design

3.2   Eye Mechanism Design

As shown in Fig. 3, eye muscles are the six muscles (also known as extraocular muscles or EOMs) that rotate the eye. Horizontal eye rotations, usually referred to as horizontal eye movements, are produced mainly by the lateral and medial rectus muscles (also known as the horizontal recti). Vertical and torsional eye movements are produced mainly by the superior and inferior rectus muscles (vertical recti) in combination with the superior and inferior oblique muscles (obliques) [13]. Since the rotation of the eyeball is small, the design only considers the left, right, up and down movements of the eyeball to save space. The range

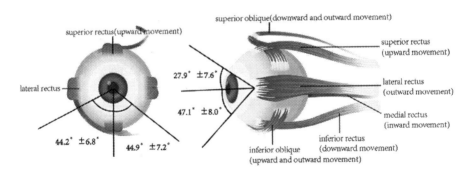

Fig. 3. Muscle structure of human eye and view range

Table 1. The normal ranges of eye movement [12]

Eye orientation	The rotation angle
Adduction	$44.9 \pm 7.2°$
Abduction	$44.2 \pm 6.8°$
Elevation	$27.9 \pm 7.6°$
Depression	$47.1 \pm 8.0°$

of eye movements is described in Table 1. In this paper, the eyeball is embedded in a support frame, which makes the eyeball able to rotate freely. The rotation of each eyeball is controlled by four cables with a diameter of 0.4 mm. The four cables are rhombus and distributed on the surface of the eyeball. By controlling the rotation of servo motor to pull the cables, to drive the eyeball to realize left, right, up and down rotation, as shown in Fig. 4.

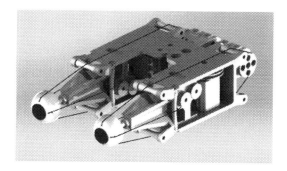

Fig. 4. Eye mechanism design

3.3 Mouth Mechanism Design

The mouth mechanism includes the jaw mechanism and the lip mechanism. The jaw is driven by a servo motor to realize the opening and closing movement of the jaw. Behind the lips, there are three sets of driving points Fig. 5(a). Each set has two driving points. As shown in Fig. 5(b), the servo motor pulls three sets of driving points to realize different mouth shapes when speaking, utilizing a flexible cable connecting the chute and the pulley block. It is worth mentioning that the reduction of the pull point is accomplished by silicone lip due to the unidirectionality of the cables.

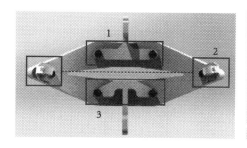   

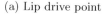

(a) Lip drive point

(b) Robot mouth mechanism design

Fig. 5. Robot mouth mechanism

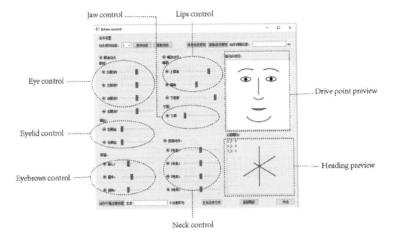

Jaw control ....   Lips control

Eye control ·········

Eyelid control ·········

Eyebrows control ·········

.... Drive point preview

.... Heading preview

Neck control

Fig. 6. The user interface of the robot system

3.4   Control System

DYNAMIXEL Servo motors are employed as actuators to provide sufficient
pulling torque and control precision. The XL-320 model from DYNAMIXEL
is selected. The precision of this servo motor is 0.29 while the speed is controllable. It is deployed in the driving mechanism of eyebrow, eye and mouth. The
servo motor with superior performance provides the hardware basis for the high
frequency and high precision motion control. For this humanoid head, a tedious
process of controlling the actuator action directly through serial port communication is needed, and the function of direct visual feedback is lack. To fulfill the
robot expression action intuitively, a software control box is developed. Inside
the software interface, a simple expression model with 9 feature points in the
eyes and 4 feature points in the mouth according to the location of each feature
point provided by OpenFace, is built to show a visible system, as shown in Fig. 6
There are three main functions in this interface, the motion control function,
the movement storage function and the facial tracking function. Among them,
the action control function is used for the debugging a single servo motor or
a specific expression. The debugger controls the position of the corresponding
action driving point by adjusting each action slider. The corresponding emoji
preview will be displayed in the emoji preview box. The action storage function
is used to assist the above action regulation function. The debugger can save
the adjusted position values of each action point in the local file so that it can
be directly read and used in the next debugging. The facial tracking function is
used for debugging the facial expression capture function of OpenFace. This program will process the captured facial feature points in the real-time, and obtain
the position values of the corresponding points after taking the position data of

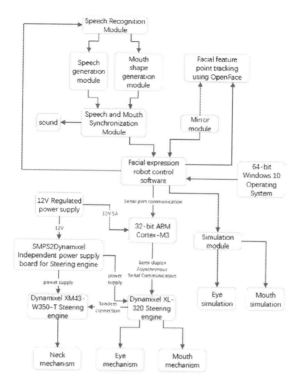

Fig. 7. The control flow chart

some key points for numerical conversion. They will be feedback to the expression preview box (see Fig. 6). Facial expression robot controls software runs on a 64 - bit Windows operating systems implementing 10 type synthesis. Speech recognition, mouth lip synchronization of speech synthesis, speech, facial feature points tracking and mirror modules are invoked in the control software(see Fig. 7). Facial expressions in the robot controlling software simulation module can generate the eyes and the mouth of the two-dimensional image simulation. The facial expression robot controlling software communicates with the 32-bit ARM Cortex-M3 kernel MCU through a serial port. A 12 V regulated voltage power supply provides power to the MCU and the servo motor. The MCU and DYNAMIXEL servo motor have the semi-duplex asynchronous serial communication, but the servo motor has the serial connection. Then the servo motors directly control the motion of the eyebrow, eye and mouth mechanism.

4   Kinematics

4.1   Eyebrows

As shown in Fig. 8, the left and right eyebrow displacement can be expressed as:

$$\Delta L = 4L_1 sin \left(\frac{a}{2}\right) \tag{1}$$

Where L_1 is the arm length driven by servo motor, and α is its rotation Angle. The left and right displacement is controlled by the rotation of servo motor.

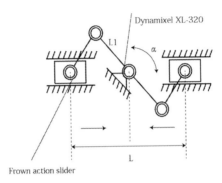

Fig. 8. The schematic diagram for driving frowning mechanism

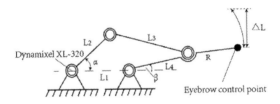

Fig. 9. The schematic diagram for driving eyebrow lifting mechanism

As shown in Fig. 9, the up and down eyebrow displacement can be expressed as:

$$L_4^2 + L_2^2 - 2 \cdot L_2 \cdot L_4 \cos\left(\alpha - \beta\right) = L_3^2 \tag{2}$$

$$\Delta L = R \cdot \beta \tag{3}$$

Where L_1, L_2, L_3, L_4 is the arm length driven by servo motor, and α is its rotation Angle, while R is the distance from the control point to the center of rotation.

4.2 Eye

As shown in Fig. 10, taking left and right rotation of the eyeball for example, the relationship of cable displacements is,

$$R \cdot \alpha = r \cdot \beta, \tag{4}$$

Where β is the rotation angle of the eyeball, while r is the radius of the eyeball. Simplifying Eq. 4, we further yields the rotation angle of the eyeball as,

$$\beta = \frac{R \cdot \alpha}{r}. \tag{5}$$

Similarly, the up and down rotations of eye is the same as the left and right ones.

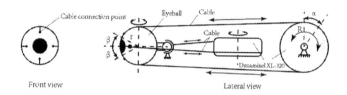

Fig. 10. The schematic diagram for driving the eye mechanism

4.3 Mouth

The driving relationship between the upper lip and the lower lip is shown in Fig. 11. The displacement of the upper/lower lip point and the rotation angle of the servo motor can be calculated as,

$$D = R \cdot \alpha \tag{6}$$

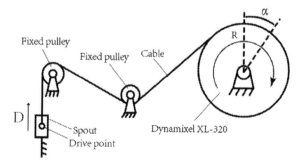

Fig. 11. The schematic diagram for driving the upper/lower lip

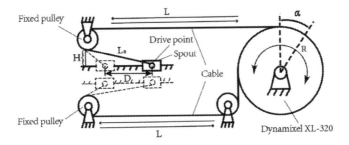

Fig. 12. The schematic diagram for driving the angulus oris

Nevertheless, the geometry relation of the mouth corner point is shown in Fig. 12. The displacement of the mouth corner point and the rotation angle of the servo motor can be calculated as,

$$D = \sqrt{L_0^2 - H^2} - \sqrt{(L_0 - R \cdot \alpha)^2 - H^2} \tag{7}$$

5   Experiments

For the eyebrow, eye and mouth mechanism of the proposed humanoid robot face, we designed several experiments to verify its feasibility. The former mechanisms constitute a humanoid robot face, as shown in Fig. 13(a). The soft elastic skin is attached to the surface of the humanoid head, see Fig. 13(b). Therefore, the head of a humanoid robot consists of three parts: internal mechanical structure, supporting headshell and soft elastic skin. Among them, the support headshell is made of 3D-printed resin material, and the elastic skin is mainly composed of silica gel. In addition, to make the elastic skin as close as possible

(a) Overall structural model   (b) With the imitation skin

Fig. 13. The designed humanoid robot face

to the supporting headshell, the mold of the elastic skin uses the same CAD model of supporting headshell.

5.1   Movement of Eyebrows

There are four degrees of freedom of the eyebrow mechanism. The outer control points of the eyebrows can move up and down independently, while the inner control points can move up and down, as well as left and right synchronously (see Fig. 14).

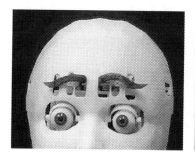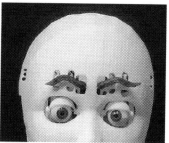

(a) Eyebrows rise   (b) Eyebrows tight knit

Fig. 14. Movement of the eyebrows mechanism

5.2   Movement of Eye

There are four degrees of freedom of the eye mechanism (see Fig. 15). Yaw and pitch of each eyeball are controlled separately. The rotation of the eyeball can be controlled by the output angle of the servo motor based on kinematics. Each eyeball is very flexible because of the usage of the cable driven in eye mechanism.

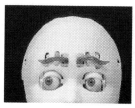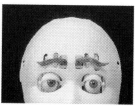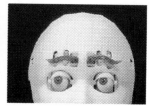

(a) Adduction   (b) Abduction   (c) Elevation

Fig. 15. Movement of the eye mechanism

5.3 Movement of Mouth

As shown in Fig. 16, to clearly show the movement effect of the mouth mechanism, silicone lips are obtained by the silicone filling mold. Silicone is good in elasticity to simulate human lips. The three driving points on the lips which can open and close are controlled to show eventual effect.

 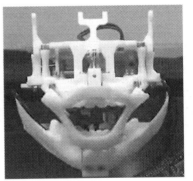

(a) The normal state   (b) The slightly open state

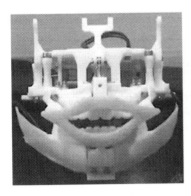

(c) The normal speaking state   (d) The limit state

Fig. 16. Movement of the mouth mechanism

5.4 Six Basic Expressions

Coordinating movements of the above mechanisms, the robot is able to express all six basic facial expressions (Happiness, Anger, Sadness, Surprise, Fear and Disgust), as shown in Fig. 17. From the figure, we can see that the expressions without soft skin are more realistic. One reason is that the soft skin does not fit well with the skull. Another reason is the current soft skin is still not soft enough.

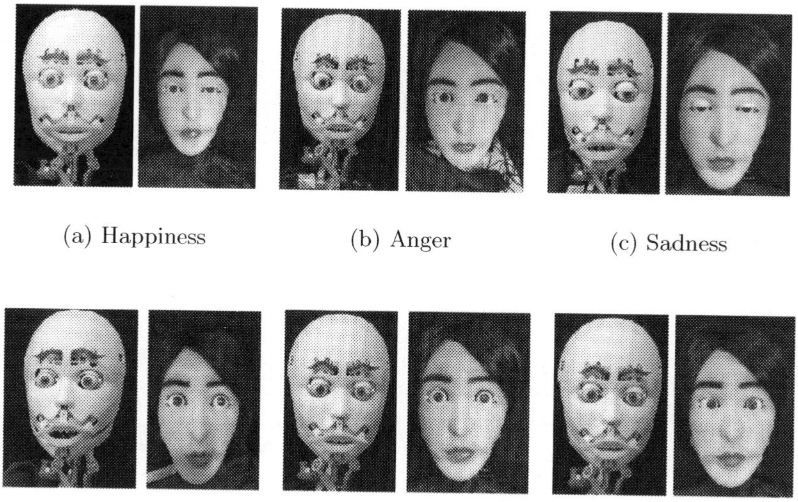

(a) Happiness   (b) Anger   (c) Sadness

(d) Surprise   (e) Fear   (f) Disgust

Fig. 17. Six basic expressions

6   Conclusion and Future Work

Our faces are important windows for us expressing emotions. To implement a humanoid robot face, this paper analyzed the muscle trend of human eyes, eyebrows and lips during the movement from the perspective of bionics and anatomy. The mechanisms and kinematics of these organs were presented. The method of using cables and pulley block not only satisfied the movement range of each part but also agreed with the structure design of bionics.

However, the presented humanoid robot face required further extensive experiments, to explore its capabilities and limitations. In the future work, the production of soft skin for the facial expression robot should be conducted, in terms of material, driving point and corresponding mechanisms, so as to realize micro-expression.

Acknowledgment. This research was funded in part by the National Natural Science Foundation of China (Grant Nos. 51605096, 51705086), the Program of Guangdong Yangfan Introducing Innovative and Entrepreneurial Teams (Grant No. 2017YT05G026), and the Program of Foshan Innovation Team of Science and Technology (Grant No. 2015IT100072).

References

1. Yang, Y., Ke, X., Xin, J., Lu, K.: Development and experiment of facial robot SHFR-III. In: 2015 IEEE International Conference on Mechatronics and Automation (ICMA), Beijing, pp. 1944–1949 (2015). https://doi.org/10.1109/ICMA.2015.7237783
2. Qingmei, M., Weiguo, W., Lin, L.: Research and development of the humanoid head portrait robot "H-Frobot-II" with expression and function of recognizing human expression. In: 2006 IEEE International Conference on Robotics and Biomimetics, Kunming, pp. 1372–1377 (2006)
3. Miwa, H., Okuchi, T., Takanobu, H., Takanishi, A.: Development of a new human-like head robot WE-4. In: IEEE/RSJ International Conference on Intelligent Robots and Systems, Lausanne, Switzerland, vol. 3, pp. 2443–2448 (2002). https://doi.org/10.1109/IRDS.2002.1041634
4. Chestnutt, J., Lau, M., Cheung, G., Kuffner, J., Hodgins, J., Kanade, T.: Footstep planning for the honda ASIMO humanoid. In: Proceedings of the 2005 IEEE International Conference on Robotics and Automation, Barcelona, Spain, pp. 629–634 (2005)
5. Beira, R., et al.: Design of the robot-cub (iCub) head. In: Proceedings 2006 IEEE International Conference on Robotics and Automation, ICRA 2006, Orlando, FL, pp. 94–100 (2006)
6. Mazzei, D., Lazzeri, N., Hanson, D., De Rossi, D.: HEFES: an hybrid engine for facial expressions synthesis to control human-like androids and avatars. In: 2012 4th IEEE RAS EMBS International Conference on Biomedical Robotics and Biomechatronics (BioRob), Rome, pp. 195–200 (2012)
7. Oh, J.H., Hanson, D., Kim, W.S., et al.: Design of android type humanoid robot albert HUBO. In: 2006 IEEE/RSJ International Conference on Intelligent Robots and Systems. IEEE (2006)
8. Kobayashi, H., Ichikawa, Y., Senda, M., et al.: Realization of realistic and rich facial expressions by face robot. In: IEEE Technical Exhibition Based Conference on Robotics, Automation. IEEE (2004)
9. Kaneko, K., Kanehiro, F., Morisawa, M., et al.: Cybernetic human HRP-4C. In: IEEE-RAS International Conference on Humanoid Robots. IEEE (2009)
10. Kobayashi, H., Ichikawa, Y., Tsuji, T., et al.: Development on face robot for real facial expressions. In: IEEE/RSJ International Conference on Intelligent Robots, Systems (2001)
11. Marur, T., Tuna, Y., Demirci, S.: Facial anatomy. Clin. Dermatol. 32(1), 14–23 (2014)
12. Shin, Y., Lim, H.W., Kang, M.H., et al.: Normal range of eye movement and its relationship to age. Acta Ophthalmol. Scand. 94, 1 (2016)
13. Eye muscle. In: Binder, M.D., Hirokawa, N., Windhorst, U. (eds.) Encyclopedia of Neuroscience. Springer, Heidelberg (2009)

LTF Robot: Binocular Robot with Laser-Point Tracking and Focusing Function

Shuang Song[1,2] and Wenzeng Zhang[1(✉)]

[1] Department of Mechanical Engineering, Tsinghua University, Beijing, China
wenzeng@tsinghua.edu.cn
[2] Department of Mechanical Science and Engineering, UIUC, Urbana, IL, USA

Abstract. A traditional binocular vision system needs matching images captured from its left camera and right camera, which leads to huge computational consumption and matching errors. This paper proposes a novel binocular vision method with laser-point tracking and focusing (LTF) function. A binocular robot with the LTF function is developed, called LTF Robot. The LTF Robot is composed of two cameras, a platform with 3 degrees of freedom, a micro controller, and a computer in which there is an application with the LTF function based on LabVIEW. This robot achieves the LTF function. When the position of the laser point changes, the intersection point of light axes of the two cameras will coincide with the laser point in the environment, and the laser point locates in the center of the images. The laser point is from a laser pointer handling by operators or LED lights mounted on targets. The LTF function is useful for many applications, e.g. guiding the robot easily in human-robot interaction or games, active monitoring and video recording.

Keywords: Robot vision · Visual control · Binocular system ·
Laser point tracking · Gazing

1 Introduction

The design aim of the robot with laser-point tracking and focusing (LTF) function is to simplify the image processing and control system of binocular vision, and apply to the humanoid visual system. Binocular vision is a very important branch of the research field of robot vision, or computer vision. A robot with binocular vision system can capture real-time environmental images through its two cameras (left camera and right camera like human eyes setup) and derive spatial coordinates and motion parameters of the target using image processing technology and computer vision analysis.

Over the last several decades, many researchers worked on the robots with binocular vision system and get a lot of breakthroughs in the research field. Yabuta [1] presented a binocular robot vision system based on shape recognition mainly for the image processing of binocular vision. This binocular vision system in the robot succeeds in computing the spatial coordinates of the object by recognizing quadrangles of the object in images captured by both of cameras and then setting up the correspondence of the recognized quadrangles between left and right images.

© Springer Nature Switzerland AG 2019
H. Yu et al. (Eds.): ICIRA 2019, LNAI 11740, pp. 39–48, 2019.
https://doi.org/10.1007/978-3-030-27526-6_4

Fan [2, 3] presented a stereo matching algorithm based on shape for binocular vision. This algorithm can calculate the 3D position of the target object easily by just registering the patterns with respect to the features in the object.

Huang [4] designed a robotic binocular vision system using the principle of image processing and edge detection algorithms. This system can capture the target quickly and accurately.

Shibata [5] discussed a control system of visual tracking of a fast-moving target using a binocular robot, which is visual feedback control only based on images. Through tuning the control parameters as PD feedback gain, visual feedback gain and image capturing frequency, the control of visual tracking was achieved.

Yu [6] designed a real-time-tracking robot based on binocular positioning. This system evaluated the color and morphological property of the target, used the Kalman filter to predict the movement, and used a simplified binocular positioning model to achieve the function of real time tracking of the target.

Kwon [7] designed a head-mounted binocular gaze tracker, which can be a human-robot interfacing device. This tracker can extract the visual attention areas in three dimensional spaces, which is selected by users. Then the robot will know the current interests of human operators. Through continuous recognition of the target, the robot can move to the target.

Wang [8] presented a learning-based strategy for action planning in robot tele-control. The remote robot was equipped with a binocular vision system, and its motion parameters can be pre-scheduled by a visual robot at the control terminal.

Zamora-Esquivel [9] presented an analysis of the kinematics and differential kinematics of a binocular head, which used conformal geometric algebra framework. It can help us to deal with mechanical problems and computer vision problems.

Coombs [10] examined the problem of tracking a moving target when the robot was also moving and presented a solution to this problem. The gaze of the robot was implemented with the pursuit system and vergence system, the former was driven by the centroid of intensity in the windowed output of a filter, the latter used a global disparity measure, which was applied to the same window to keep the foveated object at zero disparity.

Yang [11] introduced the working principle and constitutes of surgical navigation robot, which was based on binocular stereovision. They utilized this robot to solve the problem about locating the distal interlocking hole and the shortcoming of manual operation. This system made minimally invasive surgery come true.

Li [12] proposed a method to measure the distance and to track target, which was based on the binocular parallax between colors of two images. This algorithm can help with detecting and locating the target commendably.

Traditional binocular robot used the algorithms for matching based on multiply image features, which can be complex in computation and control, slow to process, and unstable in real-time applications.

Furthermore, it needs high resolution cameras and accurate parameters and it is also difficult to do some calibration experiments to get the accurate parameters, these problems make binocular robot very expensive and very difficult to use in many applications.

In order to overcome these problems of traditional binocular visions, this paper proposes a novel robotic feedback control system with binocular vision, which can be called laser-point tracking and focusing (LTF) method.

The LTF method works as follows.

In the preparatory phase, the operator captures the pictures of one laser point or a kind of assembly of several laser points, then gets the pattern of the laser point and saves this pattern into data base. When the LTF robot begins to work, the operator or active part producing laser pointer projects the combined laser point into the collective visual field of two cameras, then two cameras will capture the motion parameters according to the position of the laser point in the captured image, through a PID control process, the cameras will adjust angles until the laser point moving to reach the center of the real-time captured image, and the robot achieves the function of laser-point tracking and focusing.

2   Design of the LTF Robot

The two same cameras is mounted on the end of the robot. The robot has three kinds of movements, including shaking head, nodding and focusing. The robot has five joints. Two of the joints are associated with vertical movements could be coupled in the control system according to similar movements of a human head. The control system uses Arduino microcontroller to control. The software is built on LabVIEW platform.

The operator uses a laser pointer to project the small and clear laser spot to the object to be tested. The robot captures the image containing the laser point through its two cameras, and the 3-DOF body mechanism of the robot automatically moves accordingly to make the laser point locate at the center of both left and right captured images.

Several steps to move quickly to the center of the left and right binocular images, that is, the binocular line of sight is focused on the marker point to be tested (gazing target), and then the three-dimensional coordinates of the marker point under the robot base coordinate system are calculated in combination with the visual and kinematics understanding. Coordinate information can be used for robot control for better inter-activity and intelligence.

2.1   Structure Design of the LTF Robot

LTF Robot is shown in Fig. 1. The LTF robot has 5 rotary joints, 2 cameras. The structure of LTF robot is similar to human head. It has a neck, which can rotate in the horizontal plane. It has two vertical rotary joints, which can rotate in the vertical plane. It has two eyes, which can rotate in the horizontal plane separately. These joints are independent, which can help the robot to achieve the function of target tracking.

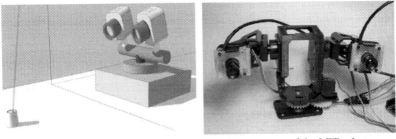

(a) Design of the LFT robot.   (b) Prototype of the LFT robot.

Fig. 1. Structure design and prototype of the LTF robot.

The proposed robot includes laser beam, horizontal rotary joint, robot head, right camera along with right horizontal rotary joint, right vertical rotary joint, left vertical rotary joint, and left camera along with left horizontal rotary joint.

2.2   Control System Design of the LTF Robot

Figure 2 describes the control system architecture of the LTF Robot. It can be divided to two phases: (1) The preparatory phase and working phase. In the preparatory phase, the operatory should get the pattern of the laser point and register it to the data base of the robot.

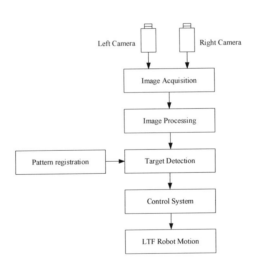

Fig. 2. The system workflow in the LTF robot.

In the working phase, the operator projects the laser point into the visual field of two cameras, the cameras will capture images under the control of the program of LabVIEW. Then the LabVIEW program will process images based on the color and shape to get the 2D coordinate of laser point on the image, which will be transmitted to control system to control the motion of the robot. The main technical functions of the proposed method are laser point detection and motor control. They will be explained in detail in the following sections.

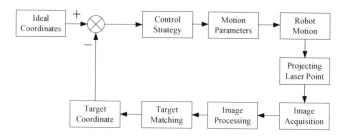

Fig. 3. Control strategy of the LTF robot.

The basic control principle of the LTF method (shown in Fig. 3) is that the binocular robot collects two images with different positions of the laser spot from two cameras. The coordinate system is set in the robot link and camera using the matrix operation method in robot kinematics. The relationship between the cameras and the world coordinate system can be obtained by establishing a coordinate system between the links and an image coordinate system. Through the transformation relationship between the two cameras and the world coordinate system and the transformation relationship between the two cameras, the position of the target point (laser spot) in the world coordinate system can be finally obtained.

3 Kinematics Analysis of the LTF Robot

Figure 4 is the sketch map of coordinate system of the LTF robot.

The 2D coordinates of the laser point on the image will be transmitted to control system after image processing. Traditional method is calculating the 3D coordinates of the laser point based on the 2D coordinates and the parameters of two cameras. But it needs to calibrate the parameters of cameras, which may be inconvenient for changing cameras and influenced by the environment.

In this paper, the control system is based on 2D coordinates, the origin of 2D coordinate system is on the upper left of the image, the horizontal right direction is the positive direction of the X axis, and the vertical downward direction is the positive direction of the Y axis. The detailed algorithm can be written as follows:

$$\theta_1 = k_1 \frac{x_L + x_R - L}{2} \tag{1}$$

$$\theta_2 = k_2 \frac{y_L + y_R - H}{2} \tag{2}$$

$$\theta_3 = k_3(x_L - \frac{L}{2})\tag{3}$$

In the equations above, x_L, x_R - x axis of the laser point on the left, right images;
y_L, y_R - y axis of the laser point on the left, right images;
k_1, k_2, k_3 - proportional coefficient;
L - the horizontal length of the image;
H - the vertical height of the image.

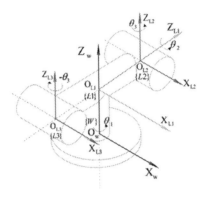

Fig. 4. The coordinate systems of the LTF robot.

As for inverse kinematics of the LTF robot, θ_1, θ_2 and θ_3 are known. Using the coordinate values of the above-mentioned target points in the world coordinate system, three rotation angles $\Delta\theta_1$, $\Delta\theta_2$, $\Delta\theta_3$ can be obtained by geometric operation.

According to the Fig. 5, one can get:

$$O_{L1}A = BJ = \sqrt{{}^wX_j^2 + {}^wY_j^2}\tag{4}$$

$$O_{L1}J = \sqrt{(d_1 - {}^wZ_j)^2 + {}^wX_j^2 + {}^wY_j^2}\tag{5}$$

$$\begin{cases} \theta_{1t} = \arctan({}^WY_j/{}^WX_j) \\ \theta_{2t} = \arctan((d_1 - {}^WZ_j)/\sqrt{({}^WX_j^2 + {}^WY_j^2)}) \\ \theta_{3t} = -\arctan(d_2/\sqrt{((d_1 - {}^WZ_j)^2 + {}^WX_j^2 + {}^WY_j^2)}) \end{cases}\tag{6}$$

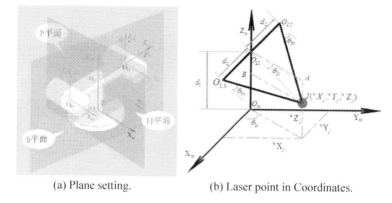

(a) Plane setting.   (b) Laser point in Coordinates.

Fig. 5. Plane setting and laser point position in coordinates.

Then one can obtain:

$$\begin{cases} \Delta\theta_{1t} = \theta_{1t} - \theta_1 \\ \Delta\theta_{2t} = \theta_{2t} - \theta_2 \\ \Delta\theta_{3t} = \theta_{3t} - \theta_3 \end{cases} \tag{7}$$

The above result is input into the control program to control the binocular robot to move to achieve the effect of gazing at the target point.

4   Experiments of the LTF Robot

Our experimental setup is shown in Fig. 6. Two cameras are used as the vision hardware, the cameras connect to the PC via an Arduino UNO controller. A laser pointer is used as the laser point source. The distance between the laser point and the cameras is about 0.2–1.5 m, which are the minimum and maximum distances. The software platform is LabVIEW (Fig. 7).

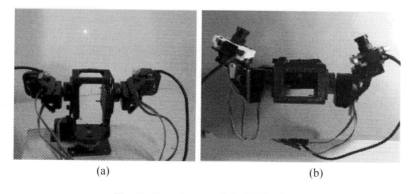

(a)   (b)

Fig. 6. Experiments of the LTF robot.

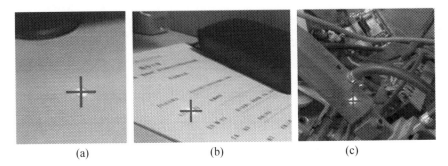

(a)   (b)   (c)

Fig. 7. The results of image processing of the laser points.

To confirm the tracking ability of the LTF robot, the experiments were examined with using our binocular robot. In the experiments, an operator moved the laser point from one side to another side in front of the LTF robot. The images were captured by the left and right cameras 5 frames per second. The size of the image was 640×480 pixels. The Robot sets up a correct correspondence between the images and the motion parameters, and achieved the function of target tracking very well, and had few mistakes. The experimental results are shown in Figs. 8 and 9.

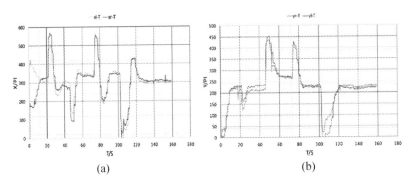

(a)   (b)

Fig. 8. The results of laser-point tracking: changing of the x position.

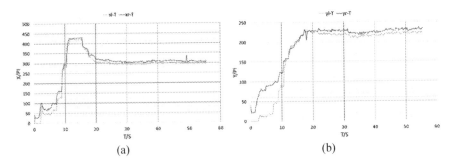

(a)   (b)

Fig. 9. The results of laser-point tracking: changing of the y position.

As can be seen from the Figs. 8 and 9, when the laser point moved, the binocular robot moved according to the visual signal, after several seconds, the coordinates of the laser point became stable gradually, which shown that the binocular robot achieved the function of target tracking.

The experimental results show that the LTF Robot can track target with structured laser point or LED light point quickly and accurately. The LTF method is effective to control the motion of the binocular robot, which can be widely used in many kinds of applications.

5   Conclusion

A laser point tracking and focusing (LTF) method is proposed to decrease computation between two cameras in binocular system. A binocular robot (the LTF Robot) with LTF function is developed. The image processing and control method of the LTF Robot are described in detail. Unlike the traditional binocular robot, the image processing is simplified by adopting laser point as the target. For the LTF Robot, it does not need to calibrate the parameters of cameras, which will be more convenient to change cameras and allow the lower installation precision. Because of its convenience, the LTF Robot will be easier to be accepted by most people, and it can be widely used in many kinds of automatic system that needs target tracking.

Acknowledgements. This Research was supported by National Natural Science Foundation of China (No. 51575302), Beijing Natural Science Foundation (No. J170005) and National Key R&D Program of China (No. 2017YFE0113200).

References

1. Yabuta, Y., Mizumoto, H.: Binocular robot vision system with shape recognition. In: SICE-ICASE International Joint Conference, Busan, South Korea, 18–21 October, pp. 5002–5005 (2006)
2. Fan, X., Wang, X., Xiao, Y.: A shape-based stereo matching algorithm for binocular vision. In: IEEE Transaction on Security, Pattern Analysis, and Cybernetic (SPAC), Wuhan, China, 18–19 October, pp. 70–74 (2014)
3. Fan, X., Wang, X., Xiao, Y.: An automatic robot unstacking system based on binocular stereo vision. In: IEEE Conference on Security, Pattern Analysis, and Cybernetic (SPAC), Wuhan, China, 18–19 October, pp. 86–89 (2014)
4. Huang, G.-S.: 3D coordinate identification of object using binocular vision system for mobile robot. In: IEEE International Automatic Control Conference (CACS), Nantou, Taiwan, pp. 91–96 (2013)
5. Shibata, M., Eto, H., Ito, M.: Image-based visual tracking to fast moving target for active binocular robot. In: IEEE 36th Annual Conference on IEEE Industrial Electronics Society (IECON), Glendale, AZ, USA, 7–10 November, pp. 2727–2732 (2010)
6. Yu, K., Bo-Wen, L.: Design of a real-time tracking robot based on simplified binocular position model. International Conference on Automatic Control and Artificial Intelligence (ACAI), Xiamen, China, 3–5 March, pp. 811–816 (2012)

7. Kwon, S.H., Kim, M.Y.: Head-mounted binocular gaze tracker as a human-robot interfacing device. In: IEEE International Conference on Robot and Human Interactive Communication (RO-MAN), Gyeongju, Korea, 26–29 August, pp. 374–375 (2013)
8. Wang, C., Chen, L., Zhang, C., et al.: Learning-based action planning for real-time robot telecontrol with binocular vision in enhanced reality environment. In: 2009 IEEE International Conference on Robotics and Biomimetics (ROBIO), Guilin, China, pp. 2041–2046 (2009)
9. Zamora-Esquivel, J., Bayro-Corrochano, E.: Kinematics and differential kinematics of binocular robot heads. In: IEEE International Conference on Robotics and Automation (ICRA), Orlando, Florida, USA, 15–19 May, pp. 4130–4135 (2006)
10. Coombs, D., Brown, C.: Real-time smooth pursuit tracking for a moving binocular robot. In: IEEE Computer Society Conference on Computer Vision and Pattern Recognition, Champaign, IL, USA, 15–18 June, pp. 23–28 (1992)
11. Yang, J., Qian, J.: Surgical navigation robot based on binocular stereovision. In: IEEE International Conference on Mechatronics and Automation, Luoyang, China, 25–28 June, pp. 2378–2382 (2006)
12. Li, B., Xie, W.: Target tracking and measuring based on binocular vision. In: IEEE International Conference on Information Science and Technology, Yangzhou, China, 23–25 March, pp. 1393–1396 (2013)

Human Biomechanics and Human-Centered Robotics

New Rigid-Soft Coupling Structure and Its Stiffness Adjusting Device

Che Liu, Hengyang Mu, Diansheng Chen[(✉)], and Min Wang

Beihang University, Beijing, China
chends@163.com

Abstract. As the core component of the robot, the dexterous hand directly determines the level of robotic dexterity. Rigid dexterous hands and soft dexterous hands have their own advantages and disadvantages, and the new rigid-soft coupling structure needs to be studied. In this paper, a new rigid-soft coupling structure is proposed, and a corresponding stiffness adjustment device is designed according to the rigid-soft coupling structure to realize the adjustment of the rigid coupling structure stiffness. According to the rigid-soft coupling structure designed in this paper, a prototype of a rigid-soft coupling dexterous hand principle was successfully fabricated, and the performance and function verification of the dexterous hand was completed through the experimental platform. The performance and reliability of the new rigid-soft coupling structure were verified.

Keywords: Dexterous hand · Rigid coupling structure · Stiffness adjustment device

1 Introduction

As early as the middle of the last century, people developed rigid dexterous hands (hereinafter referred to as rigid hands) for repetitive and heavy work. The biggest differences between rigid hands and human hands are flexibility and durability. The biggest advantage of rigid hands is that they can perform the same action for a long time and repeatedly when its mechanical structure is normal. But the shortcomings are more obvious, such as large size, high cost, single working mode, poor interactivity and high control precision requirements. And it is easy to cause damage to the item during the gripping process of the surface which is fragile or the material is very brittle.

In recent years, the soft dexterous hands which are designed and manufactured by soft materials have attracted the attention of many research institutions. They essentially solve the problems of rigid hands such as poor interaction with human, poor adaptability of complex environment, inflexibility, etc. They also provide new ideas and directions for the development of science and technology. As the research results

This research was supported by the Beijing Municipal Science and Technology Project (Z181100003118005).

H. Yu et al. (Eds.): ICIRA 2019, LNAI 11740, pp. 51–63, 2019.
https://doi.org/10.1007/978-3-030-27526-6_5

are gradually enriched, the shortcomings of the soft hands grasping force are slowly revealed. After many soft dexterous hands have been developed, they have found that their gripping force is no more than 1.0 kg [1, 2].

To solve the above problems, people think of some examples of soft structures with variable stiffness in nature: the octopus's arms, the elephant's nose, the human tongue, and the human lips can effectively interact with the environment by adjusting the stiffness. These are rigid-soft coupling structures, which also confirm the inevitability of the development of rigid-soft coupling structures.

The rigid-soft coupling structure has been applied in the direction of dexterous hands and has developed very rapidly in recent years. Its working principle is based on variable stiffness materials or structures. The body of the dexterous hand is generally designed as a soft body, and the rigidity of the structure is strengthened after approaching and surrounding the object.

The rigid-soft coupling structure can be divided into the following four categories according to its variable stiffness principle: (1) Material jamming [3, 4], which is a system consisting of an outer membrane and internal filling. By turning the interior into a vacuum, the membrane creates a depression on the filler material, reducing the flowable space of the internal filler, thereby increasing the density and stiffness of the system. Typical examples are particle jamming and layer jamming. (2) Low melting point materials [5, 6], which are readily meltable hard materials having a low melting point. When heat is input to the material, the material can be rapidly deformed after melting, that is, the rigidity becomes smaller. Typical examples are low melting point alloys and low melting point polymers. (3) Electro and magnetorheological materials [7, 8] are materials in which electric particles or magnetic particles are embedded. When subjected to an external electric or magnetic field, an interaction chain is formed between the particles, and the resistance to deformation is increased to change the stiffness. Typical examples are elastic electrorheological materials, fluid point active materials, elastic magnetorheological materials, etc. (4) Shape memory material [9, 10] is a material capable of restoring a predetermined geometric shape by inducing internal phase transformation after plastic deformation of the material. On the basis of this shape memory effect, there are different mechanical properties of two or more stable stages. Typical examples are shape memory alloys, shape memory polymers, etc.

2 Proposal of a New Rigid-Soft Coupling Structure

This paper proposes a new variable stiffness structure based on chain particle blockage. The basic principle of the structure is shown in Fig. 1. Dozens of particles are connected in series to form a chain-like particle structure in which one line passes through the hole of each particle. The proximal end of the chain-like particle structure is bound by the fixture, while the distal end is free. In the natural state, due to the influence of gravity, the chain-like particle structure will sag and exhibit a low stiffness state, as shown in Fig. 1(a). However, when an external tensile force is applied to the line of the chain-like particle structure, the chain-like particle structure "blocks" and becomes a high-stiffness state by compressing the particles together. In this state, the self-gravity of the chain-like particle structure has no significant effect on its shape, as shown in Fig. 1(b).

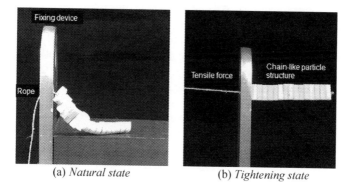

(a) *Natural state*   (b) *Tightening state*

Fig. 1. Working principle of chain-like particle structure

Furthermore, it has been observed that, within a certain range, the greater the force applied to the rigid-soft coupling structure line, the higher the stiffness that can be achieved. That is, in addition to resisting the gravity of its own sagging, it can carry more external forces. Many studies have shown that the cross-sectional shape, size and material of the particles have an effect on the stiffness properties. Based on the laboratory's existing experimental conditions, the material of the chain-like particles is selected from 3D printed PLA materials (PLA PolyPlus). The cross-sectional shape of the chain-like particle structure will be studied in the following.

3   Structural Interface Design Analysis

According to research by Jiang A. et al., commercially available spherical, cylindrical and cuboid particles can be applied to vacuum particle blocking structures. However, in the chain-like structure, spherical particles will be excluded first. It has been found experimentally that the chain-like particle structure formed by spherical particles (such as a pearl necklace) cannot overcome its own gravity without sagging, no matter how much tensile force is applied, that is, the effect of Fig. 1(b) cannot be achieved. This indicates that the variable stiffness range is small and does not meet the design requirements. According to the simple analysis, it can be found that the spherical particles are in point contact when they are in contact with each other, and the point contact is easily changed to the other two points under the driving of the external force, so the stability is poor. According to this, it can be known that the change in the stiffness of the inter-particle line contact is higher than the change in the stiffness caused by the point contact, and the change in the stiffness caused by the surface contact is higher than the change in the stiffness caused by the line contact. Therefore, in the process of designing particles, the shape of the particles has at least two parallel surfaces, which ensures that the chain-like particles can achieve surface contact, so the cuboids and cylinders are thought of as particles.

The maximum bending stiffness analysis is performed on the particles composed of the cuboid and the cylinder respectively. When a vertical downward force is applied to the distal end of the chain-like particle of Fig. 1(b), it is assumed that the square particles are ideally contacted, that is, there is no deflection angle between the two particles. At this time, the deflection of the distal end of the chain-like particles can be applied to the Timoshenko beam theory to estimate the bending stiffness of the chain-like particle structure composed of the same particles.

$$k = \frac{F}{\omega} = \frac{3EI}{L^3} \tag{1}$$

In this formula, F is the perpendicular force applied to the distal end of the beam, ω is the deflection generated by force, E is the modulus of elasticity, I is the moment of inertia and L is the length of the beam. The particle material is the same, so the elastic modulus of the chain-like particle structure is the same. Therefore, for a chain-like particle structure with the same length, it can be inferred that the bending stiffness is completely dependent on the moment of inertia. It can be known from the knowledge of material mechanics that the moment of inertia of the rectangular cross section of the cuboid or the circular cross section of the cylinder can be:

$$I_r = \frac{bh^3}{12}$$
$$I_c = \frac{\pi D^4}{64} \tag{2}$$

In this formula, b is the length of the rectangle, h is the width of the rectangle, D is the diameter of the circle. If you control the area of the cross section of the two particles is the same, and according to the finger cross-sectional size of the human hand $b > h$, you can get $I_r < I_c$. Applied to the human hand, the variable stiffness efficiency of the circular section is higher than that of the rectangular section. Considering that the chain particles will rotate a certain angle around the threading direction, and the circular shape is exactly the same as the state of no rotation, no matter how it rotates around the center of the circle. Then the variable stiffness efficiency of the moment of inertia of the rectangular cross section (a face where each particle completely overlaps the end projection) is less than the circular cross section.

4   Structural Improvement

According to the above theoretical analysis, this paper attempts a new rigid-soft coupling driver based on the combination of fiber-reinforced driver and chain-like particle structure. Although the variable stiffness efficiency of rectangular cross section chain-like particles is slightly smaller than that of circular cross section chain-like particles, since the bottom surface of the internal software driver is flat, it is less likely that the chain-like particles are designed to be circular, so we try to use the rectangle first.

The rigid-soft coupling driver consists of dozens of identical rectangular particles and a software driver. As shown in Fig. 2, the sectional dimension of the chain-like particles is 12×8 mm^2, and the height of the particles is 4 mm. In addition, the particles in the chain-like structure are arranged with a small gap between each two particles to ensure that the chain-like particle structure and the rigid-soft coupling driver can be easily bent with low rigidity in the soft state and quickly return to the soft state after changing the stiffness.

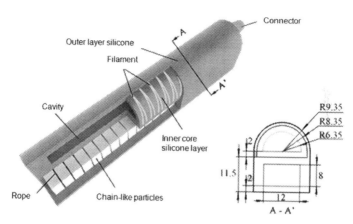

Fig. 2. Rigid-soft coupling driver configuration based on chain-like particle structure

However, it is not difficult to find through Fig. 1 that the chain-like particles will have a tendency to move to the state shown in Fig. 1(b) regardless of the state in which the tensile force is applied to the chain-like particles. If the force applied to the chain-like particle structure is sufficiently large, the chain-like particles will remain in the state of Fig. 1(b), which is also the greatest stiffness state.

According to the design structure, the force analysis of the process of grabbing the item is shown in Fig. 3. Case (a) is that no force is applied to the line of the rigid-soft coupling structure. If you want to make the rigid-soft coupling driver just touch the object and there is no squeeze between them, that is, when the interaction force between them is 0 N, it is necessary to charge the air pressure of M kPa to the inside of the rigid-soft coupling driver. Case (b) is the application of force F_T to the rope of the soft-rigid coupling structure. In this state, if the rigid-soft coupling driver and the object are just in contact and the contact force is 0 N, the air pressure charged to the inside of the rigid-soft coupling driver must be greater than M kPa (this assumes M + m kPa and m > 0). The reason is very simple. When the chain-like particles are subjected to tensile force, the movement tendency of the chain-like particles is changed toward a straight state. As shown in the Fig. 3(b), it will generate an upward force F to the rigid-soft coupling driver. In this way, a rigid-soft coupling driver that wants to touch an object must apply a higher air pressure to resist the force generated by the chain-like particles. As shown in case (c), when no force is applied to the rope of the rigid-soft coupling structure and the air pressure of M + m kPa is charged to the inside of the driver, it can be concluded that the contact force between the driver and the object must be greater than 0 N.

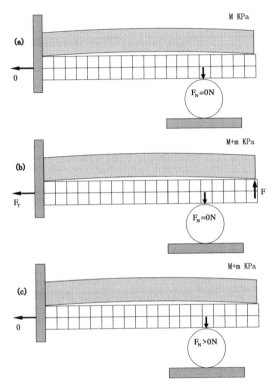

Fig. 3. Three cases of force analysis

In summary, the chain particles do have variable stiffness characteristics. However, the state of the variable stiffness is in a state where the chain-like particles are stretched, so that the application in the rigid-soft coupling driver is not suitable, so the structure needs to be improved.

In order to further improve the practicality of the chain-like particle structure, the fishbone structure shown in Fig. 4 is designed in combination with the high efficiency variable stiffness characteristics of circular cross section. The cross section of the fishbone structure approximates the shape of the human hand and is as close as possible to the circle. The middle of the fishbone structure is empty, placing the pneumatic driver inside the fishbone structure. In order to prevent the fishbone structure from covering the software driver unevenness and affecting the performance of the rigid-soft coupling driver, the chain-like particle structure near the bottom of the pneumatic driver is connected. At this time, each ring of the fishbone structure can be equivalent to one particle, and the threading hole of the fishbone structure is at the bottom. The biggest difference between the fishbone structure and the chain-like particle structure is that the maximum variable stiffness state of the fishbone structure is in a state in which the fishbone structure is completely bent. This state is advantageous for the rigid-soft coupling imitation hand to grasp the object, so the fishbone structure does not have the chain-like particle structure problems mentioned in Fig. 3.

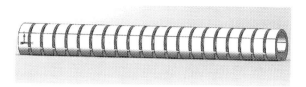

Fig. 4. Fish bone structure modeling

There is a fish bone structure design details should be noted. Figure 5 shows the bottom groove of the fishbone structure, and the picture on the right is a magnified view of the red circle on the left.

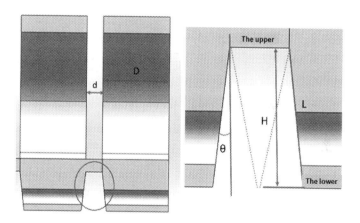

Fig. 5. Fishbone structure design detail

Suppose the number of fish bones is N, the width of the fish bone is D, the gap between the fish bones is d, the height of the bottom groove is H, the inclination angle in the groove is θ, and there is no inclination angle on the outer side of the fishbone ring at both ends. So the total length of the upper part of the groove is $ND + (N-1)d$, and the total length of the lower part is $ND + (N-1)d-2(N-1)H\tan\theta$. When the internal driver of the fishbone structure is inflated and bent, the maximum bending angle is that the end of the driver is in contact with the head of the driver. At this time, the rigid-soft coupling driver is bent into a circular shape (the bending angle is 180°), and when the upper part is closed into a circular shape, the length of the lower closing is just the maximum $ND + (N-1)d-2\pi H$. When the two are closed in a perfect circle, that is, when the upper part is closed, the lower part is just closed or not closed, so that the bending of the drive is not affected, so the range of the inclination angle is:

$$\theta > \arctan \frac{\pi}{N-1} \tag{3}$$

If the angle of θ is less than the theoretical value, the lower part first contacts together before the driver is fully bent, and the fishbone structure affects the motion of the driver and reduces the output force of the driver. When the angle of θ is more than the theoretical value, the variable stiffness strength of the fishbone has not reached the maximum when fully bent.

Fish bone structure contrast chain-like particle structure has the following advantages: (1) Realized the application in the rigid-soft coupling imitation hand. (2) The fishbone structure itself is a 3D printing one-shot molding (NinjaFlexTM), which does not require stringing individual particles, and the process flow is simplified. (3) The fishbone structure itself replaces the chain-like particle structure, non-deformation layer structure, clamping device and the fiber filament that restricts the soft body pneumatic driver, greatly reducing the size and weight of the driver. The weight of a single rigid-soft coupling driver has dropped from 36.05 g to 18.98 g, and the weight has dropped by 47.35%. (4) The fishbone structure has good function scalability, it can increase the degree of freedom on the basis of small changes in its structure. For example, the abduction and inward movement that mimics the thumb of a human hand can be achieved by opening a row of small holes on each side of the fishbone.

5   Security Monitoring Information Management System

The new rigid-soft coupling structure proposed in this paper needs to provide tension to the rope to further achieve the change of stiffness. In the first generation prototype, we used a ratchet as a manual variable stiffness device. In the development of the second generation prototype, two new variable stiffness structures are proposed, one is the tubular variable stiffness device, and the other is the spherical variable stiffness device.

5.1   Ratchet Manual Variable Stiffness Device

The ratchet is a gear with a rigid toothed surface or friction surface on the outer or inner edge. The stepping motion is performed by the pawl pushing mechanism, and the meshing motion is characterized in that the ratchet can only rotate in one direction and cannot be reversed. According to the ratchet's own motion characteristics, we wrap the rope around the shaft of the ratchet. When the ratchet rotates in one direction, the rope is tightened and locked in the opposite direction to achieve the purpose of pulling the rope and providing tension. Through the investigation of the ratchet structure device on the market, the ratchet tap wrench is found. The device is a two-way ratchet that can rotate and lock in both directions, which not only satisfies the function of pulling down and not slack in the working state, but also satisfies the purpose of free relaxation in the non-working state.

However, the ratchet manual variable stiffness device has three disadvantages: The first disadvantage is that the device is bulky. Each rigid-soft coupling imitation hand prototype can only be equipped with one ratchet tap wrench. The ropes of the rigid-soft coupling structure of the five rigid-soft coupling drivers need to be wound around the shaft of one ratchet. When the ratchet rotates, the five ropes move at the same length at the same time. However, in practical applications, the five ropes have different stretching requirements, that is, different lengths of motion are required. So the ratchet device cannot provide different stretching requirements; The second disadvantage is that the ratchet structure provides a stepping structure. For a single rigid-soft coupling driver, the pull of the rope is not in the form of a step function, but in the form of a smooth curve. Therefore, the ratchet device cannot steplessly adjust the tension of the rigid-soft coupling structure rope; The third disadvantage is that the ratchet structure needs to manually adjust its rotation every time it is working, which cannot meet the requirements of electronically controlled aerodynamic stiffness.

Based on the above problems, we put forward four requirements for the variable stiffness device of the second generation prototype: (1) Each variable stiffness device drives a rigid-soft coupling structure. (2) Can provide stepless adjustment force. (3) Aerodynamic variable stiffness can be achieved by electronic control. (4) The volume is as small as possible. In response to the above four requirements, two kinds of conjectures are proposed, and their feasibility and practicability are verified in theory.

5.2   Tubular Pneumatic Variable Stiffness Device

The tubular variable stiffness device is based on the working principle of the syringe. The syringe is composed of a nipple, an empty tube, a piston and a piston rod. When the syringe is working, the piston rod is first pushed by the external force, and the internal pressure of the empty tube is increased, but the empty tube is maintained at the same pressure as the external atmospheric pressure, so the internal liquid or gas is forced to be discharged from the nipple.

Inspired by the working principle of the syringe, we design a structure shown in Fig. 6.

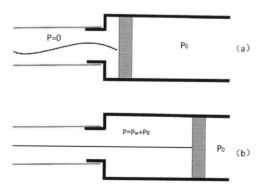

Fig. 6. Tubular variable stiffness device working principle

The normal state of the tubular variable stiffness device is the state shown in Fig. 6(a), and the rope of the rigid-soft coupling structure is in a relaxed state. When the internal pressure of the tubular variable stiffness device is charged at $P_w + P_0$, the piston of the tubular variable stiffness device moves toward the atmosphere side, and the rope of the variable stiffness device is pulled to tighten and generate a tensile force. The ideal structure is to fix the rope to the piston, and the air pipe is connected to the nipple. When the inside of the tubular variable stiffness device is inflated, the relationship between the traction force F and the inflation pressure $P_w + P_0$ is:

$$F = P_W S \qquad (4)$$

S is the cross-sectional area of the piston. If the airtightness is intact and you want to achieve 3 N traction through the input pressure of 180 kPa, a cross section of about 16.6 mm^2 is required. Considering that the stroke is at least 10 mm, the volume of the single tubular variable stiffness device is around 170 mm^3. However, the biggest problem about tubular variable stiffness devices is the tightness. Because the position of the nipple must be sealed and the rope of the rigid-soft coupling structure should be pierced in it. So it is very difficult to design.

5.3   Spherical Pneumatic Variable Stiffness Device

The ball type variable stiffness device is a structure proposed according to experiment which is found that the software structure expands in various directions when inflated. If the software structure is made into a spherical shape, it expands into a larger spherical shape when inflated, and the circumference of each cross section changes. Therefore, the rope can be pulled by the change of the maximum cross-sectional circumference difference caused by the expansion of the ball.

Based on the size of the pressure sealing element and the minimum wall thickness used in this paper, we designed the silica gel structure as shown in Fig. 7. The ball has a diameter of 16 mm and a minimum volume of about 200 mm^3. The rope is wound around a winding groove of the silicone ball, and one end is connected to the rigid-soft coupling structure, and one end is fixed. When the silicone ball is not inflated, the rope wound around the ball will not receive any force. When the silicone ball is inflated, the circumference of the circular section at the position of the entanglement becomes larger. The rope is slowly straightened and generates a pulling force. According to the size design and working principle of the silica gel, the silica gel ball structure is fabricated. The size and volume of the wound groove after the expansion of the silica gel ball were measured and calculated to obtain the data as shown in Table 1.

The maximum circular cross section of the silicone ball has a circumference difference of 10.02 mm, which satisfies the stroke demand. At this time, the volume is about 300 mm^3.

Since the structure made of the soft material is difficult to theoretically analyze, we actually test the relationship between air pressure and tension.

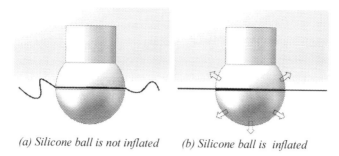

(a) Silicone ball is not inflated   *(b) Silicone ball is inflated*

Fig. 7. Spherical variable stiffness device working principle

Table 1. Silicone ball inflation measurement data

Air pressure (kPa)	Ball diameter (mm)	Rope length (mm)	Volume (mm^3)
0	19.86	62.36	197.46
60	20.24	63.55	207.03
120	20.94	65.75	225.27
180	23.02	72.38	283.98

(1) Experiment platform

We built the experimental platform shown in Fig. 8, where 1 is the SMC digital electronic pressure regulator, 2 is the Adelburg digital electronic push-pull force meter, which can read the pull force value in real time on the electronic display and display the pressure value in the silicone ball in real time. 3 is a 16 mm diameter silica gel ball, 4 is a strong magnet (The adsorption force between the magnet and the iron table is much larger than the tension generated when the silica ball expands, so it is assumed here that the magnet has no relative displacement with the table during the experiment).

Fig. 8. Silicone ball tensile test platform

(2) Experimental data

During the experiment, the silicone ball was inflated at a rate of 10 kPa/time by adjusting the pressure regulating valve. Repeat three times to obtain the experimental data shown in Table 2 below.

Table 2. Inflatable silicone ball force measurement data

Air pressure (kPa)	First pull (N)	Second pull (N)	Third pull (N)
60	0.14	0.14	0.17
70	0.2	0.2	0.23
80	0.26	0.3	0.33
90	0.37	0.36	0.4
100	0.5	0.45	0.6
110	0.52	0.63	0.75
120	0.81	0.82	0.97
130	1.19	1.14	1.27
140	1.62	1.62	1.64
150	2	2.16	2.03
160	2.42	2.5	2.36
170	2.86	2.9	2.8
180	3.11	3.2	3.01

It can be seen from the experimental data that the inflation of the silicone ball to 180 kPa can also provide a tensile force of 3 N, which is similar to the mechanical properties of the tubular pneumatic variable stiffness device. However, from the trend point of view, the growth rate of the output force of the spherical variable stiffness device changes, and the larger the inflatable pressure, the greater the growth rate. However, the growth rate of the output force of the tubular variable stiffness device is constant, so under a large air pressure, the spherical variable stiffness device can output more force than the tubular variable stiffness device.

According to the advantages and disadvantages of the two structures, although the tubular structure is small in size and the output force is linear, the shortcoming of the sealing makes the solution difficult to achieve. Therefore, the silicone ball is selected as the pneumatic variable stiffness device in this paper.

6   Conclusion

This paper analyzes existing rigid dexterous hand and soft dexterous hand. The rigid dexterous hand has a large grip force and precise control, but its safety is low and expensive. Soft dexterous hand is soft and safe, but lacks grip force. Therefore, this paper proposes a new type of rigid-soft coupling structure and designs its corresponding stiffness adjustment device to create a rigid-soft coupling dexterous hand with high flexibility, high safety, high grip force and low price to meet dexterous work requirements.

References

1. Deimel, R., Brock, O.: A novel type of compliant and under actuated robotic hand for dexterous grasping. Int. J. Robot. Res. **35**(1–3), 161–185 (2016)
2. Connolly, F., Polygerinos, P., Walsh, C.J., et al.: Mechanical programming of soft actuators by varying fiber angle[J]. Soft Robot. **2**(1), 26–32 (2015)
3. Hao, Y., Gong, Z., Xie, Z., et al.: Universal soft pneumatic robotic gripper with variable effective length. In: 35th Chinese Control Conference, pp. 6109–6114. IEEE, Piscataway (2016)
4. Brown, E., Rodenberg, N., Amend, J., et al.: Universal robotic gripper based on the jamming of granular material. Proc. Natl. Acad. Sci. **107**(44), 18809–18814 (2010)
5. Nakai, H., Kuniyoshi, Y., Inaba, M., et al.: Intelligent Robots and Systems, pp. 2025–2030. IEEE, Piscataway (2002)
6. Araromi, O.A., Gavrilovich, I., Shintake, J., et al.: Electroactive polymers as an enabling materials technology. IEEE/ASME Trans. Mechatron. **20**, 438 (2015)
7. Pettersson, A., Davis, S., Gray, J.O., et al.: Food Eng. **98**, 332 (2010)
8. Firouzeh, A., Paik, J.: Soft pneumatic actuator with adjustable stiffness layers for multi-DoF actuation. IEEE/ASME Trans. Mechatron. IEEE **22**, 2165 (2017)
9. Wang, W., Ahn, S.H.: Non-intrusive load monitoring system for anomaly detection based on energy disaggregation by cascading semi-supervised learning and deep learning methods. Soft Rob. **3**, 379 (2017)
10. Mccoul, D., Rosset, S., Besse, N., et al.: Multifunctional shape memory electrodes for dielectric elastomer actuators enabling high holding force and low-voltage multisegment addressing. Struct. **26**, 25015 (2017)

Capacitive Sensing Based Knee-Angle Continuous Estimation by BP Neural Networks

Dongfang Xu[1,3] and Qining Wang[1,2,3(✉)]

[1] The Robotics Research Group, College of Engineering, Peking University,
Beijing 100871, China
qiningwang@pku.edu.cn

[2] Beijing Innovation Center for Engineering Science and Advanced Technology
(BIC-ESAT), Peking University, Beijing 100871, China

[3] Beijing Engineering Research Center of Intelligent Rehabilitation Engineering,
Beijing 100871, China

Abstract. In this paper, we propose a capacitive sensing based method for knee joint angle continuous estimation. The motion capture system is used to record the position information of knee joint and output knee joint angel as a fitting target. Two capacitance rings are fixed on the thigh and shank to record the relaxation and contraction of muscles. Three healthy subjects participate in the study. Based on BP (back propagation) neural networks, the map relationships (i.e. model) between capacitance signals and knee joint angles are built. In the continuous estimation of angle, capacitance signals are fed into the model, and then we can get the estimated angles. The error (root mean square) and the cross-correlation coefficient are 4.4° and 97.01% between the estimated knee joint angles (based on capacitance signals) and actual keen knee-angle. The results show that capacitive sensing method is effective and feasible to estimate the joint angles.

Keywords: Capacitive sensing · Knee joint angle ·
Continuous estimation · BP neural networks

1 Introduction

Exoskeletons and prostheses can assist human motion or rehabilitation who have suffered amputation, spinal cord injury (SCI) or stroke [1–3]. These robotic devices are designed by mimicking human joint(s). Therefore the joint angle plays a very important role in the control of prosthesis and exoskeleton [4,5]. The joint angle can be measured by angle sensor, but what the angle sensor measures is the approximate equivalent information of human limbs' movement not the muscle information of human limbs. As is known, muscles behave as the actuators of the sensory-motor system and they contain abundant motion information [6–8]. Muscle signals could directly and deeply reflect human's motion

© Springer Nature Switzerland AG 2019
H. Yu et al. (Eds.): ICIRA 2019, LNAI 11740, pp. 64–72, 2019.
https://doi.org/10.1007/978-3-030-27526-6_6

intent and state. Therefore, it is meaningful to build the relationships between the muscle signals and joints' motion.

Surface electromyography (sEMG) signals can record the electrical potential of muscle which is generated by muscle cells and is widely used in robot field [9–11]. Several studies have developed the method of mapping between sEMG signals and joint angles [11–13]. Hou *et al.* have developed the continuous estimation of joint angles by using BP (back propagation) neural networks based on sEMG signals. Xi *et al.* have also conducted the continuous estimation of hip, knee and ankle joints by using deep belief networks based on sEMG signals and motion capture signals. Though they have achieved continuous joint angle estimation, there are some challenges to be solved. As is known, sEMG signals is weak and easy to be contaminated by ambient noises, motion artefact [14]. Besides, the sweats may affect signal quality in long time use for that sEMG electrodes are cling on the skin.

Our previous studies has proposed a non-contact capacitive sensing method to measure the relaxation and contraction of muscle [15]. The capacitive sensing method does not need to contact directly to the skin and can overcome the affection of sweats, besides, it has good signal repeatability and stability. The capacitive sensing method has been applied to recognize the motion mode of lower-limbs and upper-limbs [16–18]. It has also been used to estimate gait phase and achieved satisfactory performance [19]. We have also conducted pilot study and build the relationships between non-contact capacitive sensing signals and continuous grasp forces [20]. Based on the mentioned studies, we are trying to use the capacitive sensing method to find certain relationships between muscle motor signals (capacitance signals) and human joint(s). For this purpose, we continued our study and developed the knee joint estimation based on capacitive sensing method.

The study aimed to explore the map relationships between capacitance signals and human knee joint angle. BP neural networks was used to continuously estimate the knee joint angle. Three able-bodied subjects participated in the study. Motion capture system was adopted to record the position information by the markers tied on the thigh and shank. Two capacitance rings were fixed on the thigh and shank to record the relaxation and contraction of muscles. The estimation performances were evaluated.

The rest paper is organized as follows. Section 2 introduces the material and method, including capacitive sensing system and motion capture system, experimental protocol, signal processing, BP neural networks and system evaluation. Experiment results and conclusion are presented in Sects. 3 and 4.

2   Material and Method

2.1   Capacitive Sensing System and Motion Capture System

Motion capture system could record the position information (i.e. coordinate information of x, y and z axis's) of markers corresponding to (1), (2), (3), and (4) in Fig. 1. In experiments, four markers were fixed on the thigh ((1) and

(2) in Fig. 1) and shank ((3) and (4) in Fig. 1) by double faced adhesive tape. By recoding the markers' coordinate information, the knee joint angle could be calculated (i.e. the θ in Fig. 1).

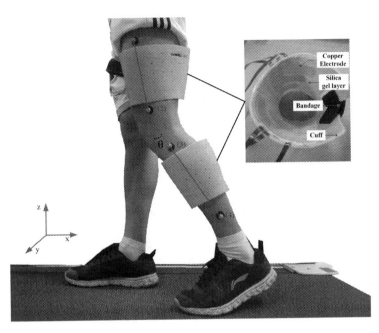

Fig. 1. The diagram of wearable systems including capacitive sensing system and motion capture system. Motion capture system consists of cameras and four markers (corresponding to (1), (2), (3), and (4)). θ denotes the knee joint angle. Capacitive sensing system includes one thigh capacitive sensing ring and one shank capacitive sensing ring. The capacitive ring is made of cuff shell, copper electrode, silica gel layer and bandage, as shown in the top right corner.

The capacitive sensing system consisted of two capacitive sensing ring, as shown in Fig. 1. Capacitive sensing ring was made of cuff shell, copper electrode, silica gel layer and bandage, as shown in the top right corner of Fig. 1. The length, width and thickness of copper electrode were 3.5 cm, 4.5 cm and 0.5 mm, respectively. The thickness of silica gel layer was 2 mm, and its functions were to protect electrodes and void contacting with human limb. The electrodes were adhered on the cuff shell. The cuff shell was made of thermoplastic material. Thermoplastic material could be reshaped at about 70 centigrade according to the limb's shape. The black bandage was used to fix the capacitive sensing ring with human limb. The human limb and the copper electrode could be viewed as the two electrodes of one capacitor. The dielectric layer was cloth and silica gel layer between the metal electrode and human limb, so human's skin could not contacted with electrodes. During human's motion, the capacitance signals would change with muscles' contraction and relaxation. In the experiments, the capacitance signals of thigh and shank were recorded.

2.2 Experimental Protocol

In the study, three healthy subjects participated in the research. The basic information of each subjects were listed in Table 1. During the experiment, the subjects would walk on the treadmill at their normal speeds. Motion capture signals and capacitance signals would be synchronized and collected.

Table 1. Basic information of the three subjects

	Gender	Age	Weight (kg)	Height (cm)
Subject 1	Male	31	78	182
Subject 2	Male	24	66	175
Subject 3	Male	29	60	181

2.3 Signal Processing

Motion capture system could record the motion position information of thigh and shank and then calculate the joint angle. The position information were collected with capacitance signals synchronously. In the study, a low-pass filter was used to filter raw signals. To acquire more effective information, some features of capacitive sensing signals were extracted by a continuous sliding window (100 ms' length) with a 10 ms' increment. Five time domain features were selected for the study. The features were defined as follows: average, standard deviation, maximum, minimum and root mean square. After feature extracting, all the feature values were concatenated together to be a feature vector with its corresponding knee joint angle value. BP neural networks were used to fit knee joint angle curves and then estimate the knee joint angle curves, as shown in Figs. 2(a) and (b).

In Fig. 2(a), feature vectors were used to fit the knee joint curves based on BP neural networks and then map relationships (i.e. the model) between capacitance signals and knee joint angle was built. The model was used to estimate the knee joint angle curves, as shown in Fig. 2(b). In Fig. 2(b), feature vectors were fed into the model and then output estimated angles.

2.4 BP Neural Networks

In this study, we adopted a multi-layer BP neural networks for knee joint angle estimation based on capacitance signals. The designed BP neural networks consist of an input layer, three hidden layers and an output layer, as shown in Fig. 3.

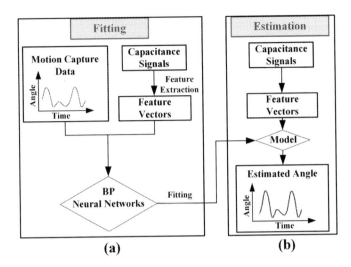

Fig. 2. Knee joint angle fitting and estimation based on BP neural networks. (a) Knee joint angle fitting. Motion capture can record the actual joint angles which is targets for fitting. Capacitance signals are used to fit the joint angles. When the fitting is finished, map relationships (i.e. a model) will be built and output for next continuous estimation of knee joint angle. (b) The continuous estimation of knee joint angle based on model.

The first layer of designed BP neural networks is input layer to accept the feature vectors. The mid hidden layers consists of three layers. The first hidden layer has 40 neurons with a sigmoid transfer function ($f(x) = \frac{1}{1+e^{-x}}$). The second hidden layer also has 40 neurons with a sigmoid transfer function ($f(x) = \frac{1}{1+e^{-x}}$). The third hidden layer has one neurons with a linear transfer function ($f(x) = w \cdot x + b$). The output layer will output the classification results. At each layer, the neurons multiply the output from the previous layer by weight vectors, apply a transfer function to compute the output values of this layer, then pass the outputs to the next layer [21]. The values in this architecture are only travel from input to output, and the weight vectors in each neuron are trained by back propagation procedure [22].

2.5 System Evaluation

In order to describe the estimation precision of knee joint angle, root mean square error θ_{RMS} between estimated and actual joint angles is used, which can be formulated as follows:

$$\theta_{RMS} = \sqrt{\sum_{i=1}^{N} \frac{(\widetilde{\theta}_i - \theta_i)^2}{N}} \qquad (1)$$

where N denotes the sample number, $\widetilde{\theta}_i$ denotes the estimated knee joint angle and θ_i is the actual knee joint angle. The smaller the θ_{RMS} is, the higher the

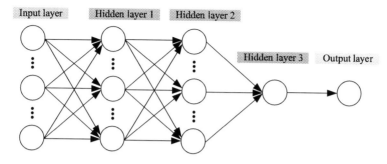

Input layer   Hidden layer 1   Hidden layer 2

Hidden layer 3   Output layer

Fig. 3. A multi-layer neural networks. The designed neural networks consist of an input layer, three hidden layers and an output layer. Feature vectors are input into the neural networks in input layer, and the output layer outputs the classification results.

estimation precision is. The cross-correlation coefficient ρ is also adopted to evaluate the estimation performance, which is defined as follows:

$$\rho = \frac{\sum_{i=1}^{N}(\widetilde{\theta}_i - \overline{\widetilde{\theta}})(\theta_i - \overline{\theta})}{\sqrt{\sum_{i=1}^{N}(\widetilde{\theta}_i - \overline{\widetilde{\theta}})^2}\sqrt{\sum_{i=1}^{N}(\theta_i - \overline{\theta})^2}} \qquad (2)$$

where N denotes the sample number, $\widetilde{\theta}_i$ denotes the estimated knee joint angle, $\overline{\widetilde{\theta}}$ is the mean of estimated knee joint angle, and θ_i is the actual knee joint angle and $\overline{\theta}$ is the mean of actual knee joint angle. ρ varies from 0 to 100%. When ρ is close to 100% in the study, it means good performance.

3 Experimental Results

Three healthy subjects participated in the research, and the corresponding data were collected. The joint angles were calculated for each subject based on motion capture data and corresponding capacitance signals were used to fit knee joint angle curve and then generated a model based on BP neural networks. In estimation, the capacitance signals were fed into the model and output the estimated angles. The estimated knee joint angle curves and corresponding actual knee joint angle curves were shown in Fig. 4. From the Fig. 4, we could see that each subject owned its specific knee joint angle curves. Though subjects had individuals' differences, the estimation of knee joint for each subject was good based on capacitance signals by using BP neural networks. The estimation performances were listed in Table 2.

The estimation errors (Root Mean Square) were 4.1°, 4.4° and 4.8° for the three subjects between the estimated and actual knee joint angles. The maximal estimated error was 4.8° for Subject 3, and Subject 1 could achieve the minimal estimation errors (4.1°). The cross-correlation coefficients between actual and

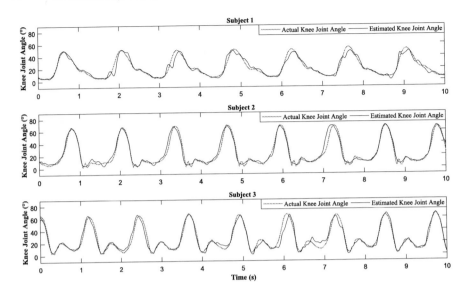

Fig. 4. The estimated and actual knee joint angle curves for the three subjects. Red lines represent the actual knee joint angle curves and the black lines represent the estimated angle curves by BP neural networks. (Color figure online)

Table 2. The root mean square error (θ_{RMS}) and cross-correlation coefficient (ρ) between estimated and actual knee joint angles.

	θ_{RMS}	ρ
Subject 1	4.1°	96.23%
Subject 2	4.4°	97.95%
Subject 3	4.8°	96.86%
Mean	4.4°	97.01%

estimated knee joint angle were 96.23%, 97.95% and 96.86% corresponding to the three subjects. The mean estimated error and cross-correlation coefficient were 4.4° and 97.01%. Our study has achieved comparable performances with some studies based on sEMG signals [11,12]. In the future, we will adopt some methods to improve the estimation performances, recruit more subjects (especially some patients) to the study and apply the study to the practical application.

4   Conclusion

The paper proposes a capacitive sensing method for the continuous estimation of knee joint angle. The motion capture system is used to record the position information of knee joint and calculate knee joint angel as a fitting target. Based on BP neural networks, the map relationships between capacitance signals and knee joint angle is built. In the continuous estimation, the root mean square is 4.4° (mean) and the cross-correlation coefficient is 97.01% (mean) between the estimated knee joint angles (based on capacitance signals) and actual keen joint angles (based on motion capture signals). The results show that capacitive sensing method is effective and feasible to estimate the knee joint angles.

Acknowledgment. This work was supported by the National Key R&D Program of China (No. 2018YFB1307302, 2018YFF0300606), the National Natural Science Foundation of China (No. 91648207, 61533001), the Beijing Nova Program (No. Z141101001814001) and the Beijing Municipal Science and Technology Project (No. Z181100009218007).

References

1. Wang, Q., Yuan, K., Zhu, J., Wang, L.: Walk the walk: a lightweight active transtibial prosthesis. IEEE Robot. Autom. Mag. **22**(4), 80–89 (2015)
2. Baunsgaard, C.B., Nissen, U.V., Brust, A.K., et al.: Exoskeleton gait training after spinal cord injury: an exploratory study on secondary health conditions. J. Rehabil. Med. **50**(9), 806–813 (2018)
3. Morone, G., Paolucci, S., Cherubini, A., et al.: Robot-assisted gait training for stroke patients: current state of the art and perspectives of robotics. Neuropsychiatr. Dis. Treat. **13**, 1303–1311 (2017)
4. Feng, Y., Wang, Q.: Combining push-off power and nonlinear damping behaviors for a lightweight motor-driven transtibial prosthesis. IEEE/ASME Transact. Mechatron. **22**(6), 2512–2523 (2017)
5. Huo, W., Mohammed, S., Amirat, Y., Kong, K.: Fast gait mode detection and assistive torque control of an exoskeletal robotic orthosis for walking assistance. IEEE Transact. Robot. **34**(4), 1035–1052 (2018)
6. Scott, S.H.: Optimal feedback control and the neural basis of volitional motor control. Nature Rev. Neurosci. **5**(7), 532–546 (2004)
7. Tucker, M.R., et al.: Control strategies for active lower extremity prosthetics and orthotics: a review. J. NeuroEng. Rehabil. **12**(1), 1 (2015)
8. Shi, J., Zheng, Y.P., Huang, Q.H., Chen, X.: Continuous monitoring of sonomyography, electromyography and torque generated by normal upper arm muscles during isometric contraction: sonomyography assessment for arm muscles. IEEE Transact. Biomed. Eng. **55**(3), 1191–1198 (2008)
9. Chen, B., Wang, Q., Wang, L.: Adaptive slope walking with a robotic transtibial prosthesis based on volitional EMG control. IEEE/ASME Transact. Mechatron. **20**(5), 2146–2157 (2015)
10. Joshi, D., Nakamura, B.H., Hahn, M.E.: High energy spectrogram with integrated prior knowledge for EMG-based locomotion classification. Med. Eng. Phys. **37**(5), 518–524 (2015)
11. Li, Q., Song, Y., Hou, Z.G.: Estimation of lower limb periodic motions from semg using least squares support vector regression. Neural Process. Lett. **41**, 371–388 (2015)
12. Chena, J., Zhang, X., Cheng, Y., Xi, N.: Surface EMG based continuous estimation of human lower limb joint angles by using deep belief networks. Biomed. Signal Process. Control **40**, 335–342 (2018)

13. Anwar, T., Aung, Y.M., Jumaily, A.A.: The estimation of knee joint angle based on generalized regression neural network (GRNN). In: Proceedings of the IEEE International Symposium on Robotics and Intelligent Sensors, pp. 208–213. Langkawi, Malaysia (2015)
14. Phinyomark, A., Quaine, F., Charbonnier, S., Serviere, C., Tarpin-Bernard, F., Laurillau, Y.: EMG feature evaluation for improving myoelectric pattern recognition robustness. Expert Syst. Appl. **40**(12), 4832–4840 (2013)
15. Zheng, E., Wang, L., Wei, K., Wang, Q.: A noncontact capacitive sensing system for recognizing locomotion modes of transtibial amputees. IEEE Transact. Biomed. Eng. **61**(12), 2911–2920 (2014)
16. Zheng, E., Wang, Q.: Noncontact capacitive sensing based locomotion transition recognition for amputees with robotic transtibial prostheses. IEEE Transact. Neural Syst. Rehabil. **25**(2), 161–170 (2017)
17. Zheng, E., Wang, Q., Qiao, H.: A preliminary study of upper-limb motion recognition with noncontact capacitive sensing. In: Proceedings of the 10th International Conference on Intelligent Robotics and Applications, Wuhan, China, pp. 251–261 (2017)
18. Xu, D., Yang, Y., Mai, J., Wang, Q.: Muscle redistribution surgery based capacitive sensing for upper-limb motion recognition: Preliminary results. In: Proceedings of the IEEE International Conference on Cyborg and Bionic Systems, Beijing, China, pp. 125–129 (2017)
19. Zheng, E., Manca, S., Yan, T., Parri, A., Vitiello, N., Wang, Q.: Gait phase estimation based on noncontact capacitive sensing and adaptive oscillators. IEEE Transact. Biomed. Eng. **64**(10), 2419–2430 (2017)
20. Zheng, E., Wang, Q., Qiao, H.: Identification of the relationships between noncontact capacitive sensing signals and continuous grasp forces: preliminary study. In: Proceedings of the Annual International Conference of the IEEE Engineering in Medicine and Biology Society, Honolulu, USA, pp. 3922–3925 (2018)
21. Min, S., Lee, B., Yoon, S.: Deep learning in bioinformatics. Brief. Bioinf. **18**(5), 851–869 (2017)
22. Goodfellow, I., Bengio, Y., Courville, A., Bengio, Y.: Deep Learning, vol. 1. MIT press, Cambridge (2016)

Concept and Prototype Design of a Soft Knee Exoskeleton with Continuum Structure (SoftKEX)

Zhihao Zhou[1,2,3], Xiuhua Liu[1], and Qining Wang[1,2,3]($\boxtimes$)

[1] The Robotics Research Group, College of Engineering, Peking University,
Beijing 100871, China
`qiningwang@pku.edu.cn`
[2] The Beijing Innovation Center for Engineering Science and Advanced Technology
(BIC-ESAT), Peking University, Beijing 100871, China
[3] The Beijing Engineering Research Center of Intelligent Rehabilitation Engineering,
Beijing 100871, China

Abstract. In this paper, we proposed a novel soft knee exoskeleton based on continuum structure. The bionic design is from the knee extension mechanism: extensor contraction stretching the patella on the gap of the femur and tibia. Concept and prototype design were presented in detail. In the continuum structure, two adjacent modules have two major degrees of freedom, which are bilateral siding and unilateral rotation. The end motion area of the continuum can meet the knee joint feature which is coupled motion with sliding and rotating between the femur and tibia. In addition, a high-power cable-driven actuator was developed to drive the exoskeleton. Tension control results indicated that the actuator can track the force quickly and accurately at fast movement. Walking experiments on two subjects wearing the proposed exoskeleton at slow, normal and fast speeds were carried out. Knee joint kinematic data show flexible and natural gait motion.

Keywords: Soft exoskeleton · Cable-driven and continuum

1 Introduction

Lower-limb exoskeletons have been proposed and developed in military or medical applications, aiming for human argumentation, motion aid and rehabilitation training [1]. Recently, soft exoskeletons as a research focus, use cables anchored to the human body by soft fabric to transfer power. They have several advantages compared with the rigid ones composed of rigid links and simplified joints. At first, no robotic joint means there is no misalignment and constrain problem between the human joint and the exoskeleton joint due to complexity and multi-degrees of freedom (DoF) of biologic joint. Secondly, the soft exoskeleton can be made lightweight and compact. These can obtain more flexible and natural motion during the human gait assistance, e.g. highly dynamic locomotion [2].

© Springer Nature Switzerland AG 2019
H. Yu et al. (Eds.): ICIRA 2019, LNAI 11740, pp. 73–82, 2019.
https://doi.org/10.1007/978-3-030-27526-6_7

However, soft ones cannot provide effective support especially in load-bearing position.

As far, soft lower-limb exoskeletons based on cable/belt-driven actuation have been studied. In [3], a biologically inspired soft multi-articular exosuit for walking assistance was proposed and can provide torques to ankle plantarflexion and hip flexion. In [4], the researchers proposed a unilateral soft robotic exosuit to supplement the paretic ankle's residual ability which could facilitate more normal walking after stroke. Agrawal et al. proposed a cable-Driven leg exoskeleton aimed at gait assistance by providing short bursts of forces to the leg during walking [5].

Soft exoskeleton structure for ankle/hip joint cannot been transferred to knee joint directly except the cable-driven actuator. To our knowledge, knee flexion will form a convex curve of leg in the sagittal plane and the apex of this curve is patella bone. If we adopt existing mode and use cable anchored to the front of human thigh and shank directly, the cable will cut the knee cab when cable stretches to provide knee extension torque. In order to avoid this problem, anchor points of cable were designed far away from body [5], but it will make the exoskeleton larger. Therefore, an extra mechanism is needed to keep comfortable, safe, small, light and effective to assist knee movement. In addition, biological nature characteristics of knee joint is needed to consider in our bionic structure design. Human knee joint is close to a crossed four-bar linage model [6], constructed by posterior cruciate ligament, anterior cruciate ligament, tibia and femur. The joint has a nonuniform geometry surface in varying articulating and a nonconstant rotation axis, which is six DoFs [7]. However, the robotic joint structure is generally simplified, e.g. a hinge with one DoF for flexion-extension e.g. Lokomat [8], LOPES [9], or pure rolling by double gears meshing, e.g. BioKEX [10], Tibion [11].

To address these challenges, we proposed a novel soft knee exoskeleton based on continuum structure in this paper. The bionic design is from the knee extension mechanism, extensor contraction stretching the patella on the gap of the femur and tibia. The end motion area of our proposed continuum structure can meet the knee joint feature which is coupled motion with sliding and rotating between the femur and tibia. Additionally, cable-driven actuator is also designed for driving the continuum structure. In order to verify their feasibility, preliminary experiments were conducted including actuator test and level-walking at different speeds.

2   SoftKEX

To our knowledge, this is the first demonstration of soft powered knee exoskeleton (SoftKEX, short for Soft Knee EXoskeleton) based on continuum structure and cable-driven actuation, as shown in Fig. 1 which can provide active extension torque in knee extension motion and resistance torque in flexion motion.

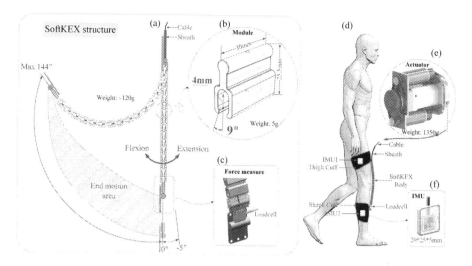

Fig. 1. SoftKEX design. (a) The continuum structure and its motion area. (b) The module design of degrees of freedom. (c) Interaction force measurement. (d) SoftKEX worn in front of human leg by the thigh belt and shank belt. (e) High-power cable-driven actuator design. (f) IMU sensors integration

2.1 Biological Requirements

In order to ensure the proposed exoskeleton performance being capable of the biological requirements of knee joint motion in daily activities, we listed and calculated those relative parameters as shown in Table 1. Thereinto, leveling and stairs walking at normal, comfortable speed are based on data in [13] and sit-to-stand transitions in [14,15]. The maximum required assistive torque for knee joint is around 1.4 Nm/kg and the average angular speed of knee joint reach up to 6.5 rad/s. To translate joint biomechanics into cable force and linear speed of actuator, the moment arm was estimated based on the design of the proposed SoftKEX (approximately 0.08m).

2.2 Bionic Structure Design

According to knee biomechanics analysis, knee extensor is doing more work than knee flexors in our daily locomotion, e.g. stair walking, ramp walking, STS transitions [13,15]. Therefore, considering unidirectional characteristic of soft actuation, the exoskeleton is designed to provide knee extension torque to assist human locomotion.

In this paper, we proposed a novel soft knee exoskeleton structure, which can make it lighter, smaller, more receptive, more easily integrated into pants, as shown in Fig. 1d. We adopted an continuum structure composed of modules (shown in Fig. 1a) and the cable pass through the holes of modules to provide force to bend this continuum. Two adjacent modules have two major degrees

Table 1. Design requirements of SoftKEX from biological data

Items	Walking	Stair[a]	STS[b]
Range of motion (Degrees)	63.8	95.4	107.5
Maximum joint velocity (rad/s)	5.4	6.5	3.2
Maximum joint Moment (Nm/kg)	0.5	1.3	1.4
Cable stroke (m)	111.4	166.5	187.6
Actuator minimum speed (m/s)	0.4	0.5	0.3
Actuator peak force (N/kg)	6.3	16.2	17.5

[a]Stair locomotion includes stair ascending and descending.
[b]STS is short for sit-to-stand and stand-to-sit transitions.

of freedom, which are bilateral siding (4 mm) and unilateral rotation (flexion 9°), as shown in Fig. 1b. 16 modules was "head-tail" connected and the end motion area is grey shaded marked in Fig. 1. So the maximum flexion range is 144° and we can easily to increase and decrease the module number as needed. We can find that the proposed kind of structure is adaptive extensively for different wearers. More importantly, end motion area can meet the knee joint feature which is coupled motion with sliding and rotating between the femur and tibia. In addition, extension range of motion can reach −5° due to the elastic deformation of long and flat structure.

From the bionic point of view, it likes a human skeletal muscle (e.g. quadriceps femoris), lies on the front of leg, cross the knee joint. Its origin connects to the femur by the thigh cuff and belts and its termination to the tibia. The modules likes the human patella and the cable stretch likes the muscle contraction. From the biological data in [16], moment-arm lengths of rectus femoris is 4 cm. In this version, SoftKEX can worn close the human body and moment Arm length is approximately 8 cm.

All the modules and thigh and shank connector are manufactured through 3D Printing. To ensure the mechanical strength and toughness of the modules, we used high performance polyamide (nylon) instead of photosensitive resin. But for the thigh and shank connector, to keep them fit the body shape well and worn comfortably, we adopt polyethylene (softness: 60). The whole weight is only about 120 g, which is felt very lightweight.

2.3   Actuator Design

According to the biological data, we designed a kind of cable actuator (as shown in Fig. 1e) with a peak force capability of 500 N (active mode) and 800 N (damping mode [17]), maximum speed of 1.90 m/s. The speed margin is for compensation of system elasticity due to suit deformation and cable. In order to obtain high power output, we used dual-motor modality (rated power 400 W). Therefore, the actuator consists of two DC-brushless motor (Maxon Motor, Switzerland) with encoders (1000 cnt) mounted on their tails. Two-class reduction structure was

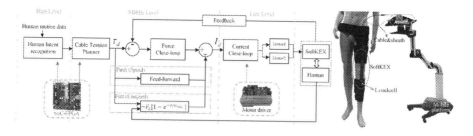

Fig. 2. The prototype of the proposed SoftKEX and its hierarchical control system design

used to increased the end tensile force. Each motor is connected to gearbox (ratio: 10/1) through a timing belt drive (ratio: 44/14), respectively. The overall reduction ration is 31.43. A 69 mm diameter cable pulley was installed on the output side of the gearbox. The pulley groove is designed to be able to wrap the Bowden cable around the pulley which is limited by two-side mechanical stop (free 280°), allowing 168.5 mm of cable travel. The whole weight of mechanic structure is about 1.3 kg (Fig. 2).

2.4 Sensory System

Except the encoders on the motor used for position and speed feedback and safety range check, we placed sensors for measurements of human-robot interaction information. In the end of cable, we integrated a force sensor (Futek, USA) into the continuum structure as shown in Fig. 1c. In order to measure the knee joint kinematic data (e.g. knee joint angle, speed) and further to detect the locomotion modes and gait phases, two IMUs were placed on the lateral side of thigh part and shank part of exoskeleton belts, respectively, as shown in Fig. 1d. The self-customized IMU (shwon in Fig. 1f) was designed based on MPU 9250 and outputs triaxial angles, angular speeds and accelerated speeds (9 channels). All signals were fed into control system with the sampling rate at 100 Hz.

2.5 Control System

According to the requirements of actuation, sensors and control, we design a hierarchical control system. In Low-level, current closed-loop control was implemented in our customized drivers with maximum 60 V supply voltage. The driver can provides continuous 30 A output and maximum 80 A (during 3 s). Middle level was based on microprocessor and used to accomplish torque trajectory generation, sensory data acquisition/analysis, torque closed-loop control and feedforward compensation. High level was a FPGA based control hardware which is used to realize human intent recognition online. It is not involved in this study, but have verified in our previous study [12] (Fig. 3).

For obtain better force control, we add feed-forward compensation on the close-loop control. In the pull phase, the cable was spool around the pulley

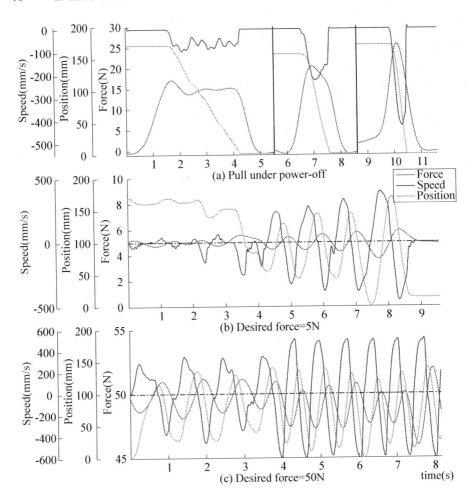

Fig. 3. Tension control performance. Cable force, speed and position were shown. (a) Backdriving force measurement. (b) Desired force 5 N.

driven by motor to provide extension torque. In the push phase, the cable was unspool around the pulley and passively dragged out while human flexes his leg. In the flexion phase, the actuator can provide resistance torque for muscle eccentric contraction or the actuator actively unspool to let wearer easily drag out. The motor driver can work on damping mode to save energy [17]. Speed direction was used to detect the push or pull phase to choose the corresponding compensation strategy.

3   Experimental Results

3.1   Tension Control Performance

Tension/force control was extensively used in the lower-limb exoskeletons. The performance of the proposed actuator and control method was tested in this experiment. At first, we test the backdriving force at different speeds. As shown in Fig. 5a, the cable was dragged out by hand from 100 mm/s to over 400 mm/s and the maximum resistance force can reach 25.7 N. The backdriving resistance is felt obviously when wearing the exoskeleton during knee flexion. In order to test the transparent control performance, SoftKEX was worn and free swing at different frequency (shown in Fig. 5b–c). The cable was pulled and pushed by knee flexion and extension. When set desired force 5 N, the maximum error is 1.4 N under about 450 mm/s. For desired force 50 N, the maximum error is 4.0 N under about 600 mm/s. In addition, force trajectory tracking experiments are also carried out. Sine curves with amplification 50 N and offset 80 N under 2 Hz, 5 Hz and 8 Hz are regarded as desired input of force controller. Real-time feedback from loadcell was record as shown in Fig. 4. The average error is 1.62 N,

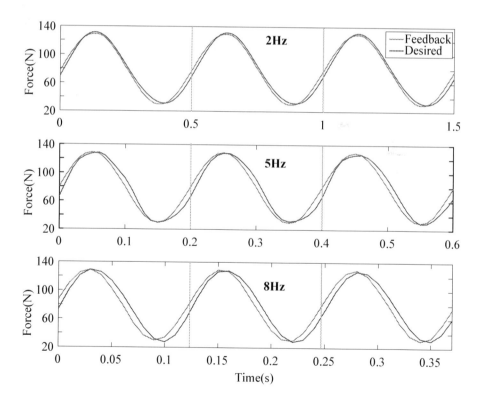

Fig. 4. Force tracking performance. Desired sine curves with amplification 50 N and offset 80 N under 2 Hz, 5 Hz and 8 Hz and corresponding feedback signal are labelled blue and red lines, respectively. (Color figure online)

3.85 N and 7.28 N for three different frequencies. The maximum delay is about 10 ms. Those results indicate that force can be controlled well at quick movement which can ensure the natural swing in fast walking or jogging.

3.2   Level-Walking Wearing SoftKEX

In order to verify feasibility of the proposed SoftKEX based on the novel continuum structure, two healthy subject (Subject 1, Male, age 30, height 168 cm, weight 72 kg and Subject 2, female, age 25, height 162, weight 46 kg) are taking level-walking experiments. They are walking on a treadmill wearing the exoskeleton in three different speeds (defined as slow, normal and fast). Each speed is needed walking at least 30 s. Joint kinematic data measured from the IMU sensors are normalized by gait cycle and averaged by all steps. As shown in Fig. 5, two subjects can freely walking on each speed under transparent mode (In order to keep cable no slack, we chose the desired force 10 N instead zero). During the stride, subjects did not feel resistance and can walk naturally. We find that the joint motion curve is similar compared with the data in [16].

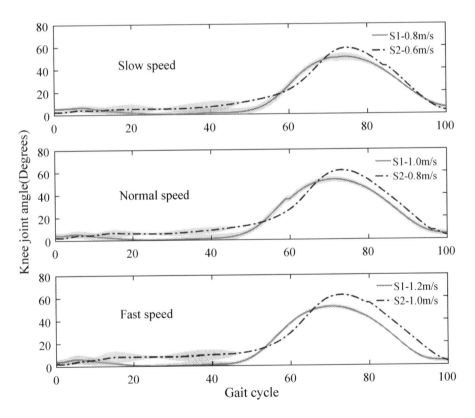

Fig. 5. Knee joint angle in gait cycle at different level-walking speed.

4 Conclusions

In this paper, we have proposed a different soft knee exoskeleton based on continuum structure and present mechatronic design of the SoftKEX prototype. Meanwhile, we also design a high-power cable-driven actuator to input force into the exoskeleton. In order to test its feasibility quickly, this study is firstly design for unilateral limbs. Preliminary experiments including tension control and level walking under transparent mode are conducted to verify its functional design successfully. In the future work, we will evaluate its assistance effect through EMG data and metabolic cost in different terrains. We also try to integrate the actuation on the human back to become a fully wearable robotic system.

Acknowledgment. This work was supported by the National Key R&D Program of China (No. 2018YFF0300606, 2018YFB1307302), the National Natural Science Foundation of China (No. 91648207, 61533001), the Beijing Natural Science Foundation (No. L182001) and the Beijing Municipal Science and Technology Project (No. Z181100009218007). The authors would like to thank Y. Zhou and T. Zhang for their contributions in prototype implementation.

References

1. Young, A.J., Ferris, D.P.: State of the art and future directions for lower limb robotic exoskeletons. IEEE Trans. Neural Syst. Rehabil. Eng. **25**(2), 171–182 (2017). https://doi.org/10.1109/TNSRE.2016.2521160
2. Asbeck, A.T., De Rossi, S.M.M., Galiana, I., Ding, Y., Walsh, C.J.: Stronger, smarter, softer: next-generation wearable robots. IEEE Robot. Autom. Mag. **21**(4), 22–33 (2014). https://doi.org/10.1109/MRA.2014.2360283
3. Asbeck, A.T., De Rossi, S.M.M., Holt, K.G., Walsh, C.J.: A biologically inspired soft exosuit for walking assistance. Int. J. Robot. Res. **34**(6), 744–762 (2015). https://doi.org/10.1177/0278364914562476
4. Awad, L.N., et al.: A soft robotic exosuit improves walking in patients after stroke. Sci. Transl. Med. **9**, eaai9084 (2017). https://doi.org/10.1126/scitranslmed.aai9084
5. Jin, X., Prado, A., Agrawal, S.K.: Retraining of human gait - are lightweight cable-driven leg exoskeleton designs effective? IEEE Trans. Neural. Syst. Rehabil. Eng. **26**(4), 847–855 (2018). https://doi.org/10.1109/TNSRE.2018.2815656
6. O'Connor, J.J., Shercliff, T.L., Biden, E., Goodfellow, J.W.: The geometry of the knee in the sagittal plane. Proc. Inst. Mech. Eng. H. **203**, 223–233 (1989). https://doi.org/10.1243/PIME_PROC_1989_203_043_01
7. Wismans, J., Veldpaus, F., Janssen, J., Huson, A., Struben, P.: A threedimensional mathematical model of the knee-joint. J. Biomech. **13**(8), 677–685 (1980). https://doi.org/10.1016/0021-9290(80)90354-1
8. Jezernik, S., Colombo, G., Keller, T., Frueh, H., Morari, M.: Robotic orthosis lokomat: a rehabilitation and research tool. J. Neurol. Neurosur. Psychiatry **6**, 108–115 (2003). https://doi.org/10.1046/j.1525-1403.2003.03017.x
9. Veneman, J.F., Kruidhof, R., Hekman, E.E.G., van Asseldonk, E.H.F., van der Kooij, H.: Design and evaluation of the LOPES exoskeleton robot for interactive gait rehabilitation. IEEE Trans. Neural. Syst. Rehabil. Eng. **15**, 379–386 (2007). https://doi.org/10.1109/tnsre.2007.903919

10. Zhou, Z., Liao, Y., Wang, C., Wang, Q.: Preliminary evaluation of gait assistance during treadmill walking with a bionic knee exoskeleton. In: Proceedings of the IEEE International Conference on Robotics and Biomimetics, pp. 1173–1178 (2016). https://doi.org/10.1109/ROBIO.2016.7866484

11. Horst, R.W.: A bio-robotic leg orthosis for rehabilitation and mobility enhancement. In: Proceedings of the Annual International Conference of the IEEE Engineering in Medicine and Biology Society, pp. 5030–5033 (2009). https://doi.org/10.1109/IEMBS.2009.5333581

12. Liu, X., Zhou, Z., Wang, Q.: Real-time onboard recognition of gait transitions for a bionic knee exoskeleton in transparent mode. In: Proceedings of the Annual International Conference of the IEEE Engineering in Medicine and Biology Society, pp. 3202–3205 (2018)

13. Riener, R., Rabuffetti, M., Frigo, C.: Stair ascent and descent at different inclinations. Gait Posture **15**(1), 32–44 (2002). https://doi.org/10.1016/S0966-6362(01)00162-X

14. Spyropoulos, G., Tsatalas, T., Tsaopoulos, D.E., Sideris, V., Giakas, G.: Biomechanics of sit-to-stand transition after muscle damage. Gait Posture **38**(1), 62–67 (2013). https://doi.org/10.1016/j.gaitpost.2012.10.013

15. Mak, M.K.Y., Levin, O., Mizrahi, J., Hui-Chan, C.W.Y.: Joint torques during sit-to-stand in healthy subjects and people with parkinson's disease. Clin. Biomech. **18**(3), 197–206 (2003). https://doi.org/10.1016/S0268-0033(02)00191-2

16. Winter, D.A.: Biomechanics and Motor Control of Human Movement. Wiley, Hoboken (2009). https://doi.org/10.1016/S0031-9406(10)63713-3

17. Wang, Q., Yuan, K., Zhu, J., Wang, L.: Walk the walk: a lightweight active transtibial prosthesis. IEEE Robot. Autom. Mag. **22**(4), 80–89 (2015). https://doi.org/10.1109/mra.2015.2408791

An Improved Model to Estimate Muscle-Tendon Mechanics and Energetics During Walking with a Passive Ankle Exoskeleton

Nianfeng Wang, Yihong Zhong[✉], and Xianmin Zhang

Guangdong Provincial Key Laboratory of Precision Equipment
and Manufacturing Technology, School of Mechanical and Automotive Engineering,
South China University of Technology, Guangzhou 510640, China
menfwang@scut.edu.cn, z749195787@163.com

Abstract. One experiment has shown that wearing an elastic ankle exoskeleton can reduce the metabolic cost of walking by $7.2 \pm 2.6\%$, and the best exoskeleton stiffness is $180\,\mathrm{Nm/rad}$. A model has evaluated the plantar flexor muscle-tendon mechanics and energetics during walking with this unpowered exoskeleton, but the optimal stiffness value is twice that of the experiment, so the simulated muscle-tendon mechanics and energetics may be somewhat biased. The purpose of this paper is to develop a model to match the simulation results to the experimental results and to better explore the muscle-tendon mechanics and energetics. The main improvements of this study are: (1) adding the modeling of dorsiflexor to match the work efficiency of plantar flexor and dorsiflexor, (2) analyzing the distribution of moments when the assistant moment is too large, and (3) updating the calculation process. By the improved model, the error of the optimal stiffness is reduced to 3.3%, and the error of the reduction rate of metabolic cost is reduced to nearly 0%.

Keywords: Ankle joint · Human walking · Muscle-tendon dynamics · Metabolic energy cost · Passive elastic exoskeleton

1 Introduction

Unlike previous exoskeletons with large weights, complex mechanical structures and the ability to achieve power amplification [1,2], studies on exoskeletons which are lightweight, miniaturized, and capable of reducing the body's metabolic consumption have been conducted by many researchers [3–5]. Among them, the special one is a passive elastic ankle exoskeleton developed by Collins [5]. The exoskeleton is simple in design, light in weight, and requires no electronic equipment or batteries to achieve a reduction in metabolic cost. Exoskeleton users with a proper spring stiffness ($180\,\mathrm{Nm/rad}$) can reduce their metabolic costs by $7.2 \pm 2.6\%$ during normal walking.

© Springer Nature Switzerland AG 2019
H. Yu et al. (Eds.): ICIRA 2019, LNAI 11740, pp. 83–96, 2019.
https://doi.org/10.1007/978-3-030-27526-6_8

There have been many computer simulations of human musculoskeletal models used to study the effects of human muscles [6, 7], but they are often too complex, and in most cases, we do not need to understand the effects on each muscle. A model built by Sawicki can evaluate plantar flexor muscle-tendon mechanics and energetics during walking with the unpowered exoskeleton developed by Collins [8]. This model combined the triceps surae group into a single, lumped uniarticular muscle-tendon with an origin and insertion locations like soles. This model assumed that the overall ankle joint kinematics and dynamics remain invariant in the context of elastic ankle exoskeleton. Using an inverse modeling framework, the model can simulate human walking at different stiffness values and evaluate the muscle-tendon mechanism and energetics. However, the stiffness reported is twice that found by Collins. They thought the mismatch in the best stiffness between model and experiments is likely due to the very rudimentary approach they took to the compensatory metabolic cost in their study, which assumed dorsiflexor and plantar flexor have the same metabolic cost per unit moment.

The goal of this study was to develop a simplified musculoskeletal model to investigate the plantar flexor and dorsiflexor muscle-tendon mechanisms and energetics during walking with different exoskeleton stiffness. First, we not only modeled plantar flexor but also modeled the dorsiflexor using the Hill-type muscle-tendon model [9]. Then, the model real-time moment arm and the experimental real-time moment arm were compared to get the model skeletal geometric parameters. The muscle dynamics and tendon dynamics were used to obtain the model biological contraction dynamics parameters, the plantar flexor and dorsiflexor evaluation moments. After that, the minimum plantar flexor muscle moment in the gait cycle was calculated. Finally, the distribution of muscle moments in various situations was analyzed, and the inverse framework was used to analyze the plantar flexor and dorsiflexor muscle-tendon mechanisms and energetics.

2   Modeling Method

2.1   Ankle Musculoskeletal Model Construction

We built a simplified ankle musculoskeletal model in the sagittal plane based on Sawicki's model [8]. The model consisted of two uniarticular muscle-tendon units (MTUs). The MTU was modeled using the Hill muscle-tendon model, which consisted of muscle and tendon. The muscle and tendon connected in series. The muscle was composed of an active contractile element (CE) and a passive element (PE). The tendon was represented by a series elastic element (SEE). As shown in Fig. 1, one MTU was the plantar flexor (PF) muscle-tendon unit to realize the plantar flexion; the other MTU was the dorsiflexor (DF) muscle-tendon unit to achieve dorsiflexion. The PF muscle was an integrated muscle composed of calf triceps (soleus, gastrocnemius) and DF muscle was the anterior tibialis.

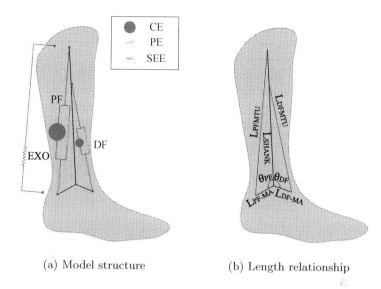

(a) Model structure   (b) Length relationship

Fig. 1. Modeling schematic.

2.2   Model Parameter Values Determination

Setting Model Parameter Values. The model was constructed based on a 170 cm, 70 kg human subject. The skeletal geometric parameters are shown in Table 1. The biological contraction dynamics parameters are shown in Table 2. The ankle model was built with a set of remaining unknown model parameters: $\Omega = [A, B, C]$, where $A = [L_{PF-MA}, L_{DF-MA}, \theta_{PF}, \theta_{DF}]$ represented the moment arm length and angle parameters corresponding to the two ankle muscles, $B = [m]$ represented the force scaling parameter corresponding to the PF, $C = [L_{PFMTU0}, L_{DFMTU0}, K_{PFSEE0}, K_{DFSEE0}]$ represented the MTU slack length and SEE linear stiffness corresponding to the two ankle muscles.

Determination of Skeletal Geometric Parameters. The Angle values similar to Maganaris's paper [13,14] were used to calculate the real-time moment arm length defined as the vertical distance from the ankle joint center to the MTU path by skeletal geometry. We found the skeletal geometric parameters to minimize the root mean squared error (RSME) between the model real-time moment arm and experimental real-time moment arm [13,14] by an optimization procedure in MATLAB. Finally, we got $A = [56, 42, 106, 100]$.

Determination of PF Force Scaling Parameter and Calculation of Distributed Muscle Moment for Evaluation. The maximum force of the muscle should be scaled to account for the different strength capabilities across people [15]. Since the DF muscle force is much smaller than the PF muscle force, only the maximum force of the PF muscle was scaled. The PF maximum muscle

Table 1. Model skeletal geometric parameters

Parameter	Value	Source
Body mass (kg)	70	Based on values used by Sawicki [8]
Body height (m)	1.70	
Shank length L_{SHANK} (cm)	40	
PF insertion point length (cm)	0.125 L_{SHANK}	
DF insertion point length (cm)	0.25 L_{SHANK}	Based on values reported in Brand [10]
PF moment arm length (mm)	L_{PF-MA}	Unknown parameters
DF moment arm length (mm)	L_{DF-MA}	
PF moment arm angle ($^\circ$)	θ_{PF}	
DF moment arm angle ($^\circ$)	θ_{DF}	

force scaling parameter m, and distributed model moments for evaluation were calculated, as shown in Fig. 2. The relative activation data [16,17], muscle length of the PF and DF [16,18], were brought into CE dynamics, and the muscle force was calculated by the following equations:

$$F_{CE} = F_{MAX} \cdot (a \cdot \tilde{F}^a_{CE}(\tilde{l}_{CE}) \cdot \tilde{F}_{CE}(\tilde{v}_{CE}) + \tilde{F}^p_{CE}(\tilde{l}_{CE})) \tag{1}$$

$$\tilde{v}_{CE} = -\frac{\Delta l_{CE}}{\Delta t} = -\frac{\Delta \tilde{l}_{CE}}{\Delta t \cdot (\frac{v_{CEMAX}}{L_{CE0}})} \tag{2}$$

where a is muscle activation ranged from 0 to1, $\tilde{l}_{CE}$ is CE length normalized by L_{CE0} and $\tilde{v}_{CE}$ is CE velocity normalized by v_{CEMAX}, $\frac{v_{CEMAX}}{L_{CE0}}$ is from Table 2, the computational detail of formulas $\tilde{F}^a_{CE}$ and $\tilde{F}^p_{CE}$ is given in [8], and the computational detail of formula $\tilde{F}_{CE}$ is given in [19].

The PF and DF muslce real-time moment arms were calculated by taking kinematic data into the skeletal geometry. The model muscle force of PF and DF multiplied by the respective model muscle arms to get the respective model muscle moments. The model muscle moment of the PF was subtracted from the model muscle moment of the DF to obtain the total model muscle moment. The PF maximum muscle force scaling parameter m was obtained by minimizing the RSME between the total model muscle moment and experimental moment by an optimization procedure in MATLAB. Then, we got B = [1.07]. The obtained DF model moment value was directly used as the DF model moment evaluation value $M_{DFTOTAL}$ for the subsequent steps. The sum of the experimental total moment value and the DF model moment evaluation value was used as the PF model moment evaluation value $M_{PFTOTAL}$ for the subsequent steps.

Determination of Biological Contraction Dynamics Parameters. The unknown biological contraction dynamics parameters (L_{PFMTU0}, K_{PFSEE0}, L_{DFMTU0}, K_{DFSEE0}) were calculated, as shown in Fig. 3. The unknown parameters of the PF and the DF were calculated separately, using the same method. The MTU full-length L_{MTU} at each time point was calculated from the skeletal geometry. L_{MTU0} was multiplied by $\frac{L_{CE0}}{L_{MTU0}}$ to get L_{CE0}. L_{CE0} was subtracted

Table 2. Model biological contraction dynamics parameters

Parameter	Value	Source
PF maximum isometric force F_{PFMAX} (N)	6000 m	Based on values used by Sawicki [8], m is the scaling parameter
DF maximum isometric force F_{DFMAX} (N)	1000	Based on values reported in Arnold [11]
PF MTU slack length (mm)	L_{PFMTU0}	Unknown parameters
DF MTU slack length (mm)	L_{DFMTU0}	
Optimal PF muscle fiber length L_{PFCE0} (mm)	$0.108 L_{\mathrm{PFMTU0}}$	Based on values used by Sawicki [8]
Optimal DF muscle fiber length L_{DFCE0} (mm)	$0.217 L_{\mathrm{DFMTU0}}$	Based on value reported in Arnold [11]
Maximum PF shortening velocity v_{PFCEMAX} (mm/s)	$8.24 L_{\mathrm{PFCE0}}$	Based on value reported in Geyer [12]
Maximum DF shortening velocity v_{DFCEMAX} (mm/s)	$12 L_{\mathrm{PFCE0}}$	
PF SEE linear stiffness (N/mm)	K_{PFSEE0}	Unknown parameters
DF SEE linear stiffness (N/mm)	K_{DFSEE0}	

from L_{MTU0} to calculate L_{SEE0}. L_{CE0} was multiplied by $\tilde{l}_{\mathrm{CE}}$ to calculate the L_{CE} at each time point. The L_{CE} at each time point is subtracted from the L_{MTU} at each time point to obtain the L_{SEE} at each time point. The slack length of the tendon L_{SEE0} was subtracted from L_{SEE} at each time point to calculate the elongation of the SEE D_{LSEE}. According to D_{LSEE}, the muscle force F_{SEE} was obtained by solving the following equation:

$$D_{\mathrm{LSEE}}(F_{\mathrm{FSEE}}) = \int_{F\mathrm{SEE}=0}^{F\mathrm{SEE}=F\mathrm{SEEMAX}} \frac{dF_{\mathrm{SEE}}}{K_{\mathrm{SEE}}(F_{\mathrm{SEE}})} \qquad (3)$$

The computational detail of formula K_{SEE} is given in [8].

The muscle force F_{SEE} was multiplied by the real-time moment arm to calculate the moment produced by the SEE. Because muscles and tendons are connected in series, the forces they produce are equal. C was obtained by minimizing the RSME between model moment produced by SEE and model moment for evaluation. Using an optimization procedure in MATLAB, we got C = [366 304 169 32].

2.3   Modeling the Function of the Elastic Ankle Exoskeleton

Calculation of Minimum PF Muscle Moment in the Gait Cycle. The minimum PF muscle moment is the passive moment generated by the PFMTU

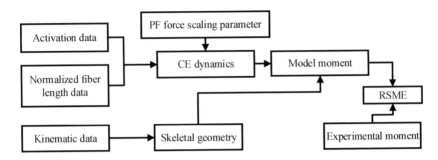

Fig. 2. The block diagram of the optimization process for B.

as a purely passive elastomer when the assistant force of the exoskeleton PF direction is too large. When the exoskeleton assistant force exceeds the force required by the PF, the PF muscle is theoretically in an inactive state [8]. At this time, the CE does not work, and the MTU becomes an elastic body composed of two elastic elements (PE and SEE) connected in series. PE is a stiffer spring, and SEE is a softer spring. In this case, the two spring forces are the same, and the PE having a higher spring stiffness are less stretched, and the SEE having a smaller stiffness are more stretched. At this point, the MTU satisfies the following binary quadratic equations:

$$\begin{cases} L_{\mathrm{MTU}} = L_{\mathrm{CE}} + L_{\mathrm{SEE}} \\ F_{\mathrm{CE}}(L_{\mathrm{CE}}) = F_{\mathrm{SEE}}(L_{\mathrm{SEE}}) \end{cases} \tag{4}$$

where L_{MTU} is calculated by taking kinematic data into the skeletal geometry, L_{CE} and L_{SEE} are unknowns, F_{CE} is a function of L_{CE} calculated by Eq. 1 (muscle activation is equal to 0), F_{SEE} is a function of L_{SEE} calculated by Eq. 3.

Solving this binary quadratic equation, the minimum muscle force at each time point was obtained, multiplied the corresponding real-time muscle moment arm to obtain the minimum muscle moment M_{MIN} for later discussion of the classification in the case of wearing exoskeleton.

Calculation of Minimum PF Muscle Moment in the Gait Cycle. The modeling of the passive exoskeleton (EXO) as shown in Fig. 1. For ease of calculation, EXO is parallel to PFMTU, the length of EXO is equal to L_{PFMTU}, and the same moment arm is used as PFMTU. The spring stiffness was multiplied by the spring elongation to calculate the assistant force generated by the EXO. The assistant force generated by the EXO was multiplied by the EXO moment arm to calculate the assistant moment generated by the EXO. The model assumed that kinematics and dynamics remain invariant under the conditions of different EXO stiffness values. The key to our model was to determine which part of the moment is applied by the PF and which part of the moment is applied by the DF. The PF and the DF muscle moment were obtained by the following formulas:

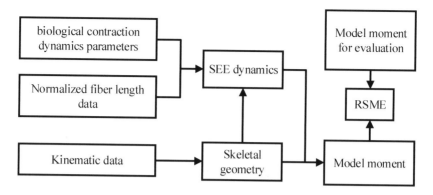

Fig. 3. The block diagram of the optimization process for C.

$$\text{when} M_{\text{EXO}} \leq M_{\text{PFTOTAL}} - M_{\text{MIN}}$$
$$M_{\text{PFmtu}} = M_{\text{PFTOTAL}} - M_{\text{EXO}}$$
$$M_{\text{DFmtu}} = M_{\text{DFTOTAL}}$$
$$\text{and} \tag{5}$$
$$\text{when} M_{\text{EXO}} > M_{\text{PFTOTAL}} - M_{\text{MIN}}$$
$$M_{\text{PFmtu}} = M_{\text{MIN}}$$
$$M_{\text{DFmtu}} = M_{\text{EXO}} + M_{\text{MIN}} - M_{\text{PFTOTAL}} + M_{\text{DFTOTAL}}$$

where M_{EXO} is the assistant moment generated by the EXO, M_{PFTOTAL} and M_{DFTOTAL} is the PF and DF model moment evaluation values, M_{MIN} is the minimum PF muscle moment.

In the first case, when the exoskeleton assistant force is small, the PF muscle needs to activate to generate a moment, and the DF muscle maintains its original moment; in the second case, when the exoskeleton assistant force is too large, the PF muscle does not need to be activated to generate a moment. At this time, the PFMTU exists as a passive unit. The DF muscle not only maintains its original torque but also produces an increase in antagonistic force to recharge the exoskeleton to produce a corresponding assistant torque. After calculating the muscle moments of PF and DF, the inverse frame of the PF muscle in the Sawicki's model was used to find PF and DF muscle-tendon mechanics and energetics.

3   Results

3.1   EXO Moment, PF and DF Muscle Moment

As shown in Fig. 4, when the exoskeleton is not worn, the PF muscle moment is higher than the net moment of the ankle joint due to the presence of antagonistic activity. When the exoskeleton is worn, the passive exoskeleton is added to the gait walking during the specific period under the action of the clutch, and the auxiliary torque is generated as the spring is extended. The exoskeleton produces an assistant moment from ∼10% to ∼60% of the walking stride, and the assistant moment exhibits a very regular increase with increasing spring stiffness. The muscle moment required by the PF gradually decreases as the assistant moment increases. When the stiffness is small, the moment generated by the DF muscle remains invariant. As the stiffness increases, the exoskeleton assistant moment exceeds the net moment required and the DF muscle produces an increase in the antagonistic moment.

3.2   Muscle Mechanical Power and Work

PF muscle only does positive work in the gait cycle, while PF tendon first does negative work to absorb energy, and then do positive work to release energy, as shown in Fig. 5. When the PF tendon releases energy, the superposition with the muscles is an explosion of the MTU's overall energy production. When the stiffness of the exoskeleton increases, the muscle force of the PF decreases, and the muscle velocity of the PF increases. Under the interaction of the muscle force and velocity, the mechanical power and the mechanical work of the muscle generated during the period do not change much. When the stiffness of the exoskeleton increases, the PF muscle strength becomes smaller, and the contraction speed and the stretching speed of the tendon become slower so that the tendon is reduced in power whether it is doing positive or negative work.

When a high stiffness is selected, the muscle strength of the DF increase, and the contraction and stretching speed of the DF muscle and tendon increase so that the mechanical power of the DF muscle and tendon become higher regardless of the negative work or the positive work. However, it should be noted that in the ∼5%–∼40% cycle, the muscle does positive work first, then does negative work, while the tendon first performs negative work and then does positive work. The time points for muscle and tendon work are similar. One is doing positive work, and the other is doing negative work. The magnitude of the power is relatively close, but one doing positive work is bigger than the other doing negative work.

3.3   Muscle Activation, Metabolic Power

As the stiffness of the exoskeleton spring increases, the degree of activation of the PF muscle regularly decreases, while the DF muscle remains invariant without increasing the antagonistic force, as shown in Fig. 6. As the stiffness of the exoskeleton continues to increase, the degree of DF muscle activation increases. The maximum spring stiffness value is ∼110 N/mm and the peak of DF muscle activation is close to the limit of 1. If this spring stiffness exceeds the maximum allowable spring stiffness value, the DF muscle activation will exceed the limit of 1, and the model has no way to achieve the corresponding gait while maintaining the same kinematics and dynamics without EXO. After the spring stiffness, humans will adjust the gait to cope with the effect of increasing the spring stiffness.

The degree of muscle activation of PF decreases with increasing stiffness, and the coverage of biological work time also narrows, but faster muscle speed leads to

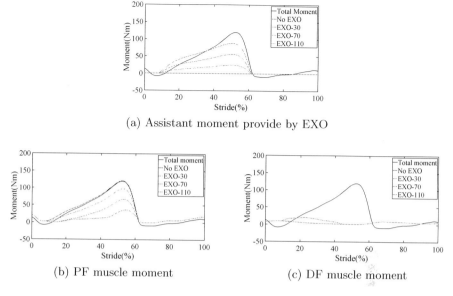

(a) Assistant moment provide by EXO

(b) PF muscle moment   (c) DF muscle moment

Fig. 4. The assistant moment, PF and DF muscle moment over a gait cycle during walking with EXO of different stiffnesses. Curves with varying line types represent different exoskeleton stiffness values ranging from no exoskeleton up 110 N/mm.

higher energy consumption. The combination of reduced activation and increased muscle speed cause the peak of PF metabolic power to increase slightly as the stiffness increases. Under the condition of high stiffness, the DF muscle speed becomes higher, so that the influence coefficient of muscle speed on the muscle metabolic power becomes higher, which makes the DF muscle to consume more energy. At the same time, the activation degree of the DF muscle becomes higher, and the superposition of the two makes the time range of the DF biological work to become larger, and the metabolic power of the DF increases.

3.4   Muscle Metabolic Cost and Muscle Efficiency

The metabolic cost of muscles is shown in Fig. 7. As the spring stiffness increases, the energy cost of PF muscles decreases in an approximately linear manner, while the metabolic energy consumption of DF muscles is almost constant when the stiffness value increases from 0 N/mm to 70 N/mm, and then gradually increases as the stiffness continues to increase; When the EXO stiffness is from 0N/mm to 74.23 N/mm, the total metabolic cost is decreasing. When the spring stiffness exceeds 74.23 N/mm, the total metabolic cost gradually increases with the increase of spring stiffness. The optimal EXO stiffness value is 74.23 N/mm (rotating spring stiffness is about 186 Nm/rad), and the spring stiffness at this time differs from the experimental spring stiffness value of 180 Nm/rad by only 3.3% [5]. When the stiffness value is optimal, the ankle joint muscle metabolism

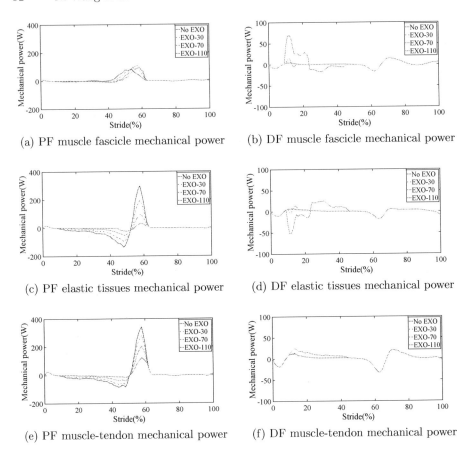

Fig. 5. The CE, SEE and MTU mechanical power curve of PF and DF during walking with the exoskeleton of different stiffnesses over a gait cycle. Curves with varying line types represent different exoskeleton stiffness values ranging from no exoskeleton up 110 N/mm.

is reduced by 21%. According to Umberger's study [20], PF muscle metabolism consumes ~27% of the total metabolic consumption of the human body during walking, and the total energy consumption of this model can be calculated. By dividing the total metabolic energy reduction of the ankle joint with the optimal stiffness by the total metabolic energy consumption without the exoskeleton, it can be concluded that the energy consumption at the optimal stiffness is reduced by 7.2% relative to the total metabolic consumption of the human body. This value is the same as the metabolic reduction of the experiment [5]. The energy efficiency of muscles was calculated by the following formula:

$$\eta = \frac{W_{\text{Mech}}^{+}}{W_{\text{Met}}} \tag{6}$$

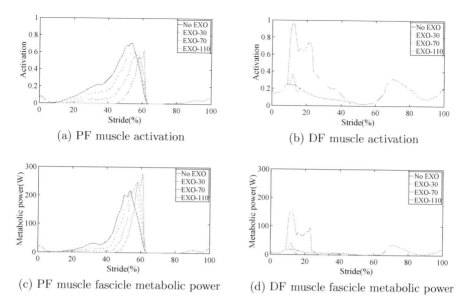

(a) PF muscle activation

(b) DF muscle activation

(c) PF muscle fascicle metabolic power

(d) DF muscle fascicle metabolic power

Fig. 6. The muscle activation and metabolic power curve of PF and DF during walking with the exoskeleton of different stiffnesses over a gait cycle. Curves with varying line types represent different exoskeleton stiffness values ranging from no exoskeleton up 110 N/mm.

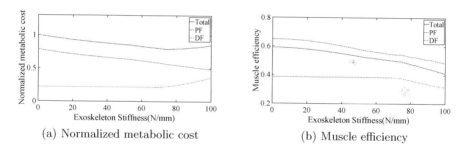

(a) Normalized metabolic cost

(b) Muscle efficiency

Fig. 7. The normalized muscle metabolic cost and muscle efficiency of PF, DF and the total ankle muscle during walking with EXO of different stiffnesses. The normalized muscle metabolic cost is normalized by the metabolic muscle cost of the total ankle muscle without EXO.

where W_{Mech}^{+} is positive mechanical work performed by MTU over a stride and W_{Met} is metabolic work performed by CE over a stride. The computational detail of formulas W_{Mech}^{+} and W_{Met} is given in [8] The PF muscle efficiency is higher than the DF muscle efficiency under all EXO stiffness conditions. The PF muscle efficiency reduced gradually in similar linearity. The DF muscle efficiency remains unchanged first, and after the exoskeleton stiffness exceeds 60 N/mm, it began to decrease gradually.

4   Discussion

The goal of this study was to develop an ankle musculoskeletal model capable of simultaneously analyzing PF and DF muscles. There are two main hypotheses: First, not only the efficiency of PF muscle but also the efficiency of DF muscle are reduced with EXO. Second, when the passive exoskeleton torque is close to or higher than the ankle moment required, the PFMTU is as a passive elastomer, at which time the muscles and tendons are stretched as two springs in series. From the matching degree between the simulation results and the experimental results, these hypotheses are convincing.

4.1   Modeling of Dorsiflexor MTU

The benefit of the modeling of DF is the ability to analyze the efficiency of DF muscles under different stiffness conditions. It allows us to distinguish inefficient muscles from high-efficiency muscles. When the DF muscle charges the EXO, the allowable increase in the antagonist is small, even at the maximum stiffness value. When the exoskeleton stiffness is low, the increase in the assisting moment does not result in an increase in antagonistic muscle strength. As the stiffness of the exoskeleton continues to increase, the muscle efficiency of DF is at a higher stage relative to itself, and the muscle efficiency of PF has decreased by a large part. At this time, from the perspective of total metabolic consumption, it is cost-effective for the DF muscles to charge EXO at this time, and the total metabolic consumption decreases with increasing stiffness. When the exoskeleton stiffness reaches the optimal value, the increase in antagonism caused by the DF muscle is very small, but the exoskeleton assistant torque is considerable. As the exoskeleton stiffness continues to increase, the DF muscle efficiency continues to decline, it becomes less cost-effective for the DF muscles to charge EXO and total metabolism begins to rise. When the stiffness value reaches the maximum allowed, the degree of muscle activation is close to the limit, and the EXO assistant moment at this time is part of the desired muscle moment rather than nearly all.

4.2   Analysis of Minimum PF Passive Moment

When the exoskeleton assistant torque is higher than the muscle torque required by the ankle joint, if the PF muscle moment is set to 0, then the tendon force, the change in tendon length, the tendon speed, and the tendon mechanical power are all equal to 0. At this condition, if the MTU is at stretching, the muscles share the stretching of the MTU and produce the passive force, at which time the muscle force and the tendon force are contradictory. Therefore, the minimum PF muscle force should not be ignored. From the simulation results, the muscle and tendon are stretched stretch simultaneously when the MTU is stretched with high EXO stiffness, and the force generated by muscle and the force generated by tendon is equal. At the same time, the force, the elongation, the velocity, and the mechanical power of the tendon are not equal to zero. For the analysis of the PF minimum passive torque, the benefit is the analysis of muscle, tendon length, velocity and energy in the case of high stiffness.

5 Conclusion

This work explores the biological mechanics and energetics of the ankle joint muscle-tendon unit under a passive ankle exoskeleton assistance in normal walking. The musculoskeletal model which model plantar flexor and dorsiflexor based on Hill-type muscle-tendon model can distinguish muscle efficiency of efficient muscles and inefficient muscles. The analysis of minimum plantar flexor passive moment can solve the contradiction between muscle force and tendon force when the exoskeleton assistant moment is at a high level. The analysis results of the improved model are more consistent with the experimental results. This makes us realize that although the dorsiflexor muscle force and the minimum passive force of the plantar flexor are relatively small, they cannot be ignored in the modeling of the ankle joint.

Acknowledgment. The authors would like to gratefully acknowledge the reviewers comments. This work is supported by National Natural Science Foundation of China (Grant Nos. U1713207), Science and Technology Planning Project of Guangdong Province (2017A010102005), Key Program of Guangzhou Technology Plan (Grant No. 201904020020).

References

1. Sankai, Y.: Leading edge of cybernics: robot suit HAL. In: 2006 SICE-ICASE International Joint Conference, pp. P–1. IEEE (2006)
2. Walsh, C.J., Endo, K., Herr, H.: A quasi-passive leg exoskeleton for load-carrying augmentation. Int. J. Humanoid Rob. **4**(03), 487–506 (2007)
3. Mooney, L.M., Rouse, E.J., Herr, H.M.: Autonomous exoskeleton reduces metabolic cost of human walking during load carriage. J. Neuroeng. Rehabil. **11**(1), 80 (2014)
4. Panizzolo, F.A., et al.: A biologically-inspired multi-joint soft exosuit that can reduce the energy cost of loaded walking. J. Neuroeng. Rehabil. **13**(1), 43 (2016)
5. Collins, S.H., Wiggin, M.B., Sawicki, G.S.: Reducing the energy cost of human walking using an unpowered exoskeleton. Nature **522**(7555), 212 (2015)
6. Rajagopal, A., Dembia, C.L., DeMers, M.S., Delp, D.D., Hicks, J.L., Delp, S.L.: Full-body musculoskeletal model for muscle-driven simulation of human gait. IEEE Trans. Biomed. Eng. **63**(10), 2068–2079 (2016)
7. Uchida, T.K., Seth, A., Pouya, S., Dembia, C.L., Hicks, J.L., Delp, S.L.: Simulating ideal assistive devices to reduce the metabolic cost of running. PLoS ONE **11**(9), e0163417 (2016)
8. Sawicki, G.S., Khan, N.S.: A simple model to estimate plantarflexor muscle-tendon mechanics and energetics during walking with elastic ankle exoskeletons. IEEE Trans. Biomed. Eng. **63**(5), 914–923 (2016)
9. Zajac, F.E.: Muscle and tendon: properties, models, scaling, and application to biomechanics and motor control. Crit. Rev. Biomed. Eng. **17**(4), 359–411 (1989)

10. Brand, R.A., Crowninshield, R.D., Wittstock, C., Pedersen, D., Clark, C.R., Van Krieken, F.: A model of lower extremity muscular anatomy. J. Biomech. Eng. **104**(4), 304–310 (1982)
11. Arnold, E.M., Ward, S.R., Lieber, R.L., Delp, S.L.: A model of the lower limb for analysis of human movement. Ann. Biomed. Eng. **38**(2), 269–279 (2010)
12. Geyer, H., Herr, H.: A muscle-reflex model that encodes principles of legged mechanics produces human walking dynamics and muscle activities. IEEE Trans. Neural Syst. Rehabil. Eng. **18**(3), 263–273 (2010)
13. Maganaris, C.N.: In vivo measurement-based estimations of the moment arm in the human tibialis anterior muscle-tendon unit. J. Biomech. **33**(3), 375–379 (2000)
14. Maganaris, C.N., Baltzopoulos, V., Sargeant, A.J.: In vivo measurement-based estimations of the human achilles tendon moment arm. Eur. J. Appl. Physiol. **83**(4–5), 363–369 (2000)
15. Wu, S., Chen, W., Xiong, C.: A simplified musculoskeletal hip model for replicating the natural human walking behavior. In: 2018 3rd International Conference on Advanced Robotics and Mechatronics (ICARM), pp. 426–430. IEEE (2018)
16. Chleboun, G.S., Busic, A.B., Graham, K.K., Stuckey, H.A.: Fascicle length change of the human tibialis anterior and vastus lateralis during walking. J. Orthop. Sport. Phys. Ther. **37**(7), 372–379 (2007)
17. Thelen, D.G., Anderson, F.C.: Using computed muscle control to generate forward dynamic simulations of human walking from experimental data. J. Biomech. **39**(6), 1107–1115 (2006)
18. Rubenson, J., Pires, N.J., Loi, H.O., Pinniger, G.J., Shannon, D.G.: On the ascent: the soleus operating length is conserved to the ascending limb of the force-length curve across gait mechanics in humans. J. Exp. Biol. **215**(20), 3539–3551 (2012)
19. Alexander, R.M.: Optimum muscle design for oscillatory movements. J. Theor. Biol. **184**(3), 253–259 (1997)
20. Umberger, B.R., Rubenson, J.: Understanding muscle energetics in locomotion: new modeling and experimental approaches. Exerc. Sport Sci. Rev. **39**(2), 59–67 (2011)

Modeling and Analysis of Human Lower Limb in Walking Motion

Huan Zhao, Junyi Cao$^{(\boxtimes)}$, and Ruixue Wang

Xi'an Jiaotong University, Xi'an 710049, China
caojy@mail.xjtu.edu.cn

Abstract. Dynamic modeling and analysis of human lower limb motion is necessary in many fields like medical, robotics and energy supplying of wearable device. As it is complex to model the human lower limb motions, a simplified plant model of human lower limb was established in this paper to explore the properties in walking motion. To present the position relation of each joints in the plant model, kinematic methods such as Denavit-Hartenberg notion and Roberson-Wittenburg algorithm were used. In addition, dynamic methods like Newton Euler, Lagrange equation and Kane equation were also applied to characterize the plant model. Simultaneously, the applicability of these methods was illustrated and compared. Furthermore, an experiment was conducted on a treadmill at a speed of 5 km/h to evaluate the validity of plant model. The Simulink model results were compared with the experiment results, which demonstrated the robustness and accuracy of the plant model.

Keywords: Human lower limb · Denavit-Hartenberg ·
Newton Euler equation · Lagrange method

1 Introduction

Modeling and analysis of human walking motion is essential in human health monitoring, medical diagnoses, design of prostheses and orthoses, humanoid robot, and energy supply to wearable devices [1–3]. Therefore, lots of efforts have been devoted to model and analysis in human walking. The walking motion requiring interaction among joints of the body, especially the hip and knee in the lower limb [4]. Therefore, the development of an appropriate human lower limb model is highly desired.

Many human lower limb models have been developed these years, such as inverted pendulum model, multiple-mass inverted pendulum model, and multi-segment-rigid body model [5, 6]. In inverted pendulum model, the body mass concentrates at one point (center of gravity), and the massless leg acts as the supporting rod. It's simple but is unable to generate natural and realistic human motion. Multiple-mass inverted pendulum model is more stable as it considered the dynamic effect of the swing leg [7]. Multi-rigid-body model shares appropriate fidelity which can produce kinematic outputs similar to natural gait [8].

The human lower limb model needs to be described by some equations to represent its moving characteristics. Generally, the equations are obtained by kinematics and dynamics. The Kinematic representations of many open-loop robotic applications are

© Springer Nature Switzerland AG 2019
H. Yu et al. (Eds.): ICIRA 2019, LNAI 11740, pp. 97–105, 2019.
https://doi.org/10.1007/978-3-030-27526-6_9

commonly based on the Denavit-Hartenberg (D-H) notion [9]. Qiu used D-H notation to calculate the position of knee and hip when the limb at the stand phase [10]. Roberson-Wittenburg (R-S) algorithm utilize the system graph theory to replace the connection of multi-rigid-body system structure [11].

As for dynamic characters analysis, there are different dynamic modeling methods to calculate the forces and moments of each joint during gait. To solve the dynamic parameters at the joint, Newton-Euler equation is applied to establish the human lower limb dynamic equations [12]. Pejhan et al. applied classical Lagrange dynamic equations to build the model of human lower limb for optimizing an above-knee prosthesis based on the kinematics of gait [13]. As Kane equation is ideally suited for the analysis of multi-body system dynamics, Mu used Kane equation in the impact prediction of human motion [14]. Nasir applied Kane equation to model the motion of human lower limb [15].

Both the kinematic and dynamic modeling methods have been widely used in human lower limb motion. However, the previous studies lack distinct comparison among these methods. This paper aims to find an applicable dynamic modeling method toward human lower limb to describe the moving characteristics during human's walking.

The rest of this paper is organized as follows. In Sect. 2, human lower limbs are simplified as a plant model which moves in the two-dimensional sagittal plane. In Sect. 3, the kinematic analysis methods are illustrated to establish relationships of human lower limb joints. Dynamic methods are displayed to exhibit the dynamic characteristics of joints. In addition, a comparison among the methods was also made. In Sect. 4, the experimental data of an adult man walking at 5 km/h are analyzed and the comparison between the torques calculated by the Lagrange equation and the simulation results is also discussed. The conclusion is drawn in the final section.

2   Plant Model of Human Lower Limb

Lower limb motion produce the walking of human. As the three joints of hip, knee and ankle play an important role in human lower limb motion, hip and knee mainly stretch and flex the thigh and shank, which acute the whole body to move. Considering the ankle presents no obvious influence in forward motion as it rotates by a slight angle, rotation of the ankle can be ignored. The swing leg can then be simplified as two rigid links, and the stance leg is simplified as a rigid rod fixed to the ground. Therefore, the structure of human lower limbs are reduced to planar rigid body model as shown in Fig. 1.

In the model, H, K and A respectively represent the hip, knee and ankle of swing leg, T and S are respectively the centers of mass of swing thigh and shank. L represents the centers of mass of stance leg. The stance foot is taken as the origin of coordinate. p_1 is the distance from origin to mass center of the stance foot, p_2 is the distance from hip to mass center of swing thigh, p_3 is the distance between mass center of swing shank and knee. l_1 is the length of stance leg, l_2 and l_3 are the length of thigh and shank of swing leg, θ_1 is the angle from Y axis to stance leg, θ_2 is the angle from Y axis to thigh, θ_3 is the angle from Y axis to shank.

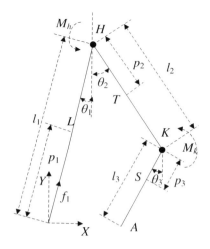

Fig. 1. A plant model of human lower limb

3 Analysis Methods of the Plant Model

3.1 Kinematic Analysis Method

Denavit-Hartenberg Notion. D-H method fixes a coordinate in each link, and then the homogeneous transformation matrix is applied to describe the space relation between two adjacent links. Based on the plant model, D-H parameters of the plant model are established as Table 1.

Table 1. D-H parameters

i	α_i/rad	a_i/m	θ_i/rad	d_i/m
1	0	0.885	θ_1	0
2	0	0.505	θ_2	0
3	0	0.38	θ_3	0

Based on Table 1, the homogeneous transformation matrix is calculated as follows,

$$T_{i,i+1} = \begin{bmatrix} \cos\theta_i & -\sin\theta_i\cos\alpha_i & \sin\theta_i\sin\alpha_i & a_i\cos\theta_i \\ \sin\theta_i & \cos\theta_i\cos\alpha_i & -\cos\theta_i\sin\alpha_i & a_i\sin\theta_i \\ 0 & \sin\alpha_i & \cos\alpha_i & d_i \\ 0 & 0 & 0 & 1 \end{bmatrix} \quad (1)$$

The kinematic equations can be derived based on the transformation matrix to obtain the position of knee and hip. The D-H method describes the position changes of each link in the plant model, which is comprehensible and convenient. In some closed-loop or tree structures, the transmission shaft may exceed one and results in the ambiguous relationship. Fortunately, modified D-H has developed and compensated this shortage [16]. For the human lower limb model, D-H is enough and concise.

Roberson-Wittenburg Algorithm. The structure and path relationship of the system are described by the incidence matrix and path matrix in graph theory. A pair of adjacent rigid bodies of each hinge is taken as the independent unit, one rigid body act as the reference, and the generalized coordinates of the hinge express the other rigid body. The generalized coordinate is usually the hinge displacement between adjacent rigid bodies, so that the position of the open loop system can be determined through the generalized coordinate matrix of all the hinges. In the plant model of human lower limb, the incidence matrix and path matrix can be shown as follow,

$$S = \begin{bmatrix} -1 & 1 & 1 \\ 0 & -1 & 1 \\ 0 & 0 & -1 \end{bmatrix} \quad T = \begin{bmatrix} -1 & -1 & -1 \\ 0 & -1 & -1 \\ 0 & 0 & -1 \end{bmatrix} \quad (2)$$

Based on the theorem of motion of mass center and theorem of momentum, the dynamic equations can be established.

3.2 Dynamic Analysis Method

Newton Euler Equation. As a classical mechanics method, Newton Euler method simplifies human body as rigid links. The plane motion of a body is decomposed as translation from a point and rotation around a point. Newton Euler equation of thigh and shank can be written as follow respectively,

$$\begin{cases} \vec{f}_1 - \vec{f}_2 + m_1 g = m_1 p_1 \ddot{\theta}_1 \\ M_1 = I_1 \ddot{\theta}_1 + \dot{\theta}_1 \times I_1 \dot{\theta}_1 \end{cases} \Rightarrow I_1 \ddot{\theta}_1 + \dot{\theta}_1 \times I_1 \dot{\theta}_1 = M_h - \vec{f}_1 \times p_1 + \vec{f}_2 \times (l_1 - p_1) \quad (3)$$

$$\begin{cases} \vec{f}_2 - \vec{f}_3 + m_2 g = m_2 p_2 \ddot{\theta}_2 \\ M_2 = I_2 \ddot{\theta}_2 + \dot{\theta}_2 \times I_2 \dot{\theta}_2 \end{cases} \Rightarrow I_2 \ddot{\theta}_2 + \dot{\theta}_2 \times I_2 \dot{\theta}_2 = M_h - M_k - \vec{f}_2 \times p_2 + \vec{f}_3 \times (l_2 - p_2)$$

$$(4)$$

$$\begin{cases} m_3 g + \vec{f}_3 = m_3 p_3 \ddot{\theta}_3 \\ M_3 = I_3 \ddot{\theta}_3 + \dot{\theta}_3 \times I_3 \dot{\theta}_3 \end{cases} \Rightarrow I_3 \ddot{\theta}_3 + \dot{\theta}_3 \times I_3 \dot{\theta}_3 = M_k - \vec{f}_3 \times p_3 \quad (5)$$

where I_1 and M_1 are the inertia tensor and moment of stance leg, I_2 and I_3 are the inertia tensor of swing thigh and shank. M_2 and M_3 are the moment of swing thigh and shank. Moreover, f_1 is the ground support force applied to stance leg, f_2 is the constraint force that thigh react to the stance leg and f_3 denotes the force that thigh act to shank in swing leg.

The moment of hip and knee can be derived as M_h and M_k respectively as follows,

$$\begin{cases} M_k = f_2 p_2 \sin\theta_2 + I_2\ddot{\theta}_2 + \dot{\theta}_2 \times I_2\dot{\theta}_2 \\ M_h = I_1\ddot{\theta}_1 + \dot{\theta}_1 \times I_1\dot{\theta}_1 + f_2 p_2 \sin\theta_2 + I_2\ddot{\theta}_2 + \dot{\theta}_2 \times I_2\dot{\theta}_2 + f_1 p_1 \cos\theta_1 - f_2(l_1 - p_1)\cos\theta_1 \end{cases} \quad (6)$$

In the Newton Euler equation, the existence of constraint reaction forces increase the dynamic analysis complexity. In addition, Newton Euler equation illustrates the dynamic characteristics of one rigid body. The human lower limb model consists of three rigid bodies, the dynamic equation of the plant model is a simultaneous equations composed of multiple equations.

Lagrange Equation. Based on the viewpoint of energy, the kinetic energy function is represented by generalized coordinates and velocity. It avoids the complicated calculation of force, velocity, acceleration and other vectors. The Lagrange equation of the plant model can be formed as follows.

$$\begin{cases} E_k = \frac{1}{2}m_1 p_1^2\dot{\theta}_1^2 + \frac{1}{2}m_2 l_1^2\dot{\theta}_1^2 + \frac{1}{2}m_2 p_2^2\dot{\theta}_2^2 + \frac{1}{2}m_2 l_2^2\dot{\theta}_2^2 + \frac{1}{2}m_3 p_3^2\dot{\theta}_3^2 \\ E_p = m_1 g p_1(1 - \cos\theta_1) + m_2 g p_2(1 - \cos\theta_2) + m_3 g p_3(1 - \cos\theta_3) + m_3 g l_2(1 - \cos\theta_2) \end{cases}$$
$$(7)$$

$$L = E_k - E_p = \frac{1}{2}m_1 p_1^2\dot{\theta}_1^2 + \frac{1}{2}m_2 l_1^2\dot{\theta}_1^2 + \frac{1}{2}m_2 p_2^2\dot{\theta}_2^2 + \frac{1}{2}m_2 l_2^2\dot{\theta}_2^2 + \frac{1}{2}m_3 p_3^2\dot{\theta}_3^2$$
$$- m_1 g p_1(1 - \cos\theta_1) - m_2 g p_2(1 - \cos\theta_2) - m_3 g p_3(1 - \cos\theta_3) - m_3 g l_2(1 - \cos\theta_2) \quad (8)$$

$$\begin{cases} M_k = \frac{d}{dt}\frac{\partial L}{\partial \dot{\theta}_3} - \frac{\partial L}{\partial \theta_3} = m_3 p_3^2\ddot{\theta}_3 - m_3 g p_3 \sin\theta_3 \\ M_h = \frac{d}{dt}\frac{\partial L}{\partial \dot{\theta}_2} - \frac{\partial L}{\partial \theta_2} = (m_2 p_2^2 + m_2 l_2^2)\ddot{\theta}_2 - (m_2 p_2 + m_3 l_2)g \sin\theta_2 \end{cases} \quad (9)$$

Compared with Newton Euler equation, Lagrange illustrates the multi-rigid-body system in one equation, and no constrain force is included. As for the plant model of human lower limb, Lagrange equation is more simple and distinct.

Kane Equation. Kane equation is established using Alembert principle and virtual displacement principle. (The system is composed of n particles, with ideal constraints and n degrees of freedom)

$$F_r + F_r^* = 0 \, (r = 1, \ldots, n) \quad (10)$$

F_r and F_r^* are generalized applied force and inertia force which depend on the generalized coordinates respectively. That is,

$$F_r = \sum_{i=1}^{N} f_i = m_1 g + m_2 g \quad (11)$$

$$F_r^* = \sum_{i=1}^{N} (-m_i a_i) = -m_1 P_1\ddot{\theta}_1 - m_2 P_2\ddot{\theta}_2 + 2m_1\dot{\theta}_1 \times P_1\ddot{\theta}_1 + 2m_2\dot{\theta}_2 \times P_2\ddot{\theta}_2 \quad (12)$$

3.3   Summary of Analysis Method

To summarize these analysis methods when they describe the plant model, Table 2 is shown as follow.

Table 2. Analysis methods comparisons

Methods	Application	Characteristics
Denavit-Hartenberg	Kinematic analysis	Concise and basic
Roberson-Wittenburg	Kinematic analysis	Features of each linkage is specific
Newton Euler equation	Dynamic analysis	Clear but complex due to constraint
Lagrange equation	Dynamic analysis	Simple to derive
Kane equation	Dynamic analysis	Convenient for numerical calculation

We can see that Lagrange method is more straightforward than Newton Euler and Kane method to characterize the dynamic features of knee and hip, and it's the reason why Lagrange method is widely used in human motion modeling and analysis.

4   Comparison Between Simulation and Experimental Results

The plant model is simulated in the Simulink to imitate the motion of human. The experiment on the treadmill is conducted to verify the plant model and the dynamic analysis method. The subject is a health man (24 years old, 65 kg, 1.78 m) without previous history musculoskeletal injury. The experiment setup is shown in Fig. 2 and the acceleration sensors (CXL04GP3) are used to collect the human walking information when the treadmill's speed is controlled at 3, 4, 5, 6, 7 km/h.

Fig. 2. Experiment setup

The torques of hip and knee are then calculated by Lagrange method based on the experiment data. This paper uses motion data at 5 km/h as it is close to the normal walking speed mostly. Both the numerical calculated torques and experiment calculated torques of hip and knee respectively are shown in Fig. 3.

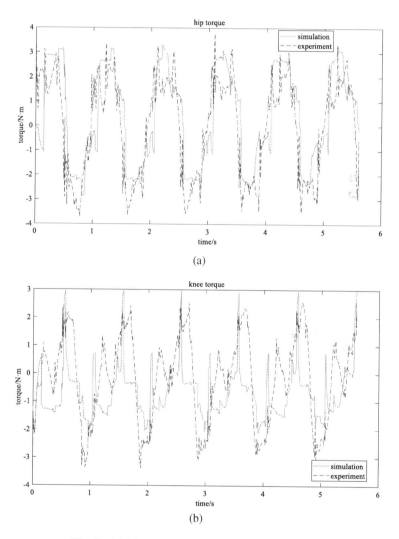

(a)

(b)

Fig. 3. (a) The torque of hip (b) The torque of knee

Some errors exist between the experimental analysis and simulation, it may result from the relative motion between clothes and human body. Compared with the simulation, the experiment result line presents many glitch impulses which come from the muscles jitter, damp characteristic and flexibility of human body. Moreover, the period of simulation and experiment at hip are totally coincide, but they are not as well at the knee. It implies that knee and hip may have relative hysteresis in the real motion, which hasn't been considered in the plant model and simulation. Aiming at these phenomena, further research work will be carried out in the future to quantify these influences.

5   Conclusion

The human lower limb was simplified to a three-rigid-link system which moves in a two-dimensional sagittal plane, and it is named as plant model. To explore the properties of the pant model in walking motion, Denavit-Hartenberg notion and Roberson-Wittenburg algorithm were used to deploy the relation of each joints. Moreover, Newton Euler, Lagrange equation and Kane equation were compared when they build the dynamic equation of the plant model. The superiority of Lagrange equation was demonstrated. Therefore, the torques of experiment data were analyzed by Lagrange equation. The comparisons of simulation and experiment results show that the dynamic properties of plant model is similar to the real human, thus the fidelity of the plant model is validated.

Acknowledgment. This work was in part by the National Key R&D Program of China (2018YFB1306100).

References

1. Rajagopal, A., Dembia, C., Demers, M., Delp, D., Hicks, J., Delp, S.: Full body musculoskeletal model for muscle-driven simulation of human gait. IEEE Trans. Biomed. Eng. **63**(10), 2068–2079 (2016)
2. Arnold, E.M., Ward, S.R., Lieber, R.L., Delp, S.L.: A model of the lower limb for analysis of human movement. Ann. Biomed. Eng. **38**(2), 269 (2010)
3. Wei, W., Cao, J., Nan, Z., Jing, L., Liao, W.H.: Magnetic-spring based energy harvesting from human motions: design, modeling and experiments. Energy Convers. Manag. **132**, 189–197 (2017)
4. Kuo, A.D.: The six determinants of gait and the inverted pendulum analogy: a dynamic walking perspective. Hum. Mov. Sci. **26**(4), 617–656 (2007)
5. Suzuki, Y., Inoue, T., Nomura, T.: A simple algorithm for assimilating marker-based motion capture data during periodic human movement into models of multi-rigid-body systems. Front. Bioeng. Biotechnol. **6** (2018)
6. Xiang, Y., Arora, J.S., Abdel-Malek, K.: Physics-based modeling and simulation of human walking: a review of optimization-based and other approaches. Struct. Multi. Optim. **42**(1), 1–23 (2010)
7. Albert, A., Gerth, W.: Analytic path planning algorithms for bipedal robots without a trunk. J. Intell. Rob. Syst. **36**(2), 109–127 (2003)
8. Sun, J.: Dynamic modeling of human gait using a model predictive control approach. Dissertations and Theses - Gradworks (2015)
9. Kim, J.H., Yang, J., Abdel-Malek, K.: A novel formulation for determining joint constraint loads during optimal dynamic motion of redundant manipulators in DH representation. Multibody Sys. Dyn. **19**(4), 427–451 (2008)

10. Qiu, S., Wang, Z., Zhao, H., Hu, H.: Using distributed wearable sensors to measure and evaluate human lower limb motions. IEEE Trans. Instrum. Meas. **65**(4), 939–950 (2016)
11. Roberson, R.E., Schwertassek, R., Huston, R.L.: Dynamics of Multibody Systems (1989)
12. Hirashima, M., Kudo, K., Ohtsuki, T.: A new non-orthogonal decomposition method to determine effective torques for three-dimensional joint rotation. J. Biomech. **40**(4), 871–882 (2007)
13. Pejhan, S., Farahmand, F., Parnianpour, M.: Design optimization of an above-knee prosthesis based on the kinematics of gait. In: International Conference of the IEEE Engineering in Medicine and Biology Society (2008)
14. Qiao, M., Yang, C., Yuan, X.: The application of Kane equation in the impact prediction of human motion. In: Duffy, V.G. (ed.) ICDHM 2007. LNCS, vol. 4561, pp. 179–188. Springer, Heidelberg (2007). https://doi.org/10.1007/978-3-540-73321-8_22
15. Nasir, N.H.M., Ibrahim, B.S.K.K., Huq, M.S., Ahmad, M.K.I.: Modelling of subject specific based segmental dynamics of knee joint. In: Advances in Electrical and Electronic Engineering (2017)
16. Khalil, W., Kleinfinger, J.F.: A new geometric notation for open and closed-loop robots. In: Institute of Electrical and Electronics Engineers 1986 IEEE International Conference on Robotics and Automation, San Francisco (1986)

A Self-calibration Method
for Mobile Manipulator

Hangbo Zou[1,2,3,4], Yinghao Li[1,2,3,4], Sijun Zhu[1,4], Kanfeng Gu[1,4],
Xinggang Zhang[1,2,3,4], and Mingyang Zhao[1,4(✉)]

[1] Shenyang Institute of Automation,
Chinese Academy of Sciences,
Shenyang 110016, China
myzhao@sia.cn
[2] Institutes for Robotics and Intelligent Manufacturing,
Chinese Academy of Sciences, Shenyang 110016, China
[3] University of Chinese Academy of Sciences, Beijing 100049, China
[4] Kunshan Intelligent Equipment Research Institute,
Shenyang Institute of Automatio, Kunshan 215347, China

Abstract. With the development of the mobile manipulator, it is
needed to have a calibration method suits for ordinary people to improve
its absolute position accuracy of the manipulator when the structure is
worn. The method should be cheap, convinence and should do not rely
on any professional equipment or external measurement. This paper proposes a self-calibration method that not only inherits the above advantages, but also is not affected by the convected motion caused by the
shifting of the mobile platform. The basic idea is that when the endpoint
of the manipulator reaches the specified target point in different configurations, if the gravity moment of the manipulator with respect to the
platform remains basically unchanged, the shift of the platform and the
influence of the convected motion can be neglected. By discretizing the
target points in Cartesian space, grouping the data based on these target
points, and combining the nonlinear least squares method, the parameters of the kinematic model can be optimized. Finally, the effectiveness
of the proposed method is verified by different methods including the use
of the laser tracker. The absolute position error of the flange center at
the end of the manipulator is reduced from 2.25 mm to 0.42 mm.

Keywords: Mobile manipulator · Self-calibration ·
Absolute position accuracy

1   Introduction

As robots and varieties of sensors have a well development, robots are gradually
be used in different fields. The mobile manipulator is the robot system consists
of a robotic manipulator arm mounted on a mobile platform, which combines
the advantages of mobile platforms and robotic manipulator arms and reduces

© Springer Nature Switzerland AG 2019
H. Yu et al. (Eds.): ICIRA 2019, LNAI 11740, pp. 106–116, 2019.
https://doi.org/10.1007/978-3-030-27526-6_10

their drawbacks. Since it can help and replace people to complete their daily housework, bring great convenience to life, and have great application value, it has become a research hotspot [2,8].

When a mobile manipulator works in the auto module, it will utilize the vision system to locate the target object first, and then control the manipulator to complete the task. However, the kinematic parameters of the manipulator will not match its current state after wear or maintenance, resulting in a decrease in absolute position accuracy. And the location error of the endpoint will be further enlarged by the end effector. At this time, a robotic calibration method is needed to have better kinematic parameters to improve the absolute position accuracy.

There are two methods to calibrate a manipulator. Usually, the open-loop kinematic calibration method [7] is a convenience choose. It will utilize the laser tracker to obtain the position of the end effector in Cartesian space, and then combine with different kinematic models or methods to realize the optimization. For example, the screw-axis measurement method [10] and the CMMK model [12]. Calibration can also be achieved by using the ballbar to compare the distance between the measuring points and the preset distance [9]. The close-loop kiematic calibration method is the other one, which is also called self-calibration [7]. By fixing precision balls on the platform and then adjusting the manipulator to make the endpoint contact balls [3], or by means of geometric characteristics of external planes can achieve the self-calibration [13]. For robots that have different types of sensors, they can calculate the geometrical relationships between manipulators and cameras by force sensors and vision sensors [1,11].

Whether it is an open-loop or close-loop calibration method, in most robot calibration processes, the geometric relationship between the robot base and external measurement equipment or physical constraints needs to be established [3,9,10,12,13]. However, as for a mobile manipulator, it is necessary to fix the mobile platform to avoid the influence of the convected motion on the endpoint due to its shift. In addition to this, the open-loop calibration method has other application conditions. Due to the need of professional measuring equipment such as laser trackers and ballbars, the calibration cost is high, the operation is complicated, and the calibration work cannot be carried out flexibly. For mobile manipulators sold to the general public, it is difficult to calibrate the manipulator using the above conventional methods. Even if the end contact sensor is used for self-calibration, since the contact point is not a sharp point, the calibration accuracy is susceptible to the end contact surface, and the locating deviation is likely to occur [1,11].

In this paper, the robotic self-calibration technology is used to realize the calibration of kinematic parameters for a manipulator on a mobile platform. Joint angles acquired by having the manipulator reaches the spatial target point in different configurations, and grouping the data according to target points to avoid the influence of the platform when the gravity moment of the manipulator with respect to the mobile platform is changed obviously. Finally, the iterative least square method is used to converge the objective function and optimize the parameters. The calibrated parameters of the manipulator are verified by means of analysis including the use of the laser tracker.

The paper is organized as follows. Section 2 presents the principle and methodology of how to calibrate the manipulator mounted on the platform. The experimental equipments and verifications are shown in Sects. 3 and 4. Section 5 is the conclusion.

2   Principle and Methodology

The mobile manipulator sold to ordinary people needs to be calibrated after its absolute position accuracy decreasing. However, due to the lack of professional measuring equipments, and the change of the gravity moment of the manipulator with respect to the platform causes the platform to shift resulting in a convected motion at the endpoint. The calibration method by establishing the geometric relationship between the robot base and the external measuring feature is no longer suitable. To avoid the disadvantages mentioned above and balance the relationship between the cost and the calibration accuracy, a new self-calibration method based on grouping the data at specified points (GDSP) is proposed.

2.1   Different Configurations at a Specified Point

In theory, the endpoint can be brought to a specified target point in different configurations without considering the pose of the end effector. The vector of joint angles $\mathbf{q}_{ij}$ and the vector of endpoint $\mathbf{P}_{ij}$ can be defined as

$$\mathbf{q} = \begin{bmatrix} q_1 & q_2 & \cdots & q_m \end{bmatrix}^{\mathrm{T}}$$
$$\mathbf{P} = \begin{bmatrix} x & y & z \end{bmatrix}^{\mathrm{T}}$$

Where q_m is the angle of the joint m. And $\mathbf{q}_{ij}$ is the vector of joint angles when the manipulator in the configuration j under the target point i; $\mathbf{P}_{ij}$ is the nominal position of the endpoint corresponding to $\mathbf{q}_{ij}$ in the Cartesian space.

In order to have the calibration result more credible globally, specified target points should be discreted in space and configurations need to be different.

Kinematic Model. To establish the kinematic model for the manipulator, there are different methods. For example, DH method [4], Hayati method [5], and POE method [6]. The paper chooses the modified DH method. The link transformation matrix is

$$^{i-1}\mathbf{T}_i = \mathbf{R}_x\left(\alpha_{i-1}\right) \cdot \mathbf{T}_x(a_{i-1}) \cdot \mathbf{T}_z(d_i) \cdot \mathbf{R}_z\left(\theta_i\right) \tag{1}$$

Where α_{i-1}, a_{i-1}, d_i, θ_i are kinematic parameters for the coordinate frame $\mathbf{O}_i$; $\mathbf{R}_*\left(\alpha\right)$ represents the homogeneous matrix that rotates α around the axis $*$; $\mathbf{T}_*\left(d\right)$ represents the homogeneous matrix that translates d around the axis $*$.

The homogeneous matrix $^b\mathbf{T}_e$ is the pose-array of the coordinate frame $\mathbf{O}_e$ on the end link respects to the base coordinate frame $\mathbf{O}_b$, it can be obtained by multiplying

$$^b\mathbf{T}_e = {}^b\mathbf{T}_1 {}^1\mathbf{T}_2 \cdots {}^{i-1}\mathbf{T}_i \tag{2}$$

Since the geometric relationship $^b\mathbf{T}_1$ between the first coordinate frame $\mathbf{O}_1$ and the base coordinate frame $\mathbf{O}_b$ will influence the nominal position of the endpoint. However, it can be ignored when there is not any external geometric relationship or measurement introduced.

In order to avoid the structure of the manipulator being scaled, it is necessary to obtain $^e\mathbf{P}_{tool}$, the position of the endpoint respect to the center of the flange. And the endpoint respect to the base of the manipulator $^e\mathbf{P}_{tool}$ is

$$^b\mathbf{P}_{tool} = {}^b\mathbf{T}_e \cdot {}^e\mathbf{P}_{tool} = f(\mathbf{q}, \phi, \psi) \tag{3}$$
$$\mathbf{P} = {}^b\mathbf{P}_{tool} \tag{4}$$

Where $f(\cdot)$ is the forward kinematic function of the manipulator; ϕ is the vector of the parameters to be calibrated; ψ is the vector of the other paremeters.

Position Error. When the endpoint reaches the specified target point, there is position error with the nominal position (Fig. 1). It contains the error $\mathbf{e}_{ij}$ caused by the deviation between the position $\mathbf{P}_{ij}$ calculated by the forward kinematic function and the position of the actual endpoint, and the error ε_{ij} caused by the deviation between the position of the actual endpoint and the specified target point $\mathbf{P}_i$.

$$\mathbf{P}_{ij} = \mathbf{P}_i + \varepsilon_{ij} + \mathbf{e}_{ij} \tag{5}$$

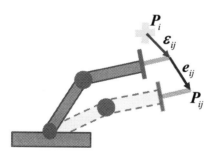

Fig. 1. Position error of the nominal position to the specified target point

Because of the parameters to be optimized are structural parameters of the manipulator itself, the error $\mathbf{e}_{ij}$ is the comprehensive reflection of the position and orientation error of the flange of the manipulator after ignoring the error of the tool coordinate frame.

2.2   Grouping the Data

When the manipulator changes its center of the gravity greatly by changing its configuration, it will lead to the change of the gravity moment of the manipulator with respect to the platform and the mobile platform will be shifted, and the convected motion will influence the endpoint of the manipulator. If the measurement is used to match a preset geometric constraint or external measurement, the calibration error will be caused.

By grouping the data based on their target points, when the endpoint reaches a specified target point in different configurations, the gravity moment of the manipulator with respect to the platform remains basically unchanged, the mobile platform of the manipulator will be little shifted and the convected motion at the endpoint can be ignored, because of the structural constrain of the manipulator. At the same time, by calculating the nominal location error, any geometric constraint among the target points or between target points and the robot base can be avoided.

If the kinematic parameters are accurate enough, the relationship between the nominal endpoints and the specified target point is

$$\sum_{j=1}^{n} \mathbf{P}_{ij} = \sum_{j=1}^{n} \mathbf{P}_i + \varepsilon_{ij} + \mathbf{e}_{ij} = n\mathbf{P}_i \tag{6}$$

$$\overline{\mathbf{P}_i} = \frac{\sum\limits_{j=1}^{n} \mathbf{P}_{ij}}{n} \tag{7}$$

Where $\overline{\mathbf{P}_i}$ is the estimate of the specified target point $\mathbf{P}_i$ and n is the number of the configurations in this group. The error ε_{ij} follows a normal distribution with a mean of zero.

The nominal location error of every endpoint is

$$\Delta\mathbf{P}_{ij} = \mathbf{P}_{ij} - \overline{\mathbf{P}_i} \tag{8}$$

2.3   Identification

If the function $f(\cdot)$ is continuous and differentiable for ϕ, a Taylor series expansion can be performed. When higher order terms are ignored, there is

$$\begin{cases} \overline{\mathbf{P}} = f(\mathbf{q}, \phi, \psi) \\ \mathbf{P} = f(\mathbf{q}, \phi + \Delta\phi, \psi) \end{cases} \tag{9}$$

$$\Delta\mathbf{P} = \mathbf{P} - \overline{\mathbf{P}} = \mathbf{J} \cdot \Delta\phi \tag{10}$$

$$\mathbf{J} = \frac{\partial f(\mathbf{q}, \phi, \psi)}{\partial \phi} \tag{11}$$

Where Jacobian $\mathbf{J}$ is a function of constants and it changes from one iteration to the next. $\Delta\phi$ is the shift vector.

In this paper, the error of the position and orientation of the flange have been unified into the position of the endpoint by the vector ${}^e\mathbf{P}_{tool}$. To improve the calibration accuracy, a calibration tool that is more compatible with the actual endeffector can be used.

For a linear model, when the sample size is greater than the size of variable, linear squares method can be used to identify parameters. If $\mathbf{y}$ is the dependent variable, $\mathbf{x}$ is the independent variable, and $\mathbf{A}$ is the observation matrix, there is

$$\begin{cases} \mathbf{y} = \mathbf{A}\mathbf{x} \\ \mathbf{x} = \left(\mathbf{A}^{\mathrm{T}}\mathbf{A}\right)^{-1}\mathbf{A}^{\mathrm{T}}\mathbf{y} \end{cases} \tag{12}$$

Combining the linear square method and the GDSP method, the kinematic parameters can be identified by iterating.

$$\begin{cases} \mathbf{y} = \left[\mathbf{y}_1{}^{\mathrm{T}}, \cdots, \mathbf{y}_n{}^{\mathrm{T}}\right]^{\mathrm{T}}, \ \mathbf{y}_i = \left[\varDelta\mathbf{P}_{i1}{}^{\mathrm{T}}, \cdots, \varDelta\mathbf{P}_{im}{}^{\mathrm{T}}\right]^{\mathrm{T}} \\ \mathbf{A} = \left[\mathbf{A}_1{}^{\mathrm{T}}, \cdots, \mathbf{A}_n{}^{\mathrm{T}}\right]^{\mathrm{T}}, \ \mathbf{A}_i = \left[\mathbf{J}_{i1}{}^{\mathrm{T}}, \cdots, \mathbf{J}_{im}{}^{\mathrm{T}}\right]^{\mathrm{T}} \end{cases} \tag{13}$$

$$\begin{cases} \varDelta\phi = \left(\mathbf{A}^{\mathrm{T}}\mathbf{A}\right)^{-1}\mathbf{A}^{\mathrm{T}}\mathbf{y} \\ \phi_0 = \phi + \varDelta\phi \end{cases} \tag{14}$$

3   Experiment

3.1   Experimental Method and Equipments

The GDSP method needs the manipulator to be mounted on a platform, and the manipulator should change its configuration to have the endpoint reach specified target point. The equipment installation and experimental states are shown in Fig. 2, and the parameters of the manipulator and the mobile platform are shown in Table 1. The position of the endpoint respect to the flange is

$$^e\mathbf{P}_{tool} = [0, 0, 55.100]^{\mathrm{T}}$$

3.2   Kinematic Parameters

The initial value of the kinematic parameters to be calibrated are their ideal parame-ters, and the nonlinear least squares based on trust region is used in matlab. Each length parameter is limited to itself with ± 3 mm, and each rotation parameter is limited to itself with $\pm 3°$. The kinematic parameters are shown in Table 2.

3.3   Verification Experiment

In order to prove the validity of the GDSP method, laser tracker (see Table 1) is used. In this experiment, UR10 is fixed to a base with foundation screws. A reflective ball is mounted on the flange and using the teach pendant to control the robot's flange to translate in space. SA (SpatialAnalyzer) software is used to analysis the absolute position accuracy.

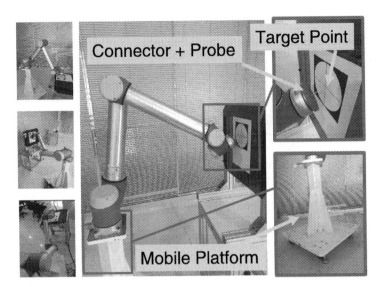

Fig. 2. Left of the figure are different states of the experiment, and right of the figure are details of the endeffector and the mobile platform. The connector is made by 3D printing. The mobile platform will shift when the gravity moment of the manipulator with respect to the platform changes obviously. The configuration of the manipulator is changed slowly by hand.

Table 1. Equipments used in the experiments

Manipulator	
Type	UR10
Payload	10 kg
Repeatability	±0.03 mm
Reach	1300 mm
Weight	28.9 kg
Laser tracker	
Type	Leica AT960
Accuracy	$U_{x,y,z} = \pm 15\,\mu m + 6\,\mu m/m$
Range accuracy	±0.5 μm/m
Angular accuracy	±15 μm + 6 μm/m
Mobile platform	
Weight	110 kg
Height	870 mm

Table 2. Kinematic parameters before and after calibration

Joint	Before-calibration				After-calibration			
	$\alpha_i(°)$	a_i(mm)	d_i(mm)	$\theta_i(°)$	$\alpha_i(°)$	a_i(mm)	d_i(mm)	$\theta_i(°)$
1	90.000	0.000	–	–	90.007	0.068	–	–
2	0.000	−612.000	0.000	0.000	−0.523	−612.605	−0.038	0.000
3	0.000	−572.300	0.000	0.000	−0.946	−571.651	−0.016	0.000
4	90.000	0.000	163.941	0.000	89.790	−0.038	163.943	0.000
5	−90.000	0.000	115.700	0.000	−89.891	−0.045	115.929	0.000
6	–	–	92.200	0.000	–	–	92.198	0.000

4 Verifications and Results

4.1 Configurations of the Manipulator

The manipulator needs to have different configurations throughout the experiment, to obtain global data. Eight target points are discrete in space and ehch target point has six different configurations. The distribution of joints are show in Fig. 3.

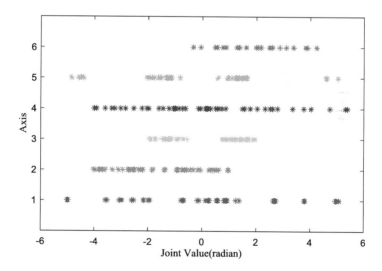

Fig. 3. The distribution of joints. The value of each joint is displayed in rows. The third axis cannot be rotated 360° because of its structural constraint.

4.2 The Norminal Deviation of the Endpoint

The norminal deviation of the endpoint is the distance between the nominal endpoint and the estimate of the specified target point (Eq. 8), the result is in

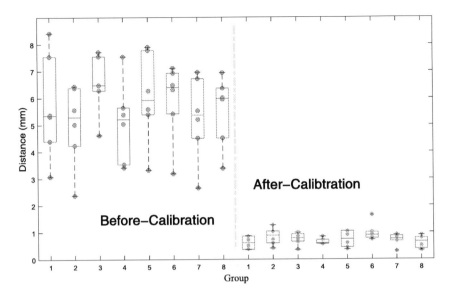

Fig. 4. The boxplot of the nominal deviation is grouped according to the target points. The left of the picture is boxplots with initation parameters and the right of the picture is boxplots with parameters after calibration.

Fig. 4. The mean nominal distance of the endpoint is reduced from 5.630 mm to 0.739 mm, and the covariance of the norminal distance is reduced from 1.508 mm to 0.268 mm. The result after calibration is consistent with the error of the manual model.

4.3   Verified by SA

The reflective ball on the flange is translated by the teach pendant. The joint angles of these configurations are used to calculate their nominal positions of the flange. And the SA software are used to analysis these nominal positions combining with the discrete spatial positions captured by the laser tracker. After the calibration, the mean norminal offset of the flange center of the manipulator is reduced from 2.25 mm to 0.42 mm. The maximum offset is 5.47 mm before the calibration and reduced to 0.94 mm after the calibration. The minimum offset is 0.75 mm before the calibration and reduced to 0.08 mm.

4.4   The Norminal Orientation of the Endeffector

The norminal orientations of the endeffector are analysised with joint angles obtained from Sect. 4.3 after the offset are analysised. During the translation of the endeffector, its posture should remain unchanged. The result of the analysis is in Table 3. The distribution of the norminal orientations after the calibration is closer.

Table 3. The analysis of the norminal orientation of the endeffector

Item	Before-calibration			After-calibration		
	Roll	Pitch	Yaw	Roll	Pitch	Yaw
Mean($^\circ$)	84.485	67.567	−2.798	84.798	66.739	−2.066
Conv.($^\circ$)	1.149	0.379	1.214	0.547	0.101	0.513

5 Conclusion

The application field of mobile manipulator is gradually expanded because of the development of robots and sensors. The mobile manipulator, which sales to the general public, needs to be calibrated when it is in a low absolute position accuracy. A calibration method with a low cost and do not need professional measuring equipments is required. Simutaneously, the method should not be affected by the convected motion when the manipulator changes its gravity moment with respect to the platform obviously during the calibration process. The GDSP method is proposed and the effectiveness of this method is verified by different methods including the use of the laser tracker. After the calibration, the norminal deviation of the endpoints in the endeffctor is more consistent with the error of the manual model during the experiment. As for the flange's translation controlled by the teach pandent, the absolute position error of the flange is reduced from 2.25 mm to 0.42 mm and the distribution of the norminal orientations is fitter the translation. To have a higher calibration accuracy, a more accurate endeffector can be used. In addition, by being more careful in the manual model and developing the semi-automatic or fully automatic calibration model with sensors can also improve the calibration accuracy.

Acknowledgments. This work is supported by the Special Research Foundation of Civil Aircraft of Ministry of Industry and Information Technology of China (No. MJ-2017-G-58) and the High-tech Industrialization Special Fund Project for Science and Technology Cooperation of Jilin Province and Chinese Academy of Sciences (No. 20170925006).

References

1. Birbach, O., Frese, U., Bäuml, B.: Rapid calibration of a multi-sensorial humanoid's upper body: an automatic and self-contained approach. Int. J. Robot. Res. **34**(4–5), 420–436 (2015)
2. Chen, T.L., et al.: Robots for humanity: using assistive robotics to empower people with disabilities. IEEE Robot. Autom. Mag. **20**(1), 30–39 (2013)
3. Gaudreault, M., Joubair, A., Bonev, I.: Self-calibration of an industrial robot using a novel affordable 3D measuring device. Sensors **18**(10), 3380 (2018)
4. Hartenberg, R.S., Denavit, J.: A kinematic notation for lower pair mechanisms based on matrices. J. Appl. Mech. **77**(2), 215–221 (1955)
5. Hayati, S.A.: Robot arm geometric link parameter estimation. In: The 22nd IEEE Conference on Decision and Control, pp. 1477–1483. IEEE (1983)

6. He, R., Zhao, Y., Yang, S., Yang, S.: Kinematic-parameter identification for serial-robot calibration based on poe formula. IEEE Transact. Robot. **26**(3), 411–423 (2010)
7. Hollerbach, J., Khalil, W., Gautier, M.: Model identification. In: Siciliano, B., Khatib, O. (eds.) Springer Handbook of Robotics. Springer, Heidelberg (2008). https://doi.org/10.1007/978-3-540-30301-5_15
8. Khokar, K., Alqasemi, R., Sarkar, S., Reed, K., Dubey, R.: A novel telerobotic method for human-in-the-loop assisted grasping based on intention recognition. In: 2014 IEEE International Conference on Robotics and Automation (ICRA), pp. 4762–4769. IEEE (2014)
9. Santolaria, J., Aguilar, J.J., Yagüe, J.A., Pastor, J.: Kinematic parameter estimation technique for calibration and repeatability improvement of articulated arm coordinate measuring machines. Precis. Eng. **32**(4), 251–268 (2008)
10. Santolaria, J., Conte, J., Ginés, M.: Laser tracker-based kinematic parameter calibration of industrial robots by improved CPA method and active retroreflector. Int. J. Adv. Manuf. Technol. **66**(9–12), 2087–2106 (2013)
11. Stepanova, K., Pajdla, T., Hoffmann, M.: Robot self-calibration using multiple kinematic chainsa simulation study on the ICub humanoid robot. IEEE Robot. Autom. Lett. **4**(2), 1900–1907 (2019)
12. Zhang, X., Zheng, Z., Qi, Y.: Parameter identification and calibration of DH model for 6-DOF serial robots. Robot **38**(3), 360–370 (2016)
13. Zhuang, H., Motaghedi, S.H., Roth, Z.S.: Robot calibration with planar constraints. In: Proceedings 1999 IEEE International Conference on Robotics and Automation (Cat. No. 99CH36288C), vol. 1, pp. 805–810. IEEE (1999)

Design and Development of a Linkage-Tendon Hybrid Driven Anthropomorphic Robotic Hand

Haosen Yang[1], Guowu Wei[2(✉)], and Lei Ren[1]

[1] School of Mechanical, Aerospace and Civil Engineering,
The University of Manchester, Manchester M13 9PL, UK
haosen.yang@postgrad.manchester.ac.uk, lei.ren@manchester.ac.uk
[2] School of Computing, Science and Engineering,
University of Salford, Salford M5 4WT, UK
g.wei@salford.ac.uk

Abstract. This paper presents the design and development of a linkage-tendon hybrid driven anthropomorphic robotic hand, i.e. MCR-Hand II. Structure design of the proposed robotic hand is presented and kinematics of the linkage and tendon driven based fingers is formulated. Then, workspace of the robotic hand is characterised and thumb opposability is investigated. Further, prototype of the robotic hand is developed, tested and evaluated.

Keywords: Anthropomorphic robotic hand ·
Kinematics and workspace · Grasping

1 Introduction

The modern robotic hand research only started since 1960s when the Belgrade hand was developed and after that a great number of various robot hands have been proposed and developed. Although most of the industrial applications still prefer two or three-fingered grippers with simple design and robust grasp, teleoperation in hazardous or unstructured environments provided much of the impulsion for developing dexterous multifingered robot hands and a number of them have been proposed by researchers in the past three decades including, to name but a few, the Stanford/JPL hand [1], the Utah/MIT hand [2], the DLR hand [3] and the UBH3 hand [4].

From the drive system, robotic hands can be classified into tendon-driven robotic hand, linkage-driven robotic hand, and gear-driven robotic hand. In tendon-driven robotic hands, tendons are usually used together with pulleys. The pulleys are often mounted on finger joints and the wrist. The tendons are twined around the pulleys with one end tied to the output shaft of actuators and another end tied to the finger joint or the phalange. By pulling the tendons, the finger joints would rotate to operate a finger phalange. One typical tendon-driven system can be found in the DIST hand [5]. The pulleys act in the role of

© Springer Nature Switzerland AG 2019
H. Yu et al. (Eds.): ICIRA 2019, LNAI 11740, pp. 117–128, 2019.
https://doi.org/10.1007/978-3-030-27526-6_11

supporters and guides as that in the Utah/MIT hand. Besides acting as supporters and guides, pulleys further help distribute forces to fingers as shown in the development of an anthropomorphic robotic hand that has 15 DOFs actuated by only one actuator using tendons and pulleys; pulleys in this hand make the most contribution to the distribution of the force among the fingers [6]. Tendon-driven system is usually used for developing under-actuated robotic hand; with the under-actuated system helps the robotic hand get a good grasp adaptability and stability [7]. The tendon-driven system can significantly minimize the dimensions of the drive-system and thus the robotic hand, but would not satisfy the situation where a large grasping force is demanded. In order to get the large grasping force the linkage-driven system is usually preferred. These include the TUAT/Karlsruhe humanoid hand [8], the HIT prosthetic hand [9], and the Kawabuchi hand [10]. The tendon-driven system has two main disadvantages that are of low speed and low resolution while the link-driven system causes increase in the size and weight of the drive-system. To avoid these problems, researchers directly mount the actuators on fingers. In this case, the drive-system used is the gear-driven system. This kind of robotic hand includes the GCUA hand [11] and the DLR-HIT hand [12].

In this research, a robotic hand which combine linkage and tendon driven system is designed and developed. Mechanical structure of the proposed robotic hand is addressed, and kinematics of the hand is presented. A physical prototype of the proposed robotic hand is then developed which is consequently validated with grasping tests.

2   Design of a Linkage-Tendon Hybrid Driven Anthropomorphic Robotic Hand

2.1   Design Rationales

Figure 1 shows a linkage-tendon hybrid driven anthropomorphic robotic hand, named as MCR-Hand II. This hand is designed according to following detailed design goals.

Size: It might be desirable for the robotic hand to imitate the human hand in size and geometry for the aim of skilful manipulation. Hence, the MCR-Hand II is designed according to the size of a real hand.

Built-in Servomotor and Control System: In order to make the robotic hand convenient to be attached to a robot arm, all joints of the MCR-Hand II are driven by built-in servomotors which are all inside the palm including the servo which control the motion of wrist (excepting the servo drive the rotation of wrist in the MCR-Hand II). As the robotic hand contains of many joints, space for the control system is another issue. In MCR-Hand II, all the control system is embedded into a short wrist require no external space. However, the control system can place into the palm by increasing the thickness of the palm.

Lightweight: The MCR-Hand II is designed as light as possible because of the payload limitation of the manipulators. Most existing robotic hands weight more

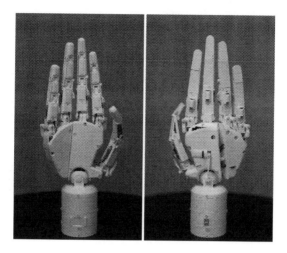

Fig. 1. A linkage-tendon hybrid driven anthropomorphic robotic hand, MCR-Hand II.

than 1 kg, might limits the allowable payload for the grasping object. The MCR-Hand II is designed to weigh less than 800 g, including electronics (except power supply).

User-Friendly: All wires and actuators are built into the palm of the MCR-Hand II. Ordinary gloves can be wear by the robotic hand to make it more close to the human hand.

Highly Bio-Mimetic: There are 18 servos been applied in the MCR-Hand II which lead to a similar motion of human hand.

2.2 Mechanical Design of the MCR-Hand II

In this section, mechanical design of the MCR-Hand II is introduced providing the design details of the fingers, the thumb, the palm, and the wrist.

Finger and Thumb. In a human hand, both the thumb and fingers have four degrees of freedom. It is not easy for humans to control the PIP and DIP joints independently. An independent joint needs an independent actuator in the robotic hand. Thus, the fingers and thumb can be simplified as a link mechanism with three joint of four DOFs (Degree of Freedom). The number of joints and number of DOFs of the MCR-Hand II are designed to imitate this characteristic of the human hand. Each finger consists of three joints as the MCP joint of 2-DOFs, the PIP joint of 1-DOF and the DIP joint of 1-DOF. Nevertheless, the joints of PIP and DIP couple each other. Furthermore, the DIP is a passive DOF that can be dictated by the PIP joint. Thus, in this design the fingers and the thumb are actuated by three servos. The locations of the servos in the hand are illustrated in the CAD model of the hand in Fig. 2.

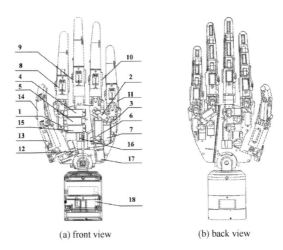

(a) front view   (b) back view

Fig. 2. The CAD model of the MCR-Hand II (without cover on the palm). There are seventeen servos located inside the palm as numbered in the front view. The servo driving the rotation of the wrist is situated inside the wrist numbered as 18.

Figure 3(a) shows the structure of a finger. In this design the MCP is a 2-DOF joint enabling both flexion/extension and abduction/adduction of the finger; a universal joint is used in the design. The MCP-1 joint abduction/adduction of each finger is actuated by servos 1 to 3, as shown in Fig. 2, through a short transmission rod; driving the universal joint. The MCP-2 joints in the fingers, providing flexion/extension, are actuated by servos 4 to 7 through cables across the palm. In this design, abduction and adduction of the middle finger was eliminated due to its limited motion range in the human hand. The PIP and DIP joints are single motion joints, with only flexion and extension motion allowed. Compared to a pure tendon driven robotic hand, a combined driven method is introduced in the MCR-Hand II. The PIP and DIP joints in the fingers are actuated by servos 8 to 11 located inside the proximal phalanges (MCP-PIP) through transmission rods. The PIP and DIP are coupled by a linkage mechanism which means that the angle of joint DIP will change with angle of joint PIP.

The trapezium bone is located at the base of the thumb; it might be considered to be the most critical part that enables the thumb to have opposability [13]. Due to the uncertain shape of the trapezium bone, there is still debate about the accurate locations of its joint axes. In this research, CMC joint is described as a saddle joint which enables the thumb to retain a flexible ROM: adduction/abduction, flexion/extension, and movement across the palm. CMC-1 joint, rotation of thumb, is driven by servo 12 through a short rod, and the CMC-2 joint (abduction/adduction) is actuated by servo 13 located inside the phalange CMC-MP. The coupled joints MP and IP (shown in Fig. 3(b)) are driven by servo 14 inside the phalange MP-IP through a rod.

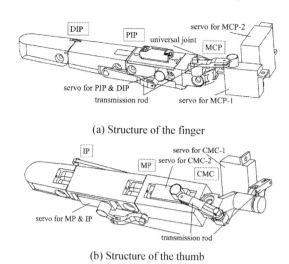

(a) Structure of the finger

(b) Structure of the thumb

Fig. 3. (a) The structure of index fingers, the DIP joint is coupled with PIP joint; the structure of fingers are similar, while the MCP joint of middle finger is only allowed for flexion/extension. (b) The driven mechanism of the thumb in the MCR-Hand II; CMC joint is capable of adduction/abduction, flexion/extension and rotation.

Palm and Wrist. Although rotation of the palm does not exist in the human hand, there might be deformation of the palm due to the flexible structure. In the design of the MCR-Hand II, the palm is built to divide into two parts. These two parts are connected by a rotary rod which allows an additional DOF of the palm; referred as PL joint. The rotation of the wrist is driven by servo 17 through a linkage.

Further, two servos (15 and 16, as shown in Fig. 2) are used to allow the wrist to swing left and right (marked as LR joint) and swing back and forth (referred as BF joint) inside the wrist in the MCR-Hand II through control cable and linkage. The DOF of rotation (referred to as RT joint) of the wrist is actuated by an additional servo 18, located in the short wrist in MCR-Hand II.

3   Kinematics of the Linkage-Based Drive System

3.1   Linkage-Based Robotic Finger

In the finger, a four-bar linkage is designed to allow the DIP joint to be coupled with the PIP joint. All the fingers and thumb are designed using this same structure. Figure 4 presents the geometry of the four-bar linkage. In the linkage, link O_2O_3 with length l_2 represents phalange from PIP to DIP; link AB with length l_b is a rod; link AO_2 with length l_a represents the distance (constant for all fingers) between one side of the linkage and the PIP joint; and BO_3 with length l_0 represents the distance between the other side of the linkage and the DIP joint.

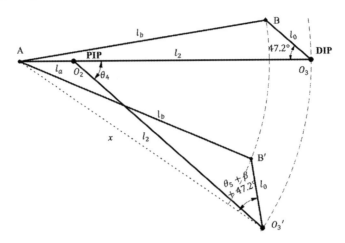

Fig. 4. Geometry of the four-bar linkage used in the finger.

Referring to Fig. 4, the initial angle between link BO_3 and link O_2 is of $47.2°$. When the angle of the PIP joint θ_4 changes, the angle of the DIP joint θ_5 follows to change due to the action of the rod AB. The relation between θ_5 and θ_4 can be derived as follows.

Referring to Fig. 4, assuming that the length of AO_3 is x, using the cosine law, it has

$$x^2 = l_a^2 + l_2^2 - 2l_a l_2 \cos(180° - \theta_4) \tag{1}$$

Let the angle of $\angle AO_3B$ which consists of $\angle AO_3O_2$, denoted as β, and θ_5 be α. As $\cos(\alpha)$ is a function of both angles θ_4 and θ_5, it can be used as an auxiliary angle to establish the relationship between θ_4 and θ_5.

From Fig. 4 there exists

$$\alpha = \theta_5 + \beta + 47.2° \tag{2}$$

Using the cosine law, Eq. (2) gives

$$\cos\alpha = \cos(\theta_5 + \beta + 47.2°) = \frac{x^2 + l0^2 - lb^2}{2xl0} \tag{3}$$

According to the cosine law, the angle β can be expressed as

$$\cos\beta = \frac{x^2 + l2^2 - la^2}{2xl_2} \tag{4}$$

Combining Eqs. (2) to (4), the relation between θ_5 and θ_4 can be derived as

$$\theta_5 = \alpha - \beta - 47.2°$$
$$= \arccos\left(\frac{l_a^2 + l_2^2 + 2l_a l_2 \cos\theta_4 + l_0^2 - l_b^2}{2l_0\sqrt{l_a^2 l_2^2 + 2l_a l_2 \cos\theta_4}}\right)$$
$$- \arccos\left(\frac{l_2 + l_a \cos\theta_4}{\sqrt{l_a^2 l_2^2 + 2l_a l_2 \cos\theta_4}}\right) - 47.2° \tag{5}$$

This equation still holds in the case that l_b crosses the joint PIP.

Using Eq. (5), the relation between angle θ_4 of PIP joint and angle θ_5 of DIP joint can be computed and illustrated as shown in Fig. 5. It indicates that the maximum angle for the DIP joint is slightly different for each four fingers. However, they are all close to 78° when the angle of the PIP joint reaches its maximum angle of 100°. In addition, Fig. 5 implies that the angle of DIP joint changes slowly when the angle of PIP joint is relatively smaller, and that the DIP joint changes relatively rapidly as the angle of PIP joint increases. This tendency is similar to the tendon-driven human finger, which indicates that this structure can imitate human finger movement to an outstanding degree.

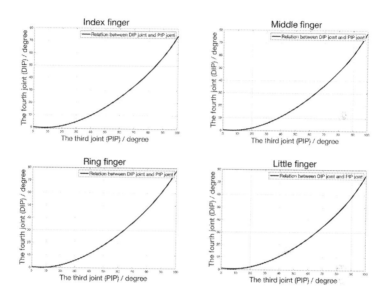

Fig. 5. The relation between PIP joint and DIP joint.

As the relation curve between the third joint and fourth joint has been presented, the movement of robotic fingers (without adduction/abduction) can be plotted in Fig. 6. When making comparison with the motion of a human finger, it is evident that the motion of the robotic finger is quite similar.

3.2   Workspace

In this section, the workspace and thumb opposability of the MCR-Hand II are investigated based on Denavit–Hartenberg method [14]. The benefit of the PL joint will be analysed by comparing with traditional rigid palm. It is widely accepted that the workspace of fingertip of each finger might be a significant index to indicate the performance of the robotic hand. Following creation of the mathematical model, the workspace of each finger and thumb of the MCR-Hand II is presented in this section. Figure 7 presents the workspace of all the

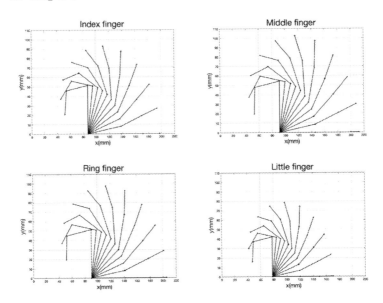

Fig. 6. The movement of PIP joint and DIP joint of the MCR-Hand II.

fingers and thumb. The shape of workspace for the index finger is a fan-shaped volume due to the MCP-1 joint (adduction/abduction). Note that the kinematic singular point of the index finger is located in the middle of its workspace. The workspace of the middle finger is a two-dimensional graphic because of the lack of MCP-1 joint. Because the move range of MCP-1 joint of human's middle finger is not as large as other fingers, the structure of middle finger was simplified in MCR-Hand II.

Figure 8(a) presents the workspace of the ring finger with the PL joint, and Fig. 8(b) presents that of MCR-Hand II without the PL joint. As there is no PL joint, the shape of workspace for the ring finger is similar to the index finger, presenting a fan-shaped volume. Due to the PL joint, the workspace of the ring finger presents an irregular volume. Meanwhile, this feature leads to a difference between the workspace volume of these two design. It is not difficult to notice that the total volume 701.5 mm³ of the workspace of the ring finger with the PL joint is much larger than that 190.8 mm³ of the traditional model without the PL joint; about 367.6% larger. It is clear that the performance of the robotic hand has been significantly improved by the PL joint.

Thumb Opposability. It is widely accepted that an opposable thumb is the key to the dexterity of human hands [15]. This can be described more specifically using the concept of the common workspace. For example, an opposable thumb may create an overload volume of workspace between fingers and thumb, which leads to the ability to control the position of grasped objects. Hence, it is reasonable to suggest that a larger common workspace could improve dexterous grasping. Figure 9 indicates the common workspace for the ring finger of the

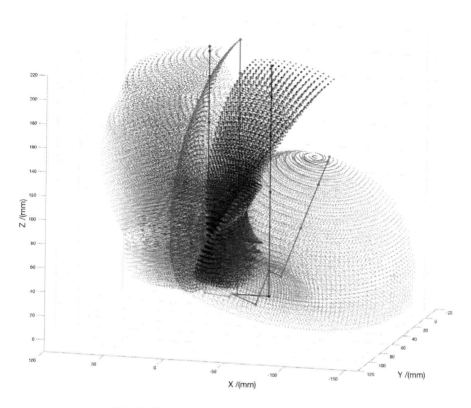

Fig. 7. Workspace of all the fingers and thumb.

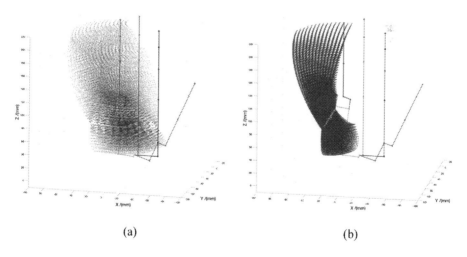

(a)   (b)

Fig. 8. Workspace of the ring finger: (a) with the PL joint; (b) without the PL joint.

MCR-Hand II. By comparing figures (a) and (b), it can be easily proved that the common volume (thumb-to-ring-finger and thumb-to-little-finger) of MCR-Hand II is much larger than that without PL joint of palm. Repeatedly, the common workspace for the little finger is also much larger than that without PL joint.

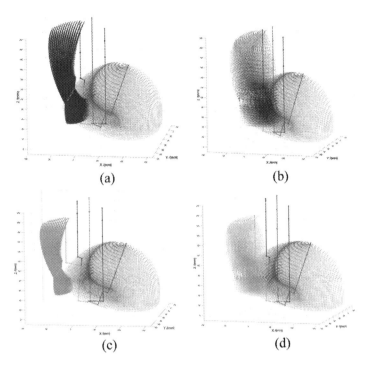

(a)   (b)

(c)   (d)

Fig. 9. Workspace of the fingers and thumb. (a) presents the common workspace for the ring finger without PL joint and (b) presents that with PL joint. (c)–(d) Common workspace of the thumb-little finger, repeatedly.

4   Prototype and Evaluation

Prototype of the proposed robotic hand in developed in this paper. All the parts of MCR-Hand II except electronic components and screws are printed by dual extrusion 3D printer Ultimaker 3. The dual extrusion allows water-soluble support material to be used to create complex mechanical parts, then result in a smooth, professional finish. Several materials are applied to print the prototype of the MCR-Hand II, including PLA, TPU 95A (soft material at fingertip), and Ultimaker Breakaway (print the supports). Integrated with low-level control system, the prototype was constructed and evaluated according to the Kamakura taxonomy test [16] as illustrated in Fig. 10. The test revealed that only the T-I type (tripod-grasp) failed due to insufficient fingertip friction. As a result, it is evident that almost all the grasp types are sufficiently well-holding,

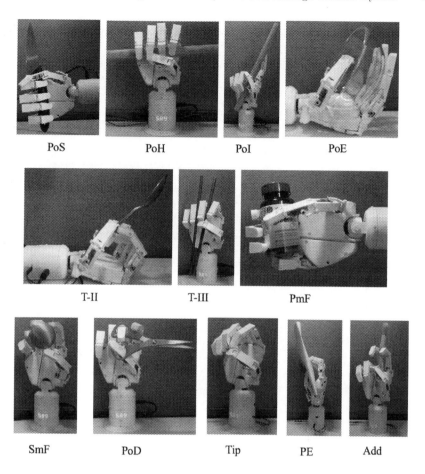

PoS   PoH   PoI   PoE

T-II   T-III   PmF

SmF   PoD   Tip   PE   Add

Fig. 10. Workspace of the fingers and thumb. (a) presents the common workspace for the ring finger without PL joint and (b) presents that with PL joint. (c)–(d) Common workspace of the thumb-little finger, repeatedly.

however, the friction of the fingertips may need to increased. Furthermore, there may also be a need to change the shape of the fingertips in the current model to mimic the flexible structure of the human fingertips, which have a soft spherical curved surface.

5   Conclusions

A linkage-tendon hybrid driven anthropomorphic robotic hand, i.e. MCR-hand II was for the first time presented in this paper. Structure design of the proposed robotic hand was firstly addressed and kinematics of the linkage-tendon driven based finger, palm and hand was presented. Workspace and thumb opposability were then computed and characterised indicating that the performance of the robotic hand was significantly improved by the PL joint. Moreover, prototype of the hand was developed leading to the tests and evaluation of the proposed linkage-tendon hybrid driven robotic hand design.

References

1. Salisbury, J.K., Craig, J.J.: Articulated hands: force control and kinematic issues. Int. J. Robot. Res. **1**(1), 4–17 (1982)
2. Jacobasen, S.C., Iversen, E.K., Knutti, D.F., Johnson, R.T., Biggers, K.B.: Design of the UTAH/MIT dexterous hand. In: IEEE International Conference on Robotics and Automation, pp. 1520–1532 (1986)
3. Grebenstein, M.: Approaching Human Performance–The Functionality-Driven Awiwi Robot Hand. Springer, Switzerland (2014)
4. Lotti, F., Tiezzi, P., Vassura, G.: UBH3: investigating alternative design concepts for robotic hands. In: IEEE International Conference on Robotics Automation, pp. 135–140 (2004)
5. Caffaz, A., Cannata, G.: The design and development of the DIST-Hand dextrous gripper. In: Proceedings of IEEE International Conference on Robotics and Automation, pp. 2075–2080 (1998)
6. Gosselin, C., Pelletier, F., Laliberte, T.: An anthropomorphic underactuated robotic hand with 15 dofs and a single actuator. In: IEEE International Conference on Robotics and Automation, pp. 749–754 (2008)
7. Kamikawa, Y., Maeno, T.: Underactuated five-finger prosthetic hand inspired by grasping force distribution of humans. In: IEEE/RSJ International Conference on Intelligent Robots and Systems, pp. 717–722 (2008)
8. Fukaya, N., Toyama, S., Asfour, T., Dillmann, R.: Design of the TUAT/Karlsruhe humanoid hand. In: Proceedings of IEEE/RSJ International Conference on Intelligent Robots and Systems, pp. 1754–1759 (2000)
9. Huang, H., Pang, Y.J., Li, J., Fan, S.W., Wang, X.Q., Liu, H.: Underactuated hand dynamic modeling, its real-time simulation, and control. Int. J. Humanoid Robot. **7**(4), 609–634 (2010)
10. Hoshino, K., Kawabuchi, I.: A humanoid robotic hand performing the sign language motions. In: Proceedings of IEEE International Symposium on Micromechatronics and Human Science, pp. 89–94 (2003)
11. Che, D., Zhang, W.: A dexterous and self-adaptive humanoid robot hand: GCUA hand. Int. J. Humanoid Robot. **8**(1), 73–86 (2011)
12. Gao, X.H., et al.: The HIT/DLR dexterous hand: work in progress. In: Proceedings of IEEE International Conference on Robotics and Automation, pp. 3164–3168 (2003)
13. Crisco, J.J., Halilaj, E., Moore, D.C., Patel, T., Weiss, A.P., Ladd, A.L.: In vivo kinematics of the trapeziometacarpal joint during thumb extension-flexion and abduction-adduction. J. Hand Surg. **40**(2), 289–296 (2015)
14. Corke, P.I.: A simple and systematic approach to assigning Denavit-Hartenberg parameters. IEEE Trans. Rob. **23**(3), 590–594 (2007)
15. Lee, D.-H., Park, J.-H., Park, S.-W., Baeg, M.-H., Bae, J.-H.: KITECH-hand: a highly dexterous and modularized robotic hand. IEEE/ASME Trans. Mechatron. **22**(2), 876–887 (2017)
16. Fukaya, N., Asfour, T., Dillmann, R., Toyama, S.: Development of a five-finger dexterous hand without feedback control: the TUAT/Karlsruhe humanoid hand. In: 2013 IEEE/RSJ International Conference on Intelligent Robots and Systems (IROS), pp. 4533–4540 (2013)

Predict Afferent Tactile Neural Signal for Artificial Nerve Based on Finite Element Human Hand Model

Yuyang Wei[1], Guowu Wei[2], and Lei Ren[1(✉)]

[1] School of Mechanical, Aerospace and Civil Engineering,
The University of Manchester, Manchester M13 9PL, UK
{yuyang.wei,lei.ren}@manchester.ac.uk
[2] School of Computing, Science and Engineering, University of Salford,
Salford M5 4WT, UK
g.wei@salford.ac.uk

Abstract. This paper aims to investigate the biomechanical aspect of human hand tactile perception by using finite element method and build the artificial neural nerve which can be interfaced with human afferent nerve. A subject-specific digital human hand finite element model (FE-DHHM) was developed based on CT and MR images. The geometries of phalanges, carpal bones, wrist bones, ligaments, tendons, subcutaneous tissue, epidermis and dermis were all included. The material properties were derived from *in-vivo* and *in-vitro* experiment results which are available in the literature, the boundary and loading conditions which were kinematic motion data and muscle forces, were captured based on the specific subject. This FE-DHHM was validated against *in-vivo* test results of the same subject based on contact pressure and contact areas. The whole active touch procedure was performed and simulated, the strain energy density near the locations of mechanoreceptors including slowly adapting type 1 (SA-I) and rapidly adapting (RA) were extracted and then used as inputs into the transduction and neural-dynamics (Izhikevivh neuro model) sub-model to predict neural spike or somatosensory information. A prototype of 'artificial nerve' which can produce the action potential signal is presented. Therefore the FE-DHHM presented in this paper can make a detailed and quantitative evaluation into biomechanical and neurophysiological aspects of human hand tactile perception and manipulation. The results obtained in this paper can be applied to design of bionic or neuro-robotic hand in the near future.

Keywords: Tactile sensing · Artificial afferent nerve ·
Finite element human hand

1 Introduction

Sense of touch or somatosensory information is essential for performing daily tasks and maintaining hand dexterity. Human can adjust the activation levels of muscle synergies based on the perceived afferent signals; lack of sensory feedback can significantly affect the performance of human hand [1–3]. The neural spike information is received and

© Springer Nature Switzerland AG 2019
H. Yu et al. (Eds.): ICIRA 2019, LNAI 11740, pp. 129–140, 2019.
https://doi.org/10.1007/978-3-030-27526-6_12

encoded by the mechanoreceptors which are mainly located under glabrous skin of the hand. To enable the next generation of prosthetic hand with tactile feedback, also to gain the deep understanding of how these biological receptors work [4], neural spike information needs to be detected or predicted. In the meanwhile, the distribution patterns of these mechanoreceptors are crucial for the placements of artificial bionic tactile sensors.

Tactile sensation is currently studied at two levels, i.e. the electrophysiological recordings level and the psychophysical responses level [5]. Microneurography technique has been applied to the single-afferent electrophysiological study by inserting a fine tungsten electrode into median or ulna nerve to detect the neural impulse signal. On the other hand, psychophysical experiments were carried out based on the assumption that the mechanoreceptors are always clustered and work at a population-level, due to unmeasurable impulse signals from hundreds of tactile fibers, the study on this level mainly focuses on subject's behavior response by measuring absolute thresholds and difference discrimination. However, it's still not achievable based on today's technologies to capture afferent signals during active touch or simple grasping, studies of human hand perception on both of the levels are restricted by time duration limitation of microneurography; for the in-vivo experiments can cause permanent neural damages to the subjects, and there are unrevealed difficulties to detect population-level signals [4].

In order to investigate human tactile sensing from both psychophysical and population-level neurophysiological aspects, and to overcome the difficulties of unrepeatable microneurography tests on a specified subject, a subject-specific and anatomically-intact finite element digital human hand model (FE-DHHM) has been developed and physically validated in this paper. Though similar FE models of human hand were developed by other researchers, none of these models has been validated and the geometry of skin layers were not included. In addition, the dexterity of previous FE model was worse than that of the human hand [6–9]. Hence, the previous developed FE hand models were not suitable for the investigations of biomechanical or neurophysiological properties of human hand. This paper for the first time presents a well-validated FE-DHHM, providing an efficient computational model for investigating hand contact and perception. Further, researchers found that the neural impulse signal could be predicted based on biomechanical parameters like strain energy density (SED) [10–12]; Gerling et al. [13] has built the mathematical model to convert SED at the location of mechanoreceptors into afferent signals. Integrating Gerling's SED mathematical model with the present FE-DHHM, the proposed digital human hand model can produce population-level impulse signals across the process of active touch or simple manipulation. This paper presents the development and validation of the proposed FE-DHHM, and the approach to predict afferent signals based on the SED model.

2 Finite Element Human Hand Model Development

2.1 3D Model Construction

Development of the proposed FE-DHHM starts from the human hand anatomic data collection. In order to construct the geometry of the hand, CT and MR scans were conducted on a specific subject, i.e. a 23-year-old healthy male, the image data was then imported into medical image processing software Mimics™ to convert 2D images into 3D mesh for rebuilding the geometry of the whole hand by applying reverse-engineering techniques. The images were segmented manually into bones (14 phalangeal bones, 5 metacarpal bones, and 8 carpal bones), subcutaneous tissue, epidermis, and dermis shown in the finite element model development in Fig. 1. The bones were rebuilt based on CT images while soft tissues were reconstructed based on MR images of the same subject. The anatomically intact human hand model and its development procedure are illustrated in the flow chart in Fig. 1.

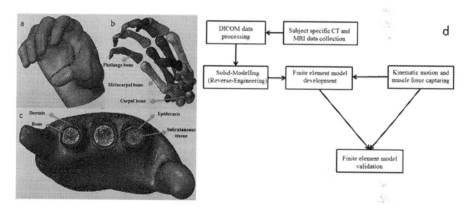

Fig. 1. Developed FE-DHHM. (a) and (b) show the hand and its corresponding bone skeleton inside, (c) shows the intersection structure of the four-layered (epidermis, dermis, subcutaneous tissue and bones) structure fingers. (d) illustrates the process for developing the FE-DHHM.

2.2 Finite Element Model Development

By importing the 3D model of the hand into ABAQUS™, finite element model was created. The 3D geometry of all the segments was assigned with first order tetrahedral mesh, mesh study was carried out and the mesh densities for different parts were optimized. In the FE model, material properties of the skin and the subcutaneous tissues were defined as isotropic hyperplastic governed by the Holzapfel-Gasser-Ogden (HGO) constitutive equation [14, 15]. Further, in this FE-DHHM, the bones were defined to be isotropic linear elastic, and the ligaments and tendons, as shown in Fig. 2 were represented by using non-linear spring elements at their corresponding anatomical positions located according to the MR images.

In addition, for kinematics the finger motion was defined as angle displacement at each interphalangeal joint, the relative constrains were defined on adjacent bone segments to restrain the relative motion, the kinematic motion was all assigned on the bone skeleton structure. There were totally 25 constrains defined at 15 joints, 20 coupling constrains were assigned to the proximal and middle phalanges to maintain the relative motion, and another 5 coupling constrains were defined on the distal phalanges for constraining the angle displacements. This FE-DHHM has the same mobility and dexterity of a real human hand.

3   Finite Element Model Validation

3.1   Loading and Boundary Conditions Defined for Grasping Simulation and the Corresponded *In-Vivo* Test

Three fundamental grasping poses, i.e. cylinder grasping, spherical grasping and precision grasping, are considered in the simulation for the purpose of validating the proposed FE-DHHM. In order to gather the kinematic and force inputs for the simulation, *in-vivo* grasping tests were carried out by the same subject who provided the hand CT and MR data for FE hand modelling. The kinematic motion or joint angles were monitored and recorded by using a VMG^{TM} data glove. This data glove has embedded bending sensors to detect joint angles, and five pressure sensors were placed at fingertips to capture the contact pressures. In addition, muscle forces were measured by using Delsys^{TM} wireless Trigno sensors; for simulating the grasping process, nine muscle forces were calculated based on electromyography (EMG) signals. The set-up of the data glove and EMG sensors are illustrated in Fig. 2g and h, and the in-vivo grasping tests are shown in Figs. 2a, b and c. The detected joint angles and calculated muscle forces were then used as inputs to drive the proposed FE-DHHM for simulating the three grasping poses as shown in Figs. 3d, e and f.

Three different objects were grasped and each grasping was repeated six times. Before the isometric grasping test, the maximum voluntary contraction (MVC) tests were carried out for all nine muscles involved by using Jamar dynamometer. The recorded EMG data were band-pass filtered (20–400 Hz) with a Butterworth filter and rectified. The muscle forces during grasping were then derived based on the maximum voluntary contraction forces and the assumption that for isometric muscle contracting, there would be a linear relationship between EMG signal and muscle force. Similar method has been employed by other researchers to calculate muscle forces of isometric contraction. In total nine muscle forces were applied as concentrated loads onto the insertion points of the corresponding ligaments or tendons. All the anatomical positions where forces are applied were determined based on MR images and the wrist joint was fully fixed.

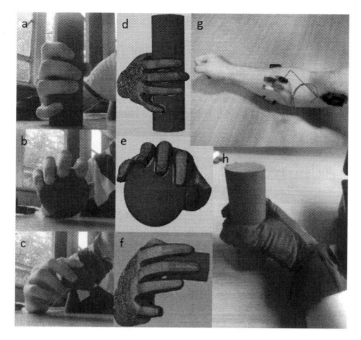

Fig. 2. Experiment setup and FE-DHHM based simulation. (a) cylindrical grasping, (b) spherical grasping, (c) precision gripping, (d)–(e) simulations in FE-DHHM model, (g) Delsys wireless trigno sensor placement for capturing electromyography signals, (h) the VMG30 data glove for capturing kinematic motion of hand.

3.2 Numerical Model Validation

The simulation results from the FE-DHHM model were then validated by comparing the predicted and experimental contact pressure and contact area. The experimental contact pressure was recorded by using VMG data glove; while for measuring contact areas, the hand of subject was daubed with red paint and the objects were covered with white papers to capture the experimental contact areas.

Figure 3 shows the comparisons between the simulated and experimental contact pressure and contact areas. It can be seen clearly from the left column of Figs. 3a, b and c that for all the three grasping poses, the contact pressures predicted from the FE simulation are all in the ranges of experimental test results; on other hand, from the right column of Figs 3a, b and c, it can be found that the difference for the contact area values detected from the FE simulation and obtained from the in-vivo experiment is below 15%. Two main sources may contribute to the difference between the predictions and experimental results. First, the anisotropic viscoelastic material behavior of the hand was simplified by employing HGO model. Secondary, the contact pressure was detected by data glove during the *in-vivo* grasping test and this data glove was not included in the FE model. Most of the predicted contact areas were smaller than the experimental results. This may due to the use of daubed paint onto the subject's hand since the wet hydration condition can significantly affect the skin's deformation and increase the contact area. Hence, the FE-DHHM proposed in this paper was physically validated and it can provide good representations of biomechanical properties of a real human hand. It would be a powerful digital tool for studying tactile sensing especially population-level coding mechanism of the mechanoreceptors or tactile fibers.

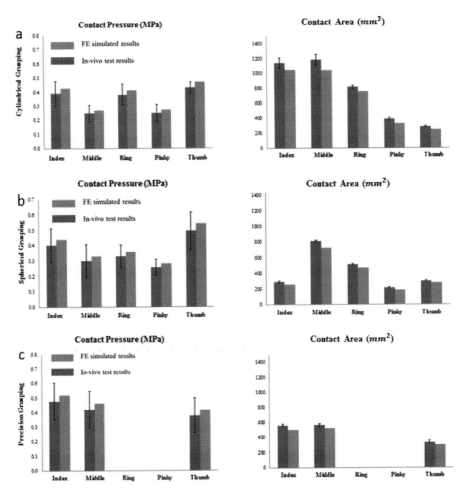

Fig. 3. Comparisons between simulated and experimental results. (a) to (c) simulation results of cylinder grasping, spherical grasping and precision gripping, respectively. The left column shows comparisons of contact pressure while the right column shows the comparisons of contact area. The grasping poses were repeated for six times for the in-vivo tests, this resulted in six corresponded predicted results and these predicted results are averaged for numerical model validation. The experimental results are presented with standard deviations.

4 Dynamic Neural Model for Afferent Signal Prediction and the *In-Vivo* Microneurography Test

After validating the proposed FE-DHHM, further mathematical models for converting simulated results such as strain energy density to neural spike information were developed. This mathematical sub-model mainly consists of bi-phasic functions to represent mechanoreceptors' transformation from stress/strain to membrane current and an Izhikevich neural dynamic model to generate timing of action potentials based on current. The transduction and neural dynamic model were derived based on *in-vivo* microneurography test results of the same subject as that of the physical grasping test. The action potential signal of single SA-I and RA afferent fiber was recorded by inserting fine tungsten electrode into subject's medial nerve while a sweep-motion stimulus was delivered by programmed robotic arm to the receptive area.

4.1 Strain Energy Density and Bi-phasic Sub Model

It has been found that the action potentials can be estimated based on the strain energy density (SED) extracted at the locations of the mechanoreceptors [10, 11, 14–16]. Impulse signals generated by slowly adapting one (SA-I) and rapid adapting one (RA) neural complexes were estimated accurately by other researchers, however, they only develop the model of a simple skin specimen, and the skeleton structure and muscle forces were not taken into consideration [10, 12, 14, 15], in other words, previous research didn't study neural potential information in a closed sensory-motor controlling loop. The first step for predict neural spike signal is to calculate the membrane current of neurite complex and then the current derived on time domain would be used as input of the Izhikevich neural model to predict spike information for different types of mechanoreceptors.

The bi-phasic sub model transforms SED near the mechanoreceptors like Merkel cell neurite complex to the current entering the tactile afferent through its membrane, also called receptor current. The formula to derive receptor current is shown in Eq. 1 [13].

$$I(U_o) = \alpha \frac{1}{1 + e^{\gamma(\lambda - U_0)}} \tag{1}$$

Where U_0 is the SED derived from the proposed FE-DHHM and the other paprmers are all constances for specifying the shape of the function. These constants need to be determined based on the specified subject's nerual response.

Izhikevich neural model was then used to predict neural spiking based on the input receptor current on time domain [17]. Izhikevich neural model combines the biological plausibility of Hodgkin-Huxley model (H-H) and the computational efficient of the Leaky-Integral-Firing model (LIF). All of the previous studies applied LIF model to predict neural spike information from SED, but this neural dynamic model cannot provide rich response spiking patterns [10, 11, 15, 16]. In this study, two types of different mechanoreceptors (SA-I and RA) are investigated, it's found that Izhikevich model is more suitable and this neural model has been used for many research to produce real-time control of neuro-robotic hand [18–20]. The regular spiking Izhike-vich neural model [20] was selected for predicting SA-I spiking information and is expressed as:

$$\frac{dv(t)}{dt} = 0.04V(t)^2 + 5V(t) - u(t) + \frac{K_1}{C_m}I(t) + 140$$
$$\frac{du(t)}{dt} = a(bv(t) - u(t))$$

$$\text{if } v \geq 30mv \begin{cases} v \leftarrow c \\ u \leftarrow u + d \end{cases}$$

(2)

Where $I(t)$ is the receptor current and u is the membrane recovery variable, a, b, c and d are all constants. C_m is the capacity of memebrane and v stands for memebrane potential. K_1 represents the gain.

4.2   Parameter Optimization

The parameters of bi-phasic model need to be determined based on the subject. For this study, the four parameters (a, b, c, d) shown in Eq. (2) were optimized against our microneurography test results by applying RSM optimization algorithm, similar RSM optimization method was applied before based neural action potential signals and achieved good accuracy [21]. Two thirds of the microneurography data was applied to optimize the parameters via response surface method while the other data was used to validate the optimized model. The same validation method has been used previously by Gerling et al. [13]. This bi-phase combined with Izhikevich neural model was then evaluated with the goodness of fit between experimental and predicted firing rates.

The SED in the vicinity of SA-I of the index fingertip was extracted, the locations of interest were determined based on Knibestol and Vallbo's semi-schematic drawings of the mechanoreceptor receptive fields and the marked receptive field during our microneurography test [22]. The synthetic output current of all mechanoreceptors connected to the single tactile fiber was derived by summing up all the currents of the receptors, this synthetic model was validated by Pham et al. in his previous study [10].

5   Results and Discussion

5.1   Predict Neural Spike Information During Active Touch

After validating this proposed FE-DHHM and neural dynamic sub model, the spiking rates of mechanoreceptors across the whole process of active touch or the fundamental grasping can be predicted by using this FE-DHHM, the active touch process to explore a small tripod was performed and simulated by using our numerical models, the spiking rate of a cluster of SA-I mechanoreceptors on index fingertips were derived. The process of active touch was divided into four parts: lateral motion, hardness test, static contact, and unsupported holding. This active touch procedure was previously defined by Lederman [25]. Figure 4 shows spiking rates of a single tactile fiber connected with SA-I mechanoreceptors. To the best of the authors' knowledge, this FE-DHHM combined with Izhikevich neural model is the only way which has been found to predict neural signals during active touch or simple manipulation procedure.

As can be seen from Fig. 4, the firing rate increased dramatically during the 'hardness test' procedure since the muscle forces and contact pressure increased. For the process of 'lateral motion' and 'static contact', the firing rate maintained at 25 and 35 spikes/second respectively because fingertips gently touched the object, expiring relatively small contact pressure, resulting less strain energy density than that of 'hardness test' procedure. While for 'unsupported holding' step, the firing rate increased by approximately 10 spikes/second at the beginning since the contact pressure needs to increase for lifting the object.

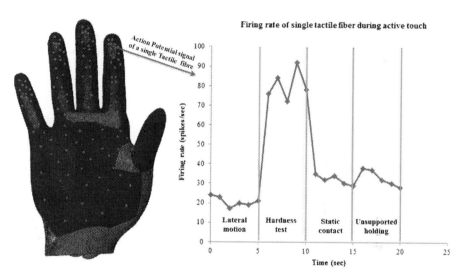

Fig. 4. Firing rate of a single tactile fiber connected with SA-I mechanoreceptors during active touch. The diagram on the left shows the distribution of SA-I mechanoreceptors (The distribution density of mechanoreceptor has been reduced in this diagram to gain a better representation).

5.2 Artificial Neural Nerve Prototype

Hardware Setup. The artificial neural nerve is consisted of three main parts as is shown in Fig. 8. A single piezo-resistive sensor (Flexiforce A201; Tekscan Inc., South Boston, MA) was employed, it responds to normal force within a range of 0 to 4.44N within the thin pressure sensing area. When load is applied onto the sensing rea, the sensor's resistance decreases making conductance increase linearly with the applied force. The force is transformed into current, similar to how stress applied at mechanoreceptors is transformed into current across its membrane. The sensor was integrated with Arduino mega 2560 board to convert analog into digital signal and then the Matlab was applied to collect the pressure data from Arduino serial port and convert it into neural spike information by using the subject-specific neural dynamic model illustrated above.

Neural Dynamic Model. The contact pressure was linearly transferred to strain energy density by using FE human hand model, the same neural dynamic model for SA-I mechanoreceptor presented in Sect. 4 was applied. This is the first human *in-vivo* microneurography test results based and validated biomimetic artificial tactile neural nerve. Figure 5 shows the predicted output SA-I neural signal over 1000 ms and the overview of the system connectivity.

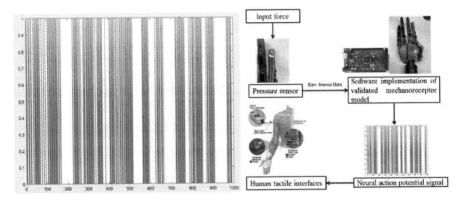

Fig. 5. Overview of system connectivity (right) and the output single SA-I afferent nerve action potential signal (left)

Previous biomimetic tactile sensors [23–26] were trained by monkey or mouse's neural spiking data and their predicted neural signal cannot be compared with the real action potential signal that generated by their corresponding subject's nerve. This effort is unique since it combines the subject-specific neural data with skin elasticity as well as the anatomically-intact FE hand model, the output signal from artificial neural can be compared with the FE model's predicted action potential in our scenario. In the future a population-leveled afferent artificial nerve can be made based on tactile sensor array by applying similar method mentioned in this research. This artificial neural nerve can also be connected with human afferent nerve through nerve interface to form a neuro-prosthetic or neuro-robotic hand.

6   Conclusion

This FE-DHHM is the first digital tool which can estimate neural spiking information by combining it with Izhikevich neural model. This FE model will help to investigate the population-level coding mechanism of tactile fibers and provide a powerful research tool for designing bionic and neuro-robotic prosthetics. The prototype of single afferent artificial neural nerve integrated engineering approach that replicate firing behavior of SA-I mechanoreceptor, it proved that the artificial neural nerve can be built through tactile pressure sensor with subject-specific microneurography data and corresponding FE human hand model. The tactile sensor array can be applied to mimic the mechanoreceptor distribution on human hand in order to create multi-fiber afferent neural nerve in the future.

References

1. Alessandro, C., et al.: Muscle synergies in neuroscience and robotics: from input-space to task-space perspectives. Front. Comput. Neurosci. **7**, 43 (2013)
2. Ajiboye, A.B., Weir, R.F.: Muscle synergies as a predictive framework for the EMG patterns of new hand postures. J. Neural Eng. **6**(3), 036004 (2009)
3. Israely, S., et al.: Muscle synergies control during hand-reaching tasks in multiple directions post-stroke. Front. Comput. Neurosci. **12**, 10 (2018)
4. Valle, G., et al.: Biomimetic intraneural sensory feedback enhances sensation naturalness, tactile sensitivity, and manual dexterity in a bidirectional prosthesis. Neuron **100**(1), 37–45. e7 (2018)
5. Kandel, E.R., et al.: Principles of Neural Science, vol. 4. McGraw-Hill, New York (2000)
6. Chamoret, D., Bodo, M., Roth, S.: A first step in finite-element simulation of a grasping task. Comput. Assist. Surg. **21**(Suppl. 1), 22–29 (2016)
7. Harih, G., Nohara, R., Tada, M.: Finite element digital human hand model-case study of grasping a cylindrical handle. J. Ergon. **07**(02) (2017)
8. Harih, G., Dolsak, B.: Recommendations for tool-handle material choice based on finite element analysis. Appl. Ergon. **45**(3), 577–585 (2014)
9. Chamoret, D., et al.: A novel approach to modelling and simulating the contact behaviour between a human hand model and a deformable object. Comput. Methods Biomech. Biomed. Eng. **16**(2), 130–140 (2013)
10. Pham, T.Q., et al.: An FE simulation study on population response of RA-I mechanoreceptor to different widths of square indenter. SICE J. Control Meas. Syst. Integr. **10**(5), 426–432 (2017)
11. Yao, M., Wang, R.: Neurodynamic analysis of Merkel cell–neurite complex transduction mechanism during tactile sensing. Cogn. Neurodyn. **13**, 293–302 (2018)
12. Gerling, G.J., Thomas, G.W.: Fingerprint lines may not directly affect SA-I mechanoreceptor response. Somatosens. Mot. Res. **25**(1), 61–76 (2008)
13. Gerling, G.J., et al.: Validating a population model of tactile mechanotransduction of slowly adapting type I afferents at levels of skin mechanics, single-unit response and psychophysics. IEEE Trans. Haptics **7**(2), 216–228 (2014)
14. Dandekar, K., Raju, B.I., Srinivasan, M.A.: 3-D finite-element models of human and monkey fingertips to investigate the mechanics of tactile sense. J. Biomech. Eng. **125**(5), 682–691 (2003)
15. Pham, T.Q., et al.: Effect of 3D microstructure of dermal papillae on SED concentration at a mechanoreceptor location. PLoS ONE **12**(12), e0189293 (2017)
16. Gong, H., et al.: Preliminary study on SED distribution of tactile sensation in fingertip. MATEC Web Conf. **45**, 04006 (2016)
17. Izhikevich, E.M.: Which model to use for cortical spiking neurons? IEEE Trans. Neural Networks **15**(5), 1063–1070 (2004)

18. Zhengkun, Y., Yilei, Z.: Recognizing tactile surface roughness with a biomimetic fingertip: a soft neuromorphic approach. Neurocomputing **244**, 102–111 (2017)
19. Oddo, C.M., et al.: Artificial spatiotemporal touch inputs reveal complementary decoding in neocortical neurons. Sci. Rep. **8**, 45898 (2017)
20. Salimi-Nezhad, N., et al.: A digital hardware realization for spiking model of cutaneous mechanoreceptor. Front. Neurosci. (2018)
21. Phillips, J.R., Johnson, K.O.: Tactile spatial resolution. II. Neural representation of bars, edges, and gratings in monkey primary afferents. J. Neurophysiol. **46**(6), 1192–1203 (1981)
22. Knibestöl, M., Vallbo, Å.B.: Single unit analysis of mechanoreceptor activity from the human glabrous skin. Acta Physiol. Scand. **80**(2), 178–195 (1970)
23. Yi, Z., Zhang, Y., Peters, J.: Biomimetic tactile sensors and signal processing with spike trains: a review. Sens. Actuators A: Phys. **269**, 41–52 (2018)
24. Bologna, L., et al.: A closed-loop neurobotic system for fine touch sensing. J. Neural Eng. **10**(4), 046019 (2013)
25. Oddo, C.M., et al.: Roughness encoding for discrimination of surfaces in artificial active-touch. IEEE Trans. Rob. **27**(3), 522–533 (2011)
26. Yi, Z., Zhang, Y., Peters, J.: Bioinspired tactile sensor for surface roughness discrimination. Sens. Actuators A: Phys. **255**, 46–53 (2017)

Screw Displacement and Its Application to the *In Vivo* Identification of Finger Joint Axes

Yiming Zhu[1], Zirong Luo[2], Guowu Wei[3(✉)], and Lei Ren[1]

[1] School of Mechanical, Aerospace and Civil Engineering,
The University of Manchester, Manchester M13 9PL, UK
{yiming.zhu,lei.ren}@manchester.ac.uk
[2] College of Mechatronic Engineering and Automation,
National University of Defense Technology,
Changsha 410073, People's Republic of China
luozirong@nudt.edu.cn
[3] School of Computing, Science and Engineering,
University of Salford, Salford M5 4WT, UK
g.wei@salford.ac.uk

Abstract. This paper provides the exponential derivation of screw displacement and its application in the identification of rotation axes of finger joints. Expressions of screw displacement, including the Rodrigues' formulae for rotation and general spatial displacement, are derived in details with matrix exponential method in a note form. Then an *in vivo* approach based on a gyroscope sensor and Arduino board is proposed to determining the joint axes of human finger. The experimental results are feasible comparison with the results obtained through traditional methods in literature.

Keywords: Screw displacement · Rodrigues formula ·
Axes of rotation · Human finger

1 Introduction

The general spatial displacement of a rigid body is a translation plus a rotation as stated by Chasles' theorem, and a stronger form of the theorem asserts that regardless of how a rigid body is displaced from one location to anther, the displacement can be regarded as a rotation and a translation along some axis; such a combination of translation and rotation is called a screw displacement [1]. There are mainly two approaches to derive the screw displacement, one is through geometric and vector interpretation, and the other is through exponential derivation. In text books [1–7] and literature [8–12], to mention but a few; derivation of screw displacement was either presented in geometric form or exponential approach, but not both. The geometric derivation stems from the Rodrigues' formulae for rotation and general spatial displacement; and the

© Springer Nature Switzerland AG 2019
H. Yu et al. (Eds.): ICIRA 2019, LNAI 11740, pp. 141–153, 2019.
https://doi.org/10.1007/978-3-030-27526-6_13

exponential derivation is based on matrix exponential. The detailed derivation of the exponential expression of screw displacement is presented in this paper in a note form; screw displacement has wide applications in engineering, computer science and biomechanics – it has been a useful tool for the identification of joint axes of human bones [15].

The axis of rotation between two bones is defined a line that does not move in relationship to either bone while the bones move around each other [15]. Knowledge of locations and directions and joint axes should help in constructing prosthetic joints and in planning re-constructive surgery such as tendon transfers. Commonly, there are two approaches used to determining the joint axes of bones, one is by using "axis finder" [16] and the other one is by camera system integrated with markers [17]. In this paper a lower cost solution in vivo approach is presented to identify the rotation axes of human finger, assisted by the screw displacement derivation.

2   Note on Exponential Derivation of Screw Displacement

2.1   Exponential Derivation for Rotation

Each rotation of a rigid body corresponds to some special orthogonal group $\mathbf{R} \in SO(3)$ that can be expressed as a function of the direction vector $\boldsymbol{\omega}$ and the rotation angle θ.

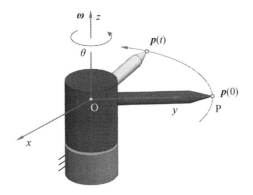

Fig. 1. Rotation of point P about axis $\boldsymbol{\omega}$ by θ

As indicated in Fig. 1, a rigid body rotates at constant unit velocity about the axis $\boldsymbol{\omega}$, the velocity of a point P, denoted as $\dot{\boldsymbol{p}}$, can be written as

$$\dot{\boldsymbol{p}}\left(t\right) = \boldsymbol{\omega} \times \boldsymbol{p}\left(t\right) = \left[\boldsymbol{\omega}\right]\boldsymbol{p}\left(t\right) \tag{1}$$

which is a time-invariant linear differential equation. It can be integrated, yielding

$$\boldsymbol{p}\left(t\right) = e^{\left[\boldsymbol{\omega}\right]t}\boldsymbol{p}\left(0\right) \tag{2}$$

with $\boldsymbol{p}(0)$ representing the initial (when $t = 0$) position of point P, and the matrix exponential of $e^{[\omega]t}$ given in the Taylor's series form as

$$e^{[\omega]t} = \mathbf{I} + [\omega]\,t + [\omega]^2\,\frac{t^2}{2!} + [\omega]^3\,\frac{t^3}{3!} + \cdots \tag{3}$$

Here, the matrix $[\omega]$ is a skew-symmetric matrix form of vector ω, it satisfies $[\omega]^T = -[\omega]$. The vector space of all 3×3 skew matrices is defined as $so(3)$ and generally the space of $n \times n$ skew-symmetric matrices is defined as $so(n) = \{\mathbf{S} \in \mathbb{R}^{n \times n} : \mathbf{S}^T = -\mathbf{S}\}$.

Considering the rotation about axis ω at unit velocity for θ units of time, $e^{[\omega]t}$ can be written as $e^{[\omega]\theta}$, hence Eq. (3) can be expressed as

$$\exp([\omega]\,\theta) = e^{[\omega]\theta} = \mathbf{I} + \theta\,[\omega] + \frac{\theta^2}{2!}\,[\omega]^2 + \frac{\theta^3}{3!}\,[\omega]^3 + \cdots \tag{4}$$

Using the formulas for powers of $[\boldsymbol{a}]$ that $[\boldsymbol{a}]^2 = \boldsymbol{a}\boldsymbol{a}^T - \|\boldsymbol{a}\|^2\mathbf{I}$ and $[\boldsymbol{a}]^3 = -\|\boldsymbol{a}\|^2\,[\boldsymbol{a}]$ and considering that $[\boldsymbol{a}] = [\omega]\,\theta$ and $\|\omega\| = 1$, Eq. (4) can be further derived as

$$e^{[\omega]\theta} = \mathbf{I} + \theta\,[\omega] + \frac{\theta^2}{2!}\,[\omega]^2 - \frac{\theta^3}{3!}\,[\omega] - \frac{\theta^4}{4!}\,[\omega]^2 + \frac{\theta^5}{5!}\,[\omega] + \frac{\theta^6}{6!}\,[\omega]^2 - \frac{\theta^7}{7!}\,[\omega] - \frac{\theta^8}{8!}\,[\omega]^2 + \frac{\theta^9}{9!}\,[\omega] + \cdots$$
$$= \mathbf{I} + \left(\theta - \frac{\theta^3}{3!} + \frac{\theta^5}{5!} - \frac{\theta^7}{7!} + \frac{\theta^9}{9!} - \cdots\right)[\omega] + \left(\frac{\theta^2}{2!} - \frac{\theta^4}{4!} + \frac{\theta^6}{6!} - \frac{\theta^8}{8!} + \cdots\right)[\omega]^2 \tag{5}$$

Taylor's series for sine and cosine functions give that $\sin\theta = \theta - \frac{\theta^3}{3!} + \frac{\theta^5}{5!} - \frac{\theta^7}{7!} + \frac{\theta^9}{9!} - \cdots$, and $\cos\theta = 1 - \frac{\theta^2}{2!} + \frac{\theta^4}{4!} - \frac{\theta^6}{6!} + \frac{\theta^8}{8!} - \cdots$. Using these, Eq. (5) can be rearranged as

$$e^{[\omega]\theta} = \mathbf{I} + \sin\theta\,[\omega] + (1 - \cos\theta)\,[\omega]^2$$
$$= \cos\theta\mathbf{I} + \sin\theta\,[\omega] + (1 - \cos\theta)\,\omega\omega^T \tag{6}$$

and thus the ration matrix of the rotational motion of a rigid body can be given as

$$\mathbf{R}([\omega], \theta) = e^{[\omega]\theta} = \mathbf{I} + \sin\theta\,[\omega] + (1 - \cos\theta)\,[\omega]^2$$
$$= \cos\theta\mathbf{I} + \sin\theta\,[\omega] + (1 - \cos\theta)\,\omega\omega^T \tag{7}$$

where the relation $[\omega]^2 = \omega\omega^T - \|\omega\|^2\mathbf{I}$ is used. Equation (7) can also be obtained through geometric approach [3].

Hence Eq. (7) gives an orthogonal matrix in $SO(3)$ as

$$\mathbf{R}([\omega], \theta) = e^{[\omega]\theta} = \begin{bmatrix} r_{11} & r_{12} & r_{13} \\ r_{21} & r_{22} & r_{23} \\ r_{31} & r_{32} & r_{33} \end{bmatrix} \tag{8}$$

where the elements r_{ij} are: $r_{11} = \cos\theta + \omega_1^2(1 - \cos\theta)$, $r_{12} = \omega_1\omega_2(1 - \cos\theta) - \omega_3\sin\theta$, $r_{13} = \omega_1\omega_3(1 - \cos\theta) + \omega_2\sin\theta$, $r_{21} = \omega_2\omega_1(1 - \cos\theta) + \omega_3\sin\theta$, $r_{22} =$

$\cos\theta + \omega_2^2\,(1 - \cos\theta)$, $r_{23} = \omega_2\omega_3\,(1 - \cos\theta) - \omega_1\sin\theta$, $r_{31} = \omega_3\omega_1\,(1 - \cos\theta) - \omega_2\sin\theta$, $r_{32} = \omega_3\omega_2\,(1 - \cos) + \omega_1\sin\theta$, $r_{33} = \cos\theta + \omega_3^2\,(1 - \cos\theta)$.

Equation (7) is known as Rodrigues' formula for rotation of an arbitrary axis passing through the origin of a reference frame. The quantity $e^{[\omega]\theta}\boldsymbol{p}$ has the effect of rotating $\boldsymbol{p} \in \mathbb{R}^3$ about the fixed-frame axis $\boldsymbol{\omega}$ by an angle θ.

Equation (7) is also called the *screw axis representation* of the rotation of a rigid body. This representation uses four parameters: three associated with the direction of the screw and one associated with the angle of rotation. However, only two of the three parameters associated with the direction of the screw axis are independent since they must satisfy the condition of a unit vector, i.e. $\boldsymbol{\omega}^T\boldsymbol{\omega} = 1$.

Hence, given the screw axis and angle of rotation, we can compute the elements of the rotation matrix from Eq. (7). On the other hand, given a rotation matrix, we can compute the screw axis and the angle of rotation. The angle of rotation is obtained by summing the diagonal elements of the rotation matrix in Eq. (7), leading to

$$\theta = \cos^{-1}\left(\frac{\mathrm{tr}\mathbf{R} - 1}{2}\right) \tag{9}$$

where $\mathrm{tr}\mathbf{R} = r_{11} + r_{22} + r_{33} = 1 + 2\cos\theta$.

The direction of the screw axis is obtained by taking the differences between each pair of two opposing off-diagonal elements:

$$\omega_x = \frac{r_{32} - r_{23}}{2\sin\theta}$$
$$\omega_y = \frac{r_{13} - r_{31}}{2\sin\theta}$$
$$\omega_z = \frac{r_{21} - r_{12}}{2\sin\theta} \tag{10}$$

which can also be obtained from the following skew-symmetric matrix as

$$[\boldsymbol{\omega}] = \begin{bmatrix} 0 & -\omega_z & \omega_y \\ \omega_z & 0 & -\omega_x \\ -\omega_y & \omega_x & 0 \end{bmatrix} = \frac{1}{2\sin\theta}\left(\mathbf{R} - \mathbf{R}^T\right) \tag{11}$$

From Eqs. (9) and (10) it appears that there are two solutions of the screw axis, one being the negative of the other. In reality, these two solutions represent the same screw since a $-\theta$ rotation about the $-\boldsymbol{\omega}$ axis produces the same result as a $+\theta$ rotation about the $\boldsymbol{\omega}$ axis.

2.2   Exponential Derivations for Spatial Rigid-Body Motion

The derivation of the rotation matrix introduced in Sect. 2.1 for $SO(3)$ can be generalized to the Euclidean group, $SE(3)$ for the spatial rigid-body motion.

Figure 2 shows a point P that is displaced from a first position P_1 to a second position P_2 by a rotation of θ about a screw axis $\boldsymbol{\omega}$ followed by a translation of d along the same axis. The rotation takes P from P_1 to P_2^r, and the translation

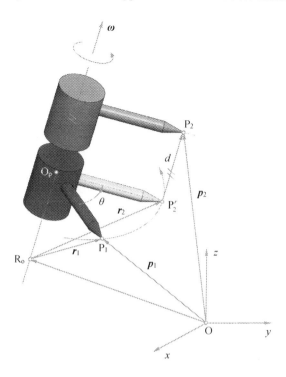

Fig. 2. Vector diagram of a general spatial displacement

takes P from P_2^r to P_2. In the figure, $\boldsymbol{\omega} = [\omega_x, \omega_y, \omega_z]^T$ is a unit vector along the direction of the screw axis, and $\boldsymbol{r}_o = [r_{ox}, r_{oy}, r_{oz}]^T$ denotes the position vector of a point lying on the screw axis. The rotation angle θ and the translational distance d are termed the screw parameters. Such a motion is called a screw motion, since it is reminiscent of the motion of a screw. By this analogy, the pitch of the screw is defined as the ratio of translation to rotation, $h = d/\theta$, assuming that $\theta \neq 0$ and hence the net translational motion after rotating by θ radians is $h\theta$. The screw axis together with the screw parameters completely define the general displacement of a rigid body. Note that for a general displacement of a rigid body, the screw axis does not necessarily pass through the origin of the fixed frame.

As aforementioned, the axis of rotation is $\boldsymbol{\omega} \in \mathbb{R}^3$, $\|\boldsymbol{\omega}\| = 1$, and $\boldsymbol{r}_o \in \mathbb{R}^3$ is the vector for a point R_o on the axis. Assuming that the rigid body rotates about $\boldsymbol{\omega}$ with angular velocity $\dot{\theta}\boldsymbol{\omega}$ together with a translational velocity $\dot{d}\boldsymbol{\omega} = h\dot{\theta}\boldsymbol{\omega}$, then the velocity of the tip point, $\boldsymbol{p}(t)$, is

$$\dot{\boldsymbol{p}}(t) = \boldsymbol{\omega} \times (\boldsymbol{p}(t) - \boldsymbol{r}_o) + h\boldsymbol{\omega} \tag{12}$$

This equation can be conveniently converted into homogeneous coordinates by defining a 4×4 matrix $[\boldsymbol{S}]$ as

$$[\boldsymbol{S}] = \begin{bmatrix} [\boldsymbol{\omega}] & \boldsymbol{v} \\ \boldsymbol{0} & 0 \end{bmatrix} \tag{13}$$

with $\boldsymbol{v} = -\boldsymbol{\omega} \times \boldsymbol{r}_o + h\boldsymbol{\omega}$. Using Eq. (13), Eq. (12) can be rewritten with an extra row appended to it as

$$\begin{bmatrix} \dot{\boldsymbol{p}} \\ 0 \end{bmatrix} = \begin{bmatrix} [\boldsymbol{\omega}] & \boldsymbol{v} \\ \boldsymbol{0} & 0 \end{bmatrix} \begin{bmatrix} \boldsymbol{p} \\ 1 \end{bmatrix} = [\boldsymbol{S}] \begin{bmatrix} \boldsymbol{p} \\ 1 \end{bmatrix} \tag{14}$$

That is

$$\dot{\bar{\boldsymbol{p}}} = [\boldsymbol{S}]\,\bar{\boldsymbol{p}} \tag{15}$$

The solution of the differential equation in Eq. (15) is given by

$$\bar{\boldsymbol{p}}\,(t) = e^{[S]t}\bar{\boldsymbol{p}}\,(0) \tag{16}$$

where $e^{[S]t}$ is the matrix exponential of the 4×4 matrix $[\boldsymbol{S}]\,t$, defined by

$$e^{[S]t} = \mathbf{I} + [\boldsymbol{S}]\,t + \frac{([\boldsymbol{S}]\,t)^2}{2!} + \frac{([\boldsymbol{S}]\,t)^3}{3!} + \cdots \tag{17}$$

If the body rotates about the axis $\boldsymbol{\omega}$ at unit velocity for θ units of time, then the net transformation is given by

$$\mathbf{T} = e^{[S]\theta} = \mathbf{I} + [\boldsymbol{S}]\,\theta + [\boldsymbol{S}]^2\,\frac{\theta^2}{2!} + [\boldsymbol{S}]^3\,\frac{\theta^3}{3!} + \cdots \tag{18}$$

where, $[\boldsymbol{S}]^2 = \begin{bmatrix} [\boldsymbol{\omega}]^2 & \boldsymbol{v} \\ \boldsymbol{0} & 0 \end{bmatrix}$, $[\boldsymbol{S}]^3 = \begin{bmatrix} [\boldsymbol{\omega}]^3 & [\boldsymbol{\omega}]^2\,\boldsymbol{v} \\ \boldsymbol{0} & 0 \end{bmatrix}$, $[\boldsymbol{S}]^4 = \begin{bmatrix} [\boldsymbol{\omega}]^4 & [\boldsymbol{\omega}]^3\,\boldsymbol{v} \\ \boldsymbol{0} & 0 \end{bmatrix}$, $\cdots$. Such that Eq. (18) becomes

$$\mathbf{T} = e^{[S]\theta} = \begin{bmatrix} e^{[\boldsymbol{\omega}]\theta} & \mathbf{Q}\,(\theta)\,\boldsymbol{v} \\ \boldsymbol{0} & 1 \end{bmatrix} = \begin{bmatrix} \mathbf{R} & \boldsymbol{q} \\ \boldsymbol{0} & 1 \end{bmatrix} \tag{19}$$

with $\mathbf{Q}\,(\theta) = \mathbf{I}\theta + [\boldsymbol{\omega}]\,\frac{\theta^2}{2!} + [\boldsymbol{\omega}]^2\,\frac{\theta^3}{3!} + \cdots$; and using the identity $[\boldsymbol{\omega}]^3 = -[\boldsymbol{\omega}]$, $\mathbf{Q}\,(\theta)$ can be simplified to

$$\begin{aligned} \mathbf{Q}\,(\theta) &= \mathbf{I}\theta + [\boldsymbol{\omega}]\,\frac{\theta^2}{2!} + [\boldsymbol{\omega}]^2\,\frac{\theta^3}{3!} + \cdots \\ &= \mathbf{I}\theta + \left(\frac{\theta^2}{2!} - \frac{\theta^4}{4!} + \frac{\theta^6}{6!} - \cdots \right) [\boldsymbol{\omega}] + \left(\frac{\theta^3}{3!} - \frac{\theta^5}{5!} + \frac{\theta^7}{7!} - \cdots \right) [\boldsymbol{\omega}]^2 \\ &= \mathbf{I}\theta + (1 - \cos\theta)\,[\boldsymbol{\omega}] + (\theta - \sin\theta)\,[\boldsymbol{\omega}]^2 \end{aligned} \tag{20}$$

Hence, considering that $\boldsymbol{v} = -\boldsymbol{\omega} \times \boldsymbol{r}_o + h\boldsymbol{\omega}$, $\mathbf{Q}\,(\theta)\,\boldsymbol{v}$ can be derived as following by using the identities that $[\boldsymbol{\omega}]^2\,\boldsymbol{\omega} = \boldsymbol{0}$ and $[\boldsymbol{\omega}]^3 = -[\boldsymbol{\omega}]$:

$$\begin{aligned} \mathbf{Q}\,(\theta)\,\boldsymbol{v} &= \left(\mathbf{I}\theta + (1 - \cos\theta)\,[\boldsymbol{\omega}] + (\theta - \sin\theta)\,[\boldsymbol{\omega}]^2 \right) (-\boldsymbol{\omega} \times \boldsymbol{r}_o + h\boldsymbol{\omega}) \\ &= \mathbf{I}\theta\,(-\boldsymbol{\omega} \times \boldsymbol{r}_o + h\boldsymbol{\omega}) + (1 - \cos\theta)\,[\boldsymbol{\omega}]\,(-\boldsymbol{\omega} \times \boldsymbol{r}_o + h\boldsymbol{\omega}) + (\theta - \sin\theta)\,[\boldsymbol{\omega}]^2\,(-\boldsymbol{\omega} \times \boldsymbol{r}_o + h\boldsymbol{\omega}) \\ &= -[\boldsymbol{\omega}]\,\boldsymbol{r}_o\theta + h\theta\boldsymbol{\omega} - (1 - \cos\theta)\,[\boldsymbol{\omega}]^2\,\boldsymbol{r}_o + 0 + (\theta - \sin\theta)\,[\boldsymbol{\omega}]\,\boldsymbol{r}_o + 0 \\ &= h\theta\boldsymbol{\omega} - (1 - \cos\theta)\,[\boldsymbol{\omega}]^2\,\boldsymbol{r}_o - \sin\theta\,[\boldsymbol{\omega}]\,\boldsymbol{r}_o \\ &= \left(\mathbf{I} - e^{[\boldsymbol{\omega}]\theta} \right) \boldsymbol{r}_o + h\theta\boldsymbol{\omega} = (\mathbf{I} - \mathbf{R})\,\boldsymbol{r}_o + d\boldsymbol{\omega} = \boldsymbol{q} \end{aligned} \tag{21}$$

with q being derived as

$$
\begin{aligned}
q_x &= dw_1 - r_{ox}(r_{11} - 1) - r_{oy}r_{12} - r_{oz}r_{13} \\
q_y &= dw_2 - r_{oy}r_{21} - r_{oy}(r_{22} - 1) - r_{oz}r_{23} \\
q_x &= dw_3 - r_{ox}r_{31} - r_{oy}r_{32} - r_{oz}(r_{33} - 1)
\end{aligned}
\tag{22}
$$

Substituting Eq. (21) into Eq. (19), it yields

$$
\mathbf{T} = e^{[S]\theta} = \begin{bmatrix} e^{[\omega]\theta} & \mathbf{Q}(\theta)\,v \\ 0 & 1 \end{bmatrix} = \begin{bmatrix} e^{[\omega]\theta} & \left(\mathbf{I} - e^{[\omega]\theta}\right) r_o + h\theta\omega \\ 0 & 1 \end{bmatrix} = \begin{bmatrix} e^{[\omega]\theta} & (\mathbf{I} - \mathbf{R})\,r_o + d\omega \\ 0 & 1 \end{bmatrix}
\tag{23}
$$

Further, considering that $\omega^T v = \omega^T(-\omega \times r_o) + h\omega^T\omega$ such that $h = \omega^T v$, and $r_o = \omega \times v$, Eq. (23) can also be written as

$$
\mathbf{T} = e^{[S]\theta} = \begin{bmatrix} e^{[\omega]\theta} & \left(\mathbf{I} - e^{[\omega]\theta}\right)(\omega \times v) + \omega\omega^T v\theta \\ 0 & 1 \end{bmatrix} = \begin{bmatrix} e^{[\omega]\theta} & \left[\left(\mathbf{I} - e^{[\omega]\theta}\right)[\omega] + \omega\omega^T\theta\right] v \\ 0 & 1 \end{bmatrix}
\tag{24}
$$

which is the same as the one obtained in Ref. [2].

In the case of pure translation which complies with $\|\omega\| = 0$, and $\|v\| = 1$, it has

$$
[S] = \begin{bmatrix} 0 & v \\ 0 & 0 \end{bmatrix}
\tag{25}
$$

which leads to $\mathbf{R} = e^{[\omega]\theta} = \mathbf{I}$, and $\mathbf{Q}(\theta) = \mathbf{I}\theta$ where $\theta = d$ is the amount of translation, such that

$$
\mathbf{T} = e^{[S]\theta} = \begin{bmatrix} \mathbf{I} & d\,v \\ 0 & 1 \end{bmatrix}
\tag{26}
$$

In the case that $h = d = 0$ and $\|\omega\| = 1$, which corresponds to the pure rotational motion, Eqs. (23) and (24) become

$$
\mathbf{T} = e^{[S]\theta} = \begin{bmatrix} e^{[\omega]\theta} & \left(\mathbf{I} - e^{[\omega]\theta}\right) r_o \\ 0 & 1 \end{bmatrix} = \begin{bmatrix} e^{[\omega]\theta} & \left(\mathbf{I} - e^{[\omega]\theta}\right)(\omega \times v) \\ 0 & 1 \end{bmatrix}
\tag{27}
$$

where r_o is the vector for a point on the screw axis as shown in Fig. 2.

The above derivation of a spatial displacement requires eight parameters: three associated with the direction of the screw axis, three associated with the location of the screw axis, one associated with the rotation angle, and one associated with the translational distance. However, only two of the three parameters associated with the direction of the screw axis are independent since they must satisfy the condition of a unit vector:

$$
\omega^T\omega = 1
\tag{28}
$$

Similarly, only two of the three parameters associated with the location of the screw axis are independent, since r_o can be any point on the screw axis. For convenience, one may choose r_o to be normal to the screw axis such that

$$
r_o^T\omega = 0
\tag{29}
$$

Given the screw axis and screw parameters, one can compute the elements of the transformation matrix by Eq. (19). On the other hand, given the spatial displacement of a rigid body in terms of a rotation matrix, $\mathbf{R}$, and a translation vector, $\boldsymbol{q}$, we can compute the angle of rotation based on Eq. (9), the direction of the screw axis based on Eqs. (10) and (11), and the translational distance is calculated by

$$d = {}^A\boldsymbol{q}^T\boldsymbol{\omega} \tag{30}$$

In addition, the screw axis location can be obtained by solving any two of the three equations in Eq. (22) together with Eq. (29). Since these equations are linear, there exists one solution corresponding to each solution set of $\boldsymbol{\omega}$, θ, and d.

From the derivation above, it appears that there are two solutions of the screw axis, one being the negative of the other. In reality, these two solutions represent the same screw, since a $-\theta$ rotation about and a $-d$ translation along the $-(\boldsymbol{\omega}, \boldsymbol{r}_o)$ screw axis produces the same result as a $+\theta$ rotation about and a $+d$ translation along the $+(\boldsymbol{\omega}, \boldsymbol{r}_o)$ screw axis.

The screw displacement derived above provides background for kinematics investigation through transform operator approach [13], which also coined as POE (product of exponentials) approach [2], involving only one reference coordinate system and one tool coordinate system. The POE method is different from the traditional Denavit-Hartenberg method [14] which is based on transform mapping among $n+1$ different coordinate systems with n being the number of links in a robotic manipulator. Further, the screw displacement is also very useful in biomechanics for investigating joint axes of bones.

3   Application of Screw Displacement in In Vivo Finger Joint Axes Identification

There are three joints in a human finger (not including the thumb), i.e., the MCP (Metacarpophalangeal), PIP (Proximal Interphalangeal) and DIP (Distal interphalangeal) joints, which can perform complex movements with their six extrinsic and intrinsic muscles. Though the irregular shape of the articulating joint surfaces, especially the MCP joint, makes the joints move in three-dimensional space [18], the PIP and DIP joints are still being widely studied by simple hinge models. Besides, most research assume that the rotation axes in PIP and DIP joint are parallel to each other, and perpendicular to the axial direction of phalanges. This simplified model may produce certain errors when we analyse the kinematic and kinetic properties of finger joints. Therefore, Scientifically and effectively orienting the rotation axes in PIP and DIP joint could be significant for the research in human fingers.

As shown in Fig. 3(a), three coordinate frames $O_p\text{-}X_pY_pZ_p$, $O_m\text{-}X_mY_mZ_m$ and $O_d\text{-}X_dY_dZ_d$ are established at the centre of the head of proximal, middle and distal phalanx, respectively. As can be seen, the radial-ulnar direction is along the x-axis, the proximal-distal direction is along the y-axis, and the dorsal-palmar direction is along the z-axis. And the radial, proximal and dorsal sides

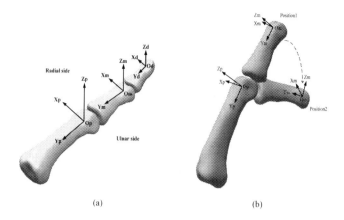

Fig. 3. (a) The coordinate frames in each phalanx of the index finger; (b) Rotation process in PIP joint.

are positive. Thus, each step of the rotation in PIP joint will generate a rotation axis in $O_p\text{-}X_pY_pZ_p$ frame, resulting in a series of axes during the whole rotation process, and the same for the DIP joint. It is expected that the average rotation axis $\boldsymbol{\omega}$ can be found in each joint through the experiment, and the Rodrigues' formula for rotation derived in Sects. refExponentialRotation can be applied to solve this problem.

Referring to Fig. 3(b), take PIP joint as an example, the reference coordinate frame $O_m\text{-}X_mY_mZ_m$ at position 1 is regarded as a fixed frame, and the coordinate $O_m\text{-}X_mY_mZ_m$ at position 2 is taken as a body coordinate frame. Based on transform mapping [13], the rotation of coordinate frame $Om\text{-}X_mY_mZ_m$ from position 1 to position 2 can be expressed with direction cosine matrix as

$$\begin{array}{c}^1_2\mathbf{R} = \begin{bmatrix} \boldsymbol{X}_{m1}\cdot\boldsymbol{X}_{m2} & \boldsymbol{X}_{m1}\cdot\boldsymbol{Y}_{m2} & \boldsymbol{X}_{m1}\cdot\boldsymbol{Z}_{m2} \\ \boldsymbol{Y}_{m1}\cdot\boldsymbol{X}_{m2} & \boldsymbol{Y}_{m1}\cdot\boldsymbol{Y}_{m2} & \boldsymbol{Y}_{m1}\cdot\boldsymbol{Z}_{m2} \\ \boldsymbol{Z}_{m1}\cdot\boldsymbol{X}_{m2} & \boldsymbol{Z}_{m1}\cdot\boldsymbol{Y}_{m2} & \boldsymbol{Z}_{m1}\cdot\boldsymbol{Z}_{m2} \end{bmatrix}\end{array} \tag{31}$$

According to Eq. (8), it has $^1_2\mathbf{R} = \mathbf{R}\,(\boldsymbol{\omega},\boldsymbol{\theta})$, such that using Eqs. (9) and (11), rotation angle θ and direction vector $\boldsymbol{\omega}$ indicated in Fig. 3(b) can be calculated as

$$\theta = \cos^{-1}\left(\frac{\mathrm{tr}^1_2\mathbf{R}-1}{2}\right) = \cos^{-1}\left(\frac{\boldsymbol{X}_{m1}\cdot\boldsymbol{X}_{m2}+\boldsymbol{Y}_{m1}\cdot\boldsymbol{Y}_{m2}+\boldsymbol{Z}_{m1}\cdot\boldsymbol{Z}_{m2}}{2}\right) \tag{32}$$

and

$$[\boldsymbol{\omega}] = \begin{bmatrix} 0 & -\omega_z & \omega_y \\ \omega_z & 0 & -\omega_x \\ -\omega_y & \omega_x & 0 \end{bmatrix} = \frac{1}{2\sin\theta}\left(^1_2\mathbf{R}-^1_2\mathbf{R}^T\right) \tag{33}$$

Hence, as long as the rotation matrix (direction cosine matrix) is known, the rotation angle θ and the rotation axis vector $\boldsymbol{\omega} = [\omega_x,\omega_y,\omega_z]^T$ can be obtained.

And in order to express the rotation axis vector $\boldsymbol{\omega}$ in the reference coordinate frames $O_p\text{-}X_pY_pZ_p$, the rotation matrix ${}^m_p\mathbf{R}$ from $O_m\text{-}X_mY_mZ_m$ to $O_p\text{-}X_pY_pZ_p$ should be found, thus the rotation axis vector $\boldsymbol{\omega}$ in the reference coordinate frames $O_p\text{-}X_pY_pZ_p$ can be expressed as

$$\boldsymbol{\omega}_p = {}^m_p\mathbf{R}\boldsymbol{\omega} \tag{34}$$

In this paper, a MPU-9250 9 Axis Sensor Module (Banggood Technology, Cyprus) is used to identify the joint axes of the PIP and DIP joints. In the test, the sensor was attached to the proximal, middle and distal phalanx, together with Arduino board, providing the angle information of each reference coordinate frames during the whole rotation process, as shown in Fig. 4. Through the IMU and AHRS sensor fusion algorithm developed by Sebastian Madgwick from the University of Bristol, the initial data gathered from MPU-9250 can be transformed and output as many quaternion groups, which can be following transformed into the direction cosine matrix in Matlab.

Fig. 4. Measurement through MPU-9250 gyroscope and Arduino board.

Using the above set-up, the mappings between frames $O_p\text{-}X_pY_pZ_p$ and $O_m\text{-}X_mY_mZ_m$, and frames $O_m\text{-}X_mY_mZ_m$ and $O_d\text{-}X_dY_dZ_d$ are obtained in the direction cosine matrix from, and the joint axes of the PIP and DIP joints are identified. As shown in Fig. 5, the blue line cluster reflects the direction change of the rotation axis during the whole rotation process, and the red line is the average direction of the rotation axis. As a result, in the coordinate frame $O_p\text{-}X_pY_pZ_p$ of PIP joint, the average rotation axis vector is $(-4.93, -0.65, -0.53)$, and in the coordinate frame $O_m\text{-}X_mY_mZ_m$ of DIP joint, the average rotation axis vector is $(-1.22, -0.53, -1.01)$.

The experiment results contain some errors due to the noise in the sensor's signals and the skin movement. Moreover, the rotation axis direction in the finger joint can be quite different between individuals. But the experiment and data processing method could provide a rational reference for the future research in human fingers.

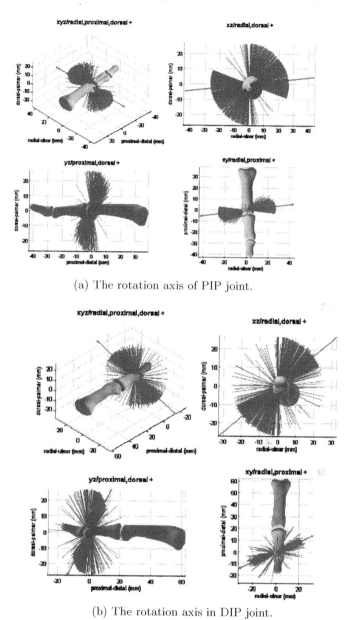

(a) The rotation axis of PIP joint.

(b) The rotation axis in DIP joint.

Fig. 5. The rotation axes in PIP and DIP joint shown in Matlab. (Color figure online)

Based on the average rotation axis in PIP and DIP joint and the length of the proximal, middle and distal phalanx, the workspace of the fingertip is shown in Fig. 6. According to the experiment data from Ref. [19], the PIP and DIP joint has a mean value of flexion of $101°$ and $73°$ respectively for the index finger.

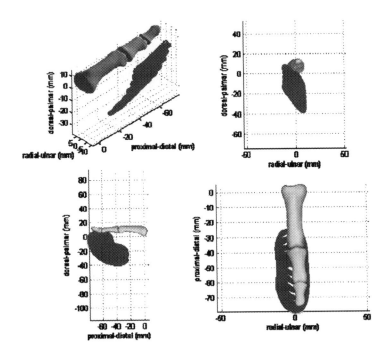

Fig. 6. Workspace of the fingertip based on the PIP and DIP joint rotation.

4   Conclusions

This paper presented the note providing the detailed derivations of screw displacement with matrix exponential formula and it application in identifying axes of rotation of human finger. The matrix exponential based derivation of screw displacement provides a comprehensive note for researchers in the fields of mechanisms and robotics. And the application of Rodrigues' formula in determining location and orientation of joint axes of human finger offered a new lower cost approach for biomechanics research community.

References

1. Bottema, O., Roth, B.: Theoretical Kinematics. North Holland Publishing Company, Amsterdam (1979)
2. Murray, R.M., Li, Z., Sastry, S.S.: A Mathematical Introduction to Robotic Manipulation. CRC Press, Boca Raton (1994)
3. Tsai, L.-W.: Robot Analysis: The Mechanics of Serial and Parallel Manipulators. Wiley, New York (1999)
4. Selig, J.M.: Geometric Fundamentals of Robotics, 2nd edn. Springer, New York (2005). https://doi.org/10.1007/b138859
5. Uicker, J.J., Sheth, P.N., Ravani, B.: Matrix Methods in the Design Analysis of Mechanisms and Multibody Systems. Cambridge University Press, New York (2013)

6. Shabana, A.A.: Dynamics of Multibody Systems. Cambridge University Press, New York (2013)
7. Lynch, K.M., Park, F.C.: Modern Robotics: Mechanics, Planning, and Control. Cambridge University Press, New York (2017)
8. Brockett, R.W.: Robotic manipulators and the product of exponentials formula. In: Fuhrmann, P.A. (ed.) Mathematical Theory of Networks and Systems. LNCIS, vol. 58, pp. 120–129. Springer, Heidelberg (1984). https://doi.org/10.1007/BFb0031048
9. Park, F.C., Eobrow, J.E., Ploen, S.R.: A lie group formulation of robot dynamics. Int. J. Robot. Res. **14**(6), 609–618 (1995)
10. Gallier, J., Xu, D.: Computing exponential of skew-symmetric matrices and logarithms of orthogonal matrices. Int. J. Robot. Autom. **17**(4), 1–11 (2002)
11. Dai, J.S.: Finite displacement screw operators with embedded Chalses' motion. J. Mech. Robot. Trans. ASME **44**, 041002 (2012)
12. Dai, J.S.: Euler-Rodrigues formula variations, quaternion conjugation and intrinsic connections. Mech. Mach. Theory **92**, 144–152 (2015)
13. Craig, J.J.: Introduction to Robotics: Mechanics and Control, 3rd edn. Pearson Education Inc., Upper Saddle River (2005)
14. Denavit, J., Hartenberg, R.S.: A kinematic notation for lower pair mechanisms based on matrices. ASME J. Appl. Mech. **77**, 215–221 (1955)
15. Brand, P.W., Hollister, A.M.: Clinical Mechanics of the Hand, 3rd edn. Mosby Inc., St. Louis (1999)
16. Hollister, A., Giurintano, D.J., Buford, W.L., Myers, L.M., Novick, A.: The axes of rotation of the thumb interphalangeal and metacarpophalangeal joints. Clin. Orthop. Relat. Res. **320**, 188–193 (1995)
17. Chang, L.Y., Pollard, N.S.: Method for determining kinematic parameters of the in vivo thumb carpometacarpal joint. IEEE Trans. Biomed. Eng. **55**(7), 1897–1906 (2008)
18. Dumont, C., Albus, G., Kubein-Meesenburg, D., Fanghänel, J., Stürmer, K.M., Nägerl, H.: Morphology of the interphalangeal joint surface and its functional relevance. J. Hand Surg. **33**(1), 9–18 (2008)
19. Chao, E.Y.S., An, K.-N., Cooney III, P.W., Linscheid, R.L.: Boimechanics of the Hand: A Basic Research Study. World Scientific Publishing Co., Pte. Ltd., Farrer Road, Singapore (1989)

Robotics for Cell Manipulation and Characterization

A Cell Manipulation Method Based on Stagnation Point of Swirl

Zhiming Ou📧, Qin Zhang$^{(\boxtimes)}$📧, and Hao Yang📧

School of Mechanical and Automotive Engineering,
South China University of Technology, Guangzhou 510640, Guangdong, China
zhangqin@scut.edu.cn

Abstract. As one of the key techniques of cell manipulation, the trapping, movement and rotation of cell are wildly applied in various areas including Bioengineering, Medicine, Chemical Analysis, Properties Evaluations and so on. One particular technique of cell manipulation based on stagnation point of swirl is brought up: Create a swirling flow field using three microtubules, and control the stagnation point of swirl through matching the jet velocities of the microtubules, so as to achieve the movement and rotation of the cell near the stagnation point. The microfluidics dynamic model of the swirling flow field is established, and the correlations among each direction of the swirl stagnation point in the field while the jet velocities of the three microtubules change are analyzed through simulation. Also, the mechanism and pattern that how the cell moves along with the stagnation point within the swirling flow field are discussed. We demonstrate that three microtubules in triangular layout jetting fluids in convectional directions can create swirl, and matching the jetting velocities of each microtubule in the swirling flow field can control the strength of the swirl and the location of the stagnation point. We further show that this approach can trap the cell using the region near the stagnation point of swirl. Overall, this technique can achieve the directional and quantitative movement and rotation of the cell along different directions in the swirling flow field.

Keywords: Cell manipulation · Swirling flow field · Stagnation point of swirl · Stagnation point control

1 Introduction

Cell manipulation and control are crucial techniques in micromanipulation, as well as the core of microfluidic chips, and are wildly applied in various areas including Bioengineering, Medicine, Chemical Analysis, Properties Evaluations and so on. The manipulation method based on microfluidics will avoid mechanical damage to cells, which shows excellent safety and maneuverability.

In the methods of movement control based on microfluidics, Aoyama et al. came up with a method of microfluidics vibrations: Control the microfluidic field generated around the cell through the vibration of the micro pipette in the fluids, then adjust the

Supported by The National Natural Science Foundation of China (Grant No. 51675187).

H. Yu et al. (Eds.): ICIRA 2019, LNAI 11740, pp. 157–165, 2019.
https://doi.org/10.1007/978-3-030-27526-6_14

movement of the cell in the fluid field, leading to the omni-bearing manipulation of the cell position and attitude [1]. Liu et al. used piezoelectric actuators to generate circular vibration of microtubules. By controlling the relative position of the microtubules and the cell, the trapping, movement and attitude adjustment of the cell were realized [2, 3]. The methods just mentioned both use the vibration of the microtubules to stimulate the fluids, and adjust the flow field around the cell, using the pressure difference around the cell and the torque formed by flow field velocity gradient to manipulate cell. However, the adjustment of vibration parameters is complex when the cell size and solution change, and it is difficult to achieve system integration. Hayakawa et al. designed a chip with micropillar array. They used the rotational vibration of the micropillar to trap, move and rotate the cell directionally [4, 5]. However, this approach can only achieve the cell movement along specific paths of the micropillar which causes problems such as weak generality of cell control and low calibration accuracy of attitude adjustment.

When it comes to micromanipulation using stagnation point of the fluids, Tanyeri et al. designed an integrated control device based on particle position of the microfluidic. It trapped and immobilized micro-nano particle contactlessly through the stagnation point of the fluid field and held it still for several minutes or even hours, but no movement [6]. Shenoy et al. developed a six-channel system to generate stagnation points by controlling the flow rates of each channel, which makes it possible to manipulate a pair of particles to move along any path [7]. Safavieh et al. designed a multi-microtubule, movable and channel-less microfluidics device which can move the stagnation point by altering the position and flow rate of the microtubules [8]. Zhang et al. raised a particle manipulation method based on opposed jets: Place two microtubules bilaterally on the two sides of the particle, jet fluids towards the particle and create an opposed-jet flow field, trap and move the particle directionally and quantitatively through the pressure containment formed on the particle's surface around the stagnation point of the opposed-jet flow field [9]. The approaches above manage to move the particle by moving the stagnation point but are still hard to control the attitude.

In Reference [10, 11], two parallel microtubules jetting fluids oppositely can create swirl and using stagnation point of the swirl can trap various shapes of particles. The particle can be moved and rotated directionally and quantitatively by controlling the stagnation point position of swirl. However, due to the constraint of the swirling flow field, the movement of stagnation point is limited on restrictive directions of the two microtubules. On the basis of previous research, this paper furtherly comes up with a method of constructing swirling flow field out of three microtubules and studies the mechanism of manipulating cell in different directions within the stagnation point of swirl. Also we establish a dynamic model of the microfluidic in the field, analyze the correlations among each direction of the swirl stagnation point in the field while the jet velocities of the three microtubules change through simulation, and discuss the pattern that how the cell moves along with the stagnation point within the swirling flow field.

2   Mechanism of Cell Manipulation Using Swirl

2.1   Constructing Swirling Flow Field

Place three identical microtubules in a plane with the end faces of the microtubules aligned with the vertexes of a triangle. When the microtubules jet fluids simultaneously, a swirl will form where the microtubules bound. The features of the swirling flow field are shown in Fig. 1, in which (a) is the contour plot of pressure and (b) is the streamlines and contour plot of velocity. From the graphs, we can tell that the distributions of the pressure and the velocity in the fluid field resemble triangle. The center of the swirl O (center of the field model) has lower pressure and smaller velocity around it. Pressure and velocity gradually raise with the distance from O increasing in radial direction. The velocity at the swirl center is zero where the pressure is also the lowest, so O is the stagnation point of the swirling flow field. Using the surrounding area of the stagnation point, the cell can be trapped and manipulated.

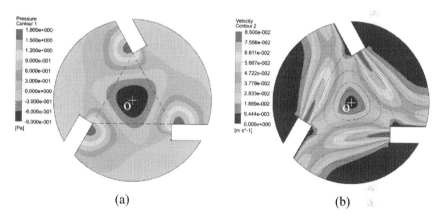

(a)   (b)

Fig. 1. Swirling flow field features. (a) Contour plot of pressure. (b) Streamlines and contour plot of velocity.

2.2   Manipulation Mechanism

Cell entering the swirling flow field is under the influence of several forces: fluid resistance, subsidiary load applied to the cell due to inhomogeneity of the fluid field and the force applied to the cell by the fluids when the cell accelerates. Cell makes corresponding movement under the combined action of these forces. First, cell in swirl rotates because of the viscosity of the fluids; then the cell will be impelled to move towards the center by swirl. If the parameters of the swirling flow field match the ones of cell, the cell will rotate on its axis under viscosity and will not leave the center of the swirl. The cell will move along with the movement of swirl stagnation point.

When the flow rates of the three microtubules unify, the pressure and velocity near the center O are shown in Fig. 2(a), the net force of the cell almost equals to zero, so under symmetric fluids, the cell will be fixed close to stagnation point. Moreover, since the fluid velocities on the two sides of the cell are in opposite directions, the cell will rotate stably near stagnation point. When the flow rates of microtubules change, the stagnation point position in the swirling flow field also changes. The changing of fluid pressures beside the cell will cause the cell deviating from its original stagnation point O and move along with the new stagnation point to O', which is the movement of cell demonstrated in Fig. 2(b). Altering microtubules jet velocities changes swirl strength, as a result the rotation speed of the cell changes too. Similarly, the rotation direction changes with the swirl direction as shown in Fig. 2(c) and (d). Therefore, controlling the jet velocities of each microtubule can gain control of the cell attitude.

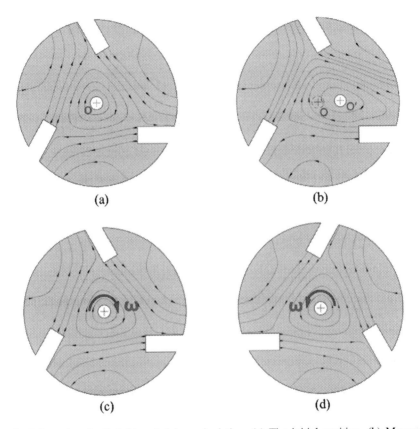

Fig. 2. Schematic of cell (white circle) manipulation. (a) The initial position. (b) Movement along with the stagnation point. (c) Clockwise rotation. (d) Counterclockwise rotation.

3   Simulation Analysis

3.1   Simulation Model

In software Fluent, we commence numerical simulation of the swirling flow field using Finite Volume Method. We analyze the generation of the swirling flow field and the correlations between microtubules jet velocities and swirl stagnation point. Then we simulate the cell movement using dynamic mesh technique. The cell properties are interpolated into the motion equation through user-defined function (UDF). And we simulate the cell movement driven by the stagnation point of swirl though Fluent unsteady solution.

Suppose the simulated fluid field model is a circle with a diameter of 5 mm (D = 5 mm). As is shown in Fig. 3, three identical microtubules are placed within the same plane with the included angels of their axis lines equal to 120°, and their end faces top points serve as vertices of an equilateral triangle (side length L = 2.5 mm). Set the center of the equilateral triangle as origin of coordinates O and set up a coordinate system $\sum$xoy. Diameters of each microtubule are 0.5 mm (d = 0.5 mm) and the fluid is set as pure water at 25 °C. The inlets of microtubules are set as velocity inlet, pipe walls of microtubules are set as wall boundary and the circular fluid field boundaries are set as pressure outlet. By loading UDF, the flow velocities at micro-tubules outlet are defined to follow parabola distribution. Laminar flow model is adopted as calculation model. We input different microtubules jet velocities to simulate the characteristics of the swirling flow field and the changes of swirl stagnation point. Through CFD-Post processing, read the coordinate of the position where the velocity is zero in this fluid field, which is the stagnation point.

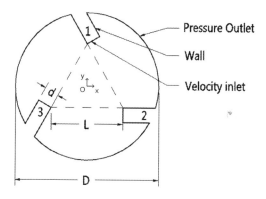

Fig. 3. Simulation model.

3.2 Stagnation Point Movement

When the flow rates of three microtubules are the same, the swirl stagnation point remains at coordinate origin O. If microtubule 1 and microtubule 2 keep the average flow velocity at v1 = v2 = 35 mm/s, while microtubule 3 changes its jet velocity, stagnation point position begins to gradually move away from the microtubule along linear direction with the flow velocity of microtubule 3 increasing, as the blue solid line shown in Fig. 4. If the average flow velocities constant of microtubule 2 and 3 are changed to v2 = v3 = 35 mm/s, then the stagnation point will move away from the microtubule 1 with the increasing jet velocity of microtubule 1, as the red dotted line shown in Fig. 4. As shown in the Figure, the direction in which the stagnation point moves will be changed by matching the average flow velocities of three microtubules.

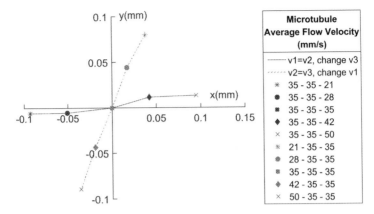

Fig. 4. Stagnation points change with different flow field parameters (Color figure online).

Considering the symmetry of the fluid field, matching the flow rates of three microtubules can control the swirl stagnation point to change position in any direction. Set up simulation parameters according to orthogonal experiment, the simulation results are shown in Fig. 5.

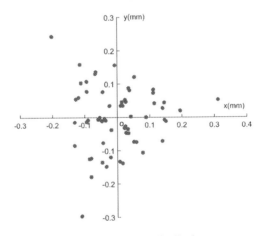

Fig. 5. Stagnation point distribution map.

As shown in the Figure, the stagnation point of the swirling flow field can be moved in any direction by matching the flow velocities of three microtubules.

3.3   Cell Movement in the Swirling Flow Field

In order to explore the relationship between cell position and stagnation point in the swirling flow field, dynamic mesh technique is applied and cell properties are loaded into UDF files. By invoking six degree-of-freedom dynamic mesh model, we attain the positions and velocities of cell's center of gravity at each moment during its movement. If the cell has a diameter of 0.6 mm, average flow velocities of microtubule 2 and 3 keep constant at 35 mm/s and microtubule 1 average flow velocity grows from 21 mm/s to 50 mm/s gradually, the correlation between cell position and stagnation point position in the x-direction is shown in Fig. 6(a), and the correlation in the y-direction is shown in Fig. 6(b). It can be told from the graph that the cell's position follows stagnation point in the swirling flow field. Figure 6(c) demonstrates cell's rotation speed under different average flow velocity. As a result, matching the swirling flow field parameters can gain control of the directional and quantitative movement and rotation of cell.

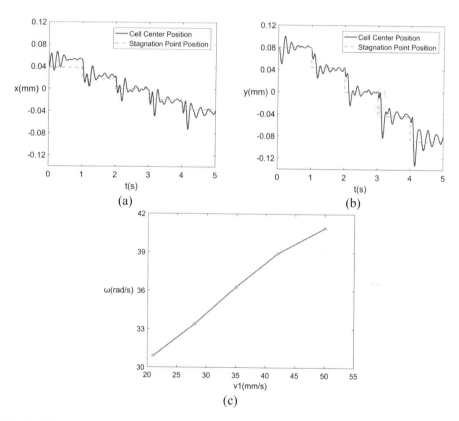

Fig. 6. Manipulation of swirl-drive cell. (a) The cell follows the stagnation point in the x-direction. (b) The cell follows the stagnation point in the y-direction. (c) Angular velocity with different average flow velocity.

Since fluid is amorphous, swirl can still drive cell to rotate when the cell shape changes. Figure 7 shows the rotation status of an elliptical cell near the stagnation point at different moments.

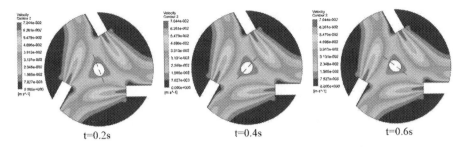

t=0.2s   t=0.4s   t=0.6s

Fig. 7. Rotation of an elliptical cell.

4   Conclusion

A technique of cell manipulation based on stagnation point of swirl is brought up: The microfluidics dynamic model of the swirling flow field is established; the correlations among each direction of the swirl stagnation point in the field while the velocities of three microtubules change are analyzed through simulation; also, the mechanism and pattern that how the cell moves along with the stagnation point within the swirling flow field are discussed. Research results show that: Three microtubules in triangular layout jetting fluids in convectional directions can create swirl; matching the jet velocities of each microtubule in the swirling flow field can control the strength of the swirl and the location of the stagnation point; cell can be trapped using the region near the stagnation point, and achieve the directional and quantitative movement and rotation of the cell along different directions in the flow field, which realizes cell manipulation. Furthermore, our future work will focus on performance analysis of cell manipulation based on stagnation point, quantitative mapping correlations between microtubules jet velocities and the cell movement coerced by stagnation point, and further experimental verification.

References

1. Aoyama, H., Chiba, N., Fuchiwaki, O., Misaki, D., Usuda, T.: Non-contact bio cell manipulation by nonlinear micro flow around the vibrated pipette on micro robot. In: 21st Annual Meeting of the American Society for Precision Engineering, ASPE (2006)
2. Liu, X., et al.: Hydrodynamic tweezers: trapping and transportation in microscale using vortex induced by oscillation of a single piezoelectric actuator. Sensors **18**(7), 18072002 (2018)
3. Liu, X., et al.: Vortex-driven rotation for three-dimensional imaging under microscopy. IEEE Trans. Nanotechnol. **17**(4), 688–691 (2018)
4. Hayakawa, T., Sakuma, S., Arai, F.: On-chip cell transportation based on vibration-induced local flow in open chip environment. In: 2015 IEEE/RSJ International Conference on Intelligent Robots and Systems, pp. 1409–1414. IEEE, Hamburg (2015)
5. Hayakawa, T., Sakuma, S., Arai, F.: On-chip 3D rotation of oocyte based on a vibration-induced local whirling flow. Microsyst. Nanoeng. **1**, 15001 (2015)

6. Tanyeri, M., Johnson-Chavarria, E.M., Schroeder, C.M.: Hydrodynamic trap for single particles and cells. Appl. Phys. Lett. **96**(22), 224101 (2010)
7. Shenoy, A., Rao, C.V., Schroeder, C.M.: Stokes trap for multiplexed particle manipulation and assembly using fluidics. Proc. Natl. Acad. Sci. U.S.A. **113**(15), 3976–3981 (2016)
8. Safavieh, M., Qasaimeh, M.A., Vakil, A., Juncker, D., Gervais, T.: Two-aperture microfluidic probes as flow dipole: theory and applications. Sci. Rep. **5**(8), 663–668 (2015)
9. Zhang, Q., Fan, J.B., Wang, H., Aoyama, H.: A particle manipulation method and its experimental study based on opposed jets. Biomicrofluidics **12**(2), 024110 (2018)
10. Zhang, Q., Wang, J.H., Huang, W.J., Aoyama, H.: Swirl-based control method of cell orientation-impact on control performance with eccentricity. Key Eng. Mater. **625**, 717–721 (2014)
11. Zhang, Q., Fan, J.B., Aoyama, H.: Manipulation of particles based on swirl. Jpn. J. Appl. Phys. **57**(1), 017202 (2017)

Adaptive Threshold Processing of Secondary Electron Images in Scanning Electron Microscope

Weiguo Bian, Mingyu Wang, and Zhan Yang[✉]

School of Mechanical and Electric Engineering, Soochow University,
Suzhou 215123, China
yangzhan@suda.edu.cn

Abstract. Observing the sample under a scanning electron microscope (SEM) requires adjustment of brightness and contrast to obtain a clear image. The traditional method is manually adjusted by the operator, which inevitably has errors. In this paper, an adaptive threshold processing method based on image-based normalized gray histogram is proposed. This method can acquire the threshold of the image according to the state of the currently obtained secondary electron images. When the brightness and contrast of the image change, the threshold can also be changed accordingly. It is concluded from a large number of tests that when the secondary electron image gray histogram has obvious double peaks and is located in the trough, the threshold obtained is optimal. Therefore, it is possible to better observe the pictures under the SEM.

Keywords: SEM · Secondary electron images · Adaptive threshold · Gray histogram · Binarization

1 Introduction

Scanning electron microscope [1, 2] can be used to observe, manipulate, and analyze micro-nano samples, which is an important tool. The imaging principle of SEM is to emit a focused high-energy electron beam through an electron gun to scan the surface of the sample and excite various signals, mainly secondary electrons [3, 4]. The electrons are then collected, amplified, and displayed by a detector to ultimately observe the sample.

However, when the sample is observed, it is necessary to continuously zoom in. Moreover, the initial image is not clear enough to judge the target object, which requires constant focus and adjustment of brightness and contrast. This brings a lot of trouble to the operator, if the observed image is not handled properly, this will directly cause inconvenience to the subsequent operations and analysis.

© Springer Nature Switzerland AG 2019
H. Yu et al. (Eds.): ICIRA 2019, LNAI 11740, pp. 166–173, 2019.
https://doi.org/10.1007/978-3-030-27526-6_15

Researchers have conducted constant research on this. Yoshihiro et al. [5, 6] used Canny edge detector to enhance the sharpness of the image edges, this method can only be applied to the edges of the image and is not suitable for the overall image. Soumik et al. [7, 8] studied the silica nanoparticles and added an image processing algorithm to obtain more clear images than unprocessed. Li et al. [9, 10] adopted an improved Otsu threshold processing algorithm, by using fiber as a material. After processing, it was found that the brightness and contrast of the image were improved, which enhanced the sharpness of the image. Different from the above methods, in this article, we adopt an adaptive threshold processing method [11–18] based on image-based normalized gray histogram. The gray histogram is obtained by this method. If two peaks appear in the figure, the optimal threshold corresponds to the trough, so that a clear image can be obtained. This facilitates subsequent operations and analysis in the scanning electron microscope, which can improve efficiency.

2 Experiment Platform and Procedure

In the experiments, a Carl Zeiss MERLIN Compact SEM was used to verify the results. An operating platform is built in the sample chamber of the scanning electron microscope (Fig. 1). Two identical operating units are mounted opposite each other on the platform. Each operating unit consists of a SmarAct operator, a Picmotor operator and an end effector AFM probe (Fig. 2). The end effector drive is provided by SmarAct and Picmotor. Among them, the SmarAct operator can provide linear translation in three directions of X, Y and Z, while the Picmotor operator can provide 360 degrees of free rotation.

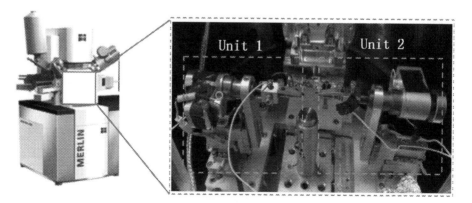

Fig. 1. Zeiss MERLIN Compact SEM and operating platform in the sample chamber.

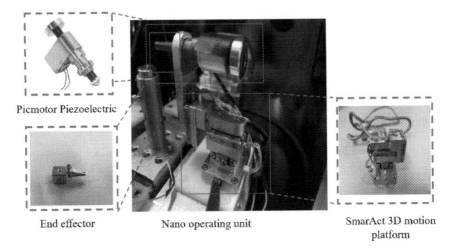

Picmotor Piezoelectric

End effector   Nano operating unit   SmarAct 3D motion
platform

Fig. 2. Micro-nano operating unit structure.

The AFM probe is then placed on the end effector of the operating unit 1, and the substrate of the carbon nanotube is placed on the end effector of the operating unit 2 for picking up the carbon nanotubes. In the process of pickup, AFM was firstly moved to the vicinity of the substrate. When there was obvious deformation in the contact between the two, EBID was conducted at the contact point. After several minutes of waiting, AFM probe was moved to pull out the carbon tube. The specific operation process is shown in Fig. 3.

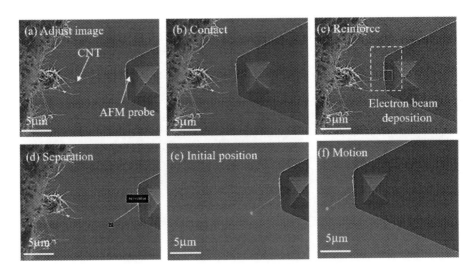

Fig. 3. Carbon nanotube picking up process.

3 Experimental Analysis and Results

In order to get a clearer image in SEM, the first step is to adjust the brightness and contrast of the image. At the same time, during the operation, the charge is accumulated due to the electron beam bombarding the surface of the sample for a long time, resulting in local sample generation. A brightening phenomenon that changes the brightness and contrast of an image.

To find out the contour of the image efficiently and get a clear image. In this experiment, the image was binarized. Binarization processing can reduce the amount of data in the image, eliminate irrelevant information in the image, highlight the target area of interest and enhance the detectability, so as to improve the reliability of target recognition and extraction.

Image binarization is to set the gray value of the pixel on the image to 0 or 255, so that the whole image presents an obvious black and white effect. Let the original image be $f(x, y)$ and the image after image segmentation be $g(x, y)$. In accordance with certain criteria, an appropriate gray value T is found in $f(x, y)$ as the threshold. For pixel points with gray value greater than or equal to T in the image, set the gray value of the pixel point to 255, otherwise set to 0.

The sample in the scanning electron microscope was observed to obtain an initial image. Due to the poor brightness and contrast of the image, a clear image cannot be obtained. In order to avoid too many human operations, this experiment adds an adaptive threshold algorithm, which can better separate the target body and get a clear image. The specific steps are shown in the flowchart (Fig. 4).

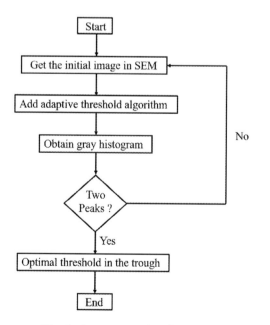

Fig. 4. Image processing flow chart.

In this experiment, two samples were selected as AFM probes and carbon nanotube substrates. They were placed under a scanning electron microscope and the initial image was obtained by the SmartSEM software provided by Zeiss. In this paper, an adaptive threshold processing method based on image-based normalized gray histogram is adopted. Since the initial image obtained by SEM is grayscale image, the image needs to be normalized only.

In the first set of experiments, an AFM probe was selected as the sample. By comparing the brightness and contrast under different parameters, after adding the adaptive threshold algorithm, two peaks can be found in the normalized gray image. The specific experimental diagram is shown in Figs. 5 and 6.

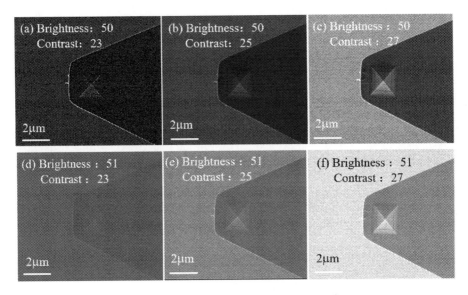

Fig. 5. Probe images under different brightness and contrast.

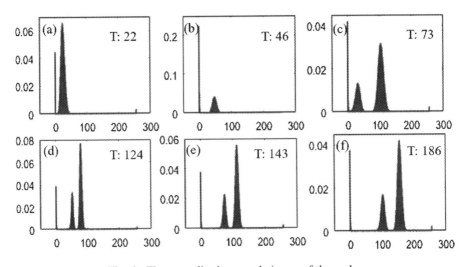

Fig. 6. The normalized grayscale image of the probe.

In order to prevent the contingency of the experiment, another set of experiments was performed in this experiment. The carbon nanotube substrate was selected as a sample and was carried out under the same brightness and contrast, and it was found that this phenomenon still existed, as shown in Figs. 7 and 8.

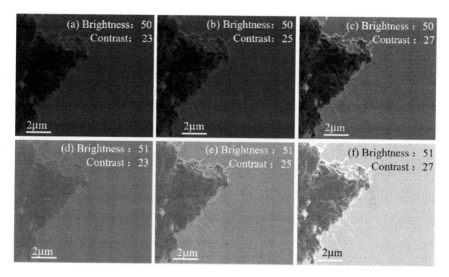

Fig. 7. Carbon nanotube substrate images under different brightness and contrast.

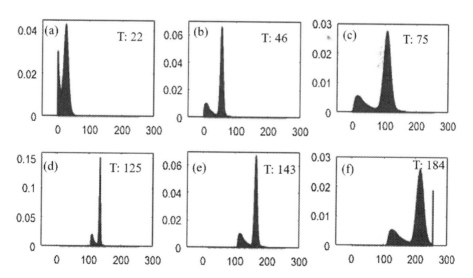

Fig. 8. The normalized grayscale image of the carbon nanotube substrate.

Through the above two sets of experiments, it can be concluded that when there are two peaks in the normalized gray histogram, the optimal threshold appears in the trough. That is to say, the threshold can separate the target body and obtain a clear image. If there are no two peaks, you need to adjust the parameters until they appear, so that you can get a clear picture for subsequent operations.

4 Conclusion

The adaptive threshold algorithm proposed in this paper can reduce the manual adjustment of brightness and contrast, and can get clear images, which can be well applied to SEM. When the image is normalized, if there are two peaks, the optimal threshold can be determined, that is, in the trough. If there are no peaks, the image is not clear at this time, so it is necessary to continue debugging and repeat the above steps. Therefore, it is possible to provide protection for other operations in the SEM.

Acknowledgments. This work is supported by National Key R&D Program of China (2018YFB1304901).

References

1. Reimer, L.: Scanning electron microscopy. Cirp Encycl. Prod. Eng. **94**(6), 756–776 (1985)
2. Jackman, H., Krakhmalev, P., Svensson, K.: Image formation mechanisms in scanning electron microscopy of carbon nanotubes, and retrieval of their intrinsic dimensions. Ultramicroscopy **124**(1), 35–39 (2013)
3. Cazaux, J.: From the physics of secondary electron emission to image contrasts in scanning electron microscopy. J. Electron Microsc. **61**(5), 261–284 (2012)
4. Würtz, P., Gericke, T., Vogler, A., et al.: Image formation in scanning electron microscopy of ultracold atoms. Appl. Phys. B: Lasers Opt. **98**(4), 641–645 (2010)
5. Midoh, Y., Miura, K., Nakamae, K., et al.: Statistical optimization of Canny edge detector for measurement of fine line patterns in SEM image. Meas. Sci. Technol. **16**(2), 477–487 (2005)
6. Pratt, W.K.: Digital Image Processing. Wiley-Interscience, Hoboken (1978)
7. Kundu, S., Jana, P., De, D., et al.: SEM image processing of polymer nanocomposites to estimate filler content. In: IEEE International Conference on Electrical. IEEE (2015)
8. Galloway, J.A., Montminy, M.D., Macosko, C.W.: Image analysis for interfacial area and cocontinuity detection in polymer blends. Polymer **43**(17), 4715–4722 (2002)
9. Li, D., Wang, Y.: Application of an improved threshold segmentation method in SEM material analysis (2018)
10. Wang, Z., Wang, Y., Jiang, L., et al.: An image segmentation method using automatic threshold based on improved genetic selecting algorithm. Autom. Control Comput. Sci. **50**(6), 432–440 (2016)
11. Lei, Y.Y., Wang, R., Yao, J.M., et al.: Research and implementation on image denoising for scanning electron microscopy. Opt. Optoelectron. Technol. **12**(5), 77–82 (2014)
12. David, S., Visvikis, D., Roux, C., et al.: Multi-observation PET image analysis for patient follow-up quantitation and therapy assessment. Phys. Med. Biol. **56**(18), 5771–5788 (2011)

13. Chao, X., Fenghua, H., Zhengyuan, M.: An improved two-dimensional Otsu thresholding segmentation method. Appl. Electron. Tech. (2016)
14. Wang, Y.Q., Zhuang, L.L., Shi, C.X.: Construction research on multi-threshold segmentation based on improved Otsu threshold method. Adv. Mater. Res. **1046**, 425–428 (2014)
15. Ni, L., Kailin, P., Yexiang, N.: An improved automatic threshold segmentation method used in PCBA vision inspection. In: Second International Symposium on Test Automation & Instrumentation (2008)
16. Solomon, A., Cassuto, Y.: Adaptive threshold read algorithms in multi-level non-volatile memories with uncertainty. In: Science of Electrical Engineering (2017)
17. Yang, Y., Li, X., Pan, X., et al.: Downscaling land surface temperature in complex regions by using multiple scale factors with adaptive thresholds. Sensors **17**(4), 744 (2017)
18. Ting, D.: Adaptive threshold sampling and estimation (2017)

Experimental Study of the Behavior of Muscle Cells on Projection Micro-stereolithography Printed Micro-structures

Qian Gao[1], Qinyi Wang[1,2], Dili Li[1,2], Weiqi Ge[1,2], Xue Meng[1,2],
Guoqing Jin[3], Haiyi Liang[4,5], Xifu Shang[6], and Runhuai Yang[1,2(✉)]

[1] School of Life Science, Anhui Medical University, Hefei 230032, China
yangrunhuai@ahmu.edu.cn
[2] School of Biomedical Engineering, Anhui Medical University,
Hefei 230032, China
[3] Robotics and Microsystems Center,
School of Mechanical and Electric Engineering, Soochow University,
Suzhou 215006, China
[4] CAS Key Laboratory of Mechanical Behavior and Design of Materials,
University of Science and Technology of China, Hefei 230027, China
[5] IAT-Chungu Joint Laboratory for Additive Manufacturing,
Anhui Chungu 3D Printing Institute of Intelligent Equipment
and Industrial Technology, Wuhu 241200, China
[6] Department of Orthopedics, The First Affiliated Hospital of USTC
(University of Science and Technology of China), Hefei 230026, China

Abstract. Recently, muscle cells were studied as a promising bioactuator for bio-syncretic robots. While projection micro-stereolithography (PµSL) can print poly (ethylene glycol) diacrylate (PEGDA) hydrogels into micro-scale 3D structures, the muscle cells based robots could be small and easy-fabricated if the muscle cells can directly grow and differentiate on PµSL PEGDA structures. However, PµSL PEGDA cannot be directly used as an extracellular environment for muscle cells without bio-functionalization; the behavior of muscle cells on modified PµSL PEGDA should also be studied. In this paper, collagen I and Matrigel were used to explore the bio-functionalization of PµSL PEGDA. By using functionalized PµSL PEGDA hydrogel structures, the adhesion, survival, differentiation of muscle cells were studied. Results show that physically crosslinked by collagen I, PµSL PEGDA was able to provide a suitable environment for adhesion of C2C12 muscle cells. Mixed with 10% Matrigel in DMEM, the condition of cells were further improved. The results of viability assay were consistent and confirmed the living condition of muscle cells on PµSL PEGDA. The differentiation test provides the evidence that the differentiated C2C12 muscle cells were able to contract. Eventually, this paper provide methods for improving the bio-functionalization of PµSL printed PEGDA, and the results proves that the functionalized PµSL printed PEGDA structures have the potential to be used as muscle cells based micro bioactuators and bio-syncretic robots.

Keywords: Biological robots · PµSL · Soft robots · Hydrogel · Muscle cell

© Springer Nature Switzerland AG 2019
H. Yu et al. (Eds.): ICIRA 2019, LNAI 11740, pp. 174–184, 2019.
https://doi.org/10.1007/978-3-030-27526-6_16

1   Introduction

Recently, biological powers are considered as promising strategy for soft robots. Compared with conventional robotics which are driven by electric power, biological based robots have much higher energy efficiency [1]. While the biological robots are similar to living beings, the robots also have desirable attributes such as high bio-compatibility, intrinsic safety, self-assemble and self-repairing capabilities [2–4]. Besides, biological robots can directly get chemical power inside human body and transform the power into mechanical movement [5]. Therefore, Biological energy sources, such as bacterials, myocardial cells and muscle cells were studied as actuators for robotics [6]. These biological actuators were used to actuate different types of robots, such as microswimmers [7], bionic jellyfish [8], tail based swimmer [9] or worm-like crawling robots [10].

Among all the biological energy sources, muscle cells are powerful and controllable [10], and thus it is considered as one of the best biological actuator [11]. Muscle cells provide precise force in uniaxial direction [12]. A single muscle cell can provide 15–20 μN force, while a single myocardial cell only can provide 1–14 μN [4]. Muscle cell based actuators and robots were developed to utilize the abilities that the muscle cells can provide force [13] and movement [10, 14].

Although muscle cells provide great applicable prospect for robotics, there still are some challenges to overcome. All the muscle cells were used as "matrix" for robotics, which restricts the size of robots. The suspended muscle cells were mixed with some natural hydrogel, and the mixture was dropped to a structure with centimeter scale. The natural hydrogel cannot be precisely printed into 3D micro scale. Therefore, all the reported muscle cells based robots cannot be micro-sized. If the muscle cell based robotics are fabricated at micro-scale, the muscle cell should be directly cultured on delicate micro structure made of appropriate materials.

Synthesis hydrogels have the ability to be fabricated into delicate micro structures. Currently, projection micro-stereolithography (PμSL) [15] provides a micro scale fabrication method for poly (ethylene glycol) diacrylate (PEGDA) hydrogel [16]. By using commercial Digital Mirror Device (DMD), LED light source and commercial lens, PEGDA hydrogel can be printed with high resolution at low-cost. Although PEGDA and PμSL have such advantages, PEGDA hydrogel cannot be directly used for muscle cell culture. The reason is that synthesized PEGDA hydrogel is inert to cell attachment, and the manufacture process of the PEGDA may also change the properties of PEGDA. Therefore, the surface of PμSL PEGDA based structures should be functionalized and studied to provide an appropriate environment for muscle cell adhesion, growth and differentiation.

Aiming at promoting the muscle cell based biological robot to be smaller, in this paper, we focused on the studying and improving of the adhesion and functionalization of PμSL printed PEGDA hydrogel for muscle cells. By using self-built PμSL system, PEGDA pre-gelling solution, collagen I, Matrigel, C2C12 muscle cells, etc., the adhesion and differentiation of muscle cells on functionalized PμSL printed PEGDA hydrogel were experimentally studied. The results show that the adhesion of C2C12 muscle cells was significantly improved by using physical crosslink of PEGDA and collagen I. Besides, cell with dilute Matrigel with DMEM further improved the adhesion. Compared with previous adhesion by high concentration Matrigel, the cultured C2C12 muscle cells were not assemble as a centimeter sized "matrix". Therefore, by this method, the muscle cells were able to adhere to PEGDA hydrogel based microstructure which was printed PμSL. The differentiation experiments also proved the driving ability of the muscle cells cultured by our method. Eventually, this paper provides a method and experimental study for improving the muscle cells adhesion on PμSL printed PEGDA hydrogel, which can be a reference for studies in the area of biological actuators and bio-syncretic robots.

2   Preparation of Functionalized PμSL PEGDA

The functionalized PμSL PEGDA was described in Fig. 1. Pre-gelling PEGDA solution (Sigma, USA) was mixed with 1% photo initiator (Phenylbis (2, 4, 6-trimethylbenzoyl) phosphine oxide) over night. A self-built PμSL system was used to provide dynamic patterned 405 nm Ultra Violet (UV) to print the pre-gelling solution to micro-scale 3D structures. The π bond inside PEGDA monomer was opened by photo initiator and UV, and then monomer-addition-polymerized with others into long polymer chains. The repeating part of a PEGDA molecular could crosslink one chain or two different polymer chains. As a result, cross-linked hydrogel was formed. Then cross-linked hydrogel was bathed in collagen I solution (5% collagen I in DMEM) for 24 h. Because of the swelling property of hydrogel, the interval space was extended and collagen flowed into the interval of grid slowly. Collagen I is a natural bio-macromolecular and has lots of hydrogen atom. Numerous hydrogen bonds were formed between collagen I and hydrogel chain, forming physical crosslink on the surface of PμSLPEGDA structures.

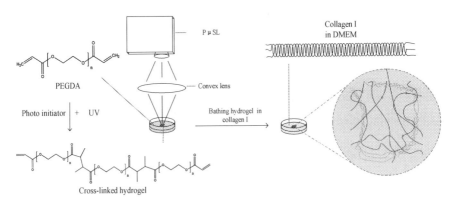

Fig. 1. The schematic of preparation of functionalized PμSL PEGDA

3   Adhesion and Viability Test of Muscle Cells on Functionalized PµSL PEGDA

3.1   Muscle Cell Culture and Behavior

We chose C2C12 cell line as the muscle cells in this paper. C2C12 which is an immortalized mouse myoblast cell line was used to study the cellular state during culture and differentiation induction. Figure 2 shows the schematic image of the adhesion and then the differentiation of C2C12 cells to form myotubes. Cellular morphology changed from almost round shape to fusiform shape rigorously showing one central nucleus when they adhered to the substrate and reached confluence, and then to elongated tubular shape with multiple nuclei due to the differentiation of C2C12 muscle cells. The muscle cells can provide actuator functions only if the cells are adhesive on the materials. Therefore, we studied the adhesion of the cells on functionalized PµSL PEGDA.

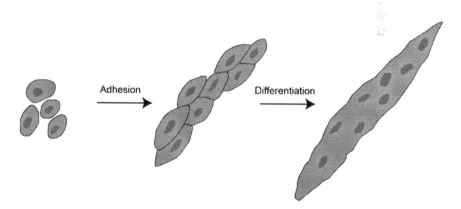

Fig. 2. Schematic image of adhesion and differentiation of C2C12 cells.

The immortalized mouse myoblast cell line C2C12 (American Type Culture Collection, Manassas, VA, USA) were maintained at 37 °C with 5% CO_2. The growth medium consisted of Dulbecco's modified Eagle's medium with 10% fetal bovine serum, 1% penicillin-streptomycin and 1 mM L-Alanyl-L-Glutamin (Biological Industries, Cromwell, CT, USA). For seeding cells on functionalized PµSL PEGDA, cells were trypsinized with 0.25% trypsin/EDTA (Biological Industries, Cromwell, CT, USA), followed by centrifugation for 3 min at 1000 rpm. For the Matrigel treated cells, in this step the cells were resuspended in growth medium containing 10% Matrigel (CORNING, Sao Paulo, Brazil). A 200 µl volume of cell suspension was dropped onto the patterned PEGDA structures laid on the bottom of the 35 mm low attachment dish. After 2 h incubation at 37 °C with 5% CO_2, 2 ml growth medium was added to the dish.

3.2 Adhesion Test

The adhesion test was performed when the suspended cells were cultured on different types of PEGDA. After 24 h, we found C2C12 cells clustered and adhered poorly to the PEGDA samples (Fig. 3A). On the other hand, C2C12 cells adhered, and spread well on collagen I coated PEGDA samples (Fig. 3B). Furthermore, matrigel treated C2C12 cells adhered and arranged in a tightly organized fashion on collagen I coated PEGDA samples (Fig. 3C). Thus, our results implied that collagen I increased the attachment of PEGDA, while Matrigel might activate the adhesion between C2C12 cells which would benefit myotubes formation.

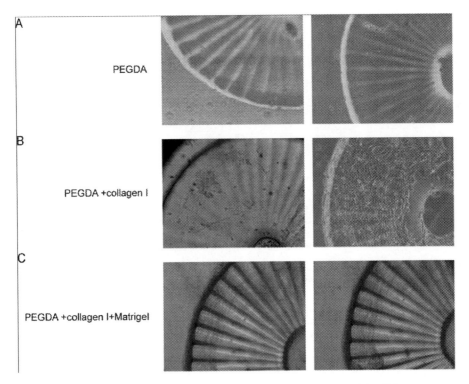

Fig. 3. Morphology of C2C12 cells grown on PEGDA coated with different agents. Representative images of C2C12 cells grown on PEGDA (A), collagen I coated PEGDA (B) and collegan I coated PEGDA when cells were pretreated with Matrigel (C). All images were captured at magnifications under 10× objectives.

3.3 Viability Assay

Viability assay was used to verify the living of muscle cells on functionalized PμSL PEGDA. C2C12 cells were cultured on the PEGDA samples for 48 h and then examined by the viability assay. Calcein-AM which produce strong green color fluorescence in a viable cell, and Propidium iodide which could not pass through a viable cell membrane and only reach the nucleus of dead cell to emit strong red color fluorescence, were added to the culture medium. As a result, live cells were stained in green, while dead cells in red under a fluorescence microscope. The green fluorescence covering all area of collagen I coated-PEGDA samples suggested good cell viability, although no fluorescence was observed from bare PEGDA sample (Fig. 4A). Most C2C12 cells cultured on collagen I coated-PEGDA samples were viable; only few dead cells were detected (Fig. 4B). These data supported the good biocompatibility of our PEGDA samples.

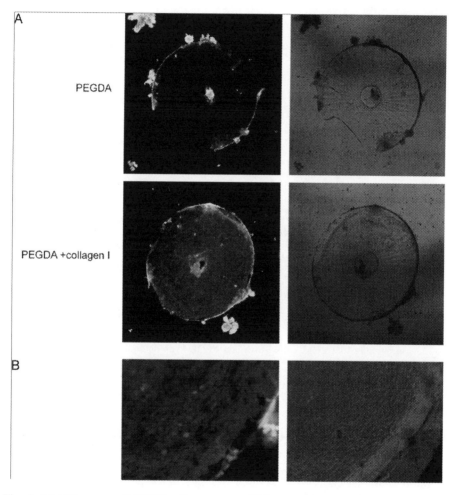

Fig. 4. Viability assay of C2C12 cells grown on PEGDA. (A) Viability staining of C2C12 grown on PEGDA (upper panels) and collagen I coated PEGDA (bottom panels). Images were captured at magnifications under 4× objectives. (B) Viability staining of C2C12 grown on collagen I coated PEGDA. Dead cells were stained in red and live cells were stained in green. Images were captured at magnifications under 10× objectives. (Color figure online)

3.4   Behavior of Muscle Cells on Functionalized PµSL PEGDA

To explore the proper pattern of PEGDA sample for C2C12 cells adhesion and growth, different shape of collagen I coated-samples were tested for cell culture. 24 h after cell seeding, the 200 µm thick samples demonstrated pretty bad cell adhesion, similar to the special low-attachment bottom. In the meantime, 80% area of 30 µm thick samples while 20% area of 100 µm thick samples were covered by confluent C2C12 cells (Fig. 5A), suggesting that C2C12 cells preferred adhering to thinner samples. In addition, inspired by groove of the 3D muscle strip, we designed the PEGDA sample of round shape with a concentric hole. As we expected, the C2C12 cells clustered and bridged the hole (Fig. 5B). These data indicated the hole in sample might arrange C2C12 cells in parallel to enable high contractile myotubes.

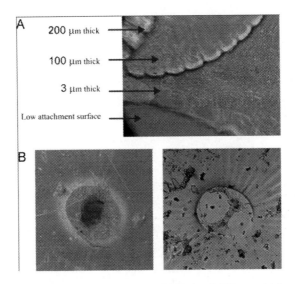

Fig. 5. Morphology of C2C12 cells grown on PEGDA of different thicknesses and shapes. Representative images of C2C12 cells grown on collagen I coated PEGDA of different thicknesses (A) and the round shape with a concentric hole (B). All images were captured at magnifications under 10× objectives.

4   Experimental Study of Differentiation of Muscle Cells

As pre-mentioned in Fig. 2, the cells can provide actuator force after differentiation. Therefore, after the adhesion and viability assay, we tested the differentiation of C2C12 muscle cells. The differentiation test was performed by using the setup as shown in Fig. 6. +10 V to −10 V voltage pulse were generated by Arduino based MCU system and amplifier, while the width and frequency of the voltage pulse were adjustable. This voltage pulse can avoid redox reaction on the electrode while the pulse duration is short and the duration of positive voltage is equal to negative voltage.

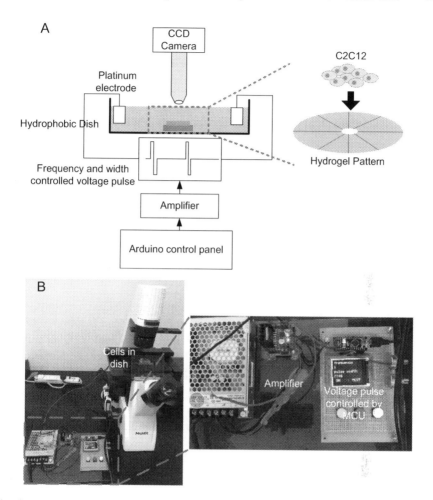

Fig. 6. The schematic and experimental setup of the recording of the motion of muscle cells.

C2C12 cells (less than ten passages) were trpsinized and seeded in petri dishes three days before differentiation induction (Fig. 7A). Then C2C12 cells adhered, spread and proliferated. When they reached 90% confluence, the differentiation was induced by special culture medium consisted of Dulbecco's modified Eagle's medium with 2% horse serum (Sangon Biotech, shanghai, China), 1% penicillin–streptomycin and 1 mM L-Alanyl-L-Glutamin after washing three times with phosphate-buffered saline (Biological Industries, Cromwell, CT, USA) (Fig. 7B). Subsequently replace the differentiation medium with fresh every two days. Striations were observed in C2C12 cells at day 4 of differentiation (Fig. 7C). At day 8 of differentiation, small myotubes could be recognized from cultures although less aligned and more branched (Fig. 7D).

Large myotubes appeared at the day 12 of differentiation (Fig. 7E). Conversely, no detectable myotube formed from non-confluent C2C12 cells even after 12 days of differentiation induction (Fig. 7F), suggesting cell contact was essential for myotube formation by C2C12 cells.

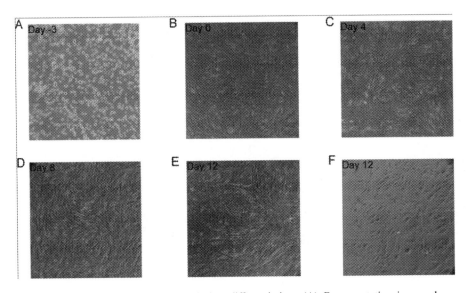

Fig. 7. Morphology of C2C12 cells during differentiation. (A) Representative image shows trypsinized C2C12 cells three days before differentiation induction (Day -3). (B, C, D and E) Representative images of confluent C2C12 cells cultured in differentiation medium for 0 days (B), 4 days (C), 8 days (D), and 12 days (E). (F) Representative images from non-confluent C2C12 cells cultured in differentiation medium for 12 days. The date was defined as Day 0 when the culture medium was switched to differentiation medium. All images were captured at magnifications under 10× objectives.

Next, we investigated the electrophysiological properties of the C2C12 myotubes with electrical pulse stimulation. The C2C12 myotubes contracted synchronously with electrical stimulation (Fig. 8). The movies showing the contractions of C2C12 myotubes in response to electrical pulse stimulation is attached as Movie 1. Taken together, the myotubes formed by differentiation of C2C12 cells were contractile and thus suitable for driving mini-robots made of PEGDA.

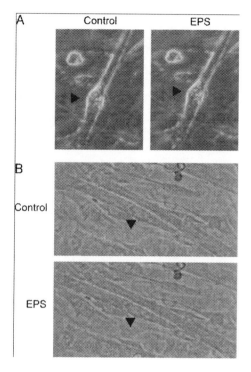

Fig. 8. Morphology of C2C12 myotubes under electrical pulse stimulation. Phase contrast images (A) and bright field images (B) showed C2C12 myotubes contracted under electrical pulse stimulation (EPS). All images were captured at magnifications under 10× objectives.

5 Discussions and Conclusion

PμSL printed PEGDA provides a low-cost and easy fabrication method for micro-sized soft robots. While muscle cells provides a promising biological power source, in this paper, we experimental studied the adhesion, survival and differentiation of the muscle cells with functionalized PμSL printed PEGDA hydrogels. Results show that physically crosslinked by Collagen I, PμSL PEGDA was able to provide a suitable environment for adhesion of C2C12 muscle cells. Pretreated with 10% Matrigel in DMEM, the adhesion of cells were further improved. The results of viability assay were consistent and confirmed the living condition of muscle cells on PμSLPEGDA. The differentiation setup in this paper provides an easy-fabrication method for muscle cells differentiation test and observation. Besides, the results of differentiation proved that the differentiated C2C12 muscle cells were able to contract. This paper provides methods for functionalizing the PμSL printed PEGDA, and provides typical methods for studying of cell based bio-syncretic actuators. Results prove that the PμSL printed PEGDA structures have the potential to be used as muscle cells driving micro robots and bio-syncretic robots. In future work, PEGDA will be printed to micro-scale specific shape, such as biomimetic crawling caterpillar, earthworm and snakes to further verify the contraction ability and controllability of C2C12 muscle cells on PEGDA based micro-sctructures.

Acknowledgments. This work was supported by the National Natural Science Foundation of China (grant nos. 61603002, 81802391and 61773274), Anhui Provincial Natural Science Foundation (1808085QH266 and KJ2017A209) and the Plan of Funding Outstanding Innovation Projects Launched by Talents Returning from Studying Overseas of Anhui Province (grant no. 2017-20).

References

1. Wang, W., Duan, W., Ahmed, S., Mallouk, T.E., Sen, A.: Small power: autonomous nano- and micromotors propelled by self-generated gradients. Nano Today **8**(5), 531–534 (2013)
2. Zhang, C., Wang, W., Xi, N., Wang, Y., Liu, L.: Development and future challenges of bio-syncretic robots. Engineering **4**, 452–463 (2018)
3. Ricotti, L., Menciassi, A.: Bio-hybrid muscle cell-based actuators. Biomed. Microdevices **14**(6), 987–998 (2012)
4. Duffy, R.M., Feinberg, A.M.: Engineered skeletal muscle tissue for soft robotics: fabrication strategies, current applications, and future challenges. Wiley Interdiscip. Rev. Nanomed. Nanobiotechnol. **6**(2), 178–195 (2014)
5. Darnton, N., Turner, L., Breuer, K., Berg, H.C.: Moving fluid with bacterial carpets. Biophys. J. **86**(3), 1863–1870 (2004)
6. Carlsen, R.W., Sitti, M.: Bio-hybrid cell-based actuators for microsystems. Small **10**(19), 3831–3851 (2014)
7. Park, B.W., Zhuang, J., Yasa, O., Sitti, M.: Multifunctional bacteria-driven microswimmers for targeted active drug delivery. ACS Nano **11**(9), 8910–8923 (2017)
8. Nawroth, J.C., et al.: A tissue-engineered jellyfish with biomimetic propulsion. Nat. Biotechnol. **30**(8), 792–797 (2012)
9. Williams, B.J., Anand, S.V., Rajagopalan, J., Saif, M.T.A.: A self-propelled biohybrid swimmer at low Reynolds number. Nat. Commun. **5**, 1–8 (2014)
10. Liu, L., Wang, W., Xi, N., Wang, Y., Zhang, C.: Regulation of C2C12 differentiation and control of the beating dynamics of contractile cells for a muscle-driven biosyncretic crawler by electrical stimulation. Soft Robot. **5**(6), 1–13 (2018)
11. Lieber, R.L.: Skeletal Muscle Structure, Function, & Plasticity, 2nd edn. Lippincott Williams & Wilkins, Baltimore (2002)
12. King, A.M., Loiselle, D.S., Kohl, P.: Force generation for locomotion of vertebrates Skeletal muscle overview. IEEE J. Ocean. Eng. **29**(3), 684–691 (2004)
13. Asada, H.H., et al.: Formation and optogenetic control of engineered 3D skeletal muscle bioactuators. Lab Chip **12**(23), 4976–4985 (2012)
14. Cvetkovic, C., et al.: Three-dimensionally printed biological machines powered by skeletal muscle. Proc. Natl. Acad. Sci. U.S.A. **111**(28), 10125–10130 (2014)
15. Han, D., Lu, Z., Chester, S.A., Lee, H.: Micro 3D printing of a temperature-responsive hydrogel using projection micro-stereolithography. Sci. Rep. **8**(1963), 1–10 (2018)
16. Yang, W., Yu, H., Li, G., Wang, B., Wang, Y., Liu, L.: Regulation of breast cancer cell behaviours by the physical microenvironment constructed: via projection microstereolithography. Biomater. Sci. **4**(5), 863–870 (2016)

Automatic Micropipette Tip Detection and Focusing in Industrial Micro-Imaging System

Xiaohui Cheng, Jiahong Xu, Xin Zhao, and Mingzhu Sun[✉]

Institute of Robotics and Automatic Information System
(Tianjin Key Laboratory of Intelligent Robotics), Nankai University,
Tianjin 300071, China
sunmz@nankai.edu.cn

Abstract. Image processing is basic but important in micromanipulation technology. In this paper, we propose automatic micropipette tip detection and focusing algorithms for an economical and portable industrial micro-imaging system. At present, there are many image processing methods which have obtained good experimental results for microscopic vision. However, there are not suitable image processing methods for images with non-uniform brightness or at different magnification rates. The proposed detection method introduces morphological black hat operator to deal with the non-uniform background and obtains the position of the pipette tip accurately in both clear and blurred images. The proposed focusing method applies a multi-scale gradient transform algorithm to evaluate the clarity of the pipette at different magnifications. A focus strategy is then selected to realize auto-focusing according to the clarity feedback. Experimental results show that the proposed methods obtain better tip detection and clarity evaluation results when the micropipette tip changes from defocusing state to focusing state at different magnifications.

Keywords: Micro-manipulation · Visual detection · Clarity evaluation · Autofocusing

1 Introduction

Microscopic imaging is widely used in biological and medical research. It enables us to observe the objects in tiny sizes. High-quality imaging provides rich image information of the objects. However, microscopes are expensive and inconvenient to carry in industrial production.

In order to improve the portability and reduce the cost, we designed an economical and portable industrial micro-imaging system, which consisted of an objective lens, an industrial zoom lens, an industrial camera, a light source and a stepper motor for automatic focusing. We will realize automatic cell micro-operation by using this system. In this paper, we focus on the automatic detection and focusing of the micro-manipulation tool, micropipette, which is used to operate the cells with 80–100 μm in diameter. In order to fulfill the fully automatic micromanipulation, the detection algorithm should be available for the micropipettes with a tilt angle or the defocusing

© Springer Nature Switzerland AG 2019
H. Yu et al. (Eds.): ICIRA 2019, LNAI 11740, pp. 185–195, 2019.
https://doi.org/10.1007/978-3-030-27526-6_17

micropipettes after being mounted, and the focusing algorithm should be used in different magnification rates of the zoom lens.

Micropipette tip detection and focusing are basic works in robotic and automatic micromanipulation system. A kind of detection algorithm based on motion history image (MHI) has been applied to adherent cell injection [1], automated aspiration of the mouse embryo limb bud tissue [2] and end-effector tip location in robotic micromanipulation [3]. However, when the micropipette tip is far from the focus plane, the detection algorithm may fail due to the low contrast between the pipette tip and the background. A binarization based identification algorithm was utilized to locate the pipette tip for automated sperm aspiration [4]. However, this method is not suitable for the case of complex background, uneven brightness or defocus images.

For auto-focusing, traditional time-domain clarity detection algorithms mainly utilize the gradient of edges to represent the clarity of the images [5]. The credibility of these algorithms depends on the credibility of the extracted edges, which is very sensitive to noise. Liu et al. evaluated and ranked 16 kinds of focusing algorithms, in which, the variance algorithm and the normalized variance algorithm provided good results for non-fluorescence microscopy applications [6]. However, this method is susceptible to noise. Improved normalized variance algorithms were generally less sensitive to noise than derivative-based algorithms [7]. However, these methods are not particularly suitable for non-uniform brightness images or defocus images under different magnifications. In patch-clamp experiment with two-photon microscope, the focusing image was selected from a sequence of images in z-axis direction by brightness calculation [8]. However, as for the non-fluorescent object, this method cannot achieve its best effect.

In this paper, we present automatic tip detection and focusing algorithms that are applicable to images with complex background and at variety of magnification rates. The detection algorithm uses the morphological black hat operator to deal with the complex background, and uses GrabCut segmentation to obtain the pipette region, so that the algorithm is available in both focusing and defocusing states. For micropipette focusing, a multi-scale gradient transform algorithm is proposed to evaluate the clarity of the pipette at different magnifications, and a focusing strategy is designed to achieve automatic focusing. The experimental results indicate that the proposed automatic tip detection and focusing algorithms are performed well in the industrial micro-imaging system at a variety of magnification rates, even if the micropipette is tilted. These algorithms are applicable for automatic cell manipulations.

2   System Design

2.1   System Architecture

The micro-imaging system consists of an objective lens (MPLAN APO 10X, Cinv-Optics, China), an industrial μm zoom lens (AFT-ZL0745X, Microvision, China), a digital camera (aca2040-25gc, B μm asler, Germany), a light source (TH2-51X51SW-PM, CSS, Japan), a stepper motor driver (TMCM-1021, TRINAMIC, Germany) for automatic focusing, as shown in Fig. 1. The pipette, which is used to manipulate the cells

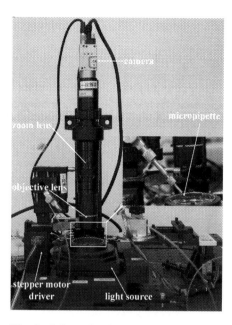

Fig. 1. Schematic of micro-imaging system.

with 80–100 in diameter, has an outer diameter of 100 μm and an inner diameter of 20. This system will be used to achieve automatic cell injection by the micromanipulators.

The zoom lens has a total of 10 different magnification rates, including 0.75, 1, 1.5, 2, 2.5, 3, 3.5, 4, 4.5 and 5 times. The total magnification of the micro-imaging system is calculated by Eq. (1):

$$TSM = OM \times OR \times ZR \tag{1}$$

Where, TSM represents the total magnification of the micro-imaging system. OM, OR, ZR represent the magnification of the objective lens, the ratio of the objective lens, and the magnification of the zoom lens respectively. In the micro-imaging system, OM is10 X, OR is 9/20, ZR is 0.75 ~ 5.

For initialization, we set the magnification of the zoom lens to 0.75X due to its wide field of view, so that the pipette tip is more easily to appear in the field of view. Figure 2(a) shows the image with 0.75X magnification. With the increase of the magnification of the zoom lens, the field of view narrows and the details of the experiment enlarge. The cell injection experiment is performed at 3X magnification of the zoom lens according to the size of the cells, as shown in Fig. 2(b). In the experiments, the brightness value of the light source is adjusted automatically according to the magnification of the zoom lens.

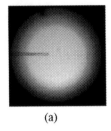 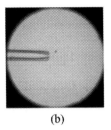

(a)   (b)

Fig. 2. The images at different magnifications. (a) The image at 0.75X. (b) The image at 3X.

In order to maximize the field of view of the micro-imaging system, we choose the camera, whose surface size is bigger than the view of the objective lens. When light passes through the objective lens and enters the camera lens, it can only form a circular spot in the center of the camera lens, which leads to a black region beyond the circular spot. As shown in Fig. 2, the brightness decreases gradually from the center to the edge of the bright circle. Common image processing methods cannot get ideal results for this kind of images. In this paper, the detection and focusing of the pipette with the magnifications of 0.75 ~ 3X will be carried out for this kind of images.

3 Key Methods

3.1 Micropipette Tip Detection

In traditional image processing, the black region and the pipette region in Fig. 2. will be both set to foreground after binarization, which makes it difficult to identify the pipette. Therefore, we propose a new detection method based on morphological black hat algorithm. This algorithm only highlights the areas that are darker than its surroundings, so it removes the black areas in the image. Although there is some background noise after black hat calculation, it has little effect on the subsequent process. The pipette detection and positioning process is listed as follows:

1. Take the maximum inner rectangle of the circle in the figure as the region of interest, which preserves the largest visual field as possible;
2. Sharpen the grayscale image and carry out the black hat calculation. The sharpening operation makes the edge of the pipette more distinct and enhances the contrast between the pipette and the background, as shown in Figs. 3(a) and (b);
3. Image binarization by adaptive threshold method, as shown in Fig. 3(c). This method is applicable for both clear and blurred images;
4. Denoise by morphological operation, as shown in Fig. 3(d);
5. Dilate the contours to highlight the pipette contour features, as shown in Fig. 3(e);
6. Perform Progressive Probabilistic Hough Transform (PPHT). Retain as many straight lines as possible in the pipette region, as shown in Fig. 3(f);
7. Adopt GrabCut algorithm to realize image segmentation. The segmentation result is used to determine whether it is a pipette or not, as shown in Fig. 3(g);
8. Calculate the circularity value after image filtering and thresholding:

$$F(i) = 4 * \pi * mu_i / mc_i^2 \qquad (2)$$

Here mu_i and mc_i are the area and perimeter of ith contour. According to the experiments, the value of the circularity of pipette is set to $0.12 \sim 0.83$.

9. Frame the pipette by a rotating rectangle. The center point on the right-side-boundary of the rotating rectangle is represented as the position of the pipette tip, as shown in Fig. 3(h).

The proposed pipette detection algorithm gets a good detection result, and it is also suitable for blurred and tilted pipettes. The combination of the morphological black hat algorithm and threshold operation can preserve the basic shape characteristics of the blurred pipettes, and the morphological process makes the characteristics more obvious. The Hough line transformation obtains the straight lines on the pipettes, even if the pipettes are tilted, so the circularity value of the pipette is not affected by the inclination of the pipettes.

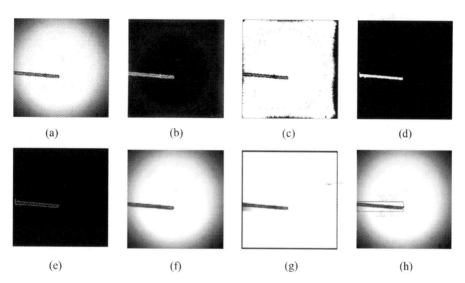

Fig. 3. Pipettes detection process. (a) Sharpening. (b) Black hat operation. (c) Adaptive threshold. (d) Denoise. (e) Contour dilation. (f) Progressive Probabilistic Hough Transform. (g) GrabCut segmentation. (h) Pipette

3.2 Micropipette Focusing

The accuracy and rapidity of focusing determines the performance of the micro manipulation system. Choosing a good focusing strategy is of vital importance. The biggest problem of microscopic imaging is the non-uniform brightness of the image and the large brightness difference between the head and the tail of the pipette. Since the morphological gradient does not involve the differential transformations, it could reduce the sensitivity to noise greatly [9]. We propose a new clarity evaluation algorithm for micropipette focusing, which uses multi-scale gradient transform to evaluate the image definition.

In morphology, the shape and the size of a structure element are called the scale of the structure element. Since the structure elements of different scales are sensitive to the features of different scales, the morphological gradient operation with structure elements of different scales is carried out in the boundary extraction process, and then the obtained edge images are weighted to obtain the final edge image, making the final edge image $G(f)$ more integral and continual [10]:

$$G(f) = p * \sum_{i}^{N} \omega_i G_i(f) \tag{3}$$

$$\sum_{i}^{N} \omega_i = 1 \tag{4}$$

Where, $G_i(f)$ is i^{th} edge image, ω_i is the weight of the results of the morphological operations, p is the proportionality coefficient.

Supposing $G(f)$ is the image with $M \times N$ in size, and the grayscale value at point (m, n) is $f(m, n)$, the mean value $\bar{G}$ of the image $G(f)$ is calculated and the variance $Var(G)$ is used as the final result of the clarity judgment:

$$\bar{G} = \frac{1}{MN} \sum_{m}^{M} \sum_{n}^{N} f(m, n) \tag{5}$$

$$Var(G) = \sum_{m}^{M} \sum_{n}^{N} [f(m, n) - \bar{G}]^2 \tag{6}$$

We use three different sizes of structure elements b_1, b_2, b_3 in the experiment. $b_1 = \{(0,0,0),(0,0,0),(0,0,0)\}$ is a square matrix of 3×3, which extracts the horizontal and vertical edges and ignores the noise to some extent. But it is not sensitive to the details. Then, we use $b_2 = \{(0,0)\}$, the 2×1 vector to extract the vertical detail edges and $b_3 = \{0,0\}$, the 1×2 vector to extract the horizontal detail edges. The vertical contour clarity of the pipette tip has a greater impact on subsequent experiments, so we set $\omega_2 > \omega_3$. After conducting many experiments at different magnification of the optical system, we find that $\omega_1 = 0.06, \omega_2 = 0.64, \omega_3 = 0.3$ and $p = 6.0$ gets a good feedback of each focal plane.

The design of the focusing strategy is shown in Fig. 4. We move the objective lens up first to prevent the collision. The focus strategy is divided into two cases:

Case 1: When the pipette is below the focal plane, objective begins to move upward in the distance of ΔZ for 3 times. If the clarity curve rises, it means that the focal plane is above the pipette. Continue to move upward in the distance of $2 * \Delta Z$, and record the maximum clarity A and the position. When the curve begins to fall, record the number M of moving and move downward with $2 * \Delta Z$ distance for $(M - 1)$ times. Then move 5 more times with $1/2 * \Delta Z$ distance near the focus plane, recording the maximum clarity B and position. When the difference between B and A is less than 10%, the position of the maximum value is the focal plane.

Case 2: When the pipette is above the focal plane, objective begins to move upward in the distance of ΔZ for 3 times. If the clarity curve falls, it means that the focal plane is below the pipette. Move down with $3 * \Delta Z$ distance to the initial position, then move down with ΔZ distance, when the clarity curve gradually rises, record the maximum definition A and the position. When the curve begins to fall, record the number M of moving and move up with $2 * \Delta Z$ distance for $(M - 1)$ times. then move 5 more times with $1/2 * \Delta Z$ distance near the focal plane, recording the maximum clarity B and the position. When the difference between B and A is less than 10%, the position of the maximum value is the focal plane.

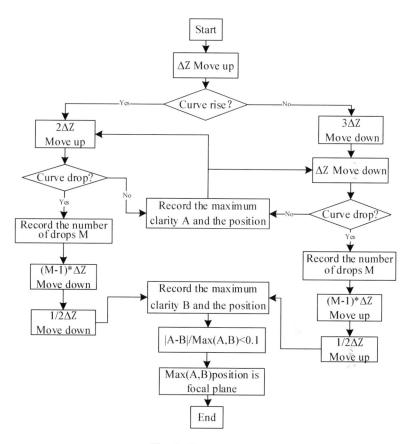

Fig. 4. Focus strategy.

4   Experiment Results

4.1   Image Capture

In the experiment, sequences of pipette images at 6 different magnification rates (0.75X to 3X) are captured. The image sequences are composed of images from defocusing state to focusing and then to defocusing at a certain step in the Z direction. The light source at different magnification rates is adjusted to get the best brightness. Figures 5 and 6 show the images at the magnifications of 0.75X and 3X, in which, the Z steps are 50 and 10 μm, respectively.

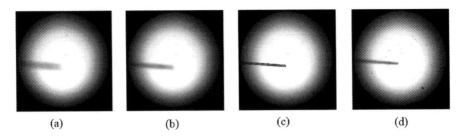

(a)   (b)   (c)   (d)

Fig. 5. Image captured in 0.75X when Z step is 50 μm. (a) 1st image. (b) 6th image. (c) 26th image. (d) 42nd image.

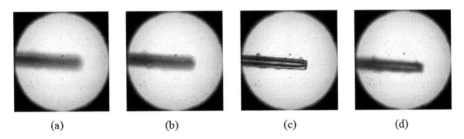

(a)   (b)   (c)   (d)

Fig. 6. Image captured in 3X when step is 10 μm. (a) 1st image. (b) 6th image. (c) 18th image. (d) 26th image.

4.2   Positioning Results

The positioning results of the pipettes at 0.75X and 3X magnifications are shown in Fig. 7. The red point on the right-side-boundary of the rectangle represents the center of the pipette tip. As the pipette gets closer to the focal plane, as shown in Figs. 7(a) and (c), the pipette becomes clear and the positioning of the pipette is accurate. When the pipette is in a blurred state, as shown in Figs. 7(b) and (d), the rotating rectangle can frame the position of the pipette in the region. The red point also shows the center of the pipette tip approximately.

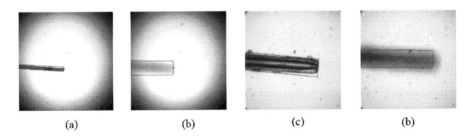

(a)   (b)   (c)   (b)

Fig. 7. Pipettes detection and positioning results in 0.75X and 3X (a) focused image in 0.75X. (b) defocused image. (c) focused image. (d) defocused image. (Color figure online)

When there are cells in the field of view, the pipette can also be identified and positioned well, as shown in Fig. 8. Table 1 shows the positioning results of the pipette with or without cells in the field of view at different magnifications.

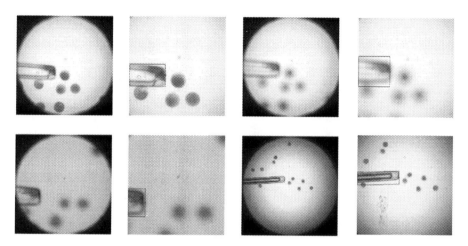

Fig. 8. Localization of the pipette when there are cells in the field.

Table 1. The positioning results of the pipette at different magnification rates.

Magnification	Number of test image	Number of detection error	Success rate
0.75	50	0	100%
1	37	1	97.3%
1.5	25	2	92%
2	32	2	93.75%
2.5	33	3	90.9%
3	47	4	93.62%

Experimental results indicate that the pipette detection algorithm has a good success rate at different magnifications. The positioning failure is mainly caused by two factors: firstly, the pipette is very blurry and short in the field of view. Secondly, when the cells are close to the pipette, parts of the cells and the pipette will be identified together, leading to a large deviation in the center of the pipette.

4.3 Focusing Results

Figure 9 shows the comparison of the clarity evaluation methods based on the propose multi-scale morphology gradient (MORPH-GRA), Laplace evaluation function (LAP-MEAN), Laplace evaluation function (LAP-VAR) and Sobel evaluation function (S-MEAN) at different magnifications of 0.75X ~ 3X.

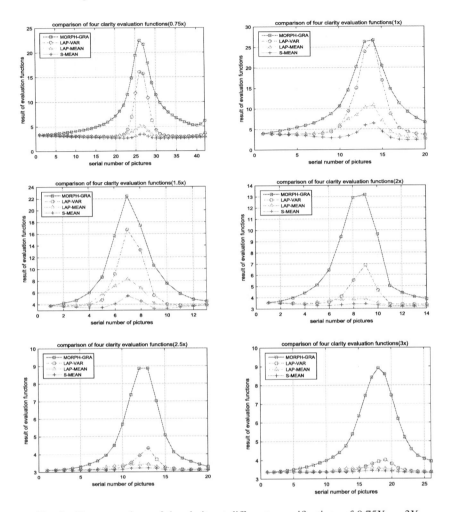

Fig. 9. The comparison of the clarity at different magnifications of 0.75X ∼ 3X.

By comparison, we find that the single-peak trend of the proposed method does not change with the increase of the magnification, while that of the other three approaches tend to flatten out. At the same time, the ratio of the maximum value to the minimum value of the proposed method is larger than the other methods. Compared with other algorithms, the clarity curve of the proposed method has a smooth trend, and there is no local maximum except for the maximum value obtained in the focused image. Experimental results indicate that this method is suitable for the clarity detection of the micro-operation images at all magnification levels with better sensitivity.

5 Conclusion

In this paper, we propose automatic micropipette tip detection and focusing algorithms for an economical and portable industrial micro-imaging system. The proposed detection method introduces morphological black hat opera-tor to deal with the non-uniform background and obtains the position of the pipette tip accurately in both clear and blurred images. The proposed focusing method applies a multi-scale gradient transform algorithm to evaluate the clarity of the pipette at different magnifications. The pipette detection and focusing algorithm has achieved good experimental results for the special microscopic images. The proposed method is suitable for detecting the pipette and judging the clarity of the pipette at different magnifications automatically and in real-time, facilitating the realization of the automation of micro-operation experiments.

Acknowledgment. This research was jointly supported by National Key R&D Program of China (2018YFB1304905), National Natural Science Foundation of China (U1813210, U1613220), Fundamental Research Funds for the Central Universities, Nankai University (63191177) and Natural Science Foundation of Tianjin (14JCZDJC31800, 14ZCDZGX00801).

References

1. Liu, J., Siragam, V., Gong, Z., et al.: Robotic adherent cell injection for characterizing cell–cell communication. IEEE Transact. Biomed. Eng. **62**(1), 119–125 (2015)
2. Wen, J., Liu, J., Lau, K., et al.: Automated micro-aspiration of mouse embryo limb bud tissue. In: 2015 IEEE International Conference on Robotics and Automation (ICRA), pp. 2667–2672. IEEE (2015)
3. Liu, J., Gong, Z., Tang, K., et al.: Locating end-effector tips in robotic micromanipulation. IEEE Transact. Robot. **30**(1), 125–130 (2014)
4. Zhang, X.P., Leung, C., Lu, Z., et al.: Controlled aspiration and positioning of biological cells in a micropipette. IEEE Transact. Biomed. Eng. **59**(4), 1032–1040 (2012)
5. Pech-Pacheco, L., Cristobal, G., Chamorro-Martinez, J., Fernandez-Valdivia, J.: Diatom autofocusing in brightfield microscopy: a comparative study. IN: Proceedings 15th International Conference on Pattern Recognition, ICPR 2000, Barcelona, Spain, vol.3, pp. 314–317 (2000)
6. Liu, X.Y., Wang, W.H., Sun, Y.: Dynamic evaluation of autofocusing for automated microscopic analysis of blood smear and pap smear. J. Microsc. **227**(1), 15–23 (2007)
7. Che, X., Li, Y., Zhao, X., et al.: Batch-targets-oriented auto-switching of view field in micro-manipulation. Nanotechnol. Precis. Eng. **8**(3), 215–220 (2010)
8. Suk, H.J., van Welie, I., Kodandaramaiah, S.B., et al.: Closed-loop real-time imaging enables fully automated cell-targeted patch-clamp neural recording in vivo. Neuron **95**(5), 1037–1047. e11 (2017)
9. Zeng, Y., He, Y.: Gear edge detection based on improved morphological gradient. Tool Technol. **51**(01), 101–103 (2017)
10. Zhao, Y., Gui, W., Chen, Z.: Edge detection based on multi-structure elements morphology. In: 2006 6th World Congress on Intelligent Control and Automation, Dalian, pp. 9795–9798 (2006)

Morphologic Reconstruction of 2D Cellular Micro-scaffold Based on Digital Holographic Feedback

Xin Li[1(✉)], Huaping Wang[1], Qing Shi[1], Juan Cui[1], Tao Sun[1],
Hongpeng Qin[2], Qiang Huang[1], and Toshio Fukuda[1]

[1] The Intelligent Robotics Institute, School of Mechatronical Engineering,
Beijing Institute of Technology, 5 South Zhongguancun Street, Haidian District,
Beijing 100081, China
18801338737@163.com
[2] Beijing TaiGeekTechnology Co., Ltd., Beijing 100022, China
z.wang@isasi.cnr.it

Abstract. The artificial 2D cellular micro-scaffold is increasingly needed in tissue engineering and biomedical engineering. Yet, the study of the influence between the scaffold physical properties and the cell behaviors during cell cultures still remains lacking. In this paper, the micro-scaffold based on the PEGDA hydrogel was fabricated by combining digital holographic microscope technique and DMD-based manipulation system. The morphology and thickness coefficients of the micro-scaffold shaped under the UV exposure was sampled in real-time by the holographic microscopy as the feedback and utilized to control the DMD-based local solidification of the micro-scaffold, which can modify and reconstruct the morphology of the scaffold to improve the fidelity of the shape. With this technique, the system can fabricate micro-scaffold with any customized shape and thickness, which can be seeded or encapsulated with cells to study the influence of substrate mechanism to the cell behaviors under micro-nano scale. The RGDS-linked (Arg-Gly-Asp-Ser) PEGDA as a typical hydrogel was utilized to fabricate the micro-scaffold to verify the effectiveness of the system. Through encapsulating NIH/3T3 cells inside scaffold with different morphologies, we cultured the cells for 7 days and evaluate the cell behaviors. As a result, the NIH/3T3 cell can maintain different proliferation speed with very high cell viability. The proposed micro-scaffold fabrication method provide novel techniques for more accurate biofabrication of microtissues for the future regenerative medicine.

Keywords: 2D cellular micro-scaffold · Cell behavior study ·
PEGDA hydrogel · Digital holographic microscope · Tissue engineering

1 Introduction

The artificial 3D model systems that can substitute specific tissues is in great demand in various applications ranging from fundamental science, clinical studies to the replacement of human organs [1]. The construction of in vitro 3D tissue model is composed of multiple cell types and extracellular matrix (ECM)-mimetic micro-scaffold [1, 2]. The stiffness, architecture, compositions and surface morphology of micro-scaffold have

© Springer Nature Switzerland AG 2019
H. Yu et al. (Eds.): ICIRA 2019, LNAI 11740, pp. 196–208, 2019.
https://doi.org/10.1007/978-3-030-27526-6_18

significant influences on cell behaviors such as differentiation, migration and proliferation [3, 4]. Fabricating the appropriate scaffold for specific application is one of the major challenges toward developing artificial tissues.

Diverse methods to fabricate micro-scaffold with different formations have been demonstrated, and a serious of modular properties including stiffness, architecture and compositions have been investigated [5, 6]. For example, Pathak and Kumar combined photolithography techniques and controlled polymerization of polyacrylamide (PA) hydrogels to construct the ECM with different stiffness, and investigated the influence of matrix stiffness on the tumor cell migration [5]. Aubin et al. used the micromolding techniques created various aspect ratio rectangular cell-laden microstructures and demonstrated the influence of matrix architecture on cell proliferation [6]. Chiang et al. constructed the heterogeneous micro-hydrogels to utilize electrowetting and dielectrophoresis and analyzed the effect of matrix compositions to the NIH/3T3 fibroblasts differentiation [2]. These methods have efficient access to the manufacture of different micro-scaffolds. However, the fabricated micro-scaffold has low fidelity due to the attributes of the biomaterial. For instance, when fabricating a quadrate micro-structure in soft materials, the height usually occurs shrinkage and the corners are round [7]. For most of the approaches, the micro-scaffold is shaped by using the predetermined mould, and the surface morphology such as the thickness can't be changed simultaneously during fabrication. Thus, modifying or reconstructing the local microscale profile features in situ is impossible.

The PEGDA (poly (ethylene) glycol diacrylate) as a biocompatible hydrogel was selected with appropriate concentration to generate ECM-mimetic micro-scaffold. Recently, employing the 3D bioprinting method to construct biomimetic scaffold based on the hydrogel is prevalent [8]. During the fabrication process, the shear stress has negative effect on cell viability [9]. Therefore, a micro-nano technology based on Digital Micro-mirror Device (DMD) has been utilized as fabricating technique of biological microstructure [10]. The optical schematic diagram DMD-based system was shown in Fig. 1. The arbitrary shaped cellular micromodules can be created by programmable photo-crosslinking reaction of hydrogel [11]. The geometry and shape of fabricated micromodules are acquired and displayed in real-time by CCD and computer, respectively. Besides, the effect of photo-crosslinking reaction on the cellular bioactivities is negligible compared to shear stress [9, 12]. But obtaining the particular parameters of surface morphology about the micro-scaffold is disabled. The modification and reconstruction for the surface local morphology in situ is extremely difficult without an efficient data feedback system.

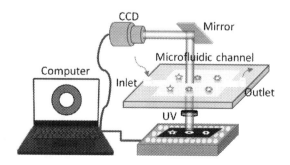

Fig. 1. Schematic of DMD-based system

To solve the above issue for a real-time and controllable microscale process in the local surface morphogenesis of micro-scaffold during the fabrication, we proposed a novel fabrication method to change the local thickness of micro-scaffold by combining the digital holographic microscope and the DMD-based manipulation system. The geometry and surface morphological parameters of fabricated micro-scaffold can be obtained in real-time, and transferred back to the DMD-based system synchronously to modify and reconstruct the micro-scaffold through repeating local fabrication in situ. Based on the above system, the 2D PEGDA cellular micro-scaffold with excellent profile features was created. Additionally, high cell viability can be achieved after long-term culture encapsulated in the microstructure. This study has huge potential to provide a novel cell scaffold fabrication method for the local study of cell behaviors with high fidelity in the tissue engineering.

2 Micro-robotic System for 2D Cellular Micro-scaffold Fabrication

2.1 Overview

Here, we designed the innovative micro-fabrication of 2D cellular micro-scaffold, which can modify and reconstruct the local surface morphology of micro-scaffold, to study the cell behavior in the micro-scaffold. The optical schematic of 2D cellular micro-scaffold fabrication was illustrated in Fig. 2. Firstly, the microfluidic channel was filled with cells mixed PEGDA and placed on the sample stage for the micro-scaffold fabrication. Through the controllable UV light pattern, the arbitrary shape of 2D cellular micro-scaffold can be created with high flexibility and efficiency. Because the PEGDA hydrogel is bioinert to cell adhesion, the RGDS (Arg-Gly-Asp-Ser) peptide sequences were incorporated into PEGDA hydrogels to induce cell adhesion and proliferation [13]. Secondly, even though the PEGDA hydrogel was cured under the once UV exposure to form 2D cellular micro-scaffold, the surface morphology of formed micro-scaffold is asymmetric. The local nonuniform thickness affects the cell behaviors such as differentiation, migration and proliferation. Therefore, the digital holographic microscope technique is employed to analyze the local surface morphology of the micro-scaffold. The digital hologram of the cured PEGDA hydrogel is captured by the high precise charge coupled device (CCD) camera, which can obtain the particular profile information of object's surface. However, the modification of micro-scaffold is impossible only by the information. The high efficient loop feedback system of graphical user interface (GUI) is utilized to automatically control DMD-based system and repeatedly cross-link PEGDA hydrogel in the micro-scale formation. Finally, through the repeating UV exposure, the surface morphology of fabricated 2D cellular micro-scaffold was modified and reconstructed.

2.2 DMD-Based Manipulation System Setup

The DMD-based fabrication system consists of programmable UV exposure components and multi-degree of freedom translation platform which can be moved on the

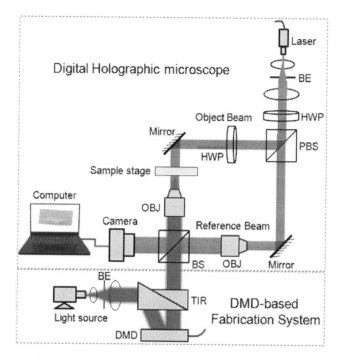

Fig. 2. Optical schematic of 2D cellular micro-scaffold fabrication

direction along X-Y-Z axes respectively, as shown in Fig. 3. The high power light source offers UV beam to solidify the liquid PEGDA hydrogel with all kinds of geometrical shapes. The microfluidic channel is fixed on the sample stage and can be moved along with the translation platform. The divergent UV beam from light source is converged by two convex lens with the 10 cm focal length to enhance the optical density. The DMD reflects the UV beam and then collected by the objective lens to pattern the PEGDA hydrogel.

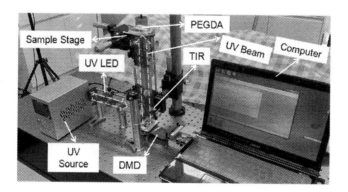

Fig. 3. DMD-based fabrication system

The DMD with 1024 * 768 micrometer-sized aluminum mirrors (micromirrors) as a digital dynamic mask is used to produce various images. Each micromirror is approximately 13.68 microns in size, and can be independently controlled to switch between two discrete angular positions: $-12°$ and $+12°$ by programming. Changing the angular positions of different micromirrors, UV beam irradiated on the DMD can be vertically reflected to the objective lens for cross-linking process. Through the programmable control of DMD, shape-specific UV beam can be generated and then the liquid PEGDA hydrogel can be cross-linked expected shape. Thus arbitrary geometrical 2D cellular micromodules can be achieved rapidly without any objective masks.

2.3   Digital Holographic Microscope System Setup

2.3.1   The Traditional Holographic Principle

The holography based on the optical interference is used to completely record the information of amplitude and phase in the optical field [14]. The principle of traditional holography is showed in Fig. 4. A beam of laser from light source is divided into two beams equally by the beam splitter (BS) to obtain coherent light with the uniform distribution of complex amplitude. One of the laser beams is reflected by the object to form object beam, and other laser beam is reference beam. As the medium is irradiated simultaneously by two laser beams, the hologram is created with the optical interference in the medium [15].

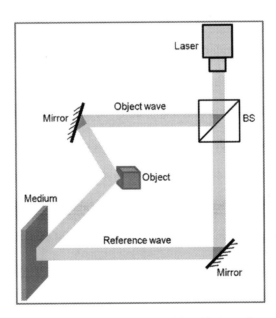

Fig. 4. Optical principle of traditional holography

2.3.2 The Digital Holographic Microscope System

In the digital holographic field, the optical interference image is generated by the linear superposition of object and reference beams, and then is digitally sampled by the CCD camera. The computer collects the digital signals from CCD to convert to an array of numbers. The propagation function of optical field is completely expressed by diffraction theory. Through the numerical reconstruction of interference image as array of complex numbers, the information of optical field about amplitude and phase can be represented accurately. The digital holography possesses numerous significant advantages including the rapid acquirement of holograms, complete data acquisition of the optical field and high efficient image processing technique [16].

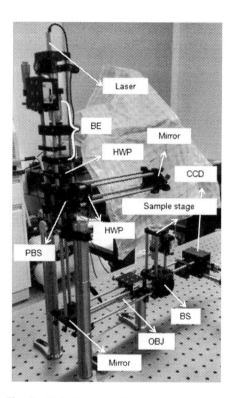

Fig. 5. Digital holographic microscope system

Figure 5 shows the optical system of the digital holographic microscope technique. The polarization beam-splitter (PBS) is employed to divide the laser beam into two perpendicular linear polarized light containing object and reference beams. The vibrational plan of linear polarized light is rotated by the half wave plate (HWP) to obtain clear stripe of holographic optical interference. The object beam and reference beam are superposed on each other by using the beam-splitter (BS) to generate optical interference pattern of holography. Through the using of CCD camera, the generated pattern can be sampled and be converted into digital signal to transfer to the computer as an array of numbers.

2.4   Principle of Loop Feedback System of GUI

The loop feedback system of GUI is utilized for the data collection from CCD camera and holographic image processing to obtain the thickness coefficients of fabricated micromodule, and then transfers simultaneously the coefficients to DMD-based system to change the local surface morphology of the micromodule.

The design of loop feedback system is based on the classic holography principle. The recorded intensity $I(x, y)$ at the hologram plane is the square module of the amplitude superposition of the object and reference beams. It is given by

$$
\begin{aligned}
I(x,y) = & |O_O(x,y)|^2 + |R_O(x,y)|^2 + O_O^*(x,y)\, R_O(x,y) \\
& + O_O(x,y)\, R_O^*(x,y)
\end{aligned}
\tag{1}
$$

where $O_O(x, y)$ and $R_O(x, y)$ are the optical field of object and reference waves, respectively. The first two terms represent the intensities of the reference and object waves. They do not provide spatial information about the object optical field and form the zero-order term. The last two terms provide spatial frequency of the recorded hologram and are responsible for the virtual and real images, respectively. We reconstructed holograms by numerically propagating the optical field along the z direction using the angular spectrum method, which has a significant advantage in that it has no minimum reconstruction distance requirement. If $E(x, y; 0)$ is the wave-front at plane $z = 0$, the angular spectrum $A(\xi, \eta; 0) = F\{E(x, y; 0)\}$ at this plane is obtained by taking the Fourier transform, where $F\{\}$ denotes the Fourier transform; ξ and η are the corresponding spatial frequencies of x and y directions, respectively; and z is the propagation direction of the object wave. The new angular spectrum A at plane $z = d$ is calculated from $A(\xi, \eta; 0)$ as:

$$
A(\xi,\eta;d) = A(\xi,\eta;0) * \exp\left\{ j\frac{2\pi d}{\lambda}\left[\begin{matrix} 1 - (\lambda\xi)^2 \\ -(\lambda\eta)^2 \end{matrix} \right]^2 \right\}
\tag{2}
$$

where λ is the wavelength. The reconstructed complex wave-front at plane $z = d$ is found by taking the inverse Fourier transform as:

$$
E(x,y;d) = F^{-1}\{A(\xi,\eta;d)\}
\tag{3}
$$

where $F^{-1}\{\}$ denotes the inverse Fourier transform. The intensity image $I(x, y; d)$ and phase image $\varphi(x, y; d)$ are simultaneously obtained from a single digital hologram by calculating the square module of the amplitude and the argument of the reconstructed complex wave-front:

$$
I(x,y;d) = |E(x,y;d)|^2
\tag{4}
$$

$$
\varphi(x,y;d) = \arctan\left(\frac{\mathrm{Im}[E(x,y;d)]}{\mathrm{Rm}[E(x,y;d)]} \right)
\tag{5}
$$

The phase diagram of fabricated micromodule can be reconstructed with the phase information, and thus a series of parameters about the thickness of morphology can be obtained. The DMD-based system receives these parameters to repeatedly control the local exposure time by programming, and then the micromodule is partly cross-linked under the multiple UV exposure to modify the thickness of surface morphology.

3   Method for Cellular Micro-scaffold Fabrication

The correct procedure of experiment determines the success of 2D cellular micro-scaffold fabrication. Firstly, using the software of XIMEA CamTool to debug the digital holographic microscope. Changing the angle of HWP or the distance between BS and CCD camera to obtain a clear optical stripe of holographic interference in the XIMEA CamTool, as shown in Fig. 6. The light and dark fringes are distributed regularly in the interference image.

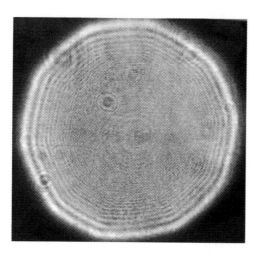

Fig. 6. Optical stripe of holographic interference

Secondly, placing the microfluidic channel filled PEGDA hydrogel mixed cells on the sample stage to cross-link the micromodule with the patterned UV exposure. Then the digital holographic microscope system records the holographic information of cured micromodule and transfers to the loop feedback system of GUI to obtain the morphologic thickness. Figure 7(a) shown the holographic image of a hollow hexagonal micromodule. Through extracting the information of amplitude and phase from the holographic image, the corresponding images can be created, as shown in Fig. 7(b) and (c), respectively. Figure 7(d) reconstructed the 3D diagram of morphologic thickness, which the local true thickness can be clearly illustrated with the data, for the fabricated micromodule.

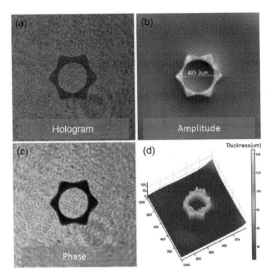

Fig. 7. Surface morphologic analysis of micromodule. (a) Holographic image of micromodule. (b) Amplitude image. (c) Phase image. (d) 3D diagram of morphologic thickness.

Finally, with the reliable data feedback of morphologic thickness in real-time, the DMD-based system is controlled to repeatedly solidify the local surface position of cross-linked micromodule. Then the surface morphology of micromodule can be modified and reconstructed to achieve specific application.

4   Experiment Result

4.1   Fabrication of 2D Cellular Micro-scaffold

The PEGDA of M_w 3400 (Sigma Aldrich, St Louis, USA) was dissolved in 1 mL DMEM without phenol red (Gibco, Carlsbad, USA) to form 60% (w/v) pre-polymer solution. The photoinitiator (PI, Irgacure 2959, USA) was dissolved in dimethyl sulfoxide (DMSO, Fisher Scientific, USA) at 50% (w/v) stock solution. The RGDS peptide sequences (M_w 433.4 Da, NJPeptide, China) were Conjugated to Acrylat-PEG-NHS (Mw 3400 Da, Ponsure Biotechnology, China) to obtain the Acrylate-PEG-RGDS, which modifying the PEGDA inadhesion of cells, and the Acrylate-PEG-RGDS was added to pre-polymer solution. The Dulbecco's Modified Eagle's Medium (DMEM, Sigma Aldrich) with NIH/3T3 cells and 10% Fetal Bovine Serum (FBS, Sigma Aldrich) were added to the pre-polymer solution in a appropriate volumetric ratio. The final pro-polymer solution contained 20% (w/v) PEGDA, 5 mM RGDS, 1% (w/v) PI and 10% FBS in DMEM [17].

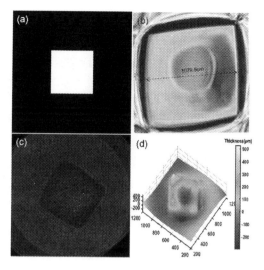

Fig. 8. Fabrication of 2D cellular micro-scaffold. (a) Quadrate image with the size 1 cm * 1 cm. (b) Microscope image of micro-scaffold. (c) Holographic image of micro-scaffold. (d) 3D diagram of morphologic thickness.

For 2D cellular micro-scaffold fabrication, the final pro-polymer solution was injected into PDMS-based microchannel which was fixed on the sample stage. Then the UV beam with the 10.8 mW/cm^2 light intensity illuminated on the microchannel to crosslink expect micro-scaffold based on the DMD mask. Simultaneously, the digital holographic microscope system acquired the holographic image of micro-scaffold and transferred the information of amplitude and phase to the loop feedback system to obtain the morphologic thickness parameters. As shown in Fig. 8(a), the quadrate image with the size 1 cm * 1 cm designed by autoCAD was loaded into the DMD-based system, and then photo-crosslinked the 2D cellular micro-scaffold with the time of UV exposure was 10 s. Figure 8(b) and (c) shown the microscope and holographic interference images of fabricated micro-scaffold. With the reconstruction of hologram, the 3D diagram of morphologic thickness about the quadrate micro-scaffold was shown in Fig. 8(d), which illustrated the left thickness is higher compared with the right part of micro-scaffold. Therefore, the DMD was controlled by programming with the image as shown in Fig. 9(a) to irradiate the right local position of cured micro-scaffold once again for 3 s. The 3D diagram of morphologic thickness about the final quadrate micro-scaffold was shown Fig. 9(b), which illustrated the thickness of micro-scaffold was uniform compared with Fig. 8(d). Thus the surface morphology of micro-scaffold was modified and reconstructed.

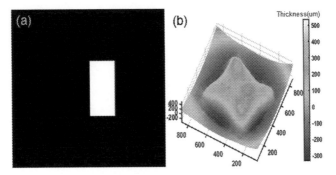

Fig. 9. Modification of 2D cellular micro-scaffold. (a) Rectangle image with the size 0.5 cm * 1 cm. (b) 3D diagram of morphologic thickness.

4.2 Cell Behavior and Viability

In order to investigate the cell behavior, the fabricated 2D cellular micro-scaffold was cultured in an incubator for 7 days. Figure 10 shows the observation of the cell behaviors for 0 h, 5 h, 24 h, 48 h, 72 h, 96 h and 7 days, respectively. The adhesion and elongation of NIH/3T3 cells in the PEGDA micro-scaffold were established in first 5 h, and these

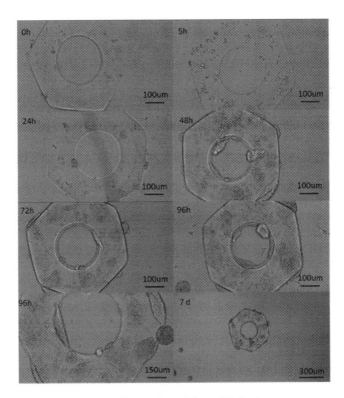

Fig. 10. Observation of the cell behaviors.

Fig. 11. Fluorescent images of live and dead cells. (Color figure online)

cells maintained rapid proliferation. The micro-scaffold was fully filled with cells after 7 days. For studying the cell viability, the NIH/3T3 cells were dyed by Calcein-AM and Prodium Iodide. The fluorescent images of live (green fluorescence) and dead (red fluorescence) cells are shown in Fig. 11, in which cell viability are nearly 95%.

4.3   Discussion

Previous studies in tissue engineering for the fabrication of 2D cellular micro-scaffold with different mechanical properties including stiffness, architecture and compositions have received repaid development. But the modification and reconfiguration of surface morphology for the various specific application have been restricted by the fabrication methods. In this study, the digital holographic microscope technique combined with DMD-based system realized the fabrication of 2D cellular micro-scaffold with PEGDA hydrogel.

Through the proposed method, not only can the micro-scaffold with different geometric shape and size be fabricated, but also the surface morphology can be modified and reconstructed.

5   Conclusion

The DMD-based manipulation system combined digital holographic microscope technique was utilized to fabricate 2D cellular micro-scaffold based on photo-crosslinking reaction of PEGDA hydrogel. The thickness coefficients of fabricated micro-scaffold ranging from 400um to 600um was obtained and the local morphology of micro-scaffold was modified and restructured for the specific demand.

Acknowledgment. This research was funded by National Key R&D Program of China under grant number 2017YFE0117000, and National Nature Science Foundation of China (NSFC) under grant number 61603044.

References

1. Chan, V., Zorlutuna, P., Jeong, J.H., et al.: Three-dimensional photopatterning of hydrogels using stereolithography for long-term cell encapsulation. Lab Chip **10**(16), 2062–2070 (2010)
2. Chiang, M.Y., Hsu, Y.W., Hsieh, H.Y., et al.: Constructing 3D heterogeneous hydrogels from electrically manipulated prepolymer droplets and crosslinked microgels. Sci. Adv. **2**(10), e1600964–e1600964 (2016)
3. Lauffenburger, D.A.: Cell migration: a physically integrated molecular process. Cell **84**(3), 359–369 (1996)
4. Klymkowsky, M.W., Parr, B.: The body language of cells: The intimate connection between cell adhesion and behavior. Cell **83**(1), 5–8 (1995)
5. Pathak, A., Kumar, S.: Independent regulation of tumor cell migration by matrix stiffness and confinement. Proc. National Acad. Sci. **109**(26), 10334–10339 (2012)
6. Aubin, H., Nichol, J.W., et al.: Directed 3D cell alignment and elongation in microengineered hydrogels. Biomaterials **31**(27), 6941–6951 (2010)
7. Kim, H.N., Kang, D.H., Kim, M.S., et al.: Patterning methods for polymers in cell and tissue engineering. Ann. Biomed. Eng. **40**(6), 1339–1355 (2012)
8. Pedde, R.D., Mirani, B., Navaei, A., et al.: Emerging biofabrication strategies for engineering complex tissue constructs. Adv. Mater. **29**(19), 1–27 (2017)
9. Bhise, N.S., Manoharan, V., Massa, S., et al.: A liver-on-a-chip platform with bioprinted hepatic spheroids. Biofabrication **8**(1), 1–9 (2016)
10. Qian, J., Lei, M., Dan, D., et al.: Full-color structured illumination optical sectioning microscopy. Sci. Rep. **5**(1), 1–13 (2015)
11. Chung, S.E., Park, W., Park, H., et al.: Optofluidic maskless lithography system. In: Transducers International Actuators & Microsystems Conference. IEEE (2007)
12. Fedorovich, N.E., Oudshoorn, M.H., Geemen, D.V., et al.: The effect of photopolymerization on stem cells embedded in hydrogels. Biomaterials **30**(3), 344–353 (2009)
13. Mann, B.K., Gobin, A.S., Tsai, A.T., et al.: Smooth muscle cell growth in photopolymerized hydrogels with cell adhesive and proteolytically degradable domains: synthetic ECM analogs for tissue engineering. Biomaterials **22**(22), 3045–3051 (2001)
14. Latychevskaia, T., Fink, H.W.: Simultaneous reconstruction of phase and amplitude contrast from a single holographic record. Opt. Express **17**(13), 10697–10705 (2009)
15. Dainty, J.C.: Optical holography: principles, techniques and applications. Opt. Acta Int. J. Opt. **32**(1), 1 (1985)
16. Kim, M.K.: Principles and techniques of digital holographic microscopy. J. Photonics Energy **1**(1), 1–51 (2009)
17. Park, K.H., Na, K., Kim, S.W., et al.: Phenotype of hepatocyte spheroids behavior within thermo-sensitive poly (NiPAAm-co-PEG-g-GRGDS) hydrogel as a cell delivery vehicle. Biotechnol. Lett. **27**(15), 1081–1086 (2005)

Field Robots

An Improved Artificial Potential Field Method for Path Planning of Mobile Robot with Subgoal Adaptive Selection

Zenan Lin[1], Ming Yue[1,2($\boxtimes$)], Xiangmin Wu[1], and Haoyu Tian[1]

[1] School of Automotive Engineering,
Dalian University of Technology, Dalian 116024, China
yueming@dlut.edu.cn
[2] State Key Laboratory of Robotics and System,
Harbin Institute of Technology, Harbin 150001, China

Abstract. As a simple and effective method, artificial potential field method is often used in robot path planning. Based on this, an improved artificial potential field model is proposed to solve the local minimum problem by using a subgoal strategy. In order to show the subgoal adaptive selection feature of the robot, an obstacle potential field function is established and the effectiveness of the adaptive feature is verified by path planning simulation. A double closed-loop control strategy is adopted to track the trajectory planned by the improved artificial potential field method, and simulation results show that the improved artificial potential method is reliable and the robot can well track the trajectory under the action of the controller.

Keywords: Path planning ·
Improved artificial potential field method · Subgoal adaptive selection ·
Trajectory tracking

1 Introduction

Path planning has always been a hot topic in robotics. As a global path planning method, artificial potential field method proposed by Khatib [1], which is simple to calculate and easy to understand. However, there are two inevitable defects in the traditional artificial potential field method: the unreachable target and the local minimum problem. This paper mainly discusses the local minimum problem.

The local minimum problem refers to that the robot is balanced by the repulsive force and gravity and falls into a stable state in the local region and cannot continue to move. To solve this problem, many scholars have proposed different solutions. Lee [2] proposed virtual obstacle to get rid of the local minimum in local path planning. Li [3] proposed an artificial potential field method based on the regression search method, which can effectively obtain a better path

© Springer Nature Switzerland AG 2019
H. Yu et al. (Eds.): ICIRA 2019, LNAI 11740, pp. 211–220, 2019.
https://doi.org/10.1007/978-3-030-27526-6_19

in the dynamic environment and solve the oscillation problem. However, these improvement strategies are all specific to some scenarios, and their applicability still needs to be improved.

In this paper, we use an subgoal strategy. When a local minimum problem is encountered, a subgoal is generated, after reaching the subgoal, the robot continues to move towards the original target point. The subgoal selection method is adaptive. When encountering the minimum problem, the robot will both judge the obstacles and the target's position information at its current position and select the appropriate subgoal punctuation.

This paper also carries out collaborative design for the trajectory tracking of the robot, builds the robot model and tracks the obstacle avoidance trajectory planned by the improved artificial potential field method with designed controller, which verifies the effectiveness and feasibility of the improved method.

2   Local Minimum Problem Description

The local minimum problem of the artificial potential field method refers to that when the robot starts from the starting point, avoids obstacles under the action of the whole situation field and moves towards the target point, it encounters some obstacles which makes the robot's gravity and repulsive force cancel each other and make it in an equilibrium state, unable to move forward or to avoid obstacles [4]. There are two main forms of local minimum problems, which are caused by a single obstacle or multiple obstacles. Although the two expressions are different, the essence is the same: the gravity acting on the robot is balanced with the repulsive force.

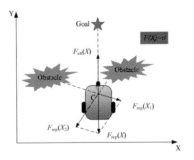

Fig. 1. The local minimum problem

For the local minimum problem, different improvement methods proposed by domestic and foreign scholars, such as redefining potential field [5] and simulated annealing [6], have their own advantages and disadvantages. This paper introduces the strategy of adding subgoal to improve the original artificial potential field method.

3   Subgoal Adaptive Selection Strategy

3.1   Improvement of Local Minimum Problem

The subgoal strategy is to get the robot out of the minimum region when it encounters the local minimum problem. Firstly, the potential field of the subgoal is minimized as the target point for the rescue. After the robot drives to the subgoal, the global potential field is restored and the robot moves from the subgoal to the original target point.

In the method of adding subgoal, the location of it is very important, because it determines whether the robot can get out of trouble and finally reach the target point. In this paper, an adaptive subgoal selection method is introduced. When encountering the minimum problem, the robot will select the appropriate subgoal punctuation position based on the obstacles and the target's current position information.

The selection criteria of subgoal: take the line connecting the target point and the position of the robot as the dividing line, set the angle between the dividing line and the X-axis as α, the angle between the line connecting the robot and the X-axis as β, and define the obstacle angle ϕ_j of the jth obstacle as $(\alpha_j - \beta_j)$, if $0 < \phi_j < \pi/2$, then the obstacle is the left-front obstacle. If $\pi/2 < \phi_j < \pi$, on the other hand, the obstacle is the right front obstacle. The obstacle potential field is defined as follows

$$O = \sum_{k=1}^{n} \frac{1}{\rho^2(X, X_g)} \tag{1}$$

X_{oi} is the position coordinate of the ith obstacle. Let the potential field of the left front obstacle be O_l and the potential field of the right front obstacle be O_r, and judge the value of them. If $O_l > O_r$, take the current position of the robot as the reference point, the subgoal is at the position of $\phi = \pi/4$, and the distance is P_0; if $O_l < O_r$, the target point is at the position of $\phi = -\pi/4$, and the distance is P_0.

There are two main reasons for choosing $|\phi| = \pi/4$ as the direction of subgoal position. First, compared with the direction of $|\phi| \in (\pi/4, \pi)$, the efficiency is higher. Because of the comparison between the "transverse" strategy $(|\phi| = \pi/2)$ and the "backward" strategy $(|\phi| \in (\pi/2, \pi))$, the selection of $|\phi| = \pi/4$ can make the robot closer to the final target point after reaching the subhead punctuation, and the total travel time and distance are less. Secondly, considering the performance constraints of the robot itself, it is possible to avoid the occurrence of large corner and angular velocity in the process of turning after the robot reaches the subgoal. For example, if the robot select $(|\phi| \in (\pi/2, \pi))$ as a subgoal direction, the rotation angle φ in the next moment is between $(\pi/2, \pi)$, which is much larger than the $|\phi| = \pi/4$ one.

3.2   The Simulation of Local Minimum Problem

In order to verify the feasibility of the improved method proposed above, map environment and other relevant elements were constructed in MATLAB, and initialization parameters were given in Table 1.

Table 1. Artificial potential field method simulation parameters

Parameters	Value	Parameters	Value
m	3 kg	P_0	1 m
v	0.1 m/s	(X_0, Y_0)	(0,0)
k_{att}	5	(X_g, Y_g)	(9,10)
k_{rep}	3		

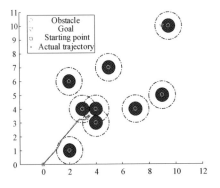

Fig. 2. Trapped in local minimum   **Fig. 3.** Escape local minimum area

As shown in Fig. 2, when the robot moves to the target point, it is surrounded by three obstacles (4,3), (4,4) and (3,4), and then falls into a local minimum point and cannot continue to move. In order to solve this problem, we adopt the solution of adding subgoal. As shown in Fig. 3, according to the distribution information of obstacles, a subgoal is selected to make the robot escape local minimum area. In order to clearly illustrate the adaptive selection of sub-goals, the target point was set as (10,10) again and only one obstacle located at (5,5) existed globally. Obviously, the robot could not move forward because the resultant force was 0 in the process of approaching the obstacle. At the same time, add two obstacles at (5,8) and (8,5), which are symmetric about the dividing line. Therefore, the obstacle avoidance direction of the robot is, obviously $O_l = O_r$. And if an obstacle located at (5,6) is added, the robot will choose the direction of $\phi = \pi/4$ as the subgoal, as shown in Figs. 4 and 5.

As for the direction choosing of subgoal, Fig. 6 shows the φ values of the robot under different ϕ. The specific values and the time to reach the final target are given in Table 2.

It can be seen from Table 2 that the planning track selected $|\phi| = \pi/4$ as a subgoal takes the shortest time to reach the target point and has the smallest turning angle. In addition, this paper adopts an extension strategy considering that the subgoal to be at the extreme position of an obstacle, or is so close to the obstacle that it will be affected by the repulsion force that tends to infinity immediately after arriving at the subgoal. If the subgoal position falls within the

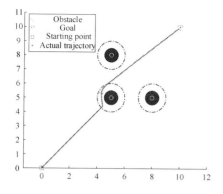

Fig. 4. Obstacle potential field $O_l = O_r$

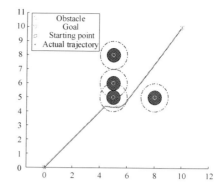

Fig. 5. Obstacle potential field $O_l > O_r$

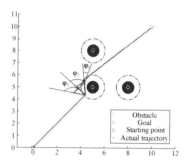

Fig. 6. Three subgoal direction strategy

range of $n = \pi/2$, the extension strategy will extend the distance of P_0 of the original subgoal in the direction of ϕ to get a new subgoal position, and so on if the above situation is still encountered.

Table 2. The turning angle and arrival time of different subtarget selection strategies

Serial number	Subtarget direction ϕ	Steering angle φ	t
1	$\pi/4$	0.3228	146
2	$\pi/2$	1.7825	154
3	$2\pi/3$	2.2681	158

As shown in Fig. 7, the planned subgoal point is located at (4.313,5.313), within the circular range of $n = \pi/2$ of the obstacle (4.5,5.5). The robot cannot reach the subgoal directly and it has to retreat to some low potential places and replan a path to the subgoal.

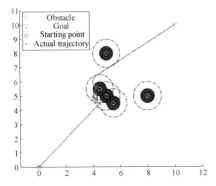

Fig. 7. Subgoal falls near the obstacle

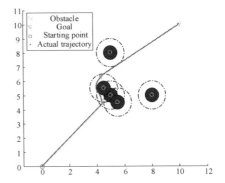

Fig. 8. Avoid obstacles via extended strategy

As can be seen in Fig. 8, after the extension strategy is adopted, the robot replans the subgoal at the new location (4.313,6.313). With the new path, the robot can reach the final target point successfully.

4   Robot Trajectory Tracking Controller

4.1   System Simulation Platform Modelling

In the geodetic coordinate system, the posture of a typical wheeled mobile robot (WMR) in Fig. 9 can be expressed by generalized coordinates with three dimensions, namely $q = [x_c, y_c, \theta]^T$, where x_c and y_c are the mass center of the robot, θ represents the angle between the robot motion direction and the X-axis of the geodetic coordinate system. The velocity of WMR can be defined as $\boldsymbol{v} = [\upsilon, \omega]^T$, where υ and ω represent the longitudinal velocity and the steering velocity. Assume that the motion of the robot wheels meet the condition of pure rolling [7].

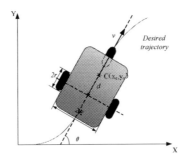

Fig. 9. A nonholonomic wheeled mobile robot

4.2   Controller Description

In this paper, a double closed-loop control strategy is used to control the dynamic behavior of mobile robot in the process of motion. The outer loop is composed of robot kinematics model and pose controller. The robot's pose under the current state can be described as $q = [x, y, \theta]^T$, and the robot's reference trajectory $q_r = [x_r, y_r, \theta_r]^T$. The function to be achieved by the outer loop is to find the appropriate pose controller to make sure $q \rightarrow q_r$ when $t \rightarrow \infty$, so that the global asymptotic stability of the robot's pose tracking can be achieved. The inner loop is composed of the dynamic model and the dynamic controller of the mobile robot. The speed of the robot in the current state can be described as $v = [v, \omega]^T$ and the desired speed as $v_d = [v_d, \omega_d]^T$. The function that the inner ring needs to achieve is to establish an appropriate dynamic controller to make sure $v \rightarrow v_d$ when $t \rightarrow \infty$. More details of the controller can found in [8].

5   Controller Simulation

5.1   Robot Path Planning Simulation

In order to verify the effectiveness of the robot trajectory tracking controller, the simulation research was carried out on MATLAB. Under the improved artificial potential field method, the robot can plan a path from the initial point to the target point. At the same time, in order to test the improvement of the IAPF method for these two problems, we set the starting point as (0,0), the target point as (9,10), the position coordinate of the intermediate obstacle as (2,3), (3,3), (4,3), (4.6,1.65), (6,8), (9.6,10), and the robot's moving speed as 0.5 m/s. Based on the above obstacle location and target location settings, the robot will plan a path to avoid obstacles via subgoal method.

The physical parameters of the robot are as follows: m = 3, d = 0.1, R = 0.25, R = 0.3. In order to better achieve the control objectives, the parameters of the controller are as follows: $c_1 = c_2 = 5$, $\lambda_1 = \lambda_2 = \lambda_3 = 1$, $\sigma_1 = \sigma_2 = 1$, $k = 5$, $\delta_1 = 5$, $\delta_2 = 3$, $\mu = 100$.

As shown in Fig. 10, under the action of the improved artificial potential field method, the robot has planned an obstacle avoidance path from the starting point (0,0) to the target point (9,10). Local minimum and unreachable problems appear in the planned path, which are solved successfully by the improved artificial potential field method.

5.2   Robot Trajectory Tracking Simulation Results

Given a certain initial error (−0.5, −0.5, 0.1), the real starting position of the robot is further away from the final target point than the starting point. The actual driving trajectory and reference trajectory are shown in Fig. 11. The simulation results show that the robot can track the planned trajectory well under the control of the initial error.

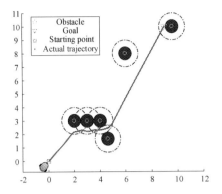

Fig. 10. Obstacle avoidance trajectory planning

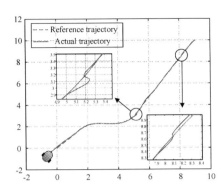

Fig. 11. Reference trajectory and actual running trajectory

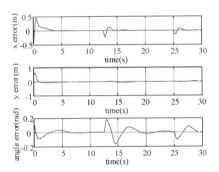

Fig. 12. Robot trajectory tracking error

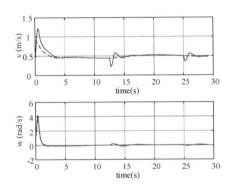

Fig. 13. Robot speed tracking

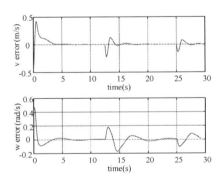

Fig. 14. Robot speed error

Figure 12 shows the trajectory tracking error of the robot. It can be seen from the figure that the tracking error gradually decreases from the initial value at the beginning and finally converges to zero. In addition, under the action of the adaptive scheme, the external disturbance used to represent the bad working conditions also decays to zero rapidly.

Figures 13 and 14 show the curves and errors of the actual and expected speeds of the robot. Under the action of the controller, the error rapidly converges to zero and remains stable.

Through the above simulation results, it is proved that the trajectory tracking controller proposed in this paper can effectively control the dynamic behavior of the robot in motion and realize the effective tracking of the desired trajectory.

6 Conclusion

Aiming at the local minimum problem of artificial potential field method in trajectory planning of mobile robot, this paper proposes a new improved artificial potential field method by using subgoal strategy for quadratic programming. The obstacle potential field function is constructed to make the selection of subgoal punctuation adaptive, which is proved by MATLAB platform simulation. Finally, the double closed-loop control strategy is adopted to track the trajectory, and the good tracking results prove the reliability of the improved artificial potential field method and subgoal adaptive selection strategy.

Acknowledgement. This work was supported by National Natural Science Foundation of China under Grant (Nos. 61873047 and 61573078), Fundamental Research Funds for the Central Universities (DUT19ZD205), and State Key Laboratory of Robotics and System Grant (SKLRS-2019-KF-17).

References

1. Khatib, O.: Real-time obstacle avoidance for manipulators and mobile robots. Int. J. Robot. Res. **5**, 90–98 (1986). https://doi.org/10.1007/978-1-4613-8997-2_29
2. Lee, M.C., Park, M.G.: Artificial potential field based path planning for mobile robots using a virtual obstacle concept. In: International Conference on Advanced Intelligent Mechatronics, pp. 735–740 (2003). https://doi.org/10.1109/AIM.2003.1225434
3. Li, G., et al.: Effective improved artificial potential field-based regression search method for autonomous mobile robot path planning. Int. J. Mechatron. Autom. **3**(3), 141 (2013). https://doi.org/10.1504/ijma.2013.055612
4. Zhu, Y., Zhang, T., Song, J.: An improved wall following method for escaping from local minimum in artificial potential field based path planning. In: IEEE Conference on Decision Control, pp. 6017–6022 (2010). https://doi.org/10.1109/CDC.2009.5399854
5. Zhu, Q., Yan, Y., Xing, Z.: Robot path planning based on artificial potential field approach with simulated annealing. In: International Conference on Intelligent Systems Design Applications, vol. 2, p. 622 (2006). https://doi.org/10.1109/ISDA.2006.253908
6. Park, M.G., Jeon, J.H., Lee, M.C.: Obstacle avoidance for mobile robots using artificial potential field approach with simulated annealing. In: IEEE International Symposium on Industrial Electronics Proceedings, vol. 3, pp. 1530–1535 (2001). https://doi.org/10.1109/ISIE.2001.931933

7. Yue, M., Wang, S., Zhang, Y.: Adaptive fuzzy logic-based sliding mode control for a nonholonomic mobile robot in the presence of dynamic uncertainties. Proc. Inst. Mech. Eng. Part C: J. Mech. Eng. Sci. **229**(11), 1979–1988 (2015). https://doi.org/10.1177/0954406214551625

8. Yue, M., Wu, G., Wang, S., An, C.: Disturbance observer-based trajectory tracking control for nonholonomic wheeled mobile robot subject to saturated velocity constraint. Appl. Artif. Intell. **28**(8), 751–765 (2004). https://doi.org/10.1080/08839514.2014.952918

Trajectory Planning for Digital Camouflage Spray Painting Robot Based on Projection Method

Zhang Xutang[1], Shi Wen[1(✉)], Wang Bohao[1], Li Jianming[2], and Zhang Ling[2]

[1] School of Mechatronics Engineering, Harbin Institute of Technology, Harbin 150001, China
630617776@qq.com
[2] Hubei Communication Technical College, Wuhan 430079, China

Abstract. At present, the digital camouflage painting is still mainly by manual spraying, the process is complicated and inefficient. In view for this situation, on the basis of the previous research on the texture mapping technology based on the octree theory, a spray trajectory planning method based on the projection method is proposed. This method takes the texture mapping result as the input. Firstly, the Mosaic boundary on the 3D model is projected to the plane; then the "scanning" raster trajectory planning is carried out on the projection plane; finally, the trajectory of spraying planning is corrected. This method transforms the 3D trajectory planning problem into the 2D trajectory planning problem, which not only greatly simplifies the difficulty of the algorithm planning, but also can adapt to different shape surfaces. The experiment verifies the feasibility of the algorithm. The research results can provide reference for the practice of digital camouflage spraying.

Keywords: Spray painting robot · Trajectory planning · Digital camouflage · Off-line programming

1 Introduction

The perception of digital camouflage is a complex process, which can confuse the enemy and achieve the effect of camouflage [1]. Due to the complexity of digital camouflage spraying process, manual spraying is still the main way. It requires some professional workers to draw the digital camouflage to the combat equipment firstly and then spray. The accuracy is difficult to guarantee. Every time spraying a new color needs to shade other areas that already sprayed, which are very cumbersome. Manual spraying has many problems such as long construction time, low work efficiency, workers exposed to toxic environment and many uncertain factors. So it is very necessary to find an automatic spraying solution for digital camouflage.

Trajectory planning is the key to realize automatic spraying. The motion trajectory of the robot is automatically generated by the algorithm rather than the traditional teaching mode, which can improve the work efficiency. Klein put forward the concept of off-line programming of spraying robot based on CAD in 1986 [2] and achieved

© Springer Nature Switzerland AG 2019
H. Yu et al. (Eds.): ICIRA 2019, LNAI 11740, pp. 221–230, 2019.
https://doi.org/10.1007/978-3-030-27526-6_20

good result in spraying some simple models, laying a foundation for the development of off-line programming. Subsequently, many scholars have carried out research on the trajectory planning method [3–8]. The existing methods usually abstract the trajectory planning problem of free-form surface spraying into a variation problem with constrain. These kinds of methods requires solving nonlinear differential equations, leading to excessively long time of trajectory planning [9].

This paper presents a new trajectory planning method for free-form surface spraying. On the basis of the existing mathematical model of airbrush [10–13], carrying out research on rapid path generation method. The validity of the method is verified by experiments in this paper.

2   Overview of Trajectory Planning Methods

Digital camouflage painting planning is dependent on the result of volume segmentation mapping and needs to be planned with Cell (Mosaic square) as the basic unit. In general, the points provided by the triangle grid model in STL format are too sparse, as shown in Fig. 1, and more points need to be interpolated before trajectory planning. The traditional method is to divide the 3D model of the original triangular face into regular quadrilateral face and use the center point as the trajectory point. However, the trajectory planning is limited by the size of the quadrangle.

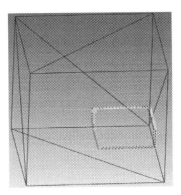

Fig. 1. The original model and cell boundaries.

In conclusion, this paper adopts the following methods for trajectory planning:

- First, space transformation is carried out to transform the ordered point boundary of Cell from the 3d model into a plane. So the 3d trajectory planning problem is transformed into a 2d problem. Which can solve the problem that the surface information in the 3d space is too little to construct the trajectory points.
- Second, the way of "scan" is used to adjust the spacing of the plane trajectory points on the plane. Then the trajectory points constructed are mapped to the 3d model surface corresponding to the Cell by means of projection.

- At last, parameters affecting the spraying quality in the spraying process are set to complete the trajectory planning.

3   Space Transformation

The main purpose of the space transformation is to transform the Cell boundary of the 3d model into a 2d plane. The space transformation is mainly divided into the following four steps:

1. Project a boundary point onto a plane. First, calculate the center point p_c, average normal direction N_a and spraying direction:

$$\begin{cases} p_c = \frac{1}{n} \sum_{i=0}^{n} p_i \\ \vec{N}_a = \frac{1}{n} \sum_{i=0}^{n} \vec{N}_i \\ \left| \vec{N}_a \cdot \vec{N}_x \right| - \left| \vec{N}_a \cdot \vec{N}_y \right| \leq 0 \quad x\text{-direction} \\ \left| \vec{N}_a \cdot \vec{N}_x \right| - \left| \vec{N}_a \cdot \vec{N}_y \right| > 0 \quad y\text{-direction} \end{cases} \quad (1)$$

Where N_x is the unit vector in the positive direction of the X-axis, and N_y is the unit vector in the positive direction of the Y-axis. N_y is the normal direction of the boundary point.

If N_a is satisfied with Eq. 3 in (1), the movement direction is set as the X-axis direction, and if N_a is satisfied with Eq. 4 in (1), the movement direction is set as the Y-axis direction. Suppose the direction of movement is the X-axis direction, then we can get the point p_{c1} according to the formula $p_{c1} = p_c + N_x$.

Construct a plane perpendicular to normal direction N_a, and project the Cell's boundary point to the plane. Suppose the distance between the center point and the projection plane is d. Then the projection formula is:

$$p_{new} = p_{old} + \left[(p_c - p_{old}) \cdot \vec{N}_a + d \right] \times \vec{N}_a \quad (2)$$

Update the boundary point according to formula (2), and the projection operation of the boundary point is completed. Then establish the coordinate system on the projection plane, and construct the rotation matrix to prepare for the subsequent transformation. The origin of the coordinate system on the projection plane is p_c', and x, y and z axes are denoted by N_x', N_y', N_z' respectively, The calculation formula is as follows:

$$\begin{cases} \vec{N}_z' = \vec{N}_a \\ \vec{N}_x' = p_{c1}' - p_c' \\ \vec{N}_y' = \vec{N}_z' \times \vec{N}_x' \end{cases} \quad (3)$$

The transformation matrix constructed is as follows:

$$T = \begin{bmatrix} n_x & o_x & a_x & p_x \\ n_y & o_y & a_y & p_y \\ n_z & o_z & a_z & p_z \\ 0 & 0 & 0 & 1 \end{bmatrix} \tag{4}$$

Where T is column vector matrix, the first three elements of column 0–3 are three components of N'_x, N'_y, N'_z, p'_c respectively.

2. Transform the boundary points on the projection plane to the x-y plane according to the following formula:

$$\begin{cases} \vec{p} = [p_x \quad p_y \quad p_z \quad 1]^{-1} \\ \vec{p}' = T^{-1}\vec{p} \\ p_{new} = [\vec{p}'_x \quad \vec{p}'_y \quad \vec{p}'_z] \end{cases} \tag{5}$$

Where p_x, p_y, p_z are the three coordinate values of point p.

3. Transform the trajectory points on the x-y plane to the projection plane according to the following formula:

$$\begin{cases} \vec{p} = [p_x \quad p_y \quad p_z \quad 1]^{-1} \\ \vec{p}' = T \cdot \vec{p} \\ p_{new} = [\vec{p}'_x \quad \vec{p}'_y \quad \vec{p}'_z] \end{cases} \tag{6}$$

4. The trajectory points on the projection plane are mapped to the surface contained in the Cell based on average normal direction. The intersection formula of ray and triangle is used to calculate the position of the trajectory point on the surface, where the ray origin O is the trajectory point on the projection plane, the ray direction is d, the intersection point *point* is the trajectory point on the surface, the distance from the point to the ray origin is t, u and v are weight factors of $\overrightarrow{AB}$, $\overrightarrow{AC}$, respectively. The calculation formula of intersection point is:

$$point = O + \vec{d} \cdot t = (1 - u - v) \cdot A + u \cdot C + v \cdot B \tag{7}$$

$$\begin{bmatrix} t \\ u \\ v \end{bmatrix} = \frac{1}{|\vec{d} \times \overrightarrow{AB} \cdot \overrightarrow{AC}|} \begin{bmatrix} \overrightarrow{AO} \times \overrightarrow{AC} \cdot \overrightarrow{AB} \\ \vec{d} \times \overrightarrow{AB} \cdot \overrightarrow{AO} \\ \overrightarrow{AO} \times \overrightarrow{AC} \cdot \vec{d} \end{bmatrix} \tag{8}$$

4 "Scanning" Grid Trajectory Planning

4.1 Trajectory Types and Bias Algorithms

In the process of trajectory planning, there are two commonly used trajectory methods: grid and spiral. The grid trajectory planning is simple, but the spray edge effect is poor.

The spiral shape has better edge uniformity than grid shape, but its calculation and control are more complicated.

The requirement of camouflage block boundary is relatively high, it needs a certain amount of painting transition, but cannot have a large range of mixed color phenomenon. This topic combines the advantages of the two trajectory methods, suing the spiral trajectory control boundary, and suing the grid to carry out trajectory planning inside of the Cell. Specific planning ideas are shown in Fig. 2.

In Fig. 2, the outermost boundary represents the boundary of Cell transformed into x-y plane. The circle represents the area covered by the spray gun, and the diameter is set as d; The direction of the arrow is the direction of the gun movement.

As can be seen from Fig. 2, the final spray-painted annular trajectory needs to be obtained by inward offsetting 0.5d.

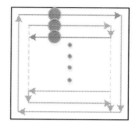

Fig. 2. Schematic diagram of trajectory planning

The trajectory offsetting algorithm can be divided into the following steps:

(1) Use cubic b-spline curve to fit the trajectory. Cubic b-splines can replace higher-order polynomials by piece-wise low-order polynomials through continuous connections, thus avoiding the instability of higher-order polynomials.
(2) Take the derivative of the fitted spline curve and calculate the normal of each point on the curve.
(3) The curve is offset by the normal direction. After curve fitting the plane contour, the offset contour can be obtained according to the normal direction of each point.

4.2 "Scanning" Trajectory Planning

In this project, the idea of "scanning" is adopted for trajectory planning, and the plane trajectory spacing is adjusted according to the spatial projection results, as shown in Fig. 3:

The so-called "scanning" means that the planning process is similar to taking a line to scan the Cell boundary from top to bottom to determine the trajectory spacing. The essential idea is to use the line segment to approximate the curve, and use the length of the line segment to replace the length of the curve.

In Fig. 3(a), the innermost ring is defined as the limiting ring, which is the boundary of the grid trajectory, and is obtained by inward offsetting 0.65d of the middle ring. p_0, p_1, p_2 are the intersection point of three top-down scanning lines and

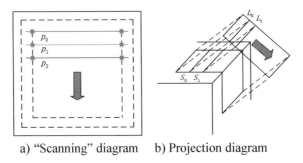

a) "Scanning" diagram   b) Projection diagram

Fig. 3. "Scanning" trajectory planning

the restriction ring and the distance between the intersection points is $L = 0.01d$. Figure 3(b) shows the trajectory on the x-y plane is transformed into the original model, and the distance between the intersection points is converted into the distance between the projection points on the original model. Finally, the actual trajectory distance is determined by the cumulative distance between each projection point. The final grid trajectory is shown in Fig. 4:

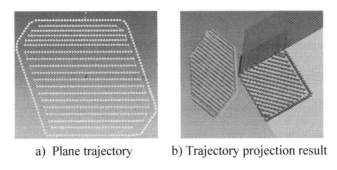

a) Plane trajectory   b) Trajectory projection result

Fig. 4. Result of trajectory planning in Cell

4.3   Trajectory Space Correction

The projected results may deviate from the planar results, so it is necessary to ensure the accuracy of trajectory points in space by means of correction. The above "scanning" planning method can only ensure that the spatial distance between the left end points of each grid meets the requirements of spraying, but there is no restriction on the interpolation points in the middle. The circular spraying trajectory is obtained by equidistant offset on the plane. Therefore, it is impossible to guarantee the equidistant between the projection and the Cell boundary, and it also needs to be corrected.

Here, the interpolation trajectory point method is used to fine-tune the space until the scanning distance of the sprayed surface meets the formula $0.6d < S < 0.7d$.

5 Parameter Setting

After the spraying trajectory is generated, the parameters that affect the spraying quality in the painting process are: the spraying gun posture, the track distance and the moving speed of the spray gun.

5.1 Determination of Spraying Gun Posture

Usually we suppose that the ideal spray posture spraying is that the gun axis and trajectory point normal are coincidence, but digital painting requires that between various pieces boundary cannot have the phenomenon of large mixed color, if two plain angle change is big, the other side may be damaged, as shown in Fig. 5(a).

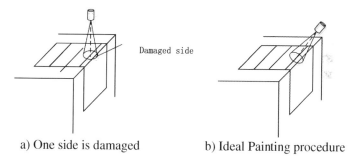

a) One side is damaged   b) Ideal Painting procedure

Fig. 5. Spraying gun posture

In view of the above situation, this paper proposes a method to determine the spraying gun posture based on local shape. In this method, the projection plane is taken as the reference plane, and the moving direction of the spraying gun is taken as the horizontal reference plane. Extend the current point in four directions respectively. The position of each extension point on the surface of the original model is determined by the projection method, then we can get the normal direction of each projection point. The normal direction of the final trajectory point is the average normal direction of the extension point.

In Fig. 5(b), it can be seen that the spraying gun is not simply perpendicular to the sprayed surface when the trajectory is near the interface of the sprayed surface, which can well avoid the large-scale color mixing of various color blocks and ensure that the surface that has been sprayed will not be damaged.

It is still impossible to determine the specific posture of the spraying gun only by determining the normal direction of the trajectory point. In addition, the freedom of the spraying gun around the z-axis needs to be limited by determining the direction of the X-axis and Y-axis. The pose of the trajectory point is determined by the above calculation, and the pose of the trajectory point is the target pose of the spraying gun.

5.2 Determination of Track Spacing and Velocity of the Gun

As mentioned in the previous section, the formula $0.6d < S < 0.7d$ is used to determine the distance between the trajectories, so as to ensure the full coverage of the sprayed surface and to ensure the uniformity of the thickness to the maximum extent.

In this experiment, when the spray gun is 50 mm away from the sprayed surface, the coverage radius is 20 mm, and the ideal thickness of the automobile surface is 20 um. According to the parabola model of Chinese scholar Zhao dean et al., the moving speed of the spray gun is 53.33 mm/s and the distance between trajectories is 25.668 mm.

6 Experiment

Determine the parameters related to the spraying process, as shown in Table 1:

Table 1. Spraying parameters

Parameters	Number
Atomizing pressure	0.05 MPa
Switch pressure	0.4 MPa
Pump pressure	0.2 MPa
Spraying distance	50 mm
Spraying width	30 mm

As can be seen in Fig. 6, the corner of the Cell boundary is not a right Angle, which is caused by the circular coverage area of the spray gun. Generally speaking, in the actual camouflage spraying process, the camouflage color block is much larger than the experimental color block, and the car will be sprayed with a layer of primer before the camouflage spraying, these two reasons make the trajectory planning scheme can be used in the actual engineering. In Fig. 6(c), it can be seen that the boundaries of each color block are obvious, and there is no large-area color mixing problem, and the position arrangement is consistent with the software generation effect. As a result of paint modulation and shooting light and other factors, there are color differences between the actual spraying results and the software generated results.

a) Spraying process   b) Software generation   c) Actual spraying effect

Fig. 6. Spraying effect

The Cell side length set in the simulation software is 20 cm, and the measurement of the experimental results is shown in Fig. 7. It can be seen from the figure that the error is within 5 mm, far less than the required 50 mm.

Fig. 7. Measurement of experimental results

By analyzing the experimental results, it can be seen that the trajectory planning results outputted in the simulation software meet the requirements of camouflage spraying, which proves the feasibility of the application of automatic spraying system in practical engineering.

7 Conclusion

This paper first describes the space transformation based on matrix method, and explains the reason and process of space transformation in detail. Then, according to the characteristics of digital camouflage spraying, a "scan" trajectory planning method is proposed. The offset algorithm was used to generate a circular trajectory to ensure the Cell boundary is clear and avoid the problem of large area color mixing. Subsequently, we determine the distance between trajectories by "scan" projection, interpolate each trajectory, and correct the trajectory points. Then the spraying parameter planning is carried out to determine the corresponding relations among the color switching mode, the posture of the spray gun passing through the trajectory point, the distance between the trajectories, the moving speed of the spray gun and the thickness of the target coating and the coverage area of the spray gun. Finally, the application of the automatic spraying system in practical engineering is verified by the experimental results. The method presented in this paper provides a new idea for trajectory planning of vehicle digital camouflage spraying.

References

1. Zhang, Y., Xue, S., Jiang, X., et al.: The spatial color mixing model of digital camouflage pattern. Defence Technol. **9**(3), 157–161 (2013)
2. Klein, A.: CAD-based off-line programming of painting robots. Robotica **5**(4), 267–271 (1987)

3. Suk, S.-H., Lee, J.-J., Choi, Y.-J.: A prototype integrated robotic painting system: software and hardware development. J. Manuf. Syst. **12**(6), 475–482 (1993)
4. Chen, H., Sheng, W., Xi, N., et al.: Automated robot trajectory planning for spray painting of free-form surfaces in automotive manufacturing. In: Proceedings of IEEE International Conference on Robotics and Automationm, ICRA, vol. 1, pp. 450–455. IEEE (2002)
5. Atkar, N.P., Greenfield, A., Conner, C.D., Choset, H., Rizzi, A.A.: Hierarchical segmentation of surfaces embedded in R3 for auto-body painting. In: Proceedings of the 2005 IEEE International Conference on Robotics and Automation, pp. 574–579 (2005)
6. Chen, H., Fuhlbrigge, T., Li, X.: A review of CAD-based robot path planning for spray painting. Microelectron. Reliab. **42**(3), 343–347 (2009)
7. Gyorfi, J.S., Gamota, D.R., Mok, S.M., et al.: Evolutionary path planning with subpath constraints. IEEE Trans. Electron. Packag. Manuf. **33**(2), 143–151 (2010)
8. Andulkar, M.V., Chiddarwar, S.S.: Incremental approach for trajectory generation of spray painting robot. Ind. Robot **42**(3), 228–241 (2015)
9. Miao, D., Wang, G., Wu, L., et al.: Trajectory planning for freeform surface uniform spraying. J. Tsinghua Univ. Sci. Technol. **53**(10), 1418–1423 (2013)
10. Chen, Y., Yan, H., Wang, L., et al.: Coating uniformity with a uniform robotic spray gun velocity. J. Tsinghua Univ. **50**(8), 1210–1213 + 1218 (2010)
11. Chen, H., Fuhlbrigge, T., Li, X.: Automated industrial robot path planning for spray painting process: a review. In: IEEE International Conference on Automation Science and Engineering, pp. 522–527. IEEE (2008)
12. Ramabhadran, R., Antonio, J.K.: Fast solution techniques for a class of optimal trajectory planning problems with applications to automated spray coating. IEEE Trans. Robot. Autom. **13**(4), 519–530 (1995)
13. Zhang, Y.: New model for air spray gun of robotic spray-painting. Chin. J. Mech. Eng. **42**(11), 226–233 (2006)

Autonomous Fault-Tolerant Gait Planning Research for Electrically Driven Large-Load-Ratio Six-Legged Robot

Hong-Chao Zhuang[1(✉)], Ning Wang[2], Hai-Bo Gao[3],
and Zong-Quan Deng[3]

[1] College of Mechanical Engineering, Tianjin University of Technology and
Education, Tianjin 300222, China
zhuanghongchao_hit@163.com
[2] College of Information Technology Engineering, Tianjin University of
Technology and Education, Tianjin 300222, China
wangning811108@163.com
[3] State Key Laboratory of Robotics and System, Harbin Institute of Technology,
Harbin 150001, China

Abstract. Gait planning is an important basis for the walking of the multi-legged robot. To improve the walking stability and to reduce the impact force between the foot and the ground, autonomous fault-tolerant gait strategies are respectively presented for an electrically driven large-load-ratio six-legged robot. Then, the configuration and walking gait of robot are designed. Typical walking ways are acquired. According to the Denavit–Hartenberg (D–H) method, the kinematics analysis is implemented. The mathematical models of articulated rotation angles are established. In view of the buffer device installed at the end of shin, an initial lift height of leg is brought into the gait planning when the support phase changes into the transfer phase. The mathematical models of foot trajectories are established. The autonomous fault-tolerant gait strategies are proposed. The prototype experiments of electrically driven large-load-ratio six-legged robot are carried out. The reasonableness of autonomous fault-tolerant gait strategy is verified based on the experimental results. The proposed strategies of fault-tolerant gait planning can provide a reference for other multi-legged robot.

Keywords: Large-load-ratio six-legged robot · Fault-tolerant gait ·
Initial lift height · Support phase · Transfer phase

1 Introduction

In nature, the legged animal utilizes the coordinated motion of leg to realize from the current location to the goal location, which is commonly called gait. As the number of legs increases, the type of gait increases. Then, the gait planning of legged robots will be more complex. The legged robot can have many types of gaits in theory, but not every gait can make the robot effectively walk. It is necessary to carry out the motion analysis and gait planning. The different mobile system structures of the legged robots often need the different gait planning strategies. The gait planning of legged robots not

© Springer Nature Switzerland AG 2019
H. Yu et al. (Eds.): ICIRA 2019, LNAI 11740, pp. 231–244, 2019.
https://doi.org/10.1007/978-3-030-27526-6_21

only directly affects the consistency and stability, but also relates to the degrees of energy dissipation. Many researchers hope to get outstanding legged robots which can independently think and work like the animal. At present, the walking of the outstanding multi-legged robots mainly depends on the sensing system, control strategy, initial gait planning, etc. The information of the robot and environment can be acquired by the sensing system. The initial gait planning can be used and repaired by the control strategy of robot. Then, the walking of legged robots can be achieved in the structure and unstructured environment.

The large-load-ratio multi-legged robot can not only carry a variety of detection equipment to carry out the scientific exploration tasks, but also play a role of the transporter. Hence, the terrain adaptability is needed for large-load-ratio multi-legged robots. To enhance the walking stability of the robot and reduce the impact force of the swing leg to the ground, the large-load-ratio multi-legged robot often is required to install the elastic cushion or the rubber tire on the end of foot. The spring and other elastic elements are often installed in the lower limb of the leg by comparing with the non-bearing small multi-legged robot. Hence, the buffer devices can be often found in many large-load-ratio multi-legged robots, such as BigDog [1], COMET-IV [2], ATHLETE [3], and so on. Generally speaking, the conventional fault-tolerant strategy means that a joint or a single leg of multi-legged robot is damaged due to its own or external reasons. When the planning strategy is adopted, the robot can work normally according to the remaining intact joints or supporting legs, and then it can complete the established tasks. In this article, the proposed autonomous fault-tolerant strategy is just the opposite of the conventional fault-tolerant idea. To reduce the energy dissipation of mobile system, the autonomous fault-tolerant gait planning in this article refers to the planned closure of a joint or a supporting leg by the multi-legged robot.

The gait planning of the multi-legged robot is concerned by many researchers. Ishikawa et al. [4] used a simplified neural network model called the associatron to deal with the gait motion planning problem on the irregular field for a six-legged robot. The availability of the proposed method was verified by the simulation and the experiments of developed robot. Estremera et al. [5] presented the crab-typed turning gaits for the hexapod robots on the uneven ground and forbidden zones. The turning gaits were tested by the SILO-6 walking robot. Satzinger et al. [6] proposed an end-to-end planning method that can achieve the teleoperated mobility of robot in the complex environments. Tedeschi and Carbone [7, 8] addressed the design and operation of hexapod walking robots. The example of gait planning was provided through kinematic and dynamic features of Cassino hexapod leg operation. Sadati et al. [9] developed a motion planning algorithm for walking with passive knees. Although many researchers have done a lot of research works in the gait planning of the legged robots and have obtained the effective planning strategies, the buffer device locating at the shin is rarely considered in the gait planning. At present, we have not found the literatures that the initial lift height of swing leg is introduced into the gait planning for large-load-ratio multi-legged robots. The autonomous fault-tolerant gait schemes are also not discovered in the recent literatures.

According to the above problems and the previous research on the legged robot [10–13], the initial lift height of the swing leg is brought forward and introduced into the research of the autonomous fault-tolerant gait planning for an electrically driven large-load-ratio six-legged robot. This article is divided into seven sections. In Sect. 2, the configuration and walking gait are designed for the electrically driven large-load-ratio six-legged robot. The typical walking ways are acquired. In Sect. 3, the kinematics analysis is executed based on the D-H method. The mathematical models are built for the articulated rational angles. In Sect. 4, the initial lift height of the swing leg is incorporated into the analysis of the fault-tolerant gait planning. The mathematical models of the feet trajectories are established. In Sect. 5, the autonomous fault-tolerant gait strategies are presented. In Sect. 6, a prototype of the electrically driven large-load-ratio six-legged robot is developed. The experiments of the walking speed are actualized to verify the reasonableness of the autonomous fault-tolerant gait strategies. In the final section, the conclusions are presented.

2 Configuration and Walking Gait of Robot

2.1 Configuration of Large-Load-Ratio Six-Legged Robot

To conveniently carry out the analysis of the gait planning, the electrically driven large-load- ratio six-legged robot is called the large-load-ratio six-legged robot for short. The leg of robot is designed based on the walking leg of hexapod. Each leg has three joints: abductor joint, hip joint, and knee joint. The abductor joint, hip joint, and knee joint are respectively defined as $A_i, H_i,$ and $K_i (i = 1, \ldots, 6)$. Each leg is made up of three linkages: a coxa, thigh, and shin. To maintain the characteristics of universal walking, the configuration of robot body is designed as a regular polygon. The mechanism of robot and structure of leg are respectively shown in Fig. 1. The lengths of the coxa, thigh, and shin are set as $l_c, l_t,$ and l_s. The rotation angle of the abductor joint is set as θ_i. $\beta_i\prime (i = 1, \ldots, 6)$ is regarded as the included angle between the coxa of leg i and the thigh of leg i. $\gamma_i (i = 1, \ldots, 6)$ is regarded as the included angle between the thigh of leg i and the shin of leg i. The included angle between the coxa of leg i and the shin of leg i is defined as $\beta_i (i = 1, \ldots, 6)$. Then, the relations among $\beta_i\prime, \gamma_i$ and β_i can be obtained; they are $\beta_i = \beta_i\prime + \gamma_i$ and $0° \leq \beta_i\prime \leq \beta_i \leq 90°$.

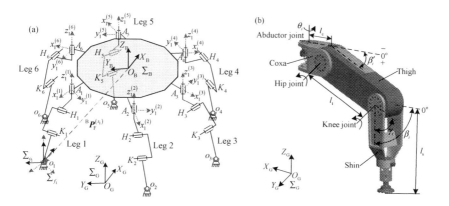

Fig. 1. Electrically driven large-load-ratio six-legged robot: (a) schematic diagram of mechanism; and (b) top view of mechanism.

In Fig. 1, the body coordinate system of robot is set as $\sum_B$ locating at the center of body. The ground coordinate system is defined as $\sum_G$. The abductor joint coordinate system of leg i is regarded as $\sum_{A_i}$, including $z_1^{(i)}$-axis, $x_1^{(i)}$-axis, and $y_1^{(i)}$-axis. The $z_1^{(i)}$-axis is parallel to the Z_B-axis of the body coordinate system. The $x_1^{(i)}$-axis keeps parallel with the coxa of leg i. The leg i lies in the plan $z_1^{(i)} x_1^{(i)}$. The foot coordinate system $\sum_{o_i}$ of leg i is parallel to the body coordinate system $\sum_B$. The foot coordinate system $\sum_{f_i}$ of leg i is parallel to the abductor joint coordinate system $\sum_{A_i}$ of leg i. The foot position matrix of leg s_k is set as $^B P_F^{(s_k)}$ in the body coordinate system. The coordinate system, which locates at the body and connects the body to the leg i, is regarded as $\sum_{o_i}$. The coordinate system $\sum_{o_i}$ and the coordinate system $\sum_{A_i}$ are coincident with each other, when the rotating angle θ_i of the abductor joint is zero degrees.

2.2 Walking Ways of Large-Load-Ratio Six-Legged Robot

The gait of six-legged robot is the static gait. The number of legs in the support phase should be no less than 3 at any time. The gait is called u foot gait when the number of legs is u in the support phase. The duty ratio is set as β_R. The range of the duty ratio is from 0.5 to 1 for the six-legged robot. It can be concluded that the three foot gait (or tripod gait) has the maximum walking speed than the four foot gait (or quadrangular gait, tetrapod gait) and the five foot gait (or pentagon gait) when the walking speed and step pitch are the constants. According to the configuration of the large-load-ratio six-legged robot, the walking ways can be divided into the crab type, ant type, crab–ant mixed type I, and crab–ant mixed type II; they are shown in Fig. 2.

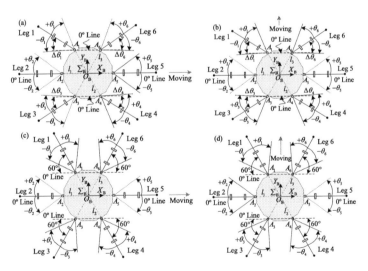

Fig. 2. Four kinds of typical walking ways for large-load-ratio six-legged robot: (a) crab type; (b) ant type; (c) crab–ant mixed type I; and (d) crab–ant mixed type II.

In Fig. 2, the $0°$ lines keep parallel with the X_B-axis of the $\sum_B$ and pass the origins of the coordinate systems of abductor joints. The included angle $\Delta\theta_i$ between the $0°$ line and leg i is defined as the initial angle of abductor joint. The initial angle $\Delta\theta_i$ can be used to set the initial position of the abductor joint when the robot begins to walk. The range of $\Delta\theta_i$ is limited from $0°$ to $60°$. θ_i is the rotation angle of the abductor joint based on the initial angle $\Delta\theta_i$. The initial angles $\Delta\theta_2$ and $\Delta\theta_5$ are always zero degrees for the legs 2 and 5. The initial angles $\Delta\theta_1$, $\Delta\theta_3$, $\Delta\theta_4$, and $\Delta\theta_6$ can vary within their range, and they are equal to each other when the robot begins to walk. The initial attitudes of robot under the crab type and ant type can be arbitrarily set though the abductor joint initial angles of the legs 1, 3, 4, and 6. The crab type and ant type can be respectively change into the crab–ant mixed type I and crab–ant mixed type II, when condition is $\Delta\theta_1 = \Delta\theta_3 = \Delta\theta_4 = \Delta\theta_6 = 60°$. $+\theta_i$ and $-\theta_i$ are defined as the front swing angle and rear swing angle on the basis of the $\Delta\theta_i$. The straight lines l_1, l_2 and l_3 are orthogonal to the relevant axes of abductor joints. To keep the stability of robot, the condition is set as $\Delta\theta_1 = \Delta\theta_3 = \Delta\theta_4 = \Delta\theta_6$. Then, the homogeneous joint on the legs 1, 3, 4 and 6 has the same contribution to the walking speed of robot.

According to Fig. 2, it can be concluded that the walking speed of robot is directly provided by the hip joints and knee joints of the legs 2 and 5 under the crab type and crab–ant mixed type I. The abductor joints of the legs 2 and 5 do not contribute for the walking of robot. When the articulated actuating devices output the large torques under the constant power, the walking speed of robot is limited by the hip joints and knee joints of the legs 2 and 5. Then, we can know that the crab type and crab–ant mixed type I are not conducive to the high-speed walking of robot, but they are suit for climbing the slope and other tasks. Based on the ant-typed walking way, the walking speed of robot is mainly provided by the abductor joints. The hip joints and knee joints only play an auxiliary role. It can be concluded that the maximum walking speed of robot is beneficial to be realized under the ant type. The crab–ant mixed type I and crab–ant mixed type II are more stable than the crab type and ant type through analyzing the stability margin of robot.

3 Kinematics Analysis of Large-Load-Ratio Six-Legged Robot

The D-H model and posture of the leg i is shown in Fig. 3. To elaborate the kinematics analysis of robot, the coordinate systems of the abductor joint A_i, hip joint H_i, and knee joint K_i are further defined as $\sum_{A_i}\left(A_i - x_1^{(i)}y_1^{(i)}z_1^{(i)}\right)$, $\sum_{H_i}\left(H_i - x_2^{(i)}y_2^{(i)}z_2^{(i)}\right)$, and $\sum_{K_i}\left(K_i - x_3^{(i)}y_3^{(i)}z_3^{(i)}\right)$. In Fig. 3, H expresses the distance from the body centroid O_B to the ground. So it can be known that the relation is $h_i = H$. The axes of the abductor joints keep parallel with the Z_G-axis when the body bottom is parallel to the ground. The $y_1^{(i)}$-axis keeps parallel with the axes of the hip joint and knee joint of leg i.

$\sum_{0_i}$ is coincident with $\sum_{A_i}$ when the value of the abductor joint is zero degrees for the leg i. h_i represents the distance from the coordinate origin of the $\sum_{A_i}$ to the ground. L_{pi} is defined as the span which is the projection length of the leg i in the coordinate system $\sum_{A_i}$ of the abductor joint. ${}^{G}P_{F}^{(i)}$ is the position matrix from the foot of leg i to the coordinate system $\sum_{G}$ of the ground. The position matrix ${}^{G}P_{0}^{(i)}$ is from the coordinate system $\sum_{0_i}$ to the coordinate system $\sum_{G}$ of the ground, ${}^{0}P_{F}^{(i)}$ is the position matrix of the foot of leg i in the coordinate system $\sum_{0_i}$.

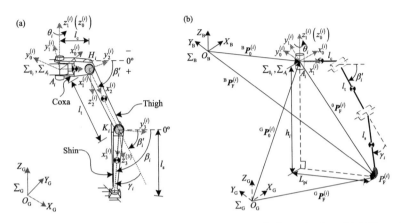

Fig. 3. D-H model and posture of leg i for large-load-ratio six-legged robot: (a) D-H model of leg i; (b) posture of leg i.

Through the kinematics analyses, the rotation angles of the abductor joint, hip joint, and knee joint are solved for the leg i. Then

$$
\begin{cases}
\theta_i = \arctan\left(\left({}^{B}P_{Fy}^{(i)} - {}^{B}P_{0y}^{(i)}\right) \Big/ \left({}^{B}P_{Fx}^{(i)} - {}^{B}P_{0x}^{(i)}\right) \right) - \Phi_i \\[2mm]
\gamma_i = \arccos\left(\left(\xi - l_{t}^{2}\right)/2l_{s}l_{t} \right) \\[2mm]
\beta_i' = \arcsin\left(\dfrac{2l_t\left({}^{B}P_{Fz}^{(i)} - {}^{B}P_{0z}^{(i)}\right)}{\sqrt{\left(\xi+l_t^2\right)^2 + 4l_s^2 l_t^2 - \left(\xi - l_t^2\right)}} \right) - \arctan\left(\dfrac{\sqrt{4l_s^2 l_t^2 - \left(\xi - l_t^2\right)}}{\xi + l_t^2} \right) \\[4mm]
\xi = \left(\sqrt{\left({}^{B}P_{Fx}^{(i)} - {}^{B}P_{0x}^{(i)}\right)^2 + \left({}^{B}P_{Fy}^{(i)} - {}^{B}P_{0y}^{(i)}\right)^2} - l_c \right)^2 + \left({}^{B}P_{Fz}^{(i)} - {}^{B}P_{0z}^{(i)}\right)^2 - l_s^2
\end{cases} \tag{1}
$$

4 Gait Planning of Large-Load-Ratio Six-Legged Robot

The anterior extreme position (AEP) and posterior extreme position (PEP) are brought into the gait planning. s is defined as the step pitch. The organization principles of the gait planning are set up for the support phase and transfer phase. Firstly, the foot that has the shortest distance from the PEP is the first to enter the transfer phase. Secondly, the support phase and the transfer phase are periodic alternation. Actually, the AEP and PEP can be exchanged with each other, and they depend on the reference position of foot and motion vector a. The AEP is the reference position of foot plus the motion vector a. The PEP is the reference position of foot minus the motion vector a. The length of the motion vector a is half of the step pitch s.

To reduce the impact force between the foot and the ground, the end of each shin is installed a buffer device. The initial lift height of leg is introduced to eliminate the influence of buffer mechanism when the support phase changes into the transfer phase. The mopping phenomenon of foot can be prevented. The initial lift height of leg is favorable for striding over the larger obstacles and improving the terrain trafficability of robot. The maximum swing height and initial lift height of the leg are respectively defined as $h_{T\text{-max}}$ and h_{TB}. The relation between the $h_{T\text{-max}}$ and the h_{TB} is $0 \leq h_{TB}$ $h_{T\text{-max}}$. The coordinates of foot, reference position, and motion vector a are respectively set as $\left({}^{B}P_{Fx1}^{(i)}, {}^{B}P_{Fy1}^{(i)}, {}^{B}P_{Fz1}^{(i)} \right)$, $\left({}^{B}P_{Fx0}^{(i)}, {}^{B}P_{Fy0}^{(i)}, {}^{B}P_{Fz0}^{(i)} \right)$, and $({}^{B}a_x, {}^{B}a_y, {}^{B}a_z)$ in the coordinate system $\sum_B$ of the body.

4.1 Motion Planning of Tripod Gait

The number of legs is 3 in the support phase. The duty ratio β_R is 0.5. The legs 2, 4, and 6 are located in the support phase when the legs 1, 3, and 5 are in the transfer phase, and vice versa. The feet trajectories of the leg i between the AEP and the PEP are shown in Fig. 4 for the support phase and transfer phase. Based on Fig. 4, the foot of leg i in the transfer phase swings from the current position to the AEP. Then, the foot of leg i in the support phase supports from the current position to the PEP along the opposite direction of the motion vector a. To ensure the support foot not crossing the PEP in the first gait period of robot, the first support distance in the support phase can be calculated from the current position to the PEP. To maintain the same support distance in the later gait period, the next support distance in the support phase is obtained based on the motion vector a.

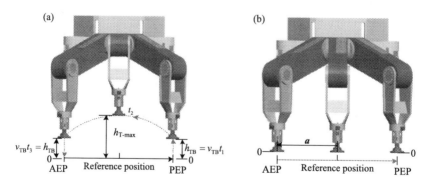

Fig. 4. Feet trajectories of leg i in tripod gait: (a) transfer phase; and (b) support phase.

4.1.1   Motion Planning of Transfer Phase

The foot of the transfer phase swings along a curve from the PEP to the AEP. Due to the arbitrary initial state for the swing leg, the moving trajectory of leg i in the transfer phase is the curve from the arbitrary position to the AEP. Two constraint conditions need to be considered in the motion planning of the transfer phase. Firstly, the velocity value of foot is zero at the AEP and the PEP. Secondly, the acceleration curve of foot has no the jump in the swing process of leg. Generally, the energy consumption of the support phase is much larger than that of the transfer phase when the walking speed of robot is not high. Based on the research results of Lin [14], we can find that there is little difference between the foot trajectory of swing leg and the cosine curve. Hence, the cosine programming is employed for the gait planning in this article.

Owing to the initial lift height h_{TB}, the foot trajectory of the leg i can be divided into three parts in the transfer phase. In the first part, the foot of the leg i chooses the velocity v_{BT} to uplift from 0 to h_{TB} along the direction of Z_B in the time $0 - t_1$. In the second part, the foot of the leg i moves to the AEP along the cosine curve in the time $t_1 - t_2$. In the third part, the foot of the leg i selects the velocity v_{BT} to fall from h_{TB} to 0 along the direction of Z_B in the time $t_2 - T/2$. Then, the leg i is completely turned into the support leg.

In the first part, the mathematical model of the foot trajectory can be written for the leg i in a period of the tripod gait. Then,

$$
\begin{cases}
{}^{B}X_{T1} = {}^{B}P_{Fx1}^{(i)} \\
{}^{B}Y_{T1} = {}^{B}P_{Fy1}^{(i)} \\
{}^{B}Z_{T1} = v_{TB}t + {}^{B}P_{Fz1}^{(i)} \\
0 \leq t \leq t_1
\end{cases}
\tag{2}
$$

In the second part, the mathematical model of the foot trajectory can be written for the leg i in a period of the tripod gait. Then,

$$
\begin{cases}
{}^{B}X_{T2} = \left({}^{B}P_{Fx0}^{(i)} + {}^{B}a_x - {}^{B}P_{Fx1}^{(i)}\right)\Big/2 \times (\cos(\pi(t + t_2 - 2t_1)/(t_2 - t_1)) + 1) + {}^{B}X_{T1} \\
{}^{B}Y_{T2} = \left({}^{B}P_{Fy0}^{(i)} + {}^{B}a_y - {}^{B}P_{Fy1}^{(i)}\right)\Big/2 \times (\cos(\pi(t + t_2 - 2t_1)/(t_2 - t_1)) + 1) + {}^{B}Y_{T1} \\
{}^{B}Z_{T2} = -(h_{T-max} - h_{TB})/2 \times (\cos(2\pi(t + t_2 - 2t_1)/(t_2 - t_1)) - 1) + {}^{B}Z_{T1} \\
t_1 \leq t \leq t_2
\end{cases}
\tag{3}
$$

In the third part, the mathematical model of the foot trajectory can be written for the leg i in a period of the tripod gait. Then,

$$
\begin{cases}
{}^{B}X_{T3} = {}^{B}X_{T2} \\
{}^{B}Y_{T3} = {}^{B}Y_{T2} \\
{}^{B}Z_{T3} = {}^{B}Z_{T2} - v_{TB}t \\
t_2 \leq t \leq T/2
\end{cases}
\tag{4}
$$

4.1.2 Motion Planning of Support Phase

The foot of the support phase supports from the AEP to the PEP. The motion direction of the support phase is opposite to that of the transfer phase. To make the robot in any state quickly enter the support phase, the support distance of foot is set as $2a$ along the opposite direction of the motion vector $\boldsymbol{a}$. The cosine programming is also selected for the support phase. The mathematical model of the foot trajectory in the support phase can be written for the leg i under the tripod gait. Then,

$$
\begin{cases}
{}^B X_S = -{}^B a_x (\cos(2\pi t/T) + 1) + {}^B P_{Fx1}^{(i)} \\
{}^B Y_S = -{}^B a_y (\cos(2\pi t/T) + 1) + {}^B P_{Fy1}^{(i)} \\
{}^B Z_S = {}^B P_{Fz1}^{(i)} \\
T/2 \le t \le T
\end{cases}
\tag{5}
$$

4.2 Motion Planning of Quadrangular Gait

The cosine programming is employed for the foot trajectory of robot. The leg which has the minimum distance from the PEP is stipulated to first enter the transfer phase. The duty ratio β_R is 2/3. Each leg needs to fulfill a swing task and two support tasks in a period of the quadrangular gait. The foot trajectory of the leg i can be divided into three parts in the transfer phase. In the first part, the foot of the leg i chooses the velocity v_{BT} to uplift from 0 to h_{TB} along the direction of Z_B in the time $0 - t_1$. In the second part, the foot of the leg i moves to the AEP along the cosine curve in the time $t_1 - t_2$. In the third part, the foot of the leg i selects the velocity v_{BT} to fall from h_{TB} to 0 along the direction of Z_B in the time $t_2 - T/3$. The motion planning of the leg i under the quadruped gait is the same as that of the tripod gait in the transfer phase. Although the mathematical models of the foot trajectories under the tripod gait can be directly applied to the quadruped gait, the total swing time $T/2$ of leg i under the tripod gait needs to be changed to $T/3$ under the quadrangular gait.

When the motion vector $\boldsymbol{a}$ is constant, the support distance of leg i is changed from $2a$ under the tripod gait to a under the quadrangular gait. The total support distance of the support phase is $2a$ along the opposite direction of the motion vector $\boldsymbol{a}$. The mathematical model of the foot trajectory in the support phase can be written for the leg i under the quadrangular gait. Then,

$$
\begin{cases}
{}^B X_S = {}^B a_x (\cos(3\pi t/2T - \pi/2) - 1) + {}^B P_{Fx1}^{(i)} \\
{}^B Y_S = {}^B a_y (\cos(3\pi t/2T - \pi/2) - 1) + {}^B P_{Fy1}^{(i)} \\
{}^B Z_S = {}^B P_{Fz1}^{(i)} \\
T/3 \le t \le T
\end{cases}
\tag{6}
$$

4.3 Motion Planning of Pentagon Gait

Each leg needs to finish a swing task and five support tasks in a period of the pentagon gait. The duty ratio β_R is 5/6. Then, each leg can be regarded as a group. The leg which has the minimum distance from the PEP is stipulated to first enter the transfer phase. The cosine programming is employed for the motion planning of the pentagon gait. The foot trajectory of the leg i can be divided into three parts in the transfer phase. In the first part, the foot of the leg i selects the velocity v_{BT} to uplift from 0 to h_{TB} along the direction of Z_B in the time $0 - t_1$. In the second part, the foot of the leg i moves to the AEP along the cosine curve in the time $t_1 - t_2$. In the third part, the foot of the leg i uses the velocity v_{BT} to fall from h_{TB} to 0 along the direction of Z_B in the time $t_2 - T/6$. Then, the leg i is completely turned into the support leg. The motion planning of the leg i under the pentagon gait is the same as that of the tripod gait in the transfer phase. Although the mathematical models of the foot trajectories under the tripod gait can be directly applied to the pentagon gait, the total swing time $T/2$ of leg i under the tripod gait needs to be changed to $T/6$ under the pentagon gait.

When the motion vector $\boldsymbol{a}$ is constant, the support distance of the leg i is changed from $2a$ under the tripod gait to $2a/5$ under the pentagon gait. The total support distance of the support phase is $2a$ along the opposite direction of the motion vector $\boldsymbol{a}$. The mathematical model of the foot trajectory in the support phase can be written for the leg i under the pentagon gait. Then,

$$
\begin{cases}
{}^{B}X_S = -{}^{B}a_x(\cos(6\pi t/5T + 4\pi/5) + 1) + {}^{B}P^{(i)}_{Fx1} \\
{}^{B}Y_S = -{}^{B}a_y(\cos(6\pi t/5T + 4\pi/5) + 1) + {}^{B}P^{(i)}_{Fy1} \\
{}^{B}Z_S = {}^{B}P^{(i)}_{Fz1} \\
T/6 \leq t \leq T
\end{cases}
\tag{7}
$$

5 Autonomous Fault-Tolerant Gait Strategies of Large-Load-Ratio Six-Legged Robot

The conventional fault tolerant of the legged robot means that a joint or a single leg is damaged due to its own or external reasons. When the planning strategy is adopted, the robot can work normally based on the remaining intact joints or supporting legs, and then it can complete the established tasks. The proposed autonomous fault-tolerant strategy in this article is just the opposite of the conventional fault-tolerant idea. To reduce the energy dissipation of mobile system, the autonomous fault-tolerant gait planning refers to the planned closure of a joint or a supporting leg by the robot itself.

According to the research results in the Sect. 4, the fault-tolerant gait strategies can be employed based on the robot's self-state and external working conditions. The flow chart of autonomous fault-tolerant gait strategies is shown in Fig. 5. Firstly, the external environment and load carried information are acquired through the robot perception system. The large-load-ratio six-legged robot can determine whether it can pass through the rugged terrain by judging its own state and external working conditions. If it can traverse the terrain, the robot prepares to implement the self-planning ways of walking and gait through the terrain. Otherwise, the robot walks and explores other walking paths. Next, different fault-tolerant strategies are used according to the stability of robot and working condition requirements.

6   Experiments of Large-Load-Ratio Six-Legged Robot

According to our previous research results, a prototype of electrically driven large-load-ratio six-legged robot is developed. Then, the experiments of the walking speed and surmounting obstacle are respectively actualized. The robot takes the 0.4 times of the maximum walking speed as the goal speed to execute the walking speed test. The body of robot carries the load of 1519 N. The parameter TM is set as 100 in the motion control card PMAC. The support distance of the leg i is set as 0.2 m in the support phase. The experiment of the walking speed $2v_{\text{max}}/5$ under the load of 1519 N is shown in Fig. 6.

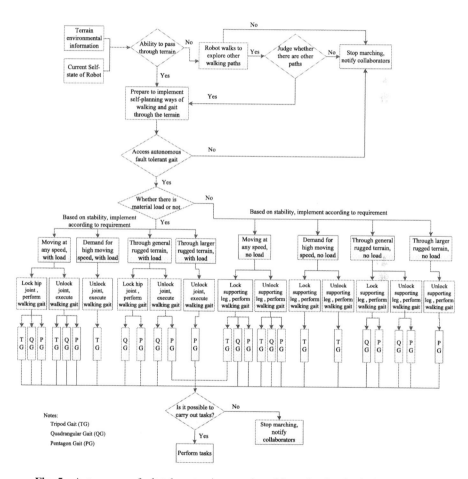

Fig. 5. Autonomous fault-tolerant gait strategies of large-load-ratio six-legged robot.

Based on robot's own state and external working conditions, the ant-typed tripod gait is employed to walk in Fig. 6. The actual walking speed of robot is calculated though the walking distance l_b and time t. The contrastive analysis is implemented between the actual walking speed of robot and the theoretical walking speed $2v_{max}/5$. The contrastive result shows that the above both data is the same.

When the leg 4 is lifted, the articulated servomotors in the leg 4 are powered off and locked. The prototype of the large-load-ratio six-legged robot employs the quadrangular gait to climb the slope of 35° under the no load. The climbing experiment of the fault-tolerant gait is shown in Fig. 7. According to Fig. 7, it is found that the large-load-ratio six-legged robot can climb the slope of 35° under the quadrangular gait. The impact phenomenon does not appear between the foot and the ground. The reasonableness of the autonomous fault-tolerant gait strategies are verified for the large-load-ratio six-legged robot.

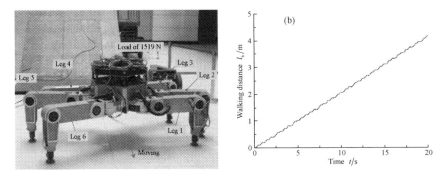

Fig. 6. Experiment of walking speed $2v_{max}/5$ under load of 1519 N: (a) experiment of walking speed $2v_{max}/5$ of prototype; and (b) cure of walking speed for robot body.

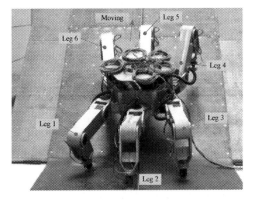

Fig. 7. Climbing experiment of fault-tolerant gait for large-load-ratio six-legged robot.

7   Conclusions

In this article, the autonomous fault-tolerant gait strategies are presented for an electrically driven large-load-ratio six-legged robot. The body structure of robot is designed as the regular polygon to make the robot maintain the characteristics of universal walking. The six legs are evenly distributed around the robot body. The conventional gaits and walking ways are designed based on the configuration of robot. The typical walking ways are obtained. The D-H model of leg i is established. The kinematics analyses are implemented. The mathematical expressions of the rotation angles are respectively gained for the abductor joint, hip joint, and knee joint.

The initial lift height of leg is brought into the autonomous fault-tolerant gait planning. The mathematical models of the foot trajectories are respectively established. The prototype of electrically driven large-load-ratio six-legged robot is developed. The experiments of robot are implemented. The experimental results show that the autonomous fault-tolerant gait strategies are reasonable and can be conducive to reducing the impact force and energy dissipation of robot mobile system. The proposed autonomous fault-tolerant gait strategies can provide a reference for the large-load-ratio multi-legged robots.

Acknowledgments. This work was supported by the National Natural Science Foundation of China (Grant No. 51505335) and the Doctor Startup Projects of TUTE (Grant No. KYQD 1903, KYQD 1806).

References

1. Playter, R., Buehler, M., Raibert, M., Boston Dynamics: BigDog. In: International Society for Optical Engineering, Bellingham, USA, pp. 1–6 (2006)
2. Irawan, A., Nonami, K.: Optimal impedance control based on body inertia for a hydraulically driven hexapod robot walking on uneven and extremely soft terrain. J. Field Robot. **28**, 690–713 (2011)
3. SunSpiral, V., Wheeler, D.W., Chavez-Clemente, D., Mittman, D.: Development and field testing of the footfall planning system for the ATHLETE robots. J. Field Robot. **29**, 483–505 (2012)
4. Ishikawa, T., Makino, K., Imani, J., Ohyama, Y.: Gait motion planning for a six legged robot based on the associatron. J. Adv. Comput. Intell. Intell. Inf. **18**, 135–139 (2014)
5. Estremera, J., Cobano, J.A., de Gonzalez Santos, P.: Continuous free–crab gaits for hexapod robots on a natural terrain with forbidden zones: an application to humanitarian demining. Robot. Auton. Syst. **58**, 700–711 (2010)
6. Satzinger, B.W., Lau, C., Byl, M., Byl, K.: Tractable locomotion planning for RoboSimian. Int. J. Robot. Res. **34**, 1541–1558 (2015)
7. Tedeschi, F., Carbone, G.: Hexapod walking robot locomotion. In: Carbone, G., Gomez-Bravo, F. (eds.) Motion and Operation Planning of Robotic Systems. MMS, vol. 29, pp. 439–468. Springer, Cham (2015). https://doi.org/10.1007/978-3-319-14705-5_15. (1st edn.)

8. Tedeschi, F., Carbone, G.: Design of hexapod walking robots: background and challenges. In: Handbook of Research on Advancements in Robotics and Mechatronics, 1st edn. Idea Group: Hershey, USA (2014)
9. Sadati, N., Dumont, G.A., Hamed, K.A., Gruver, W.A.: Hybrid Control and Motion Planning of Dynamical Legged Locomotion, 1st edn. Wiley-IEEE Press, Hoboken (2012)
10. Zhuang, H.C., Gao, H.B., Deng, Z.Q., Ding, L., Liu, Z.: Method for analyzing articulated rotating speeds of heavy-duty six-legged robot. J. Mech. Eng. **49**, 44–52 (2013)
11. Zhuang, H.C., Wang, N., Gao, H.B., Deng, Z.Q.: Quickly obtaining range of articulated rotating speed for electrically driven large-load-ratio six-legged robot based on maximum walking speed method. IEEE Access **7**, 29453–29470 (2019)
12. Zhuang, H.C., Gao, H.B., Deng, Z.Q., Ding, L., Liu, Z.: A review of heavy-duty legged robots. Sci. China Technol. Sci. **57**, 298–314 (2014)
13. Zhuang, H.C., Gao, H.B., Deng, Z.Q.: Analysis method of articulated torque of heavy-duty six-legged robot under its quadrangular gait. Appl. Sci. **6**, 1–21 (2016)
14. Lin, B.S., Song, S.M.: Dynamic modeling, stability, and energy efficiency of a quadrupedal walking machine. J. Robot. Syst. **18**, 657–670 (2001)

Long-Term Real-Time Correlation Filter Tracker for Mobile Robot

Shaoze You[1,2], Hua Zhu[1,2(✉)], Menggang Li[1,2], Lei Wang[1,2], and Chaoquan Tang[1,2]

[1] School of Mechanical and Electrical Engineering,
China University of Mining and Technology, Xuzhou 221116, China
zhuhua83591917@163.com
[2] Jiangsu Collaborative Innovation Center of Intelligent Mining Equipment,
China University of Mining and Technology, Xuzhou 221008, China

Abstract. Computer vision has received a significant attention in recent years, which is one of the important parts for robots to apperceive external environment. Discriminative Correlation Filter (DCF) based trackers gained more popularity due to their efficiency, however, most of the-state-of-the-art trackers are effective for short-term tracking, not yet successfully addressed in long-term scene. In this work, we tackle the problems by introducing Long-term Real-time Correlation Filter (LRCF) tracker. First, fused features only including HOG and Color Names are employed to boost the tracking efficiency. Second, we used the standard principal component analysis (PCA) to reduction scheme in the translation and scale estimation phase for accelerating. Third, we learned a long-term correlation filter to keep the long-term memory ability. Finally, we update the filter with interval updates. The extensive experiments on popular Object Tracking Benchmark OTB-2013 datasets have demonstrated that the proposed tracker outperforms the state-of-the-art trackers significantly achieves a high real-time (33FPS) performance in our mobile robot hardware. The experimental results show that the novel tracker performance is better than the-state-of-the-art trackers.

Keywords: Object tracking · Correlation filter · Long-term tracking · Robot

1 Introduction

Visual Object Tracking (VOT) is one of the most important fundamental problems in computer vision, which also plays an important role in real-time vision applications such as intelligent monitoring system, automatic driving, robotics and so on [1–3]. The target is to select the target from the first frame and track it in the subsequent frame by inputting the video frame or real-time image.

In recent years, Discriminative Correlation Filter (DCF) based methods have significantly advanced the state-of-the-art in short-term tracking. Such as MOSSE [4], KCF [5], CSR-DCF [6], BACF [7] and ECO [8] performed good effective for short tracking. Due to the online nature of tracking and in practical applications, an ideal tracker should be accurate and robust under a longer period of time and real-time vision

© Springer Nature Switzerland AG 2019
H. Yu et al. (Eds.): ICIRA 2019, LNAI 11740, pp. 245–255, 2019.
https://doi.org/10.1007/978-3-030-27526-6_22

systems. Moreover, because the complexity of environment, such as appearance deformation object occlusion, illumination change, motion blur and out of view are encountered, the performance of trackers is limited, which can cause the tracker to drift easily in the long-term tracking.

Mobile robot is one of the research hotspots in science and technology in recent years. The path planning, positioning and navigation, obstacle avoidance and other aspects of mobile robot are inseparable from the help of vision [9–11]. Owing to the mobile robot is limited by the endurance, volume and flexibility of the mobile robot. The hardware configuration of the robot is usually based on the low power consumption, so the algorithm of running the large amount of computation can seriously affect the real-time performance of the robot.

Hence, we propose to learn Long-term Real-time Correlation Tracker (LRCT) for long-term object tracking. Our method can learning/update filters from real negative examples densely extracted from the back-ground. The SVM classifier is used as a heavy detector to obtain the possibility of long-term tracking, which has better tracking accuracy and robust performance. Finally, using a new update strategy for filters to further improve the speed of the algorithm.

The paper is organized as follows. Section 2 discusses previous work related to our tracking framework. We introduce the classical DCF tracking formulation and our approach in Sect. 3. The experimental results are analyzed and discussed in Sect. 4. Conclusion is given in Sect. 5.

2 Related Work

In this section, we describe the recent achievements related to our work. For a comprehensive overview of existing tracking methods, readers can refer to the following surveys and evaluations.

Tracking-by-Detection. The tracking detection method regards the target tracking in each frame as a detection problem in a local search window and usually separates the target from its surrounding background by an incremental learning classifier [12, 13]. In this work every frame is regarded as once target detection process, which is the most commonly used method in visual object tracking.

Correlation Filters Tracker. In 2011, Bolme et al. learned the MOSSE [4] filter to tracking with an impressive speed of more than 600 Frames Per Second (FPS) and shows the potential of correlation filter. Discriminant correlation filter-based (DCF-based) trackers have emerged in endlessly. Numerous improved DCF-based trackers [4–8] have been proposed with more precise and robust tracking performance by sacrificing the tracking speed. By using the property of fast Fourier transform (FFT) and inverse fast Fourier transform (IFFT), the DCF-based tracker reduces a lot of computing time by means of correlation operation on image features.

CNN-Based Tracker. In recent years, Deep Learning (DL) has been widely concerned. As a representative architecture, Convolutional Neural Network (CNN) has achieved remarkable results in visual tracking with its powerful feature expression ability [14–16]. They can get a surprising high-precision result with the support of the graphics card, but its huge amount of computation limits its development on mobile devices.

Long-Term Tracker. Long-term tracking is different from short-term tracking, which has long-term occlusion and field-of-view situations. In order to solve the problem of long-term tracking, Zdenek et al. proposed the tracking framework TLD [17] and decomposed the long-term tracking task into three parts: tracking, learning and detection. After the correlation filter-based tracker has become a hotspot, Ma et al. proposed LCT [18] and LCT+ [19] which added re-detector and long-time memory templates to the short-term tracker. Zhu et al. proposed a novel collaborative correlation tracker (CCT) [20] using Multi-scale Kernelized the Correlation Tracking (MKC) and Online CUR Filter for long-term tracking.

3 Our Approach

3.1 Discriminative Correlation Filter

In this section, we adopt the fast Discriminative Scale Space Tracker (fast DSST) tracker proposed in [21] as our baseline due to its outstanding performance in VOT. It learns two independent correlation filters for target translation locating (2-dimensional) and scale estimation (1-dimensional) in a new frame. For translation estimation, given a new frame size of W $\times$ H, the goal is to learn a multi-channel correlation filter $f_t \in \mathbb{R}^{W \times H \times D}$ based on the sample sets $\{(x_t, y_t)\}_{t=1}^{l}$. Where $x_t \in \mathbb{R}^{W \times H \times D}$ represents the feature extracted from the sample of t-th frame, and the $l \in \{1, \ldots, D\}$ is defined as the feature layer of $\{\cdot\}_t^l$. The joint desired output $y_t \in \mathbb{R}^{M \times N}$ is a scalar value function, which is used to evaluate the correlation between samples and targets. This is achieved by the ridge regression formula which minimizes the correlation response of the correlation filter f^l.

$$\varepsilon(f) = \left\| \sum_{l=1}^{D} x_t^l \circledast f^l - y_t \right\|_2^2 + \lambda \sum_{l=1}^{D} \left\| f^l \right\|^2. \tag{1}$$

where $\circledast$ donates circular convolution and λ is a regularization weight. The response label y_t is usually expressed by Gaussian function. Equation 1 is a linear least squares problem, which can be quickly solved by transforming Parseval formula into Fourier domain. Therefore, the filter that minimizes (1) is given by

$$\varepsilon(F) = \left\| \sum_{l=1}^{D} \overline{X^l} \odot F^l - Y \right\|_2^2 + \lambda \sum_{l=1}^{D} \left\| F^l \right\|^2. \tag{2}$$

Here, the capital letters denote the discrete Fourier transform (DFT) of the corresponding quantities. The bar $\overline{\bullet}$ denotes complex conjugation. The $\odot$ donate Hadamard product. So, in first frame we can solution Eq. 2 to

$$F^l = \frac{\bar{Y} \odot X^l}{\sum_{k=1}^{D} \bar{X}^k \odot X^k + \lambda}, l = 1, \ldots, D. \tag{3}$$

Then define the numerator A_t^l and the denominator B_t for the t-th frame. An optimal update strategy for the filter F_t^l to new sample x_t as follows

$$A_t^l = (1 - \eta)A_{t-1}^l + \eta\bar{Y} \odot X_t^l. \tag{4}$$

$$B_t = (1 - \eta)B_{t-1} + \eta \sum_{k=1}^{D} \bar{X}_t^k \odot X_t^k. \tag{5}$$

where η denotes the learning rate. To detect the variations of position in a new frame t, the correlation scores y_t for a new test sample z_t can be computed in the Fourier domain

$$y_t = \mathcal{F}^{-1}\left\{\frac{\sum_{l=1}^{D} \bar{A}_{t-1}^l \odot Z^l}{B_{t-1} + \lambda}\right\}. \tag{6}$$

where Z^l denotes the l-dimensional features extracted from the frame of pending detection. $\mathcal{F}^{-1}$ is the Inverse Fast Fourier Transform (IFFT). Equation 6 determines the current position of the target by finding the maximum correlation score.

In order to estimate the scale, we construct the image feature pyramid of the current sample in a rectangular area and learn the scale filer $S = \{\alpha^n | \lfloor -\frac{N-1}{2} \rfloor, \ldots, \lfloor \frac{N-1}{2} \rfloor \}$. The current target region with a size of $W \times H$ is reconstructed to form a series scale patch I_n of size $\alpha^n W \times \alpha^n H$ based on N scale levels. The scale filter with a 1-dimensional Gaussian score y_s. The max value $S_t(n)$ of the training sample $x_{t,scale}$ for I_n is the current scale.

Principal component analysis (PCA) dimensionality reduction is a frequently used acceleration method in engineering applications. In our approach, the computing speed of FFT can be improved effectively by reducing the dimension of the extracted target features. Construction of projection matrix $P_t \in \mathbb{R}^{d \times D}$ for μ_t based on updating formula of target template $\mu_t = (1 - \eta)\mu_{t-1} + \eta x_t$, d is the dimension of the compressed feature. The current test sample z_t via the compressed training sample $\mathcal{X}_t = \mathcal{F}\{P_{t-1}x_t\}$ can be obtained by Eq. 7

$$y_t = \mathcal{F}^{-1}\left\{\frac{\sum_{l=1}^{d} \bar{\mathcal{A}}_{t-1}^l \odot \mathcal{Z}_t^l}{\mathcal{B}_{t-1} + \lambda}\right\}. \tag{7}$$

where $\mathcal{Z}_t = \mathcal{F}\{P_{t-1}z_t\}$ is the new compressed sample, the $\bar{\mathcal{A}}_{t-1}^l$ and the $\mathcal{B}_{t-1}$ are the updated numerator and denominator of the template after feature compression, respectively. Note that the projection matrix P_t is not calculated explicitly, it can be quickly obtained by the QR-decomposition.

3.2   Long-Term Memory

In practical applications, trackers often work for a long time, during this period, out of view and occlusion have been the main problems in long-term tracking, because when the target disappears, the reappearance of the position is often not the vanishing position. So, the tracker needs to re-detect the location of the target, and it also needs to store memories of the historical appearance of the target to prevent the trace from failing.

In order to avoid the tracking failure caused by the noise pollution of the model in the long-term tracking, we have been inspired by the work of LCT [18], learned a long-term filter f_{Long}. Unlike the LCT, we do not use the kernel trick [5] for f_{Long} to calculate the response score R (Eq. 8), we use a DSST-like approach to directly calculate the correlation response between the test sample $x_{t,Long}$ and the filter f_{Long}. The re-detection module is an important part of improving the robustness and long-term tracking ability of the tracker. It is used to find the target quickly after the target is lost. The online SVM classifier is used as the detector and it only training the translated samples.

$$R(z) = \mathcal{F}^{-1}\left\{ \bar{K}^{\bar{x}z} \odot \frac{\bar{Y}}{\bar{K}^{xx'} + \lambda} \right\}. \tag{8}$$

where the K is defined as the Fourier transform of Gauss kernel correlation matrix $\mathbf{k}$, which general form is as follows,

$$\mathbf{k}^{xx'} = \exp\left\{ -\frac{\|x\|^2 + \|x'\|^2}{\sigma^2} - 2\mathcal{F}^{-1}\left(\sum_{l=1}^{d} X_l \odot \bar{X}'_l \right) \right\}. \tag{9}$$

3.3   Confidence Function and Update Strategy

Tracking confidence parameter is an important index for judging whether the target is lost or not. Most CF-based trackers use maximum response $R_{\max}$ to locate the target in the next frame, but in a complex scene only in this way the treatment effect is not ideal. Wang et al. proposed LMCF [22] with Average Peak-to-Correlation Energy (APCE, 9), which can effectively deal with the target occlusion and loss. Zhang et al. proposed a tracker MACF [23] based on Confidence of Squared Response Map (CSRM, 10).

$$APCE = \frac{|R_{max} - R_{min}|^2}{mean\left(\sum_{w,h} \left(R_{w,h} - R_{min} \right)^2 \right)} \tag{10}$$

$$CSRM = \frac{|R_{max}^2 - R_{min}^2|^2}{mean\left(\sum_{w,h} \left(R_{w,h}^2 - R_{min}^2 \right)^2 \right)} \tag{11}$$

where the R_{max}, R_{min} and $R_{w,h}$ are denote the maximum, the minimum, the w-th row h-th column elements of the peak value of the response respectively. In order to determine whether the combination of multiple confidence parameters will improve the performance of the tracker, we conducted a comparative experiment in Sect. 4. The flow chart of our method is shown on Fig. 1.

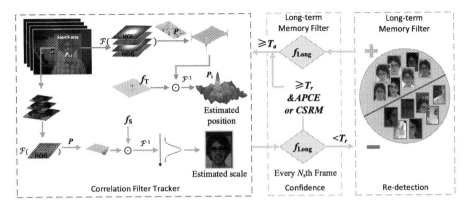

Fig. 1. The flow chart of our method. We applied the projection matrix P to the LCT [18] architecture to reduce the amount of computation.

In the DCF-based tracker, the general practice is to train a sample and filter at each frame and update it, so that the iterative search can be done very well, but because the optimization calculation of the filter is the core calculation step in the whole algorithm. Update filter in each frame has a serious impact on the computing load. In order to improve the computational efficiency, we adopt an ECO-like [8] method to reduce the computational complexity by updating the filter template in every N_Sth frame. It can not only improve the running speed, but also effectively prevent over-fitting. Similar to ECO, we update the target sample in each frame.

4   Experimental

4.1   Implementation Details

We implement our LRCF in MATLAB 2016b on our mobile robot, the Industrial Personal Computer (IPC) with Intel i7 3.70 GHz CPU and Nvidia GeForce GTX 1080 GPU (But we didn't need GPU in practice, so we removed it during the experiment). In order to improve the real-time performance of the operation, we have not applied the CNN feature, and only used the Hand-Craft features (HOG and Color Names). The dataset adopted to evaluate our method is Online Tracking Benchmark (OTB) [24], which is an authoritative dataset that compares with other state-of-the-art trackers. It contains 50 sequences with many challenging attributes.

We set the regularization parameter to $\lambda = 0.01$ and the learning rate to $\eta = 0.025$. The standard deviation of the Gaussian function output y is set to 1/16 of the translation target size. The padding of filter is set to two times size of the initial target size. The scale filters interpolate from $N = 17$ scales to $N^* = 33$ scales by interpolation and the scale factor of $a = 1.02$. We set the re-detection threshold $T_r = 0.2$ for the activation detection module and $T_a = 0.4$ for the detection result. Note that the threshold setting here is only the corresponding fraction of the long-term filter f_{Long}. The confidence parameters of response of LCT are set to two types, 0.9 times the maximum response and 0.75 times the APCE (or CSRM), respectively. Update the long-term memory template when both parameters of it exceed the set threshold.

4.2   Update Strategy Comparison

We set up the update gap $N_S = 1, 3, 5$ and compared the performance AUC with the running speed. The experimental results are shown in Table 1 and Fig. 2, we found that it is best to update filter when $N_S = 3$, but the running speed will be significantly improved when $N_S = 5$.

Table 1. Update strategy comparison

N_S	AUC	FPS
1 (per frame)	58.6	29.5
3	61.3	32.8
5	60.6	37.5
Fast DSST	60.0	173

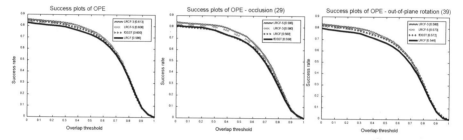

Fig. 2. OTB-2013 benchmark test for interval update strategy. The effect is obviously improved after adding long-term memory filter. In occlusion environment, the performance is not as good as $N_S = 5$ when $N_S = 3$, presumably because of occlusion time, occlusion object is trained as a sample.

4.3   Overall Performance

We evaluate our method with trackers in [7] and other trackers including the baseline trackers TLD [17], LCT [18] and fast DSST [21] et al. Figure 3 shows the comparison of our method with the baseline. Through comparison, we can find that our method is superior in experiment. Our method outperforms the baseline tracker (fast DSST) with 1.0% in TRE success rate and 0.7% in TRE precision. Our method has an average running speed of 33 FPS ($N_S = 3$) which can run in real time.

Figure 4 shows the superiority of our method in difficult tracking scenarios such as low resolution, fast motion, scale variation and occlusion. Compared with fast DSST, our method is improved by 12.3%, 2.0%, 1.4% and 6.6% on distance precision, respectively. And we found that using multiple confidence parameters in filter updates can lead to performance degradation.

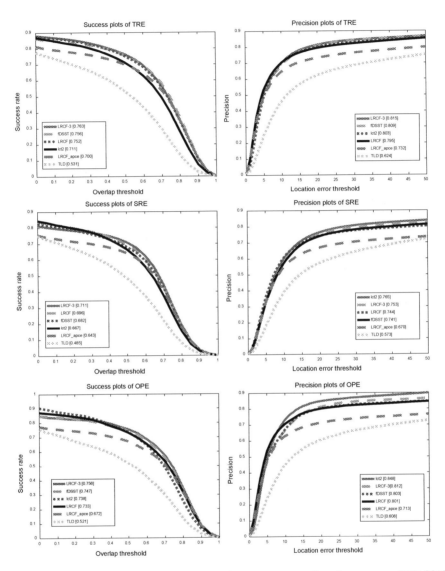

Fig. 3. Distance precision and overlap success plots average overall performance on OTB-2013 dataset. One pass evaluation (OPE), Spatial robustness evaluation (SRE), and Temporal robustness evaluation (TRE) are shown in this figure. OPE refers to the success threshold of calculating the proportion of successful tracking frames in the total video frames in the evaluation dataset. SRE and TRE refers to the success threshold of calculating the proportion of successful tracking frames in the total video frames after 20 different sampling areas (deviation around the target).

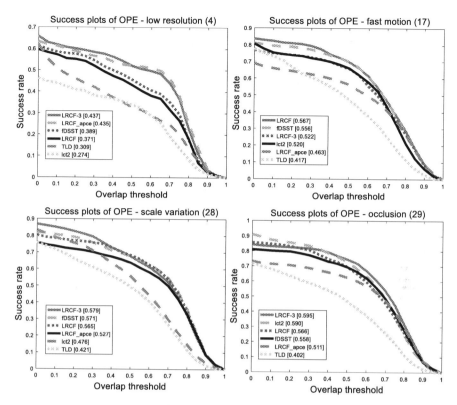

Fig. 4. The comparison results about our method and baseline in different types of challenges under. The area-under-the-curve (AUC) score for each tracker is reported in the legend.

5 Conclusions

In this paper, we propose an effective tracker LRCF for long-term Real-time visual tracking based fast DSST framework. We improved fast DSST from two aspects: long-term tracking and updating strategy. We also carried out experiments on the use of confidence parameters which concluded that careful use of confidence parameters has a great impact on the performance of the tracker. Finally, we compare our tracker with the baseline tracker. The experimental results show that LRCF has good robustness and effectiveness for the benchmark.

Acknowledgments. This work has been supported by grant of the National Key Research and Development Program of China (No. 2018YFC0808000) and the Priority Academic Program Development of Jiangsu Higher Education Institutions (PAPD), China.

References

1. Yilmaz, A., Javed, O., Shah, M.: Object tracking: a survey. ACM Comput. Surv. (CSUR) **38**(4), 13 (2006)
2. Li, X., Hu, W., Shen, C., et al.: A survey of appearance models in visual object tracking. ACM Trans. Intell. Syst. Technol. (TIST) **4**(4), 58 (2013)
3. Xu, K., Chia, K.W., Cheok, A.D.: Real-time camera tracking for marker-less and unprepared augmented reality environments. Image Vis. Comput. **26**(5), 673–689 (2008)
4. Bolme, D.S., Beveridge, J.R., Draper, B.A., et al.: Visual object tracking using adaptive correlation filters. In: 2010 IEEE Computer Society Conference on Computer Vision and Pattern Recognition, pp. 2544–2550. IEEE (2010)
5. Henriques, J.F., Caseiro, R., Martins, P., et al.: High-speed tracking with Kernelized correlation filters. IEEE Trans. Pattern Anal. Mach. Intell. **37**(3), 583–596 (2015)
6. Lukezic, A., Vojir, T., Cehovin Zajc, L., et al.: Discriminative correlation filter with channel and spatial reliability. In: Proceedings of the IEEE Conference on Computer Vision and Pattern Recognition, pp. 6309–6318 (2017)
7. Kiani Galoogahi, H., Fagg, A., Lucey, S.: Learning background-aware correlation filters for visual tracking. In: Proceedings of the IEEE International Conference on Computer Vision, pp. 1135–1143 (2017)
8. Danelljan, M., Bhat, G., Shahbaz Khan, F., et al.: ECO: efficient convolution operators for tracking. In: Proceedings of the IEEE Conference on Computer Vision and Pattern Recognition, pp. 6638–6646 (2017)
9. Zhang, M., Liu, X., Xu, D., et al.: Vision-based target-following guider for mobile robot. IEEE Trans. Ind. Electron. **PP**(99), 1 (2019)
10. Bedaka, A.K., Vidal, J., Lin, C.Y.: Automatic robot path integration using three-dimensional vision and offline programming. Int. J. Adv. Manuf. Technol. **8**, 1–16 (2019)
11. Wang, X.: Autonomous mobile robot visual SLAM based on improved CNN method. In: IOP Conference Series Materials Science and Engineering, vol. 466, p. 012114 (2018)
12. Henriques, J.F., Caseiro, R., Martins, P., Batista, J.: Exploiting the circulant structure of tracking-by-detection with Kernels. In: Fitzgibbon, A., Lazebnik, S., Perona, P., Sato, Y., Schmid, C. (eds.) ECCV 2012. LNCS, vol. 7575, pp. 702–715. Springer, Heidelberg (2012). https://doi.org/10.1007/978-3-642-33765-9_50
13. Danelljan, M., Khan, F.S., Felsberg, M., et al.: Adaptive color attributes for real-time visual tracking. In: 2014 IEEE Conference on Computer Vision and Pattern Recognition. IEEE (2014)
14. Zhang, Z., Xie, Y., Xing, F., et al.: MDNet: a semantically and visually interpretable medical image diagnosis network (2017)
15. Bertinetto, L., Valmadre, J., Henriques, J.F., Vedaldi, A., Torr, P.H.S.: Fully-convolutional siamese networks for object tracking. In: Hua, G., Jégou, H. (eds.) ECCV 2016. LNCS, vol. 9914, pp. 850–865. Springer, Cham (2016). https://doi.org/10.1007/978-3-319-48881-3_56
16. Valmadre, J., Bertinetto, L., Henriques, J., et al.: End-to-end representation learning for correlation filter based tracking. In: Proceedings of the IEEE Conference on Computer Vision and Pattern Recognition, pp. 2805–2813 (2017)
17. Kalal, Z., Mikolajczyk, K., Matas, J.: Tracking-learning-detection. IEEE Trans. Pattern Anal. Mach. Intell. **34**(7), 1409–1422 (2012)
18. Ma, C., Yang, X., Zhang, C., et al.: Long-term correlation tracking. In: Proceedings of the IEEE Conference on Computer Vision and Pattern Recognition, pp. 5388–5396 (2015)
19. Ma, C., Huang, J.B., Yang, X.: Adaptive correlation filters with long-term and short-term memory for object tracking. Int. J. Comput. Vis. **126**(8), 771–796 (2018)

20. Zhu, G., Wang, J., Wu, Y., et al.: Collaborative correlation tracking (2015)
21. Danelljan, M., Häger, G., Khan, F.S.: Discriminative scale space tracking. IEEE Trans. Pattern Anal. Mach. Intell. **39**(8), 1561–1575 (2017)
22. Wang, M., Liu, Y., Huang, Z.: Large margin object tracking with circulant feature maps. In: Proceedings of the IEEE Conference on Computer Vision and Pattern Recognition, pp. 4021–4029 (2017)
23. Zhang, Y., Yang, Y., Zhou, W.: Motion-aware correlation filters for online visual tracking. Sensors **18**(11), 3937 (2018)
24. Wu, Y., Lim, J., Yang, M.H.: Online object tracking: a benchmark. In: Proceedings of the IEEE Conference on Computer Vision and Pattern Recognition, pp. 2411–2418 (2013)

IMU-Aided Ultra-wideband Based Localization for Coal Mine Robots

Meng-gang Li[1,2], Hua Zhu[1,2(✉)], Shao-ze You[1,2], Lei Wang[1,2], Zheng Zhang[1,2], and Chao-quan Tang[1,2]

[1] School of Mechanical and Electrical Engineering, China University of Mining and Technology, Xuzhou 221116, Jiangsu, China
zhuhua83591917@163.com
[2] Jiangsu Collaborative Innovation Center of Intelligent Mining Equipment, China University of Mining and Technology, Xuzhou 221008, Jiangsu, China

Abstract. Robotic mining equipment is playing an increasingly important role in coal mine operations. Due to the complexity of underground occlusion environment, the localization methods available are limited, which restricts the development of coal mine robots (CMRs). Ultra Wideband (UWB) is a promising positioning sensor with accurate ranging capacity, but it needs to overcome the transient signal loss caused by multipath effect and metal block in coal mine. Range measurements from UWB can only provide 3 degrees of freedom (DOF) position without orientation, which is not enough to operation for CMRs under space-constrained coal mine. In this paper, a pseudo-GPS positioning system composed by UWB range measurements is proposed to provide the position of CMRs. Additionally, an Error State Kalman Filter (ESKF) is used for fusing measurements from Inertial Measurement Unit (IMU) and UWB positioning system. The complete 6 DOF state estimation is established, and the biases of IMU and the calibration parameters of IMU w.r.t. the UWB mobile node are also estimated online to accommodate the long-term operation in underground harsh environment. Experiments in different motion conditions show that our approach can provide robust and precise 6 DOF state estimation for CMRs.

Keywords: UWB · IMU · EKF · ESKF · State estimation

1 Introduction

The robotization of coal mine equipment is conducive to reducing the labor intensity and danger of workers, at the same time improving production efficiency [1]. Tracked and wheeled mobile vehicles are widely used in excavation, mining, transportation, security control and rescue in coal mine. Accurate localization is the basis for the intelligent realization of these equipment. Unlike terrestrial and space robots, the working conditions of CMRs are extremely complicated. Ground mining vehicles use RTK-GPS technology [2] to achieve high-precision positioning, but this method can't be used in the downhole where is GPS-denied. VICON [3] is often used in high-precision positioning for indoor robots, but the price is expensive and not suitable for

© Springer Nature Switzerland AG 2019
H. Yu et al. (Eds.): ICIRA 2019, LNAI 11740, pp. 256–268, 2019.
https://doi.org/10.1007/978-3-030-27526-6_23

dim and damp scenes. The research of visual [4] and laser [5] SLAM is a striking field, but the robustness and accuracy still need to be further improved in degraded scene and low illumination with less structure environment of downhole.

The positioning technology is mainly applied to the shearer [6] and Load Haul Dump (LHD) [7] in underground coal mine. High-precision inertial sensors, RFID [8] and Zigbee [9], WiFi-based wireless network [10] are commonly used in underground mine. Compared with them, UWB has the advantages of low power consumption, high measurement accuracy, strong robustness for multipath effect and NLOS environment. These make it be the most promising sensor that can be widely used to build communication and location network in underground coal mine [11].

Conventional wireless sensor networks need to receive four non-coplanar distance observations at the same time to obtain a unique position in 3D space without orientation. Strict time synchronization and signal loss induce such location networks fragile, especially when distance observations contain a lot of noise due to multipath and NLOS effects. In this paper, a downhole pseudo-GPS system is constructed by UWB based on Two-Way TOF (TW-TOF). Considering the motion model of CMRs, the noisy range measurements from available UWB anchors are used to update the EKF to achieve position estimation. Furthermore, the IMU is used to provide short-term high-precision state propagation, combining with UWB positioning results for correction to achieve 6DOF pose estimation under the loose coupling framework. The IMU biases and calibration parameters of IMU w.r.t. the mobile UWB node are also estimated online, which are essential for long-term underground operations with harsh conditions. The recommended method enables robust pose estimation for CMRs even in the circumstance of signal loss and uneven terrain.

2 Preliminaries

2.1 Coordinate Systems

The choice of navigation reference system is an important issue, especially when using multiple sensors for data fusion. Figure 1 shows a possible coordinate established in a tunnel-link laneway. Professional surveying instruments such as an electronic total station can determine the spatial location of UWB anchors, based on the original control points in the laneway. The UWB positioning system is then established as the navigation frame (n), which is based on the UWB anchors and aligned with gravity direction (g). The estimated state of the proposed algorithms are relative to this frame. The body frame of the robot is fixed to the IMU (Fig. 1), its xb axis is aligned to the robot's longitudinal axis, and its zb axis is perpendicular to the robot's body. The mobile UWB node coordinate frame is constructed on the position of the mobile UWB node which is aligned with the body coordinate frame. There is an extrinsic sensor transformation between the IMU and mobile UWB node. The East-North-Up (ENU) coordinate is recommended as the navigation coordinate system (n) because it is convenient to use the magnetometer to achieve initial rough alignment between the CMR and the UWB positioning system. As illustrated in Fig. 1, four non-coplanar anchors are required in the system initialization area. Aside from installation convenience and remaining within the line of sight between adjacent nodes, there are no special requirements for anchors installed in other parts of the laneway. The optimal deployment of anchors in the laneway is discussed further in Sect. 3C.

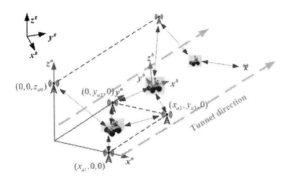

Fig. 1. Coordinate frames definition: earth gravity vector aligned inertial frame (g), the body frame (b), and the UWB anchor coordinate (n). A possible initial configuration of anchors is shown: ID0 $(0, 0, z_{a0})$, ID1 $(x_{a1}, 0, 0)$, ID2 $(0, y_{a2}, 0)$, ID3 $(x_{a3}, y_{a3}, 0)$.

2.2   UWB Range Measurements

UWB signals have good penetration capacity for ordinary walls and fragmentary occlusion, which result in good resistance to multipath effects compared to other shortwave signals. Because TOA, TDOA et al. require strict time alignment between station-station and station-mobile node, it is not conducive to the rapid establishment of the system. So we use the TW-TOF principle for range measurement, which only need time alignment between station and mobile node. The P440 module which we use can achieve the accuracy of time synchronization in picosecond, so it can be assumed that the time of the requester and responder is strictly synchronized.

Figure 2 shows the principle of TW-TOF range measurements. The time interval between signal sending t_i^{Tx} and receiving t_i^{Rx} is composed of transmission time f and anchor's delay δ.

$$f = (t_i^{Tx} - t_i^{Rx} - \delta)/2 \tag{1}$$

Formula 2 is the range measurements, where c is the propagation speed of light:

$$d = f \cdot c \tag{2}$$

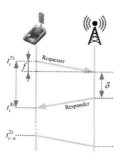

Fig. 2. Timestamp and TW-ToF range measurement between mobile node and anchor node

UWB ranging accuracy will be affected by many factors such as antenna installation method, temperature, obstacle type around and so on. The downhole environment is very complex. The interference of metal equipment and the occlusion in the laneway lead to signal loss especially under NLOS scenes. The values of UWB observation need to be calibrated in practical application [12].

2.3   System Architecture

The workflow of the system is shown in Fig. 3. The system starts by the initialization operation to determine the initial value of the state estimator. A trilateration process will be conducted first within the signal coverage of four non-coplanar anchors to determine initial position in 3D space. The orientation of the robot can be obtained by a magnetometer or manually specified to realize initial alignment. The initial value above have a great impact on the convergence performance for ESKF process.

The motion model of CMR in 3D space is established to propagate the state, which is then updated by the range measurements after outlier detection. Consequently the initial position and velocity estimation of the robot are obtained by the EKF process in the first stage, which can provide position measurements acting as a pseudo-GPS system. Based on the ESKF framework, the measurement of the IMU and the position output by the UWB positioning System are integrated to achieve the complete 6-DOF state estimation, as well as the online calibration of the biases of IMU and the calibration parameters of IMU w.r.t. the UWB mobile node.

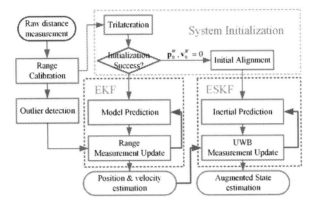

Fig. 3. System workflow.

3   UWB Positioning System

The function of the UWB positioning system is to replace the GPS system in underground environment and provide positioning for the CMRs under the navigation reference system.

3.1   Trilateration

There have different trilateration approach in the literature. Traditional triangulation directly calculates three sets of distance differences without redundant information [13]. Compared with their method, we construct a loss function to determine the best fitting set of $\mathbf{x} = [x, y, z]^T$:

$$f_{loss}(\mathbf{x}) = \min \sum_{n=1}^{N} \sum_{i=1}^{4} \{ d_{a_i}^n - \sqrt{(x - x_{a_i}^n)^2 + (y - y_{a_i}^n)^2 + (z - z_{a_i}^n)^2} \}^2 \tag{3}$$

Using a gradient descent approach like Gauss Newton in Ceres [14], the suitable set can be found quickly by iteratively with good initial values. Because in the initial stage the robot stay still, the asynchronous measurements retrieved in a cyclic fashion from the available anchors can be directly used to trilateration, generating accurate position estimates.

3.2   UWB Localization Based on EKF

The UWB mobile node is attached on the robot, whose position $\mathbf{p} = (p_x, p_y, p_z)^T$ and velocity $\mathbf{v} = (v_x, v_y, v_z)^T$ are the state variables to be estimated. Under the navigation coordinate system (Fig. 4), the following motion model can be established using the robot's angular velocity and acceleration information:

$$\begin{cases} \mathbf{p}^n_{k+1} = \mathbf{p}^n_k + \mathbf{v}^n_k \Delta T + \frac{1}{2}\mathbf{a}^n_k(\Delta T)^2 \\ \mathbf{v}^n_{k+1} = \mathbf{v}^n_k + \mathbf{a}^n_k \Delta T \end{cases} \tag{4}$$

where ΔT is the sampling interval between time instant k to $k+1$. The acceleration item $\mathbf{a}^n_k$ is treated as a noise item. The initial alignment and effect of gravity, as well as the biases and so on are carried out directly by assigning a large covariance to realize conservative estimation. The propagation equation of the system state can be obtained:

$$\mathbf{x}_{k+1} = \mathbf{A}_k \mathbf{x}_k + \mathbf{w}_k$$
$$\mathbf{P}_{k+1} = \mathbf{A}_k \mathbf{P}_k \mathbf{A}^T_k + \mathbf{Q}_k \tag{5}$$

The corresponding system matrix $\mathbf{A}_k = \begin{bmatrix} \mathbf{I}_{3\times3} & \Delta T \mathbf{I}_{3\times3} \\ \mathbf{0}_{3\times3} & \mathbf{I}_{3\times3} \end{bmatrix}$ and noise term $\mathbf{w}_k \sim N(0, Q)$ can be obtained. The covariance of noise term $\mathbf{Q}_k$ is generated by random acceleration:

$$\mathbf{Q}_k = E(\mathbf{w}_k \mathbf{w}^T_k) = \begin{pmatrix} \frac{(\Delta T)^4}{4}\mathbf{I}_{3\times3} & \frac{(\Delta T)^3}{2}\mathbf{I}_{3\times3} \\ \frac{(\Delta T)^3}{2}\mathbf{I}_{3\times3} & \Delta T^2 \mathbf{I}_{3\times3} \end{pmatrix} \otimes \begin{pmatrix} \sigma^2_x & & \\ & \sigma^2_y & \\ & & \sigma^2_z \end{pmatrix} \tag{6}$$

where $E(\mathbf{a}_k \mathbf{a}^T_k) = diag(\sigma^2_x, \sigma^2_y, \sigma^2_z)$. σ is the conservative estimate of the maximum acceleration in the corresponding direction.

The position of an UWB anchor denote as $(p_{A_x}, p_{A_y}, p_{A_z})$. The observation equations of UWB is:

$$\mathbf{z} = \sqrt{(p_x - p_{A_x})^2 + (p_y - p_{A_y})^2 + (p_z - p_{A_z})^2} + \mathbf{n}_k \tag{7}$$

The corresponding observation matrix is:

$$\mathbf{H}_{k+1} = \frac{\partial \mathbf{h}(\mathbf{x}_k, 0)}{\partial \mathbf{x}_k}\bigg|_{\mathbf{x}=\mathbf{x}_{k+1}} = \begin{bmatrix} \frac{p_{x_{k+1}} - p_{A_x}}{d_{k+1}} & 0 & \frac{p_{y_{k+1}} - p_{A_y}}{d_{k+1}} & 0 & \frac{p_{z_{k+1}} - p_{A_z}}{d_{k+1}} & 0 \end{bmatrix} \tag{8}$$

The complete EKF process of UWB positioning system is shown in Table 1. Note that the step 6 is used to detect outlier by calculating Mahalanobis distance and compared with a predefined threshold which comes from the measurements calibration in Sect. 2.2.

Table 1. The principle UWB positioning system

Algorithm1: EKF-based Pose Estimation
0   **Input**: $(\mathbf{p}_0, \mathbf{v}_0)$
1   **Output**: $(\mathbf{p}, \mathbf{v})$
2   while (new UWB range)
3     $\hat{\mathbf{x}}_{k+1} = \mathbf{A}_k \hat{\mathbf{x}}_k$
4     $\hat{\mathbf{P}}_{k+1} = \mathbf{A}_k \hat{\mathbf{P}}_k \mathbf{A}_k^T + \mathbf{Q}_k$
5     $\mathbf{S}_{k+1} = \mathbf{H}_{k+1} \hat{\mathbf{P}}_{k+1} \mathbf{H}_{k+1}^T + \mathbf{R}$
6   if ($\sqrt{(d_{k+1} - \hat{d}_{k+1})^T \mathbf{S}_{k+1}^{-1}(d_{k+1} - \hat{d}_{k+1})} > Threshold$)
7   return ;
8   else
9        $\mathbf{K}_{k+1} = \hat{\mathbf{P}}_{k+1} \mathbf{H}_{k+1}^T \mathbf{S}_{k+1}^{-1}$
10       $\hat{\mathbf{x}}_{k+1} \leftarrow \hat{\mathbf{x}}_{k+1} + \mathbf{K}_{k+1}[d_{k+1} - \hat{d}_{k+1}]$
11       $\hat{\mathbf{P}}_{k+1} \leftarrow (\mathbf{I} - \mathbf{K}_{k+1} \mathbf{H}_{k+1}) \hat{\mathbf{P}}_{k+1}$
12   end

4 Full State Estimation by ESFK

Although the position and velocity of the CMR can be obtained basing on the UWB positioning system, the attitude estimation cannot be directly obtained. In order to realize accurate and continuous state estimation, we develop an iterative ESKF method based on loose coupling. The state prediction is driven by the observation of the IMU, using UWB positioning system to conduct position updating. Full 6 DOF of state estimation can be realized, as well as the online calibration of the IMU's biases and the transformation parameters of the IMU relative to the UWB mobile node.

4.1 State Propagation

The coordinate system is built with gravity aligned. The IMU accelerometer bias $\boldsymbol{b}_a$ and gyroscope bias $\boldsymbol{b}_w$ are modeled as random walk driven by white noise of $\boldsymbol{n}_w$ and $\boldsymbol{n}_a$. The actual value of linear acceleration $\mathbf{a}$ and angular velocity $\boldsymbol{\omega}$ can be expressed as:

$$\mathbf{a}^W = \mathbf{C}(\bar{\mathbf{q}}_I^W)(\mathbf{a}_m - \mathbf{b}_a - \mathbf{n}_a) - \mathbf{g}^W \tag{9}$$

$$\boldsymbol{\omega} = \boldsymbol{\omega}_m - \mathbf{b}_\omega - \mathbf{n}_\omega \tag{10}$$

Denote nominal state as $\mathbf{x}$ and the error state as $\delta\mathbf{x}$. The error state can be established by

$$\delta\tilde{\mathbf{x}} = \begin{bmatrix} \delta\mathbf{p}^W & \delta\mathbf{v}^W & \delta\boldsymbol{\theta}^W & \delta\mathbf{b}_a & \delta\mathbf{b}_\omega & \delta\mathbf{p}_I^U \end{bmatrix}^T \tag{11}$$

The system's error state dynamics Eq. (12) can be derived from the nominal kinematics:

$$\delta\dot{\mathbf{x}} = \begin{bmatrix} \delta\dot{\mathbf{p}}^W \\ \delta\dot{\mathbf{v}}^W \\ \delta\dot{\boldsymbol{\theta}}^W \\ \delta\dot{\mathbf{b}}_a \\ \delta\dot{\mathbf{b}}_\omega \\ \delta\dot{\mathbf{p}}_I^U \end{bmatrix} = \begin{bmatrix} \delta\mathbf{v}^W \\ -\mathbf{C}(\bar{\mathbf{q}}_I^W)\lfloor \mathbf{a}_m - \hat{\mathbf{b}}_a \rfloor_\times \delta\boldsymbol{\theta} - \mathbf{C}(\bar{\mathbf{q}}_I^W)\delta\mathbf{b}_a - \mathbf{C}(\bar{\mathbf{q}}_I^W)\mathbf{n}_a \\ -\lfloor \boldsymbol{\omega}_m - \mathbf{b}_\omega \rfloor_\times \delta\boldsymbol{\theta} - \delta\mathbf{b}_\omega - \mathbf{n}_\omega \\ \mathbf{n}_{b_a} \\ \mathbf{n}_{b_\omega} \\ \mathbf{0} \end{bmatrix} \tag{12}$$

The above differential equations need to be integrated into a difference equations to apply to discrete time system. There are usually two integration methods: exact closed-form solutions and numerical integration. Euler numerical integration is used to propagate the error state here. The state propagation Eq. (13) and error covariance Eq. (14) can be obtained:

$$\delta\hat{\mathbf{x}} \leftarrow \mathbf{F}_x\delta\hat{\mathbf{x}} + \mathbf{G}_x\mathbf{n} \tag{13}$$

$$\mathbf{P} \leftarrow \mathbf{F}_x\mathbf{P}\mathbf{F}_x^T + \mathbf{G}_x\mathbf{Q}\mathbf{G}_x^T \tag{14}$$

where $\mathbf{n} = [\mathbf{v}_{\mathbf{n}_a}^T, \boldsymbol{\theta}_{\mathbf{n}_\omega}^T, \mathbf{a}_{\mathbf{n}_{b_a}}^T, \boldsymbol{\omega}_{\mathbf{n}_{b_\omega}}^T]$,

$$\mathbf{F}_x = \begin{bmatrix} \mathbf{I} & \mathbf{I}\Delta t & \mathbf{0} & \mathbf{0} & \mathbf{0} & \mathbf{0} \\ \mathbf{0} & \mathbf{I} & -\mathbf{C}(\bar{\mathbf{q}}_I^W)\lfloor \mathbf{a}_m - \hat{\mathbf{b}}_a \rfloor_\times \Delta t & -\mathbf{C}(\bar{\mathbf{q}}_I^W)\Delta t & \mathbf{0} & \mathbf{0} \\ \mathbf{0} & \mathbf{0} & \mathbf{C}(\bar{\mathbf{q}}_I^W)^T\{(\boldsymbol{\omega}_m - \boldsymbol{\omega}_b)\Delta t\} & \mathbf{0} & -\mathbf{I}\Delta t & \mathbf{0} \\ \mathbf{0} & \mathbf{0} & \mathbf{0} & \mathbf{I} & \mathbf{0} & \mathbf{0} \\ \mathbf{0} & \mathbf{0} & \mathbf{0} & \mathbf{0} & \mathbf{I} & \mathbf{0} \\ \mathbf{0} & \mathbf{0} & \mathbf{0} & \mathbf{0} & \mathbf{0} & \mathbf{I} \end{bmatrix}_{18\times18}$$

$$\mathbf{G}_x = \begin{bmatrix} \mathbf{0} & \mathbf{0} & \mathbf{0} & \mathbf{0} \\ \mathbf{I} & \mathbf{0} & \mathbf{0} & \mathbf{0} \\ \mathbf{0} & \mathbf{I} & \mathbf{0} & \mathbf{0} \\ \mathbf{0} & \mathbf{0} & \mathbf{I} & \mathbf{0} \\ \mathbf{0} & \mathbf{0} & \mathbf{0} & \mathbf{I} \\ \mathbf{0} & \mathbf{0} & \mathbf{0} & \mathbf{0} \end{bmatrix}_{18\times12} \qquad \mathbf{Q} = \begin{bmatrix} (\sigma_a\Delta t)^2\mathbf{I} & \mathbf{0} & \mathbf{0} & \mathbf{0} \\ \mathbf{0} & (\sigma_\omega\Delta t)^2\mathbf{I} & \mathbf{0} & \mathbf{0} \\ \mathbf{0} & \mathbf{0} & (\sigma_{b_a}\Delta t)^2\mathbf{I} & \mathbf{0} \\ \mathbf{0} & \mathbf{0} & \mathbf{0} & (\sigma_{b_\omega}\Delta t)^2\mathbf{I} \end{bmatrix}_{12\times12}$$

4.2   Measurements Update

UWB positioning system constructed by EKF in Sect. 3 provides observation updating and corresponding uncertainty covariance. The observation equation obtained by UWB considering both position and velocity is:

$$\mathbf{y} = h(\mathbf{x}) + \mathbf{v} = \begin{bmatrix} \mathbf{p}^W - C(\bar{\mathbf{q}}_I^W)^T \mathbf{p}_U^I \\ C(\bar{\mathbf{q}}_U^I)^T C(\bar{\mathbf{q}}_I^W) v^W + C(\bar{\mathbf{q}}_U^I)^T \left(\lfloor \boldsymbol{\omega} \rfloor_\times \mathbf{p}_U^{I^T} \right) \end{bmatrix} + \mathbf{v} \qquad (15)$$

Here only the position and the corresponding covariance from the UWB positioning system will be used in the updating process. The measurements matrix $\mathbf{H}$ can be calculated by chain rule:

$$\mathbf{H} = \frac{\partial h}{\partial \delta \mathbf{x}}\bigg|_{\mathbf{x}} = \frac{\partial h}{\partial \mathbf{x_x}} \frac{\partial \mathbf{x}}{\partial \delta \mathbf{x_x}} \qquad (16)$$

where

$$\frac{\partial h}{\partial \delta \mathbf{p}} = \mathbf{I}_{3\times3} \quad \frac{\partial h}{\partial \delta \boldsymbol{\theta}} = \frac{\partial h}{\partial \boldsymbol{\theta}} \frac{\partial \boldsymbol{\theta}}{\partial \delta \boldsymbol{\theta}} = -C(\bar{\mathbf{q}}_I^W)^T \lfloor \mathbf{p}_U^I \rfloor_\times \quad \frac{\partial h}{\partial \delta \mathbf{p}_U^I} = \frac{\partial h}{\partial \mathbf{p}_U^I} \frac{\partial \mathbf{p}_U^I}{\partial \delta \mathbf{p}_U^I} = C(\bar{\mathbf{q}}_I^W)^T$$
$$(17)$$

Then we can obtain the residual:

$$\mathbf{r} = \hat{\mathbf{y}} - \mathbf{p}^W + C(\bar{\mathbf{q}}_I^W)^T \mathbf{p}_U^I \qquad (18)$$

The correction process is similar to the update process in EKF from step 9–11 in Table 1. After the state propagate and measurement update, the updated errors will be injected into the nominal state and the error state mean will get reset.

5   Experiment

Simulation experiments are performed using the Gazebo engine. Three common motion forms of CMRs including linear motion, S-type motion, and the movement on uneven terrain are simulated, whose nonlinear are gradually enhanced. The simulation environment shows in Fig. 4. The parameters used in the simulation shows in Table 2.

Table 2. Parameters used in the simulation

Parameter	Value	Units	Description
σ_g	0.0013	$\frac{rad}{s}\frac{1}{\sqrt{Hz}}$	Gyroscope noise density
σ_a	0.083	$\frac{m}{s^2}\frac{1}{\sqrt{Hz}}$	Accelerometer noise density
σ_{b_g}	0.00013	$\frac{rad}{s^2}\frac{1}{\sqrt{Hz}}$	Gyroscope random walk
σ_{b_a}	0.0083	$\frac{m}{s^3}\frac{1}{\sqrt{Hz}}$	Accelerometer random walk
σ_{UWB}	0.02^2	m^2	UWB range measurements noise
f_{UWB}	40	Hz	UWB measurements frequency
f_{IMU}	200	Hz	IMU output frequency

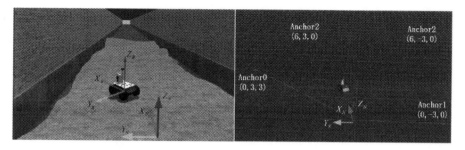

Fig. 4. Gazebo simulation environment: (*N*) is navigation coordinate and (*B*) is body coordinate. The initial pose assumes at the origin of (*N*) and initial velocity is 0.

Scenario 1: Flat ground

Firstly, the robot is driven along the laneway direction (the x-axis of navigation coordinate system) to travel approximately in a straight line of 20 m and then return back. The average speed is about 0.4 m/s and the maximum angular velocity is 0.2 rad/s. The proposed position measurements from the UWB positioning system, EKF-based IMU/odometer fusion [15] and the proposed ESKF-based fusion approach are compared to evaluate positioning capacity.

As can be seen from Fig. 5a, both absolute positioning error provided by UWB positioning system (ekf_UWB) and ESKF-fusion (eskf) are smaller than 0.5 m. ESKF-fusion convergence ability is affected by UWB positioning system, but convergent faster than EKF and has better accuracy. Compared with Fig. 5b, it also shows that in the case of sharp corners, the error of both systems increase. This is due to the reduced adaptive capacity of both EKF and ESKF to nonlinear increasing. The orientation error shown in Fig. 5c and d indicates that the proposed eskf algorithm can be used to estimate the attitude accurately even when the motion state changes dramatically.

Figure 6 gives the changing trend of transformation between IMU and UWB mobile node. The correct initial transformation values make the estimation of the parameters change very little, which also indicates that the proposed filter is stable.

Scenario 2: Uneven ground

In order to simulate the real working conditions of CMRs, we set up the simulation environment of uneven ground in gazebo, which has dramatic changes of movement status in all directions. Figure 7a shows that the UWB positioning system provide more accuracy position estimation than the proposed ESKF-fusion approach. This is due to the dramatically changes in the acceleration and angular velocity of IMU under uneven ground conditions make the reliable state propagation difficult. The performance of ESKF decreases under such strong nonlinear condition. Nevertheless, the system still achieves high positioning in x-axis and attitude (Fig. 7b–d). This is because the movement in the x-axis direction is closer to the uniform speed. Thanks to the correction of UWB positioning system, errors does not continue to accumulate with the distance increasing.

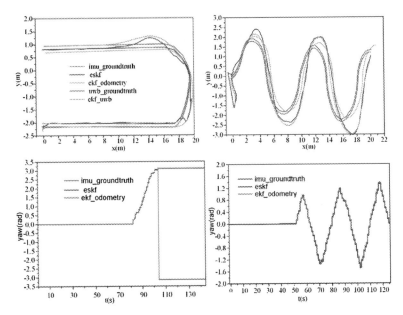

Fig. 5. (a–b) are the trajectory in the x-y plane when the robot moves along approximately straight line and S-shape respectively. (c–d) are the changes in the yaw direction of the robot during operation. The red line (imu_groundtruth) represents the ground-truth of IMU which is provided by the gazebo environment. The blue line (eskf) is the eskf fusion approach proposed by this paper. The green line (ekf_odometry) indicate the ekf-based imu/odometer fusion proposed by [15]. The ground-truth of UWB is shown in magenta line (uwb_groundtruth) which is retrieved from the IMU ground-truth by a static transformation. The UWB positioning system provides the trajectory in orange line (ekf_uwb). (Color figure online)

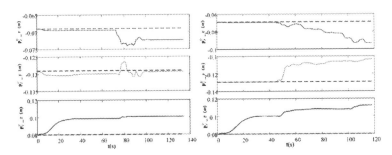

Fig. 6. The transformation between IMU and UWB mobile node in x-y-z axis. The dashed lines represent initial values, which are the true values.

Figure 8 shows that the transformation between IMU and UWB mobile node is still in a stable state, indicating that the system has a strong adaptability even in such an uneven ground, which has promising practicality for state estimation of CMRs.

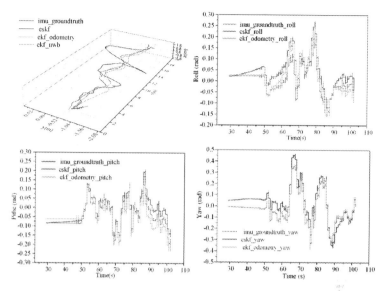

Fig. 7. (a) is the motion trajectory of the robot in 3D space. (b–d) reflects the attitude change of the robot in roll, pitch, yaw respectively.

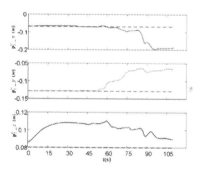

Fig. 8. The transformation between IMU and UWB mobile node in x-y-z axis. The dashed lines represent initial values, which are the true values.

6   Conclusion

This paper proposed a pseudo-GPS positioning system for underground coal mine by UWB range measurements. Furthermore, ESKF is used for fusing measurements from IMU and UWB. The complete 6 DOF state estimation is established, while the biases of IMU and the calibration parameters of IMU w.r.t. the UWB mobile node are also estimated online. The experiments in different motion forms and terrain conditions show that the proposed approach can provide accurate and robust 6 DOF state estimation for the application of coal mine robots.

Acknowledgment. This work is supported by the National Key Research and Development Program of China (No. 2018YFC0808000) and the Priority Academic Program Development of Jiangsu Higher Education Institutions (PAPD), China.

References

1. Siciliano, B., Khatib, O.: Springer Handbook of Robotics. Springer, Cham (2016). https://doi.org/10.1007/978-3-319-32552-1
2. Aghili, F., Salerno, A.: Driftless 3-D attitude determination and positioning of mobile robots by integration of IMU with two RTK GPSs. IEEE/ASME Trans. Mechatron. **18**(1), 21–31 (2013)
3. Kushleyev, A., Mellinger, D., Powers, C., Kumar, V.: Towards a swarm of agile micro quadrotors. Auton. Robots **35**(4), 287–300 (2013)
4. Kanellakis, C., Nikolakopoulos, G.: Evaluation of visual localization systems in underground mining. In: 2016 24th Mediterranean Conference on Control and Automation (MED), pp. 539–544. IEEE(2016)
5. Menggang, L., Hua, Z., Shaoze, Y., Lei, W., Chaoquan, T.: Efficient laser-based 3D SLAM for coal mine rescue robots. IEEE Access **7**, 14124–14138 (2019). https://doi.org/10.1109/access.2018.2889304
6. Einicke, G.A., Ralston, J.C., Hargrave, C.O.: Longwall mining automation an application of minimum-variance smoothing [Applications of Control]. IEEE Control Syst. Mag. **28**(6), 28–37 (2008)
7. Paraszczak, J., Gustafson, A., Schunnesson, H.: Technical and operational aspects of autonomous LHD application in metal mines. Int. J. Surf. Min. Reclam. Environ. **29**(5), 391–403 (2015)
8. Liu, Z., Li, C., Wu, D.: A wireless sensor network based personnel positioning scheme in coal mines with blind areas. Sensors **10**(11), 9891–9918 (2010)
9. Longkang, W., Baisheng, N., Ruming, Z.: ZigBee-based positioning system for coal miners. Proc. Eng. **26**, 2406–2414 (2011)
10. Bulin, M. A., Fan, Y.: The design and implementation of WiFi localization GIS for mine. J. Xi'an Univ. Sci. Technol. **3** (2012)
11. Yang, H., Luo, T., Li, W., et al.: A stable SINS/UWB integrated positioning method of shearer based on the multi-model intelligent switching algorithm. IEEE Access **7**, 29128–29138 (2019)
12. Fang, X., Wang, C., Nguyen, T.M., et al.: Model-free approach for sensor network localization with noisy distance measurement. In: 2018 15th International Conference on Control, Automation, Robotics and Vision (ICARCV), pp. 1973–1978. IEEE (2018)
13. Zhou, Y.: An efficient least-squares trilateration algorithm for mobile robot localization. In: IEEE International Conference on Intelligent Robots and Systems, IROS 2009, pp. 3474–3479. IEEE/RSJ (2009)
14. Agarwal, S., Mierle, K.: Ceres solver (2013). https://github.com/ceres-solver/ceres-solver
15. Moore, T., Stouch, D.: A generalized extended Kalman Filter implementation for the robot operating system. In: Menegatti, E., Michael, N., Berns, K., Yamaguchi, H. (eds.) Intelligent Autonomous Systems 13. AISC, vol. 302, pp. 335–348. Springer, Cham (2016). https://doi.org/10.1007/978-3-319-08338-4_25

Analysis and Optimization of the Drive System of the Mobile Robot Arm in Unmanned Mining Working Face

Lijuan Zhao, Zuen Shang$^{(\boxtimes)}$ (iD), Bin Wang, and Xionghao Liu

Liaoning Technical University, 88 Yulong Road, Fuxin 123000, China
shangzuen@gmail.com

Abstract. The function of the mining patrol robot arm is to assist or even replace the staff to operate and maintain the equipment when the underground equipment fails, so as to reduce the possibility of potential accident safety hazards. Different from the conventional design process of the drive system, the structure of the mobile robot arm is analyzed firstly in this paper to obtain the design requirements of the drive system of the mobile robot arm. Then, according to the design requirements, the optimization performance indexes of the time and vibration are taken as the objective function, and the working performance of the motor, the reliability of the reducer and the weight of the motor reducer are taken as the constraint functions. The genetic algorithm is used to solve the multi-variable optimization problem. The data results show that the optimization model and method are feasible, and the working performance of the mobile robot arm is improved overall.

Keywords: Unmanned mining working face · Patrol robot ·
Mobile robot arm · Optimization of the drive system

1 Introduction

In recent years, in order to solve the problem of frequent accidents in the underground coal mine and improve the efficiency of the coal mining, the concept of "unmanned mining working face" [1, 2] has been put forward internationally.

Based on the background of "unmanned mining working face", special robots are gradually applied to the coal mining industry. Most of the research hotspots of underground robots in the world are on the obstacle climbing of mobile platforms, so the functions of the product are mostly designed for patrol [3, 4] and rescue [5, 6], however, the research of the robotic arm installed on them, which can realize auxiliary work, holding of the repeater (Extending the transmission distance of the signal) and equipment maintenance, is negligible, because there are too many factors to consider in order to design a mobile robot arm [7, 8] that can be suitable for the underground work.

The underground is different from the ground. No matter from the endurance, portability and maneuverability of the robot, the underground robot cannot be too large, which seriously affects the performance of the mobile robot arm. Therefore, the analysis and optimization of the dynamic performance of the mobile robot arm are

© Springer Nature Switzerland AG 2019
H. Yu et al. (Eds.): ICIRA 2019, LNAI 11740, pp. 269–281, 2019.
https://doi.org/10.1007/978-3-030-27526-6_24

focused on in this paper, so as to improve the performance of the mobile robot arm as much as possible while meeting various constraints.

Different from the previous methods which only consider the characteristics of a single joint [9, 10], this paper changes from the design with local performance as the criterion to the dynamic design based on the overall performance of the robot arm [11], taking into account the properties of the drive system itself. The optimization problem of discrete variables is realized by the genetic algorithm, which improves the performance of the drive system [12].

The rest of this paper is organized as follows: The whole mobile robot arm is analyzed in Sect. 2. Then, the optimization model of the drive system is established in Sect. 2.4. In Sect. 3, the simulation results are compared and analyzed. Finally, the conclusion is drawn in Sect. 4.

2   Optimization Model of the Drive System

2.1   Analysis of Design Requirements of the Drive System

In order to shorten the work completion time of the mobile robot arm, it is necessary to optimize the shortest work completion time of the mobile robot arm with the shortest working time as the objective function and in accordance with all the constraints of the mobile robot arm. The scaling of the time that the mobile robot arm completes the specified task can be achieved by the coefficient $1/\lambda$, thereby the Eq. (1) is established as the optimization index of the time.

$$\lambda = \min\left\{ \frac{v_{\max}}{|\tilde{p}^{(1)}(u)|_{\max}}, \sqrt{\frac{a_{\max}}{|\tilde{p}^{(2)}(u)|_{\max}}}, \sqrt{\frac{\tilde{\tau}_{s,i}(t')}{\tau_{s,i}(t)}}, \sqrt[3]{\frac{j_{\max}}{|\tilde{p}^{(3)}(u)|_{\max}}} \right\} \tag{1}$$

Among them, $\tilde{p}^{(1)}(u)$, $\tilde{p}^{(2)}(u)$ and $\tilde{p}^{(3)}(u)$ are respectively the velocity, acceleration and jerk equations of the trajectory. $V_{\max}$, $a_{\max}$ and $j_{\max}$ are the speed constraint, acceleration constraint and jerk constraint. $\tau_{s,j}(t)$ represents the item related to the position, velocity, and acceleration in the output torque of the ith motor, and $\tilde{\tau}_{s,j}(t)$ represents a new equation (where t is a time variable) obtained by scaling the trajectory scaling equation t = $\sigma(t')$.

Due to the small weight of the designed body of the mobile robot arm, the vibration mode of the mobile robot arm itself is relatively complex. In addition to the complex working environment in the coal mine underground, the improvement of the natural frequency is beneficial to improve the stability and rapid response of the system, reduce the errors caused by various factors and improve the anti-interference ability. Thereby the Eq. (2) is established, which is the vibration performance optimization index.

$$f = \frac{\sqrt{\omega^2}}{2\pi} \tag{2}$$

Among them, f represents the vibration frequency of the robot system corresponding to the modal vector U.

The constraints of the drive system are analyzed as follows:

1. Consider the lightweight factor of the motor reducer

Considering the energy consumption of the actual mobile robot arm and the convenient carrying of the staff, it is necessary to carry out the lightweight design of the mobile robot arm. In addition, due to the environmental characteristics of the coal mine underground, the explosion-proof treatment of the motor also makes the mass of the motor increase, while the mass of the articulated arm is mostly concentrated on the motor and the reducer, so the mass of the motor and the reducer needs to be constrained.

2. Consider the working life factor of the reducer

The air humidity is high in the coal mine underground, the content of the floating impurities in the air is high, such as coal dust, and the content of the corrosive gas is relatively high, Moreover, the reducer is worn in the working process. It is necessary to ensure the reliability of the mobile robot arm. Therefore, the working life of the reducer is restricted.

3. Consider the performance factor of the motor

By limiting the RMS of the rated torque, it is ensured that the motor can work under the best operating condition. The constraint of the locked torque ensures the starting performance of the motor. The motor cannot start because the load torque is too large. The constraint on the maximum allowable speed ensures the normal operation of the motor. Once this value is exceeded, the motor will be in danger of burning down and there will be a safety risk in the coal mine underground. Therefore, the maximum allowable speed must be limited. Constraining the performance of the motor ensures the stability and working efficiency of the motor.

2.2 Optimization Process

The model of the mobile robot is shown in Fig. 1(a) and Its structure schematic diagram is shown in Fig. 1(b). In the past, the conventional design of mobile robots was usually judged by whether the motor and reducer of a particular joint had good performance to judge whether it met the design requirements of the drive system. However, this design process was not considered comprehensively enough. Because the influences of the coupling of the whole system, the working environment and other factors on the mobile robot arm were not taken into account. Therefore, the dynamic model is taken as the performance index and many factors are taken as constraints to optimize the system in this optimization process. The design process of the drive system is shown in Fig. 2.

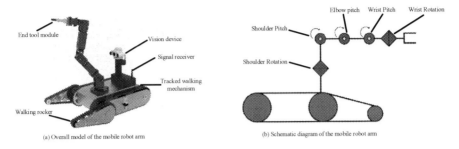

(a) Overall model of the mobile robot arm

(b) Schematic diagram of the mobile robot arm

Fig. 1. Model introduction of the mobile robot arm

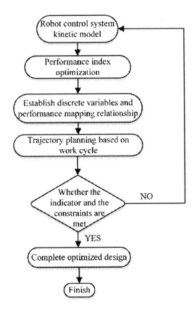

Fig. 2. Drive system design flow chart of the mobile robot arm

2.3 Mathematical Model of Design Indexes of the Drive System

Based on the analysis, the following optimization model is established:

$$\min\left(\alpha \cdot \frac{1}{\lambda} + \beta \cdot \frac{1}{f}\right) \tag{3}$$

s.t.:

$$\alpha + \beta = 1 \tag{4}$$

$$\tau_{m,rated} \geq \sqrt{\frac{1}{t}\int_0^t \left((J_m + J_g)\ddot{q}_a \cdot N + \frac{\tau_l}{N}\right)^2 dt} \tag{5}$$

$$\tau_{m,peak} \geq \max \left|(J_m + J_g)\ddot{q}_a \cdot N + \frac{\tau_l}{N}\right| \tag{6}$$

$$\omega_{m,peak} \geq \max|\dot{q}_{a,i}| \cdot i \tag{7}$$

$$L_{life} = 6000 \times \frac{N_0}{N_m} \times \left(\frac{T_0}{T_m}\right)^{\frac{10}{3}} \geq 20 \text{ million cycles} \tag{8}$$

$$\sum_i^3 \left(m_{motor.i} + m_{gearbox.i}\right) \leq 17.5kg \tag{9}$$

$$\lambda \leq \min\left\{\frac{v_{max}}{|p^{(1)}(u)|_{max}}, \sqrt{\frac{a_{max}}{|p^{(2)}(u)|_{max}}}, \sqrt{\frac{\tilde{\tau}_{s,i}(t')}{\tau_{s,i}(t)}}, \sqrt{\frac{j_{max}}{|p^{(3)}(u)|_{max}}}, \cdots\right\} \tag{10}$$

In the objective function formula (3), λ is the coefficient of the proportional term of the working time scaling function. Set the initial working time T to complete the specified trajectory. By solving the maximized λ and scaling T proportionally, the efficiency of the robot will be improved. The Eq. (10) is a constraint function of time scaling ratio. In the optimization process, the minimum working time should meet the constraints of the maximum speed, maximum acceleration and joint torque of each joint. f represents the minimum natural frequency of the robot in the working space, and the optimal calculation will improve the natural frequency of the robot itself. In the objective function, α and β represent the weighted values of the objective function of the working efficiency and the objective function of the frequency index respectively. The constraint functions (5)–(7) are the performance constraints of the motor. The formulas (8) and (9) correspond to the life constraint of the reducer and the total mass constraint of the motor and the reducer respectively.

2.4 Hybrid Variable Optimization of the Drive System

Since the optimization variables of the drive system include not only continuous variables but also discrete variables, it is necessary to optimize the mixed variables. Take the motor of the second joint as an example: According to the dynamic model of the mobile robot arm, several suitable primary motors are selected (here, in order to ensure the diversity of the collection, 8 motors with similar parameters are selected) as the parent. The corresponding variables of the motors of the 2nd, 3rd, and 4th joints are x1, x2 and x3. The corresponding variables of the reducers of the 2nd, 3rd, and 4th joints are x4, x5 and x6. The variables corresponding to a model of motor include the mass, inertia, peak torque and rated torque. Therefore, it is necessary to establish the mapping relationship between the optimization variables and the properties of the motor and the reducer itself. The function of the mapping relationship in the optimization is shown in Fig. 3.

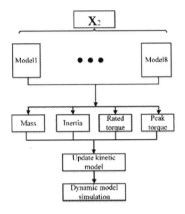

Fig. 3. Schematic diagram of genetic variables

Due to the coupling between the optimization parameters, a clear mapping relationship between the optimization variables and the system variables needs to be defined:

$$x_{sp} = u(x) \tag{11}$$

Where x denotes the models of the motor and reducer can be selected. In the optimization process, different system variables x_{sp} are used for each iteration, such as the mass, inertia, and other parameters of the motor and reducer. Then, according to the system variables, the dynamic model of the robot is simulated, and the performance characteristics of the system (Root mean square value of the torque of the motor, the life of the reducer, etc.) are calculated. The characteristic expressions are as follows:

$$y_{sc} = v(x_{sp}) \tag{12}$$

Calculate the value of the objective function g according to the above formula.

$$g = g(y_{sc}) \tag{13}$$

The dynamic optimization process is shown in Fig. 4. According to the value of the objective function, a new group of new optimization variables are selected and a new iteration process is started until a certain convergence criterion is met. A complete optimization problem can be expressed as:

$$g = \min g(v(u(x))) \tag{14}$$

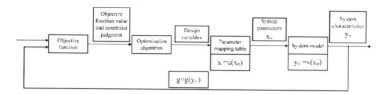

Fig. 4. Dynamic optimization process based on robot dynamic model simulation

3   Comparison and Analysis of Optimization Results

The design optimization variables $x_1, x_2, x_3, x_4, x_5, x_6, x_7$, where x_{1-3} and x_{4-6} are discrete variables, representing the selectable models of the motors and reducers of the 2nd, 3rd, and 4th axes of the robot, and x_7 is a continuous variable, representing the coefficient of the proportional term of the working time scaling function. The maximum load capacity of the designed robot is 15 kg, and the initial working time T is set to 15 s. The genetic algorithm is adopted, the number of population is 100, the evolutionary algebra is set to 50 generations, and the weighted values of the working efficiency of the objective function and the natural frequency of the robot are respectively selected as $\alpha = 0.52$ and $\beta = 0.48$. The value change of the objective function in the optimization process is shown in Fig. 5. The variation trend of the discrete optimization variables $x_1, \cdots, x_6$ in the iteration process is shown in Fig. 6. Finally, the optimal value of the optimization discrete variable is $x_1, \cdots, x_6$, and the scaling coefficient of the continuous optimization variable working time scaling function is $x_7 = 1.211$.

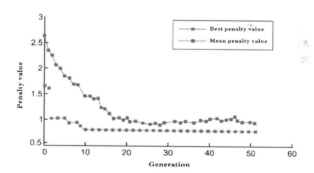

Fig. 5. Penalty function values in the iteration process

From the comparison in Fig. 7, it can be seen that for the first-order natural frequency index, the optimized parameter group is greatly improved compared with the initial parameter group. The minimum natural frequency of the whole working space under the original parameter is 22.45 Hz, and the minimum natural frequency of the robot after optimization is 29.85 Hz, which is 33% higher than that before the optimization. The improvement of the natural frequency of the robot also means that the ability of the stability and anti-interference of the robot itself to low-frequency vibration is improved.

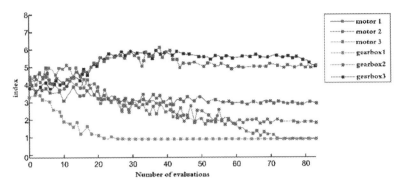

Fig. 6. Discrete optimization variable values in the iteration process

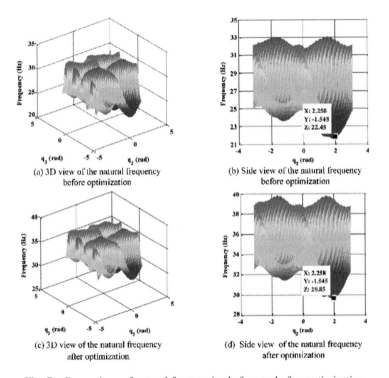

(a) 3D view of the natural frequency
before optimization

(b) Side view of the natural frequency
before optimization

(c) 3D view of the natural frequency
after optimization

(d) Side view of the natural frequency
after optimization

Fig. 7. Comparison of natural frequencies before and after optimization

It can be seen from Fig. 8 that the same working trajectory is completed under the condition of meeting the dynamic constraints, after optimization, the zooming time is reduced from 17.49 s to 15 s, which is reduced by 16.6%, and the purpose of improving the working efficiency of the robot is achieved.

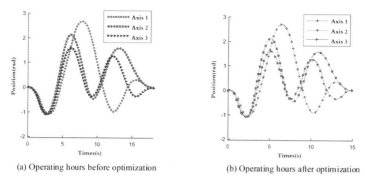

(a) Operating hours before optimization   (b) Operating hours after optimization

Fig. 8. Comparison of working efficiency before and after optimization

It can be seen from the output torque curves of the motors in Fig. 9 that although the working efficiency is remarkably improved. However, the requirements for the driving torque of each axis after optimization has not been significantly improved with the improvement of working efficiency, which proves the effectiveness of the optimization method.

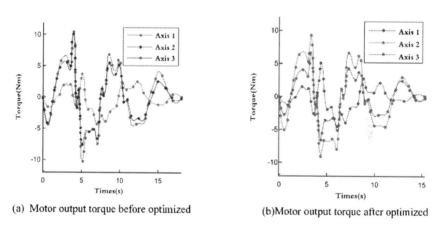

(a) Motor output torque before optimized   (b)Motor output torque after optimized

Fig. 9. Comparison of output torque before and after optimization

Figure 10 shows the change of the peak torque and rated torque of the motor in the optimization process. The results show that the motor after optimization meets the constraint function formulas (5)–(6).

278   L. Zhao et al.

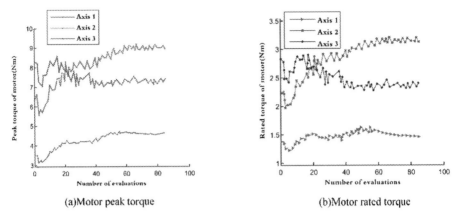

(a)Motor peak torque   (b)Motor rated torque

Fig. 10. Peak torque and rated torque changeing diagram of the motor

Figure 11 shows the changing trend of the life of the reducer in the optimization process. The reduction of the life of the reducer is because the mass of the reducer of each joint is greater than that of the motor. To improve the natural frequency of the robot, the overall mass of the robot needs to be reduced, so the reducer with lower mass is selected in the optimization process, and the value of the rated torque of the reducer decreases with the reduction of the mass of the reducer. Therefore, the life of the reducer calculated by the formula (8) also decreases. Although the life of the reducer is reduced, it still meets the constraint function formula (8).

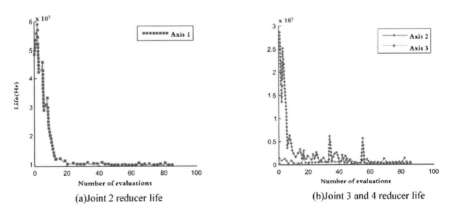

(a)Joint 2 reducer life   (b)Joint 3 and 4 reducer life

Fig. 11. Changing diagram of the working life of the reducer

It can be seen from Fig. 12 that although the overall mass of the control system is reduced, it does not fully meet the requirements of the constraint function formula (9). The main reason is that the strong nonlinearity of the optimization model of the drive system and the dynamics model of the robot result in the strong coupling relationship between the indexes, which makes the multi-objective optimization not all achieve the desired effect. But the goal of lightweight design of the robot is still partially realized.

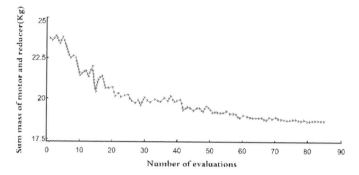

Fig. 12. Total mass changing diagram of the drive system

In order to further prove the effectiveness of the optimization method, the root mean square value of the torque required to complete the work of the motors of the second and third axes in the optimization process is compared with the rated torque corresponding to the optimization variables. It can be seen from Fig. 13 that the rated torque of the optimization variable gradually approaches the root mean square value of the torque required to complete the work in the optimization process due to the constraint function formula (5), which proves the effectiveness of the design method.

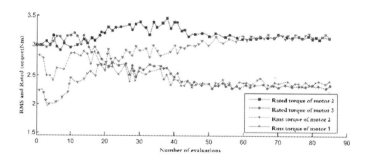

Fig. 13. Changing diagram of the rated torque and root mean square value of the motor

To sum up, the whole optimization model and optimization method are feasible, reasonable and effective. Taking the working efficiency and vibration frequency of the mobile robot arm as the main goal, taking into account the performance constraints of the motor and reducer of the robot, the loss factor and load-weight ratio of the reducer and other performance indexes, the hybrid variable optimization algorithm is used, the time is reduced from 17.49 s to 15 s after scaling the working efficiency, the working efficiency is improved by 16.6%, the minimum natural frequency is reduced from 29.85 Hz to 22.45 Hz. The natural frequency is improved by 33%, and the weight is reduced from 23.75 kg to 19 kg by 20% under the premise of meeting the constraint conditions.

4   Conclusion

In this paper, a new optimization design method of the drive system of the mobile robot arm is proposed based on the background of unmanned mining working face. The optimization model of the drive system is established, which takes the working efficiency and low-order natural frequency as objective functions and constraints on dynamic performance including system performance limit, loss and load-weight ratio and other indexes. According to the discrete characteristics of the optimization variables of the drive system, the relationship between the performance indexes of the system and optimization variables is established. According to the dynamic simulation results, it is analyzed whether the value of the objective function and the constraint condition meet the performance requirements. The hybrid variable genetic algorithm is used to solve the optimization model. The results show that the lightweight design of the mobile robot arm is realized to a certain extent while improving the working efficiency and the low-order natural frequency, so that the overall performance of the underground mobile robot arm is improved.

Acknowledgement. The author first thanks the doctoral supervisor for his support and guidance. Then thanks to the financial and technical support provided by the foreign robotics project (No. 2018LNGXGJWPY-ZD001), and also to the help of laboratory researchers.

References

1. Wang, X., Meng, F.: Statistical analysis of large accidents in China's coal mines in 2016. Nat. Hazards **92**(1), 311–325 (2018)
2. Jinhua, W.Z.H.: The recent technological development of intelligent mining in China. Eng. Engl. **3**(4), 439–444 (2017)
3. Zhao, J., et al.: A search-and-rescue robot system for remotely sensing the underground coal mine environment. Sensors **17**(10), 2426 (2017)
4. Deyong, S., Jianwei, Z., Xun, F.: Design and mechanics analysis of moving mechanism of inspection robot for thin coal seam. Open Mater. Sci. J. **9**(1), 43–48 (2015)
5. Schwarz, M., et al.: NimbRo rescue: solving disaster-response tasks with the mobile manipulation robot momaro. J. Field Robot. **34**(2), 400–425 (2017)
6. Ito, K., Maruyama, H.: Semi-autonomous serially connected multi-crawler robot for search and rescue. Adv. Robot. **30**(7), 489–503 (2016)
7. Deepak, B., Parhi, D.R.: Control of an automated mobile manipulator using artificial immune system. J. Exp. Theor. Artif. Intell. **28**(1-2), 417–439 (2016)
8. Korayem, M.H., Esfeden, R.A., Nekoo, S.R.: Path planning algorithm in wheeled mobile manipulators based on motion of arms. J. Mech. Sci. Technol. **29**(4), 1753–1763 (2015)
9. Benath, K.: Advanced design rules for the energy optimal motor-gearbox combination in servo drive systems. In: 2014 International Symposium on Power Electronics, Electrical Drives, Automation and Motion, SPEEDAM, pp. 94–99 (2014)
10. Giberti, H.: Drive system sizing of a 6-DOF parallel robotic platform. In: ASME 2014 12th Biennial Conference on Engineering Systems Design and Analysis, ESDA, pp. 124–129 (2014)

11. Johansson, C., Ölvander, J., Derelöv, M.: Multi-objective optimization for safety and reliability trade-off: Optimization and results processing. Proc. Inst. Mech. Eng. Part O J. Risk Reliab. **232**(6), 661–676 (2018)
12. Kim, E., Seki, K., Iwasaki, M.: Motion control of industrial robots by considering serial two-link robot arm model with joint nonlinearities. J. Mech. Sci. Technol. **28**(4), 1519–1527 (2014)

Compliant Mechanisms

A Flexure-Based XY Precision Positioning Stage with Integrated Displacement PVDF Sensor

Mingxiang Ling[(✉)]

Institute of Systems Engineering, China Academy of Engineering Physics,
Mianyang 621999, China
ling_mx@163.com

Abstract. A piezo-actuated XY precision positioning stage with integrated piezoelectric displacement sensor is developed. The displacement sensing is realized by bonding a semi-rectangular shaped polyvinylidene fluoride (PVDF) film on the surface of the guiding flexible beam. The measuring principle is based on the simple kinematic relationship and the 'clamped-sliding' boundary condition of the guiding flexible beam, both of which are widely available in compliant mechanisms. The sensing concept is experimentally verified with high precision and sensitivity, resulting in a comparative precision with the commercial optical displacement meter but with smaller waveform distortion at high frequencies. The presented precision positioning stage is measured with a maximum stroke range of 138 μm × 138 μm. The feature of the sensing method lies in its very compactness with high precision, fast frequency response, low cost, fine resolution and simplicity, thus opening up interesting opportunities for volume displacement measuring of precision positioning stages or other flexible manipulators with confined interspaces and harsh environments where integrating a bulky transducer is hard.

Keywords: Compliant mechanisms · PVDF · Nanopositioner · Flexure hinge · Piezoelectric sensor

1 Introduction

Piezo-actuated compliant mechanisms are drawing more and more attentions in the field of precision driving/positioning for scanning probe microscope, biological cell manipulation, optical fiber alignment, and so forth [1, 2]. Piezo-actuated flexure-based precision positioning stages can be advantageous in several aspects. For example, high resolution, large output force and fast dynamic response of piezoelectric actuators (PZT) along with the merits of no friction, no wear, no requirement of assembling and compact structure of compliant mechanisms, which transmit force and motion through elastic deformations and are usually fabricated in a monolithic form.

Because of hysteresis of piezoelectric materials and lightly damping of compliant mechanisms, feedback precise control is usually designed for piezo-actuated flexure-based precision positioning stages, also including other flexible manipulators [3]. However, accurately measuring the motion information of a precision positioning stage

© Springer Nature Switzerland AG 2019
H. Yu et al. (Eds.): ICIRA 2019, LNAI 11740, pp. 285–295, 2019.
https://doi.org/10.1007/978-3-030-27526-6_25

to perform precise feedback control of tracking, vibration suppression and hysteresis compensation becomes intractable for confined interspaces and for harsh environment (e.g. under liquid or in temperature box) where it is difficult to assemble a bulky and separate transducer. Thus, a compact sensor with high precision, fine resolution, high frequency response is critical.

In this paper, the compact motion sensing of flexure-based precision positioning stages is implemented by integrating a structurally shaped PVDF film on the surface of the guiding flexible beam based on simple kinematical relations and 'clamped-sliding' boundary conditions widely available in compliant mechanisms. The distinct compactness of the sensor and the characteristics of resonant frequency-dependence on the measurand suggesting it's superiority for confined inter-spaces and high-frequency applications. PVDF is a piezoelectric polymer with low-Q response, high sensitivity and flexibility, commercially available as thin sheets (usually less than 0.11 mm). As a piezoelectric material, PVDF film can generate charges when it is mechanically deformed. The past applications of PVDF mainly focused on various force sensors, strain sensors, vibration accelerometers, vibration mode filtering [4–7], etc.

To the best of our knowledge, there are few cases applying PVDF into compliant mechanisms or flexible manipulators for measuring volume displacement. The motion sensing method we pursue here for a two-DOF precision positioner is based on two pieces of semi-rectangular shaped PVDF films and the distinct kinematic relations and boundary condition widely available in compliant mechanisms [8]. Features of the concept include compactness, low cost, light weight, high frequency response, fine resolution and especially suitable for narrow interspaces.

The remainder of the paper is organized as follows. Design of the precision positioning stage with a novel PVDF sensor is described in Sect. 2. Motion sensing principle and signal processing circuit are presented in Sect. 3. Calibration of the sensor and comparative experiments are performed in Sect. 4. Finally, concludes are provided in Sect. 5.

2 Design of the XY Precision Positioner with PVDF Sensor

2.1 Configuration Design and Kinematical Relations for Sensing

The schematic of the presented XY precision positioning stage is illustrated in Fig. 1. The parallel configuration enables the same kinematical and dynamic performance in the *x*- and *y*-directions. The small displacements of piezoelectric actuators are amplified by two rhombus-type compliant mechanisms with suitable geometric parameters. The translational motions in the two DOFs are decoupled by flexible beams. Distributed-compliance configuration but not flexure hinge is used to avoid stress concentration and to reduce fatigue effect under dynamic loading conditions.

As shown in Fig. 1, the guiding flexible beams, which have much larger axial stiffness with respect to their weak transverse deflection stiffness, are utilized to transmit and decouple the motions in the *x*- and *y*-directions. Taking the DOF in the *x*-direction as the study object, one end port of the guiding flexible beam 'AB' is rigidly connected to the output port (Point 'B' in Fig. 1) of the rhombus amplifier '1', while another port is mounted on the fixed block. Obviously, the rigid tip end 'B' of the guiding flexible beam 'AB' has the same displacement as the output port of the rhombus amplifier '1' due to the symmetric configuration. On the other hand, since the axial stiffness of the guiding flexible beam 'BC' is very large compared to its transverse deflection, its axial deformation can be ignorable when the rhombus amplifier '1' is actuated. Therefore, displacement of the platform in the x-direction approximately equals to the output displacement of the rhombus amplifier '1' and also equals to the tip deflection of the guiding flexible beam 'AB'. That's to say, if the tip deflection of the guiding flexible beam 'AB' is measured, the output displacement of the precision positioner in the x-direction can be obtained. Similar analysis can be applicable for the motion in the y-direction.

Based on the above analysis of kinematical relations, two pieces of semi-rectangular shaped PVDF films are respectively designed on the surface of two guiding flexible beams to measure their tip deflections. Orange segments in Fig. 1 represent the PVDF sensor.

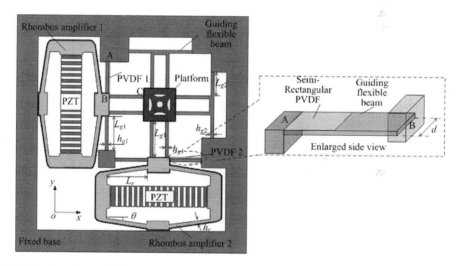

Fig. 1. The schematic illustration and enlarged side view of the structure of the presented XY precision positioning stage including shaped PVDF sensor.

2.2 Kinematical and Natural Frequency Evaluation

Taking one DOF in Fig. 1 as the study object, the output displacement of the precision positioning stage can be described as Eq. (1) according to the analytical kinematics model in our previous theoretical work [9]. Here, the limited stiffness effect of the piezoelectric actuator is considered

$$x_{out} = \frac{1}{1+\delta} \cdot \frac{k_{out}}{k_{out}+k_{load}} \cdot R_{amp} \cdot \frac{k_{PZT}}{k_{in}+k_{PZT}} \cdot K_v \cdot V \tag{1}$$

where K_v is the piezoelectric constant relating to the strain, k_{PZT} is the axial stiffness of the piezoelectric actuator, V is the input voltage. k_{in}, k_{out}, R_{amp} are respectively the input stiffness, the output stiffness and the displacement amplification ratio of the rhombus-type amplifier. k_{load} is the total transverse deflection stiffness of the guiding flexible beams in one motion direction.

Variable δ in Eq. (1) is a non-dimensional coupling factor among the piezoelectric actuator, the rhombus-type amplifier and the guiding flexible beams and is equal to the following Eq. (2) according to our previous study [9]

$$\delta = \frac{R_{amp}^2 \cdot k_{out} \cdot k_{load}}{(k_{out}+k_{load}) \cdot (k_{in}+k_{PZT})} \tag{2}$$

Based on the definition of geometric parameters in Fig. 1, theoretical models of R_{amp}, k_{in}, k_{out} for the rhombus-type amplifier are directly given out here as Eqs. (3), (4) and (5). More details are available in our previous theoretical paper on kinematical modeling of rhombus-type amplifier [9]

$$R_{amp} = \frac{K_l L_r^2 \sin\theta\cos\theta}{12K_\theta \cos^2\theta + K_l L_r^2 \sin^2\theta} \tag{3}$$

$$k_{in} = \frac{24K_l K_\theta}{12K_\theta \cos^2\theta + K_l L_r^2 \sin^2\theta} \tag{4}$$

$$k_{out} = \frac{2(12K_\theta \cos^2\theta + K_l L_r^2 \sin^2\theta)}{L_r^2} \tag{5}$$

where translational and rotational stiffness K_l and K_θ are equal to Ebh_r/L_r and $Ebh_r^3/12L_r$, respectively.

The guiding flexible beams are constant section with 'clamped-sliding' boundary condition, therefore total transverse deflection stiffness of the guiding flexible beams in one motion direction, k_{load}, can be easily deduced as

$$k_{load} = 6 \times \frac{Edh_{g1}^3}{L_{g1}^3} + 2 \times \frac{Edh_{g2}^3}{L_{g2}^3} \tag{6}$$

With the geometric and material parameters listed in Table 1, the displacement amplification ratio when considering the limited stiffness of the piezo-actuator (defined as $x_{out}/K_v V$ in Eq. (1)) is calculated versus sensitive angle θ. As shown in Fig. 2, the presented kinematical model well describes the change trend of the displacement amplification ratio with the change of angle θ, where seven sets of finite elemental results by ANSYS with the same physical parameters are calculated as the benchmark of verification. Importantly, the optimal angle corresponding to the largest displacement amplification ratio can be easily and clearly confirmed by the calculating results of the theoretical model.

Besides, it can be seen from Fig. 2 that the displacement amplification ratio of the whole stage (Blue solid curve in Fig. 2) is much reduced compared to that of the rhombus-type amplifier in Eq. (3) (Black dashed curve in Fig. 2). It means that the attenuation effects of the limited stiffness of the piezoelectric actuator and the transverse deflection stiffness of the guiding flexible beams on the output displacement of the stage are strong and can't be ignored.

Table 1. Key geometric and material parameters.

Symbol	Quantity	Symbol	Quantity
L_r	15.5 mm	ρ	2770 kg/m^3
L_{g1}	14.5 mm	K_v	0.32 µm/V
L_{g2}	13.5 mm	K_{PZT}	100 N/µm
h_r	1.0 mm	θ	Variable
h_{g1}	0.4 mm	d	10 mm
h_{g2}	0.5 mm	E	71 GPa

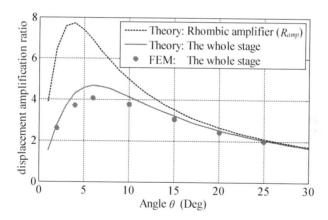

Fig. 2. Theoretical results of the displacement amplification ratio versus sensitive angle of the rhombus-type amplifier. (Color figure online)

Based on the theoretical calculation results, optimal angle $\theta = 6°$ is designed for the rhombus-type amplifier, which corresponds to the displacement amplification ratio of 4.6 in the theoretical model and about 4.1 in FEM. If piezoelectric actuator with a stroke of 36 µm is selected, then maximum motion range of 165.6 µm and 147.6 µm can be respectively predicted by the theoretical model and FEM. Compared with the results from FEM, the theoretical model has a maximum prediction error of about 12%. However, the theoretical model is accurate to predict the optimal geometric parameters, as illustrated in Fig. 2. Modal analysis with ANSYS Workbench 14.0 is carried out to evaluate the natural frequency of the designed precision positioning stage. With the optimal geometric parameters confirmed by the theoretical model and Table 1, the first and second modes of vibration are shown in Fig. 3. These two vibration modes are exactly the target translational motions in the x and y directions and are equal to 1198 Hz and 1199 Hz, respectively.

It should be noted that the PVDF film is very thin and softly flexible, whose mass and bending stiffness are insignificant compared to that of the guiding flexible beams and has little influence on the kinematical and dynamic performance of the stage. Therefore, the coupling effect of the PVDF film is not included in the above theoretical calculation of kinematics and ANSYS analysis of dynamics.

(a) 1st mode: 1198 Hz   (b) 2st mode: 1199 Hz

Fig. 3. The first and second vibration modes of the stage

3   PVDF Displacement Sensor Design

In order to measure the output displacement of the platform, two pieces of semi-rectangular shaped PVDF films with the same properties are respectively bonded to the surface of two guiding flexible beams [8], as illustrated in Fig. 1. In the design, a PVDF sheet of 110 μm thickness with silver ink electrodes on both sides from the Measurement Specialties Inc. was tailored into the semi-rectangular shape. Polyvinyl chloride (PVC) film of 100 μm thickness is used for insulating layer to avoid charge leakage, bonding on both sides of the shaped PVDF film by double-sided adhesive tape from 3 M Scotch Ltd. Then, the PVDF sensors are bonded on the surface of the guiding flexible beams by fast-cure elastic epoxy.

Here, it is assumed that different layers are well bonded to one another and there are no gaps between each layer. The working principle of the displacement sensing for the precision positioning stage is based on the bending deformation of the guiding flexible beams when actuated by the piezoelectric actuators, which in turn mechanically stimulates the PVDF film to generate electrical signals. PVDF film is a strain sensitive material, and as such, it provides local strain measurements. The output displacement of the stage can be obtained by relating these local strain signals to a displacement-related quantity via the kinematic relationship of the guiding flexible beams.

When the PVDF film bends with the guiding flexible beam, there are transient charges generated on the surface electrode. The induced charges can be measured by a charge amplifier, as shown in Fig. 4. The charge amplifier is based on the operational amplifier AD8659 with a high input impedance and very low bias current.

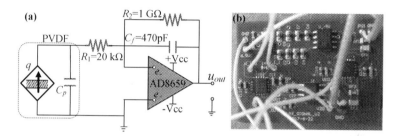

Fig. 4. The charge amplifier. (a) Schematic circuit diagram. (b) Prototype.

PVDF is represented as a charge source with capacitor C_p in parallel. The circuit is an effective charge amplifier as a high pass filter with the low cutoff frequency of $1/2\pi R_2 C_f$. Besides, the capacitor C_p and the resistance R_1 form a low pass filter with a high cutoff frequency of $1/2\pi R_1 C_p$. By defining $\tau_p = R_1 C_p$, $\tau_f = R_2 C_f$, the transfer function between the output voltage and the PVDF charge can be expressed as

$$H(\omega) = \frac{V}{Q} = \frac{-j\omega R_2}{(1+j\omega\tau_f)(1+j\omega\tau_p)} \tag{7}$$

To accommodate the working bandwidth of the precision positioning stage (1 Hz–2 kHz in the present design), the values of R_2 and C_f in the circuit are properly chosen so that the cutoff frequency of the charge amplifier is sufficiently low. By picking $R_2 = 1$ GΩ and $C_f = 470$ pF, a cut-off frequency of 0.34 Hz is achieved. From Eq. (7), it is apparently that a larger R_2 corresponds to a lower cutoff frequency limit. However, in the circuit, R_2 cannot be infinitely large because the bias current of the operational amplifier AD8659 will saturate the signal output. Besides, a small R_1 should be chosen for broadening the high frequency limit. Here, $R_1 = 20$ kΩ is set and a high cut-off frequency of about 5 kHz is achieved, which is larger than the natural frequency of the precision positioning stage.

The output of PVDF sensors are connected to a shield cable with low capacitance to prevent electrical noises and a 6.5 V battery is served as the electrical power supply for the operational amplifier. After charge amplification, the processed analog voltage signal is directly fed into a data acquisition system and then processed through a computer.

4 Experimental Results

4.1 Experimental Setup

The designed precision positioning stage is shown in Fig. 5. The prototype was monolithically fabricated by electrical discharge machining technique with a whole size of 90 mm × 90 mm × 10 mm. Aluminium alloy 7A04 was selected as the material for its large ratio of modulus to density and small input stiffness. Piezo-stacks from PI were used as motion generators and were installed into the rhombus-type amplifier with a certain preload force. It has a dimension of 10 mm × 10 mm × 36 mm, axial stiffness of 100 N/μm and an output displacement of 36 μm at the driving voltage of 120 V.

As shown in Fig. 5(a), the shaped PVDF sensor was bonded on the surface of the guiding flexible beam by fast-cure elastic epoxy. The signal is transmitted by a shield cable. Also, a precision optical displacement meter from KEYENCE with a 50 nm resolution was used as an independent observer to calibrate and verify the feasibility of the PVDF sensor, as shown in Fig. 5(b). Since the inter-space of the planar precision positioning stage is too small to receive the laser beam of the optical displacement meter, a rigid block with the smooth surface was bonded on the output port of the precision positioning stage to receive the laser beam. Apparently, additional mass of the block will greatly reduce the dynamic frequency of the stage, which indicates the limits of the bulky optical displacement meter.

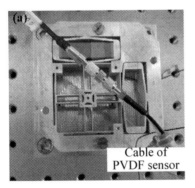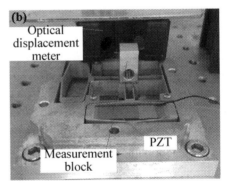

Fig. 5. Picture of the prototype. (a) Measuring by the PVDF sensor. (b) Measuring by the optical displacement meter.

4.2 Experimental Results

The Up to 120 V non-negative sine voltages with 5 Hz were applied to the piezo-stacks. The output displacement of the precision positioning stage was measured respectively by the PVDF sensor and the commercial laser displacement meter. The output voltages obtained from the laser displacement meter were plotted against the output voltages of the PVDF sensor. In this way, the outputs of the PVDF sensor can be calibrated to the amplitude of the laser displacement meter. The reason of performing the calibration is that the piezoelectric constants do not have to be known exactly. Figure 6 (a) provides the calibration results in the x direction, and the sensitivity coefficient of the PVDF sensor is 133 μm/V. It can be seen from Fig. 6 (a) that the output waveform of the PVDF sensor well matches that of the laser displacement meter with the calibrated sensitivity coefficient. Similarly, the sensitivity coefficient of the PVDF sensor in the y direction was measured and calibrated to be 132 μm/V.

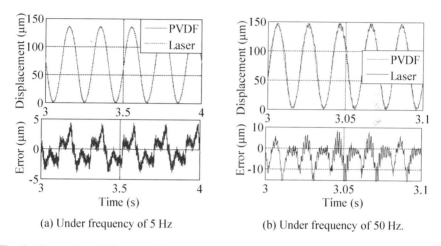

(a) Under frequency of 5 Hz   (b) Under frequency of 50 Hz.

Fig. 6. Comparison of the measuring results in the x direction by PVDF and laser displacement meter under different frequencies.

The output displacement in the y direction was further measured by the laser displacement meter and the PVDF sensor under 120 V sine voltages at the frequencies of 5 Hz and 20 Hz, shown in Fig. 7. Measured maximum displacement in the y direction is about 138 μm at the frequency of 5 Hz and becomes a little large with the increase of the actuating frequency measured by the PVDF sensor. The reason may be that the charge leakage of the PVDF sensor at a lower frequency is more heavy than that at a higher frequency. It can also be seen that the anti-noise interference capability of the PVDF sensor is superior to that of the laser displacement meter with the increase of the actuating frequency. Besides, the experimental output displacement is nonlinear with a maximum hysteresis error of about 15% and 23% at the frequencies of 5 Hz and 20 Hz due to the hysteresis effect of the piezoelectric materials.

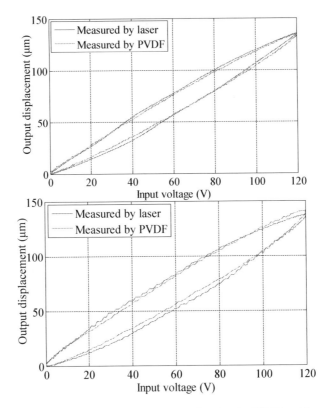

Fig. 7. Comparison of the measuring results in the y direction by PVDF and laser displacement meter under actuating frequencies of 5 Hz (top) and 20 Hz (bottom).

5   Conclusions

This paper develops a piezo-actuated two-DOF XY precision positioning stage with a new sensing concept of displacement. It has a motion range of 138 μm × 138 μm and a fundamental frequency of 1.2 kHz with a compact dimension of 80 mm × 80 mm × 10 mm. The feasibility of designing a very compact sensor based on semi-rectangular shaped PVDF to measure the displacement of the precision positioning stage is demonstrated experimentally. The sensing principle is proposed with some practical implementation issues. The results measured by the PVDF sensor well match that by a commercialized laser displacement meter. The advantages of the presented sensing concept lie in its very compactness with high precision, large bandwidth, simplicity and low cost, rendering it is promising for applications in small interspaces and harsh environment where integrating a bulky transducer is difficult. Future works include further improving the leakage of charges and designing a more reliable insulation technique; applying the PVDF sensor to perform a precise feedback control for precision positioning stages will also be the focus of our future research.

References

1. Chen, F., Liu, L., Li, Q., et al.: Experimental and theoretical analysis of a smart transmission mechanism system. Smart Mater. Struct. **27**(9), 095022 (2018)
2. Wei, H., Shirinzadeh, B., Li, W., et al.: Development of piezo-driven compliant bridge mechanisms: General analytical equations and optimization of displacement amplification. Micromachines **8**(8), 238 (2017)
3. Clark, L., Shirinzadeh, B., Bhagat, U., et al.: Development and control of a two DOF linear–angular precision positioning stage. Mechatronics **32**, 34–43 (2015)
4. Shen, Y., Xi, N., Lai, K.W.C., et al.: A novel PVDF microforce/force rate sensor for practical applications in micromanipulation. Sens. Rev. **24**(3), 274–283 (2004)
5. Shapiro, Y., Kósa, G., Wolf, A.: Shape tracking of planar hyper-flexible beams via embedded PVDF deflection sensors. IEEE/ASME Trans. Mechatron. **19**(4), 1260–1267 (2014)
6. Choi, S., Jiang, Z.: A novel wearable sensor device with conductive fabric and PVDF film for monitoring cardiorespiratory signals. Sens. Actuators A Phys. **128**(2), 317–326 (2006)
7. Lee, C.K., Moon, F.C.: Modal sensors/actuators. J. Appl. Mech. **57**(2), 434–441 (1990)
8. Ling, M.X., Cao, J.Y., Zhuang, J., et al.: Design, pseudo-static model and PVDF-based motion sensing of a piezo-actuated XYZ flexure manipulator. IEEE/ASME Trans. Mechatron. **23**(6), 2837–2848 (2018)
9. Ling, M.X., Cao, J.Y., Jiang, Z., et al.: Modular kinematics and statics modeling for precision positioning stage. Mech. Mach. Theory **107**, 274–282 (2017)

A Generalized Mathematical Model for the Bridge-Type and Lever-Type Mechanism

Fangxin Chen, Jingnan Cai, Wei Dong[✉], and Zhijiang Du

Harbin Institute of Technology, Harbin, China
dongwei@hit.edu.cn

Abstract. The bridge-type amplifier and the lever-type amplifier are the two frequently used displacement amplifiers in the precision engineering. However, to the knowledge of the authors, a generalized mathematical model appropriate for the both types mechanism was not frequently reported, which is instrumental in selecting and designing of the displacement amplifiers in the practice application. To this end, the compliance matrix method based on screw theory is employed to establish a generalized mathematical model for the two amplifiers to offer an easy and objective way to analyze them. In addition, the performances of the amplifiers under external loads are presented in this paper. Theoretical and finite elemental analysis results shown that the prediction errors of the established model for the displacement amplification ratio is within 4.5%, which is so accurate to predict the performance of the two kinds of amplifiers. Finally, the analytical model are confirmed by finite element analysis and by experimental testing of a bridge-lever-type amplifier.

Keywords: Piezoelectric actuation · Displacement amplifiers · Compliance matrix method

1 Introduction

The widely used displacement amplifiers are the bridge-type amplifier and the lever-type amplifier, as illustrated in Fig. 1. The former is well-known for the compact and symmetrical structure while the latter is superior in the simple and flexible structure. To date, the two amplifiers were analyzed applying various methods individually. For instance, Lobontiu [1] formulated an analytical model for amplification ratio and stiffness calculation of bridge-type mechanisms using Castigliano's displacement theorem. Ma [2] derived the ideal and actual amplification ratios based on kinematic theory and virtual work principle respectively. Qi [3] adopted elastic beam theory to analyze the deformation of the hinge and established a concise formula of the bridge-type mechanism's amplification ratio. Friedrich [4] proposed a modeling approach based on beam element to model the bridge-type mechanism, which is more accurate in both static and dynamic analysis. Xu [5] investigated a flexure-based compound bridge-type mechanism which features large lateral stiffness applying Euler-Bernoulli beam theory. Chen [6] modeled a three-dimension bridge type mechanism applying the screw theory. Regarding to the lever-type amplifier, for example, Tang [7] proposed a

© Springer Nature Switzerland AG 2019
H. Yu et al. (Eds.): ICIRA 2019, LNAI 11740, pp. 296–309, 2019.
https://doi.org/10.1007/978-3-030-27526-6_26

multiple-stage lever-type amplifier and predicted its amplification ratio via the geometric model, where all the flexure hinges are considered as ideal pivots. Jouaneh [8]
proposed a general approach for the lever-type mechanism, where all the flexure hinges
are replaced by two springs along two axial directions, thus the motion loss caused by
the flexure hinges stretching can be accurately predicted. Choi [9] presented an
experimentally-validated approach for designing the lever type mechanism. Su [10]
systematically studied the design theory and the synthesis of compliant micro-leverage
mechanism, where the compliance-match theory is proposed to design and analyze the
mechanism. To sum up, although various methods are applied to analyze the two
amplifiers, it is hard to find a systematical work for analyzing and comparing the two
amplifiers under a generalized modeling method. In additional, the load capacity of the
displacement has not been drawn enough attention.

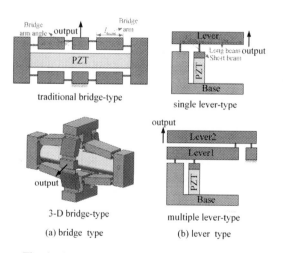

Fig. 1. Schematic of the two types of amplifiers

A generalized mathematic model based on the compliance-matrix method with
screw theory [11–13] are established for the two amplifiers in this paper. In particular,
the amplification ratio based on the geometrical structure will be described in Sect. 2.
And then, the generalized model will be detailedly presented in Sect. 3. In Sect. 4, the
analytical model are confirmed by finite element analysis and by experimental testing
of a bridge-lever-type amplifier. Finally, Sect. 5 concludes this paper.

2 Theoretical Modeling

2.1 Theoretical Model Based on Geometric Structure

The bridge-type mechanism can be considered as a center symmetrical Scott-
mechanism. According to the principle of triangular amplification, the amplification
ratio of the bridge type amplifier with ideal pivots can be calculated via the bridge arm
angle α [2]:

$$da\_Bridge = \cot(\alpha) \tag{1}$$

Based on the lever principle, the magnification of the lever-type is the rate of the long beam to the short beam.

$$da\_lever = \frac{L_{long}}{L_{short}} \tag{2}$$

Although the geometrical ratio is easy to obtain via Eqs. (1) and (2), it can only be used for preliminary design due to the neglect of the influence from the flexure hinges. To improve the accuracy of the model, the deformation of the flexure hinges should be considered in the theoretical model.

2.2 Compliance Modeling of Flexure Hinges

With the development of the compliant mechanisms, the majority of the flexure hinges' compliance matrices can be easily obtained in analytical solution [14–17]. Therefore, many approaches based on the matrix method were proposed to model the compliant mechanisms [18, 19]. On the other hand, to formulate the model in a concise and unified way, the screw theory can be employed to describe the force and displacement of the flexure hinges and the coordinate transformation of the compliance matrix [16, 25–27]. Therefore, in this paper, the two methods will be combined to model the bridge-type mechanism and the lever-type mechanism.

The geometry of a flexure hinge is illustrated in Fig. 2. One end of the flexure hinge is assumed as fixed while the other is free. The coordinate frame is assigned at the geometry center of the free end where a point load is subjected to. The force acting on the free end of the flexure hinge can be denoted by a six-vector termed as a wrench

$$W = (\begin{array}{cccccc} F_x & F_y & F_z & M_x & M_y & M_z \end{array}). \tag{3}$$

The deformation can also be dented by the same way which is termed as a twist

$$\varepsilon = (\begin{array}{cccccc} \theta_x & \theta_y & \theta_z & \delta_x & \delta_y & \delta_z \end{array}) \tag{4}$$

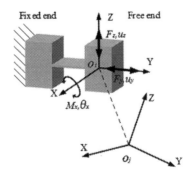

Fig. 2. Flexure hinge with free-end loads and coordinates transformation

When the wrench and the twist need to be transformed from one coordinate (i.e., Oi) to another (i.e., Oj), the adjoint transformation matrix [Ad] can be used

$$[Ad] = \begin{bmatrix} R & 0 \\ DR & R \end{bmatrix} \tag{5}$$

where R is a 3×3 rotation matrix and D is a skew-symmetric matrix defined by the translational vector. Thus Wj and εj in coordinate Oj can be expressed as below

$$W_j = \begin{bmatrix} Ad_{ij} \end{bmatrix} W_i; \quad \varepsilon_j = \begin{bmatrix} Ad_{ij} \end{bmatrix} \varepsilon_i \tag{6}$$

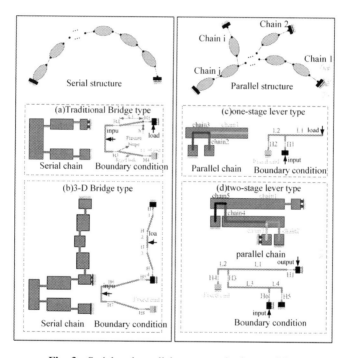

Fig. 3. Serial and parallel structures in the amplifier

According to the elastic beam theory and small deformation assumption, the relation of the wrench and the twist can be formulated as below

$$\Delta \cdot \varepsilon = CW \tag{7}$$

where Δ is a 6×6 matrix used to exchange the first and last three elements of the six-vector, which can be written as below

$$\Delta = \begin{bmatrix} O_{3\times3} & I_{3\times3} \\ I_{3\times3} & O_{3\times3} \end{bmatrix} \tag{8}$$

where $I_{3\times3}$ and $O_{3\times3}$ are 3×3 identity and zero matrices respectively. In Eq. (7), C is the compliance matrix of the flexure hinge which can be uniformly expressed as below

$$C = \begin{bmatrix} c_1 & 0 & 0 & 0 & 0 & 0 \\ 0 & c_2 & 0 & 0 & 0 & c_3 \\ 0 & 0 & c_4 & 0 & c_5 & 0 \\ 0 & 0 & 0 & c_6 & 0 & 0 \\ 0 & 0 & c_7 & 0 & c_8 & 0 \\ 0 & c_9 & 0 & 0 & 0 & c_{10} \end{bmatrix} \tag{9}$$

Combing Eqs. (6) and (7), the force or the displacement in the new coordinate can be obtained as follows

$$\varepsilon_j = \left[Ad_{ij}\right]^{-1} \Delta C \left[Ad_{ij}\right] W_j \tag{10}$$

2.3   Compliance Modeling of the Two Type Amplifiers

According to the basic theory of mechanism synthesis, all the mechanisms can be classified into two configurations, i.e., serial structure and parallel structure, as shown in Fig. 3, where the parallel structure always can be decomposed into a quantity of serial chains. Taking the traditional bridge-type mechanism as an example, this amplifier is comprised of two symmetric serial chains that are connected of several flexure hinges and rigid beams. The three-dimensional bridge-type mechanism can also be simplified as a planar serial chain, as shown in Fig. 3(b), thus only a serial chain needs to be analyzed when the bridge-type mechanism is modeled. As for the lever-type mechanism, the fixed end on the lever (which is marked in orange in Fig. 3(c) and (d)) can be considered as a branched serial chain, so the lever-type mechanism is a typical parallel structure, which should be sub-structured into simpler serial chains.

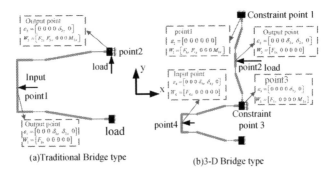

Fig. 4. The point of interest at bridge type mechanism chains and their twists/wrenches

Generally, there are two forces applied on the serial chain simplified from the bridge-type mechanism, i.e., input force and external load. In addition, the boundary conditions can also be replaced by the reaction forces. Therefore, the simplified model is a serial chain with multiple point loading, whose twists and wrenches are presented in Fig. 4. According to the small deformation assumption, the displacement on the calculated point is a summation of the displacements produced individually by all the loads over the relevant flexures, which can be formulated as below.

$$\varepsilon_c = \varepsilon_c^{f_1} + \varepsilon_c^{f_2} + \cdots + \varepsilon_c^{f_i} + \cdots + \varepsilon_c^{f_k} = \sum_{i=1}^{k} \varepsilon_c^{f_i} \tag{11}$$

where the superscript denotes the applied forces (loads) and the subscript represents the calculated point. For the same reason, the displacement individually produced by each force can be calculated by superimposing the displacements produced by the flexure hinges situated on the serial chain that are situated between the force applied point and the fixed end

$$\varepsilon_c^{f_i} = \varepsilon_{H_1}^{f_i} + \varepsilon_{H_2}^{f_i} + \cdots + \varepsilon_{H_j}^{f_i} + \cdots + \varepsilon_{H_k}^{f_i} = \sum_{j=1}^{k} \varepsilon_{H_j}^{f_i} \tag{12}$$

where the subscript represents the calculated flexure hinges. Combining Eqs. (10)–(12), the displacement on each point in the serial chain can be formulated as below.

$$
\begin{aligned}
\varepsilon_c &= \left(\sum_{j=1}^{k} [Ad_{1j}]^{-1} \Delta C [Ad_{1j}] \right) W_1 + \cdots \\
&+ \left(\sum_{j=1}^{k} [Ad_{mj}]^{-1} \Delta C [Ad_{mj}] \right) W_m \\
&= \sum_{i=1}^{m} \left(\sum_{j=1}^{k} [Ad_{mj}]^{-1} \Delta C [Ad_{mj}] \right) W_m
\end{aligned}
\tag{13}
$$

Regarding to the traditional bridge-type mechanism, the main concerned points are the input point (point 1 illustrated in Fig. 4(a)) and the output point (point 2 in Fig. 4 (a)), whose formulations are presented in Fig. 5, where three constraint equations can be obtained while the number of the unknown parameters is only two. Therefore, all the displacements and forces can be solved out by the two matrix equations.

In the same way, the matrix equations for the 3-D bridge-type mechanism can also be obtained. Differently, there are four points should be calculated (i.e., four matrix equations should be written) and the numbers of the constraint equations obtained and the unknown parameters are seven and five respectively. Thus all the parameters of the four points can be solved out.

In the same way, the matrix equations for the 3-D bridge-type mechanism can also be obtained. Differently, there are four points should be calculated (i.e., four matrix

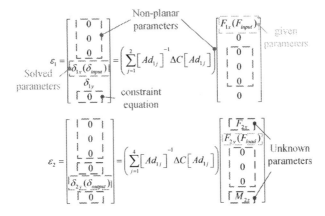

Fig. 5. The matrix equations for the traditional bridge-type mechanism

equations should be written) and the numbers of the constraint equations obtained and the unknown parameters are seven and five respectively. Thus all the parameters of the four points can be solved out.

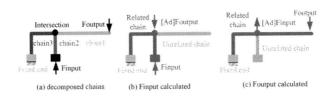

(a) decomposed chains   (b) Finput calculated   (c) Foutput calculated

Fig. 6. Illustration of the lever type amplifier's modeling process

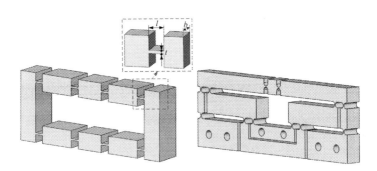

Fig. 7. Three-dimensional models of the two type amplifiers

For the lever-type mechanism, several serial chains can be decomposed. When the displacement of the interested point is calculated, only the chains between the point and the fixed end (which are termed as related chains while the others are termed as unrelated chains in the paper) should be taken into account. Taking the displacement at the input end of the one-stage lever-type amplifier as an example, the deformation of flexure hinges in chain 2 and chain 3 illustrated in Fig. 6(a) should be added in Eq. 11 but the flexure hinges in chain 1 should not be included. On the other hand, although the deformation of the flexure hinges in the unrelated chains don't contribute to the displacement of the calculated point, the force applied on those chain will influence the deformation of the flexure hinges in the related chains, therefore the force applied on the unrelated chain should be transformed to the intersection of the related chain and unrelated chain, as illustrated in Fig. 6(b). The displacement at each point on the parallel chain can be formulated as below.

$$
\varepsilon_c = \sum_{i=1}^{m} \left(\sum_{j=1}^{k} [Ad_{ij}]^{-1} \Delta C [Ad_{ij}] \right) W_i^R
$$
$$
+ \sum_{i=1}^{m} \left(\sum_{j=1}^{k} [Ad_{ij}]^{-1} \Delta C [Ad_{ij}] \right) W_i^U
$$

(14)

where superscript "R" denotes the related chain and "U" represents the unrelated chain. When the matrix equations of the lever-type mechanism are obtained, the process to get the solution of the equation is the same as the bridge-type mechanism.

When the mechanism suffers from elastic load, the load in the equations should be written in another way

$$
F_{load} = -k_{load} \cdot \delta_{out}
$$

(15)

where k load is the stiffness coefficient of the elastic load. The minus sign means the direction between the load force and the displacement is opposite.

3 Validation by FEA and Precious Experiment

In this section, the FEA simulation and the previous experimental studies are used to validate the accuracy of the established model, where the traditional bridge-type amplifier and two-stage lever-type amplifier are taken as examples whose three-dimensional models are illustrated in Fig. 7 and the structure parameters are listed in Table 1.

Table 1. The parameters of the amplifiers (unit mm)

	L_1	$L_2(h)$	L_3	L_4	t	l	b
B	12.5	2	–	–	0.6	3	10
L	7.5	12.5	10	25	0.6	5	10

The relation of the arm beam angle and the amplification ratio of the traditional bridge-type amplifier using different methods are shown in Fig. 8(a), while the results of the two-stage lever-type amplifier are demonstrated in Fig. 8(b), where the FEA is regarded as the nominal reference value. We can see the results from the proposed model and the FEA match very well, where the maximum error between both is about 4.5%. Therefore, it can be concluded that the proposed method can be employed to model both type mechanisms.

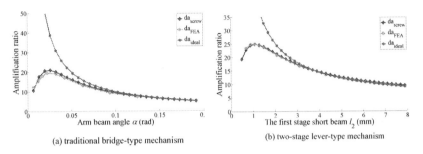

(a) traditional bridge-type mechanism   (b) two-stage lever-type mechanism

Fig. 8. Result comparisons based on different methods

Table 2. Comparison of the results from the modeling and the experiment

Traditional bridge type amplifier			Two-stage lever-type amplifier		
Screw	[22]	Error	Screw	[9]	Error
5.83	5.51	5.5%	19.78	20	1.1%

To further validate the accuracy of the modeling, the comparison of the results from the modeling and previous experimental study is presented in Table 2. Chen designed a highly efficient bridge-type amplifier in [22], where a traditional bridge-type amplifier is tested with the amplification ratio of 5.51, which is 5.83 calculated by the theoretical model in this paper. A two-stage lever-type amplifier is tested with the amplification ratio of 20 in [9] and the theoretical value calculated in this paper is 19.78. The maximum deviation between the theoretical model and the experiment is 5.5% which mainly come from the machining error and the inaccuracy of the compliance matrix of the flexure hinge. The good qualitative agreement between the modeling and the experiments confirms the effectiveness of the modeling method.

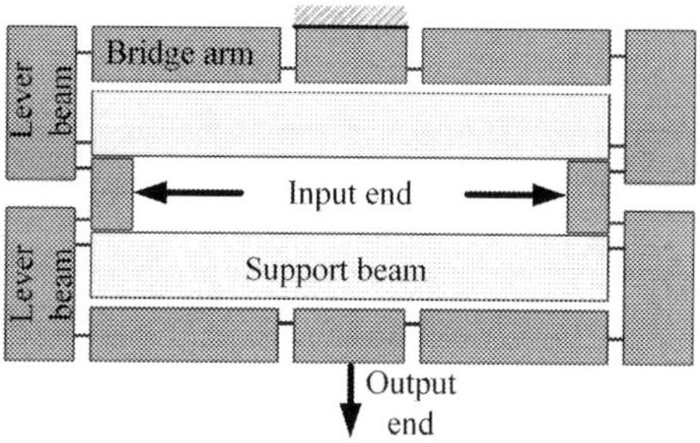

Fig. 9. Bridge-lever-type mechanism

4 Bridge-Lever-Type Mechanism

4.1 Mechanism Design

The concept of the bridge-lever-type mechanism is proposed to design a displacement amplifier inherent the merits of the two type amplifiers, i.e., compact, symmetry, and large magnification, as shown in Fig. 9. To validate the effectiveness of the proposed modeling method, the bridge-lever-type mechanism with be analyzed by the theoretical model, finite element analysis, and experiment study.

Thanks to the symmetry of the mechanism, only a quarter of the amplifier needs to be analyzed when the amplification ratio is calculated. Figure 10 is the skeleton representation of the half amplifier with boundary conditions and the coordinate systems at the links. Under the action of force produced by a piezoelectric stack, the output end will be pulled vertically.

According to Eq. (14), the input end displacement and the output end displacement can be written as below:

$$\varepsilon_c = \left(\sum_{j=1}^{3} [Ad_{iA}]^{-1} \Delta C [Ad_{iA}] \right) F_A^R$$
$$+ [Ad_{AB}]^{-1} \Delta C [Ad_{AB}] F_D^U \tag{16}$$

$$\varepsilon_c = \left(\sum_{j=3}^{6} [Ad_{iA}]^{-1} \Delta C [Ad_{iA}] \right) F_D^R$$
$$+ [Ad_{DB}]^{-1} \Delta C [Ad_{DB}] F_A^U \tag{17}$$

According to the boundary conditions, Eqs. (15) and (16) offer four homogeneous equations, which can be used to solve out the four unknown parameters in the force vectors, i.e., f_{ax}, m_a, f_{by}, and m_b. Therefore, the input displacement δ_{ay} and output displacement δ_{dx} can be obtained by substituting the solved parameters into Eqs. (15) and (16). The following numerical parameters are utilized: $l_1 = 9$ mm, $l_2 = 32$ mm, $l_3 = 68$ mm, $h = 5$ mm, $l_0 = 6$ mm, $t = 0.6$ mm, $b = 30$ mm, $E = 7.2e10$ N/m^2, $\mu = 0.3$, $\alpha_f = 1.2$.

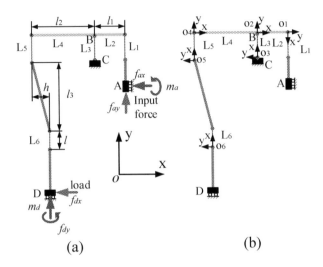

Fig. 10. Skeleton representation of the half amplifier with: (a) the lengths and boundary conditions of the actual links; (b) the coordinate systems at the links

It should be noted that this design variant is not optimized to generate the maximum displacement amplification as the main purpose of the analyzed design is to help illustrate the application of the analysis model developed in previous sections. However, the calculation procedure introduced in this paper can be used to carry an optimization study over the design parameters defining the dimensions and orientation of the flexure hinges and of the adjoining rigid links

4.2   Experiment and Simulation

First the finite element analysis based on commercial software Workbench is presented, where the meshing model is created by the Automatic Method, and a small enough smart size is adopted to mesh the flexure hinges. During the simulation, a fixed constraint applied on the base of the amplifier, and two identical force were applied at the input ends of the amplifier. Figure 11 is the FEA model of the amplifier.

Fig. 11. FEA model of the amplifiers

To further validate the effectiveness of the proposed model, an experiment study based on a prototype of the bridge-lever-type have been conducted. The prototype was fabricated via the wire-EDM process using a piece of Al 7075 alloy. A 160 μm-stroke piezoelectric actuator (PSt-150/10/160-VS15, Piezomechanik, Inc) is used to actuate the mechanism. Due to the hysteresis of the PZT, the displacements at both the input end and output end of the amplifier need to be measured by displacement sensors. Particularly, the input displacement is measured by a capacitive sensor (Micro-Epsilon Company) with the resolution of 50 nm and the measuring range of 0.5 mm, while the output displacement is measured by a computer vision system, as shown in Fig. 12, where a CCD camera (MER-200-20GM/C-P) with 1628 × 1236 pixels and 5.6 μm 5.6 μm resolution is used. To test the load capacity of the amplifier, the weights are hung at the output of the mechanism.

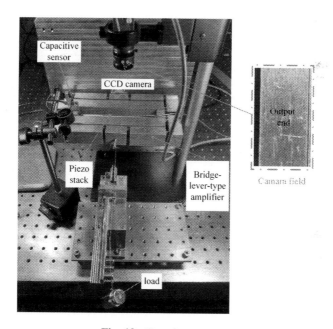

Fig. 12. Experiment setup

Figure 13 shows the amplification ratio of the mechanism in the case of four different external loads applied (i.e., 0 N, 10 N, 20 N, and 30 N). The amplification ratio of the mechanism is 46.5 tested in the experiment when the load is zero and the amplification ratio is 35.5 when the load is up to 30 N. In addition, it can be seen that the amplification ratio calculated by the geometry based model is not related to the external load, while the results from other methods show that the amplification ratio decreases linearly with the load increase. Furthermore, the deviation between the geometry based model and the experiment result is 13.1%, while the matrix model is within 2%.

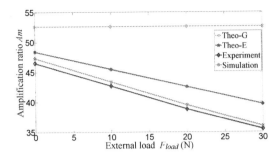

Fig. 13. The results comparison among the theoretical model, the experiment and the simulation

5   Conclusions

A generalized mathematical modeling based on compliance matrix model with screw theory is established for displacement amplifiers analysis and design. The modeling is beneficial to simplify the modeling process for the two displacement amplifiers and offers an easy and objective way to compare their working performances. The accuracy of the model is validated by the FEA simulation and previous experimental studies. Based on the model, amplification ratio and load capacitive of the bridge-lever-type amplifier is designed and analyzed. The errors between the analysis result and the experiment result tell us that the established model is accurate enough for the displacement amplifier performance prediction.

References

1. Lobontiu, N., Garcia, E.: Analytical model of displacement amplification and stiffness optimization for a class of flexure-based compliant mechanisms. Comput. Struct. **81**, 2797–2810 (2003)
2. Ma, H., Yao, S., Wang, L., Zhong, Z.: Analysis of the displacement amplification ratio of bridge-type flexure hinge. Sens. Actuators A Phys. **132**, 730–736 (2006)
3. Qi, K., Xiang, Y., Fang, C., Zhang, Y., Yu, C.: Analysis of the displacement amplification ratio of bridge-type mechanism. Mech. Mach. Theory **87**, 45–56 (2015)
4. Friedrich, R., Lammering, R., Rösner, M.: On the modeling of flexure hinge mechanisms with finite beam elements of variable cross section. Precis. Eng. **38**, 915–920 (2014)
5. Xu, Q., Li, Y.: Analytical modeling, optimization and testing of a compound bridge-type compliant displacement amplifier. Mech. Mach. Theory **46**, 183–200 (2011)
6. Chen, F., Du, Z., Yang, M., Gao, F., Dong, W., Zhang, D.: Design and analysis of a three-dimensional bridge-type mechanism based on the stiffness distribution. Precis. Eng. **51**, 48–58 (2018)
7. Tang, H., Li, Y., Xiao, X.: A novel flexure-based dual-arm robotic system for high-throughput biomanipulations on micro-fluidic chip. In: 2013 IEEE/RSJ International Conference on Intelligent Robots and Systems (IROS), Tokyo, Japan, pp. 1531–1536 (2013)
8. Jouaneh, M., Yang, R.: Modeling of flexure-hinge type lever mechanisms. Precis. Eng. **27**, 407–418 (2003)

9. Choi, S.B., Han, S.S., Han, Y.M., Thompson, B.S.: A magnification device for precision mechanisms featuring piezoactuators and flexure hinges: design and experimental validation. Mech. Mach. Theory **42**, 1184–1198 (2007)
10. Su, X.S., Yang, H.S.: Design of compliant microleverage mechanisms. Sens. Actuators A Phys. **87**, 146–156 (2001)
11. Su, H., Shi, H., Yu, J.: A symbolic formulation for analytical compliance analysis and synthesis of flexure mechanisms. J. Mech. Des. **134**, 051009 (2012)
12. Rouhani, E., Nategh, M.J.: An elastokinematic solution to the inverse kinematics of microhexapod manipulator with flexure joints of varying rotation center. Mech. Mach. Theory **97**, 127–140 (2016)
13. Hao, G., Li, H.: Constraint-force-based approach of modelling compliant mechanisms: principle and application. Precis. Eng. **47**, 158–181 (2017)
14. Tian, Y., Shirinzadeh, B., Zhang, D.: Closed-form compliance equations of filleted V-shaped flexure hinges for compliant mechanism design. Precis. Eng. **34**, 408–418 (2010)
15. Chen, G., Shao, X., Huang, X.: A new generalized model for elliptical arc flexure hinges. Rev. Sci. Instrum. **79**, 095103 (2008)
16. Kang, D., Gweon, D.: Analysis and design of a cartwheel-type flexure hinge. Precis. Eng. **37**, 33–43 (2013)
17. Lobontiu, N., Paine, J.S., Garcia, E., Goldfarb, M.: Corner-filleted flexure hinges. J. Mech. Des. **123**, 346–352 (2001)
18. Noveanu, S., Lobontiu, N., Lazaro, J., Mandru, D.: Substructure compliance matrix model of planar branched flexure-hinge mechanisms: design, testing and characterization of a gripper. Mech. Mach. Theory **91**, 1–20 (2015)
19. Lobontiu, N.: Compliance-based matrix method for modeling the quasi-static response of planar serial flexure-hinge mechanisms. Precis. Eng. **38**, 639–650 (2014)
20. Selig, J.M., Ding, X.: A screw theory of static beams. In: 2001 Proceedings of the IEEE/RSJ International Conference on Intelligent Robots and Systems, Maui, HI, USA, vol. 1, pp. 312–317 (2001)
21. Ling, M., Cao, J., Zeng, M., Lin, J., Inman, D.J.: Enhanced mathematical modeling of the displacement amplification ratio for piezoelectric compliant mechanisms. Smart Mater. Struct. **25**, 75022–75032 (2016)
22. Dong, W., Chen, F., Yang, M., Du, Z., Tang, J., Zhang, D.: Development of a high-efficient bridge-type mechanism based on negative stiffness. Smart Mater. Struct. (2017)

A Novel Giant Magnetostrictive Driven-Vibration Isolation Stage Based on Compliant Mechanism

Xiaoqing Sun[1($\boxtimes$)], Jun Hu[1], Jiuru Lu[1], and Zhilei Wang[2]

[1] Department of Mechanical Engineering, Donghua University,
Shanghai 201620, China
sunxq@dhu.edu.cn
[2] Shanghai Institute of Satellite Engineering, Shanghai 201109, China

Abstract. For aim of providing a stable working environment for those sensitive payloads on-orbit, typically the space telescope and laser communication equipment and so on, micro-vibrations generated by those instruments should be taken measures to suppress. Therefore, this article proposes a novel vibration isolation stage for controlling the low frequency vibration caused by solar arrays, which is difficult to suppress by traditional methods. By adoption of compliant mechanism embedded multilevel amplifiers and giant magnetostrictive actuator, not only the large working stroke with nano-precision could be achieved, but also the required stable output capability in low frequency is obtained. The conceptual scheme and working principle are presented firstly in this paper. And then the theoretical amplification ratio model is constructed and static analysis and dynamic analysis are carried out by ANSYS. Finally, experimental tests are conducted for verifying the related performance. It proves that the proposed stage is capable of suppressing low frequency disturbance.

Keywords: Giant magnetostrictive actuator · Compliant mechanism · Vibration isolation · FEA

1 Introduction

Micro-vibrations in space environment are mainly generated by the CMG, the reaction wheel and the solar arrays [1]. Traditionally, the middle and high frequency vibrations could be suppressed by passive vibration isolation which utilizes the function of spring-damping system. However, to the low frequency vibration, the passive approach is powerless. Thus, the active vibration suppression method should be adopted for handling this. Up to now, there is no effective way to deal with the low frequency micro-vibration, typically caused by the solar arrays. Even though a 3 DOF stage has been proposed in our previous research [2], the actual isolation effect in ultra-low frequency is less efficient, meanwhile the adoption of multi-actuators increases the weight of payload which is unacceptable in aerospace field, when considering the vibration from only one degree of freedom. Therefore, developing a targeted vibration isolation stage is of great significance.

© Springer Nature Switzerland AG 2019
H. Yu et al. (Eds.): ICIRA 2019, LNAI 11740, pp. 310–318, 2019.
https://doi.org/10.1007/978-3-030-27526-6_27

In view of the characteristics of the micro-vibration in low frequency, not only the amplitude is relatively larger than the middle and high frequency, but also the scale still lies in micro-nano level. Thus, for the vibration isolation stage, a large stroke should be ensured, meanwhile micro-nano level precision should be achieved according to the requirements of sensitive payloads. Making a comprehensive view on the research on vibration isolation stage, most attentions are put on these stages with multi-degree of freedoms, typically the Stewart platform [3, 4]. Less researches focus on the active vibration control in one degree of freedom in low frequency. Further analyzing the requirements, it can be found that the compliant mechanism and the smart material actuator are essential to realize the vibration isolation function in required scale. Through the combination of compliant mechanism and smart material actuator, not only the output stroke could be amplified so as to shield the defect of small output displacement from the actuator, but also the transmission accuracy could be guaranteed due to the introduction of flexure hinges, which owns the advantages of no friction and wear, without lubricating and etc. As for the compliant mechanism, a lot of researches have been conducted for developing various of stages, such as the positioning stage [5], the micro-gripper [6] and so on. Similarly, the piezoelectric actuator [6] and the giant magnetostrictive actuator [7] both have been applied in those fields. Without doubt, those contributions could provide a solid foundation for our research.

Therefore, the main contribution of this paper is to develop a targeted vibration isolation stage for suppressing the low frequency disturbance. Through elaborate design of the compliant mechanism, two level amplification mechanism could be embedded in the scheme. In addition, for aim of resisting the static deformation of compliant mechanism caused by the payload, an unloading device is constructed and symmetry design are adopted in the whole scheme of the stage. In order to validate the performance of the developed stage, theoretical modeling, finite element analysis and experimental tests are carried out, respectively. Further comparative analysis is conducted for revealing the future research scope.

2   Conceptual Scheme of Vibration Isolation Stage

Considering the micro-vibration generated by the solar arrays behaves the characteristics of large amplitude and low frequency, we propose the conceptual scheme of the vibration isolation stage, as shown in Fig. 1. It mainly consists of a giant magnetostrictive actuator (GMA) [8], a first amplification mechanism and a second amplification mechanism based on compliant mechanism, an unloading device, a base plate and a payload plate. The GMA generates output displacement which possesses a stable output capability and excellent response characteristics in low frequency. The unloading device based on the combination of linear bearing and spring, could provide adjustable support force for balancing mechanism gravity of the payload. Hence, for the first amplification mechanism and the second amplification mechanism, no significant impact could be introduced. In addition, the first and second amplification mechanisms are designed to enlarge the output displacement. Undoubtedly, the symmetry design could meanwhile provide a stronger support and balance capability.

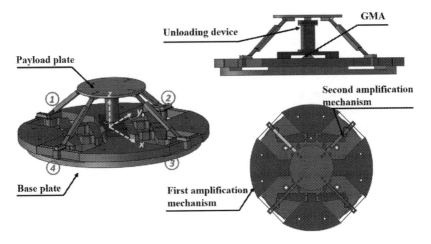

Fig. 1. Conceptual scheme of the vibration isolation stage.

By deep analysis of the first amplification mechanism, it in fact is based on the principle of crank-slider mechanism. The input from the GMA is transmitted to the lever-type crank, finally the enlarged displacement is presented in the compliant slider which is designed according to double parallel four-bar mechanism. And then, the second amplification mechanism plays the role of transition of motion direction. Meanwhile, output displacement could be further enlarged by skillfully adopting the quarter bridge-type amplifier mechanism. Attributing to the adoption of compliant mechanism, not only the stage has a compact size within $\varnothing 240 \times 60$ mm, but also the output precision could be ensured without clearance influence which is commonly found in the traditional hinge. Therefore, based on above-mentioned scheme, when a driving current is introduced to the GMA, the two ends are stretched and push the first and second amplification mechanisms forward, finally the payload plate could generate the required movement for suppressing the disturbance from the base plate. Without doubt, to actively suppress the micro-vibration, the feedback signal should be collected and closed-loop control strategy should be constructed in advance.

3   Theoretical Model and Finite Element Simulation

3.1   Displacement Amplification Ratio

Attributing to the symmetry design, a quarter model of the stage is adopted to evaluate the output performance. As depicted in Fig. 2, the velocity diagram of the stage is mainly decomposed into two parts. Thus, according to pseudo rigid body model method and velocity projection theorem [9], to the first amplification mechanism, the amplifier ratio λ_1 is,

$$\lambda_1 = \frac{\sin\theta}{\cos\left(\theta - \frac{\pi}{4}\right)} \cdot \frac{L_2}{L_1} \tag{1}$$

where θ is the transmission angle of the linking bar.

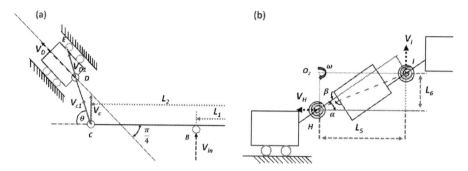

Fig. 2. Velocity diagram of the stage: (a) the first amplification mechanism, (b) the second amplification mechanism

On the other hand, to the second amplification mechanism, its amplifier ratio could be evaluated by,

$$\lambda_2 = \frac{v_I \cdot \partial t}{v_H \cdot \partial t} = \cot(\alpha - \beta) \tag{2}$$

where α and β are the inclination angle of the connecting link and inclination angle of the connecting line of the two rotary shafts, respectively. Therefore, the theoretical displacement amplification ratio of the stage λ is,

$$\lambda = \frac{\sin\theta}{\cos\left(\theta - \frac{\pi}{4}\right)} \cdot \frac{L_2}{L_1} \cdot \cot(\alpha - \beta) \tag{3}$$

3.2 Finite Element Analysis

In order to verify the related output performance, the finite element model is built primarily through ANSYS 16.0. For improving the computing efficiency, some irrelevant details are simplified and the unloading device is also deleted in view of the micro-nano level movement. Thus, the finite element model is shown in Fig. 3. It should be noted that because of the adoption of flexure hinges, local finite element mesh should be refined elaborately.

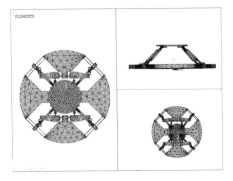

Fig. 3. The finite element model of the stage.

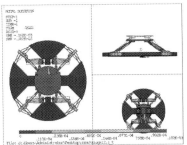

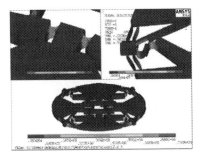

Fig. 4. Displacement nephogram of the stage.

Fig. 5. Stress nephogram of the stage.

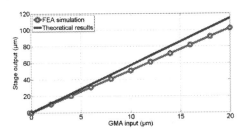

Fig. 6. Amplification ratio calculated by theoretical method and FEA method.

First, static analysis is conducted for verifying the output performance and structural strength. When a series of input displacements from 1 μm to 20 μm, which could represent the driving displacements from the GMA, are applied to the input section, the corresponding output responses could be observed. Hence, we collect and further analyze the analysis results. Typically, Fig. 4 shows the response nephogram of the stage with 20 μm driving input. Obviously, nearly 102 μm output displacement could be achieved by the amplification function of the two compliant mechanisms. In addition, a much larger driving input with 40 μm is supplied to the input section for safety, the corresponding von Mise stress is just 75.2 MPa, which is far smaller than the permissible stress of the aluminum alloy materials, as shown in Fig. 5. Meanwhile, it can be found that the maximum stress occurs in the flexure hinge of the lever fulcrum of the first amplification mechanism. Then for further analyzing the amplification ratio of the stage, the input and output displacements are re-drawn in Fig. 6. It could be found that the amplification ratio from the theoretical model and finite element simulation is 5.72 and 5.1, respectively. Nearly 10% error exists between the two results which is not taken into consideration in the theoretical model.

Finally, the modal analysis is conducted for evaluating the dynamic performance of the vibration isolation stage. As shown in Fig. 7, the first six modal shapes are presented and the first natural frequency is 333 Hz, which proves that the disturbance in low frequency could be unlikely to cause resonance, therefore a good performance could be guaranteed from the control point of view.

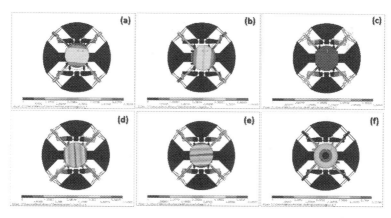

Fig. 7. The first six modal shapes of the vibration isolation stage: (a) 1st modal shape, (b) 2nd modal shape, (c) 3rd modal shape, (d) 4th modal shape, (e) 5th modal shape, (f) 6th modal shape.

4   Experimental Research

4.1   Output Response Tests

According to the proposed design scheme, a prototype is processed through wire electro discharge machining. Subsequently, we construct the experimental test system which mainly consists of two current sources (NF corporation, BP4610), two laser displacement sensors (Keyence corporation, LK-G80) and a vibration excitation system (Lavworks corporation, LW139.138-40). To begin with, the open loop tests are carried out to demonstrate the output performance. Specifically, an optical table (Zhong-hangshiji, ZPT-G-Y) should be adopted for providing the test base. One current source is utilized to supply sinusoidal driving current with peak to peak values ranging from 1 A to 12 A to the GMA. Then the response results occurred in the end of the GMA and the center of the payload plate are collected and then are drawn in Fig. 8. It can be found that the test amplification ratio is nearly to 5.1 which is similar with the FEA results. Meanwhile, it also should be noted that the amplification ratios are both slightly smaller than the theoretical result, and thus demonstrate that the theoretical model should be further revised to better predict the performance. In addition, based on the conclusions above, the designed stage possesses the potential of large stroke output capability which provides a guarantee of output requirements of vibration isolation.

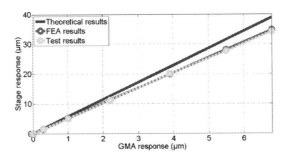

Fig. 8. Comparison of experimental amplification ratio.

4.2 Vibration Isolation Tests

In order to discuss the vibration isolation performance in low frequency, we firstly build the test system and control scheme, as shown in Figs. 9 and 10, respectively. Another current source is used to supply driving current to the vibration excitation system. The laser displacement sensors are utilized to collect the vibration amplitude before and after active control, respectively. In addition, we select the least mean square algorithm as the core of the proposed feedforward controller [10]. Then a harmonic disturbance with low frequency of 0.1 Hz, 1 Hz and 2 Hz are generated by the shaker. Through the active control function of the vibration isolation stage, the final response of the equivalent payload is recorded. Furthermore, the results are analyzed by Matlab 2013a and the corresponding vibration isolation effects are presented in Figs. 11 and 12. According to Fig. 11, it can be found that the vibration response after active control is obviously smaller than disturbance, i.e., the vibration response before active control. Meanwhile, from Fig. 12, we can find that the vibration in 0.1 Hz can be reduced more than 84%, which means at least −15.8 dB vibration suppression effect could be achieved by this stage. In addition, the vibration isolation effects in 1 Hz and 2 Hz are slightly weaker which in fact could be further improved by adjusting the control algorithm. Therefore, based on above research, we can preliminarily conclude that the proposed stage has the capability of suppressing the micro-vibration with low frequency. In future, further tests should be carried out to verify its performance.

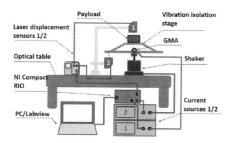

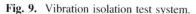

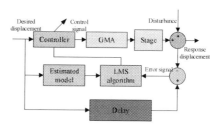

Fig. 9. Vibration isolation test system.   **Fig. 10.** The active control scheme.

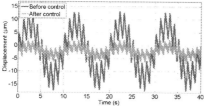

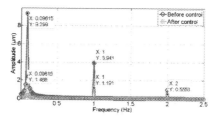

Fig. 11. Time domain results of the stage.   **Fig. 12.** Frequency domain results of the stage.

5   Conclusions

A novel vibration isolation stage driven by giant magnetostrictive actuator is developed in this paper. And theoretical modeling, FEA simulation and experimental tests are conducted for detailedly investigating its performances. The static and dynamic simulation prove that the stage has a better amplification capability and output response capability. Finally, through experimental tests the factual vibration isolation effects are validated and a better attenuation effect is just presented in 0.1 Hz, which means the control strategy might has room for further improvement. Meanwhile, based on the test results, it's not difficult to find that the proposed vibration isolation stage possesses the required function preliminarily. In future, more tests could be carried out and the control strategy could be improved for obtaining a better performance.

Acknowledgments. This research was supported by "the Fundamental Research Funds for the Central Universities (NO. 2232019D3-37)", the Initial Research Funds for Young Teachers of Donghua University (NO. 103-07-0053049) and the research grant (USCAST2015-05) from Shanghai Aerospace Fund.

References

1. Hur, G.: Isolation of micro-vibrations due to reaction wheel assembly using a source-path-receiver approach for quantitative requirements. J. Vibr. Control **25**(8), 1424–1435 (2019)
2. Sun, X.Q., Yang, B.T.: Optimal design and experimental analyses of a new micro-vibration control payload-platform. J. Sound Vibr. **374**, 43–60 (2016)
3. Duan, X.C., Qiu, Y.Y.: On the mechatronic servo bandwidth of a stewart platform for active vibration isolating in a super antenna. Robot. Comput.-Integr. Manuf. **40**, 66–77 (2016)
4. Yang, X.L., Wu, H.T.: Dynamic modeling and decoupled control of a flexible Stewart platform for vibration isolation. J. Sound Vibr. **439**, 398–412 (2019)
5. Wang, P.Y., Xu, Q.S.: Design of a flexure-based constant-force XY precision positioning stage. Mech. Mach. Theory **108**, 1–13 (2017)
6. Liu, P.B., Yan, P.: Design and trajectory tracking control of a piezoelectric nano-manipulator with actuator saturations. Mech. Syst. Sig. Process. **111**, 529–544 (2018)
7. Zhang, H., Zhang, T.L.: Design of a uniform bias magnetic field for giant magnetostrictive actuators applying triple-ring magnets. Smart Mater. Struct. **22**, 1–6 (2013). 115009
8. Sun, X.Q., Wang, Z.L.: Integrated design of actuator for thin plate optical reflector. Aerosp. Shanghai **3**, 60–66 (2018)
9. Sun, X.Q., Yi, S.C.: A new bi-directional giant magnetostrictive-driven compliant tensioning stage oriented for maintenance of the surface shape precision. Mech. Mach. Theory **126**, 359–376 (2018)
10. Yi, S.C., Yang, B.T.: Microvibration isolation by adaptive feedforward control with asymmetric hysteresis compensation. Mech. Syst. Sig. Process. **114**, 644–657 (2019)

Topological Synthesis of Compliant Mechanisms Using a Level Set-Based Robust Formulation

Benliang Zhu[1(✉)], Mohui Jin[2], Xianmin Zhang[1], and Hongchuan Zhang[1]

[1] Guangdong Key Laboratory of Precision Equipment
and Manufacturing Technology, South China University of Technology,
Guangzhou 510642, China
meblzhu@scut.edu.cn
[2] College of Engineering, South China Agricultural University,
Guangzhou 510642, China

Abstract. Topology optimized compliant mechanisms have been widely utilized as the microdevices in microelectromechanical system. In applying topology optimization to design compliant mechanisms, one of the longstanding problems is that the obtained mechanisms often have highly localized compliance regions which make them very difficult to fabricate. In order to obtain manufacturable topology optimized compliant mechanisms, this paper presents a robust formulation based on the level set method. In the formulation, the goal is to maximize the objective for the worst case of three different structural configurations which are represented by three different level set functions. Not only the formulation can eliminate the highly localized compliance regions, it also can precisely control the minimum length scale in the obtained mechanisms. The validity and different aspects of the proposed formulation are demonstrated on several benchmark problems.

Keywords: Compliant mechanisms · Topology optimization ·
Level set method · Robust design

1 Introduction

Compliant mechanisms that can transmit forces/torques through the elastic deformation of the comprising material have received considerable attention for micro-electro-mechanical system (MEMS) [6,14]. The reason is that, in compliant mechanisms, the system is generally monolithic which is essential for miniaturization. For the micro/nano-scale compliant mechanisms, the most commonly used design method is the so-called topology optimization, which is an iterative process where the aim is to seek the optimum distribution of material in a given design domain that minimizes a given cost function while fulfilling prescribed constraints.

© Springer Nature Switzerland AG 2019
H. Yu et al. (Eds.): ICIRA 2019, LNAI 11740, pp. 319–332, 2019.
https://doi.org/10.1007/978-3-030-27526-6_28

Since the pioneer work of [9], several continuum topology optimization methods have been applied to the design of compliant mechanisms, including the density-based approaches, the evolutionary structural optimization method, the moving morphable component(MMC)-based approach, and the level set-based approaches. Among them, level set methods have been paid much attention during the past few years since they can provide smooth boundaries of the obtained structures and inherently free of several numerical difficulties of the density-based methods, e.g., checkerboard patterns [8, 16].

In applying topology optimization to design compliant mechanisms, one of the main difficulties is that the resulted mechanisms often have highly localized compliance regions. This feature makes the obtained mechanisms very difficult to fabricate. Accordingly, a variety of strategies have been developed to alleviate such hinge-regions by controlling the minimum length scale of the resulted mechanisms. In the density-based topology optimization, density/sensitivity based filtering techniques have been proven to be effective approaches to avoid hinges [2]. Stress constraints have been also used to avoid the formulation of weak regions [3]. In order to precisely control the minimal length scale, Guest et al. [4] proposed a Heaviside projection method to control the minimum thickness. The robust formulations [10, 11] have been developed by taking the eroded, dilated and intermediate topologies into account at the same time.

Within level set-based topology optimization, energy function based scheme and special feature constraint have been developed to restrict the geometry thickness of created mechanisms. For example, a quadratic energy functional-based formulation have been used in [7] for the systematic design of hinge-free compliant mechanisms. An intrinsic characteristic stiffness method has been developed by Wang and Chen [13]. However, this method can also lead to point flexures when a large objective is needed. Taking both input and output mean compliances into account also has been verified as a valid method to avoid highly localized compliance regions [16]. Guo [5] suggested a skeleton-based idea to impose minimum and maximum length scale in the optimized Compliant mechanisms.

In this paper, in order to obtain manufacturable topology optimized compliant mechanisms, we presents a robust formulation based on the level set method. In the formulation, the goal is to maximize the objective for the worst case of three different structural configurations. The formulation can eliminate the highly localized compliance regions. Furthermore, it also can precisely control the minimum length scale in the obtained mechanisms.

The remainder of the paper is organized as follows. In Sect. 2, the basic idea of the level set-based topology optimization is introduced. In Sect. 3, the proposed level set-based robust formulation is presented. The minimum length features are discussed. In Sect. 4, sensitivities are presented along with the optimization algorithm for solving the robust formulation. In Sect. 5, several numerical examples are shown to demonstrate the validity of the proposed method. Conclusions and future works are provided in Sect. 6.

2   Level Set Method

Level set method has become a favourite approach to solve topology optimization problems. The underlying idea of the level set method is to represent the structural boundaries Γ as the zero level set of one higher dimensional function ϕ. The relationship between the level set function and the structure can be illustrated as

$$
\begin{cases}
\phi(\mathbf{x}, t) > 0 \text{ if } \mathbf{x} \in \Omega \\
\phi(\mathbf{x}, t) = 0 \text{ if } \mathbf{x} \in \Gamma \\
\phi(\mathbf{x}, t) < 0 \text{ if } \mathbf{x} \in D\backslash\Omega
\end{cases}
\tag{1}
$$

where D is the design domain that completely contains the structural material domain Ω, $D\backslash\Omega$ represents the void area, $\mathbf{x}$ is a point in the design domain, and t is the pseudo-time [1,12]. The optimization process can be described as the evolving of the level set function under the following equation

$$
\frac{\partial \phi}{\partial t} + V_n |\nabla \phi| = 0
\tag{2}
$$

where V_n determines the motion of the interface. To avoid the level set function becoming too flat or steep, a re-initialization procedure can be implemented during the optimization process by solving the following equation

$$
\frac{\partial \phi}{\partial t} + sign(\phi)(1 - |\nabla \phi|) = 0
\tag{3}
$$

where $sign(\cdot)$ is the sign function.

3   Level Set-Based Robust Design of Compliant Mechanisms

The general design domain for topology optimization of compliant mechanisms with single input-output behaviour can be illustrated in Fig. 1. The design domain is fixed at Γ_d. Both its input port and output port are attached with a spring. An input force F is applied at the input port. The goal of the optimization is to maximize the output displacement u_{out}. Incorporating with level set method, a general design model can be illustrated as [2]

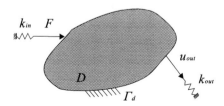

Fig. 1. Design domain of compliant mechanisms.

$$\text{min}: \quad J = -u_{out}(\phi)$$

$$\text{s.t.}: \quad \frac{m(\phi)}{m^*} = \frac{\int_D H(\phi)d\Omega}{m^*} \leq \alpha \qquad (4)$$

$$a_\phi(u, v) = l_\phi(v)$$

where the mass of the mechanism is constrained by using a ratio $0 < \alpha < 1$ between the allowable material usage m and the whole material usage m^* which means the whole design domain is occupied by solid material. H is the Heaviside function defined as

$$H(\phi) = \begin{cases} 1 \text{ if } \phi \geq 0 \\ 0 \text{ if } \phi < 0. \end{cases} \qquad (5)$$

In practice, it is often replaced with a differentiable function defined as

$$H_\epsilon(\phi) = \begin{cases} \epsilon & \text{if } \phi < -\Delta \\ 0.75(1-\epsilon)(\frac{\phi}{\Delta} - \frac{\phi^3}{3\Delta^3}) + \frac{1+\epsilon}{2} & \text{if } -\Delta \leq \phi \leq \Delta \\ 1 & \text{if } \phi > \Delta \end{cases} \qquad (6)$$

where ϵ is a small value and is set to 10^{-3}. Δ is set to $0.75\Delta x$, where Δx is the mesh size. $a_\phi(u,v)$ and $l_\phi(v)$ are the energy bilinear form and linear form respectively and can be expressed as

$$a_\phi(u, v) = \int_D E_{ijkl}\varepsilon_{ij}(u)\varepsilon_{ij}(v)H(\phi)d\Omega \qquad (7)$$

$$l_\phi(v) = \int_D bvH(\phi)d\Omega + \int_D fv\delta(\phi)|\nabla\phi|d\Omega \qquad (8)$$

where E_{ijkl} and ε_{ij} are the elasticity tensor and the strain tensor respectively. b and f are the body force and the boundary traction on the boundary $\Gamma \equiv \partial\Omega$, respectively. $\delta(\phi)$ is the Dirac delta function defined as

$$\delta(\phi) = \frac{\partial H(\phi)}{\partial \phi} \qquad (9)$$

3.1 Robust Formulation

It has been well demonstrated that the optimization problem (4) introduces de facto hinges into the obtained mechanisms, making them function essentially as rigid-body mechanisms. A variety of strategies have been developed to deal with de facto hinge regions. One notable approach is to use a so-called robust formulation which has shown some promise in the density approach to topology optimization [10]. However, extra filtering methods have to be added since there are gray transition and mesh dependence problems need to be considered simultaneously [15]. In the level set topology optimization, it is much easier to adopted this idea. In the following, we introduce how to formulate the robust formulation in the level set-based framework.

In the level set method to topology optimization, the structural configuration is described by a level set function ϕ. In the robust formulation, two extra structural configurations, ϕ^e and ϕ^d, are taken into consideration. ϕ^e and ϕ^d denote the eroded and dilated level set functions, respectively. The optimization problem is formulated by taking into account all the three level set functions and the goal is to maximize the objective function for the worst case of the three configurations. Therefore, the optimization problem can be expressed as

$$\min : \quad J = \max(-u_{out}(\Phi))$$

$$\text{s.t. :} \quad \frac{m(\phi)}{m^*} = \frac{\int_D H(\phi)d\Omega}{m^*} \leq \alpha \tag{10}$$

$$a_\Phi(u,v) = l_\Phi(v)$$

where the energy bilinear form and linear form can be expressed as

$$a_\Phi(u,v) = \int_D E_{ijkl}\varepsilon_{ij}(u(\Phi))\varepsilon_{ij}(v)H(\Phi)d\Omega \tag{11}$$

$$l_\Phi(v) = \int_D bvH(\Phi)d\Omega + \int_D fv\delta(\Phi)|\nabla\Phi|d\Omega \tag{12}$$

and Φ takes the form ϕ^e, ϕ or ϕ^d.

The above formulation requires solving of three independent finite element analysis, one for the eroded structure represented by ϕ^e, one for the original structure represented by ϕ and one for the dilated structure represented by ϕ^d. This for sure will increase the amount of calculation. In future studies, we will investigate whether it is possible to directly operate the sensitivities to avoid solving extra finite element problem and thereby speed up the computations.

As seen, for the proposed formulation, the key is to set the eroded and dilated level set functions, i.e, ϕ^e and ϕ^d. In the density topology optimization, several filter operates have been developed [2]. However, they cannot be directly adopted since in the density topology optimization the operator is used to project all the density values below a threshold to 0 which represent void area. In the level set topology optimization, however, the void area is actually represented by the level set function where its value is smaller than 0.

Here we use the following function to obtain ϕ^e and ϕ^d from ϕ

$$\Phi = c\frac{\tanh(\beta\xi) + \tanh(\beta(\phi/c + 0.5 - \xi))}{\tanh(\beta\xi) + \tanh(\beta(1 - \xi))} - \frac{c}{2} \tag{13}$$

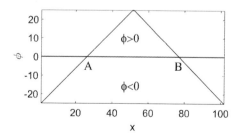

Fig. 2. A signed distance function ϕ and the corresponding structural regions.

324　B. Zhu et al.

where $\xi \in (0,1)$, $\beta > 0$ and

$$c = \max(\phi). \tag{14}$$

This function governed by two continuation parameters ξ and β can be used to shrink or enlarge the structural dimension feature and therefore obtain ϕ^e and ϕ^d. With a fixed β, ϕ^e and ϕ^d are obtained by using different ξ according to

$$\Phi = \begin{cases} \phi^e & \text{if} \quad 0 < \xi < 0.5 \\ \phi^d & \text{if} \quad 1 - \xi \end{cases} \tag{15}$$

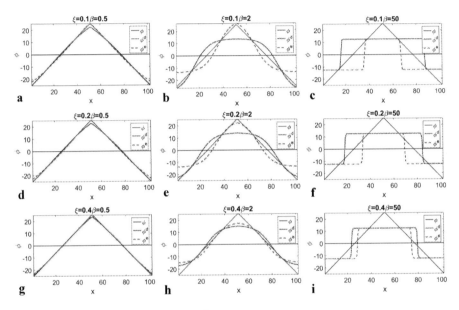

Fig. 3. Level set functions ϕ^e and ϕ^d obtained by using different values of ξ and β.

As seen in Fig. 2 where a signed distance function defining the solid region $\phi > 0$ and void region $\phi < 0$. It can be seen as a structural section which means that the distance $|AB|$ between points A and B represents the structural dimension feature. Figure 3 shows the eroded and dilated level set functions ϕ^e and ϕ^d obtained from ϕ by using different values of ξ and β. It can be seen that for a fixed ξ, the gradient of the level set function will become steep with an increase of β. With a fixed β, the value of ξ can be used to control the variation of distance $|AB|$ and thereby control the variation of ϕ^e, ϕ and ϕ^d. For the examples presented in this study, we have found that a maximum value of $\beta = 2$ is sufficient. The value of β is increased from 0.1 to 2 gradually during the optimization process in order to avoid numerical instabilities.

3.2   Minimum Length Features

This section is devoted to further explain how the choice of the parameters in Eq. (13) can be linked with the length scale. For the using the robust formulation (10), the topologies of the eroded, intermediate and dilated designs are the same [11]. With a fixed β, the minimum length scale b is estimated as a function of ξ and c. The following analysis on the minimum length scale uses an interval in 1D as an example. However, the obtained results are also valid for 2D and 3D problems. For example, in 2D the minimum length scale is defined as the diameter of a circle equals to the length scale in 1D.

As can be seen from Fig. 4(a) where $\phi > 0$ indicates the solid material and $\phi < 0$ indicates the void regions. By using Eq. (13), a solid point with length zero in the eroded design ϕ^e is suppressed to be a solid interval for the intermediate design with finite length $b = |AB|$ which is larger than zero. Similarly, as can be seen from Fig. 4(b), a point with length zero in the dilated design is suppressed to a void interval with finite length $|AB|$ as well.

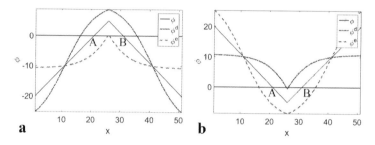

Fig. 4. (a) A solid point in ϕ^e and the corresponding ϕ and ϕ^d, (b) a point in ϕ^d and the corresponding ϕ and ϕ^e.

The minimum length b can be obtained by using Eq. (13) as

$$b = 2c \left(\frac{\text{atanh}(0.5(-\tanh(\beta\xi) + \tanh(\beta(1-\xi))))}{\beta} + \xi - 0.5 \right) \qquad (16)$$

where $0 < \xi < 0.5$. Since c is depended on the design problem, we can use b/c as a normalized length scale on the intermediate design as a function ξ with a fixed β. For example, $\beta = 2$ is used for all the numerical tests in this study, then the relation between b/c and ξ can be shown in Fig. 5 which indicates that the choice of ξ determines uniquely the minimum length features in the obtained design.

4   Sensitivity Analysis and Optimization Algorithm

The optimization requires the sensitivities of the objective function with respect to all the three level set functions. For the original structural configuration ϕ

one can find the shape sensitivities $\frac{\partial J}{\partial \phi}$ in the usual way as in [12] which means that, for the design problem illustrated in Fig. 1, $\frac{\partial u_{out}}{\partial \phi}$ can be obtained as

$$\frac{\partial u_{out}(\phi)}{\partial \phi} = -\int_{\Gamma} E_{ijkl}(\phi)\varepsilon_{ij}(\mathbf{u}(\phi))\varepsilon_{ij}(\mathbf{u}_a(\phi))V_n ds \qquad (17)$$

where $\mathbf{u}$ is the displacement vector due to the input load F, $\mathbf{u}_a$ is the adjoint displacement vector.

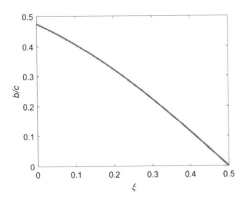

Fig. 5. Normalized length scale on the intermediate design as a function ξ with a fixed $\beta = 2$.

For the eroded and dilated structural configurations, we can use the chain role to obtain the sensitivities. Take the eroded structural configuration as an example, we can get

$$\frac{\partial u_{out}(\phi^e)}{\partial \phi} = \frac{\partial u_{out}(\phi^e)}{\partial \phi^e} \frac{\partial \phi^e}{\partial \phi} \qquad (18)$$

where

$$\frac{\partial \phi^e}{\partial \phi} = \beta \frac{(\mathrm{sech}(\beta(\phi/c + 0.5 - \xi)))^2}{\tanh(\beta\xi) + \tanh(\beta(1 - \xi))} \qquad (19)$$

The sensitivity of the material usage constraint can be simply found as

$$\frac{\partial m}{\partial \phi} = \int_{D} \delta(\phi)d\Omega \qquad (20)$$

After obtaining all the sensitivities, we define a Lagrangian function L as

$$L = J + \lambda(\frac{m(\phi)}{m^*} - \alpha) \qquad (21)$$

where λ is the Lagrange multiplier for the constraint and changes with each iteration k of the optimization algorithm using the scheme [7]

$$\lambda^{k+1} = \lambda^k + \frac{1}{\Lambda^k}(\frac{m(\phi)}{m^*} - \alpha) \qquad (22)$$

where Λ is updated using $\Lambda^{k+1} = \chi\Lambda^k$ where $\chi \in (0,1)$ is a fixed parameter and is set to 0.9. The shape derivative of L at Ω (ϕ) is defined as $L' = \int_{\partial\Omega} lV_n ds$ where l is known as the shape gradient density. To update the level set function, the velocity field can be simply set to be the negative of the shape gradient density, i.e., $V_n = -l$ and this choice guarantees a decreasing of L until the optimized topology is found.

Algorithm 1

1: Make an initial guess ϕ_k; Set ξ, $k = 0$, $\beta = 0$ and $\beta_{\max} = 2$
2: **while** Not convergent **do**
3:    $k = k + 1$
4:    Calculate ϕ_k^e, ϕ_k and ϕ_k^d
5:    Solve three finite element problems based on ϕ_k^e, ϕ_k and ϕ_k^d
6:    Calculate shape sensitivities related to three structural configurations and obtain velocity V_n
7:    Update level set function $\phi_{k+1} = \phi_k + V_n\Delta t$
8:    Re-initialization
9:    Check convergence
10:   **if** mod$(k,5) == 0$ and $\beta < \beta_{\max}$ **then**
11:      $\beta = \min(0.04k, 2)$
12:   **end if**
13: **end while**

Based on the above analysis, a simplified optimization algorithm can be illustrated in pseudo code as in Algorithm 1. For the convergence criteria, the optimization terminates if either of the following two conditions are satisfied:

(1) The difference between the current volume and the required value Vol_{max} is within 0.001. At the same time, the previous five objective function values are all within a 1% tolerance of the current objective value;
(2) The current loop number equals a pre-defined number of steps $k_{\max}$. Unless stated, k_{max} is set to 1000.

5   Examples

In this section, several examples are presented to demonstrate the validity of the proposed method. The artificial material properties are described as follows: Young's modulus for solid material is $E_0 = 1$, and Poisson's ratio is $v = 0.3$. The void area is assumed with a Young's modulus $E_{\min} = 0.001$ and the same Poisson's ratio $v = 0.3$.

5.1   Displacement Inverter

The design domain of displacement inverter is shown in Fig. 6. The input force F is set to 1. The input and output spring stiffnesses are $k_{in} = 1$ and $k_{out} = 0.001$, respectively. The material usage constraint is set to $\alpha = 0.3$. The maximum value of the level set function is artificially set to 7. The design domain is discretized using 100×50 bilinear quadrilateral elements.

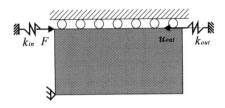

Fig. 6. The design domain (half part) of the displacement inverter.

To demonstrate the validity of the proposed method on eliminating the de facto hinges, the objective function (10) with $\xi = 0.1$ is utilized. The obtained topology and its deformed configuration are both shown in Fig. 7. The robust formulation can prevent the appearance of de facto hinges in the design. Distributed compliant deformations can be obviously observed in the topology shown in Fig. 7(b).

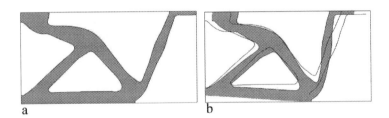

Fig. 7. The final design of the displacement inverter (a) and its corresponding deformed configuration (b).

Contours plots of some intermediate designs of the displacement inverter problem are shown in Fig. 8 in which the contours of the eroded and dilated designs are also shown. Since β is gradually increased from 0 to 2, in the first several steps, contours of eroded, intermediate and dilated designs all sit together. After 50 steps, β will be remained unchange. Topologies of eroded, intermediate and dilated designs can be clearly seen for the rest of iterations.

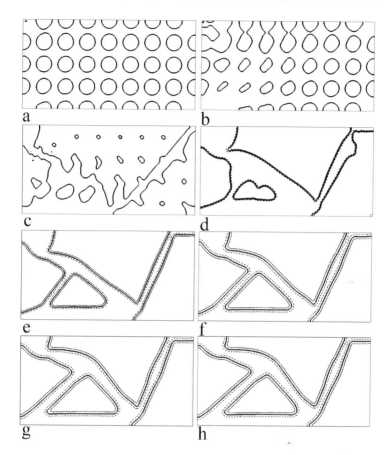

Fig. 8. Contours plots of some intermediate designs of the displacement inverter problem: (a) initial configuration, (b) step 10, (c) step 50, (d) step 100, (e) step 150, (f) step 200, (g) step 250, and (h) step 336. The bold solid lines denote the contour of the intermediate design, the dashed lines denote the contour of the eroded design, and the dot dashed lines denote the dilated design.

The optimization process runs 336 steps before a convergence. The convergence histories of the output displacement u_{out} and volume fraction α of the intermediate design are shown in Fig. 9. The actual material usage α can meet the constraint exactly because the Lagrange multiplier is adapted iteratively.

330   B. Zhu et al.

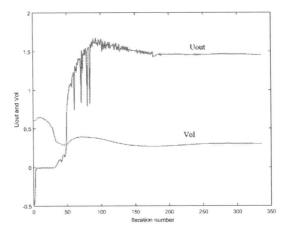

Fig. 9. Convergence histories of the output displacement u_{out} and the volume fraction α.

5.2 Gripper

To further demonstrate the proposed method, we here address another benchmark example, push gripper. The design domain of the push gripper design problem is shown in Fig. 10 where only the top half of the design domain is considered due to symmetry. It is discretized by using 100×50 bilinear quadrangle elements for the elastic analysis. Other parameters are the same with the displacement inverter problem.

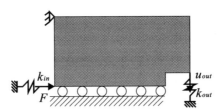

Fig. 10. The design domain (half part) of the push gripper.

The purpose of the examples presented in this section is to illustrate the effect of the volume fraction constraint on the topology of the optimized solution. Two cases are studied in which the volume fraction α is set to 0.3 and 0.2. The optimized topologies of the studied two cases are shown in Fig. 11. The optimized topologies for two values of volume fraction are slightly different. The value of the material resource constraint can directly impact the topology of the optimized mechanism. However, the proposed method can lead to a hinge-free compliant mechanism, regardless of the value of the volume constraint.

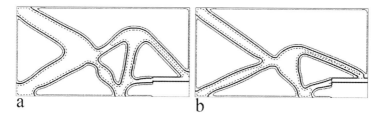

Fig. 11. The final design of the push gripper with different α: (a) $\alpha = 0.3$, (b) $\alpha = 0.2$.

6   Conclusions

This paper has proposed a method for optimizing the topology of compliant mechanisms by considering the minimum length scale control. A robust formulation has been proposed by considering several different configurations at each of the optimization iterations. A new optimization model has been proposed based on the level set method. Several numerical examples have been presented to demonstrate the validity of the proposed method. It is shown that the proposed method can achieve minimum length scale control thereby obtaining hinge-free compliant mechanisms. Future works can be illustrated as follows. The deflections experienced by the compliant mechanisms can easily exceed the linear range. Therefore, a nonlinear finite element analysis method can be incorporated to improve the analysis.

Acknowledgements. This research was supported by the Pearl River Nova Program of Guangzhou (No. 201906010061), the National Natural Science Foundation of China (Grant Nos. 51605166, 51820105007).

References

1. Allaire, G., Jouve, F., Toader, A.M.: Structural optimization using sensitivity analysis and a level set method. J. Comput. Phys. **194**(1), 363–393 (2004)
2. Bendsoe, M.P.: Topology Optimization: Methods, and Applications, 2nd edn. Springer, Heidelberg (2004). https://doi.org/10.1007/978-3-662-05086-6. Corrected printing
3. de Assis Pereira, A., Cardoso, E.L.: On the influence of local and global stress constraint and filtering radius on the design of hinge-free compliant mechanisms. Struct. Multidiscip. Optim. **58**, 1–15 (2018)
4. Guest, J.K., Prévost, J.H., Belytschko, T.: Achieving minimum length scale in topology optimization using nodal design variables and projection functions. Int. J. Numer. Methods Eng. **61**(2), 238–254 (2004)
5. Guo, X., Zhang, W., Zhong, W.: Explicit feature control in structural topology optimization via level set method. Comput. Methods Appl. Mech. Eng. **272**, 354–378 (2014)
6. Howell, L.L.: Compliant Mechanisms. Wiley, Hoboken (2001)

7. Luo, J., Luo, Z., Chen, S., Tong, L., Wang, M.Y.: A new level set method for systematic design of hinge-free compliant mechanisms. Comput. Methods Appl. Mech. Eng. **198**(2), 318–331 (2008)
8. Rozvany, G.I.N.: A critical review of established methods of structural topology optimization. Struct. Multidiscip. Optim. **37**(3), 217–237 (2009)
9. Sigmund, O.: On the design of compliant mechanisms using topology optimization. Mech. Based Des. Struct. Mach. **25**(4), 493–524 (1997)
10. Sigmund, O.: Manufacturing tolerant topology optimization. Acta Mechanica Sinica **25**(2), 227–239 (2009)
11. Wang, F., Lazarov, B.S., Sigmund, O.: On projection methods, convergence and robust formulations in topology optimization. Struct. Multidiscip. Optim. **43**(6), 767–784 (2011)
12. Wang, M., Wang, X.M., Guo, D.M.: A level set method for structural topology optimization. Comput. Metheds Appl. Mech. Eng. **192**(1–2), 227–246 (2003)
13. Wang, M.Y., Chen, S.: Compliant mechanism optimization: analysis and design with intrinsic characteristic stiffness. Mech. Based Des. Struct. Mach. **37**(2), 183–200 (2009)
14. Zhang, X., Zhu, B.: Topology Optimization of Compliant Mechanisms. Springer, Singapore (2018). https://doi.org/10.1007/978-981-13-0432-3
15. Zhou, M., Lazarov, B.S., Wang, F., Sigmund, O.: Minimum length scale in topology optimization by geometric constraints. Comput. Methods Appl. Mech. Eng. **293**, 266–282 (2015)
16. Zhu, B., Zhang, X., Wang, N.: Topology optimization of hinge-free compliant mechanisms with multiple outputs using level set method. Struct. Multidiscip. Optim. **47**(5), 659–672 (2013)

Design and Modeling of a Continuous Soft Robot

Wenbiao Wang, Hailiang Meng, and Guanjun Bao$^{(\boxtimes)}$

College of Mechanical Engineering, Zhejiang University of Technology,
Hangzhou 310023, China
1203739892@qq.com, gjbao@zjut.edu.cn

Abstract. Due to their high flexibility, ductility, adaptability and safety, soft robots attract wide interests from robotics field as well as related areas. While the large deform able nature of the material and structure of soft robot, rises the great challenge for the control and modeling. In available literatures, research work on soft robot modeling was limited to piecewise constant curvature assumption, which will result the disagreement between the mathematical curve and practical results. In this paper, we proposed the method of continuous modeling via calculus on the active face and restricted face of the developed continuous soft robot. Considering the influence of the robot mass on the motion, the virtual work principle and beam theory are used to establish the quasi-steady state model. Subsequently, the kinematic model between the inflated air pressure and bending angle of the robot was obtained. Experimental results verified the proposed model with average distance error of 10.2%, which is quite for soft robot.

Keywords: Soft robot · Continuous robot · Pneumatic muscle · Mathematic model

1 Introduction

In recent years, with the development of new materials and rapid prototyping technology, the research boom of soft robot has been launched around the world. The design of soft robot is mainly inspired by the imitation of natural soft organisms It is one of the hot research topics of robot for the inherent adaptability to unaware objects and complex environments [1]. His team developed a variety of continuous robots employing pneumatics. In 2001, Hannan and Walker developed a super-redundant pictographic robot [2] consists of 16 2-DOF U-joints with a total length of 82.32 cm. It can be divided into four sections of different lengths, each consisting of four joints. In 2005, Walker and McMahan developed the continuous robot Air-Octor [3, 4], who has a total length of 50 cm and a diameter of 10 cm. In 2006 Walker and Jones developed a continuous robot that mimicked the octopus tentacles. The robot uses pneumatic artificial muscle (PMA) as the driver, with a total length of 110 cm. It can be divided into four segments. Each segment is driven by 3–6 wheels and can bend in two degrees

© Springer Nature Switzerland AG 2019
H. Yu et al. (Eds.): ICIRA 2019, LNAI 11740, pp. 333–345, 2019.
https://doi.org/10.1007/978-3-030-27526-6_29

of freedom. The entire robot has 12 degrees of freedom. It enables the capture of complex shapes and powerful navigation and obstacle avoidance in complex environments. In 2011, Festo in Germany developed a new biomimetic machine processing system based on the characteristics of the elephant trunk, a "bionic operation assistant" [5]. From a design point of view, the above systems exhibited flexibility in the actuator and used a fully flexible material. Therefore, they are completely soft and continuous. On the other hand, the modeling of such robots is challenging due to the large nonlinear deformation of all dimensions [6]. Unlike the kinematics of traditional rigid-link robots, the pose of any point on a rigid-body robot can be precisely defined by the link length and joint angle, while continuous robots need to consider their own elasticity. In order to accurately define the point of interest on the robot, the forces and moments applied to the robot must be characterized by its own actuator and external environment. The most commonly used models were described in [7–10]. Many teams are currently applying beam theory intended to create kinematic models of continuous robots [7, 11–13]. In these mathematic work, constant curvature approximation was adopted to build various simplified modeling [12, 14, 15]. The aforementioned research is based on the analysis principle of beam theory combined with the individual structure. The beam theory has higher precision and reliability in dealing with small bending deformation no high stiffness objects. However, this method has a large error in the cases of dealing with large deformation materials. Thus, the beam theory has certain limitations in practicality for soft robot. Furthermore, the fixed curvature approximation took the bended robot as a fixed-radius circular arc which disagrees with the fact that the soft robot shows a variable curvature when bending. Under the small bending condition, the curvature approximation can generate acceptable theoretical deformation curve. However, more appropriate curve model is needed in the large deformation stage.

In this paper, the proposed continuous soft robot used pneumatic artificial muscles as the actuators. The pneumatic artificial muscle is an elastic rubber sealing structure with a braided mesh sleeve. For the developed continuous soft robot, we made the spiral motion hypothesis by analyzing the overall force of the robot. The overall force analysis of the continuous soft robot were executed to build the kinematic model, using the principle of virtual work and energy conservation.

2 Structure of the Continuous Soft Robot

2.1 Design of Pneumatic Muscles

Pneumatic muscles are composed of super-elastic silicone tube, corrugated woven mesh, air inlet joint and closed joint, as shown in Fig. 1. The main source of power for pneumatic muscles comes from the air pressure inside the silicone tube. When the silicone tube is inflated with compressed air, the tube has a forward extension force that urges the tube to stretch, due to the expansion of the closed tube and constraints provided by the braided mesh sleeve.

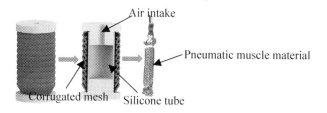

Fig. 1. Pneumatic muscle diagram

The traditional pneumatic muscle uses a double-helical woven mesh structure, and the elongation of the pneumatic muscle depends on the knitting angle of the double-helical woven mesh. When the knitting angle is 75°, the pneumatic muscle can reach the ultimate elongation of 75%. The woven mesh used in the pneumatic muscle designed in this paper is completely different from the traditional woven mesh structure, and its structure is corrugated structure. As shown in Fig. 2(a), when the corrugated structure is pressed, the thickness of each corrugated structure is 2 mm, the inner laminated portion is 3 mm, the inner diameter is 10 mm, and the outer diameter is 18 mm after pressing. The pneumatic muscle is filled with air pressure, as shown in Fig. 2(b), when the corrugated woven mesh is subjected to the radial expansion force of the silicone tube, the corrugated structure is opened. Continue to fill the silicone tube with air pressure, the radial force of the silicone tube on the woven mesh is increasing, and the corrugated structure is gradually expanded, until the corrugated structure is completely straightened as shown in Fig. 2(c), and then into the silicone tube. Pressurized, pneumatic muscles will no longer produce elongation, but its stiffness is constantly increasing.

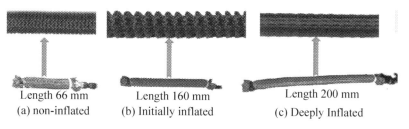

| Length 66 mm | Length 160 mm | Length 200 mm |
| (a) non-inflated | (b) Initially inflated | (c) Deeply Inflated |

Fig. 2. Inflatable test

2.2 Continuous Soft Robot

As shown in Fig. 3, the proposed continuous soft robot is mainly composed of upper end cover, lower end cover and pneumatic muscles. The upper end cap is connected to the three pneumatic muscles through the joint, and the joint holes are evenly distributed on the surface of the end cap. The three pneumatic muscles are evenly distributed between the upper and lower end caps at an angle of 120°. Controlling the internal air pressure of the three new pneumatic flexible actuators independently can realize bending in three-dimensional space. Table 1 shows the design parameters of the continuous soft robot.

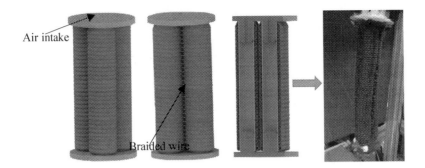

Fig. 3. Continuous soft robot diagram and prototype

Table 1. Parameters of the continuous soft robot

Description	Parameter	Value
Pneumatic tendon length	L(mm)	150
The original radius of the silicone tube	R(mm)	5
Silicone tube wall thickness	d(mm)	2
Woven mesh corrugated layer	n	80
Soft arm quality	M(g)	118

3   Kinematic Model of the Soft Robot

In order to reveal the motion trajectory of the continuous soft robot, the mathematical model is built in this section.

The proposed soft robot has three independent control air passages. When compressed air is filled into one of the air passages, the robot will bend in the corresponding direction. The inflatable tendon provides the driving force. Here we name it as the "active face", and the two un-inflated tendons provide binding force by the braided wire to limit the elongation movement of the inflatable tendon. They work as one component. Correspondingly, it is named as "restricted face". Thus, when the soft robot is inflated and bends toward an air passage, we can use Fig. 4 to demonstrate the movement.

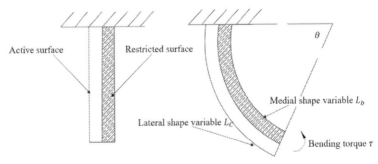

(a) Uninflated state   (b)Filing the power surface with pressure

Fig. 4. Continuous robot structural equivalent diagram

The method of piecewise constant curvature can be used in kinematics modeling. Take any micro-segment in the simplified model of the pneumatic flexible drive shown in Fig. 4, as shown in Fig. 5. To simplify any micro-segmentation during the bending process of the model. Curve AA_1 is used to represent the overall bending curve, A is the coordinate origin to establish the Cartesian coordinate system, a(s) is the unit tangent vector of the curve crossing point A, the micro-segment θ is the bending angle, ρ is the torsion angle, and r is the bending radius of the differential end. The vector a(s) can be obtained from Fig. 5:

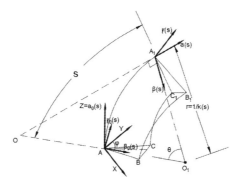

Fig. 5. Curved differential structure diagram

$$a(s) = \begin{pmatrix} \frac{\sin\varphi\left(\frac{r}{\cos\theta}-\cos\theta\right)}{\tan\theta} \\ \frac{\sin\varphi\left(\frac{r}{\cos\theta}-\cos\theta\right)}{\tan\theta} \\ \cos\theta \end{pmatrix}^T \tag{1}$$

The points of the expandable space curve can also be parameterized as follows:

$$\overline{\chi} = \int_0^S \xi(\sigma)a(\sigma)d\sigma \tag{2}$$

$\xi(s)$ is a scaling factor that controls the tangent length of the curve. The rotation matrix at point S is:

$$Q(s) = \begin{pmatrix} \cos\varphi & \sin\varphi\cos\theta & \sin\varphi\sin\theta \\ -\sin\rho & \cos\theta\cos\varphi & -\cos\varphi\sin\theta \\ 0 & \sin\varphi & \cos\theta \end{pmatrix} \tag{3}$$

The vertex coordinates of curve AA_1 can be described by a homogeneous matrix

$$H = \begin{pmatrix} Q(\text{s}) & \overline{\chi(s)} \\ 0 & 1 \end{pmatrix} \tag{4}$$

4 Dynamic Model

The overall dynamics model of the system according to the principle of virtual work:

$$\delta U + \delta V = 0 \tag{5}$$

where δU includes input pressure and elastic force, and δV is external torque. And they can be expressed as:

$$\delta U = P \delta V_S + L_C \delta W \tag{6}$$

$$\delta V = \int_0^\theta \tau d\theta \tag{7}$$

where $P\delta V_s$ is the work performed by the active face of the input air pressure, δW is the strain energy of the limit face, τ is the deformation length of the external moment L_c which is the "restricted face", and δa surrounds the angle of rotation of the actuator.

According to the conservation of energy, we can get:

$$W_S = W_b + W_C \tag{8}$$

where, W_s is the work done by the single-section muscle after filling a certain pressure, W_b continuous soft robot "active surface" is filled with the work done by the same pressure, W_c is the work of "restricted surface".

$$\delta U = W_S \qquad P\delta V_S = W_b \qquad L_C \delta W = W_C$$

It can be seen from Fig. 6 that the "active surface" arc length is L_c after the soft continuous soft robot is inflated, and the "restricted surface" arc length is L_b. When the air is not inflated, the original length of the pneumatic muscle is L, wall thickness is d, the inner radius is R, and the inner radius is R_C, wall thickness changes as d_C after the bending motion. After the air pressure is filled into the tendon, the radius R_C is:

$$R_C = \frac{(R+d)^2 L - R_C^2 L_C}{2L_C d_C} \tag{9}$$

$$R_C = \frac{-2L_C d_C + \sqrt{(2L_C d_C)^2 + 4L_C(R+d)^2 L}}{2L_C} \qquad (10)$$

The wall thickness of the silicone tube after expansion is expressed as follows:

$$d_C = \frac{Ld}{L_C - L} \qquad (11)$$

Substituting (8) into (7), we can get the relationship between the radius of the inner cavity of the pneumatic silicone and the length of the muscle according to the Hagen-Poiseuille equation:

$$\delta U = \frac{\left(P_1 - \frac{8\tau L_S Q}{\pi R_S^4}\right)}{\pi R_S^4} \qquad (12)$$

$$P\delta V_S = \frac{\left(P_1 - \frac{8\tau L_C Q}{\pi R_C^4}\right)}{\pi R_C^4} \qquad (13)$$

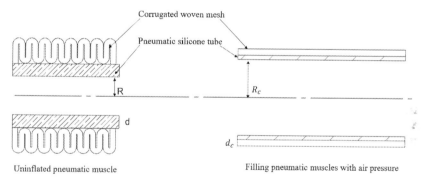

Fig. 6. Pneumatic muscle inflation expansion diagram

where, L_S elongation of a single pneumatic muscle after filling the same air pressure and R_S is its inner radius.

Since the pneumatic pipe is made of silicon material, the deformation process is nonlinear. Here, it is considered as a nonlinear spring system whose force equation is $F = KV$, where K is the experimental measurement coefficient, V is the volume change. This method is used to fit the nonlinearity of the silicon material.

$$KV_SL_S = 2K\pi R_S d_S L_S \tag{14}$$

$$KV_CL_C = 2K\pi R_C d_C L_C \tag{15}$$

$$\delta W = 2K\pi R_b d_b L_b \tag{16}$$

where, K is the experimental measurement coefficient. It can be concluded from Fig. 6 that the bending moment of the continuous soft robot is generated by the interaction of the "restricted surface" and the
"active surface":

$$\delta V = \int_0^\theta (2K\pi R_S d_S L_S - 2K\pi R_C d_C L_C)d\theta \tag{17}$$

Substituting Eqs. (15), (16) and (17) into (4) will produce the relationship between the air pressure and the length of the "restricted face" and the thickness of the "active face" tendon length silicone tube:

$$P_1 = 2K\pi^2(R_C d_C L_C + R_b d_b L_b) + \frac{8\tau L_S Q}{\pi R_S^4} \tag{18}$$

Substituting Eqs. (12), (13) and (14) into (7) gives the relationship between the inflation pressure and the bending angle θ:

$$\theta = \frac{R_C d_C L_C - R_b d_b L_b}{R_C d_C L_C - R_S d_S L_S} \tag{19}$$

5 Experiments and Discussion

In this section, the bending length and the bending angle of the end of the pneumatic tendon are measured by filling the individual muscles with different air pressures.

5.1   Experiment Platform

The experimental platform is shown in Fig. 7. The continuous soft robot is fixed on the aluminum alloy beam by means of a clamp, and three wire-type encoders are mounted on the fixture to measure the bending length of the three pneumatic muscles. The MPU6050 shaft sensor is attached to the end to measure the bending angle of the end of the pneumatic muscle. Three cable codes and MPU6050 data are transmitted to the industrial computer through the STM32 controller.

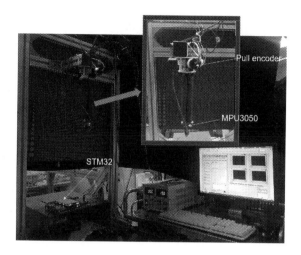

Fig. 7. Experiment platform

5.2   Model Verification

In order to verify between the proposed model and the prototype, the proposed soft robot was inflated with compressed air from 0.042 MPa to 0.182 MPa in the experiment for sampling of 20 reference points. The bending length and bending angle of the three pneumatic muscles under different air pressures were recorded respectively. Repeatedly experiments with the soft robot were executed to take the average value. Comparison between the experimental data and the model simulation is shown in Fig. 8. Figure 8(a) shows the relationship between the inflation pressure and the length of the "active surface", Fig. 8(b) shows the relationship between the inflation pressure and the bending angle. And Fig. 8(c) shows the relationship between the "active surface" bending length and the bending angles.

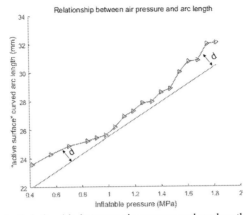

(a)   Relationship between air pressure and arc length

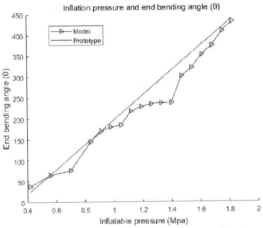

(b)   Inflation pressure and end bending angle (θ)

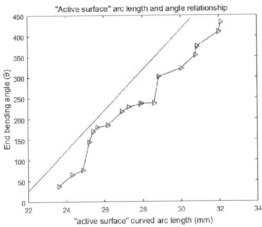

(c)   Relationship between arc length and end angle

Fig. 8. Soft robot pressure test diagram

5.3 Use of Continuous Soft Robots

Based on the continuous soft robot introduced above, a soft tentacle robot as shown in Fig. 9 is designed. The soft tentacle robot consists of three sections with a total length of 740 mm. Three individually controllable airways in each section, can achieve bending in any direction in the space and, end bending angle is greater than 360°, maximum lateral load is greater than 500 N. Figure 10 shows a soft tentacle robot grabbing objects of different shapes.

Fig. 9. Soft tentacle robot

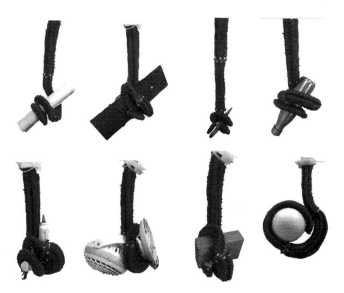

Fig. 10. Soft tentacle robot grabbing objects of different shapes

6 Conclusions

This article describes a continuous soft robot made up of silicon material. The continuous soft robot is composed of a new type of pneumatically elongated muscle developed by independent research and development, this new pneumatic elongation is greater than 300%. Firstly, the kinematics model is established, and the statics of soft robots were analyzed based on the principle of virtual work. Then, the conservation of energy and the Hagen-Poiseuille equation were employed to analyze the deformation process. Finally, the bending arc lengths of the three pneumatic muscles were obtained by using three wire-type encoders, and the bending angle was obtained by the MPU6050. Different from typical method, the proposed model and experiment show that it is possible to use the energy-based method to estimate the deformation of this kind of soft robot based on the principle of virtual work and minimum potential energy. This modeling method avoids complex stress analysis of continuous robots, the model has certain versatility.

References

1. Rucker, D.C., Jones, B.A., Webster, R.J.: A model for concentric tube continuum robots under applied wrenches. In: 2010 IEEE International Conference on Robotics and Automation (ICRA), pp. 1047–1052. IEEE (2010)
2. Connolly, F., Polygerinos, P., Walsh, C.J., et al.: Mechanical programming of soft actuators by varying fiber angle. Soft Robot. **2**(1), 26–32 (2015)
3. McMahan, W., Jones, B.A., Walker, I.D.: Design and implementation of a multi-section continuum robot: Air-Octor. In: 2005 IEEE/RSJ International Conference on Intelligent Robots and Systems, IROS 2005, pp. 2578–2585. IEEE (2005)
4. Sun, L., Hu, H., Li, M.: Continuous robot research. Robots **32**(5), 688–691 (2010)
5. http://tech.sina.com.cn/d/2011-01-20/07425111493.shtml
6. Rus, D., Tolley, M.T.: Design, fabrication and control of soft robots. Nature **521**(7553), 467–475 (2015)
7. Ivanescu, M., Florescu, M.C., Popescu, N., Popescu, D.: Coil function control problem for a hyperredundant robot. In: IEEE/ASME International Conference on Advanced Intelligent Mechatronics, pp. 1–6, September 2007. https://doi.org/10.1109/AIM.4412492
8. Gravagne, I.A., Rahn, C.D., Walker, I.D.: Large-deflection dynamics and control for planar continuum robots. IEEE/ASME Trans. Mechatron. **8**(2), 299–307 (2003). https://doi.org/10.1109/TMECH.812829
9. Chirikjian, G.S.: Hyper-redundant manipulator dynamics: a continuum approximation. Adv. Robot. **9**(3), 217–243 (1995)
10. Jones, B.A., Gray, R., Turlapati, K.: Real-time statics for continuum robots. In: IEEE/RSJ International Conference on Intelligent Robots and Systems, pp. 2659–2664 (2009)
11. Camarillo, D.B., Milne, C.F., Carlson, C.R., Zinn, M.R., Salisbury, J.K.: Mechanics modeling of tendon-driven continuum manipulators. IEEE Trans. Robot. **24**(6), 1262–1273 (2008)
12. Webster III, R.J., Romano, J.M., Cowan, N.J.: Mechanics of precurved-tube continuum robots. IEEE Trans. Robot. **25**(1), 67–78 (2009)
13. Trivedi, D., Lotfi, A., Rahn, C.D.: Geometrically exact models for soft robotic manipulators. IEEE Trans. Robot. **24**(4), 773–780 (2008)

14. Harada, K., Bo, Z., Enosawa, S., Chiba, T., Fujie, M.G.: Bending laser manipulator for intrauterine surgery and viscoelastic model of fetal rat tissue. In: IEEE International Conference on Robotics and Automation, pp. 611–616 (2007)
15. Jones, B.A., Walker, I.D.: Kinematics for multisection continuum robots. IEEE Trans. Robot. **22**(1), 43–55 (2006)

Flexure-Based Variable Stiffness Gripper for Large-Scale Grasping Force Regulation with Vision

Haiyue Zhu[1]([⊠]), Xiong Li[1], Wenjie Chen[1], and Chi Zhang[2]

[1] Singapore Institute of Manufacturing Technology, Singapore, Singapore
{zhu_haiyue,wjchen}@simtech.a-star.edu.sg
[2] Ningbo Institute of Materials Technology and Engineering,
Chinese Academy of Sciences, Ningbo, China

Abstract. This paper presents a vision grasping force sensing and regulation approach for a flexure-based variable stiffness gripper to handle broad-range objects from fragile/soft to rigid/heavy. The proposed vision approach can achieve high-precision grasping force sensing/regulation in large scale without any force sensor, which is realized base on the predictable and adjustable stiffness property of the gripper finger in our structure-controlled variable stiffness gripper, so that the deflection angle of the fingers can be detected from the vision to estimate the corresponding grasping force. Different with traditional vision-based approaches that require tedious manual calibration between the camera and target to retrieve spatial information, our approach incorporates the self-calibration algorithm to calibrate the vision system by employing the specifically-designed visual marks, so that the vision source can be placed with large flexibility in practical operation. Benefited from the large-ratio stiffness variation range of our gripper, the grasping force regulation can be achieved in a large scale, which makes it a universal gripper to handle broad-range objects with different material properties. Various experiments have been conducted to evaluate the force grasping performance using the proposed approach, including force regulation accuracy and grasping of extremely delicate objects (thin potation chip and plastic cup of water) to heavy industrial components.

Keywords: Flexure · Force grasping · Gripper · Variable stiffness · Vision

1 Introduction

Grasping of broad-range objects with different properties (size, weight, rigidity, etc.) using one gripper is an attractive goal for the robotics society, which is especially emphasized on the grasping applications with indeterministic and variational objects in industrial sorting, daily service robots, etc.

To achieve robust handling of various objects with different material properties, force-regulated grasping is an essential function for the modern robots to

© Springer Nature Switzerland AG 2019
H. Yu et al. (Eds.): ICIRA 2019, LNAI 11740, pp. 346–357, 2019.
https://doi.org/10.1007/978-3-030-27526-6_30

prevent excessive deformation, damage, or even crush on the objects. Traditionally, implementing such force regulation for the rigid grippers requires the aid of additional force sensor for direct force measurement [3,7,15,25], so that force control can be applied to adjust the gripper finger to suitable position for reaching the target force. However, there are some limitations on such solution. First, the force regulation loop requires the actuation of gripper finger to be accurate with fast response to prevent overshoot, which is not always available due to the cost, dimension, and load ability. Furthermore, the commercially available force sensor may lead to bulky design in gripper [13] and the voltage amplification mechanism in the force gauge makes the sensor either noisy in signal or expensive in cost [5], especially when the case that one gripper is designed to handle large-scale grasping force regulation concurrently. Instead of direct measurement by conventional sensors, force and tactile sensing can also be achieved by estimation [6] or integrated design for compact size, e.g. using optical fibre [30], optical waveguide [13], capacitive transduction [17], flexure mechanism [19,28], etc. soft [9,11,22,31] or compliant [4,8,21] gripper is another promising area for its intrinsic safety, Various mechanisms are explored to realize the soft grippers, e.g. granular jamming [2], dielectric elastomer [24], fluid actuation (liquids or gases) [12], and etc. Variable stiffness gripper [10,20,29] are proposed that enables both the low-stiffness mode and high-stiffness mode by mechanical approaches [14,16,20,26,27] or material property [1,2,18,23], etc.

In this work, we present a vision-based force sensing and regulation approach by utilizing the special feature of our structure-controlled variable stiffness gripper, where its finger stiffness is predictable and controllable in a large variation range. Consequently, the grasping force can be estimated from the deflection information of the gripper finger retrieved from the robot vision, where no additional force sensor is needed to sense/regulate the grasping force in real-time and also in large scale. As a result, this enables our variable stiffness gripper to handle board-range objects including soft/fragile and rigid/heavy with precision force regulation capability. In addition, our vision approach incorporates the self-calibration algorithm to automatically retrieve the accurate deflection angle for the gripper, which enables the camera placement in large flexibility and avoids tedious manual calibration. Furthermore, the algorithm is also able to correct the bias error on the deflection angle which results from the mechanical assembly and gear backlash.

The rest of the paper is organized as follows. Section 2 briefs the basic principle of the variable stiffness robotic gripper, the vision-based grasping force regulation method is detailed in Sect. 3, and then Sect. 4 presents the various grasping experiments. Finally, a conclusion is drawn in Sect. 5.

2   Structure-Controlled Variable Stiffness Gripper for Grasping Force Estimation

To enable grasping of broad-range objects, we employ a variable stiffness robotic gripper [20] for this work, which is based on the structure-controlled principle

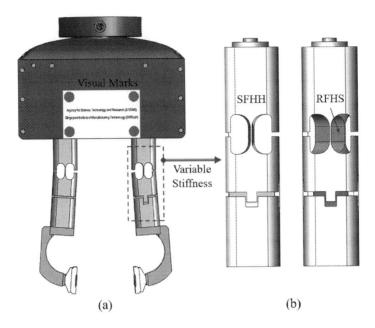

Fig. 1. (a) Variable stiffness robotic gripper and (b) the illustration of variable stiffness mechanism using structure-controlled principle.

to adjust its stiffness in a large range. Figure 1(a) shows the 2D concept of our gripper, which is actually quite similar like a traditional 2-finger gripper that the grasping is fulfilled by closing the fingers to contact the objects. The specialty of our gripper is its inside variable stiffness mechanism on each finger, which is illustrated on Fig. 1(b) that the variable stiffness finger body has two components, i.e. a Stationary Flexure Hinge Housing (SFHH) and a Rotary Flexure Hinge Shaft (RFHS). The SFHH is a constant but low stiffness (compliant) mechanism with 2-DOF, and the RFHS is coaxially inside the SFHH which also incorporates 2-DOF flexure hinges in series. The controllable stiffness variation is achieved by rotating the RFHS along its center axis so that the effective second moment of area of the finger body is changed to adjust the overall stiffness, which is termed as structure-controlled principle. In this gripper, the stiffness variation and finger opening/closing are controlled by two motors separately inside the gripper body, denoted as Stiffness Adjustment Motor and Grasping Motor, respectively.

Intuitively from Fig. 1(b), it can be seen that when the case $\alpha = 0°$, the gripper finger is most compliant with the lowest stiffness, and while the $\alpha = 90°$ case exhibits the largest stiffness almost behave like a rigid gripper. Between $0°$ to $90°$, the stiffness can be continuously adjusted by rotating α, and this stiffness adjustment is almost immediate in high time efficiency. Furthermore, this variable stiffness mechanism is extremely compact that it highly utilizes the inner space of the finger body.

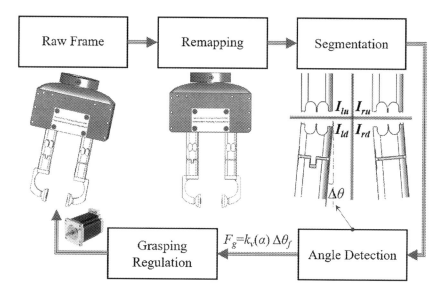

Fig. 2. Flow diagram of the proposed vision-based grasping force sensing and regulation algorithm for our variable stiffness gripper.

Although the variable stiffness gripper is inherently suitable for handling delicate objects, precision force regulation is an addon desired function which makes the gripper able to fulfill more challenging tasks in grasping and manipulation. Since the stiffness of our gripper is embodied by the flexure, it provides us a possibility to sense the grasping force from the spatial deformation of the gripper finger as the stiffness is predictable. Furthermore, since the stiffness variation range is large for the gripper, the grasping force sensing/regulation can also be achieved in a large range for handling broad-range objects. The principle of grasping force sensing is illustrated in Fig. 1(a), where the grasping force F_g can be calculated through the deflection angle $\Delta\theta_f$ of the gripper finger with the predictable and controllable stiffness $k_v(\alpha)$. The real-time detection of the deflection angle $\Delta\theta_f$ will be obtained from the vision, which will be detailed in the next section.

3   Vision-Based Grasping Force Sensing and Regulation

It is well known that a vision system requires delicate calibration to accurately retrieve the spatial information e.g. distance, deflection angle, etc. In this work, to enable automatic vision calibration, four visual marks are designed on the gripper as shown in Fig. 1(a), which allows the camera to be placed with large flexibility. Figure 2 shows the flow diagram of the vision-based grasping force sensing and regulation algorithm, the main purpose of this algorithm is to detect the deflection angle of the flexure-based gripper finger so that the grasping force can be estimated and regulated base on the angle-force relationships.

After the raw frame captured by the camera, the algorithm first localizes the positions of four visual marks, and then the raw frame is remapped into a rectified view through the projective transformation. In this work, a coarse-fine localization procedure is applied to accurately find the center positions of the visual marks, as the inaccuracy in these coordinates will incur the dithering in the rectified images, which affects the accuracy of force sensing. The coarse localization is fulfilled by the Hue Saturation Value (HSV) thresholding, as the HSV color representation is more robust and fairly invariant to illumination. The coarse localization outputs four small Regions of Interest (ROIs) containing the circular marks for fine localization, which is achieved by the parametric ellipse fitting on the edge image. As a result, the coordinates of four visual marks can be found in subpixel resolution.

The four identified coordinates will be assigned into four points: p_1 (top left), p_2 (top right), p_3 (button left), and p_4 (button right) using the corresponding logics to make sure that in different views the point assignment will always be correct. The remapping is performed to map these four points to four constant positions in the new rectified image as,

$$
\begin{aligned}
p_1 &\longmapsto P_1(125, 50), \\
p_2 &\longmapsto P_2(410, 50), \\
p_3 &\longmapsto P_3(125, 200), \\
p_4 &\longmapsto P_4(410, 200),
\end{aligned}
\tag{1}
$$

where $P_i(a, b)$ denotes a point with (a, b) coordinate in the rectified image with resolution of 535×900. The following projective transformation is utilized to remap the raw frame,

$$
\begin{bmatrix} X \\ Y \\ 1 \end{bmatrix} = \begin{bmatrix} h_{11} & h_{12} & h_{13} \\ h_{21} & h_{22} & h_{23} \\ h_{31} & h_{32} & h_{33} \end{bmatrix} \begin{bmatrix} x \\ y \\ 1 \end{bmatrix},
\tag{2}
$$

where the projective transformation matrix H can be determined from (1). Figure 3 shows the remapping process from the raw frame I_{raw} to rectified image I_{rec}, where the four corresponding points are indicated using different colors.

In the rectified image I_{rec}, it can be seen that the gripper body is almost in constant position no matter how the original view is in the raw frame, which facilitates our segmentation to segment out the gripper finger portions for estimating grasping force. In this work, four regions are chosen, which are the up (upper to flexure) and down (lower to flexure) portions of the both two gripper fingers, denoted as I_{lu}, I_{ru}, I_{ld}, and I_{rd} as indicated in Fig. 2, which are segmented based on the pixel locations as,

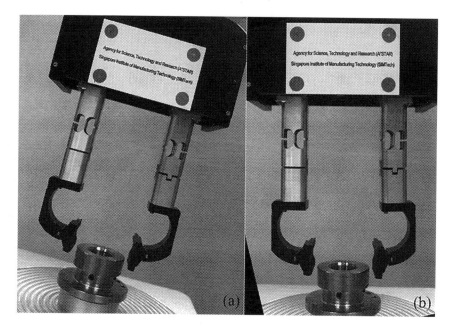

Fig. 3. Illustration of the remapping process from the (a) raw frame I_{raw} to (b) rectified image I_{rec}.

$$I_{lu} = I_{rec}[0:267,\ 280:365],$$
$$I_{ld} = I_{rec}[0:267,\ 375:535],$$
$$I_{ru} = I_{rec}[268:535,\ 280:365],$$
$$I_{rd} = I_{rec}[268:535,\ 375:535].$$

(3)

The reasons for using four portions for calculating angle are: (1) to eliminate the bias errors caused by different original view angles; (2) to eliminate the errors introduced by the mechanical sources, i.e. gear backlash and assembly misalignment, which makes the whole finger has a bias angle on the up portion. Such bias errors can be removed by subtracting the up portion angles from the down portion angles.

Base on the four segments of the finger portions, the deflection angle can be estimated by applying Hough Transform to detect the lines on the edge image of each segment. In Hough Transform, the line detection is achieved by voting the line parameters (ρ, θ) on each measurement point (x_i, y_i) in the edge space with the following form,

$$\rho = x_i \cos\theta + y_i \sin\theta,$$

(4)

where ρ is the perpendicular distance from the origin to the line, and θ is the angle between the x axis and the line connecting the origin with that closest point. In this work, in order to speed up the Hough Transform, we limit the θ in an interval $\theta \in [-20°\ 20°]$ as the gripper fingers cannot be bended excessively. For calculating the deflection angles, the ten top voted line parameters

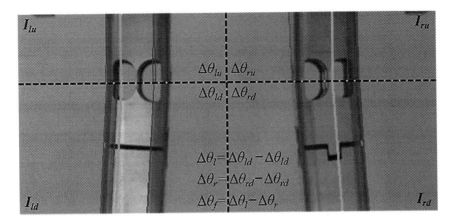

Fig. 4. Four segments of the gripper finger portions with the detected lines. (Color figure online)

in each segment are utilized to obtain the mean values by sorting and eliminating the extreme values. The estimated deflection angle of each portion in Fig. 4 are denoted as $\Delta\theta_{ul}$, $\Delta\theta_{dl}$, $\Delta\theta_{ur}$, and $\Delta\theta_{dr}$, respectively, where the blue lines show the originally detected lines on edges, and the red line indicates the mean deflection angle for each segment. Consequently, the deflection angles of the left and right gripper fingers and the overall deflection angle are calculated as,

$$\Delta\theta_l = \Delta\theta_{ld} - \Delta\theta_{lu}$$
$$\Delta\theta_r = \Delta\theta_{rd} - \Delta\theta_{ru}, \tag{5}$$
$$\Delta\theta_f = \Delta\theta_l - \Delta\theta_r$$

respectively. Once the deflection angle $\Delta\theta_f$ is detected from the vision algorithm, the corresponding grasping force can be estimated through the relationship $F_g = k_v(\alpha)\Delta\theta_f$. In this variable stiffness gripper, since the stiffness $k_v(\alpha)$ can be adjusted in large scale from soft to rigid by controlling α, the grasping force estimation of F_g can also be achieved in large scale.

4   Experiments and Discussions

This section presents the grasping experiments for the proposed force-regulated grasping algorithm with the variable stiffness gripper. The gripper is installed on a UR10 robot from Universal Robots, which is shown in Fig. 5(a), where a USB camera from The Imaging Source is placed randomly in front of the gripper to fulfill the vision-based grasping algorithm. The entire algorithm is implemented on a PC, which can achieve more than 25 FPS, and both the robot motion and gripper are controlled by this PC using TCP/IP and DAQ device, respectively.

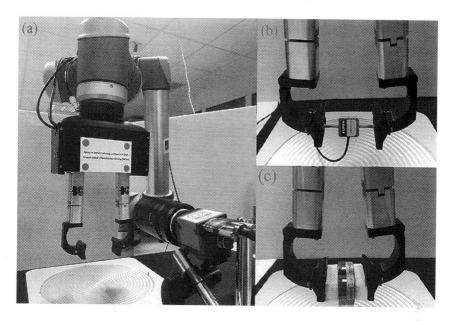

Fig. 5. (a) Experimental setup for variable stiffness gripper, (b) FUTEK LSB200 force sensor, and (c) ATI F/T Mini40 force sensor.

To demonstrate the proposed approach can execute a gentle grasping and handle delicate objects, the experiments are conducted to grasp a thin potato chip (fragile) and a plastic cup of water (soft) in Fig. 6, where three different target grasping forces are used for both cases continuously. In this experiment, the variable stiffness is on the lowest stiffness mode, so that its fingers are quite

Data: Target Grasping Force F_d, Camera Frame
Result: Grasping Force Regulation
Initialization;
$\alpha_d, \Delta\theta_d = \Phi(F_d)$;
Controlling α to α_d (Stiffness Adjustment Motor);
while *Ture* **do**
    Capture Frame;
    Frame Remapping;
    Finger Segmentation;
    Finger Deflection Angle Detection ($\Delta\theta_f$);
    if $\Delta\theta_f < \Delta\theta_d$ **then**
       | Closing Gripper Fingers (Grasping Motor);
    else
       | Stop Algorithm;
    end
end

            Algorithm 1. Vision-Based Force-Regulated Grasping

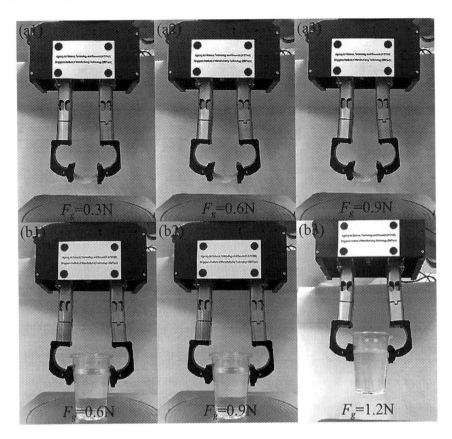

Fig. 6. Grasping of (a) thin potato chip and (b) plastic cup of water with different target grasping force.

compliant to handle the delicate objects without damage or excessively deformation. For the potato chip (weight less 1 g), it can be seen that all three forces can grasp it, but the lower force will be more safer to prevent the crush. For the plastic cup of water, the water can be lifted up when applies 1.2 N, which we can see that there are almost no visible deformations on the plastic cup. The plastic cup is not able to lift up in the first two cases, and once the grasping force large than 1.5 N, the plastic cup begin to deform largely.

Furthermore, the experiments are also conducted to demonstrate its load ability to handle broad-range objects in daily life and industry, which traditional compliant grippers specifically for delicate objects are hard to have. Figure 7 shows the grasping of three daily objects and three industrial components, i.e. (a) stainless steel scourer, (b) toy, (c) multi adapter plug, (d) PCB board, (e) metal flange, (f) Li-ion battery, where the largest piece weight is around 400 g for the metal flange. The maximal load ability is around 600 g for this variable stiffness gripper, where this load constraint is limited by the current low-cost

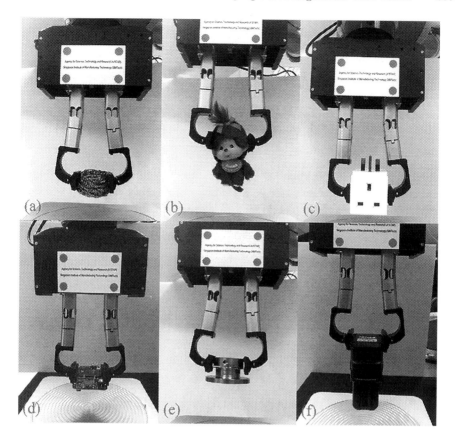

Fig. 7. Grasping of various daily objects and industrial components: (a) stainless steel scourer, (b) toy, (c) multi adapter plug, (d) PCB board, (e) metal flange, (f) Li-ion battery.

slow-dynamics Grasping Motor which is chosen considering the compactness and lightweight for this prototype. It is noted that the load ability can be improved simply by replacing a more powerful motor, and this will not sacrifice the gentle grasping ability to handle delicate objects for the proposed approach.

5   Conclusions

In this paper, we present a vision-based grasping force regulation approach for the structure-controlled variable stiffness gripper, which enables the gripper to achieve precise force regulation purely from the vision for handling broad-range objects including fragile, soft, rigid, heavy objects, etc. Our future work includes using the same vision source to achieve more functions for the grasping, e.g. optimal stiffness/force suggesting for the variable stiffness gripper, optimal grasping pose estimation, etc.

References

1. Agarwal, A., Viswanathan, V., Maheshwari, S., y Alvarado, P.V.: Effects of material properties on soft gripper grasping forces. In: 2018 IEEE International Conference on Soft Robotics (RoboSoft), pp. 437–442, April 2018

2. Amend, J.R., Brown, E., Rodenberg, N., Jaeger, H.M., Lipson, H.: A positive pressure universal gripper based on the jamming of granular material. IEEE Trans. Robot. **28**(2), 341–350 (2012)

3. Becedas, J., Payo, I., Feliu, V.: Two-flexible-fingers gripper force feedback control system for its application as end effector on a 6-DOF manipulator. IEEE Trans. Robot. **27**(3), 599–615 (2011)

4. Bykerk, L., Liu, D., Waldron, K.: A topology optimisation based design of a compliant gripper for grasping objects with irregular shapes. In: 2016 IEEE International Conference on Advanced Intelligent Mechatronics (AIM), pp. 383–388, July 2016

5. Calandra, R., et al.: More than a feeling: learning to grasp and regrasp using vision and touch. IEEE Robot. Autom. Lett. **3**(4), 3300–3307 (2018)

6. Chen, C.C., Lan, C.C.: An accurate force regulation mechanism for high-speed handling of fragile objects using pneumatic grippers. IEEE Trans. Autom. Sci. Eng. **15**, 1–9 (2017)

7. Chen, F., Sekiyama, K., Di, P., Huang, J., Fukuda, T.: i-hand: an intelligent robotic hand for fast and accurate assembly in electronic manufacturing. In: 2012 IEEE International Conference on Robotics and Automation, pp. 1976–1981, May 2012

8. Liu, C.-H., et al.: Optimal design of a soft robotic gripper for grasping unknown objects. Soft Robot. **5**(4), 452–465 (2018)

9. Deimel, R., Brock, O.: A novel type of compliant and underactuated robotic hand for dexterous grasping. Int. J. Robot. Res. **35**(1–3), 161–185 (2016)

10. Firouzeh, A., Paik, J.: Grasp mode and compliance control of an underactuated origami gripper using adjustable stiffness joints. IEEE/ASME Trans. Mechatron. **22**(5), 2165–2173 (2017)

11. Homberg, B.S., Katzschmann, R.K., Dogar, M.R., Rus, D.: Robust proprioceptive grasping with a soft robot hand. Auton. Robots **43**, 681–696 (2018)

12. Ilievski, F., Mazzeo, A.D., Shepherd, R.F., Chen, X., Whitesides, G.M.: Soft robotics for chemists. Angew. Chem. Int. Ed. **50**(8), 1890–1895 (2011)

13. Jamil, B., Kim, J., Choi, Y.: Force sensing fingertip with soft optical waveguides for robotic hands and grippers. In: 2018 IEEE International Conference on Soft Robotics (RoboSoft), pp. 146–151, April 2018

14. Kajikawa, S., Abe, K.: Robot finger module with multidirectional adjustable joint stiffness. IEEE/ASME Trans. Mechatron. **17**(1), 128–135 (2012)

15. Kappassov, Z., Corrales, J.-A., Perdereau, V.: Tactile sensing in dexterous robot hands—review. Robot. Auton. Syst. **74**, 195–220 (2015)

16. Kim, B.S., Song, J.B.: Object grasping using a 1 DOF variable stiffness gripper actuated by a hybrid variable stiffness actuator. In: 2011 IEEE International Conference on Robotics and Automation, pp. 4620–4625, May 2011

17. Kim, U., Lee, D.H., Yoon, W.J., Hannaford, B., Choi, H.R.: Force sensor integrated surgical forceps for minimally invasive robotic surgery. IEEE Trans. Robot. **31**(5), 1214–1224 (2015)

18. Kobayashi, F., Ueno, S., Nakamoto, H., Kojima, F.: Vision based grasping system with universal jamming hand. In: 2015 10th Asian Control Conference (ASCC), pp. 1–4, May 2015

19. Komati, B., Clévy, C., Lutz, P.: High bandwidth microgripper with integrated force sensors and position estimation for the grasp of multistiffness microcomponents. IEEE/ASME Trans. Mechatron. **21**(4), 2039–2049 (2016)
20. Li, X., Chen, W., Lin, W., Low, K.H.: A variable stiffness robotic gripper based on structure-controlled principle. IEEE Trans. Autom. Sci. Eng. **15**, 1–10 (2017)
21. Liu, Y., Zhang, Y., Xu, Q.: Design and control of a novel compliant constant-force gripper based on buckled fixed-guided beams. IEEE/ASME Trans. Mechatron. **22**(1), 476–486 (2017)
22. Manti, M., Hassan, T., Passetti, G., D'Elia, N., Laschi, C., Cianchetti, M.: A bioinspired soft robotic gripper for adaptable and effective grasping. Soft Robot. **2**(3), 107–116 (2015)
23. Nakai, H., Kuniyoshi, Y., Inaba, M., Inoue, H.: Metamorphic robot made of low melting point alloy. In: IEEE/RSJ International Conference on Intelligent Robots and Systems, vol. 2, pp. 2025–2030 (2002)
24. Shintake, J., Schubert, B., Rosset, S., Shea, H., Floreano, D.: Variable stiffness actuator for soft robotics using dielectric elastomer and low-melting-point alloy. In: 2015 IEEE/RSJ International Conference on Intelligent Robots and Systems (IROS), pp. 1097–1102, September 2015
25. Su, J.Y., et al.: Design of tactile sensor array on electric gripper jaws for wire gripping recognition. In: 2014 IEEE International Conference on Automation Science and Engineering (CASE), pp. 1014–1019, August 2014
26. Tamamoto, T., Koganezawa, K.: Multi-joint gripper with stiffness adjuster. In: 2013 IEEE/RSJ International Conference on Intelligent Robots and Systems, pp. 5481–5486, November 2013
27. Tamamoto, T., Sayama, K., Koganezawa, K.: Multi-joint gripper with differential gear system. In: 2014 IEEE/RSJ International Conference on Intelligent Robots and Systems, pp. 15–20, September 2014
28. Xu, Q.: Design and development of a novel compliant gripper with integrated position and grasping/interaction force sensing. IEEE Trans. Autom. Sci. Eng. **14**(3), 1415–1428 (2017)
29. Wei, Y., et al.: A novel, variable stiffness robotic gripper based on integrated soft actuating and particle jamming. Soft Robot. **3**(3), 134–143 (2016)
30. Zarrin, P.S., Escoto, A., Xu, R., Patel, R.V., Naish, M.D., Trejos, A.L.: Development of an optical fiber-based sensor for grasping and axial force sensing. In: 2017 IEEE International Conference on Robotics and Automation (ICRA), pp. 939–944, May 2017
31. Zhou, X., Majidi, C., O'Reilly, O.M.: Soft hands: an analysis of some gripping mechanisms in soft robot design. Int. J. Solids Struct. **64–65**, 155–165 (2015)

Kinetostatic Modeling of Redundantly Actuated Planar Compliant Parallel Mechanism

Miao Yang[1,2], Chi Zhang[1,2], Hongtao Yu[1,3], Xiaolu Huang[1,3],
Guilin Yang[1,2(✉)], and Zaojun Fang[1,2(✉)]

[1] Ningbo Institute of Materials Technology and Engineering,
Chinese Academy of Sciences, Ningbo 315201, Zhejiang, China
{glyang, fangzaojun}@nimte.ac.cn
[2] Zhejiang Key Laboratory of Robotics and Intelligent Manufacturing
Equipment Technology, Ningbo 315201, Zhejiang, China
[3] College of Materials Science and Opto-Electronic,
University of Chinese Academy of Sciences, Beijing 100049, China

Abstract. This paper presents the concept design of a novel three degrees of freedom (DOF) redundantly actuated planar compliant parallel mechanism (CPM). The developed CPM is a 4-PPR configuration mechanism based on leaf type flexures and actuated by four voice coil motors (VCMs). The distribute compliance design and the rotation-symmetric configuration guarantees large motion range, translation decouple as well as high structural compactness of the CPM. The stiffness model and kinetostatic model of the CPM are established via the compliance matrix method. Finite element analysis (FEA) is conducted to validate the established models. Numerical results show that the proposed CPM can achieve a workspace of ± 2.5 mm $\times \pm 2.5$ mm $\times \pm 2.5°$ in its three working directions. Moreover, the actuation forces of VCMs in the CPM can be decreased significantly by apply the redundantly actuated configuration.

Keywords: Compliant mechanism · Redundant actuation ·
Stiffness modeling · Kinetostatics

1 Introduction

Precision planar positioning stages with nanometer scale motion resolution are highly demanded in biomedical science, optical engineering, precision manufacturing and deep space exploration [1, 2]. CPMs transmit displacements and forces by means of elastic deformations of the compliant members in their structures, which can overcome a lot of shortcomings existing in conventional precision positioning stages with sliding and rolling bearings, such as friction, wear and backlash [3, 4]. Therefore, CPMs are especially suitable for applications where high resolution and high repeatability are required. However, traditional lumped compliance CPMs based on notched flexure hinges and actuated by piezoelectric actuators can only provide small travel ranges with hundreds micrometers, which cannot meet the increasing requests of motion ranges for modern precision engineering [5].

© Springer Nature Switzerland AG 2019
H. Yu et al. (Eds.): ICIRA 2019, LNAI 11740, pp. 358–369, 2019.
https://doi.org/10.1007/978-3-030-27526-6_31

Many distribute compliance CPMs that adopting leaf spring flexure hinges and actuated by VCMs have been proposed to enlarge the motion range of CPMs. Since the cross-axis coupling effect in the planar CPM will increase the complexity in modeling and controlling of the system, CPMs with decoupled kinematic configuration have attracted great attention in recent years. Awtar [6] designed a decoupled XY positioning stage based on double parallelogram flexure modules (DPM), which can not only achieve a large motion range but also decouple the output motion between the two major axis of the CPM. Wan [7] proposed a double layers CPM by applying the Roberts mechanism to guide and decouple the output motion of the VCMs, the workspace of the CPM up to 20 mm × 20 mm. Hao [8] also designed a large motion range decoupled XY CPM using 4-PP-E configuration, which increase the out of plane stiffness of the CPM significantly. Nevertheless, the inevitable manufacture error and parasitic motion in a practical CPM may cause undesirable rotation of the stage, and it cannot be corrected by the two VCMs [9, 10].

Compared with the XY CPM, the planar 3-DOF CPM add a DOF in rotation about z-axis, which make it possible to correct the undesired rotation motion. Moreover, a CPM with a large rotation range is also helpful for adjusting the posture of the end-effector. There are a few of planar 3-DOF CPMs were proposed and manufactured in the literature [11–13], but they are often subjects to strong cross-coupling between each moving axis, which challenges the closed-loop controller design of the system. Therefore, a 3-DOF planar CPM with translation decoupling property should be proposed.

Typically, a relative larger output stiffness is beneficial to the improvement of response speed and natural frequency of the CPM. However, the stiffness of the distribute compliance CPMs are always restricted in very low levels to obtain sufficient workspace. In addition, the thrust forces of VCMs are much lower than piezoelectric actuators, in order to actuate the CPM, the stiffness of the CPM should also be restricted. Inspired by the design of rigid parallel mechanisms, a capable way to solve this contradiction is constructing the redundantly actuated parallel mechanism, which can improve the dynamic performance and decrease the actuation force of the CPM simultaneously.

In this paper, we proposed a novel redundantly actuated 3-DOF planar CPM. The CPM features a 4-PPR configuration and actuated by four VCMs. The output stiffness and kinetostatic model of the CPM are established by applying the compliance matrix method. The established models are further verified by FEA, and the static performances of the CPM are also analyzed. The remaining parts of the paper are organized as follows. Firstly, the mechanism design of the proposed CPM is presented in Sect. 2. Then, the stiffness modeling of the CPM is investigated in Sect. 3. Thereafter, the kinetostatic model of the CPM is formulated in Sect. 4. The model verification via ANSYS Workbench and the performance discusses are presented in Sect. 5. Finally, this paper will end with a conclusion in Sect. 6.

2 Mechanical Design of the CPM

The mechanical structure of the proposed planar CPM is shown in Fig. 1. The CPM can be regarded as a 4-PPR configuration mechanism, where P and R denote the prismatic joint and the revolute joint, respectively. The four PPR kinematic legs of the CPM are rotation-symmetry configured around the center point of the moving stage, and each PPR leg composes of an active P joint, a passive P joint and a passive R joint in series. In order to obtain a large motion range, the P joint is performed by the DPM, and the R joint is performed by the triangle flexure hinge [14]. For the active P joint, two parallel connected DPMs (DPM-1 and DPM-2 in each leg) are applied to guider the output motion of the VCM.

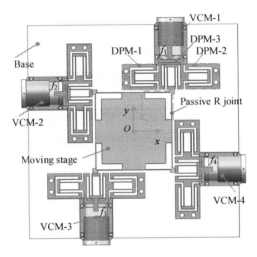

Fig. 1. Mechanical structure of the planar CPM

The operating principle of the designed planar CPM can be briefly described as follows. When the VCM-1 and VCM-3 move in opposite direction synchronously, the moving stage of the CPM will move in x-axis (Dx). In the same way, the moving stage will move in y-axis by actuating VCM-2 and VCM-4 in opposite direction synchronously (Dy). When all the VCMs move in the same direction synchronously, the moving stage will rotate around z-axis (Rz). Therefore, the planar 3-DOF motion with large stroke can be realized by actuation the VCMs.

Regarding the desired 3-DOF output motions, the adopted four VCMs construct the redundant actuation configuration for the proposed CPM. This configuration may complicate the design of the mechanical design of the CPM, however, it will facilitate the design of controller, since the translation of the moving stage are decoupled.

3 Stiffness Modeling

For the design and the static performance analysis of the proposed CPM, it is crucial to establish an accurate theoretical model to describe the stiffness and kinetostatic of the CPM. There are many approaches available to model the static behavior of the proposed CPM, e.g., pseudo rigid body method [15], elastic beam method [16], and linear finite element method [17]. In this paper, we adopted the compliance matrix method for its simplicity [18].

3.1 Stiffness of the DPM

Leaf spring flexure hinges are utilized as elastic element in the CPM to obtain relative large motion range. The geometric description of the leaf spring is shown in Fig. 2, and the compliance matrix of leaf spring is given as below

$$\xi = \mathbf{CF} \tag{1}$$

where $\xi = [\,\delta_x \quad \delta_y \quad \delta_z \quad \theta_x \quad \theta_y \quad \theta_z\,]^T$ is the output displacement at the end of the leaf spring flexure hinge, $\mathbf{F} = [\,f_x \quad f_y \quad f_z \quad M_x \quad M_y \quad M_z\,]^T$ is the end load, and $\mathbf{C}$ is the 6×6 compliance matrix expressed under the coordinate system located at the end of the leaf spring.

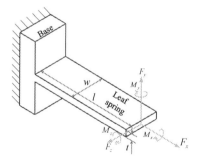

Fig. 2. The geometric description of the leaf spring

In order to model the stiffness of the CPM, the compliance matrix $\mathbf{C}$ of a leaf spring flexure hinge with respect to the local coordinate system O_l need to be expressed in the global coordinate O_g by

$$\mathbf{C}_g = \mathbf{T}_l^g \mathbf{C} \left(\mathbf{T}_l^g \right)^T \tag{2}$$

where $\mathbf{T}_l^g$ is the transformation matrix and it can be given as:

$$\mathbf{T}_l^g = \begin{bmatrix} \mathbf{R}_l^g & \mathbf{S}(\mathbf{r}_l^g)\mathbf{R}_l^g \\ \mathbf{0}_{3\times3} & \mathbf{R}_l^g \end{bmatrix} \tag{3}$$

where $\mathbf{R}_l^g = \mathbf{R}_x(\alpha)\mathbf{R}_y(\beta)\mathbf{R}_z(\gamma)$ is the 3×3 rotation matrix of coordinate O_l with respect to coordinate O_g, $\mathbf{r}_l^g = (r_x, r_y, r_z)$ is the position vector of point O_l expressed in coordinate system O_g, and $\mathbf{S}(\mathbf{r}_l^g)$ is the a skew-symmetric matrix,

$$\mathbf{S}(\mathbf{r}_l^g) = \begin{bmatrix} 0 & -r_z & r_y \\ r_z & 0 & -r_x \\ -r_y & r_x & 0 \end{bmatrix} \tag{4}$$

The DPM is a frequently used flexure guider model in complaint mechanisms to allow translation perpendicular to the length direction of the leaf spring. As it is depicted in Fig. 3, leaf-1 and leaf-4 are parallel connected to form flexure parallelogram, leaf-2 and leaf-3 are parallel connected to form anther flexure parallelogram, and finally the two flexure parallelograms are connected in series, thus the output compliance of the DPM expressed in the coordinate system O_{pa} is given as

$$\begin{aligned} \mathbf{C}_{pa} &= \mathbf{C}_{pa1} + \mathbf{C}_{pa2} \\ &= \left[\left(\mathbf{T}_1 \mathbf{C}(\mathbf{T}_1)^T \right)^{-1} + \left(\mathbf{T}_4 \mathbf{C}(\mathbf{T}_4)^T \right)^{-1} \right]^{-1} \\ &\quad + \left[\left(\mathbf{T}_2 \mathbf{C}(\mathbf{T}_2)^T \right)^{-1} + \left(\mathbf{T}_3 \mathbf{C}(\mathbf{T}_3)^T \right)^{-1} \right]^{-1} \end{aligned} \tag{5}$$

where $\mathbf{C}_{pa1}$ and $\mathbf{C}_{pa2}$ are the compliance matrix of the two flexure parallelograms in coordinate system O_{pa} respectively, and the element in the transformation matrix is given as below,

$$\mathbf{R}_1 = \mathbf{R}_z(\pi) \quad \mathbf{R}_2 = I_{3 \times 3} \quad \mathbf{R}_3 = I_{3 \times 3} \quad \mathbf{R}_4 = \mathbf{R}_z(\pi)$$

$$\mathbf{r}_1 = \left[-l, \frac{h_1}{2}, 0 \right], \quad \mathbf{r}_2 = \left[0, \frac{h_2}{2}, 0 \right]$$

$$\mathbf{r}_3 = \left[0, -\frac{h_2}{2}, 0 \right], \quad \mathbf{r}_4 = \left[-l, -\frac{h_1}{2}, 0 \right] \tag{6}$$

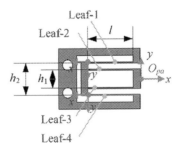

Fig. 3. The geometric description of the double parallelograms model

3.2   Stiffness of a the CPM

Since the structure of the proposed CPM is rotation-symmetry, only a quarter of the structure is chosen to model the stiffness of the CPM. The local coordinates of every flexure module are shown in Fig. 5.

For the active P joint, DPM-1 and DPM-2 are parallel connected, and the compliance of this module can be given as

$$C_{ap} = \left[\left(\mathbf{T}_{p1}^{ap} \mathbf{C} \left(\mathbf{T}_{p2}^{ap} \right)^T \right)^{-1} + \left(\mathbf{T}_{p2}^{ap} \mathbf{C} \left(\mathbf{T}_{p2}^{ap} \right)^T \right)^{-1} \right]^{-1} \tag{7}$$

where $\mathbf{T}_{p1}^{ap}$ and $\mathbf{T}_{p2}^{ap}$ are the transformation matrix of DPM-1 and DPM-2 to the coordinate system O_{ap} respectively (Fig. 4).

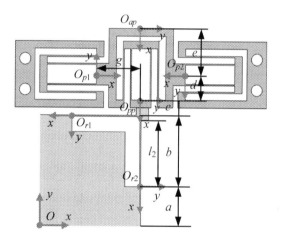

Fig. 4. The geometric description of the kinematic limb

The compliance of the kinematic limb $\mathbf{C}_l$ can be expressed as

$$\mathbf{C}_l = \mathbf{T}_{ap}^o \mathbf{C}_{ap} \left(\mathbf{T}_{ap}^o \right)^T + \mathbf{T}_{pp}^o \mathbf{C}_{pp} \left(\mathbf{T}_{pp}^o \right)^T + \mathbf{C}_{pr} \tag{8}$$

where $\mathbf{C}_{pp} = \mathbf{C}_{pa}$ is the compliance passive P joint, and $\mathbf{C}_{pr}$ is the compliance of the passive R joint, which can be formulated as

$$\mathbf{C}_{pr} = \left[\left(\mathbf{T}_{r1}^o \mathbf{C} (\mathbf{T}_{r1}^o)^T \right)^{-1} + \left(\mathbf{T}_{r2}^o \mathbf{C} (\mathbf{T}_{r2}^o)^T \right)^{-1} \right]^{-1} \tag{9}$$

where $\mathbf{T}_{r1}^o$ and $\mathbf{T}_{r2}^o$ are the transformation matrix of local coordinate system O_{r1} and O_{r2} respected to the global coordinate system.

The CPM consists of four kinematic legs connected in parallel, so the output stiffness of the CPM $\mathbf{K}_m$ is

$$\mathbf{K}_m = \sum_{i=1}^{4} (\mathbf{C}_{li})^{-1} \tag{10}$$

Therefore, the output compliance of the CPM $\mathbf{C}_m$ is

$$\mathbf{C}_m = (\mathbf{K}_m)^{-1} \tag{11}$$

4 Kinetostatic of the CPM

For a single kinematic leg, $\mathbf{F}_{pi} = \{f_i, 0, 0, 0, 0, 0\}^T$ is the actuated force generated by VCM-i ($i = 1, 2, 3, 4$) under local coordinate system O_{ap}, $\mathbf{G}_{li}$ is the internal force of the moving stage at point O. Thus, the displacement at point O δ_o can be given as

$$\delta_o = \mathbf{C}_{li}\mathbf{G}_i + \mathbf{T}_{pi}^o\mathbf{C}_{pi}\mathbf{F}_{pi} \tag{12}$$

where $\mathbf{T}_{pi}^o$ is the transformation matrix of point P_i respected to point O.

According to the static equilibrium relationship at point O, the sum force for the internal forces should be zero, i.e.,

$$\sum_{i=1}^{4} \mathbf{G}_i = \mathbf{0} \tag{13}$$

Substituting Eq. (12) into Eq. (13) yields

$$\sum_{i=1}^{4} \mathbf{C}_{li}^{-1}\delta_o - \sum_{i=1}^{4} \mathbf{C}_{li}^{-1}\mathbf{T}_{pi}^o\mathbf{C}_{pi}\mathbf{F}_{pi} = 0 \tag{14}$$

According to Eqs. (11) and (14) can be rewritten as

$$\delta_o = \mathbf{C}_m \sum_{i=1}^{4} \left(\mathbf{C}_{li}^{-1}\mathbf{T}_{pi}^o\mathbf{C}_{pi}\mathbf{F}_{pi} \right) \tag{15}$$

Equation (15) presents the relationship between the actuation force and the end displacement of the CPM. Since the major output motion of the CPM is the three in-plane motion, Eq. (15) can be simplified as

$$\delta_e = \mathbf{C}'_m\mathbf{J}_F\mathbf{F}_i \tag{16}$$

where $\boldsymbol{\delta}_e = [\delta_x \ \ \delta_y \ \ \theta_z]$ is the output displacement at the center of the moving stage, $\mathbf{C}'_m$ is the planar output compliance matrix of the CPM, $\mathbf{J}_F$ is the Jocabin matrix of the input force and $\mathbf{F}_i = [f_1, f_2, f_3, f_4]$ is the input force of the CPM, and they can be given as

$$\mathbf{C}'_m = \mathbf{T}_e \mathbf{C}_o \mathbf{T}_e \text{ where } \mathbf{T}_e = \begin{bmatrix} 1 & 0 & 0 & 0 & 0 & 0 \\ 0 & 1 & 0 & 0 & 0 & 0 \\ 0 & 0 & 0 & 0 & 0 & 1 \end{bmatrix}$$

$$\mathbf{J}_F = \sum_{i=1}^{4} \left(\mathbf{T}_e \mathbf{C}_{li}^{-1} \mathbf{T}_{pi}^o \mathbf{C}_{pi} \mathbf{T}_e^T \mathbf{L}_0 \mathbf{L}_i \right) \text{ where } \mathbf{L}_0 = \begin{bmatrix} 1 & 0 & 0 & 0 \\ 0 & 0 & 0 & 0 \\ 0 & 0 & 0 & 0 \end{bmatrix}, \ \mathbf{L}_i \text{ is a } 3 \times 3$$

matrix which is applied to perform column transformation of $\mathbf{L}_0$.

According to Eq. (16), if we know the input force vector generated by the VCMs, the output motion of the CPM can be obtained. However, given the desired posture of the moving stage, there are infinite feasible force allocation ways to the input forces that satisfying Eq. (16), since the CPM is redundantly actuated. Assume that $f_4 = 0$, the input displacement vector can be given as

$$\mathbf{F}_{i0} = (\mathbf{C}'_m \mathbf{J}'_F)^{-1} \boldsymbol{\delta}_e \tag{17}$$

where $\mathbf{J}'_F$ is the first three column of $\mathbf{J}_F$.

As it is shown in Fig. 1, simultaneously increasing the input forces of the four VCMs as $\lambda[1 \ \ -1 \ \ 1 \ \ -1]^T$ does not contribute to the output motion of the CPM, since the structural of the CPM is rotation-symmetric, λ is a variable which used to adjust the input forces of the VCMs. Therefore, the general solution for Eq. (16) can be given as

$$\mathbf{F}_i = \mathbf{F}_{i0} + \lambda[1 \ \ -1 \ \ 1 \ \ -1]^T \tag{18}$$

5 FEA Simulation and Discussion

5.1 Validation of the Output Stiffness

In order to verify the established stiffness model and kinetostatic model, FEA of the CPM is carried out by the widely adopted ANSYS Workbench software. The main geometric parameters of the CPM are listed in Table 1, and the CPM is assumed to be fabricated by Aluminum 7075-T6, which has a large reversible strain and is widely used for this application, the material properties are also listed in Table 1.

Table 1. Parameters of the CPM

Geometric parameters/mm						Material parameters	
Para.	Value	Para.	Value	Para.	Value	Para.	Value
l	30	a	18	d	15	E	71.7 GPa
h_1	22	b	32	e	23	μ	0.33
h_2	16	c	6	g	22	σ_p	503 MPa
l_2	30						

In the FEA model, an external force of 10 N is applied to the center of the moving stage in x-axis direction to test the output stiffness of the CPM. The simulation result is shown in Fig. 5. It can be seen that, the obtained translation displacement is 0.506 mm. Thus, the x-axis output stiffness of the CPM can be computed. Similarly, by applying a force and a moment to the center of the moving stage in y-axis direction and z-axis direction respectively, the translation stiffness in y-axis and rotation stiffness in z-axis can be obtained. Since the structure of the CPM is rotation-symmetric, the stiffness in y-axis is the same as x-axis. Figure 6 shows the total deformation of the CPM under a moment 1 Nm, and the rotation stiffness of the CPM is calculate as 109.17 Nm/rad. All the output stiffness obtained from the theoretical model and FEA are listed in Table 2. It is shown that the maximum deviation is 1.09%, which indicates the accuracy of the established stiffness model of the CPM.

Table 2. Output stiffness of the CPM

Axis	Output stiffness		Error
	Theory	FEA	
x (N/mm)	19.8807	19.7628	0.60%
y (N/mm)	19.8807	19.7628	0.60%
θ (Nm/rad)	109.17	107.99	1.09%

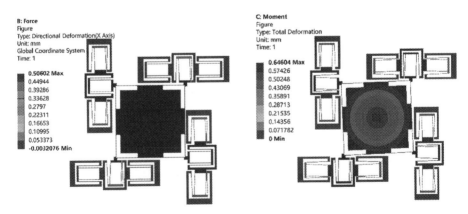

Fig. 5. F = 20 N was applied along x axis   **Fig. 6.** M = 1Nm applied about z axis

5.2   Validation of the Kinetostatic Model

The kinetostatic model describes the relationship between the output motion and the input forces of the VCMs. Given an object posture of the end-effector as [2.5 mm, 2.5 mm, 2.5°], Fig. 7 shows the calculated actuation forces of the VCMs for λ ranges from 0 to 60. It can be seen that, when $\lambda = 0$, i.e., the VCM-4 is redundant, the output forces are [−97.44 N, 49.77 N, −47.68 N, 0 N], where the maximum actuation force is generated by VCM-1, and sum of the absolute value of the VCMs is 194.89 N. Based on Eq. (18), it can be calculated that when $\lambda = 48.72$, the actuation forces of the VCMs are [−48.72 N, 1.045 N, 1.045 N, −48.72 N]. The maximum actuation force of the VCMs is only half of that in the non-redundant case. The sum of the absolute value of the VCMs is 99.53 N, which decreases 48.93% than the non-redundant case. The above analysis suggests that by adding a redundant kinematic leg in the CPM, the actuation forces for VCMs can be decreased significantly.

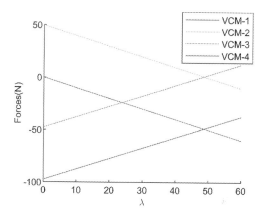

Fig. 7. The actuation forces for different lambda

In order to verify the kinetostatic model of the CPM established in this paper, the actuation forces obtained from the kinetostatic model are set as the inputs in the FEA model, the resulting posture of the moving stage obtained by FEA is [2.495 mm, 2.495 mm, 2.476°]. The maximum relative errors between the posture obtained from FEA and the given posture is 0.96%, which indicates the accuracy of the established kinetostatic model. In addition, the maximum stress of on the CPM for the given posture is 303.34 MPa, which is much less than the yield stress of the material. It suggests that the proposed CPM has a workspace larger that ±2.5 mm × ± 2.5 mm × ± 2.5°.

6 Conclusions

This paper presents an orthogonal 4-PPR redundant actuated planar CPM by leaf spring flexure hinges and VCMs. The CPM can achieve 3 DOF of planar motion (Dx, Dy, Rz) with a workspace larger than ± 2.5 mm $\times \pm 2.5$ mm $\times \pm 2.5°$. Moreover, the translation motions of the CPM are decoupled since the two adjacent kinematic legs of the CPM are arranged perpendicular to each other, which will facilitate the design of controller. The output stiffness and kinetostatic model of the CPM are established by applying the compliance matrix method. The established models are further verified by FEA, and the static performances of the CPM are also analyzed. The results show that the addition of redundant kinematic leg decreases the maximum actuation force of the VCMs significantly. In the future, we will fabricate a prototype of the proposed CPM and perform the close-loop control to obtain high precision planar motion.

Acknowledgement. The authors acknowledge funding provided by the NSFC-Zhejiang Joint Fund for the Integration of Industrialization and Informatization (U1609206, U1509202), China Postdoctoral Science Foundation under Grant 2019M652152, Natural Science Foundation of Zhejiang Province (2018C01072), and Innovation Team of Key Components and Key Technology for the New Generation Robot under Grant 2016B10016 for this research.

References

1. Lobontiu, N.: Compliance-based matrix method for modeling the quasi-static response of planar serial flexure-hinge mechanisms. Precis. Eng. **38**(3), 639–650 (2014)
2. Yang, M., Du, Z., Chen, F., Dong, W., Zhang, D.: Kinetostatic modelling of a 3-PRR planar compliant parallel manipulator with flexure pivots. Precis. Eng. **48**, 323–330 (2017)
3. Yang, M., Du, Z., Dong, W.: Modeling and analysis of planar symmetric superelastic flexure hinges. Precis. Eng. **46**, 177–183 (2015)
4. Yang, M., Du, Z., Chen, F., Dong, W.: Deformation modeling and analysis of variable thickness flexure pivots. J. Mech. Des. **130**(5), 52302–52309 (2018)
5. Naves, M., Brouwer, D.M., Aarts, R.G.K.M.: Multibody-based topology synthesis method for large stroke flexure hinges. In: ASME 2016 International Design Engineering Technical Conferences and Computers and Information in Engineering Conference, pp. 1–8 (2016)
6. Awtar, S., Parmar, G.: Design of a large range XY nanopositioning system. J. Mech. Robot. **5**(2), 21008–21010 (2013)
7. Wan, S., Xu, Q.: Design and analysis of a new compliant XY micropositioning stage based on Roberts mechanism. Mech. Mach. Theory **95**, 125–139 (2016)
8. Hao, G., Kong, X.: A novel large-range XY compliant parallel manipulator with enhanced out-of-plane stiffness. J. Mech. Des. **134**(6), 061009 (2012)
9. Zhang, L., Yan, P.: Design of a parallel XYθ micro-manipulating system with large stroke. In: Proceedings of 28th Chinese Control Decision Conference, CCDC 2016, pp. 4775–4780 (2016)
10. Xu, Q.: Design and development of a compact flexure-based XY precision positioning system with centimeter range. IEEE Trans. Ind. Electron. **61**(2), 893–903 (2014)
11. Yu, H., Zhang, C., Yang, B., Chen, S., Yang, G.: Design and analysis of a large-range flexure-based parallel mechanism based on matrix method. In: IEEE/ASME International Conference on Advanced Intelligent Mechatronics, AIM, July 2018, pp. 762–767 (2018)

12. Lum, G.Z., Pham, M.T., Teo, T.J., Yang, G., Yeo, S.H., Sitti, M.: An XY θz flexure mechanism with optimal stiffness properties. In: IEEE/ASME International Conference on Advanced Intelligent Mechatronics, AIM, pp. 1103–1110 (2017)
13. Al-Jodah, A., Shirinzadeh, B., Ghafarian, M., Tian, Y., Clark, L.: Design and analysis of a novel 3-DOF large range micropositioning mechanism. In: IEEE/ASME International Conference on Advanced Intelligent Mechatronics, AIM, July 2018, pp. 991–996 (2018)
14. Shusheng, B., Hongzhe, Z., Jingjun, Y.: Modeling of a cartwheel flexural pivot. J. Mech. Des. 131(6), 061010 (2009)
15. Su, H.-J.: A pseudorigid-body 3R model for determining large deflection of cantilever beams subject to tip loads. J. Mech. Robot. 1(2), 021008 (2009)
16. Liu, P., Yan, P., Zhang, Z., Leng, T.: Modeling and control of a novel X-Y parallel piezoelectric-actuator driven nanopositioner. ISA Trans. 56, 145–154 (2015)
17. Friedrich, R., Lammering, R., Rösner, M.: On the modeling of flexure hinge mechanisms with finite beam elements of variable cross section. Precis. Eng. 38(4), 915–920 (2014)
18. Chen, F., Du, Z.J., Yang, M., Gao, F., Dong, W., Zhang, D.: Design and analysis of a three-dimensional bridge-type mechanism based on the stiffness distribution. Precis. Eng. 51, 48–58 (2018)

Design of Screw Fastening Tool Based on SEA

Liming Tan[✉], Cheng Sun, Muye Pang, Kui Xiang, and Biwei Tang

The School of Automation, Wuhan University of Technology,
Wuhan, Hubei Province, China
tanliming@whut.edu.cn

Abstract. Screw fastening is often involved in industrial automation assembly processes. During the automatic assembly process in the industry, utilizing the electric screwdriver improves greatly the assembly efficiency. However, the powered screwdriver produces a large impact force on the work piece as he downward screwing speed and rotational speed are fast, which results in fatal damage to the work piece. This paper mainly designs a screw fastening tool to decrease the large impact force between the screw head and the work piece when the screw is driven at fast downward speed and the high speed rotation. This tool designed is based on SEA (Series Elastic Actuators) and adopts two-stage control strategy. By analyzing the experimental data, the tool can complete the function of screw fastening and can basically achieve the effect that the control strategy expects in the bolt fastening process. Within the tolerance of the error, the deformation of the rubber in the SEA has a good linear relationship with its output torque.

Keywords: Screw fastening · Electric screwdriver · SEA · Control strategy · Contact impact

1 Introduction

In the field of industrial automation, screw fastening is applied in many situations for assembling and disassembling, for instance, the large machine assembly, fixing some tools and so on. Screw fastening is also essential in our daily life to joint one component to another or fix a component, such as fixing photo frames, connecting two pieces of plastic and so on.

In the screw fastening application for daily life, considering the convenience of use, an unpowered screwdriver is generally selected to meet lower requirements. The user tightens the work piece or fixes something through the personal experience and the feeling of the reaction torque which is generated in the screw fastening process. As a consequence, the damage rate of the screw and the work piece is relatively low. However, the process is inefficient and consumes time. Compared with the unpowered tools, hand-held electric screwdrivers are adopted in the industry applications. A general shape of the powered screwdriver is shown in Fig. 1. The button (1) is to control the direction of rotation; The power switch (2) can adjust its rotational speed according to the pressure on it; The handle (3) is convenient for people to grab it when it works; The adapter (4) can connect with different model screwdriver bit. The vibration of the power tool is large, which brings harm to the user's arm and is not conducive to screw

H. Yu et al. (Eds.): ICIRA 2019, LNAI 11740, pp. 370–381, 2019.
https://doi.org/10.1007/978-3-030-27526-6_32

fastening. Moreover, the damage rate of screws and work piece increases by using powered screwdriver, although the speed of screw fastening is improved.

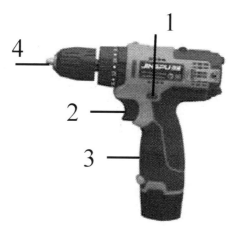

Fig. 1. The general shape of the hand held powered screwdriver includes a button (1), a power switch (2), a handle (3) and an adapter (4).

In order to reduce the damage rate of screws and work pieces, many methods have been adopted for powered screwdrivers. In the alignment stage of screw fastening process, the industry generally adopts robotic arm to ensure the accuracy of the alignment to reduce the damage rate. In the insertion and fastening stage, there are many ways to decrease the damage rate. For example, position control strategy for the fast screw-tightening is proposed in [2], which not only control the rotational torque but also control the thread angular depth of the thread; [1] analysis three control strategy by checking if the motor current reaches the pre-set threshold; the strategy of monitoring torque-angle and torque rate is also proposed in [3]; Fuzzy logic control is proposed in [4]; Compliant control is adopt in [5].

This paper focuses on the design of the electric screwdriver whose unique advantage is to reduce the impact force on the work piece when the electric power screwdriver works at high rotational speed and fast downward speed. In order to solve the above existing problem that the electric screwdriver generates the impact force in the screw fastening process, many methods are introduced in last paragraph. These methods include mainly two aspects, which includes different control strategies and improvement on the mechanism structure. Some control strategies set the current threshold and detect the motor current. If the current reaches the threshold, the motor is stopped to rotate. Some control strategies set two current thresholds: the first current threshold is set at the point in which screw head just touches the surface of the fastener (the surface of the fastener bear a little pressure from the screw screw), and the second current threshold is set to restrict the final screw tightening torque [1]. Some electric screwdrivers are precision torque controlled. A torque sensor is needed to detect the tightening torque of screw, but this method increases the commercial cost, weight and the difficulty of loading and unloading the electric screwdriver. Some electric screwdrivers are precise position controlled, and the final position of the screwdrivers bit is controlled by detecting the depth of the screw insertion. Some electric screwdrivers add electric clutch or spring to reduce the impact force. This paper presents a SEA-based electric screwing tool. This tool possesses following advantages:

1. Using series elastic component to replace the torque sensor decreases the cost and the weight of this tool, which is convenient to repairing.
2. There is accurate torque control of the final tightening.
3. Using SEA based on rubber can buffer the impact force during tightening stage and reduce the reacting force on the user's arm.
4. This tool can dynamically control the torque between this tool and the work piece.

The structure of this paper is as follows: the second section describes the screw model and mechanical model; the third section introduces control strategy based on this tool; the fourth section presents the results of some experiment; the fifth section describes the summary on the tool.

2   Screw Fastening Model and Screwdriver Mechanical Model

2.1   Screw Fastening Modeling

There are two types of external threaded fasteners: screws and bolts. A bolt is intended for use with a nut or a threaded hole to create a high clamping force, while a screw is intended for use with a preformed internal thread (machine screws) but may also form its own thread (self-tapping screws). The terms of screw and bolts are often used interchangeably [6].

The screw fastening model is generally divided into the following three processes: alignment, insertion, and fastening, as shown in Fig. 2. In the alignment process, the screw stem and the screw hole are forced to align in the same axis in order to prevent the screw from tilting into the screw hole. In the insertion process, the screw is quickly screwed into the screw hole with a constant torque until the bolt nut touches the work piece and the surface of the work piece that sustains a slight torque from the screw nut. In the fastening process, the screw is effectively tightened with a large torque to complete the screw fastening. When the screw is finally tightened, the torque between the screw nut and the fastener is approximately half of the final tightening torque. The torque on the work piece during the tightening process of the screw is shown in Fig. 3. As can be seen shown in Fig. 3, the torque on the work piece is fluctuating but does not change much in the first process and then quickly increases in short time in the second process. The screw stem generates axial tension and produces required torque according to international standard to accomplish the screw fastening.

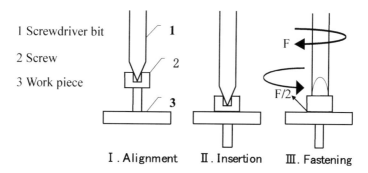

1 Screwdriver bit

2 Screw

3 Work piece

I. Alignment   II. Insertion   III. Fastening

Fig. 2. Screw fastening process

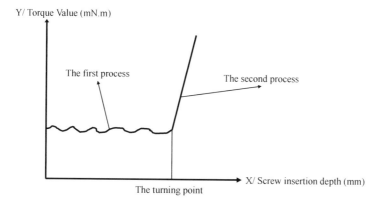

Fig. 3. Torque on the work piece during the screw fastening process

2.2 Mechanical Modeling

The continuous output power of the driving motor transfers to the screwdriver bit by means of series elastic element, which is the major part of SEA. The SEA structure is different from the traditional method of rigid drive commonly used in factory room automation. By adding an elastic element between motor drive and screwdriver bit, the tool output impedance can be changed. Compared to rigid actuators, the spring element provides several unique properties for SEA, including low mechanical output impedance, resistance to shock loads, increased peak power output and providing passive mechanical energy storage [7]. These features meet the tool requirement of robust, interaction safety and energy efficiency. The structure of the series elastic is shown in Fig. 4. Two output shafts (1) can be used to connect other parts; Two photosensitive resins (2) are used to connect cylindrical rubber and output shaft; Cylindrical rubber (3) severs as an elastic element.

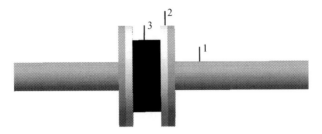

Fig. 4. The structure of the series elastic includes two output shafts (1), two photosensitive resins (2) and a cylindrical rubber (3).

The SEA designed in this article can withstand a certain mechanical torque output and has a small and lightweight shape. The output torque of the rubber in the SEA has a linear relationship with its deformation variable within its reasonable deformation range:

$$F_O = K \cdot \theta \tag{1}$$

where K is the radial elastic modulus of the rubber, and θ is the angle of the rubber rotation.

The physical diagram of the SEA-based bolt fastening tool is shown in Fig. 5. Its structure is shown in Fig. 6. It contains a motor (3) to generate mechanical power, a planetary gear (4) to amplify motor torque, two compliant elements ((2) and (5)) to connect every part, and an adapter (9) to route mechanical power to the rear output and to connect different types of screwdriver bits (10). These components can be chosen and configured in many different ways. In order to reduce the impact force on the work piece and the use's arm and to make the final clamping torque easier to control, the electric screwdriver specially adds the series elastic (7), two optical encoders composed of grating 1 (6), encoder 2 (13), grating 2 (8) and encoder 1 (12), rotary photoelectric encoder (1) and a spring (11) embedded in the adapter (9). In the fastening process of screw fastening model, adding the series elastic and the spring give more respond time for user to stop immediately the screwing to avoid the work piece to be damaged. Two optical encoders can detect the deformation of the rubber in the SEA. The rotary photoelectric encoder can detect the rotational speed of the motor. If the screw to be driven by the tool is in touch with the work piece, the axial feed of the tool will be blocked. The axial feed speed of the tool will gradually slow down, so the tool buffers the impact force of the tool's axial feed on the work piece through the spring. This unique characteristic can increase usability and controllability when implemented at the start, during or end process of screwing.

Fig. 5. The physical picture of the electric screwdriver

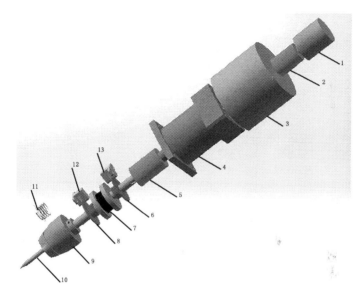

Fig. 6. The structure of the electric screwdriver tool consists of rotational encoder (1), coupling 1 (2), motor (3), reducer (4), coupling 2 (5), grating 1 (6), series elastic (7), grating 2 (8), adapter (9), screwdriver bit (10), spring (11), encoder 1 (12) and encoder 2 (13).

3 Control Strategy

During the insertion of the screw fastening model, the screws remain at a high speed. The bolt nut touches the surface of the work piece, which causes the axial feed speed and the rotational speed of the screw to drop rapidly. Most of the kinetic energy of the high speed screw will be converted into the elastic potential energy of the work piece, so it is easy to damage the work piece.

Screwing the screw into the screw hole and forming an effective pre-tightening torque is the core of the screw fastening. The tool adopts a two-stage control strategy:

the tool uses impedance control in the first stage, and the tool quickly screws the screw into the screw hole until the bolt nut is in touched with the surface of the work piece (the torque on the work piece from the tool is small); the tool adopts torque control in the second stage, and the tool uses a large torque to make the screw generate effective tension and complete the screw fastening. If the speed or position control is adopted in the first stage, it will be difficult to prejudge the expected speed or position due to the mechanical error of the screw and the work piece. If the torque control is used, the current will be suddenly cut off or the electrical screwdriver is locked when the pre-tightening torque is reached. But if the tool working in high speed is suddenly braked, it is easy to generate a large overshooting torque, which causes damage to the work piece and the operator. At present, electrical screwdrivers generally adopt a method of adding an elastic element in the axial direction to buffer the impact force and the rotational torque, but which still cannot completely solve this problem.

Impedance control is a better candidate that renders a lower inertia [8]. Impedance control is to maintain a reasonable dynamic relationship between a system output position or speed and the interaction force between the system and environment by controlling the output impedance of the system. The traditional control strategy generally takes the environmental factor as the disturbance of the system, such as speed control and position control and so on. However, the impedance control regards an act as the interaction process between the system and the environment. The screw fastening modeling is to let the high-impedance bolt nut to touch with the high-impedance work piece, which is easy to generate large impact force and to cause damage to the work piece. The impedance control makes the tool to output low-impedance to the external environment. When a low-impedance object is in touch with a high-impedance object, the impact force on the work piece is greatly reduced. However, the impedance control cannot precisely control the torque and the tool cannot generate the final prejudged tightening torque. Therefore, the control second stage uses precise torque control to achieve the precise tightening torque that the actual situation needs.

The final tightening torque in the second control stage is determined not only by the screw type, but also by the material property of the work piece. The final tightening torque of each type of screw has a uniform international standard. However, the final tightening torque also has a little change according to practical applications.

The impedance control that this designed tool adopted is based on the output speed of the tool. The impedance control block diagram is shown in Fig. 7. The inner control loop includes two traditional control methods (the current loop and the speed loop). The speed loop reduces the output speed error when the tool stably rotates, which improves robustness property of this tool. During the tool startup process, the current loop not only ensures that the tool obtains the maximum current, but also accelerates the dynamic response process of the tool. Current loop can strengthen the anti-interference ability to the power supply voltage fluctuation. When the tool is blocked, it will limit the maximum value of the armature current. These two control loops are integrated in the motor driver. Based on the above two loops, the middle loop adopts the torque control and torque controller uses the integral separation PID control. During the tool startup process, there is a big difference between the feedback torque and the input torque, the feedback torque is calculated as follow:

$$T_r = K \cdot (\theta_1 - \theta_2) \tag{2}$$

where K is the radial elastic modulus of the rubber, θ_1 and θ_2 is respectively read by Encoder 1 and Encoder 2.

Thus, the torque controller output torque is also large and the tool startup speed is very fast. Using integral separation PID control, the accumulation of the torque error can be avoided, which not only ensure that the practical torque does not exceed the maximum of torque that the motor can allow, and also reduces the overshoot caused by the integral accumulation effect. When the feedback torque is close to the set torque, the integral term could eliminate static errors and improve the accuracy of the final bolt tightening torque; The outermost loop adopts the impedance control and impedance controller adopts PI control. The output torque of the impedance controller is calculated as follow:

$$T_d = m \cdot (V_t - V_{rr}) + k \cdot \int (V_t - V_{rr}) \tag{3}$$

where m and k is respectively the virtual mass and the virtual elastic coefficient of the tool, V_t is the constant speed in the screw insertion process, V_{rr} is the feedback speed, which is calculated as follow:

$$V_{rr} = \frac{d\theta_2}{dt} \tag{4}$$

where θ_2 is read by Encoder 2, t is the time.

Because the feedback speed of the bolt is zero when the tool is started, the speed input and large torque output of the impedance controller is very large at the tool beginning stage. When the bolt head is in touch with the work piece, the bolt speed becomes slower. The difference between the feedback bolt speed and the target speed becomes larger and the feedback torque is larger, which makes the input of the torque controller be smaller. Thus, the speed of the motor decreases.

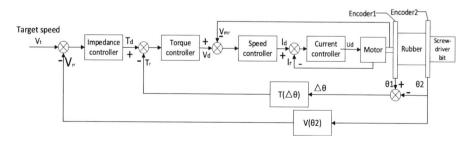

Fig. 7. Impedance control block diagram

4 Experiment and Analysis

4.1 Experiment Platform

In order to verify the practical performance of the electric screwdriver tool and evaluate the linearity of the rubber in the SEA, a set of experimental platform is built, which is shown as Fig. 8. The bracket (1) can support the electric screwdriver tool, the handle (2) can control the ascending and descending of the electric screwdriver. The three-D printing work piece (4) conveniently connects with the torque sensor, which is easy to do experiment and to collect data; the torque sensor (5) is the DF-30 type torque sensor that is produced by Lorenz, Germany. The measuring range of torque sensor is plus or minus 10 Nm, the sensitivity of torque sensor is 0.500 mVN.

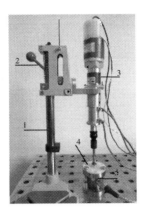

Fig. 8. The experiment platform structure includes an electric drill bracket (1), a handle (2), an electric screwdriver tool (3), a three-D printing work piece (4), and a torque sensor (5).

4.2 Experimental Results Analysis

Rubber Linearity Experiment
Since the tool is based on SEA and needs to detect the output torque of the tool, the linearity of the elastomer in the SEA needs to meet the tool requirements. If the linearity of the elastomer does not meet the tool requirements, the tool will don't work properly and will bring possibly about a series of unpredictable behaviors. The bolt fastening process is achieved through the above experimental platform. The data of the rubber deformation and tool end output torque is collected by the grating encoder and torque sensor and is stored in the SD card and then is processed with the Matlab. The processed results are shown in the Fig. 9. It can be seen from the figure that the rubber-shaped variable has a linear relationship with the tool end output torque within a certain error, and their correlation coefficient is calculated by Matlab to be 0.9929. The slope of the fitted curve in the figure is the rubber rotational elastic coefficient K, which is approximately equal to 15 N/°.

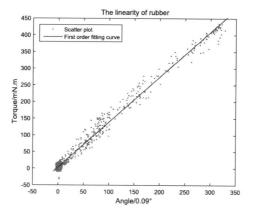

Fig. 9. The linearity relationship curve between the deformation of rubber and tool end output torque

Screw Fastening Experiment

This tool is controlled by a micro controller to complete bolt fastening. When the screw is tightened by this tool, the torque on the surface of the work piece is shown in Fig. 10a. The experimental result apparently shows the two-stage control effect. When the bolt head touches the surface of the work piece, the torque on the work piece fluctuates and the change rate is not large due to impedance control. The second stage of control strategy adopts torque control which generates a precise torque in order to let the bolt to reach the pre-tightening torque. The work piece does not burden almost impact force from the screw head during bolt insertion process.

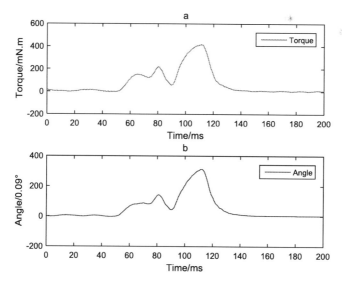

Fig. 10. The curve a represents the torque on the work piece in the screw fastening process. The curve b represents the deformation curve of rubber in the screw fastening process.

In the bolt fastening process, the deformation of rubber in the SEA is shown in Fig. 10b. The rubber deformation value was multiplied by the rubber elastic modulus K that is obtained by the above rubber linearity experiment. The data processing results are compared with Fig. 10a, and the comparison chart is shown in Fig. 11a. As can be seen from the Fig. 11a, the change trends of the torque and the rubber deformation are synchronized. The error among them is calculated by Matlab, and the error curve is shown in Fig. 11b. As can be seen from the Fig. 11b, the curve that the range is from 50 to 90 ms represents the stage that the bolt nut is just in touch with the work piece. The torque measured by torque sensor is larger than the calculated value by formula (2) because of the impact force. The curve that the range is from 90 to 110 ms represents the fastening stage of screw fastening process. The calculated value by formula (2) can be larger than the torque measured by torque sensor because the elastic coefficient K of the rubber is not accurate. However, the maximum error does not exceed 50 mNm.

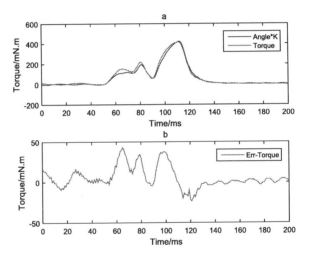

Fig. 11. The curve a represents the comparison curve between the torque measured by torque sensor and the calculated value of rubber. The curve b represents the torque difference between the torque measured by torque sensor and the calculated value of rubber.

5   Conclusion

This article mainly introduces the mechanical and control strategy design of a screw fastening tool based on SEA. The powered screwdriver uses two-stage control method to control the start, rotation and stop of the screw fastening tool in order to reduce the impact force on the work piece. The experimental results show that the tool can complete the function of screw fastening and achieve the target that the control strategy expects. Within the allowable error range, the rubber in the SEA has linearity within a certain deformation range. The advantages of this tool compared with other electric screwdrivers are lower cost, small output impact force, precise torque control and friendly to user. But, its disadvantages are that the rubber is aged in the air for a long time and the linearity of the rubber is more and more bad. In the future, there are two methods to improve the performance of this tool. First, the series elastic element in SEA can be sealed. Second, the material of the elastic element in the SEA can be replaced.

Acknowledgment. This research was funded by National Natural Science Foundation of China, grant number 61603284. The author would also like to acknowledge Cheng Sun, Muye Pang, Kui Xiang and Biwei Tang who are with School of Automation, Intelligent System Research Institute, Wuhan University of Technology, Wuhan, Hubei, China.

References

1. Althoefer, K., Seneviratne, L.D., Shields, R.: Mechatronic strategies for torque control of electric powered screwdrivers. Proc. Inst. Mech. Eng. Part C J. Mech. Eng. Sci. **214**(12), 1485–1501 (2000)
2. Ogawa, S., Shimono, T., Kawamura, A., et al.: Position control in normal direction for the fast screw-tightening. In: 41st Annual Conference of the IEEE Industrial Electronics Society, IECON 2015, pp. 003429–003433. IEEE (2015)
3. Seneviratne, L.: On the use of mechatronics for intelligent screw insertions. In: Proceedings 1996 IEEE Conference on Emerging Technologies and Factory Automation, ETFA 1996, vol. 1, pp. 193–198. IEEE (1996)
4. Dhayagude, N., Gao, Z., Mrad, F.: Fuzzy logic control of automated screw fastening. Robot. Comput. Integra. Manuf. **12**(3), 235–242 (1996)
5. Nicolson, E.J., Fearing, R.S.: Compliant control of threaded fastener insertion. In: Proceedings IEEE International Conference on Robotics and Automation, pp. 484–490. IEEE (1993)
6. Jia, Z., Bhatia, A., Aronson, R.M., et al.: A survey of automated threaded fastening. IEEE Transactions on Automation Science and Engineering (99), pp. 1–13 (2018)
7. Paine, N., Oh, S., Sentis, L.: Design and control considerations for high-performance series elastic actuators. IEEE ASME Transact. Mechatron. **19**(3), 1080–1091 (2014)
8. Keemink, A.Q.L., van der Kooij, H., Stienen, A.H.A.: Admittance control for physical human–robot interaction. Int. J. Robot. Res. **37**(11), 1421–1444 (2018)

Design of Morphing Wing Leading Edge with Compliant Mechanism

Ziang Zhang, Wenjie Ge$^{(\boxtimes)}$, Yaqing Zhang, Rongyi Zhou,
Haijun Dong, and Yonghong Zhang

Northwestern Polytechnical University, Xi'an 710072, Shaanxi, China
gwj@nwpu.edu.cn

Abstract. This paper describes a design process of morphing wing leading edge with a compliant mechanism. A bending-shape design method by thickness optimization of variable cross-section beam is proposed to solve the maximum curvature move in the leading edge of morphing wings. The leading edge is simplified into a four beam elements model with different rectangular sections. The variable cross-section leading edge is optimized by a genetic algorithm. A linear finite element analysis is added to the optimization when the non-convergence occurs. Two driving forces are determined by the same method, which are the conditions of topology optimization. The transmission mechanism is a compliant mechanism designed by topology optimization method based on non-linear structure. The simulation result is given to demonstrate the effectiveness of the proposed method.

Keywords: Morphing wing · Bending-shape design method ·
Compliant mechanism · Topology optimization

1 Introduction

In aviation, morphing wing aircraft has become a hotspot in recent years. By emulating flying animals such as birds and insects, morphing wings modify the airfoil shapes to improve the aerodynamic performance. Either smart materials like shape memory alloys [1] or transmission mechanisms [2, 3] are applied to change the shape of aircraft wings in various investigations. This paper is focused on the transmission mechanisms, which functionally deliver the force of the actuators to morphing wings.

Compliant mechanisms refer to a new type of mechanisms that transfer or transform motion, force or energy through elastic deformation of materials [4]. Compared with rigid mechanisms, compliant mechanisms have a better performance with simple structure, elimination of assembly and absence of friction, which are applicable as transmission mechanisms for morphing wings. Kota et al. [2] designed a flexible adaptive wing by changing the shape of the wing ribs through a compliant mechanism. Tong et al. [3] proposed an approach to design a compliant leading edge with composite material based on topology optimization. Although these wings were tested and verified in the wind tunnel or flight, they are not able to deal with the maximum curvature move caused by the large deformation of the leading edge.

© Springer Nature Switzerland AG 2019
H. Yu et al. (Eds.): ICIRA 2019, LNAI 11740, pp. 382–392, 2019.
https://doi.org/10.1007/978-3-030-27526-6_33

Several common design methods of compliant mechanisms have been developed, such as pseudo-rigid-body model method [5] and topology optimization method [6–10]. Frecker et al. [6] proposed a multi-criteria approach of continuum topology optimization for compliant mechanism design. Sigmund [7] designed a compliant gripper and inverter by taking multi-criteria objective function based on the solid isotropic material with penalization (SIMP) method. Zhang proposed a direct coupling method between meshless and finite element method for the analysis of structure response, which not only improved the efficiency but also ensured the accuracy. Zhang also proposed a meshless-based topology optimization for large displacement problems of nonlinear hyper-elastic structure [8–10].

In this study, a framework of designing the morphing wing leading edge with a compliant mechanism is described. A bending-shape design method by thickness optimization of variable cross-section beam is proposed to solve the problem of the maximum curvature move in the leading edge of a morphing wing. The variable cross-section wing skin is obtained by this method. The driving forces of the leading edge which are the input condition of the topology optimization are also taken with the same method. A compliant mechanism with a topology optimization method based on a non-linear structure is introduced. Finally, an experiment verified the result in the simulation.

2 Leading Edge Skin with Variable Cross-Sections

In the literature [11], the wing skin is cut through the aluminum mold, that includes stringer position and cut ends for the manufacture of the skin. The skin shows high efficiency and low cost, but it is not suitable for the large deforming of the leading edge as the skin has plastic deformation during manufacturing, which makes the skin unable to return to its original shape. The curvature of the skin curve will not change greatly, which is not applied to the morphing wing that has a large deformation. As shown in Fig. 1, the position of the maximum curvature of the wing moved after deformation.

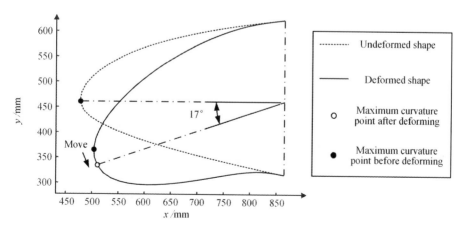

Fig. 1. Curvature move phenomenon in the deformation of the leading edge.

Considering this phenomenon, a bending-shape design method by thickness optimization of variable cross-section beam is proposed in this paper. This method takes a rectangular beam with high yield strength materials. The skin that is fixed one end and applied a moment at the other end is bent to the target shape by changing the thickness of each section of the beam. The advantage of this method is that only elastic deformation occurs in the leading edge during deforming, which satisfies the move of the maximum curvature.

2.1   Bending-Shape Design Method

A model for bending-shape design method is established to simplify the leading edge. Several assumptions are made here: (1) The leading edge could be approximated as several groups of beams with different rectangular cross-sections; (2) These rectangular beams conform to Timoshenko beam theory; (3) In the bending process, only elastic deformation occurs; (4) After deformation, the length of the leading edge does not change.

The model of the leading edge is built through the following steps. First of all, the leading edge curve is divided into four rectangular beams with different cross-sections according to the distribution of curvature. The curvature distribution is shown in Fig. 2. Three stationary points on the fitted curve of curvature are taken as the separating points, which cut the leading edge into four parts (l_1, l_2, l_3, l_4).

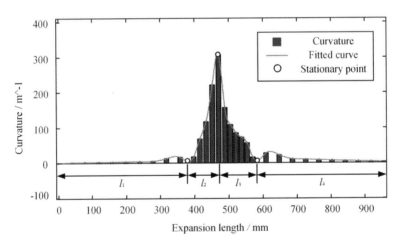

Fig. 2. Curvature distribution of the undeformed shape of the leading edge.

Next, the finite element analysis is performed on the rectangular beams by ANSYS. To change the parameters of cross-section more conveniently, the beam188 element is applied in this work. Beam188 has a better performance in large rotation and non-linear large deformation. In ANSYS, beam188 can define the shape and size of cross-section automatically. Whenever the cross-section size changes, there is no need to re-divide the mesh manually. Beam188 is based on Timoshenko beam theory, which considers the effect of transverse shear deformation on the basis of Euler-Bernoulli beam theory.

Six equidistant key points are selected separately on both undeformed and deformed shapes. The objective function of the model is the minimum displacement error of the key points. The residual sum of squares of the key points is taken as the target, and the model is as follow,

$$
\begin{aligned}
\min_{x} obj &= \sum_{i=1}^{6} \left(u_i' - u_i\right)^2 \\
\text{s.t. } u_j &= f(M, A) \\
u_i' &= int\left(u_j\right) \\
j &= 1, 2, \ldots, \text{n} \\
A &= b \cdot \boldsymbol{x} \\
x_{\min} &\leq x_{1,2,3,4} \leq x_{\max}
\end{aligned}
\tag{1}
$$

where u_j is the node displacement of beam element; u_i' is the key point displacement interpolated by node displacement; u_i is the target displacement of the key point; M is the bending moment, which is applied to the end of the beam; A is the cross-section area; b is the width of the cross-section; $\boldsymbol{x}$ is the thickness of the cross-section, and is also the design variable for this model; $x_{\min}$ and $x_{\max}$ are the upper and lower limit of design variables respectively (Fig. 3).

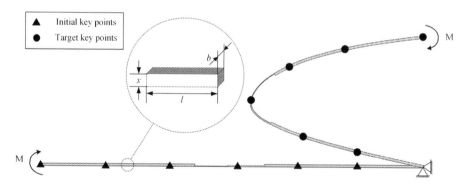

Fig. 3. Optimization model based on beam element and the relationship of key points.

2.2 Optimization of Cross-Section Thickness

Since the finite element analysis process is completed in ANSYS, the variables of displacement in the objective function can be exported directly. However, it results in the failure of getting the sensitivity of the objective function, which makes the sensitivity -based optimization method unable to solve such problems. On contrast, genetic algorithm, a method to search for optimal solutions by simulating natural evolution, which doesn't need the sensitivity of the objective function, is suitable for solving such problems.

The genetic algorithm toolbox in MATLAB is applied to solve the optimization model. The ANSYS batch program is opened by the MATLAB code "!ANSYS 170 -b -p ane3 fl -i -o". In ANSYS, the rectangular beam model is established and discretized into beam188 elements. The material and the beam section parameters are defined. The boundary conditions are constrained, and the bending moments are applied. The nodal displacement of the beam element is solved, and the ANSYS parametric design language (APDL) code providing convenient access to finite element analysis is generated. The design variables which are updated by the genetic algorithm are rewritten into the APDL code to solve the new node displacement.

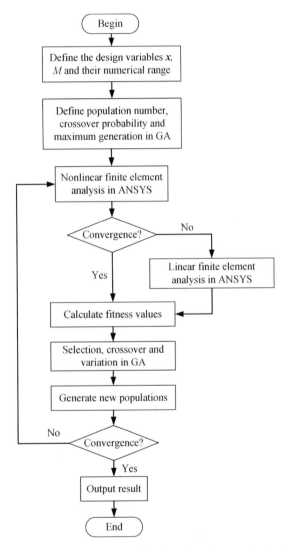

Fig. 4. Flow chart of model solution based on the genetic algorithm.

When the beam model has a large deformation during bending, the result will be inaccurate without considering geometric nonlinearity. Thus the large deformation analysis module in ANSYS is used. However, as the nonlinear solution may not converge when the force is huge, ANSYS would consider it as an error and stops the finite element analysis, which terminates the genetic algorithm optimization. To avoid this phenomenon, a linear finite element analysis is added to the optimization when the non-convergence occurs. The result of the linear solution is multiplied by a penalty coefficient p $(p > 1)$. The solution steps of the model are shown in Fig. 4.

2.3 Results and Simulation

The initial and target curves of the leading edge are shown in Fig. 5. Since only the proportion between the cross-section thickness is required here, the elastic modulus $(E = 100$ MPa$)$ and the cross-section width $(b = 10$ mm$)$ are assumed. The genetic algorithm relies on the selection of initial value largely. According to our experiment, the value range of the thickness x and moment M are set to be [1, 30] and [1, 10] respectively. The deformed shape described by the optimal solution is shown in Fig. 5.

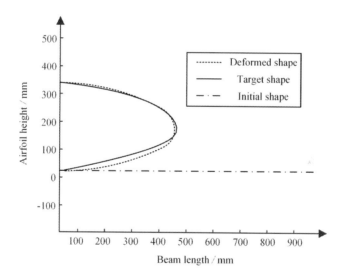

Fig. 5. Geometric relationship between the initial shape, target shape, and deformed shape.

The final optimization result and its error are shown in Table 1. The maximum error of the displacement is 3.57%.

Table 1. The initial parameters and optimal thicknesses of the leading edge model.

Beam number	Beam length (mm)	Section thickness (mm)	Rounding	Max error
1	397.33	6.08	6.0	3.57%
2	91.28	2.61	2.5	
3	81.38	2.90	3.0	
4	387.73	5.93	6.0	

The thicknesses are rounded to simplify the finite element model. The simulation result is shown in Fig. 6. There are some errors in the bottom of the leading edge, as the inaccuracy of the finite element model by rounding the thicknesses of the beam cross-section.

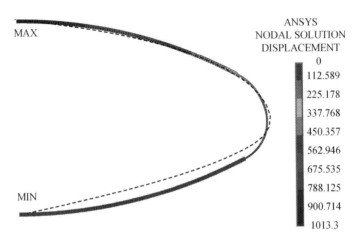

Fig. 6. Displacement result of the leading edge.

3   Optimization of Driving Forces for Leading Edge Skin

The morphing of the leading edge is driven by two forces in this paper. Our goal is to find these two forces on the initial shape to drive the leading edge skin to deform to the target shape. The initial and target shape is shown in Fig. 7.

A method for finding the skin driving force was proposed in the literature [9]. It is only applied for the case of small deformation of the leading edge skin, as it does not consider the pre-stress in skin due to buckling. Our proposed method is improved for the large deformation case in this paper. The model of skin driving force is based on the deformed shape described by the optimal solution in Sect. 2. Firstly, the bending moment is applied to bend the skin to the initial airfoil, in which the pre-stress in the skin is taken into account. Next, two driving forces drive the skin to the target shape.

The optimization model is similar to the model in Sect. 2. The difference between them is the change of the initial shape and target shape of the leading edge. The objective function of the model is the minimum displacement error of the key points. Each driving force has three design variables in the model, i.e. the action point, size and direction of the force. The genetic algorithm is still adopted to solve the model as in Sect. 2. The x directional force is set to be $[-10, 10]$ and the y directional force is set to be $[-20, 0]$. The result of the two driving force is shown in Fig. 7. The final optimization results and its errors are shown in Table 2.

Table 2. The optimal results and error of two driving forces.

Force number	Coordinates (mm)	F_x (N)	F_y (N)	Max relative error
1	(641.14, 584.13)	−10	0	0.46%
2	(534.41, 383.03)	−5	−11	

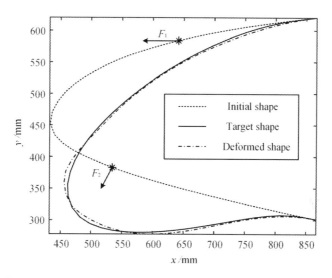

Fig. 7. Position and direction of the driving forces on the leading edge skin.

4 Compliant Mechanism for Leading Edge

4.1 Topology Optimization of Compliant Mechanism

Chen et al. [12] proposed a topology optimization method by combining ANSYS with MATLAB, which accelerates the speed of non-linear solution and improves the stability of calculation. This method is adopted as the design method of transmission mechanism in this paper.

The objective function of topology optimization of compliant mechanisms is to maximize the displacement of output nodes. The optimization model is as follows,

$$\min_{0.001 \leq x \leq 1} u_{out} = -l^T u$$
$$s.t. \quad V(x) < V^* \tag{2}$$
$$R = f^{ext} - f^{int}(u, x) = 0$$

where u_{out} is the displacement of output nodes; l is the matrix, which is a unit length vector against the direction of the anticipated output displacement; u is the nodal displacement; V^* is the volume fraction; R is the residual force; f^{ext} is the external load; f^{int} is the internal load; The SIMP model is adopted as the material interpolation model. The scheme which is derived from the Kuhn-Tucker optimality condition (OC) is applied to update the design variables.

4.2   Results and Simulation

The driving forces as the displacement output node of the compliant mechanism have been obtained in the first two sections. The objective function is to maximize the displacement at the output node, and the constraint is volume. The design domain and boundary conditions are shown in Fig. 8.

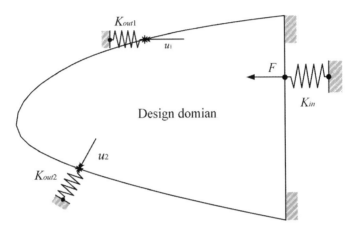

Fig. 8. Compliant mechanism model of the leading edge.

The design domain is discretized into 2883 elements in ANSYS. The volume constraint is set to be 0.4. According to results of Sect. 3, the virtual stiffness of the spring model, K_{in}, K_{out1} and K_{out2} are set to be 0.5 N/mm, 0.1 N/mm and 0.15 N/mm, which are the same as the definition in the reference [7]. The external load, f^{ext} is set to be 40 N. After 54 steps of iteration, the optimization result is shown in Fig. 9.

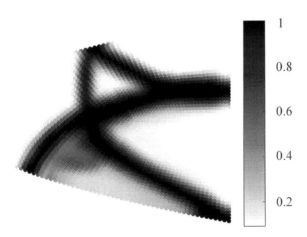

Fig. 9. Configuration of a compliant mechanism.

The static simulation experiment is carried out in ANSYS, and the results are shown in Fig. 10. The results in the simulation satisfy the target deformation well, which shows the effectiveness of this method. At the top of the leading edge, an interference caused by excessive contact area exists during morphing. A flexure hinge will be adopted to decrease the contact area in the future. The compliant mechanism is not in contact with the skin in the lower left of the leading edge, may as the inaccuracy of the finite element model by extracting the vague result of topology optimization.

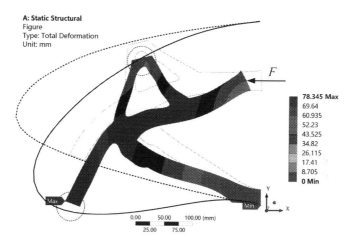

Fig. 10. Total deformation of the compliant mechanism in the simulation.

5   Conclusion

A leading edge of the morphing wing is designed in this paper. In order to solve the problem of maximum curvature move in the leading edge of a morphing wing, a bending-shape design method is proposed. In light of the distribution of curvature, the leading edge is simplified into four beam element models with different rectangular sections. The optimal solution is obtained by a genetic algorithm. Two driving forces are determined by the same method, as the input condition of the topology optimization. The drive mechanism is designed by a compliant mechanism with a non-linear topology optimization method, combining ANSYS with MATLAB. The compliant mechanism of the leading edge can let the skin deformed to the target shape in the simulation, which proves the effectiveness of the proposed method in this paper.

Acknowledgement. This work was supported in part by the National Key Research and Development Program of China under Grant 2017YFB1300102 and National Natural Science Foundation of China under Grant Nos. 51375383.

References

1. Barbarino, S., Flores, E.S., Ajaj, R.M., Dayyani, I., Friswell, M.I.: A review on shape memory alloys with applications to morphing aircraft. Smart Mater. Struct. **23**, 063001 (2014)
2. Kota, S., Osborn, R., Ervin, G., Maric, D., Flick, P., Paul, D.: Mission adaptive compliant wing–design, fabrication and flight test. In: RTO Applied Vehicle Technology Panel (AVT) Symposium. RTO-MP-AVT-168, Evora, Portugal (2009)
3. Tong, X., Ge, W., Sun, C., Liu, X.: Topology optimization of compliant adaptive wing leading edge with composite materials. Chin. J. Aeronaut. **27**, 1488–1494 (2014)
4. Howell, L.L.: Compliant Mechanisms. Wiley, Hoboken (2001)
5. Howell, L.L., Midha, A., Norton, T.: Evaluation of equivalent spring stiffness for use in a pseudo-rigid-body model of large-deflection compliant mechanisms. J. Mech. Des. **118**, 126–131 (1996)
6. Frecker, M., Ananthasuresh, G., Nishiwaki, S., Kikuchi, N., Kota, S.: Topological synthesis of compliant mechanisms using multi-criteria optimization. J. Mech. Des. **119**, 238–245 (1997)
7. Sigmund, O.: On the design of compliant mechanisms using topology optimization. J. Struct. Mech. **25**, 493–524 (1997)
8. Zhang, Y., Ge, W., Tong, X., Ye, M.: Topology optimization of structures with coupled finite element–Element-free Galerkin method. Proc. Inst. Mech. Eng. Part C: J. Mech. Eng. Sci. **232**, 731–745 (2018)
9. Zhang, Y., Ge, W., Zhang, Y., Zhao, Z.: Topology optimization method with direct coupled finite element–element-free Galerkin method. Adv. Eng. Softw. **115**, 217–229 (2018)
10. Zhang, Y., Ge, W., Zhang, Y., Zhao, Z., Zhang, J.: Topology optimization of hyperelastic structure based on a directly coupled finite element and element-free Galerkin method. Adv. Eng. Softw. **123**, 25–37 (2018)
11. Vasista, S., Riemenschneider, J., Monner, H.P.: Design and testing of a compliant mechanism-based demonstrator for a droop-nose morphing device. In: 23rd AIAA/AHS Adaptive Structures Conference, pp. 1049 (2015)
12. Chen, Q., Zhang, X., Zhu, B.: A 213-line topology optimization code for geometrically nonlinear structures. Struct. Multi. Optim. **59**, 1863–1879 (2019)

A Novel Flexure Deflection Device with Damping Function: Towards Laser Reflector of 3D Lithography

Guixin Zhang, Hui Tang$^{(\boxtimes)}$, Xun Chen$^{(\boxtimes)}$, Xiaohui Guo, Jiedong Li, Haoyu Pan, and Shuo Li

State Key Laboratory of Precision Electronic Manufacturing Technology and Equipment, Guangdong University of Technology, Higher Education Mega Center, Guangzhou, China
{huitang,xunchen}@gdut.edu.cn

Abstract. 3D lithography processing technology is widely used in micromaterial processing, biological medicine and semiconductor industry because of its fast processing speed and high precision. However, the difficulty of this technology lies in overcoming the inertial vibration of laser and realizing the control of nanosecond time and nanospace. In order to solve the problem, this paper innovatively designs a laser reflection deflection mechanism with vibration reduction function. Compared with the traditional deflection device, the displacement amplifier is designed by combining with the flexible amplification mechanism, which increases the damping coefficient of the device and dissipates the vibration energy rapidly in the flexible mechanism to achieve the purpose of vibration reduction. Then we theoretically derive the energy reduced by each vibration from the theory of mechanical vibration. Finally, the frequency domain and time domain analysis of the deflection device proves that the deflection device can reduce the inertia amplitude by 31% without the control system.

Keywords: 3D lithography · Deflection device · Flexible · Vibration reduction

1 Introduction

3D lithography processing technology is a new type of microstructure processing technology, which is widely used in micromaterial processing, biomedical and semi-conductor industries Due to its high processing speed and high precision [1, 2]. However, when processing micromaterials, the equipment is working, due to the influence of the motor or the external environment, the carrier platform has slight vibration [3], especially in the fast processing state, the resin-mounted slide will also vibrate, resulting in laser focus. The positioning accuracy is reduced, which affects the machining accuracy. The current method is to reduce the vibration at the bottom of the device to reduce the vibration of the load platform and to use effective control methods to improve the performance of the platform [4]. This method can effectively reduce the vibration of the load platform, but cannot solve the inertial vibration generated when the laser deflection device is swung rapidly. The laser beam of the processed material is reflected by the deflection device. Under the high-speed, high-acceleration and

© Springer Nature Switzerland AG 2019
H. Yu et al. (Eds.): ICIRA 2019, LNAI 11740, pp. 393–400, 2019.
https://doi.org/10.1007/978-3-030-27526-6_34

high-precision positioning requirements of the deflection device, High-speed and high-acceleration movements often have large thrusts and shocks, at the same time, under the precise operation requirements, the small and difficult to observe small disturbances and jitters will have a crucial impact on the precise positioning of the laser beam focus, for which will cause the laser beam to also vibrate, affecting the processing accuracy [5].

The traditional deflection device has no damping function. These years, some scholars launched researches on flexure mechanisms with self-reducing vibration function. Sun proposed a flexure mechanism with single-layer bracket, which possesses satisfactory property of vibration reduction [10]. Based on Sun's mechanism, Liu designed a flexure mechanism with two-layer brackets, extending the function of the mechanism into three-dimensional space and reducing vibration much further [11]. However, these flexure mechanisms with bracket structure cannot meet the requirement of a deflection device on account of its low stiffness and low natural frequency which weaken the dynamic characteristics of the deflection device under high speed. In order to reduce the vibration and improve the dynamic characteristics of the laser beam of the three-dimensional lithography apparatus, this paper designs a deflection device with self-reducing vibration function, as shown in the Fig. 1.

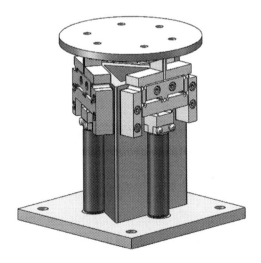

Fig. 1. Schematic of the proposed deflection device.

2   Mechanical Design

The purpose of this section is to design a tip/tilt platform with large optical beam deflection range, sub-micrometer/nanometer scale position accuracy and considerable vibration reduction performance.

The schematic of the developed tip/tilt platform is depicted in Fig. 2. Flexure mechanisms are adopted as the transmission mechanisms of the tip/tilt platform for their excellent properties such as compact structure, no friction and no assembly gap

[6]. In addition, piezoelectric actuators are selected as the actuators of the tip/tilt platform for their advantages such as nanometer resolution, fast response and small size. However, the limited strokes of the piezoelectric actuators restrict the applications of the tip/tilt platform [7]. In order to extend the displacement generated from the piezoelectric actuators so that the optical beam deflection range of the tip/tilt platform can be larger, lever mechanisms with high displacement amplification ratios are employed. Compared with bridge mechanisms which can also amplify displacement, lever mechanisms have smaller sizes for the reason that the piezoelectric actuators can be placed perpendicular to the objective platform. A lever mechanism consists of several straight levers and circular flexure hinges, where the latter possesses high motion precision [8]. The mechanisms as shown in Fig. 2(c) and (d) bring about the first and the second stages of the displacement amplification, respectively. Aiming to obtain decoupled output displacement along the z-axis, the lever mechanisms are designed to be symmetric.

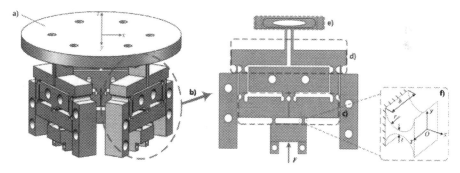

Fig. 2. The schematic of the developed tip/tilt platform, (a) the objective platform (on which a mirror is assembled), (b) a two-stage lever mechanism for displacement amplification, (c) the first and (d) the second stage of the displacement amplification of the two-stage lever mechanism, (e) the vibration reduction mechanism and (f) the circular flexure hinge.

To achieve three-degrees-of-freedom motion including tip, tilt, and translation along the z-axis, three piezoelectric actuators and corresponding three lever mechanisms are utilized. The three output points of the lever mechanisms are positioned on the three vertices of a regular triangle on the bottom of the objective platform, in which case the effects of the three outputs on the motion of the objective platform are equal. Besides, the three lever mechanisms are connected in parallel, guaranteeing high stiffness and natural frequency of the tip/tilt platform.

The key components of the tip/tilt platform are vibration reduction mechanisms which act as the links between the lever mechanisms and the objective platform, as depicted in Fig. 2(e), which is designed to reduce the vibration of the objective platform. In the middle of a vibration reduction mechanism is a through-hole in the shape of an elliptical cylinder, whose parameters determine the vibration reduction performance of the tip/tilt platform directly and can be topologically optimized by software.

What's more, aluminum 7075 is adopted to fabricate the prototype to ensure the superior static and dynamic performance of the tip/tilt platform [9].

3   Vibration Theory

Under the high-speed movement of the deflection device, inertial vibration is generated due to inertia during positioning and the generated vibration energy gradually decays to a steady state according to a certain law. When the impact velocity is small, the vibration amplitude generated is small, and the time to reach the vibration steady state under the adjustment of the mechanism itself is relatively short. When the impact velocity is fast and the inertial vibration amplitude is large, a passive damping mechanism combined with a flexible amplifying mechanism is designed. The flexible mechanism absorbs the energy generated by the inertial vibration during compression, and achieves the purpose of restoring the inertial vibration to a steady state in a short time. In the following, the energy absorption and vibration reduction of the mechanism will be theoretically derived according to the law of inertial vibration. The simulation diagram of vibration reduction is shown in Fig. 3.

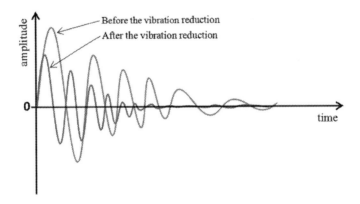

Fig. 3. Vibration simulation diagram.

Set the displacement of the deflection device after the nth energy absorption as follow:

$$x_n = B_n \sin(\omega t_n + \varphi_n) \tag{1}$$

So:

$$v_n = \omega B_n \cos(\omega t_n + \varphi_n) \tag{2}$$

where B_n is the amplitude after the nth energy absorption; φ_n is the phase of the vibration response after the nth energy absorption. In the energy transfer process of the amplifying mechanism and the energy absorption process of the damping mechanism, the relationship between the velocity before and after the vibration energy absorption is described by the material's recovery coefficient q:

$$\alpha q = \frac{v_n^+}{v_n^-} \tag{3}$$

where α is derived from the ratio of the volume of the flexible mechanism to the volume of the unprocessed monolith. The value is $\alpha = 1.5–1.8$. The initial time, $t = 0$, $x_0 = 0$, $\varphi_0 = 0$, it can be obtained:

$$x_0 = B_0 \sin(\omega t_0 + \varphi_0) \tag{4}$$

In the first energy absorption, the vibration displacement at the moment t_1^- before absorption can be expressed as:

$$\mu = B_0 \sin(\omega t_1 + \varphi_0) \tag{5}$$

Therefore:

$$\omega t_1 = \arcsin(\frac{\mu}{B_0}) \tag{6}$$

At time t_1^+ after energy absorption, the vibration displacement is:

$$\mu = B_1 \sin(\omega t_1 + \varphi_1) \tag{7}$$

So:

$$\varphi_1 = \pi - \arcsin(\frac{\mu}{B_1}) - \arcsin(\frac{\mu}{B_0}) \tag{8}$$

During inertial vibration, the energy at the highest amplitude in the vibration response is:

$$\begin{cases} E_1^- = \frac{1}{2}KB_0^2 = \frac{1}{2}K\mu^2 + \frac{1}{2}mv_1^{-2} \\ E_1^+ = \frac{1}{2}KB_1^2 = \frac{1}{2}K\mu^2 + \frac{1}{2}mv_1^{+2} \end{cases} \tag{9}$$

It can get:

$$B_1 = \sqrt{\mu^2 + (\alpha q)^2(B_0^2 - \mu^2)} \tag{10}$$

In the second energy absorption, the same method can be used to obtain the parameters of the second energy absorption:

$$\begin{cases} \omega t_2 = \pi + 2\arcsin(\frac{\mu}{B_1}) + \arcsin(\frac{\mu}{B_2}) \\ \varphi_2 = 2\pi - \arcsin(\frac{\mu}{B_2}) - 2\arcsin(\frac{\mu}{B_1}) - \arcsin(\frac{\mu}{B_0}) \\ B_2 = \sqrt{\mu^2 + (\alpha^2 q^2)^2 (B_0^2 - \mu^2)} \end{cases} \tag{11}$$

Based on the laws of the first energy absorption and the second energy absorption, we introduce the parameter expression for the nth energy absorption:

$$\begin{cases} \omega t_n = (n-1)\pi + \arcsin(\frac{\mu}{B_{n-1}}) + \sum_{i=1}^{n-1} \arcsin(\frac{\mu}{B_i}) \\ \varphi_n = 2\pi - \sum_{i=0}^{n} \arcsin(\frac{\mu}{B_i}) - \arcsin(\frac{\mu}{B_1}) \\ B_n = \sqrt{\mu^2 + (\alpha^2 q^2)^n (B_0^2 - \mu^2)} \end{cases} \tag{12}$$

Thus, the vibration energy that is reduced each time the compression is obtained is:

$$\Delta E_n = E_{n-1} - E_n = (\alpha^2 q^2)^{n-1}(1 - \alpha^2 q^2)\left[\frac{1}{2}K(B_0^2 - \mu^2)\right] \tag{13}$$

where μ is the compression limit of the damping mechanism when the first energy absorption is complete, the value of which can be measured by the damping mechanism, and B_0 is the inertia amplitude when there is no damping mechanism.

When $q = 0.56$, $\alpha = 1.75$, can get:

$$\sum_{n=1}^{100} \Delta E_n = 0.31\left[\frac{1}{2}K(B_0^2 - \mu^2)\right] \tag{14}$$

4   Analysis and Verification

In order to verify the rationality of the above theory, we used ANSYS and MATLAB software to analyze the deflection device in the frequency domain and the time domain. In the frequency domain analysis, only analyzed the frequency of 0–500 Hz according to the processing frequency. The result is shown in Fig. 4. The data before and after vibration reduction at 100 Hz, 200 Hz, 400 Hz, and 500 Hz are selected and the relative error is calculated. It is shown in Table 1; In the time domain analysis, since the three drive axes of the deflection device are symmetrically distributed, only one of the axes is selected for analysis, and the input is an instantaneous impact force, and the result is shown in Fig. 5.

It can be seen from Table 1 that in the frequency domain analysis, the relative errors of the degree of vibration reduction of the deflection mechanism at 100 Hz, 200 Hz, 400 Hz, and 500 Hz and the theoretically deduced vibration damping degree are respectively: −10.6%, −5.5%, −1.9% and −7.4%. The results are close to the theoretical values.

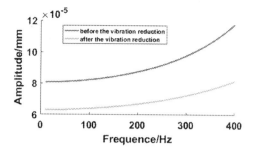

Fig. 4. Comparison of amplitude before and after vibration reduction in frequency domain.

Table 1. The data of amplitude before and after vibration reduction.

Frequency/Hz	100	200	400	500
Before VR/mm	8.4087×10^{-5}	8.5678×10^{-5}	9.2716×10^{-5}	9.8848×10^{-5}
After VR/mm	6.0794×10^{-5}	6.0574×10^{-5}	6.4344×10^{-5}	7.0478×10^{-5}
Amplitude reduction	27.7%	29.3%	30.6%	28.7%
Relative error	-10.6%	-5.5%	-1.9%	-7.4%

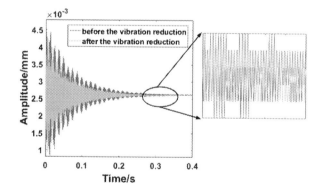

Fig. 5. Comparison of amplitude before and after vibration reduction in time domain.

5 Conclusions

According to the problem that 3D lithography processing technology causes the laser focus to be poor and the machining accuracy is impaired due to the inertial vibration. In my paper, designs a deflection device with vibration reduction function. The core component of the device is a flexible mechanism. The function of amplifying displacement and reducing amplitude is driven by three PZT respectively. From the theoretical deduction of mechanical vibration, it can be concluded that the deflection device can absorb part of the vibration energy after several vibrations, so that the mechanism is fast and stable. The frequency domain and time domain analysis of ANSYS and MATLAB also show that the deflection device has good vibration damping effect. Our next step is to design a dedicated controller to perform closed-loop control of the deflection of the mechanism for better control.

Acknowledgements. This work is supported in part by Natural Science Foundation of China (51605102, 51675106, U1601202), Guangdong Programs for Science and Technology (2016A030308016, 2015A030312008, 201804020040).

References

1. Zeng, H., Martella, D., Wasylczyk, P., et al.: High-resolution 3D direct laser writing for liquid-crystalline elastomer microstructures. Adv. Mater. **26**(15), 2319–2322 (2014)
2. Jang, D., Meza, L.R., Greer, F., et al.: Fabrication and deformation of three-dimensional hollow ceramic nanostructures. Nat. Mater. **12**(10), 893–898 (2013)
3. Divliansky, I.B., Weaver, G., Petrovich, M., et al.: CAD-integrated system for automated multi-photon three-dimensional micro-and nano-fabrication. In: MOEMS-MEMS Micro & Nanofabrication, pp. 196–203. International Society for Optics and Photonics (2005)
4. Sun, G.: Research on 3D micro-nano processing system based on femtosecond laser two-photon absorption. Jilin University (2012)
5. Zhang, L.Y., Gao, J., Tang, H.: Development and modeling of a macro/micro composite positioning system for microelectronics manufacturing. Key Eng. Mater. **679**, 135–142 (2016)
6. Zhu, X., Xu, X., Wen, Z., Ren, J., Liu, P.: A novel flexure-based vertical nanopositioning stage with large travel range. Rev. Sci. Instrum. **86**, Article no. 105112 (2015)
7. Wang, F., Liang, C., Tian, Y.: A flexure-based kinematically decoupled micropositioning stage with a centimeter range dedicated to micro/nano manufacturing. IEEE/ASME Trans. Mechatron. **21**(2), 1055–1062 (2016)
8. Tang, H., Gao, J., Chen, X., et al.: Development and repetitive-compensated PID control of a nanopositioning stage with large-stroke and decoupling property. IEEE Trans. Ind. Electron. **65**(5), 3995–4005 (2018)
9. Kim, J.-J., Choi, Y.-M.: A millimeter-range flexure-based nanopositioning stage using a self-guided displacement amplification mechanism. Mech. Mach. Theory **50**, 109–120 (2012)
10. Sun, J.: Analysis of the dynamic characteristic and sound radiation of the periodic array flexible structure. The Master thesis of Dalian University of Technology (2012). (in Chinese)
11. Liu, D.: Analysis of the dynamic characteristics and damping properties of 3-dimensional periodic flexible structures. The Master thesis of Dalian University of Technology (2013). (in Chinese)

Design and Analysis of a Planar 3-DOF Large Range Compliant Mechanism with Leaf-Type Flexure

Bao Yang[1,2], Chi Zhang[1(✉)], Hongtao Yu[1,2], Miao Yang[1],
Guilin Yang[1], and Silu Chen[1]

[1] Key Laboratory of Robotics and Intelligent Manufacturing
Equipment Technology, Ningbo Institute of Materials Technology &
Engineering, CAS, Ningbo 315201, China
zhangchi@nimte.ac.cn
[2] University of Chinese Academy of Sciences, Beijing 100043, China

Abstract. This paper presents a novel 3-degree-of-freedom (DOF) large range compliant parallel mechanism (CPM) with a 3-PPR configuration. Each PPR chain is constituted of two mutually perpendicular prismatic (P) joints and one revolute (R) joint. These joints are composed of leaf-type hinges to realize large motion range with the existence of distributed compliance. Based on the compliant parallelogram mechanism, two kinds of optimized translational joints with high cross-axis stiffness and one precise rotary pivot are proposed. Pseudo-body method is implemented to establish the quantitative kinematic model of the proposed mechanism. Finite element analysis is carried out to validate the correctness of the model and analyze the modal of the CPM. Utilizing the VCMs as the actuators, experimental tests are conducted to reveal the dynamic performance of the CPM with PID controller. The results demonstrate that the proposed platform can realize precise positioning within a large $XY\theta z$ motion range and possess a high bandwidth about 35 Hz.

Keywords: Compliant parallel mechanism · Large range · PID control

1 Introduction

With the rapid development of ultra-precision technologies, compliant mechanisms have been widely used in various industrial and scientific research fields. These mechanisms are mainly made up of notch hinges or leaf-type hinges and can be fabricated by wire Electrical Discharge Machining (EDM). It provides convenience for guaranteeing the compactness and decreasing assembly error of design. Possessing the merit of no friction and backlash, compliant hinges are usually applied as a guiding mechanism in specific direction to provide precise motions as compared to the conventional joints in the fields of nanoimprint lithography, optical instruments and measurement systems [1]. Compliant mechanisms designed by using notch hinges are normally actuated by piezoelectric actuators (PEAs) to realize high resolution. But they also suffer from the limitation of motion range and the nonlinear behaviors of hysteresis and creep, which will bring difficultness and complexity to control system. Instead,

H. Yu et al. (Eds.): ICIRA 2019, LNAI 11740, pp. 401–412, 2019.
https://doi.org/10.1007/978-3-030-27526-6_35

utilizing the voice coil motors (VCMs) as the actuators, compliant mechanisms composed by leaf-type hinge can deliver a large rang (up to centimeter level) and possess a precise motion accuracy (down to nanometer level) at the same time. This kind of large range compliant mechanisms can satisfy the requirement of micro-positioning system such as atomic force microscopy, biological cell manipulation and attract a lot of research interest.

Compliant parallel mechanisms (CPMs) adopt the parallel-kinematic configuration to provide the advantages of small inertia, none cumulative error and large structural stiffness, which are critical properties in ultra-precision applications. Multiple DOF CPMs utilized in the micro/nano-positioning applications usually consist of a fixed base, several parallel flexure-based chains and a motion stage. Over the past decades, they are intensively researched and there are many relatively previous prototypes regarding to the mechanical design and performance analysis [2–4]. Awtar [5] proposed a planar XY planar-motion CPM (PCPM) driven by two VCMs and the key performance characteristics of the XY mechanism were discussed. Based on the structure of compound multi-stage, Xu [6] designed an XY positioning platform that can realize centimeter-scale stroke. The two-layer arrangement was used to reduce the overall mechanism size and provide decoupling between two major motion directions, but it also increased the nonlinearity of the stiffness in motion directions. Based on nonlinear modeling analysis of parallelogram mechanism, Hao [7] proposed a XYZ decoupling spatial-motion CPM (SCPM) which considered the parasitic movement, the off-axis coupling effects in prime design. But this mechanism was complicated and difficult to be fabricated. By optimized the parameters of C-T beam configuration based on Bezier curve, a compliant parallel manipulator driven by VCM was presented in [8]. The designed prototype can achieve a working space about $\pm 3° \times \pm 3° \times \pm 2$ mm with a natural resonant frequency of 84.4 Hz. But it shows significant nonlinearity of compliance when the direction motion exceeds 1 mm or 2°.

Very limited interest has been shown to the design of VCM driven 3-DOF XYθz PCPM which can enhance the orientation of the sample in the X-Y plane [9–13]. Combining rigid body replacement method and structural topology techniques, Lum [14] proposed a new structure optimization algorithm to obtain the optimized results of the flexure-based branches and subsequently obtained a 3-DOF XYθz stage. The overall size of this mechanism was large because the mechanism was optimized towards optimal stiffness only. Based on Leaf-type Flexure, a rotationally symmetric micromanipulator was delivered in [15] with built-in VCMs. The R-shaped leaf springs and the π-shaped leaf springs were utilized with low enough stiffness to get a large range, but that will lead to a lower bandwidth and cause the vibration more easily. In addition, four sets of VCMs required to drive this 3-DOF mechanism increased the cost and control difficulty.

To this end, the motivation of this work is to design a new compliant 3-DOF XYθz mechanism which can overcome the problems mentioned above. By integrating VCMs, a compact 3-DOF PCPM is proposed to realize large motion range, including translations along x and y axes and rotation about z axis. The precise motion accuracy is ensured by three novel joints designed based on compliant parallelogram mechanism.

The remaining parts of this paper is organized as follow. The mechanical design is described in details in Sect. 2. The analytical kinematic model is derived based on pseudo-body method in Sect. 3 and verified in Sect. 4. And the modal analysis is conducted with FEA simulation in Sect. 4 and experimentally tested in Sect. 5. Driven by VCMs, the experimental tests of positioning accuracy and tracking control are carried out in Sect. 5. Finally, the conclusion is drawn in last section with future works indicated.

2 Mechanism Design

Compared with rotary joints, prismatic joints can produce larger stroke and more precise motions in PCPMs [16]. Therefore, the 3PPR configuration is selected in this work and the first prismatic joint will be actuated by the connected VCM. By using the rigid body replacement method, the designed monolithic 3-DOF PCPM is presented in Fig. 1. It is seen that the stage is mainly composed of three kinematic chains, a moving platform and a base. Each chain is arranged 120° apart from others and consists of a pair of dual basic parallel guiding mechanisms (DBPGMs) connected with the base, double compound parallel guiding mechanism (DCPGM) and a "X" type serial rotary module (XSRM) linked with the moving platform.

Fig. 1. The proposed 3-DOF PCPM.

The main criteria of this PCPM is to: (a) get a large and linear workspace, (b) ensure a precise motion accuracy. The basic parallelogram mechanism (BPM) made up of two leaf-type hinges connected in parallel is widely used in lots of literatures to realize a long stroke. But accompanying the motion in the major direction, the undesired additional rotary angle and parasitic displacement along other directions will be produced. And as a result, the accuracy will decrease significantly. This negative effects can be eliminated by the means of combining two BPGM in parallel, but the stiffness along motion direction will become two times. It means though the lateral load carrying capacity increases, the motion range will be halved when the VCM has been designed or selected. And then, serial method is utilized to compensate the lost range.

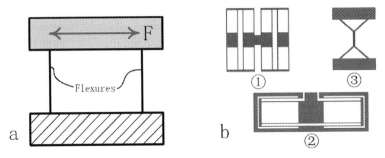

Fig. 2. Compliant Modules (a) BPM, (b): ① DBPGM, ② DCPGM, ③ XSRM

Based on the analysis above, the DBPGM, DCPGM and XSRM are designed and served as three compliant joints respectively, as shown in Fig. 2. In each chain, they are employed to ensure the large linear stroke in the specific axis for the intrinsic distributed compliance and decrease the coupling effects among joints because of the augmented stiffness in other axes. The overall dimension is limited to $300 \times 260 \times 20$ mm³. The exact geometry parameters are listed in Table 1.

Table 1. Geometry parameters of the PCPM.

Parameters	l_1	l_2	l_3	l_4	t_1	t_2
Value (mm)	37	32	3	2	0.44	0.44
Parameters	t_3	t_4	w	u_1	u_2	u_3
Value (mm)	0.4	0.6	20	6	31.5	43.5
Parameters	h_1	s_1	s_2	s_3	s_4	r
Value (mm)	13	107.5	10	30	20	55

3   Kinematic Modeling

As depicted in Fig. 3, the kinematic analysis is conducted to evaluate the relationship between input displacements forced by VCMs and the terminal position in global coordinate frame. Pseudo-body method is involved here for its significantly simple and suitable for the derivation of kinematic of PCPM, which means the prismatic and revolute joints are assumed to have purely translational and rotational motions.

The global coordinate frame EXY is located at the geometric center of the initial position of the terminal stage, while the coordinate frame MXY is the follow-up coordinate frame. The local coordinate frame QXY is fixed at the center point of the first prismatic joint of each chain and its orientation is consistent with the chain. Therefore, the prismatic joints driven by VCMs can only move along the x-axis of its corresponding coordinate frame. A_i represents the ideal rotational center of rotary joints. d_i is denoted as the active displacements while s_i is indicated as the passive displacements. By equaling the different expressions of the point A_i in the same coordinate frame, we can get the kinematic relationship of the proposed PCPM.

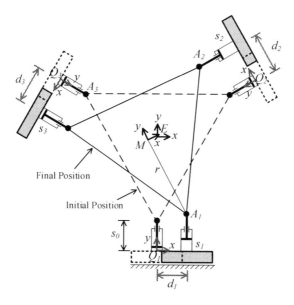

Fig. 3. Schematic diagram of 3-DOF PCPM.

The coordinates of point A_i expressed in frame MXY can be given by:

$$^MA_1 = (0, -r), {}^MA_2 = \left(\sqrt{3}r\big/2, r/2\right), {}^MA_3 = \left(-\sqrt{3}r\big/2, r/2\right) \tag{1}$$

The coordinate transformation matrix from frame j to frame k is shown as:

$$^k_jT = \begin{bmatrix} c\varphi & -s\varphi & t_x \\ s\varphi & c\varphi & t_y \\ 0 & 0 & 1 \end{bmatrix} \tag{2}$$

Where $c\varphi = \cos\varphi; s\varphi = \sin\varphi$. $p = (t_x, t_y)$ and φ represents the distance and clockwise rotation respectively from frame j to k. And the transformation matrix from frame MXY to frame EXY can be derived as:

$$^E_MT = \begin{bmatrix} c\theta & -s\theta & x \\ s\theta & c\theta & y \\ 0 & 0 & 1 \end{bmatrix} \tag{3}$$

Where $\delta = \{x, y, \theta\}$ represents the terminal position relative to the initial position. In addition, the coordinates of point A_i expressed in frame QXY are obtained as:

$$^{Q_1}A_1 = (d_1, s_1 + s_0), {}^{Q_2}A_2 = (d_2, s_2 + s_0), {}^{Q_3}A_3 = (d_3, s_3 + s_0) \tag{4}$$

And, the transformation matrix can be derived as:

$$\substack{E\\Q_i}T = \begin{bmatrix} c\phi_i & -s\phi_i & {}^E x_{Q_i} \\ s\phi_i & c\phi_i & {}^E y_{Q_i} \\ 0 & 0 & 1 \end{bmatrix}, \; i = 1,2,3 \tag{5}$$

Where

$$\phi_1 = 0, \phi_2 = 2\pi/3, \phi_3 = 4\pi/3 \tag{6}$$

$$\substack{E\\Q_1}t = (0, -r_0, 0), \substack{E\\Q_2}t = (\sqrt{3}r_0/2, r_0/2, 0), \substack{E\\Q_3}t = (-\sqrt{3}r_0/2, r_0/2, 0) \tag{7}$$

$$r_0 = r + s_0 \tag{8}$$

The corresponding item of coordinate of A_i derived in different way should be equal expressed in the frame *EXY*, therefore, we have:

$$^E A_i = \begin{bmatrix} E\\M T \end{bmatrix} \begin{bmatrix} {}^M A_i, 1 \end{bmatrix}^T = \begin{bmatrix} E\\Q_i T \end{bmatrix} \begin{bmatrix} {}^{Q_i} A_i, 1 \end{bmatrix}^T = {}^E A_i \tag{9}$$

Since the rotation displacement of the 3-DOFstage designed in this paper is not exceeded 3° at most, it can be considered that there is the following approximate expression: $c\theta = 1, s\theta = \theta$. And then, the displacement relationship between active prismatic joint and terminal position can be derived as:

$$d_1 = x + r\theta, d_2 = -\frac{x}{2} + \frac{\sqrt{3}}{2}y + r\theta, d_3 = -\frac{x}{2} - \frac{\sqrt{3}}{2}y + r\theta; \tag{10}$$

Which can be written in matrix form:

$$\begin{bmatrix} d_1 \\ d_2 \\ d_3 \end{bmatrix} = \begin{bmatrix} 1 & 0 & r \\ -1/2 & \sqrt{3}/2 & r \\ -1/2 & -\sqrt{3}/2 & r \end{bmatrix} \begin{bmatrix} x \\ y \\ \theta \end{bmatrix} = J^{-1} \begin{bmatrix} x \\ y \\ \theta \end{bmatrix}; \tag{11}$$

Where *J* is the inverse Jacobian matrix.

4 FEA Evaluation

The 3D model is established in SOLIDWORKS and imported to WORKBENCH in ANSYS software through the interface embedded in SOLIDWORKS. Aluminum 7075-T651 is selected as the material. The parameters of material are: a Young's modulus of 72 GPa, Poisson's ratio 0.33 and a yield strength in excess of 503 MPa.

4.1   Kinematic Model Verification with FEA Simulation

FEA is utilized here to validate the correctness of the derived kinematic modeling. The expected object position is set to {3 mm, 3 mm, 3°}, through the above inverse kinematic model, input displacement along the X-axis of frame QXY can be derived as {5.87, 3.97, −1.21} mm. And then, the displacements are set as the inputs in the FEA model. The results are drawn in Fig. 4.

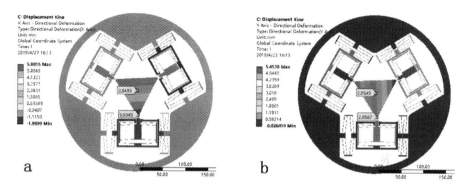

Fig. 4. Deformation along (a) X-axis; (b) Y-axis.

The displacements results of analytical model and FEA are tabulated in Table 2. Regarding FEA result as the benchmark, the discrepancy of analytical model results are all less than 2%. It reveals that the proposed kinematic model can predict the motion of the stage accurately. And the deviation is mainly due to the model simplification introduced by the pseudo-body method.

Table 2.   The results of kinematic evaluation.

Displacements	FEA	Analytical value	Deviation
X(mm)	2.95	3	1.69%
Y(mm)	2.955	3	1.52%
θ_Z(deg)	2.963	3	1.25%

4.2   Dynamic Performance Analysis with FEA Simulation

The dynamic performance of the PCPM is evaluated by modal analysis in ANSYS. Figure 5 shows the results. It can be found that the first three natural frequency are 35.3 Hz, 35.3 Hz and 42.9 Hz regarding to the corresponding mode shape as the translational motion along x and y axes and rotational motion about z-axis. Since the values of first three natural frequency of the PCPM are close, the dynamic performance of the stage is similar in the three working directions. And the natural frequency 4–6

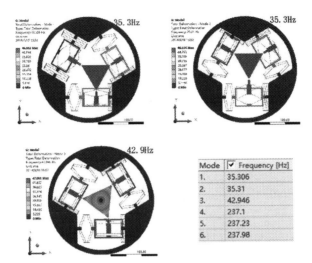

Fig. 5. Modal FEA simulation results of the 3-PPR stage

are 237.1 Hz, 237.2 Hz and 238 Hz respectively as about 5.5 times of the first three, which indicates the designed planar 3-DOF stage can effectively resist external disturbance.

5   Experiment and Results

A series of experiments are implemented to verify the feasibility of the proposed $XY\theta z$ stage.

5.1   Experiment Test of Dynamic Performance

The experiment is conducted to evaluate the natural frequency by using the LMS vibration testing equipment. It contains an impact hammer (086C03 with the sensitivity of 8.7 mV/N), an XYZ ICP accelerometer (356A16 with the sensitivity of 98.0 mV/g in x-axis, 99.9 mV/g in y-axis and 104.6 mV/g in z-axis) attached to the top surface of the end effector, and a signal acquisition equipment LMS Scadas Mobile. The received data is processed in the LMS Test.lab 13A software. Figure 6 shows the experimental setup and the resonance frequency result of the modal analysis.

It is observed that the first two natural frequency of the stage achieve 34.5 Hz in the X and Y axes. Moreover, the third natural frequency in the Z-axis is obtained as 41 Hz which is may be due to the higher stiffness of the compliant revolute joint in each chain. It is observed that the experimental result of the natural frequency is lower than the simulation value in ANSYS, the discrepancy is mainly caused by the manufacturing errors of the stage.

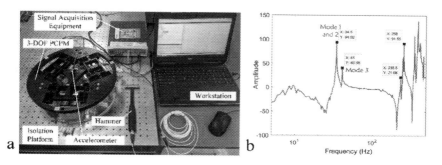

Fig. 6. (a) Modal testing setup, (b) Frequency response of the stage

5.2   Experimental Study with PID Control

In order to further validate the kinematic model and analysis the dynamic performance of the proposed 3-DOF stage, the prototype was machined monolithically using EDM process. Al7076 T6 with high ratio of E/ρ was adopted as the material of the stage. The home-made VCMs with lightweight mover were used to provide a driven displacement about ±6 mm. The structure of lightweight mover can decease the lateral parasitic displacement and improve the bandwidth of the 3-DOF stage. Three Encoders (Mercury II 6000, with a resolution of 20 nm) are used to measure the feedback displacement signal of the motor, and a differential interferometer (10715A/10770A, from Keysight Corporation, with a resolution up to 5 nm/0.03μrad) is installed for real time terminal displacement measurement as well. A dSPACE control system (MicroLab-Box) is adopted to produce control signals into three amplifiers (LA 210S, TRUST TA310) accurately, and these signals are amplified and converted into current signals to drive the VCMs. Cause the output displacements of end-effector measured by interferometer is more difficult to be served as a position feedback signal, a closed loop Proportional-Integral-Differential (PID) controller is designed to control each VCM. Figure 7 shows the control diagram of the system. Figure 8 shows the experimental setup for performance evaluation.

To study the positioning performance of the stage, three point-to-point experiments are carried out separately along X/Y axis and about Z axis. It is noted that the rotary displacements can't be measured exceed 0.5° because of the limitation of the plane measuring mirrors of interferometer. The desired translational/rotational displacement is set to 2.5 mm from the position of 2 mm and then back. The value of the desired

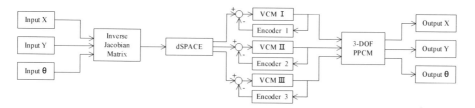

Fig. 7. Control block diagram.

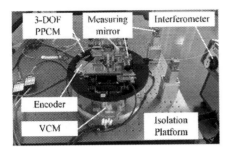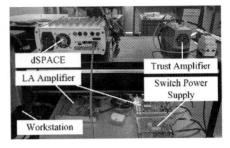

Fig. 8. Experimental setup.

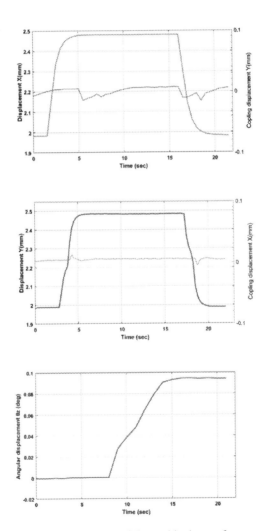

Fig. 9. Experiment test of the positioning performance.

rotational displacement is 0.1° by moving the end effector from the initial position. The displacement results and coupled motion measured by interferometer are plotted in Fig. 9. It reveals the maximum positioning error in three working directions are 0.8%, 0.7% and 6.6%, respectively. Therefore, the experimental results are in good agreement of theoretical analyses. The cross-axis coupling ratio is below 1% (0.58% in the X axis, 0.55% in the Y axis). It may be due to the mutual coupled effects produced by three parallel chains when three VCMs drive simultaneously.

In addition, a circular trajectory with a radius of 1 mm in XY plane is used to examine the tracking performance. The experimental trajectory are depicted in Fig. 10. As compared with given circle, the tracking errors are observed. The error is within ±7.1 μm in the x axis and ±15.9 μm in the y axis as well, which indicates that the stage can deliver a good performance with less than 1.59% tracking error. This tracking errors may be owing to the open-loop control strategy, manufacturing error, and assembly error of measuring apparatus.

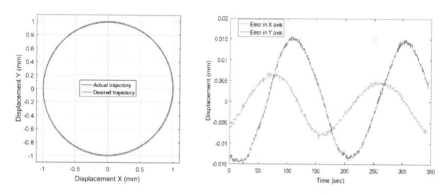

Fig. 10. The result of circular motion tracking.

6 Conclusions

In this work, a 3-DOF PCPM is designed using the leaf-type hinge for the advantage of its distributed compliance. Based on the basic parallelogram guiding mechanism, two optimized translational joints and one novel rotary pivot are presented to ensure the large linear stroke in specific axis and decrease the coupling effects in other axes. Pseudo-body method is utilized to get the kinematic model of the stage and its correctness is validated by FEA in ANSYS. Limited by measuring conditions, a large range is obtained up to ±2.5 mm × ±2.5 mm × ±0.5°. By using a PID controller to control VCMs, precise positioning motions are delivered with low cross-axis coupling ratio as 0.58% in the X axis and 0.55% in the Y axis. Moreover, a circular trajectory tracking experiment is conducted with 1.59% tracking error, which indicates that the stage can achieve good tracking performance. In addition, a high bandwidth about 35 Hz is obtained via FEA simulation and experimental test. In future works, the study of dynamic and advanced control model of the mircro-positioning stage will be presented.

Acknowledgment. This work is supported by NSFC-Zhejiang Joint Fund for the Integration of Industrialization and Informatization (U1609206), Ningbo Natural Science Foundation (No. 2018A610150) and the Innovation Team of Key Components and Technology for the New Generation Robot under Grant 2016B10016.

References

1. Howell, L.L.: Compliant Mechanisms. Springer, Netherlands, Dordrecht (2016)
2. Yu, J., Lu, D., Xie, Y.: Constraint design principle of large-displacement flexure systems. In: International Conference on Manipulation, Manufacturing and Measurement on the Nanoscale, pp. 255–260 (2014)
3. Xu, Q.: Design and development of a compact flexure-based XY precision positioning system with centimeter range. IEEE Trans. Industr. Electron. **61**(2), 893–903 (2014)
4. Lu, S.-S., Yan, P.: A stiffness modeling approach for multi-leaf spring mechanism supporting coupling error analysis of nano-stages. Int. J. Precis. Eng. Manuf. **18**(6), 863–870 (2017)
5. Awtar, S., Slocum, A.H.: Constraint-based design of parallel kinematic XY flexure mechanisms. J. Mech. Des. **129**(8), 816–830 (2007)
6. Wan, S., Zhang, Y., Xu, Q.: Design and development of a new large-stroke XY compliant micropositioning stage. J. Mech. Eng. Sci. **231**(17), 3263–3276 (2016)
7. Hao, G., Li, H.: Design of 3-legged XYZ compliant parallel manipulators with minimised parasitic rotations. Robotica **33**(04), 787–806 (2014)
8. Pham, M.T., Teo, T.J., Yeo, S.H., Wang, P., Nai, M.L.S.: A 3D-printed Ti-6Al-4 V 3-DOF compliant parallel mechanism for high precision manipulation. IEEE/ASME Trans. Mechatron. **22**(5), 2359–2368 (2017)
9. Ding, B., Li, Y., Xiao, X., Tang, Y., Li, B.: Design and analysis of a 3-DOF planar micromanipulation stage with large rotational displacement for micromanipulation system. Mech. Sci. **8**(1), 117–126 (2017)
10. Bhagat, U., et al.: Design and analysis of a novel flexure-based 3-DOF mechanism. Mech. Mach. Theory **74**, 173–187 (2014)
11. Cai, K., Tian, Y., Wang, F., Zhang, D., Shirinzadeh, B.: Development of a piezo-driven 3-DOF stage with T-shape flexible hinge mechanism. Robot. Comput.-Integr. Manuf. **37**, 125–138 (2016)
12. Qin, Y., Zhao, X.: A novel method for measuring the coupled linear and angular motions of XYΘ-type flexure-based manipulators. In: 2015 IEEE International Conference on Robotics and Automation (ICRA), pp. 2722–2727 (2015)
13. Wang, R.Z., Zhang, X.M.: Optimal design of a planar parallel 3-DOF nanopositioner with multi-objective. Mech. Mach. Theory **112**, 61–83 (2017)
14. Lum, G.Z., Pham, M.T., Teo, T.J., Yang, G., Yeo, S.H., Sitti, M.: An XYθz flexure mechanism with optimal stiffness properties. In: IEEE International Conference on Advanced Intelligent Mechatronics, pp. 1103–1110 (2017)
15. Zhang, L., Yan, P.: Design of a parallel XYθ micro-manipulating system with large stroke. In: 2016 Chinese Control and Decision Conference (CCDC), pp. 4775–4780 (2016)
16. Kucuk, S.: A dexterity comparison for 3-DOF planar parallel manipulators with two kinematic chains using genetic algorithms. Mechatronics **19**(6), 868–877 (2009)

Robotic Grasping and Manipulation with Incomplete Information and Strong Disturbance

Video-Guided Sound Source Separation

Junfeng Zhou, Feng Wang, Di Guo, Huaping Liu$^{(\boxtimes)}$, and Fuchun Sun

State Key Laboratory of Intelligent Technology and Systems, TNLIST,
Department of Computer Science and Technology, Tsinghua University,
Beijing, People's Republic of China
hpliu@tsinghua.edu.cn

Abstract. A major aim of separating sound source is to separate the sound of interest out of mixture, such as the sound of objects on the screen. In this paper we put forward a method incorporating sound-indicated object detection and using the detection result to separate the *on screen* sounds and the *off screen* ones. After training, the object detection network could recognize which object is sounding just like human learns what object making what sound. And then using the temporal information of sounds in a video segment, we separate out sound of the object that is not shown in the video. At last, experiments are carried out in data from AudioSet and we demonstrate that the method works well in given scenarios.

Keywords: Sound-source separation · Video-guided

1 Introduction

Sound source separation gains great interest over the years. Separation in single channel cases remains a difficult problem as the spacial information cannot be obtained. However, with the development and popularity of mobile devices, single channel audio processing gains growing importance. So methods to solve the problem are in badly need.

It is useful to get single source sound in many cases. For example, in an interview, we only want to hear the talk between people as in Fig. 1, or when we shooting a natural environment, we only want the chirping of the bird and bleating of the goat other than other visitor's talking. Moreover, robots or other human-machine voice interaction system could recognize orders more precisely if there is no disturbing sound. However there are some interferences occasionally, such as surrounding talking, sound of airplane passing by or abruptly barking. Specific equipments or buildings could eliminate the effect, but they are usually expensive or hardly available.

Sounds and images have deep relation in human recognizing the world [1, 13,18]. On one hand, everything has its specific sound. So after we learn the

---

This work was supported in part by the National Natural Science Foundation of China under Grant U1613212.

H. Yu et al. (Eds.): ICIRA 2019, LNAI 11740, pp. 415–426, 2019.
https://doi.org/10.1007/978-3-030-27526-6_36

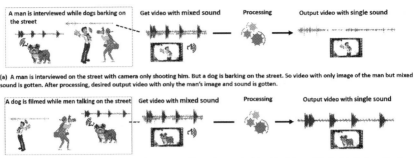

(a) A man is interviewed on the street with camera only shooting him. But a dog is barking on the street. So video with only image of the man but mixed sound is gotten. After processing, desired output video with only the man's image and sound is gotten.

(b) A dog is captured on the street with camera. But there are men talking on the street. So video with only image of the dog but mixed sound is gotten. After processing, desired output video with only the dog's image and sound is gotten.

Fig. 1. Here we show the cases when we need to get single source. (a) and (b) are two cases that the cameraman need shoot different filming targets. Similar to the cases, we usually need film with only single sound of the object in camera

correlation, we can distinguish them. For example, before we learn birds chirping, we only know this is a kind of sound, but we have no idea what it is and we also don't know if different chirps are from the same bird or different ones. After learning, we link the sound with the object and we can correctly classify the sounds by sources. Even we do not see the objects, we can imagine them. On the other hand, motions are highly related to sounds. Lips moving, string stirring, ball bounding and so on, all indicate sounds initialing. It is a strong indication but sometimes it's not easy to observe the motions for reasons that our visual field may be blocked or we are not focusing on the object when sounding.

The relation between sounds and images can also be used in the well-known cocktail party effect problem. The famous effect [22] is the ability that human has to focus his attention on particular sound while filtering out other stimuli. It provides an inspiration for sound separation [24]. Visual images can provide more information. It will be easier if you know what the man's voice is like. For example, if you see a man, you can remember what his voice is. Similarly, in the object level, you can predict what that object may sound. The visual and audio information usually jointly help human's recognition. Motivated by the fact that human can use visual information separating sound sources better, we intend to guide sound source separation with visual information.

Inspired by [?], [11], we present in this paper a video-guided sound separation framework. Our method based on sounding object detection and nonnegative matrix factoring (NMF) method. We show that with the help of visual information, object level sounds could be separated. The main contributions are summarized as the following:

1. A novel *on/off screen* sound separation method is established.
2. A method to connect the visual and audio modalities is developed and used for sound separation.
3. A dataset is constructed from the AudioSet to validate the effect of proposed method.

The paper is organized as the follow structure. We review the related works in sound separation in Sect. 2. In Sect. 3, we present an overview and in Sect. 4 the technical details are demonstrated. Then we show experimental validation and conclusion in the last two sections.

2 Related Work

There are many works focusing on denoising and speech enhancement [19–21]. At the first glance, they deal with the same problem as we propose. However, In most cases, these works actually solve a different one. The environmental sounds in their scenarios are sometimes assumed stationary [19] like crowd sounds and brook sounds or trained non-stationary sounds [20,21]. But in our scenarios, the background sounds are not absolutely "background" sounds and they can also be "foreground" ones. The only difference between the sounds is whether they are captured by the camera.

[9,12] use NMF method with some constraint. They are quite simple and easy to implement. But they need the sounds having particular structure like temporal continuity to be separated. Without special structure, there should be other extra information to separate the sounds, as we using visual clues to guide the separation.

Some other researchers also use visual clues to guide the separation [3,13, 14]. In [13], they come up with a framework, namely multi-instance multi-label learning framework. They train the network with the images and the dictionary matrix which are factored by NMF method. It results in a good separation ability comparing with plenty of methods. However, since their method uses over-complete dictionary, they may meet difficulties in sounds that varies from one to another like speech. In [3,14], they capture the relationship between action and sound. It leads to a good effect but also limitation that they need to see the motion clearly.

Other information also be used in NMF, such as music score [15], text [16], internet [23] and so on. They all need users listen to the sound and help with the separation. In [11,17], they even need the users directly annotate on the spectrogram of the sound. But those methods require users having at least basic knowledge of audio processing, which makes the methods only practicable for professional users. Our method is inspired by them, but need not the help of users. So it makes sound separation feasible for everyone. Sound detection by algorithm can be more accurate than human annotation when mixed sound is quite complex. The proposed method can also avoid the uncertain separation effect caused by different users.

3 Overview

In this section, we summarize the object detection-guided audio source separation framework. A representative algorithm architecture is presented in Fig. 2. Briefly, the audio of the video is extracted and used to detect what and when objects are sounding with the sound-indicated object detection network. That results in discrimination of *on/off screen* sounds and an activation mask. Taking the mask and the audio as input, the proposed approach can separate the *on/off screen* sound.

The separation relies on the temporal differences of the objects' sound, which give clues on how the matrix should be decomposed. Then decomposed matrix can be segmented and recovered into separated sound sources. The temporal differences are given by a network we develop that detects sounding objects in videos and uses sound as indicator. In the whole process the sound is first used to indicate object detection, and then the result of visual detection is used to direct separation of the sound. It embodies the reciprocal relation between sounds and images, that they help the cognition of each other.

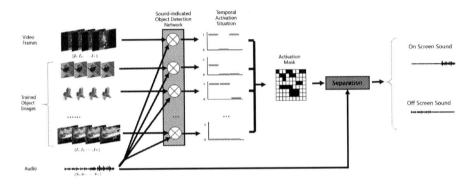

Fig. 2. The overview of the proposed architecture.

4   Sound Separation

Firstly, for *on screen* sound indication, we input a video into the sound-indicated visual object detection network. Then we get the $d_{nk}^{(i)}$ as output that evaluates the correlation between the detected objects and the sound. Next, the $d_{nk}^{(i)}$ that are higher than the threshold are considered active and setted to 1 whereas those lower than the threshold to 0. Assuming that there is one object detected active in the video, according to STFT of the sound, the matrix $M0$ which is composed of $d_{nk}^{(i)}$ can be reshaped into a matrix of $1 \times N$, where N denotes the time frames of STFT coefficients.

To detect *off screen* sound, we input the audio extracted from the same video in *on screen* sound indication. And then we calculate the $d_{nk}^{(i)}$ of the input audio and sounds of all the sample objects that are trained before (given totally J). As a result, we can get all the active time segments of all the objects that sound in the audio. The $d_{nk}^{(i)}$ higher than the threshold are setted to 1 and the others are setted to 0, which is the same as the manipulation of *on screen* sound indication. According to STFT of the sound, we reshape the matrix into $J \times N$ as $M1$.

Taken $M0$ ($1 \times N$) and $M1$ ($J \times N$) obtained above, we construct a activation mask named M with the following steps: (1) we choose from $M1$ a line, which is most similar to the line in $M0$ and delete it; (2) we combine $M0$ and $M1$ in vertical, and get a matrix with shape $J \times N$; (3) we expand the row vectors jth to K_j, making it in corresponding to the NMF model.

Then the audio extracted from the video and the activation mask M should be put into detection-guided sound separation framework. The separated sounds will be output.

The following sections will introduce the mixed sound-indicated visual object detection and detection-guided sound separation framework used in the architecture.

4.1   Mixed Sound-Indicated Visual Object Detection

The sound-indicated visual object detection follows the network we developed before. Briefly, it is composed of three main modules: preprocessing, feature projection network and localization network. The feature projection network can find a common representation space that the video features and sound features can be projected to [7,8]. The localization network inputs the image and sound features in the common space and calculates the target sound and each region in the corresponding images.

In preprocessing step, multiple visual-audio pairs $\{I_n^{(i)}, S_n^{(i)}\}$ are fed into the network to train the parameters. For video images the Faster RCNN [5] is firstly used to detect objects in each visual frame $I_n^{(i)}$. For the corresponding audio signal $S_n^{(i)}$, VGGish model [4] is used to extract 128-dimension high level sound feature $g_n^{(i)} \in \mathbb{R}^{128}$. After the preprocessing stage, the visual features are formed as a $N \times K \times 2048$ block, a binary mask with the size of $N \times K$ and the sound feature is formed as a $N \times 128$ block. The proposed network is demonstrated in Fig. 3.

In the feature projection network, visual features and sound features are dealt with in a parallel manner. We use two fully-connected layers to transform the visual and sound features. Firstly, visual and sound features are separately fed into fully-connected layers, respectively. Then we feed both of the intermediate representations into the following shared fully-connected layer, which encourages the visual and sound features to be represented in a common space [6]. For visual modality, the features are represented in object level and the visual feature $f_{nk}^{(i)}$ is transformed to a new feature annotated as $t_{nk}^{(i)} \in \mathbb{R}^{128}$. At the same time, the audio feature $g_n^{(i)}$ is transformed to a new feature annotated as $s_n^{(i)} \in \mathbb{R}^{128}$. The visual feature $t_{nk}^{(i)}$ for each object and the sound feature $s_n^{(i)}$ are comparable due to the previous shared fully-connected layer and the later common loss function.

For now the comparable visual and sound features are extracted by the feature projection network. The localization network calculates the similarity

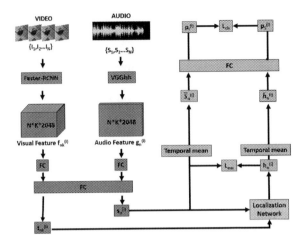

Fig. 3. The architecture of the proposed network.

between the sound feature $s_n^{(i)}$ and each visual feature $t_{nk}^{(i)}$ for $k = 1 \ldots K$, in an object level.

The similarity $d_{nk}^{(i)}$ evaluates the correlation between the sound segment $S_n^{(i)}$ and the k-th detected object in the image frame $I_n^{(i)}$. Using the similarity, we can form the new feature vector about the image frame $I_n^{(i)}$ as

$$h_n^{(i)} = \sum_{k=1}^{K} \alpha_{nk}^{(i)} \cdot t_{nk}^{(i)},$$

where $\alpha_{nk}^{(i)}$ is the normalized similarity which is defined as

$$\alpha_{nk}^{(i)} = \frac{d_{nk}^{(i)}}{\sum_{k=1}^{K} d_{nk}^{(i)}}.$$

We called $h_n^{(i)}$ as the sound indicated image representation. It combines both the information of sound and frame regions to produce a representation that is relevant to the sound content.

To make sure that the capability of intra-modal discrimination in samples is preserved after the feature projection, we deploy a classifier to predict the semantic labels of the features projected in the common representation space. A temporal mean operation is firstly performed which takes visual and sound common space features of every time step namely $h_n^{(i)}$ and $\bar{s}_n^{(i)}$ as input like in [2], producing outputs annotated as

$$\bar{h}^{(i)} = \frac{1}{N} \sum_{n=1}^{N} h_n^{(i)}, \ \bar{s}^{(i)} = \frac{1}{N} \sum_{n=1}^{N} s_n^{(i)}.$$

Then a shared fully-connected layer activated by softmax operations are added following the representation space temporal mean representations [7]. We denote the output vectors of the fully-connected layer as $\boldsymbol{p}_I^{(i)} \in \mathbb{R}^C$ and $\boldsymbol{p}_S^{(i)} \in \mathbb{R}^C$, and the classification loss for the i-th video is defined as

$$\mathcal{L}_{cls}^{(i)} = -\boldsymbol{c}^{(i)T}(log(\boldsymbol{p}_I^{(i)}) + log(\boldsymbol{p}_S^{(i)})).$$

On the other hand, we employ a Euclidean distance loss to encourage the distance between $\boldsymbol{h}_n^{(i)}$ and $\boldsymbol{s}_n^{(i)}$ to be small. The corresponding loss function is defined as

$$\mathcal{L}_{euc}^{(i)} = \sum_{n=1}^{N} ||\boldsymbol{h}_n^{(i)} - \boldsymbol{s}_n^{(i)}||_2^2.$$

Although there exist situations that the content of the image frame may not correlate to the content of the paired sound, the loss $\mathcal{L}_{euc}$ can guide the training process to go to a place where the similar concepts representations of the two different modalities are closed to each other.

The final loss function for the i-th video is defined as

$$\mathcal{L}^{(i)} = \mathcal{L}_{cls}^{(i)} + \lambda \mathcal{L}_{euc}^{(i)},$$

where λ is a balancing parameter. In this combined loss function, $\mathcal{L}_{cls}^{(i)}$ uses the semantic category information to guide the network to learn the useful semantic parts and $\mathcal{L}_{euc}^{(i)}$ encourages the visual and audio modalities to share a common representation space.

4.2   Detection-Guided Sound Separation

Assuming there are $\boldsymbol{J}$ sources, and after short-time fourier transform, there are $\boldsymbol{M}$ frequency bins and $\boldsymbol{N}$ time frames. We let $\boldsymbol{X}_{fn} \in \mathbb{C}^{M \times N}$ and $\boldsymbol{S}_{j,fn} \in \mathbb{C}^{M \times N}$ be short-time fourier transform coefficients of the single channel mixture signal and the j-th source, respectively. The model writes

$$\boldsymbol{X}_{fn} = \sum_{j=1}^{J} \boldsymbol{S}_{j,fn}$$

The power spectrogram of the mixture is expressed as $\boldsymbol{V}_{fn} = |\boldsymbol{X}_{fn}|^{\cdot 2}$, where $\boldsymbol{X}^{\cdot p}$ denotes an element-wise operation of the matrix. Then the algorithm of nonnegative matrix factoring aims to factorize the $\boldsymbol{M} \times \boldsymbol{N}$ matrix $\boldsymbol{V}_{fn} \approx \hat{V} = \boldsymbol{WH}$, where $\boldsymbol{W}$ and $\boldsymbol{H}$ are nonnegative matrices. Given that the STFT coefficients follow zero-mean Gaussian distribution, with linear model $\hat{V} = \sum_j \hat{V}_{j,fn}$, we can get $\hat{V}_{j,fn} = [\boldsymbol{W}_j \boldsymbol{H}_j]_{fn}$, where $\boldsymbol{W} = [\boldsymbol{W}_1, \ldots, \boldsymbol{W}_J]$ and $\boldsymbol{H} = [\boldsymbol{H}_1^T, \ldots, \boldsymbol{H}_J^T]^T$.
Then we seek the minimization of cost function

$$D(\boldsymbol{V}|\boldsymbol{WH})$$

which is defined as

$$D(V|WH) = \sum_{M=1}^{M} \sum_{N=1}^{N} d(V_{fn}|WH)$$

Here we use Itakura-Saito (IS) divergence as the cost. Then the parameter estimation is written as:

$$H \leftarrow H \cdot \frac{W^T ((WH)^{\cdot -2} \cdot V)}{W^T (WH)^{\cdot -1}}$$

$$W \leftarrow W \cdot \frac{((WH)^{\cdot -2} \cdot V) H^T}{(WH)^{\cdot -1} H^T}$$

where $\cdot$ denotes the Hadamard entrywise product and the division is entrywise.

In the user-guided approach, parameter estimation can be guided by temporal annotation that what time segments of each source is active. The initialization of the activation matrix H that the corresponding segments remain unchanged while other regions are setted 0. In this work, we multiply H with the active mask M to get the result. Under the rules of MU, the 0 will not be changed through the update. For sounds that not active simultaneously, the method can provide quite useful information for separation.

After the update, the single source STFT coefficients can be computed as

$$\hat{S}_{j,fn} = \frac{\hat{V}_{j,fn}}{\hat{V}_{fn}} \cdot X_{fn}$$

then the single source sound estimation can be obtained via the inverse short-time fourier transform.

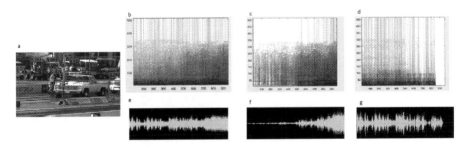

Fig. 4. In this scenario, there is a car racing and a man talking in the background. As shown in (a), cars are detected sounding. (b), (c), (d) show the spectrogram of the sound of the origin one, separated *on screen* sound and separated *off screen* sound. (e), (f), (g) are their corresponding waveform.

5   Experiment

5.1   Data for Training

We construct a sound-indicated object detection dataset derived from AudioSet. We choose 10 classes in the AudioSet containing 32469 video clips, among which 31469 are for training and 1000 are for evaluation. The 10 classes are speech, dog, cat, pig, guitar, car, motorcycle, train, helicopter and alarm clock, which are often seen and heard in real life.

5.2   Data for Separation

For qualitative results, we choose from AudioSet videos that containing two different sounds but only show images of one of them. For example the commentary of a race with camera focusing on the cars. Additionally, a realistic scene experiment that we filmed the video at home has been carried to simulate a real-world application.

To facilitate the quantitative evaluation, we construct a new dataset, which contains videos with only a single sounding object. We manually examine raw videos in AudioSet and get several such videos of 9 s as foreground videos and some of 5 s as background videos. The images of background videos are discarded to generate the background sounds. We then compound the foreground videos with the background sounds of different objects. The sounds of the foreground videos and background sounds are referred to as *on screen* sound and *off screen* sound. The videos are resized to 640 * 480 and audios resampled at 48 kHz. Three pairs of sounds are used to evaluate the proposed method, mimicking common scenarios that need sound separation in real life. They are guitar-helicopter, speech-car and guitar-cat.

5.3   Evaluation Criteria

To evaluate the quality of source separation, we use the BSS-EVAL toolbox [10], mainly the Normalized Signal-to-Distortion Ratio (NSDR) in the toolbox. The NSDR is the difference between two SDRs. One is SDR of the separated signals and the ground truth signals, and the second is SDR of the mixture signals and the ground truth signals. That is: $NSDR(\hat{v}, v, \hat{s}) = SDR(\hat{v}, v) - SDR(\hat{s}, v)$, where $\hat{v}$ is the separated signals, v is the ground truth signals, and $\hat{s}$ is the mixture signals.

5.4   Baseline

We compare to the $NMF\text{-}MFCC$ method and oracle method. $NMF\text{-}MFCC$ is a sound separation method [9], where the mixed sounds are first transformed into Mel frequency cepstrum coefficients (MFCC), and then separated channels are grouped with K-means clustering. It is used in many literature for comparation and the code is available publicly. Since the algorithm could not distinguish *on* and *off screen* sounds, after separation, we pick up the *on screen* ones manually.

The oracle method is the user-guided source separation approach [11]. Human can identify the sources of sounds more easily in most cases, resulting in a better temporal annotation and thus a better separation result.

5.5   Result

Figure 4 shows some representative qualitative results. The detected objects are marked with boxes. Here we can see that the sounds are separated into two parts. Detail result can be seen in video at https://junfengzzzzhou.github.io/websiteOFpaper/.

Quantitative result is shown in Table 1. In the cases, there are some interesting results. In the scenario of guitar-helicopter, our method surpasses *NMF-MFCC* method and even the Oracle ones, while in the case of speech-car, Oracle gets the best result. In guitar-cat scenario, all the methods gets negative results, meaning that they make the sounds more different to the ground truth than mixed sound, and our method gets closest to zero, meaning a smallest deterioration.

Table 1. NSDR of different methods

NSDR	Our method	Oracle	NMF-MFCC
guitar-helicopter	4.73	4.49	1.93
speech-car	3.94	7.50	1.91
guitar-cat	−0.82	−2.23	−4.42

Our method makes use of the temporal information of different sounds, while NMF-MFCC uses the frequency characters of the sounds. As a result, when sounds to be separated have distinguished frequency discrepancy, NMF-MFCC sometimes gets a good result. The discrepancy of our method and oracle method is due to the recognize ability of the sound-indicated network. It can be inferred that with the improvement of the sound-indicated network, we can get oracle result.

In most common scenes like speech-car, the oracle one can surpass our method because of its better detection ability. However, in the cases of guitar-helicopter and guitar-cat, our method surpasses the oracle. That is because human can easily detect different object sounding but hardly indicate it in detail, for example in frames. So even though oracle method has the best theoretical separation effect, the best result need professional people spend plenty of time dealing with the annotation. Limited by our experiment condition, the experiments of oracle method cannot get the best result. In guitar-cat scenario, all the methods seem to deteriorate the sound. That is because the interference is comparatively too small, so on one hand they are not easily separated and on the other hand the separation with even a little mistake can lead to a deterioration. When a sound is hardly heard and affects other sound, our method would not detect it, thus making less mistakes. It seems like a shortcoming, but actually it is useful in application: when the interference is weak, a separation is not worthwhile.

Admittedly, the method has some drawbacks. Our method can separate sounds that have temporal differences. But in the cases that the two sounds are highly simultaneously active, the algorithm cannot complete the task.

6   Conclusion

In this work, by jointly using the sound-indicated object detection and the NMF method, we develop a novel video *on screen* sound separation method, which could be widely used in real-life scenarios. Experimental results have demonstrated that the proposed method can successfully separate the *on* and *off screen* sound. Due to the complicated relationships between video and audio signals, there still exist many limitations of this work. For example, the detection ability still need improvement to get the oracle result and this method could not separate sounds that happen simultaneously all the time. Those tasks will be our next work.

References

1. Zhao, H., Gan, C., Rouditchenko, A., Vondrick, C., McDermott, J., Torralba, A.: The sound of pixels. arXiv preprint arXiv:1804.03160 (2018)
2. Owens, A., Efros, A.A.: Audio-visual scene analysis with self-supervised multisensory features. arXiv preprint arXiv:1804.03641 (2018)
3. Segev, D., Schechner, Y.Y., Elad, M.: Example-based cross-modal denoising. In: 2012 IEEE Conference on Computer Vision and Pattern Recognition (CVPR), pp. 486–493. IEEE (2012)
4. Gemmeke, J.F., et al.: Audio set: an ontology and human-labeled dataset for audio events. In: 2017 IEEE International Conference on Acoustics, Speech and Signal Processing (ICASSP), pp. 776–780. IEEE (2017)
5. Ren, S., He, K., Girshick, R., Sun, J.: Faster R-CNN: towards real-time object detection with region proposal networks. In: Advances in Neural Information Processing Systems, pp. 91–99 (2015)
6. Aytar, Y., Castrejon, L., Vondrick, C., Pirsiavash, H., Torralba, A.: Cross-modal scene networks. IEEE Trans. Pattern Anal. Mach. Intell. **40**(10), 2303–2314 (2018)
7. Wang, B., Yang, Y., Xu, X., Hanjalic, A., Shen, H.T.: Adversarial cross-modal retrieval. In: ACM on Multimedia Conference, pp. 154–162 (2017)
8. Hardoon, D.R., Szedmak, S., Shawe-Taylor, J.: Canonical correlation analysis: an overview with application to learning methods. Neural Comput. **16**(12), 2639–2664 (2004)
9. Spiertz, M., Gnann, V.: Source-filter based clustering for monaural blind source separation. In: Proceedings of the 12th International Conference on Digital Audio Effects (2009)

10. Vincent, E., Gribonval, R., Févotte, C.: Performance measurement in blind audio source separation. IEEE Trans. Audio Speech Lang. Process. **14**(4), 1462–1469 (2006)

11. Ozerov, A., Févotte, C., Blouet, R., Durrieu, J.L.: Multichannel nonnegative tensor factorization with structured constraints for user-guided audio source separation. In: 2011 IEEE International Conference on Acoustics, Speech and Signal Processing (ICASSP), pp. 257–260. IEEE (2011)

12. Virtanen, T.: Monaural sound source separation by nonnegative matrix factorization with temporal continuity and sparseness criteria. IEEE Trans. Audio Speech Lang. Process. **15**(3), 1066–1074 (2007)

13. Gao, R., Feris, R., Grauman, K.: Learning to separate object sounds by watching unlabeled video. arXiv preprint arXiv:1804.01665 (2018)

14. Parekh, S., Essid, S., Ozerov, A., Duong, N.Q., Pérez, P., Richard, G.: Guiding audio source separation by video object information. In: 2017 IEEE Workshop on Applications of Signal Processing to Audio and Acoustics (WASPAA), pp. 61–65. IEEE (2017)

15. Hennequin, R., David, B., Badeau, R.: Score informed audio source separation using a parametric model of non-negative spectrogram. In: Proceedings of IEEE International Conference on Acoustics, Speech, and Signal Processing (ICASSP) (2011)

16. Le Magoarou, L., Ozerov, A., Duong, N.Q.: Text-informed audio source separation. Example-based approach using non-negative matrix partial co-factorization. J. Signal Process. Syst. **79**(2), 117–131 (2015)

17. Duong, N., Ozerov, A., Chevallier, L., Sirot, J.: An interactive audio source separation framework based on non-negative matrix factorization. In: IEEE International Conference on Acoustics Speech and Signal Processing (2014)

18. Barzelay, Z., Schechner, Y.Y.: Harmony in motion. In: IEEE Conference on Computer Vision and Pattern Recognition, CVPR 2007, pp. 1–8. IEEE (2007)

19. Innami, S., Kasai, H.: NMF-based environmental sound source separation using time-variant gain features. Comput. Math. Appl. **64**(5), 1333–1342 (2012)

20. Xu, Y., Du, J., Dai, L.R., Lee, C.H.: A regression approach to speech enhancement based on deep neural networks. IEEE/ACM Trans. Audio Speech Lang. Process. (TASLP) **23**(1), 7–19 (2015)

21. Duong, T.T.H., Nguyen, P.C., Nguyen, C.Q.: Exploiting nonnegative matrix factorization with mixed group sparsity constraint to separate speech signal from single-channel mixture with unknown ambient noise. EAI Endorsed Trans. Context-Aware Syst. Appl. **4**(13), 154342 (2018)

22. Arons, B.: A review of the cocktail party effect. J. Am. Voice I/O Soc. **12**(7), 35–50 (1992)

23. El Badawy, D., Duong, N.Q., Ozerov, A.: On-the-fly audio source separation. In: 2014 IEEE International Workshop on Machine Learning for Signal Processing (MLSP), pp. 1–6. IEEE (2014)

24. Chen, X., Liu, G., Shi, J., Xu, J., Xu, B.: Distilled binary neural network for monaural speech separation. In: 2018 International Joint Conference on Neural Networks (IJCNN), pp. 1–8. IEEE (2018)

In-hand Manipulation for Active Object Recognition

Xiang Dou[1], Xinying Xu[1], and Huaping Liu[2]($\boxtimes$)

[1] College of Electrical and Power Engineering,
Taiyuan University of Technology, Taiyuan 030024, China
douxiang6677@163.com
[2] State Key Laboratory of Intelligent Technology and Systems,
Department of Computer Science and Technology, Tsinghua University,
Beijing 100084, China
hpliu@tsinghua.edu.cn

Abstract. Visual object recognition systems mounted on the automatic mobile agents face the challenge of unconstrained data, but simultaneously can realize the object recognition task in the human robot interactive environment by actively exploring. In this paper, we propose an active object recognition method to actively explore the more interesting positions of observation to reduce the uncertainty of object recognition. We propose to use the bayesian formula to iteratively accumulate the experience of image perception, and actively explore better recognition positions through control strategies. It is similar to humans actively exploring in the cognitive process, establishing the coupling relationship between perception and action, which is conducive to selecting the suitable posture to predict the labels. Furthermore, the effects of inhibiting action exploration behavior are analyzed with passive strategies. The results from the recognition of GERMS confirm that the proposed method successfully learns the effective category identification strategy, and the active selection action further boosts the recognition performance.

Keywords: Active object recognition · Bayesian perception ·
Visual recognition

1 Introduction

The research of visual object recognition aims to better perceive key information and identify a visual scene or object of interest. It has been widely used in industrial and commercial informatics, such as industrial visual inspection, assisted driving, and face recognition. Such agents (e.g., industrial cameras, self-driving cars) have made significant developments in recent years [1–5]. However, modern visual recognition still faces the problem of incomplete information in the research of unknown object recognition in complex environments, the loop of its perception and action is relatively independent. For this reason, it is crucial to allow intelligent agents to interact with the surrounding environment to actively perceive.

© Springer Nature Switzerland AG 2019
H. Yu et al. (Eds.): ICIRA 2019, LNAI 11740, pp. 427–438, 2019.
https://doi.org/10.1007/978-3-030-27526-6_37

Active object recognition refers to problems in which an agent interacts with the world and controls its sensor parameters to maximize the speed and accuracy with which it recognizes objects [6]. As Gibson would say [7], the complete animal visual system consists not only of the eyes, but also the head to which those eyes are attached, and further still, the body to which that head is attached. In this paper, we propose an active recognition method combined with bayesian perception, which combines perception and action, allowing the agent to automatically explore the interesting observation position and obtain more accurate information to improve recognition efficiency.

In this work, our approach consists of state estimation and control decision strategies. The state estimate is responsible for "perception", and the current state is calculated using the probabilistic bayesian formula based on the actions and observations taken at each time step. Furthermore, the bayesian filter maintains a probabilistic distribution of environmental conditions for the agent, and provides a powerful platform for dealing with environmental dynamics. In particular, it also provides a corresponding unstructured environment for dealing with uncertainties in measurement [8, 9]. The control decisions are responsible for "actions", it infer state and control actions at each time step based on the acquired agent status. Combined with perception and action, the agent actively explores the state of the environment that is conducive to observation.

In general, we recommend using the bayesian probabilistic approach to learn and perform effective active object recognition. The contributions of this work can be summarized as follows:

- Combine the bayesian formula with the control decision strategy to achieve the interaction between perception and action, and move in the 3D simulation environment to produce accurate classification results.
- We evaluated our model on the GERMS dataset and compared it to sequential and random strategies. The results demonstrate that the method is more advantageous than the traditional passive perception method in the environment of active object recognition.

This paper is organized as follows: first, a description of related work is presented in Sect. 2. Second, our proposed methods for the visual active object recognition is described in Sect. 3, including the basic concepts and theories of the bayesian model and active decision strategy. Third, the experiment and results are shown in Sect. 4. Finally, the conclusion is found in Sect. 5.

2   Related Work

2.1   Active and Passive Perception

The difference between active and passive perception is shown in Fig. 1. The comparison between the two ideas has always received much attention [10], including the field of information processing [11], machine learning [12, 13], tactile perception [14]. In the context of visual object recognition, the input state of passive perception is a single static image generally, and the output is represented as the estimated value of the category label. The development of passive perception has also made significant progress, such as the excellent results in the ImageNet challenge [15]. However, the input of a single image can cause ambiguity, in many recognition environments, such as the inevitable factors of posture, perspective, and light angle. In order to cope with this challenge, active perception can overcome this shortcoming. In the process of operation, the agent needs to make full use of its own cognitive characteristics and establish the coupling relationship between perception and action. It can take advantage of the important role of motion to overcome the uncertainty brought by the open environment in visual recognition, and thus improve the recognition accuracy. This paper adopts the active perception model based on the bayesian formula. Through this model, we can perform actions under the factors of posture uncertainty, change the angle of view and observe the recognition.

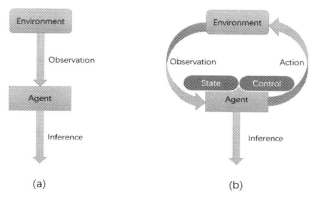

Fig. 1. The difference between active and passive perception in the field of visual recognition: (a) passive perception; (b) active perception. In passive perception, it predict category labels by extracting features on a single static image, while the methods of active perception can establish a coupling relationship between perception and motion, indicating that the autonomous mobile visual agent obtains more views through the camera to facilitate object recognition.

2.2   Bayesian in Perception

In the context of perception of bayesian, the forward generation model is an internal mental model, as shown in Fig. 2, which describes and simulates the process of sensory observations occurring in the world [16]. The bayesian model can be formalized by a

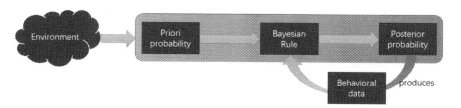

Fig. 2. Bayesian perception model.

likelihood term that describing the probability of observation of certain sensory data P (priori) for a given state of the object, and the observer infers the belief value of the possible state of the environmental object based on the sensory data P (priori).

3   Methods

3.1   Model Architecture

We consider active object recognition as a probability problem, and solve this problem by bayesian probability method. Our model consists of a bayesian formula and an active control strategy. As shown in Fig. 3, the joint position and track information of the corresponding image of the robot provides a more accurate information framework for object recognition.

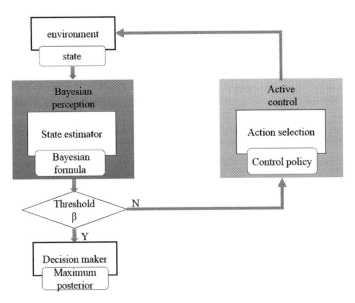

Fig. 3. The architecture of the active object recognition model. It consists of bayesian perception and active control strategies. The active control layer explores favorable positions with high levels of interest to boosts perception. The exploration and perception process is repeated until a predefined belief threshold is exceeded to make a decision about the object being explored.

3.2   Bayesian Perception in Vision

Bayesian Formula Update. Our bayesian formula recursively updates the posterior probability distribution of the environmental state. In Algorithm 1, we show the training of a single image at a time. In practice, the training algorithm uses small batches containing images from different given and accepted trials. In each training iteration, the process updates the parameters based on the prediction error.

We define the representation of the object class as c_n, each class c_n consists of the location and orbit information of the recognition object, o_t is defined as the observation result, and the t time step is at each time step t = 1; 2;..., T to predict each object instance. The bayesian formula used in this paper is described as follows:

$$P(c_n|o_t) = \frac{P(o_t|c_n)P(c_n|o_{t-1})}{P(o_t|o_{t-1})} \tag{1}$$

The formula can be understood as the posterior probability is the product of the prior probability and the adjustment factor. Where $P(c_n|o_t)$ is the "posterior probability". The "prior probability" is represented by $P(c_n|o_{t-1})$. $P(o_t|c_n)/P(o_t|o_{t-1})$ is called "adjustment factor" or "probability function", where $P(o_t|o_{t-1})$ is the edge probability, which is the normalization factor in the application of the bayesian formula. The settings of the various components in the formula are described in detail below.

Prior Probability. We set a uniform initialization probability for all categories in the experiment and define the initial prior probabilities of all identified objects as follows:

$$P(c_n) = P(c_n|o_0) = \frac{1}{N} \tag{2}$$

Where N is the number of object classes used to observe the data.

Adjustment Factor. Similar to the previous work of Martinez-Hernandez et al. [17], we used a histogram-based nonparametric estimation method to obtain a measurement model. The histogram is constructed evenly by merging the information into the spacing position s with $N_{bins} = 100$ intervals. We use these histograms to estimate the likelihood of the perceptual class c_n:

$$P(o_t|c_n) = \frac{h_n(s(j))}{\sum_{s=1}^{N_{bins}} h(s(j))} \tag{3}$$

Where j is the object instance, *and* $h_n(s(j))$ is the instance count of all training data in c_n, $\sum_{b=1}^{N_{bins}} h(s(j))$ is the normalization factor that makes it have the appropriate probability that the sum is 1. The correct normalized value is ensured by the marginal probability of previous contact conditions:

$$P(o_t|o_{t-1}) = \sum_{n=1} P(o_t|c_n)P(c_n|o_{t-1}) \tag{4}$$

Threshold. The process of object recognition can be controlled by setting the threshold. Within the scope of the system, Within the threshold range, the system continues to iteratively update and accumulate experience, and the recognition is stopped if the threshold is exceeded. Obtain the corresponding belief value according to the maximum posterior probability:

$$if \quad any \quad P(c_n|o_t) > \beta_{threshold} \quad then \quad \hat{c} = arg\,max_{c_n}\,P(c_n|o_t) \tag{5}$$

The object estimated at time t is represented by c. We used a set of belief thresholds $\beta_{threshold} = \{0.0, 0.01, \ldots, 0.99\}$ to observe their effect on the accuracy of the object recognition process. The belief threshold $\beta_{threshold}$ allows adjustment of the confidence level of the decision process.

Algorithm 1 Training state estimator layer

PROCEDURE TRAIN
    initialize prior information A
    t ← 1
    while not exceed the threshold β do
        $I_c \leftarrow I_t$
        $I_c \leftarrow$ Next-Image(t-1)
        $A_t \leftarrow$ priori(I_c)
        $B_t \leftarrow$ bayesian formula((A_t, I_c))
        NormalizeB_t
        $a_t \leftarrow$ Action-Value(B_t)
        $I_t \leftarrow$ Action-Selection(a_t)
        t ← t+1
    end while
end PROCEDURE

3.3 Active Control Strategy

We combine the bayesian formula with the active control strategy to control the choice of actions, which allows the system to actively select more interesting positions for observation. Bayesian perception transforms images into belief values, and uses active control strategy to convert the accumulated beliefs of action values to obtain action values.

Active Control Strategy Formula. In this paper, we set the prediction event to R, I indicates the degree of interest, and the active control strategy formula is as follows:

$$I(R(t)) = e_I(t-1) \cdot e_I(t) \tag{6}$$

Where I(R(t)) is the degree of interest of the predicted event R at time t, and $e_I(t-1)$ and $e_I(t)$ represent the prediction errors of the past and current times $t-1$ and t. The settings of the components in the formula are described in detail below.

Prediction Errors. We use the distance between the bayesian formula and the posterior as the prediction error. The prediction Object classification error at time t is:

$$e_I(t) = P(c_n|o_t) - \beta_{threshold} \tag{7}$$

Where $P(c_n|o_t)$ is the posterior probability of updating the state of the environment.

Degree of Interest. Based on the accumulated historical predictions and current prediction errors, combined with the idea of the intrinsic motivation model [18–20], the interest degree formula is as follows:

$$a = arg\,max_R\,I(R(t)) \tag{8}$$

4   Experiments

In order to evaluate our object recognition method, the system needs to select the movement mode in the 3D environment, and change the observation position based on the degree of interest to obtain more accurate recognition results. We trained each of these models with the Nvidia RTX2080 (4 cards with 8g memory each) machine. Each model's training takes about 10 h.

4.1   Dataset

The Germs dataset comes from the RUBI project aimed at developing robots that interact with young children in early childhood education environments [6]. The Germs dataset consists of images captured by a head-mounted camera that can be used to simulate a 3D environment using 2D images, which use 136 different bacterial toys as observation objects. Figure 4 shows the toy models of all kinds of these bacterial toys, including human cells, microorganisms, viruses and other related organisms.

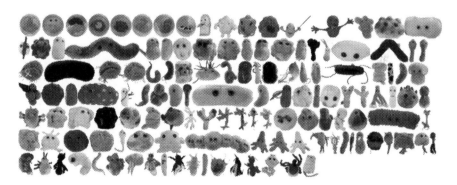

Fig. 4. Object set used in GERMS dataset [6].

Each time a RUBI is submitted to a bacterial toy, RUBI grabs the object and takes it to the center of the field of view and rotates it 180° and then returns. During the rotation, the camera continuously records at 30 frames per second, each recorded image. The capture time and joint position will be recorded accordingly, and the data will be stored in the track. Each track contains 265 snapshots of shooting and shooting experiments.

4.2   Experimental Results

First, we present the accuracy curve of the model tested on the GERMS dataset and compare it with the passive strategies of sequential strategy and stochastic strategy. Second, we list the sequence of actions used in our experimental approach.

Recognition Results. The GERMS data set consists of the left and right arms. We use the training set corresponding to the two arms to train the model, then measure the performance on the test set as a function of the number of actions. Each test is replaced with a new object for testing. The object recognition results are shown in Fig. 5 (green line), and the performance of the model is averaged over the entire test set. At the same time, we conducted comparative experiments using two passive strategies: sequential strategy and stochastic strategy. In the experiment, the sequential strategy means that each experiment starts from the same position and selects the next operation action according to the same sequence rule, as shown in Fig. 5 (blue line), and the random strategy selects a random operation action with uniform probability, such as Fig. 5 (Orange line) shows.

We report the accuracy of predicting the correct label as a function of the number of actions. The experimental results demonstrate that our method can make more accurate predictions of the corresponding view of a series of test objects. And compared to sequential and random methods, the proposed method can achieve higher recognition accuracy with fewer steps. When the number of actions reaches 15, the recognition accuracy can reach a relatively high level and the model performance remains stable.

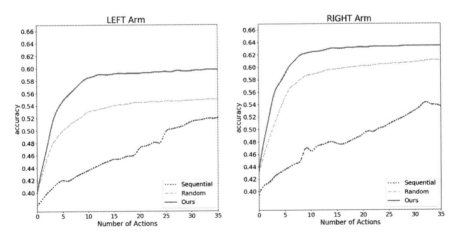

Fig. 5. Performance comparison between proposed strategies, sequential and random strategies on the GERMS dataset Left Arm (left) and Right Arm (right) test images. (Color figure online)

To more specifically illustrate the performance and characteristics of our proposed method in terms of recognition efficiency, we compared the number of steps required to achieve the same level of label prediction accuracy for all object categories (136 types) in the GERMS data set, as shown in Table 1. Compared with the other two methods, the proposed method uses significantly fewer steps to achieve the same accuracy in the test. In the experiment of the left arm test set, our method can achieve 55% accuracy in 5 steps, which is obviously better than the sequential method and the random method, and the random method can not reach this in 35 steps. Accuracy. In the experiment of the right arm test set, our method can achieve 55% accuracy in 3 steps, while the random method requires 5 steps. The sequential method cannot achieve this accuracy even in 35 steps. More importantly: our method achieved peak performance of 60% accuracy in the left-arm experiment and peak performance of nearly 64% accuracy in the right-arm experiment, which is superior to the performance baseline on the GERMS dataset [6].

Table 1. Number of steps required for random, sequential, and recommended strategies to achieve the same label prediction accuracy on GERMS data.

Method	Dataset									
	Left arm					Right arm				
	Prediction accuracy (%)									
	48	52	55	58	63	48	52	55	58	63
Sequential	22	33	-	-	-	16	27	-	-	-
Random	4	8	19	-	-	2	4	5	8	-
Ours	2	4	5	9	-	1	2	3	4	15

Action Sequence. In order to more directly and accurately indicate the characteristics of our method, Fig. 6 lists the action pictures taken by our method on the object. From left to right: The sequence of actions selected by the bayesian active sensing method, which means that we select these actions to actively recognize the object. The model system tends to return to a large rotation angle after reaching one end of the joint rotation range, and then repeat this operation. It does not repeat at the same joint position, and the wide range of actions can be used to ensure that the trained model has higher generalization performance.

Fig. 6. From left to right: continuous actions selected by the proposed method. (a) action sequence of training dataset for the left arm; (b) action sequence of training dataset for the right arm; (c) action sequence of test dataset for the left arm; (d) action sequence of test dataset for the right arm.

5   Conclusion

In this paper, we propose a model that combines a bayesian formula and an active control strategy for active object recognition. Our framework learns that future observation sequences change under their possible conditions of action, enabling them to successfully explore and recognize object. Object recognition experiments with the GERMS dataset demonstrate that our proposed active method is superior to sequential and random action selection strategies. The results demonstrate that our method has the potential to enable the robotic hand to perceive and autonomously determine the future observation position in order to obtain more favorable prediction information for active object recognition.

Acknowledgements. This work was supported in part by the National Natural Science Foundation of China under Grant 61673238.

References

1. Weimer, D., Scholz-Reiter, B., Shpitalni, M.: Design of deep convolutional neural network architectures for automated feature extraction in industrial inspection. CIRP Ann. **65**(1), 417–420 (2016)
2. Urmson, C.P., Dolgov, D.A., Nemec, P.: Driving pattern recognition and safety control. U.S. Patent No. 8,634,980, 21 January 2014
3. Fleck, S., Straßer, W.: Smart camera based monitoring system and its application to assisted living. Proc. IEEE **96**, 1698–1714 (2008)
4. Schroff, F., Kalenichenko, D., Philbin, J.: FaceNet: a unified embedding for face recognition and clustering. In: Proceedings of the IEEE Conference on Computer Vision and Pattern Recognition (2015)
5. Kendoul, F., Nonami, K., Fantoni, I., Lozano, R.: An adaptive vision-based autopilot for mini flying machines guidance, navigation and control. Auton. Robots **27**, 165 (2009)
6. Malmir, M., Sikka, K., Forster, D., Movellan, J.R., Cottrell, G.: Deep Q-learning for Active Recognition of GERMS: baseline performance on a standardized dataset for active learning. In: BMVC (2015)
7. Gibson, J.J.: The Ecological Approach to Visual Perception: Classic Edition. Psychology Press, London (2014)
8. Thrun, S., Burgard, W., Fox, D.: Probabilistic Robotics. MIT Press, Cambridge (2005)
9. Thrun, S.: Probabilistic algorithms in robotics. AI Mag. **21**, 93 (2000)
10. Lloyd, J.: Goal-based learning in tactile robotics. Diss. Faculty of Environment and Technology, University of West of England, Bristol (2016)
11. Bajcsy, R., Aloimonos, Y., Tsotsos, J.K.: Revisiting active perception. Auton. Robots **42**, 177–196 (2018)
12. Willett, R., Nowak, R., Castro, R.M.: Faster rates in regression via active learning. In: Advances in Neural Information Processing Systems (2006)
13. Settles, B.: Active Learning. Morgan & Claypool Publishers, San Rafael (2012)
14. Ward-Cherrier, B., Cramphorn, L., Lepora, N.F.: Tactile manipulation with a TacThumb integrated on the open-hand M2 gripper. IEEE Robot. Autom. Lett. **1**, 169–175 (2016)
15. Russakovsky, O., et al.: ImageNet large scale visual recognition challenge. Int. J. Comput. Vis. **115**, 211–252 (2015)

16. Vincent, B.T.: A tutorial on Bayesian models of perception. J. Math. Psychol. **66**, 103–114 (2015)
17. Martinez-Hernandez, U., Dodd, T.J., Prescott, T.J.: Feeling the shape: active exploration behaviors for object recognition with a robotic hand. IEEE Trans. Syst. Man Cybern.: Syst. **48**, 1–10 (2017)
18. Oudeyer, P.-Y., Kaplan, F., Hafner, V.V.: Intrinsic motivation systems for autonomous mental development. IEEE Trans. Evol. Comput. **11**, 265–286 (2007)
19. Gottlieb, J., Oudeyer, P.Y., Lopes, M., Baranes, A.: Information-seeking, curiosity, and attention: computational and neural mechanisms. Trends Cogn. Sci. **17**, 585–593 (2013)
20. Fortenberry, B., Chenu, J., Movellan, J.R.: RUBI: a robotic platform for real-time social interaction. In: Proceedings of the International Conference on Development and Learning, ICDL 2004. The Salk Institute, San Diego (2004)

Designing Bionic Path Robots to Minimize the Metabolic Cost of Human Movement

Jing Fang and Jianping Yuan[(⊠)]

Science and Technology on Aerospace Flight Dynamics Laboratory,
Northwestern Polytechnical University, Xi'an, China
jyuan@nwpu.edu.cn

Abstract. Despite great successes in wearable robotics, designing assistive devices that are portable like clothes and could reduce the metabolic cost of human movement remains a substantial challenge. Inspired by the driving mechanism of human body, we proposed a class of bionic path (BP) robots in this paper. The BP robots could assist human limbs along arbitrary paths pre-designed on the limb surface, and could be driven by various soft path actuators (the active, quasi-active or passive). Additionally, to minimize the metabolic cost of human movement, a human-in-the-loop optimization method for designing BP robots was also developed in this paper. As practical examples, 18 BP robots with 3 different types of path actuators along 6 different paths were designed to help people reduce their metabolic cost during walking. Each of the 18 robots combined with the human body separately to form a coupled dynamic system. The metabolic power, muscle excitations and optimal control profiles for these coupled systems were analyzed using the simulation-based method. Simulation results showed that, 13 of these 18 BP robots decreased the whole-body metabolic energy consumption, and the maximum reduction was up to 55% relative to the unassisted scenarios.

Keywords: Wearable robotics · Human-in-the-loop design · Biomechanics · Human energetics

1 Introduction

During the evolutionary process, human musculoskeletal structures have been continuously optimized to perform various movements with as little metabolic energy as possible [1–3]. However, there are still many uncontrollable factors that could weaken the optimized human bodies, such as the increasing ages, neuromuscular diseases, physical collisions, etc. In real life, many people need to further improve their musculoskeletal structures, even young and healthy athletes. To meet the need, researchers have studied many solutions, for example, the surgery, drug treatment, rehabilitation training and targeted training programs for athletes. Despite the good effectiveness of above traditional methods, most of them are time-consuming, costly and could have harmful side effects. Therefore, in recent years, scientists have begun to explore the wearable robotics as a solution to enhance human movement abilities.

Early wearable robots to enhance human movement were in the form of rigid exoskeletons consisting of rigid mechanical structures and servos or rigid hydraulic

© Springer Nature Switzerland AG 2019
H. Yu et al. (Eds.): ICIRA 2019, LNAI 11740, pp. 439–449, 2019.
https://doi.org/10.1007/978-3-030-27526-6_38

actuators [4, 5]. For example, the first power exoskeleton designed to lift heavy loads [5], the exoskeletons for soldier enhancement [6], and the upper extremity robotic exoskeletons [7], etc. Despite their great progress, rigid exoskeletons were limited by their inherent rigidity and other structural characteristics. Firstly, their fixed axis could not always align with the flexible human joints, which would apply unwanted forces to human skeletons and lead to unnatural and unhealthy human movement forms [8]. Secondly, their huge weight increased the inertia of human body, and that could change the natural dynamics and metabolic energetics of human body [9, 10].

Soft wearable robots may be an alternative option to enhance the human movement while avoiding the disadvantages of traditional rigid exoskeletons. As we all known, soft actuators are the key enablers for soft wearable robots. Researchers have made many attempts to apply the existing soft actuators to wearable robots, such as the ankle-foot rehabilitation robot actuated by Mckibben pneumatic artificial muscles [11], the wearable robotic hand actuated by a polymer-based actuator [12], the soft orthotic devices actuated by modular hyper-elastic actuators [13]. Bowden cables have also been used as the soft actuators for wearable robots to assist healthy people and to rehabilitate patients after stroke [14–16]. Current soft wearable robots are light and flexible, nevertheless, their complex and obvious geometric structures still limit their practical generalization. We need to further explore novel soft wearable robots that are powerful, comfortable, beautiful, and can be hidden under clothes.

Additionally, the coupled dynamics and energetics of the human and wearable robot combinations are rarely considered in the design process. Most researchers applied the proof-of-concept method and performed the posteriori analysis of the biomechanical effects to human body by physical prototype manufacturing and subject testing. These traditional design methods are time-consuming and expensive, because they require many iterations to get a better design profile. And sometimes designers could do a lot of useless work and end up with an ineffective wearable robot. It is necessary to develop a human-in-the-loop optimized design method that considering the coupled dynamics and energetics of the combination to predict the biomechanical effects of wearable robots to human bodies.

Therefore, in this study, we proposed a class of bionic path (BP) robots and developed a human-in-the-loop optimization design method for these robots. The concepts of BP robots and the human-in-the-loop optimal design were described in detail in Sects. 2.1 and 2.2. Then, the design and simulation evaluation of 18 specific BP robots were introduced in Sect. 2.3. These simulations were performed on the human biomechanical software OpenSim [17, 18]. Finally, the results, discussions and a conclusion of this study were presented in Sects. 3 and 4.

2   Methods and Materials

2.1   The Concept of BP Robots

Over millions of years of evolution, human beings have been constantly optimizing their body structures to reduce the metabolic energy consumption in various activities [1]. However, to trade off versatile movement forms, the human structure is not the optimal for a specific motion form. Athletes usually do some targeted training for their specific sports to improve their musculoskeletal structure properties, especially the mechanical properties of their muscles, tendons and ligaments (MTL). Inspired by the biomechanical principle of athlete training, we proposed a class of bionic path (BP) robots to enhance human motion abilities, while optimizing the energy consumption of human muscle metabolism.

The BP robot consists of one or more path actuators and some fiber materials for comfortable human-robot interaction. Path actuators are laid out along arbitrary paths predesigned on the limb surface and could apply forces along their paths, like the human MTL distributing on the skeleton. Better than the human MLT structures, BP robots could provide bidirectional forces along the preset paths by adopting different active, quasi-active or passive path actuators. Various soft materials could be used as the path actuators for BP robots, such as the electric or pneumatic artificial muscles, the passive elastic fabrics or rubber-like materials, the clutched soft springs, etc. Therefore, the BP robots could be hidden under the clothes, and would be more acceptable to users than traditional wearable exoskeletons.

2.2   Human-in-the-Loop Optimal Design of BP Robots

Traditional designing methods for wearable robots are mostly based on the continuous iterations of prototype manufacture and human subjects testing, which are time-consuming and lack advanced analysis to human body biomechanics and energetics. In this section, we propose a human-in-the-loop optimal design method for BP robots. This method is based on the dynamic and CMC simulations of a complex system coupled by the human body and BP robots.

The optimum design variables for this nonlinear problem are the geometrical and mechanical parameters and control profiles of specific path actuators embodied in BP robots. And the objective of the optimization is to minimize the metabolic energy consumption of human movement.

According to the human muscle energy expenditure research performed by Umberger et al. [19], the instantaneous power $\dot{E}(t)$ of muscle metabolic energetic expenditure can be expressed by

$$\dot{E}(t) = \dot{h}_A(t) + \dot{h}_M(t) + \dot{h}_{SL}(t) + \dot{w}_{CE}(t) \tag{1}$$

in which $\dot{h}_A(t), \dot{h}_M(t), \dot{h}_{SL}(t)$ are the heat rate of activation, maintenance and shortening/lengthening, $\dot{w}_{CE}(t)$ is the mechanical work rate of the muscle contractile element. Obviously, the instantaneous metabolic power $\dot{E}(t)$ is significantly correlated with the muscle activation. It is reasonable to use the square of the muscular instantaneous activation $\dot{e}(t)$ to determine the muscle metabolic power level.

$$\dot{E}(t) \propto \dot{e}^2(t) \tag{2}$$

Therefore, the dynamic and metabolic simulations of this complex coupled system could be performed by Inverse kinematic, Inverse dynamic and CMC tools embedded in the OpenSim software platform [17, 18].

2.3   Application to Human Walking

Considering that walking is the most common form of human movement, we have studied in-depth the impact of BP robots on human biomechanics and metabolism energetics during walking.

We explored three different types of BP robots that were driven by the active path actuators (APA), the quasi-active clutched path spring actuators (QAPA) and the passive path spring (PPS), respectively. The geometry paths for these actuators were defined by a set of points wrapped over lower limb surfaces. The forces produced by these path actuators are expressed by

$$f(\mathrm{t}) = \begin{cases} c(\mathrm{t}) \cdot f_{\max} & APA \\ k \cdot c(\mathrm{t}) \cdot z(\mathrm{t}) \cdot \left(1 + d \cdot \dot{l}(\mathrm{t})\right) & QAPA \\ k \cdot (l(\mathrm{t}) - l_0) \cdot \left(1 + d \cdot \dot{l}(\mathrm{t})\right) & PPS \end{cases} \tag{3}$$

in which $c(t)$ is the control signal to each path actuator, $f_{\max}$ is the maximum force APA could produce, k is the elastic stiffness, d is the spring's dissipation factor, $\dot{l}(t)$ is the lengthening speed of paths, $l(t)$ and l_0 are the instantaneous and the original length of path springs, respectively, $z(t)$ is the stretch of QAPA and follows the dynamics:

$$\dot{z}(t) = \begin{cases} \dot{l}(t) & c(t) > 0 \\ -\frac{1}{\lambda} \cdot z(t) & otherwise \end{cases} \tag{4}$$

where λ is a decay parameter for $z(t)$.

For each type of BP robots, we considered 6 possible path topologies for its path actuators (Fig. 1): I. only spanning the hip joint in each lower limb (SH), II. only spanning the knee joint in each lower limb (SK), III. only spanning the ankle joint in each lower limb (SA), IV. spanning the hip and knee joints in each lower limb (SHK), V. spanning the knee and ankle joints in each lower limb (SKA), VI. spanning the hip, knee and ankle joints in each lower limb (SHKA). Totally, we explored 18 BP robots in this study.

The 18 BP robots mentioned above were coupled to a musculoskeletal model with 10 degrees of freedom and 18 muscles, respectively. The musculoskeletal model without the assistance of BP robots is shown in Fig. 2, which could be found in the model library of the OpenSim platform. After adding these ideal and massless BP robots to musculoskeletal model, CMC tool in OpenSim was performed to find the change of muscle excitations and the optimal control profiles to minimize the sum of squared muscle activations.

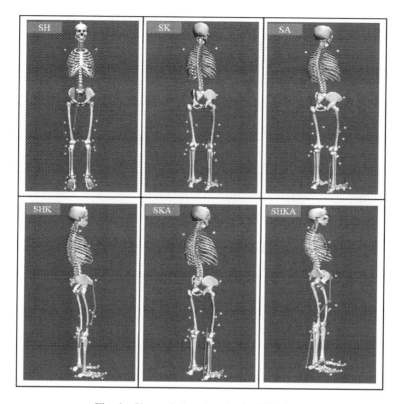

Fig. 1. Six predesigned paths for BP robots

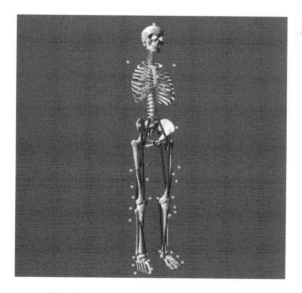

Fig. 2. The human musculoskeletal model

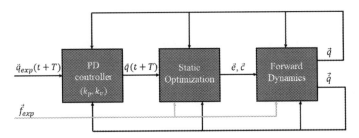

Fig. 3. The CMC workflow

The workflow for CMC algorithm [20] in OpenSim is shown in Fig. 3. Firstly, the generalized accelerations $\ddot{q}(t+T)$ which we desired are computed by the PD controller. Secondly, to achieve desired accelerations, the Static Optimization algorithm is performed to compute the excitation $\vec{e}$ for muscles and the control signal $\vec{c}$ for path actuators. Thirdly, a standard forward dynamic simulation is conduct to compute the generalized coordinate $\vec{q}$ and velocity $\dot{\vec{q}}$ at the next time step. Finally, these three steps are repeated until the end time of CMC simulations.

In the running process of CMC algorithm, the Static Optimization algorithm could weigh and balance the recruitment of path actuators and that of muscles to minimize the following objective function:

$$J(\mathrm{t}) = \sum_{i=1}^{m} e_i^2(\mathrm{t}) + \sum_{j=1}^{p} c_j^2(\mathrm{t}) \tag{5}$$

where m and p are the number of muscles and path actuator, $e_i(t)$ is the instantaneous excitation for the *ith* muscle, $c_j(t)$ is the instantaneous control signal for the *jth* path actuator. The weighing and balancing standard could be determined by different mechanical parameters of muscles and actuators.

Table 1. Settings in CMC simulations

APA			QAPA				PPS	
f_{max} (kN)	c_{min}	c_{max}	k (kN/m)	c_{min}	c_{max}	$d(t)$	k (kN/m)	$d(t)$
10	−1	1	10	−1	1	0.01	10	0.01

The detailed settings in our CMC simulations are given in the Table 1, and the original lengths for PPS along the six paths are 0.35, 0.15, 0.30, 0.7, 0.4 and 1.1 m, respectively.

Additionally, the instantaneous metabolism power $\dot{E}(t)$ and the total metabolic energy consumption E for each muscle during a gait cycle T were also calculated by Eq. (1) and the following equation:

$$E = \int_{0}^{T} \dot{E}(t) \, dt \qquad (6)$$

3   Results and Discussion

As shown in Fig. 4, all BP robots actuated by APA significantly decreased the whole-body metabolic energy consumption during a walking gait cycle (red block). The metabolic energy consumption of human with APA-SKA robot was even reduced by 55% relative to the unassisted condition (green block). Also, five QAPA-actuated (blue block) and two PPS-actuated BP robots (pink block) in our simulations could help people to save their metabolic energy.

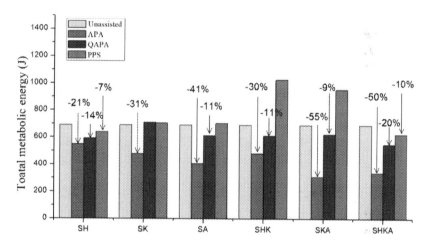

Fig. 4. The whole-body metabolic energy consumption during a gait cycle (Color figure online)

To understand the influence of BP robots on human biomechanics and energetics, we picked three of the most effective BP robots for analysis: the APA-actuated BP robot with SA path (APA-SA), the APA-actuated BP robot with SA path (APA-SKA) and the APA-actuated BP robot with SA path (APA-SHKA).

The optimal control signal computed by CMC for these three robots are shown in Fig. 5. Obviously, all the control signals reach their peak at the late stance stage, in which the peak signal of APA-SKA is more than twice that of the other two. On the one hand, this phenomenon shows that the human needs more external assistance in the late stance stage of a walking gait, on the other hand, it explains the reason why APA-SKA works best.

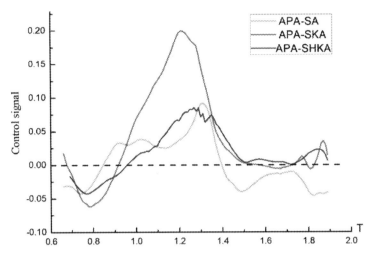

Fig. 5. The control signal of APA-actuated BP robots

The instantaneous metabolic power and muscle excitations of human with APA-SA, APA-SKA and APA-SHKA are also showed in Figs. 6 and 7. Figure 7 depicts the excitation signals for nine primary skeletal muscles that drive the movement of the right lower extremity. They are hamstrings, biceps femoris, gluteus, iliopsoas, rectus femoris, vastus intermedius, gastrocnemius, soleus and tibialis anterior, respectively. From these two figures, we can see that the APA-SA, APA-SKA and APA-SHKA actuated BP robots could reduce the human metabolic energy consumption throughout the whole gait cycle, especially in the stance stage.

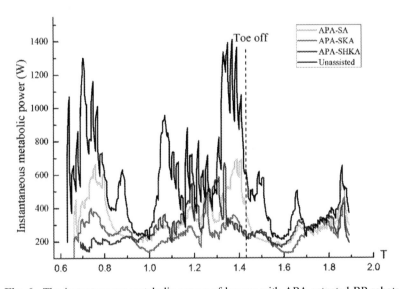

Fig. 6. The instantaneous metabolic power of human with APA-actuated BP robots

Additionally, in order to provide a theoretical reference for quasi-active BP robots designing, we also plot the optimal control signals for five effective QAPA-actuated BP robots in Fig. 8. They are the QAPA-actuated BP robot with SH path (QAPA-SH), the QAPA-actuated BP robot with SHK path (QAPA-SHK), the QAPA-actuated BP robot with SKA path (QAPA-SKA), and the QAPA-actuated BP robot with SHKA path (QAPA-SHKA).

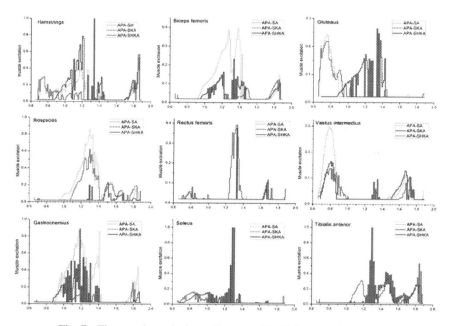

Fig. 7. The muscle excitation of human with APA-actuated BP robots

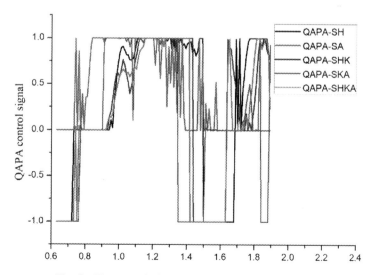

Fig. 8. The control signal of QAPA-actuated BP robots

4   Conclusion

In this paper, we developed a class of BP robots to minimize human metabolic energy consumption during movement, with the inspiration of the biomechanical principle of athlete training. The BP robots could be actuated by various soft path actuators (the active, quasi-active or passive) along arbitrary paths pre-designed on the limb surface. Also, a human-in-the-loop design method was proposed, which considered the coupling biomechanics of human bodies and BP robots. To verify the practicability of this study, 18 specific BP robots were designed to help people reduce their metabolic energy consumption during walking. The CMC simulations were also performed to obtain the biomechanical and energetical effects of these robots to human bodies. The optimal control profiles for each robot were also presented. Results showed that most BP robots designed in this paper could reduce the metabolic cost of human walking, and the largest reduction was 55% relative to the unassisted condition. Considering the optimization of geometric parameters for BP robots may obtain better results, which we will further explore in the future.

References

1. Rodman, P.S., McHenry, H.M.: Bioenergetics and the origin of hominid bipedalism. Am. J. Phys. Anthropol. **52**(1), 103–106 (2016)
2. Uchida, T.K., Seth, A., Pouya, S., et al.: Simulating ideal assistive devices to reduce the metabolic cost of running. PLoS ONE **11**(9), e0163417 (2016)
3. Dembia, C.L., Silder, A., Uchida, T.K., et al.: Simulating ideal assistive devices to reduce the metabolic cost of walking with heavy loads. PLoS ONE **12**(7), e0180320 (2017)
4. Viteckova, S., Kutilek, P., Jirina, M.: Wearable lower limb robotics: a review. Biocybern. Biomed. Eng. **33**(2), 96–105 (2013)
5. Bogue, R.: Exoskeletons and robotic prosthetics: a review of recent developments. Ind. Robot. **36**(5), 421–427 (2009)
6. Jansen, J., Richardson, B., Pin, F., et al.: Exoskeleton for soldier enhancement systems feasibility study. University of North Texas Libraries, Digital Library (2000)
7. Gopura, R.A.R.C., Kiguchi, K., Bandara, D.S.V.: A brief review on upper extremity robotic exoskeleton systems. In: 2011 6th International Conference on Industrial and Information Systems, Kandy, pp. 346–351 (2011)
8. Singer, J.C.: Lamontagne M, The effect of functional knee brace design and hinge misalignment on lower limb joint mechanics. Clin. Biomech. **23**(1), 52–59 (2008)
9. Browning, R.C., Modica, J.R., Kram, R., et al.: The effects of adding mass to the legs on the energetics and biomechanics of walking. Med. Sci. Sports Exerc. **39**(3), 515–525 (2007)
10. Phillips, B., Zhao, H.X.: Predictors of assistive technology abandonment. Assist. Technol. **5**(1), 36–45 (1993)
11. Park, Y.L., Chen, B.R., Pérez-Arancibia, N.O., et al.: Design and control of a bio-inspired soft wearable robotic device for ankle-foot rehabilitation. Bioinspir. Biomim. **9**(1), 016007 (2014)
12. Kang, B.B., Lee, H., In, H., et al.: Development of a polymer-based tendon-driven wearable robotic hand. In: 2016 IEEE International Conference on Robotics and Automation (ICRA), Stockholm, pp. 3750–3755 (2016)

13. Park, Y., Chen, B., Majidi, C., et al.: Active modular elastomer sleeve for soft wearable assistance robots. In: 2012 IEEE/RSJ International Conference on Intelligent Robots and Systems, Vilamoura, pp. 1595–1602 (2012)
14. Quinlivan, B.T., Lee, S., Malcolm, P., et al.: Assistance magnitude vs. metabolic cost reductions for a tethered multiarticular soft exosuit. Sci. Robot. **2**, eaah4416 (2017)
15. Ding, Y., Kim, M., Kuindersma, S.: Human-in-the-loop optimization of hip assistance with a soft exosuit during walking, Sci. Robot. **3**, eaah5438 (2018)
16. Awad, L.N., Bae, J., O'Donnell, K., et al.: A soft robotic exosuit improves walking in patients after stroke. Sci. Transl. Med. **9**, eaai9084 (2017)
17. Seth, A., Hicks, J.L., Uchida, T.K., et al.: OpenSim: simulating musculoskeletal dynamics and neuromuscular control to study human and animal movement. PLoS Comput. Biol. **14** (7), e1006223 (2018)
18. Delp, S.L., Anderson, F.C., Arnold, A.S., et al.: OpenSim: open-source software to create and analyze dynamic simulations of movement. IEEE Trans. Biomed. Eng. **55**, 1940–1950 (2007)
19. Umberger, B.R., Gerritsen, K.G.M., Martin, P.E.: A model of human muscle energy expenditure. Comput. Methods Biomech. Biomed. Eng. **6**(2), 99–111 (2003)
20. Thelen, D.G., Anderson, F.C.: Using computed muscle control to generate forward dynamic simulations of human walking from experimental data. J. Biomech. **39**(6), 1107–1115 (2006)

Adaptive Whole-Arm Grasping Approach of Tumbling Space Debris by Two Coordinated Hyper-redundant Manipulators

Wenya Wan[1], Chong Sun[1(✉)], Jianping Yuan[1], Xianghao Hou[1],
Yufei Guo[1], Yinong Ou-yang[1], Qixin Li[1], Liran Zhao[1], Hao Shi[2],
and Dawei Han[3]

[1] National Key Laboratory of Aerospace Flight Dynamics,
Northwestern Polytechnical University, 127 West Youyi Road, Beilin District,
Xi'an, Shaanxi, China
sunchong@nwpu.edu.cn
[2] North Automatic Control Technology Institute, Sports Road No. 351,
Xiaodian District, Tai Yuan, Shanxi, China
[3] Aerospace System Engineering Shanghai, Shanghai, China

Abstract. Space debris generally has unknown motion information, which brings great challenge for space debris capture and removal. In this paper, we propose an adaptive whole-arm grasping approach of tumbling space debris by two coordinated hyper-redundant manipulators. Firstly, the dynamic model of the tumbling target is derived and its motion characteristics are analyzed. Secondly, a complementary grasping strategy is proposed for tumbling space debris capture, in which two coordinated hyper-redundant manipulators are utilized to wrap around the space debris together. The grasping strategy includes two steps (1) determining the twining curve for each hyper-redundant manipulator and (2) searching algorithm for feasible grasping configuration that could match with the twining curve. Specifically, the second step involves the capture occasion determination and the pre-planning technique. The main advantages of the proposed method lie in its grasping efficiency and adaptivity to grasped objects. Finally, two examples to verify the effectiveness of the proposed method are presented.

Keywords: Space debris capture ·
Coordinated hyper-redundant manipulators · Complementary grasping strategy ·
Twining curve

1 Introduction

The Earth orbit is in a serious predicament caused by millions of space debris. Operational satellite vital for mankind infrastructure are threatened to be destroyed by space debris. Thus, active debris removal is of great relevance [1]. However, most space debris are in the tumbling state and there are not any handles to be grasped on these un-controlled objects, which makes the capture and removal of space tumbling targets more challenging.

© Springer Nature Switzerland AG 2019
H. Yu et al. (Eds.): ICIRA 2019, LNAI 11740, pp. 450–461, 2019.
https://doi.org/10.1007/978-3-030-27526-6_39

Space robotics is considered as one of the most promising approaches for on-orbit servicing missions such as docking, repairing and orbital debris removal [2]. Robotic arm technology has been applied in many on-orbit servicing missions [3–7]. According to the number of arms, it can be divided into single-arm capture [3, 4] and multi-arm capture [6, 7]. Compared with a single-arm space robot, a dual-arm or multi-arm system has much more dexterity and flexibility, and can complete more complex tasks [6]. However, the existing researches mainly focus on utilizing the end-effector located at the tip of arms to grasp the target where grappling points are required. As a result, the variety of grasped objects is limited.

Unlike the capture using fingertips, whole-arm capture can be more adaptive and can provide better grasping efficiency. Vividly, the whole-arm capture is carried out by wrapping the arms and torso around an object, which is in the same manner as an octopus [8]. Early work on robotic whole-arm capture started in 1988 [9], but has not received much interest until recently [10–13]. In terms of the whole-arm capture, the ratio of object size to robot size is larger which is useful in many applications especially those involving hazardous environments such as search and rescue, underwater and space exploration [10, 11]. Devereux's work developed methods that allowed serial chained manipulators to explore, analyze and plan whole arm grasps for a wide variety of objects [12]. Anders used methods from continuous-state reinforcement-learning to solve for whole-arm grasping policies [13].

Borrowing experiences from whole-arm capture, an adaptive whole-arm grasping approach of space tumbling targets by two coordinated hyper-redundant manipulators is presented in this paper, in which the grasping handles are not required and the variety of grasped objects is allowed. We first analyze the motion characteristics of the tumbling space debris. Then, a complementary grasping strategy is proposed mainly including the determination of the twining curve, the optimal capture occasion determination and grasping configuration design based on rapidly-exploring random tree (RRT) algorithm [14]. The main advantages of the proposed method lie in its grasping efficiency and adaptivity to grasped targets.

The remainder of this paper is organized as follows. Section 2 establishes the attitude motion model of the tumbling target, and analyzes its motion characteristics. In Sect. 3, the grasping strategy and grasping configuration design algorithm are presented. An example to verify the effectiveness of the proposed method is shown in Sect. 4. Finally, the conclusive remarks are given in Sect. 5.

2   Analysis of an Un-controlled Spacecraft

There are no requirements for the geometry of grasped objects as our proposed approach encircles around the object's surface to grasp it. Besides, the size of the grasped object is determined by the given specific manipulators' length. Further, the orbital motion between the grasped object and the servicing satellite system usually is synchronous, and the relative distance between the grasped object and the hyper-redundant manipulator is very small, which means that we could only focus on the caging motion of the hyper-redundant manipulator. Therefore, the analysis of an un-controlled spacecraft can focus on its attitude motion.

2.1   Dynamic Modeling of an Un-controlled Spacecraft

Under the action of space perturbation moments, most space debris often exhibit complex tumbling motion, which brings difficulties to the implementation of active debris removal mission. The possible rotation patterns of space debris can be divided into three groups: spin motion around the minimum axis of inertia I_z, spin motion around the maximum axis of inertia I_x, and the tumbling motion with nutation angle. Assume the external toque acted on the target is $\tau = [\tau_x, \tau_y, \tau_z]^T$, its equation of motion satisfies Eq. (1).

$$
\begin{cases}
I_x\dot{\omega}_x - I_{xy}\dot{\omega}_y - I_{xz}\dot{\omega}_z + (I_z - I_y)\omega_y\omega_z - I_{yz}(\omega_y^2 - \omega_z^2) - I_{xz}\omega_x\omega_y + I_{xy}\omega_x\omega_z = \tau_x \\
I_y\dot{\omega}_y - I_{xy}\dot{\omega}_x - I_{yz}\dot{\omega}_z + (I_x - I_z)\omega_x\omega_z - I_{xz}(\omega_z^2 - \omega_x^2) - I_{xy}\omega_y\omega_z + I_{yz}\omega_x\omega_y = \tau_y \\
I_z\dot{\omega}_z - I_{xz}\dot{\omega}_x - I_{yz}\dot{\omega}_y + (I_y - I_x)\omega_x\omega_y - I_{xy}(\omega_x^2 - \omega_y^2) - I_{yz}\omega_x\omega_z + I_{xz}\omega_y\omega_z = \tau_z
\end{cases}
$$

$$(1)$$

here, $I = [I_x, I_{xy}, I_{xz}; I_{xy}, I_y, I_{yz}; I_{xz}, I_{yz}, I_z]$ and $\omega = [\omega_x, \omega_y, \omega_z]^T$ are the inertia and angular velocity of the target in the frame $oxyz$, respectively. The attitude transformation matrix $A(q)$ from the target's fixed frame $oxyz$ to the inertial frame is as follows:

$$
A(q) = \begin{bmatrix}
q_0^2 + q_1^2 - q_2^2 - q_3^2 & 2q_1q_2 - 2q_0q_3 & 2q_1q_3 + 2q_0q_2 \\
2q_1q_2 + 2q_0q_3 & q_0^2 - q_1^2 + q_2^2 - q_3^2 & 2q_2q_3 - 2q_0q_1 \\
2q_1q_3 - 2q_0q_2 & 2q_2q_3 + 2q_0q_1 & q_0^2 - q_1^2 - q_2^2 + q_3^2
\end{bmatrix}
\tag{2}
$$

where, $q = [q_0, \hat{q}]^T = [q_0, q_1, q_2, q_3]^T$ is the unit quaternion representing the target's attitude, whose derivative are the functions of q and ω:

$$
\begin{bmatrix} \dot{q}_0 \\ \dot{q}_1 \\ \dot{q}_2 \\ \dot{q}_3 \end{bmatrix} = \frac{1}{2}
\begin{bmatrix} -q_1 & -q_2 & -q_3 \\ q_0 & -q_3 & q_2 \\ q_3 & q_0 & -q_1 \\ -q_2 & q_1 & q_0 \end{bmatrix}
\begin{bmatrix} \omega_x \\ \omega_y \\ \omega_z \end{bmatrix} = \frac{1}{2}S(q)\omega
\tag{3}
$$

For an arbitrary point on the target, its position vector in body-fixed frame and inertial frame are respectively denoted by r_a^I and r_a^I satisfying following relationship:

$$
r_a^I = A(q)r_a^I
\tag{4}
$$

2.2   Analysis of an Un-controlled Spacecraft

In real cases, the space target could be affected by external perturbations. However, since external forces/torques acting upon a free-floating object in space are usually small, it is reasonable here to assume that the target in space is free from any external forces and torques. Assume the grasped target is a cube with side length 0.7 m and it rotates along the principal axes of inertia, the initial attitude quaternion is $q_0 = [1, 0, 0, 0]^T$, the mass of the target is $m_t = 929.53$ kg, the inertia matrix is $I = diag(75.912,$

75.912, 75.912) (kg m^2), and the initial angular velocity of the tumbling target is $\omega_0 = [2, 1, 1]^T$ (°/s). According to the theoretical calculation, the 3D trajectory of an arbitrary point or close curve of the grasped target during 500 s is shown in Fig. 1.

According to the results, the trajectory of an arbitrary point on the surface of space debris targets is a circle, but the trajectory of a closed curve is more complex. Therefore, the tumbling space targets capture by traditional point capture is difficult.

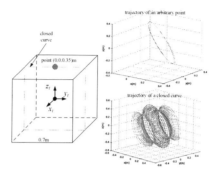

Fig. 1. The 3D trajectory of an arbitrary point and close curve of the grasped target.

3 Grasping Approach by Two Coordinated Hyper-redundant Manipulators

3.1 Grasping Strategy

In this paper, a complementary grasping strategy is proposed for the capture of space tumbling targets, in which the two coordinated hyper-redundant manipulators use their own whole arm to wrap around the grasped target together. The flow chart of the whole-arm grasping strategy is shown in Fig. 2.

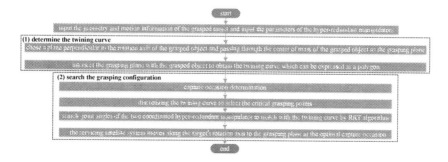

Fig. 2. The flow chart of the whole-arm grasping strategy.

The grasping strategy includes two main steps: the first step is to determine the twining curve, and the second is to search a feasible grasping configuration that could match with the twining curve by two coordinated hyper-redundant manipulators. In terms of the first step, there are two concrete sub-steps: (1) randomly chose a plane perpendicular to the rotation axis of the grasped object and passing through the center of mass of the grasped object as the grasping plane; (2) intersect the grasping plane with the grasped object to obtain the twining curve which can be expressed as a polygon. The black and red dotted lines in Fig. 3 represent the grasping plane and twining curve, respectively. In practice, the grasping plane usually is chosen as the plane determined by the two hyper-redundant manipulator to reduce the maneuver of the servicing satellite. As for the second step, RRT algorithm is adopted too search joint angles of the two coordinated hyper-redundant manipulator that can match with the twining curve. We will discuss how to plan a path for the two coordinated hyper-redundant manipulators that can realize the grasping configuration in detail in the following sections.

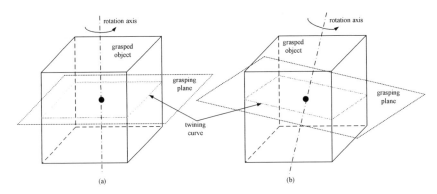

Fig. 3. Illustration of the determination of the twining curve where (a) and (b) are the cases where the grasped object rotates around the principal inertia axis and an arbitrary axis, respectively. (Color figure online)

3.2 Grasping Configuration Design

In this subsection, the kinematic motion equations of a dual-arm space robot is derived first; then the grasping configuration searching algorithm is designed.

The Kinematic Motion Equations of a Dual-Arm Space Robot

A two coordinated hyper-redundant manipulators is used to capture a tumbling target. The space robotic system is composed of a robot base, a n_1-link serial manipulator (called arm-1) and a n_2-link serial manipulator (called arm-2). Further, the universal joint structure with two orthogonal degree of freedoms (DOFs) is adopted in this paper. The model is shown in Fig. 4.

For convenience of discussion, some symbols are defined in Table 1. The coordinate transformation matrix between two adjacent coordinate frame $O_j\, x_j\, y_j\, z_j$ and $O_{j-1}\, x_{j-1}\, y_{j-1}\, z_{j-1}$ of arm-i ($i = 1, 2$) can be expressed in Eq. (5). Here, Trans(x, y, z)

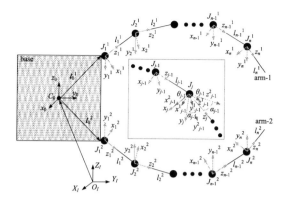

Fig. 4. A general model of the two coordinated hyper-redundant space robot system.

Table 1. Some important symbols used in this paper.

Symbol	Representation
C_0	The mass center of the base
l_0^i	The vector from C_0 to the first joint J_1 of arm-i, $i = 1, 2$
J_j^i	The jth joint of arm-i, $i = 1, 2$, $j = 1, 2, \dots, n_i$
l_j^i	The length of the jth link of arm-i, $i = 1, 2$, $j = 1, 2, \dots, n_i$
θ_j^i	The rotation angle about y_j axis of the jth joint of arm-i, $i = 1, 2$, $j = 1, 2, \dots,$ n_i
α_j^i	The rotation angle about x_j axis of the jth joint of arm-i, $i = 1, 2$, $j = 1, 2, \dots,$ n_i
$O_I X_I Y_I Z_I$	The inertial coordinate system
$C_0 x_0 y_0 z_0$	The fixed coordinate system of the base
$O_j^i x_j^i y_j^i z_j^i$	The fixed coordinate system of the jth joint and link of arm-i, $i = 1, 2$, $j = 1, 2,$ $\dots, n_i$
$^i T_j$	The coordinate transformation matrix from $O_j x_j y_j z_j$ to $O_i x_i y_i z_i$

is the translational transfer matrix; Rot(y, θ) is the rotational transfer matrix around the y axis; and Rot(x, α) is the rotational transfer matrix around the x axis. Further, the pose (position and attitude) of the jth link arm-i $^i T_j^i$ can be obtained according to Eq. (6).

$$
\begin{aligned}
^{j-1}T_j &= \text{Trans}(0, 0, l_{j-1}) \cdot \text{Rot}(y_{j-1}^1, \theta_{j-1}) \cdot \text{Rot}(x_{j-1}^2, \alpha_{j-1}) \\
&= \begin{bmatrix}
\cos\theta_{j-1} & \sin\theta_{j-1}\sin\alpha_{j-1} & \sin\theta_{j-1}\cos\alpha_{j-1} & 0 \\
0 & \cos\alpha_{j-1} & -\sin\alpha_{j-1} & 0 \\
-\sin\theta_{j-1} & \cos\theta_{j-1}\sin\alpha_{j-1} & \cos\theta_{j-1}\cos\alpha_{j-1} & l_{j-1} \\
0 & 0 & 0 & 1
\end{bmatrix}
\end{aligned}
\tag{5}
$$

$$^I T_j = {}^I T_0 {}^0 T_1 {}^1 T_2 \cdots {}^{j-1} T_{j-2} {}^{j-1} T_j \tag{6}$$

Grasping Configuration Searching Algorithm Based on RRT Algorithm

The two coordinated hyper-redundant manipulators work together to realize the match of the twining curve as shown in Fig. 5. In the beginning, the links are straightened out ready to be twining around the target. Then, the manipulators sweep around the entire target by adjusting the joint orderly from the most proximal joint to the most distal joint.

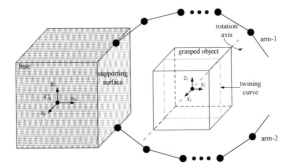

Fig. 5. Task description of grasping a tumbling space target by the two coordinated hyper-redundant manipulators.

Assume the hyper-redundant manipulators have been located in a plane parallel to the grasping plane before starting the grasping operation which can be obtained easily by adjusting the torsion angle of the first universal joint. Besides, the hyper-redundant manipulators could arrive at the grasping plane rapidly when the optimal capture occasion occurs. Then, the problem can be simplified to the planar grasping problem. Given that the twining curve is movable along with the grasped target, to grasp the target firmly, the capture occasion determination and the pre-planning technique are included in our proposed grasping configuration searching algorithm.

Capture Occasion Determination
Considering the capture of a tumbling target should be safe and reliable, the occasion where the attitude synchronization of the serving satellite and the grasped target is achieved, is chosen as the alternative occasion. In other words, the relative attitude of the twining curve to the servicing satellite is **0** when the capture is implemented, just as the configuration shown in Fig. 5. Further, taking account of the rapidity of the capture, the first or the second synchronous occasion is usually chosen as the optimal capture occasion according to the initial relative attitude as shown in Fig. 6. Therefore, we can plan the joint angles according to the state of the twining curve at the optimal capture occasion in advance.

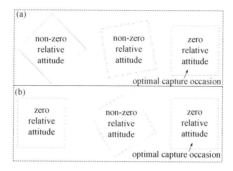

Fig. 6. Illustration of the capture occasion determination: (a) and (b) are cases where the first and the second synchronous occasion are selected as the optimal capture occasion, respectively.

Pre-planning Technique Based on RRT Algorithm

In the beginning, the critical grasping points are selected by discretizing the twining curve. As shown in Fig. 7, the critical grasping points are usually chosen as the vertexes of the twining curve to guarantee a firm capture; besides, an additional critical grasping point is selected on the wrapping demarcation edge of the twinning curve as the wrapping demarcation point of two hyper-redundant manipulators. It must be pointed out the whole-arm capture will take advantage of the surface of the base of the satellite system that is directly facing the grasped target (for example, the surface marked reseda in Fig. 5), and this surface works as a supporting surface during the grasping process. Then, the critical grasping points are divided into two groups for the two hyper-redundant manipulators bounded by the wrapping demarcation point. Now, the problem is how to realize the match of the corresponding critical grasping points for the two hyper-redundant manipulators independently while simultaneously.

Specifically, the proposed method attempts to find valid connections between two adjacent critical grasping points by RRT algorithm as shown in Table 2. The inputs of the algorithm are the joint number that coincides with the first critical grasping point j_s^i, the total number of critical grasping points for arm-i k^i, the link number of arm-i n^i, the initial configuration of arm-i q_{ini}^i, the link length l_j^i, the joint angle range $\theta_j^i \in \left[\theta_{jl}^i, \theta_{ju}^i\right]$ and $\alpha_j^i \in \left[\alpha_{jl}^i, \alpha_{ju}^i\right]$. The output of the algorithm is the joint angles q of the valid grasping configuration. A connection is valid if the manipulator can move between the two adjacent critical grasping points with a positive integral number of links and without breaking the joint angle limitation. A connection between two adjacent critical grasping points attempts to increase the number of links until the number is greater than a user specified maximum or a connection is successful. This process continues until either the algorithm has planned a path around the entire circumference of the twining curve.

The grasping configuration is calculated in advance, and the hyper-redundant manipulator has adjusted its configuration from the initial configuration to the grasping configuration before the optimal capture configuration occurs. Then, the hyper-redundant manipulators move along the target's rotation axis to the grasping plane when the optimal capture configuration occurs. Finally, the tumbling space target can be grasped firmly.

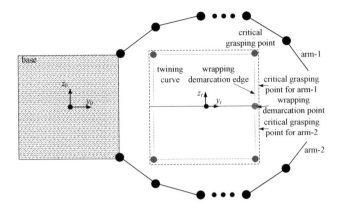

Fig. 7. Illustration of the pre-planning technique.

Table 2. Procure of grasping configuration searching algorithm based on RRT algorithm.

Step	Content
1	Input j_s^i, k^i, n^i, q_{ini}^i, l_j^i, $\theta_j^i \in [\theta_{jl}^i, \theta_{ju}^i]$, $\alpha_j^i \in [\alpha_{jl}^i, \alpha_{ju}^i]$ where $i=1,2$, set the rand seeds number N
2	For $i'=1:k^i-1$
3	$j=j_s^i$
4	While $j<=n^i$
5	For $N^i<=N$
6	Set an initial value of the j_s^i th~jth joints$\leftarrow q_{ini}$
7	Generate a random configuration q_{rand}
8	Find the nearest configuration q_{near} in the current configuration path branches
9	Generate a candidate of new configuration q_{cand} located between q_{rand} and q_{near}
10	Examine whether the hyper-redundant manipulators collide with the object; when no collision is detected, q_{cand} becomes a new configuration q_{new} and be added to the configuration path branches
11	Check if the jth joint with joint values q_{new} could match with the i' th critical grasping points; if a valid match is found: $q(j_s^i:j)= q_{new}, j_s^i=j$, go to line 2
12	End
13	If a valid match is found: $q(j_s^i:j)= q_{new}, j_s^i=j$, go to line 2
14	End
15	End
16	Output the joint angles q of the valid grasping configuration

4 Simulations

The structure configuration of the simulation example is shown in Fig. 5, which consists of two 11-universal-joint manipulators mounted on a free-floating servicing satellite and a tumbling space target. Further, assume the base of the servicing satellite system is a cube with side length 1 m, each link of the hyper-redundant manipulator is same with length $l = 0.2$ m, and the joint angles range is also same satisfying $\theta \in [-180°, 180°]$ and $\alpha \in [-180°, 180°]$. The grasped targets are two cubes with angular velocity is $\omega = [2°, 0°, 0°]$. Then, the simplified model is shown in Fig. 7. Further, assume the initial time $t_0 = 0$ s. In addition, all the initial joints angles of the two hyper-redundant manipulator are $\alpha^i_{j0} = 0°$ and $\theta^i_{j0} = 0°$ ($j = 1, 2, \ldots , 11$ and $i = 1, 2$).

Case 1: the cube with side length $a = 0.7$ m
In this case, the size of the grasped target is smaller than the base of the servicing satellite system. Assume the initial relative attitude between the grasped target and the servicing satellite is $A = Rot(x, -30°)$. Thus, the first synchronous occasion is chosen as the optimal capture occasion just as the case shown in Fig. 6(a). The capture time $t_f = 165$ s, which means that there are 165 s for the servicing satellite system to calculate the grasping configuration. The process of one possible grasping configuration design is shown in Fig. 8. The joint angles $\alpha^i_{j0} = 0°$ ($j = 1, 2, \ldots , 11$ and $i = 1, 2$) which coincides with the planar grasping case. As for the joint angles rotating around the y axis are shown in Table 3. Then, the servicing satellite system moves along the target's rotation axis to the grasping plane at the optimal capture occasion as shown in Fig. 9.

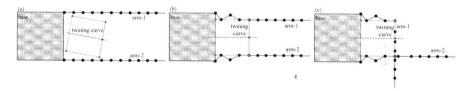

Fig. 8. The process of one possible grasping configuration design for Case 1where (a), (b) and (c) are the initial configuration, the middle configuration and final grasping configuration, respectively.

Case 2: the cube with side length $a = 1.2$ m
In this case, the size of the grasped target is larger than the base of the servicing satellite system. Assume the initial relative attitude between the grasped target and the servicing satellite is $\mathbf{0}$. Thus, the second synchronous occasion is chosen as the optimal capture occasion just as the case shown in Fig. 6(b). The capture time $t_f = 180$ s. The process of one possible grasping configuration design is shown in Fig. 10. The joint angles $\alpha^i_j = 0°$ ($j = 1, 2, \ldots , 11$ and $i = 1, 2$) and the joint angles rotating around the y axis are shown in Table 4. Then, the servicing satellite system also moves along the target's rotation axis to the grasping plane, which is similar to the process shown in Fig. 9.

Table 3. Joint angles rotating around the y axis for Case 1.

Arm	$\theta_1(°)$	$\theta_2(°)$	$\theta_3(°)$	$\theta_4(°)$	$\theta_5(°)$	$\theta_6(°)$	$\theta_7(°)$	$\theta_8(°)$	$\theta_9(°)$	$\theta_{10}(°)$	$\theta_{11}(°)$
1	48.59	−71.77	46.36	−23.18	90	0	0	0	0	0	0
2	48.59	−71.77	46.36	−23.18	0	0	0	0	0	0	0

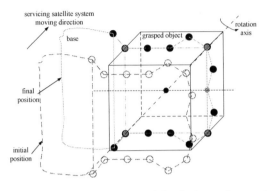

Fig. 9. Illustration of the achievement of the final grasping configuration.

In addition, It must be pointed out that our proposed method is also applicable for 3-dimensional capture because the universal joint has two orthogonal DOFs.

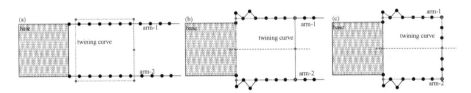

Fig. 10. The process of one possible grasping configuration design for Case 2 where (a), (b) and (c) are the initial configuration, the middle configuration and final grasping configuration, respectively.

Table 4. Joint angles rotating around the y axis for Case 2.

Arm	$\theta_1(°)$	$\theta_2(°)$	$\theta_3(°)$	$\theta_4(°)$	$\theta_5(°)$	$\theta_6(°)$	$\theta_7(°)$	$\theta_8(°)$	$\theta_9(°)$	$\theta_{10}(°)$	$\theta_{11}(°)$
1	−90	120	−85.46	110.92	−55.46	0	0	0	90	0	0
2	−90	120	−85.46	110.92	−55.46	0	0	0	90	0	0

5   Conclusions

In this paper, an adaptive whole-arm grasping approach of tumbling space debris by two coordinated hyper-redundant manipulators is proposed. Firstly, we has analyzed a space un-controlled target' motion characteristics based on its dynamic modeling.

Then, a complementary grasping strategy is proposed for the capture of space tumbling targets. Using proposed approach, it can determine the twining curve and search a feasible grasping configuration that could match with the twining curve using rapidly-exploring random tree. To verify the effectiveness of the proposed method, examples of failed Cube-Sat capture are presented to verify the proposed method, and the simulation results have shown that the grasped targets can be grasped firmly. In future, the grasping path planning and control will be studied.

Acknowledgment. This Research was supported by National Natural Science Foundation of China (No. 11802238).

References

1. Shan, M., Guo, J., Gill, E.: Review and comparison of active space debris capturing and removal methods. Prog. Aerosp. Sci. **80**, 18–32 (2016)
2. Flores-Abad, A., Ma, O., Pham, K., et al.: A review of space robotics technologies for on-orbit servicing. Prog. Aerosp. Sci. **68**, 1–26 (2014)
3. Reintsema, D., Thaeter, J., Rathke, A., et al.: DEOS—the German robotics approach to secure and de-orbit malfunctioned satellites from low earth orbits. In: Proceedings of the i-SAIRAS, Sapporo, Japan (2010)
4. Debus, T.J., Dougherty, S.P.: Overview and performance of the front-end robotics enabling near-term demonstration (FREND) robotic arm. In: AIAA Aerospace Conference, Reston, VA, USA (2009)
5. Chong, S., Jianping, Y., Wenya, W., Yao, C.: Outside envelop grasping method and approaching trajectory optimization for tumbling malfunctional satellite capture. Acta Aeronauticaet Astronautica Sinica **39**(11), 322192–322203 (2018)
6. Peng, J., Xu, W.W., Pan, E.Z., et al.: Dual-arm coordinated capturing of an unknown tumbling target based on efficient parameters estimation. Acta Astronautica (2019)
7. Ellery, A.: A robotics perspective on human space flight. Earth Moon Planets **87**(3), 173–190 (1999)
8. Walker, I.D., Dawson, D.M., Flash, T., et al.: Continuum robot arms inspired by cephalopods. In: Proceedings of SPIE-The International Society for Optical Engineering, vol. 5804, pp. 303–314 (2005)
9. Salisbury, K.: Whole arm manipulation. In: International Symposium on Robotics Research. MIT Press (1988)
10. Braganza, D., Mcintyre, M.L., Dawson, D.M., et al.: Whole arm grasping control for redundant robot manipulators. In: American Control Conference. IEEE (2006)
11. Oki, T., Nakanishi, H., Yoshida, K.: Whole-body motion control for capturing a tumbling target by a free-floating space robot. In: Proceedings of the 2007 IEEE/RSJ International Conference on Intelligent Robots and Systems. IEEE, San Diego (2007)
12. Devereux, D.: Control strategies for whole arm grasping. The University of Manchester (2010)
13. Anders, A.: Learning a strategy for whole-arm grasping. Massachusetts Institution of Technology (2014)
14. LaValle, S.M.: Rapidly-exploring random trees: a new tool for path planning. TR98–11, Department of Computer Science, Iowa State University (1998)

Development of Bolt Screwing Tool Based on Pneumatic Slip Ring

Qi Zhang, Zongwu Xie$^{(\boxtimes)}$, Yechao Liu$^{(\boxtimes)}$, and Hong Liu

State Key Laboratory of Robotics and System, Harbin Institute of Technology,
Harbin 150001, China
{xiezongwu,yechaohit}@hit.edu.cn

Abstract. End-effector tools with low weight, multiple degrees of freedom have significant application significance. At present, motor-driven robot operating tools generally have more complicated transmission systems as well as actuators, and the weight is also heavy. In this paper, a bolt-screwing tool based on a pneumatic slip ring structure is designed, which can realize two-DOF motion of clamping-releasing and rotating. The tool consists of a pneumatic slip ring with sealed structure and a cylinder driven gripper. This article also introduces the control strategy required to screw the bolt, and describes the configuration of the experiment. Finally, the bolt is screwed into the thread hole in the experiment to verify the reliability of the screw assembly tool and the effectiveness of the corresponding control scheme.

Keywords: Bolt screwing · Pneumatic slip ring · Sealing structure

1 Introduction

Robot end-effector can custom different function according to various demands, such as cutting tools, multi-function operating tools, jam nut removal tools, fuel adding tools, socket wrench tools [1,2], etc.

The robot end-gripper is a device with which the robot directly contacts the work pieces and performs tasks. In industrial applications, end-grippers usually are provided with two or three finger. However, these tools could hardly generate rotation motion at the same time. Bolt screwing is a widespread assembly task, and this work requires that the tool can not only clamp the bolt, but also can supply the rotation motion to screw the bolt. Thus, there is the need to develop an end-effector to generate these two motion simultaneously.

According to the driving form, the end-effector can be divided into pneumatic drive, motor drive and mechanical passive tool. Lopes et al. [3] present an end-effector that contact with uncertain environments of unknown stiffness. Liu et al. [4] design a tool holder that may provide various degrees of compliance and use it to attach an electric hand grinder to the spindle of a machine center.

As for the pneumatic tool, Ryuh et al. [5] adopt the cylinder to ensure the stable contact force of the polishing tool, and that the rotation motion of spindle

© Springer Nature Switzerland AG 2019
H. Yu et al. (Eds.): ICIRA 2019, LNAI 11740, pp. 462–469, 2019.
https://doi.org/10.1007/978-3-030-27526-6_40

drives the rotation motion of the polishing tool simplifies design complexity. Liao et al. [6] propose a tool-head with a pneumatic spindle that can be extended and retracted by three pneumatic actuators to provide tool compliance, and this tool-head can be used for polishing and deburring by integrating a pressure sensor and a linear encoder. Ahn et al. [7] propose a pneumatic polishing head that improves the surface quality of sculptured die surfaces.

In this paper, a pneumatic robot end-effector is proposed, which possesses the function of clamping-loosening as well as screwing the bolt. Firstly, the pneumatic structure is introduced. While this structure could generate the rotatory motion for screwing the bolt, it also transmits two passages of airflow to drive the cylinder used for clamping or loosening the bolt. Besides, the sealing structure is key to avoid gas leak and supply stable pressure for controlling the cylinder gripper. At last, bolt screwing assembly experiment from the bolt entering the thread hole to the bolt tightened reveals the validity of the developed bolt screwing assembly tool.

2 Design Scheme

2.1 Technical Specification Requirement

The bolt screwing tool is mounted at the end of the manipulator, with a 6-axis force sensor between them. As the force sensor is utilized to collect the force signals during the process of screwing bolt, light weight of the assembly tool will be beneficial to the screwing assembly work. The designed bolt screwing tool is applied for fine manipulation task in flexible robot as an end-effector. Three functions are needed for the bolt screwing tool: the tool can clamp or loosen the bolt as needed; the tool can screw the bolt into the thread hole with the bolt clamped; the tool can operate different types of hexagon socket head cap bolt. Technical specification requirements are illustrated in Table 1.

Table 1. Technical specification requirements

Design specifications	Tool weight	Output torque	Bolt scope
	<0.5 kg	>20 N·m	M4–M8

2.2 Design Scheme Selection

According to the functional requirements, the bolt screwing assembly tool requires two degrees of freedom, one for screwing the bolt, the other one for gripping or loosening the bolt. Since screwing the bolt requires certain torque and controllable whirling velocity, the rotation motion is achieved by the structure of the motor and reducer. On the other hand, if the tightening and the loosening motion is conducted by gear motor, then the motor and transmission mechanism will occupy plenty of space and increase the weight substantially, which is inconsistent with design original intention. Thus, the pneumatic transmission structure is applied to drive the cylinder to tighten and loosen the bolt.

During the process of the screwing assembly task, the tool needs to rotate 20–30 rounds to tighten the bolt. If the air pipe is connected to the cylinder directly, then it will twine round the cylinder. Therefore, we need to design a structure that can transmit the high pressure gas to the cylinder with the tool rotated.

It is rotating connector device that can afford to transmit fluid medium ensuring pressure supply of subsequent equipment when the device is rotating continuously. The slip ring structure can form a stable and reliable rotating connector system by ingenious structure and sealing structure design, precise parts manufacturing and matching, and suitable material selection. As long as the slip ring is attached to the rotating device, then the fluid medium can be supplied to gripper continuously, which helps to perform other motion.

As stable output torque is required for bolt assembly tool to screw the bolt, we use light-weight and small-volume modular joint which is same with the manipulator joints to output the rotating motion. This will simplify the electric connection between the tool and the robot controller, so the same control system can regulate both manipulator joints and end-effector.

Since the transporting medium is pressure gas, sealing should be considered seriously when designing the slip ring structure. Besides, the cylinder is utilized to clamp and loosen the bolt, so two separate air passages are required in the slip ring structure.

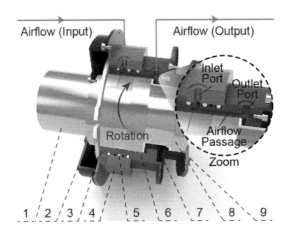

Fig. 1. Working principle of the pneumatic slip ring. ① fixed part of the rotating joint ② connection flange ③ retaining ring ④ fixed part of slip ring ⑤ sealing ring ⑥ rotating part of the slip ring ⑦ connecting flange ⑧ output part of the rotating joint ⑨ connecting flange

3   Structure Design of Bolt Assembly Tool

3.1   Working Principle of the Pneumatic Slip Ring

According to mission requirements and the design scheme, a novel pneumatic slip ring structure is developed to supply rotatory motion, torque and transmit high pressure gaseous media. The working principle diagram is shown in Fig. 1.

The high pressure airflow enters from the input port of the fixed slip ring. After passing through the airflow channel of the rotating slip ring, the high pressure airflow is exported from the output port of the rotatory slip ring. The rotatory slip ring rotates with the rotating joints, and a groove in rotatory slip ring is processed at position corresponding to the input airflow passage of the fixed slip ring. Then, the tunnel is processed in rotatory slip ring to connect the air path and transport the high pressure gas.

3.2   Sealing Principle of the Pneumatic Slip Ring

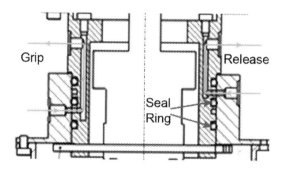

Fig. 2. Airflow and seal ring arrangement of the pneumatic slip ring

As shown in Fig. 2, two distinct direction motion, clamping and loosening, is achieved by cylinder with high pressure airflow. Two air passages are required to perform this two motion separately, and the two movements are switched by a manual valve. Therefore, it is necessary to process two channels on surface of the rotatory slip ring, which could not connect with each other and leak gas. To solve this problem, three channels are also processed to mount the sealing ring, then, the airflow is strictly constrained within different space.

3.3   Physical Display of Bolt Assembly Tool

Figure 3 shows physical diagram of the bolt screwing tool and the manipulator. The end-effector includes fixed slip ring, rotatory slip ring, cylinder gripper and JR3 6-axis force sensor.

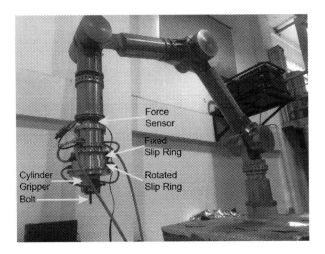

Fig. 3. Physical display of bolt assembly tool ring (Color figure online)

The fixed slip ring is connected to the airflow input by the red air pipe, and then the airflow output from the port of rotatory slip ring to drive the cylinder gripper through the blue air pipe. This pneumatic slip ring structure avoids the problem that the cylinder gripper is twined round by air pipe, and the cylinder gripper can clamp the bolt firmly with screwing torque exerted stably.

4 Experiment

In this paper, a bolt screwing experiment is conducted to verify the validity of the proposed tool. This article only discusses the function of the bolt assembly tool, regardless of the problem of aligning the bolt and the thread hole, so the initial condition of this experiment is that the bolt has entered the thread hole, and its axis has also aligned the axis of the thread hole.

4.1 Control Scheme

During the process that the bolt clamped by end-effector of the manipulator contact with the environment, on one hand, excessive contact force would damage the end-effector and the joints of the manipulator, and oversized contact force would produce large friction force during searching process, which is unbeneficial to searching motion. On the other hand, certain contact force between the bolt and the environment helps judge the contact state of them. Hence, hybrid position control scheme could meet this demand well.

Similarly, after the bolt entering the thread hole, excessive contact force between the bolt and the thread hole will result in the damage of the end-effector and the manipulator joints, while proper contact force will make for the screwing process.

A control scheme diagram (see Fig. 4) is illustrated, which include trajectory generator, force controller, position controller, and form a closed loop through the force feedback.

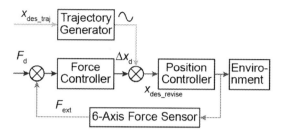

Fig. 4. Hybrid force/position control scheme

In this paper, the force controller adopts proportional control strategy (see Eq. 1):

$$\Delta X_d = K_f \cdot (F_d - F_{ext}) \tag{1}$$

Thus, the corrected robot position control vector is:

$$X_{des\_revise} = X_{des\_traj} + \Delta X_d \tag{2}$$

In the screwing process, position control strategy is required in the direction of rotation around the Z-axis, and the force control scheme is utilized in the remaining directions. The desired force can be set as:

$$\begin{aligned} F_{d\_Fx} = 0, F_{d\_Fy} = 0, F_{d\_Fz} = 5N, \\ F_{d\_Mx} = 0, F_{d\_My} = 0 \end{aligned} \tag{3}$$

4.2   Bolt Screwing Experiment

A bolt screwing assembly experiment is conducted using the control scheme in Sect. 3.1, and trajectory of manipulator end-effector and force/torque signals of the 6-axis force sensor are recorded from the bolt entering the thread hole to the bolt tightened.

Figure 5 illustrates the position of the robot end-effector during the screwing bolt process. 3-dimensional force during this period is shown in Fig. 6a, while the 3-dimensional torque is displayed in Fig. 6b at the same time.

After the bolt entering the thread hole (from 0 to A moment), there exists certain contact force along the horizontal direction. This results from bias between the bolt and the thread hole, and can be adjusted according to the force control strategy in Sect. 3.1. Moreover, the proposed method can regulate the force and torque during the screwing process by adjusting the position and attitude of the manipulator. In Fig. 6b, torques, Mx and My, are regulated to around 0 from the moment A to the moment B, and meanwhile, force signals, Fx and

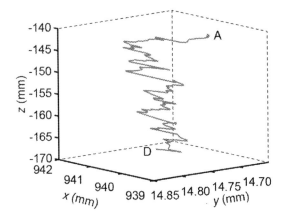

Fig. 5. End-effector position trajectory during the bolt screwing process

Fy, are regulated within 5N (see Fig. 6a). It can be seen from the Fig. 5 that manipulator end-effector move from point A to point D. As the feed depth of the manipulator end-effector coincide with the bolt length, this illustrates that the bolt screwing assembly tool accomplish the task successfully. Also, effective control result is revealed by adjusting the pose of the manipulator end-effector (see Fig. 6a and b). It could be found from the Fig. 6b that torque along the Z-axis increases suddenly at C moment when the cylinder gripper and the bolt emerge relative slide at the moment. Since the torque generated from the tool could not rotate the bolt any more, it could be inferred that the bolt has been tightened. However, this variation is not reflected explicitly in Fig. 6a, so this sudden change in torque helps to judge whether the bolt has been tightened.

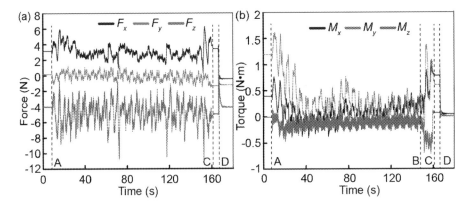

Fig. 6. (a) 3-dimensional force during the bolt screwing process, (b) 3-dimensional torque during the bolt screwing process

5   Conclusions

A bolt screwing assembly tool based on pneumatic slip ring for robotic bolt assembly is developed in this paper. The designed mechanical structure could perform two degrees of freedom motion, clamping-loosening and rotating, which satisfy the motion demands of tool. Besides, this paper also introduce the control scheme for bolt screwing and force sensor configuration. Also, condition for judging the bolt being tightened is also obtained from the experiment data. Finally, a bolt screwing assembly experiment, from the bolt entering the thread hole to the bolt being tightened, reveals the reliability of the bolt screwing assembly tool and the effectiveness of the proposed control scheme.

Acknowledgement. This work was supported by the National Natural Science Foundation of China under grant 91848202, and the project was supported by the Foundation for Innovative Research Groups of the National Natural Science Foundation of China (Grant No. 51521003).

References

1. Roberts, B.: Using the international space station as a precursor to in-orbit robotic servicing. In: AIAA Space Conference and Exposition (2010). https://doi.org/10.2514/6.2010-8898
2. Spinler, A.B.: ISS operations for the special purpose dexterous manipulator (SPDM) experiences from the robotic systems evaluation laboratory (RSEL). In: AIAA Annual Technical Symposium (1999)
3. Lopes, A., Almeida, F.: A force-impedance controlled industrial robot using an active robotic auxiliary device. Robot. Comput. Integr. Manuf. **24**(3), 299–309 (2008). https://doi.org/10.1016/j.rcim.2007.04.002
4. Liu, C.H., Chen, C.C.A., Huang, J.S.: The polishing of molds and dies using a compliance tool holder mechanism. J. Mater. Process. Technol. **166**(2), 230–236 (2005). https://doi.org/10.1016/j.jmatprotec.2004.08.021
5. Ryuh, B.S., Park, S.M., Pennock, G.R.: An automatic tool changer and integrated software for a robotic die polishing station. Mech. Mach. Theory **41**(4), 415–432 (1999). https://doi.org/10.1016/j.mechmachtheory.2005.06.004
6. Liao, L., Xi, F., Liu, K.: Modeling and control of automated polishing/ deburring process using a dual-purpose compliant toolhead. Int. J. Mach. Tools Manuf. **48**(12–13), 1454–1463 (2008). https://doi.org/10.1016/j.ijmachtools.2008.04.009
7. Ahn, J.H., Lee, M.C., Jeong, H.D.: Intelligently automated polishing for high quality surface formation of sculptured die. J. Mater. Process. Technol. **130**(02), 339–344 (2002). https://doi.org/10.1016/S0924-0136(02)00821-X

Deep Grasping Prediction with Antipodal Loss for Dual Arm Manipulators

Yunlong Dong[1], Xiangdi Liu[1], Bidan Huang[2], Chunlin Ji[3], Jianfeng Xu[4], Han Ding[4], and Ye Yuan[1(✉)]

[1] School of Artificial Intelligence and Automation and State Key Laboratory
of Digital Manufacturing Equipment and Technology,
Huazhong University of Science and Technology, Wuhan 430074, China
yye@hust.edu.cn
[2] Tencent Robotics X, Shenzhen 518000, China
[3] Kuang-Chi Institute of Advanced Technology, Shenzhen 518000, China
[4] School of Mechanical Science and Engineering and State Key Laboratory
of Digital Manufacturing Equipment and Technology,
Huazhong University of Science and Technology, Wuhan 430074, China

Abstract. The cooperative manipulators can execute a wide range of
tasks, such as carrying large or heavy payloads, which are difficult for
a single manipulator. Dual arm manipulators are in typically opera-
tive configuration to mimic human, which are of highly flexibility and
dexterity. In this paper, we propose a novel coarse-to-fine deep learning model along with investigating the grasp prior loss based on the
well-known antipodal force-closure property. The proposed deep learning model predicts the contact configurations in grasping over-loaded
and over-sized objects for dual arm manipulators directly from raw RGB
images. We first apply detection network to locate the coarse bounding
box of objects, further apply a fine-predicting network on the bounding
box clipped images to precisely generate two contact configurations via
minimizing regression loss and the antipodal grasp prior loss. Extensive
experimental results under dense clutter and occlusion strongly demonstrate the effectiveness and robustness of the proposed method.

1 Introduction

Robotic grasping has been widely applied in many areas and there have been a
recent surge of interests [7,10,12,22] that employ deep learning models to generate grasping location by feeding visual sensory information. In the literature,
the objects involved in the grasping are almost daily used small objects. But
as a matter of fact, robotics grasping often gets involved in the condition that
the objects are of over-loaded or over-sized which introduce the challenging difficulties to those methods mentioned above, cause they are designed intended
to manipulate objects via small and single gripper. Indeed [6] suggests that
cooperative manipulators can manipulate large machine parts with a load distribution property. And dual arm manipulators [20] are in typically cooperative

© Springer Nature Switzerland AG 2019
H. Yu et al. (Eds.): ICIRA 2019, LNAI 11740, pp. 470–480, 2019.
https://doi.org/10.1007/978-3-030-27526-6_41

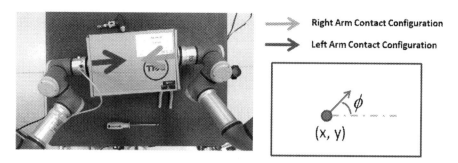

Fig. 1. Our experimental platform consists of two 6-DOF UR3 manipulators and a RGB camera mounted above viewed towards downside to capture the image. Each contact configuration stands for a tuple (x, y, ϕ) illustrated in the figure, where (x, y) presents the pixel coordinate and ϕ is the contact direction angle. Two contact configurations should complete a candidate grasp for the dual arm manipulator. The depth information of the object on the table is assumed to be known following [15].

configuration like humans, which have been applied in space robotics [21], assemblying [1,13] and valve turning [9].

In this paper, we propose a novel deep learning model to predict the grasping location comprising of two contact configurations, which are then passed to the dual arm manipulators to finish grasping in a cooperative scheme shown in Fig. 1. Due to the cooperative designation of dual-arm manipulator and the effectiveness of our proposed predicting model, grasping over-loaded or over-sized objects can be solved properly. The proposed approach consists of establishing a labeled dataset, training the deep learning model and conducting the dual arm manipulation. We gather several typical over-loaded and over-sized objects and take images in various clutter environments in order to train a robust model. On each image we label two contact configurations composed of x, y, θ, where x, y stand for the pixel coordinates and θ presents the contact direction. The detail meaning of the contact configuration and our experimental platform specifics are illustrated in Fig. 1. In order to promote performance in grasping, we adopt a coarse-to-fine strategy to generate contact configurations. First, we apply YOLO-v2 [17], a real-time and accurate object detection deep learning network, to detect the bounding box of grasped objects. Indeed, the bounding box is a coarse description of grasped objects and cannot be directly applied for grasping. Further, based on the bounding box image clip of grasped objects, another fine-predicting deep learning network is applied to precisely predict the contact configurations. The scheme of our proposed coarse-to-fine strategy can be seen in Fig. 2.

In order to achieve robust and steady grasping performance which is of essential for over-loaded and over-sized objects, we investigate the antipodal force-closure grasping [3] shown in Fig. 3 into antipodal grasp prior loss. Minimizing antipodal grasp prior loss would enforce the two contact configuration in opposite direction, which promotes the robustness in cooperative grasping tasks. We apply both regression loss (Mean Square Error) and proposed antipodal grasp prior loss to train the fine-predicting network simultaneously.

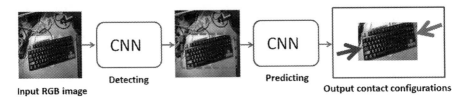

Fig. 2. The coarse-to-fine-strategy. The input is RGB image and output is contact configurations after coarse bounding box detection and fine-predicting.

In what follows, we shall introduce related works in Sect. 2. Next, we present the details about our proposed method in Sect. 3. Next we spread out and discuss the extensive experimental results in Sect. 4, and finally conclude this paper in Sect. 5.

2   Related Works

In this section we discuss the related works on applying deep learning models to robotic grasping tasks. [10] proposes a two-step cascaded network in a re-evaluated scheme to predict oriented rectangle for grasping daily objects over RGB-D images. Yet it suffers from a long searching time in candidate rectangles and background reduction in detecting objects, which is sensitive to noise and changing environment. [7] applies deep learning to form a grasp function rather than grasping location to handle with gripper pose uncertainty which is intended for parallel-jaw gripper resulting in difficulties in generalizing to other grippers. [12] uses deep learning models to evaluate the quality of grasping in a large 3D object dataset and then adopt greedy policy to choose the optimal grasping with highest quality in terms of antipodal grasp which is not efficient and time-consuming. [4] characterizes the local geometry and appearance of graspable surfaces of objects in point cloud via deep learning to evaluate whether an antipodal grasp could exist, which heavily relies on the geometry of objects and suffers from inefficient searching time of candidate grasps. On the contrary of using antipodal grasp as criterion to evaluate the candidate grasps in [4,12], we further investigate the antipodal grasp into differentiable antipodal grasp prior loss to train our proposed deep learning models to directly regress predicted grasping configuration.

Also it should be mentioned that the methods above cannot be extended to the case of over-loaded and over-sized objects. Indeed the grasping prediction must match the ability of the gripper attached on the manipulators which constraints the scope of grasping objects. As depicted in Sect. 1, cooperative manipulators are the considerable solution to handle with over-loaded and over-sized objects grasping. Deep learning models applied in cooperative grasping have been rarely conducted. The most relevant work may be [22], which exerts deep learning models to predict finger correlationship of a three-finger gripper, which is relatively limited in a specific gripper and cannot deal with over-loaded and over-sized objects.

In this paper, we propose a deep learning model along with cooperative dual arm manipulators in a coarse-to-fine strategy to handle with the over-loaded and over-sized objects grasping tasks.

3   Method

The details of our proposed method are illustrated in this section. The coarse-to-fine strategy, network architecture, loss function design and training details are stated here respectively.

3.1   Coarse-to-Fine Strategy

Directly predicting grasping contact configurations for dual arm manipulators is sensitive to changing environments and scale of objects in view. Instead we adopt a coarse-to-fine strategy which refines the coarse results to produce precise and better ones. Firstly we use a detecting network to find the object in the representation of bounding box which can coarsely reflect the location of detected object in view. Once the coarse bounding box detection is finished, a fine-predicting network generates the precise contact configurations from the clipped image within the bounding box. Finally behind the coarse-to-fine strategy, the contact configurations for left arm and right arm respectively can be stated as follows:

Definition 1. *Contact Configurations.*

$$\begin{bmatrix} C_L \\ C_R \end{bmatrix} = \begin{bmatrix} x_L \ y_L \ \phi_L \\ x_R \ y_R \ \phi_R \end{bmatrix}, \tag{1}$$

where C_L, C_R are the contact configurations already depicted blue and red in Fig. 1. Here we make assumption that the objects' distance to camera is known and stationary, so we can reconstruct the contact configurations into cartesian coordinates by:

$$\begin{bmatrix} P_L \\ P_R \end{bmatrix} = \begin{bmatrix} f(x_L, y_L, \phi_L) \\ f(x_R, y_R, \phi_R) \end{bmatrix}, \tag{2}$$

where $f(\bullet)$ stands the transform function from camera pixel coordinates to Cartesian coordinates. The whole coarse-to-fine strategy can be seen in Fig. 2.

In the grasping process, cartesian coordinates P_L, P_R in Eq. (2) is set to be the desired position of dual arm manipulators end-effectors. In order to improve the reaction speed, we devise an inverse Jacobian speed control law conducted from [2], which is stated by:

$$\begin{bmatrix} \dot{\theta}_L \\ \dot{\theta}_R \end{bmatrix} = \begin{bmatrix} -\lambda_L J_L^\dagger(\theta_L)(P_L - T_L(\theta_L)) \\ -\lambda_R J_R^\dagger(\theta_R)(P_R - T_R(\theta_R)) \end{bmatrix}, \tag{3}$$

where L, R represent the left arm and right arm respectively, $\theta_L, \theta_R \in \mathbb{R}^6$ stand for the joint angle positions of dual arm manipulators, $J_L^\dagger, J_R^\dagger : \mathbb{R}^6 \to \mathbb{R}^6$ present the pseudo inverse Jacobian matrix of manipulators detailed in [18], $T_L, T_R : \mathbb{R}^6 \to \mathbb{R}^6$ are the forward kinematics of manipulators and $\lambda_L, \lambda_R \in \mathbb{R}$ are scalars relevant to the convergence speed in the control process.

3.2   Network Architecture

Detecting Network. The input of detecting network is raw RGB image which contains the to-be-grasped objects in view and the output of the detecting network is the predicted bounding box which covers the coarse location of objects to be grasped. The detecting network is following YOLO-v2 [17], which is light-weighted and real-time by directly regressing the bounding box coordinates of objects. We adopt YOLO-v2 to coarsely predict the bounding box of the to-be-grasped objects in images to perform the coarse strategy. The details of parameters and network architecture can be found in the original YOLO-v2 [17]. It is noted that the detecting network is trained on our custom to-be-grasped objects datasets.

Fine-Predicting Network. The fine-predicting network is designed to generate contact configurations based on the predicted bounding box from detecting network. Our proposed fine-predicting network comprises of vgg16 [19] feature extractor and residual-learning blocks [5]. In order to handle with different resolution of objects in view which is very common and resizing to a fixed resolution will cause loss in information, Global Average Pooling [11] is added before the last fully-connect layer. The fine-predicting network architecture is detailed in Table 1. The convolutional layers in the fine-predicting network can automatically extract the color and geometry informations relative to the grasping contact configurations by training on the hand-labeled grasping datasets which contain various over-loaded and over-sized objects.

Table 1. Configuration of our proposed fine-predicting network. "Conv" denotes the convolution layer. "Res" denotes the residual block, "Gap" denotes Global Average Pooling [11]. "Tanh" denotes the non-linear Tanh layer, and "Fc" denotes the fully-connect layer.

Layer	vgg16 [19]	Res2-4	Conv5	Res6-8	Conv9	Gap10	Fc11	Fc12	Tanh
In_channels	3	64	64	128	128	256	1	1	1
Out_channels	64	64	128	128	256	1	1	1	1
Kernel size	7	-	5	-	3	-	-	-	-
Stride	1	-	2	-	2	-	-	-	-
Pad	3	-	1	-	1	-	-	-	-
In_dimension	-	-	-	-	-	-	256	128	6
Out_dimension	-	-	-	-	-	256	128	6	6

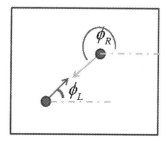

Fig. 3. Illustration of the proposed antipodal grasp prior. The two contact configuration would have opposite contact direction to form antipodal property.

3.3   Loss Function Designation

The loss function in detecting network is the same as YOLO-v2 [17]. Here we mainly discuss the loss function in training the fine-predicting network. The loss function of fine-predicting network consists of two terms, regression loss and regularization loss. The regression loss reflects the error between the predicting contact configurations and labeled ground-truth in follows:

$$\mathcal{L}_{regression} = \sum_{i \in \{L,R\}} \|\hat{C}_i - C_i^*\|_2^2, \tag{4}$$

where $\hat{C}_i$ is the predicted contact configuration and C_i^* is the labeled ground-truth. Grasping over-loaded and over-sized objects can often meet int the cases with severe slippery and unbalanced pose especially the contact configurations do not match or even conflict. To avoid this, antipodal grasp prior loss is investigated that we devise a regularization term to constraint the grasping direction ϕ in the contact configurations to have opposite directions to from antipodal force-closure by:

$$\mathcal{L}_{antipodal} = (\phi_R - \phi_L - \pi)^2, \tag{5}$$

which means the contact configurations should have opposite direction that can restrain the slippery and unbalanced cases. The illustrative explanation of the proposed antipodal grasp prior regularization term can be viewed in Fig. 3. It should be noted that the proposed antipodal grasp prior loss $\mathcal{L}_{antipodal}$ is differentiable with ϕ_L, ϕ_R, which makes it possible to conduct gradient descent to optimize the parameter of the fine-predicting network as follows:

$$W_i \leftarrow W_i - \alpha \frac{\partial \mathcal{L}_{antipodal}}{\partial W_i},$$

where W_i presents the weights of ith layer in the fine-predicting network and α stands for the learning rate. By minimizing $\mathcal{L}_{antipodal}$, one can force the predicted contact configurations to have antipodal property especially when the labeled ground-truth is not valid enough to perform robust and steady cooperative grasping.

(a) The input RGB image   (b) Prediction w/o $L_{antipodal}$ (c) Prediction w/ $L_{antipodal}$

Fig. 4. The effectiveness of the proposed antipodal grasp prior loss. (a) indicates the input RGB image to be predicted on, (b) is the predicted results from the network w/o antipodal grasp prior loss and (c) presents the results w/antipodal grasp prior loss. It can be easily seen that the proposed antipodal grasp prior loss can effectively promote the predicted results to produce antipodal property further improving the grasping results.

To be noted that the antipodal grasp prior loss is in an unsupervised scheme cause it does not rely on the labeled datasets. Further the final loss function with penalty on both regression loss and antipodal grasp prior loss can be formalized as follows:

$$\mathcal{L} = \mathcal{L}_{regression} + \mu\mathcal{L}_{antipodal}, \tag{6}$$

where μ weights $\mathcal{L}_{antipodal}$. It is intuitive to find that our proposed loss function is of semi-supervised cause $L_{regression}$ is of supervised while $L_{antipodal}$ is unsupervised. Our extensive experiments in Sect. 4 can strongly demonstrated the effectiveness of our proposed semi-supervised loss function.

3.4   Training Details

In this paper, we use PyTorch [14] to implement our networks and loss functions during training and inference. First, we train the detecting network, YOLO-v2 on our custom to-be-grasped objects detecting datasets until convergence. Then the fine-predicting network is trained on our labeled grasping datasets consisting of 10 objects in total 2000 images with augmentation. During the training procedure, Adam [8] optimizer with parameters $\beta_1 = 0.9, \beta_2 = 0.99$ is applied to minimize the semi-supervised loss in Eq. (6) with setting $\mu = 0.1$ and learning rate $lr = 1e - 4$. Convergence is achieved after 200 epochs.

To be noted that in the training time the vgg16 feature extractor is kept fixed while other layers is in active mode to update parameters. Convergence is achieved in 120 epochs. All the programs are conducted in Intel Xeon E3 1230-v3 @3.4 Ghz, Nvidia GTX 1080 GPU, 32 GB RAM, Ubuntu 16.04. And in inference step it takes about 90 ms to finish one predicting on $1920 * 1080 * 3$ input RGB image, which is considerably effective and real-time.

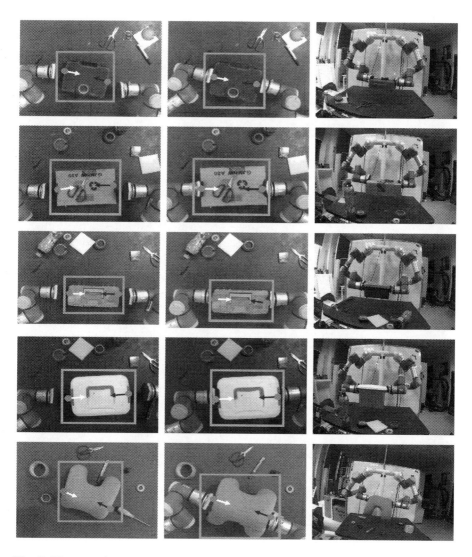

Fig. 5. The grasping experimental results are shown here. The first column shows the detecting results before grasping, the second column illustrates the detecting results even after final grasping configuration which are still robust and reasonable and the last column is the frontal view of dual arm manipulators after successful grasping and lifting in a cooperative scheme. The bounding boxes of detected objects and predicted contact configuration are plotted in the figure in the first and second column respectively. In the experiments we manually place many other small tools to generate a clutter environments and occlusion on the detected objects with different unseen orientations in training to verify the proposed method's generalization and robustness to uncertainty. The experimental results strongly demonstrated the effectiveness and robustness of our proposed method in clutter and unstructured environments.

4   Experimental Results

In this section we experiment our proposed method in different and complicated environments to verify the effectiveness. The experimental platform comprises of two UR3 6-DOF manipulators and a camera mounted above already depicted in Fig. 1. All the components of the platform are featured by ROS (Robotics Operating System) [16]. And the communication between manipulators and computers are through TCP/IP protocol to ensure the real-time reaction property. Here we discuss the grasping and lifting experiments with our proposed method and further analyze the effectiveness of our proposed antipodal grasp prior loss.

4.1   Grasping and Lifting Experiments

In what follows, we choose five over-sized or over-loaded categories of objects to conduct the grasping and lifting experiments which requires the dual arm manipulators to detect the two contact configurations for both arms respectively, successfully grasp the object and lift the object above off the table in a cooperative scheme. Dual arm manipulators cooperative grasping and lifting is very challenging requiring the precise predicted contact configurations which shall not cause slippery and unbalance. In experiments, we manually and randomly place objects with unseen pose, orientation and surroundings unseen in training and make occlusion on the detected objects in view to verify the effectiveness and robustness of our proposed method. The successful grasping and lifting experiments are shown in Fig. 5. The successful rate of grasping and lifting experiments is reported in Table 2.

Table 2. The Successful Rate (SR) of grasping and lifting experiments. SR is represented by "success number/trial number".

Objects	SR w/o $L_{antipodal}$	SR w/ $L_{antipodal}$
	54 / 89	**79** / 89
	42 / 82	**72** / 82
	56 / 101	**91** / 101
	64 / 91	**73** / 91
	58 / 71	**59** / 71
Average (%)	63.1%	**86.2** %

4.2 Effectiveness of Antipodal Grasp Prior

In this part, we further investigate the effectiveness of our proposed antipodal grasp prior loss in the experiments. We trained another model without penalty in antipodal grasp prior loss $\mathcal{L}_{antipodal}$ while keeping other hyper-parameters and settings the same. Extensive experiments are conducted on five over-sized and over-loaded objects with two models, w/ $\mathcal{L}_{antipodal}$, w/o $\mathcal{L}_{antipodal}$ respectively. From the experiments shown in Fig. 4, we can see that the proposed antipodal grasp prior loss can effectively improve the grasping quality and success rate via antipodal contact configurations, especially when the labeled ground-truth is not valid enough. Further grasping and lifting experiments are conducted sufficiently on five diverse objects with unseen orientations in training and occlusion to verify the effectiveness of $\mathcal{L}_{antipodal}$, which is listed in Table 2. The large margin over w/o $\mathcal{L}_{antipodal}$ cases does demonstrate the extremely effectiveness of the proposed antipodal grasp prior loss.

5 Conclusion

In this paper, we propose a novel deep learning models based on coarse-to-fine strategy to perform cooperative grasping of over-loaded and over-sized objects for dual arm manipulators. To eliminate the slippery and unbalanced contact configurations in grasping, we further investigate the antipodal grasp prior loss to constrain the predicted contact configurations in antipodal case to improve the robustness and steadiness in grasping. The extensive experimental results conducted in dense clutter and severe occlusion have strongly demonstrated our proposed method, which further improve the application of deep learning models and classical antipodal force-closure grasp in cooperative robotics.

Acknowledgement. This work is supported by National Natural Science Foundation of China under Grant 91748112. The authors would like to thank Wei Li, Xiuchuan Tang and Linan Deng in the School of Artificial Intelligence and Automation, Huazhong University of Science and Technology for helping in the experiments.

References

1. Almeida, D., Karayiannidis, Y.: Folding assembly by means of dual-arm robotic manipulation. In: 2016 IEEE International Conference on Robotics and Automation (ICRA), pp. 3987–3993. IEEE (2016)
2. Chaumette, F., Hutchinson, S.: Visual servo control. I. Basic approaches. IEEE Robot. Autom. Mag. **13**(4), 82–90 (2006)
3. Chen, I.M., Burdick, J.W.: Finding antipodal point grasps on irregularly shaped objects. IEEE Trans. Robot. Autom. **9**(4), 507–512 (1993). https://doi.org/10.1109/70.246063
4. Gualtieri, M., ten Pas, A., Saenko, K., Platt, R.: High precision grasp pose detection in dense clutter. In: 2016 IEEE/RSJ International Conference on Intelligent Robots and Systems (IROS), pp. 598–605. IEEE (2016)

5. He, K., Zhang, X., Ren, S., Sun, J.: Deep residual learning for image recognition. In: Proceedings of the IEEE Conference on Computer Vision and Pattern Recognition, pp. 770–778 (2016)
6. Hsu, P.: Coordinated control of multiple manipulator systems. IEEE Trans. Robot. Autom. **9**(4), 400–410 (1993)
7. Johns, E., Leutenegger, S., Davison, A.J.: Deep learning a grasp function for grasping under gripper pose uncertainty. In: 2016 IEEE/RSJ International Conference on Intelligent Robots and Systems (IROS), pp. 4461–4468. IEEE (2016)
8. Kinga, D., Adam, J.B.: A method for stochastic optimization. In: International Conference on Learning Representations (ICLR), vol. 5 (2015)
9. Korpela, C., Orsag, M., Oh, P.: Towards valve turning using a dual-arm aerial manipulator. In: 2014 IEEE/RSJ International Conference on Intelligent Robots and Systems, pp. 3411–3416, September 2014. https://doi.org/10.1109/IROS.2014.6943037
10. Lenz, I., Lee, H., Saxena, A.: Deep learning for detecting robotic grasps. Int. J. Robot. Res. **34**(4–5), 705–724 (2015)
11. Lin, M., Chen, Q., Yan, S.: Network in network. arXiv preprint arXiv:1312.4400 (2013)
12. Mahler, J., et al.: Dex-Net 2.0: deep learning to plan robust grasps with synthetic point clouds and analytic grasp metrics. In: Robotics: Science and Systems (RSS) (2017)
13. Park, C., Park, K.: Design and kinematics analysis of dual arm robot manipulator for precision assembly. In: 6th IEEE International Conference on Industrial Informatics, INDIN 2008, pp. 430–435. IEEE (2008)
14. Paszke, A., et al.: Automatic differentiation in pytorch (2017)
15. Pinto, L., Gupta, A.: Supersizing self-supervision: learning to grasp from 50k tries and 700 robot hours. In: 2016 IEEE International Conference on Robotics and Automation (ICRA), pp. 3406–3413. IEEE (2016)
16. Quigley, M., et al.: ROS: an open-source robot operating system. In: ICRA Workshop on Open Source Software (2009)
17. Redmon, J., Farhadi, A.: Yolo9000: better, faster, stronger. arXiv preprint arXiv:1612.08242 (2016)
18. Siciliano, B., Sciavicco, L., Villani, L., Oriolo, G.: Robotics: Modelling, Planning and Control. Springer, Heidelberg (2010). https://doi.org/10.1007/978-1-84628-642-1
19. Simonyan, K., Zisserman, A.: Very deep convolutional networks for large-scale image recognition. arXiv preprint arXiv:1409.1556 (2014)
20. Smith, C., Karayiannidis, Y., Nalpantidis, L., et al.: Dual arm manipulation: a survey. Robot. Autonom. Syst. **60**(10), 1340–1353 (2012)
21. Uchiyama, M., et al.: Development of a flexible dual-arm manipulator testbed for space robotics. In: Proceedings of the IEEE International Workshop on Intelligent Robots and Systems, Towards a New Frontier of Applications, IROS 1990, pp. 375–381. IEEE (1990)
22. Varley, J., Weisz, J., Weiss, J., Allen, P.: Generating multi-fingered robotic grasps via deep learning. In: 2015 IEEE/RSJ International Conference on Intelligent Robots and Systems (IROS), pp. 4415–4420. IEEE (2015)

Artificial Neural Network Based Tactile Sensing Unit for Robotic Hand

Dong-Kyo Jeong[1], Dong-Eon Kim[1], Li Ailimg[1],
and Jang-Myung Lee[2(✉)]

[1] Department of Electrical and Computer Engineering,
Pusan National University, Busan 609-735, Korea
{dongkyo1696,dongeon1696,liailing1696}@pusan.ac.kr
[2] Department of Electronic Engineering, Pusan National University,
Busan 609-735, Korea
jmlee@pusan.ac.kr

Abstract. Unlike the conventional haptic detection with the tactile sensor or Force Sensing Resistor (FSR) sensor, this paper proposes a new algorithm for tactile sensing unit that air pressure sensors are implemented to represent the tactile degree of the robot hand which can play more accurate haptic feedback. Meanwhile, in order to optimize the performance of the tactile sensing unit, several target objects are trained with the help of Artificial Neural Network (ANN) that gives the linear output values according to the constant mass when the robot hand holds different target objects. In addition, Arrival of Time (A.o.T) algorithm is utilized for recognizing the touch points of the robot hand when the target object is compressed by the tactile sensing device. The optimal output positions can be selected through amounts of tests with various grasp positions in the haptic sensing part for the reason that different pressure-points distribution facilitates the optimization mapping. Experiments show that the proposed method can be applied for Human Robot Interaction (HRI) effectively and efficiently.

Keywords: Artificial neural network · Air pressure sensor ·
Tactile sensing unit · Grasp positions

1 Introduction

Hand tactile degree is one of the important perceptions for human beings, which is used to perform various tasks, such as sensing the danger. The tactile degree is mainly used to determine the stiffness of the haptic or to detect the temperature under the various environments. When the temperature exceeds a certain range, the avoiding action occurs autonomously. The strength of the grasping force is controlled according to the temperature expansion of the object. Meanwhile, the grasping force is automatically controlled by the rigidity of object compression.

In this paper, in order to apply human tactile sense to robots, tactile sensing unit by self-manufacture is cheaper than the existing commercial expensive tactile sensors. Also, it can make more sensitive performance than the force sensing. We propose a

© Springer Nature Switzerland AG 2019
H. Yu et al. (Eds.): ICIRA 2019, LNAI 11740, pp. 481–487, 2019.
https://doi.org/10.1007/978-3-030-27526-6_42

method that can be applied for selection of the massive optimal touch positions by the ANN. The developed tactile sensing unit is mounted on the finger tip of the robot hand that detects the touch sensitivity and temperature of the target object. Final output data is intuitively processed for HRI with the optimized touch map.

Currently, lots of tactile equipment in robot hand feel the objects using tactile sensors or FSR sensors. They can be attached to curved fingers so that similar experimental environment to a real human hand can be provided [1–4]. FSR sensors have been traditionally used for force sensing, but the range of sensing is set in a narrow range due to the natural limitation of the sensor. Comparing with the tactile sensing part through the air pressure sensor, FSR has a relatively inferior detection range [5, 6].

The proposed tactile sensing part involves air pressure sensor with the wider sensing range which makes it possible to describe the tactile situation of the touching surface more functions of performance, such like temperature feedback. In order to differentiate the touch detection through the developed sensor according to the position of the object, we propose the A.o.T algorithm in Sect. 3.

2   System Configuration

2.1   Touch Sensing Unit

The structure of the robot hand used in this paper is shown as follows. In the case of the robot's hand, 3 Finger gripper is applied that each gripper type has Dynamixel. This is a kind of thumb based structure, also same to the index and middle finger which are most commonly used in real human grasping [7–9]. Dynamic sensation for holding the object exists in the whole tactile sensing process. Three tactile sensors are installed by inserting three pressure sensors of BMP 180 in the fingertip position. It enables points grasping effectively when the robot hand touch the object.

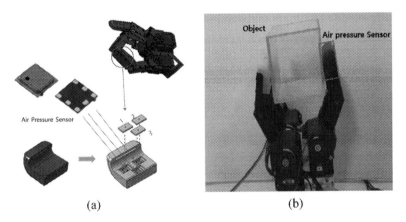

(a)   (b)

Fig. 1. Tactile pressure sensor. (**a**) Touch sensing unit with air pressure sensor located on fingertip of 3 Finger robot hand. (**b**) Object mass detection experiment using air pressure sensor.

2.2 Machine Learning Through Artificial Neural Network for Mass Detection

The object is firstly grasped. And then pick & place work is performed to measure the stable grasp success rate. Pick & place work consists of grasping, lifting, holding and moving. During lifting and holding, lots of rotations or drops depend on the occurrence of gravity. Therefore, it should be controlled by the appropriate force for the stable grasp according to grasp position with low hardness. It is necessary to perform soft grasping work by grasping. When holding an object, it is possible to perform stable grasping by sensing the mass and applying a proper amount of force.

For this, we grasp the object through the air pressure sensor to know the mass of the object by force in the touch surface between the tactile sensor and the object. Experiments are performed to predict the mass of an object through artificial neural network learning using the sensor's output value. In this experiment, it is necessary to detect that the mass of the object is constantly increased under the same conditions of temperature and touch surface. Therefore, the mass of the object is constantly increased by adding 10 g of mass continuously using a transparent cube box. The mass of this object is used as the ground truth data and used as a label. The mass detection experiment is shown in Fig. 1(b) [10].

2.3 Touch Sensing Unit Data Regression

As a result of comparing the object mass when the mass was linearly increased and the output of the air pressure sensor, there is a part where the output value of the air pressure sensor due to the linear mass increase of the object is not linear. In order to solve this problem, the output value of the sensor is learned by Artificial Neural Network through linear mass increase of the object having constant touch point, and the mass predicted value of the object is derived. The structure of the artificial neural network is shown in Fig. 2 [11–14].

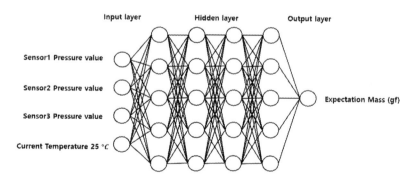

Fig. 2. Artificial Neural Network learning structure according to output value of air pressure sensor.

In this case, the artificial neural network learning method learns the function $y = f(x)$ that outputs the mass y of the object with respect to the input value x of the air pressure sensor. The training sample $\{x_i y_i\}_{i=1}^{n}$ is learned and the mass $f(x_i)$ of the actual object is used as a general output sample y_i.

$$J_{LS}(\theta) = \frac{1}{2}\sum_{i=1}^{n}(f_\theta((x_i)) - y_i))^2 \tag{1}$$

The Least Squares Method learns the parameter θ that minimizes the square error between the output $f_\theta(x_i)$ of the model and the target value $\{y_i\}_{i=1}^{n}$. Here 'LS' is an acronym for Least Squares.

$$\hat{\theta}_{LS} = arg_\theta minJ_{LS}(\theta) \tag{2}$$

The coefficient 1/2 in Eq. (1) is used to cancel the 2 multiplied by differentiating J_{LS}, and the loss minimization technique is used.

$$f_\theta(x) = \sum_{j=1}^{b} \theta_j \emptyset_j(x) = \theta^T \emptyset(x) \tag{3}$$

Using the same linear model as Eq. (3), the training error was used as $J_{LS}(\theta) = \frac{1}{2}\| \phi\theta - y \|^2$. Rectified Linear Unit (ReLU) and Sigmoid function were used for the activation function of the hidden layer, through repeated experiments. We determined layout configuration and its parameters that constitute optimal output values, a multi-layer perceptron composed of four layers of hidden layer was constructed to derive the output value of linearized air pressure sensor for each constantly increased object.

Table 1. Output value of air pressure sensor and result of mass prediction by artificial neural network learning.

Object (gf)	Sensor 1	Sensor 2	Sensor 3	Expectation Mass (gf)
0	0.2	0.7	0.8	0.96
100	1.5	9.23	3.65	99.85
110	2.3	8.28	4.32	110.84
120	2.95	8.91	4.35	116.99
130	3.81	9.1	4.9	129.85
140	4.7	9.86	5.34	143.11
150	5.32	10.6	5.69	153.47
160	6.12	10.8	6.1	164.62
170	6.88	11.2	6.47	175.45
180	7.01	11.34	6.55	177.67
190	7.61	11.65	7.1	189.27
200	8.1	11.75	7.18	193.87
210	8.74	13.85	7.4	205.66

The results of the study are shown in Table 1. At that compares the object mass and the expectation mass of the object from the learning. This shows that the air pressure sensor can function as a touch detection sensor.

3   A.o.T Position Detection Algorithm

The proposed tactile sensing unit can detect the touch position of an object in addition to predicting the mass value. When the robot hand grasps an object, the touch position of the fingertip is different, and the A.o.T algorithm is proposed using the characteristics of the air pressure sensor constituting the touch sensing unit, thereby realizing the touch position.

As a method to grasp the sensing point through the sensing time of each sensor and the distance between each sensor as shown in Fig. 3, the sensing unit is divided into nine equal rectangles. The rectangles of each of the divided sensing units are divided into Arr_n. In other words, (1, 1) the square at the top left corner is Arr_1 and the number of Arr_n is increased to the right. Arr_5, which constitutes the middle of this nine-divided rectangle, constitutes the air pressure sensors 1 and 2 on the upper left corner, and the third sensor is arranged in the middle of the base to load the sensor in the triangular shape.

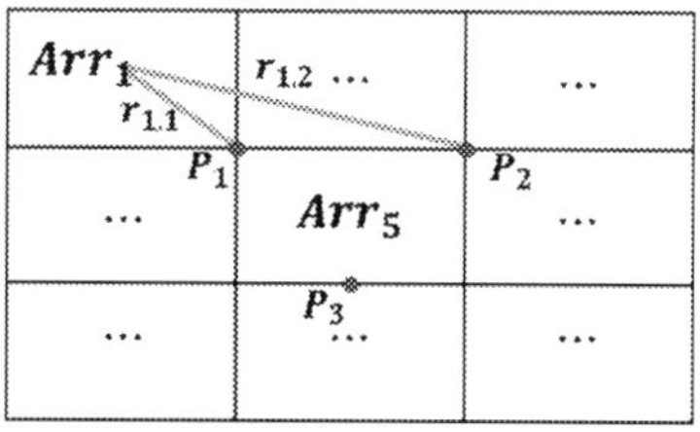

Fig. 3. Touch sensing unit configuration and mass detection experiment with air pressure sensor.

The A.o.T algorithm configuration is shown in Eq. 4. The air pressure value of the position of the object contacting the sensing unit is divided by the difference between the distances of the divided portions and the time at which the sensor corresponding to the touch position is recognized. The area of the touch sensing part is divided into nine parts and represented by Arr_n, and the three pressure sensors in the touch sensing part are represented by P_n. According to the contact point of arrn, the distance difference is calculated with P_n as the origin, and the contact map is expressed by a method of varying the contact pressure in consideration of the time difference. Through this, touch position can be sequentially recognized by the time difference and the distance difference according to the touch position by multiplying the sum of the recognized times of all the sensors.

$$Arr_n = \sum\nolimits_{k=1}^{3} \left(\frac{P_k}{r_{n,k}} \frac{\sum_{x=1}^{3} t_x}{t_k} \right) \qquad (4)$$

P_k: The air pressure value measured at the kth air pressure sensor
$r_{n,k}$:   The kth air pressure sensor and the Arr_n and the straight line distance
t_x: Sensing time of air pressure sensor.

4   Experiments

The experimental results of the proposed algorithm are shown in Fig. 4. According to various touch positions of the tactile sensing unit, tactile pressure map of those points are gives by the A.o.T algorithm. We give different colorful rectangle (24 regions) to represent this pressure perception. The touch surfaces of the tactile sensing unit are tested several times in different grasping ways. The red dot points are the focus of the mass. Meanwhile, the level of red color gives the various pressure representations that depend on the pressure expression. It is confirmed that A.o.T algorithm is applied and the concentration by contact area according to pressure and distance is expressed differently with time.

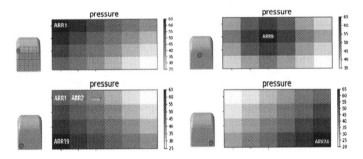

Fig. 4. Sensing expression according to touch point of touch sensing unit.

5   Conclusion

The touch sensing unit is fabricated with the air pressure sensor. Meanwhile, the values of the object mass are calculated by the A.o.T algorithm. And then, ANN training process locates the optimal touch positions of the sensing part that can be grasped stably and mapped accurately. Such optimal structure is very basic and crucial technology that enables robots to perform high level activities in HRI. It promotes the robot increasingly humanized with data driven by such tactile feed-back unit. Also, the improved tactile sensing development can help human to pursuit for more suitable operations under various terrible environments. In the future, we will try to perform different grasping operations by calculating appropriate grasping force for each object according to the mass, various strength, and temperature of the object with the touch sensing unit and deep learning methods.

Acknowledgment. This research is based upon work supported by the Ministry of Trade, Industry & Energy (MOTIE, Korea) under Industrial Technology Innovation Program. No.10073147.

References

1. Cramphorn, L., Ward-Cherrier, B., Lepora, N.F.: Tactile manipulation with biomimetic active touch. In: 2016 IEEE International Conference on Robotics and Automation (ICRA). IEEE (2016)
2. Nathan, L., Alex, C., Conrad, K., Raia, H., John, L.: From pixels to percepts: highly robust edge perception and contour following using deep learning and an optical biomimetic tactile sensor. IEEE Robot. Autom. Lett. **4**(2), 2101–2107 (2019)
3. Schmitz, A., et al.: Tactile object recognition using deep learning and dropout. In: 2014 IEEE-RAS International Conference on Humanoid Robots. IEEE (2014)
4. Baishya, S.S., Bäuml, B.: Robust material classification with a tactile skin using deep learning. In: 2016 IEEE/RSJ International Conference on Intelligent Robots and Systems (IROS). IEEE (2016)
5. Claudio, C., Vikram, R.: A wearable low-cost device based upon force-sensing resistors to detect single-finger forces. In: IEEE RAS & EMBS International Conference on Biomedical Robotics and Biomechatronics (BioRob) (2014)
6. Bahadır, S.K.: Identification and modeling of sensing capability of force sensing resistor integrated to E-textile structure. IEEE Sens. J. **18**(23), 9770–9780 (2018)
7. Dang, H., Allen, P.K.: Stable grasping under pose uncertainty using tactile feedback. Auton. Robot. **36**(4), 309–330 (2014)
8. Vinicius, F., Thiago, E.O., Katerina, E., Emil, M.P.: Stable grasping and object reorientation with a three-fingered robotic hand. In: IEEE International Symposium on Robotics and Intelligent Sensors (IRIS2017) (2017)
9. Wan, Q., Adams, R.P., Howe, R.D.: Variability and predictability in tactile sensing during grasping. In: IEEE International Conference on Robotics and Automation (ICRA) (2016)
10. Kim, D.E., Kim, K.S., Park, J.H., Ailing, L., Lee, J.M.: Stable grasping of objects using air pressure sensors on a robot hand. In: International Conference on Control, Automation and Systems (ICCAS 2018) (2018)
11. Chang, C.-H.: Deep and shallow architecture of multilayer neural networks. IEEE Transact. Neural Netw. Learn. Syst. **26**(10), 2477–2486 (2015)
12. Gong, M., et al.: A multiobjective sparse feature learning model for deep neural networks. IEEE Transact. Neural Netw. Learn. Syst. **26**(12), 3263–3277 (2015)
13. Păvăloiu, I.B., et al.: Feedforward multilayer phase-based neural networks. In: 12th Symposium on Neural Network Applications in Electrical Engineering (NEUREL). IEEE (2014)
14. Rika, A., Mia, K., Johannes, A.S., Danica, K.: Global search with bernoulli alternation kernel for task-oriented grasping informed by simulation. In: 2nd Conference on Robot Learning (CoRL 2018) (2018)

Bounded Recursive Optimization Approach for Pose Estimation in Robotic Visual Servoing

Yuchen Zhang[1], Bo Chen[1,2(✉)], Li Yu[1], and Haiyu Song[3]

[1] Department of Automation, Zhejiang University of Technology,
Hangzhou 310023, People's Republic of China
[2] Institute of Cyberspace Security, Zhejiang University of Technology,
Hangzhou 310023, People's Republic of China
[3] College of Information, Zhejiang University of Finance and Economics,
Hangzhou 310018, People's Republic of China
{bchen,lyu}@zjut.edu.cn

Abstract. Pose estimation problem is concerned with determining position and orientation of an object in real time using the image information, and has found applications in many fields such as object recognition and robotic visual servoing. Most of vision-based pose estimation schemes are derived from extended Kalman filter, which requires that the noises obey the Gaussian distribution under known covariance. However, the statistical information in robot control may not be accurately obtained or satisfied. In this paper, a novel bounded recursive optimization approach is proposed to solve the pose estimation problem in visual serving, where the addressed noises do not provide any statistical information, and the bounds of noises are also unknown. Finally, the pose estimation simulation is conducted to show the advantages and effectiveness of the proposed approach.

Keywords: Pose estimation · Visual servoing ·
Bounded recursive optimization approach

1 Introduction

As one of the important issues in robotic visual servoing (RVS), pose estimation has attracted considerable research interest during the past few decades. The major concern of pose estimation in RVS is to determine the position and orientation of an object for real-time control of robot motion. Most solutions to pose estimation problem rely on sets of 2-D-3-D correspondences between geometric features and their projections on the image plane. Particularly, point features are typically used for pose estimation due to their ease of availability in many objects [1].

The work was supported by the National Natural Science Foundation of China under Grant 61673351 and 61603331.

H. Yu et al. (Eds.): ICIRA 2019, LNAI 11740, pp. 488–497, 2019.
https://doi.org/10.1007/978-3-030-27526-6_43

Recently, there are three major methods for pose estimation have been investigated extensively, i.e., camera-calibration based methods, iterative methods and extended Kalman filter (EKF) based methods. The camera-calibration based methods rely on the geometric relationship between noncollinear feature points and the corresponding feature points on grid body plane. Solutions for three points and more than three points have already been presented [2,3]. However, the related results will be drastically affected by the points configuration and noise in the points coordinates [2]. Iterative methods formulate the pose estimation problem as a nonlinear least-squares problem, and their solutions rely on nonlinear optimization techniques, such as Gauss-Newton method [4]. The major problem for this class of methods is their convergence difficulty to guarantee [5]. EKF is a kind of recursive method and can provide near-optimal estimation for pose parameters. EKF-base platform has been proposed in reference [6] to integrate range sensor with vision sensor for robust pose estimation in RVS. However, when the assumption of local linearity is not satisfied, the linearization of measurement equations in EKF can generate unstable filters. Moreover, the statistical information of dynamic and measurement noises in EKF are always assumed to be known in advance and to remain constant, which is not possible for pose estimation problem in practice.

To overcome the drawback of EKF on noise assumptions, several methods have been proposed in the literature. Combined with the idea of adaptive filter, an adaptive EKF was proposed in reference [7] to update the dynamic noise covariance in pose estimation. This approach was then extended to iterative adaptive EKF [8] by integrating mechanisms for noise adaptation and iterative-measurement linearization. However, both adaptive EKF and iterative adaptive EKF require the assumption of Gaussian noises and the linearization error remains a problem.

Without Gaussian assumption of noise, the energy-bounded noises [9] and bounded noises [10,11] have been considered in filter designing. It should be pointed out that the bounded noises, which do not need any statistical information and bounds of noises, can be easily satisfied in practical RVS systems. Inspired by the idea of bounded recursive optimization (BRO) in reference [10,11], the pose estimation problem under bounded noises is converted into a recursive convex optimization problem in this paper that can be easily solved by standard software packages.

2 Problem Formulation

Consider the problem of estimating position and orientation of an object in robotic visual servoing, the projection model [8] of feature points is shown in Fig. 1. $O^C - (X^C, Y^C, Z^C)$, $O^I - (X^I, Y^I, Z^I)$ and $O^O - (X^O, Y^O, Z^O)$ are coordinate systems of camera frame, image frame and object frame, respectively. The X^I-axis and Y^I-axis of image frame are parallel to that of camera frame, and O^I is located F (i.e., effective focal length) from Z^C-axis. It is considered that the camera frame is fixed, while position parameters $T \triangleq [X, Y, Z]^T$ and

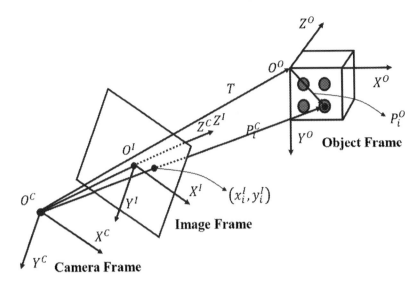

Fig. 1. Perspective projection model of camera.

orientation parameters $\Theta \triangleq [\alpha, \beta, \gamma]^T$ of an object in camera frame need to be estimated. For pose estimation, both pose and velocity parameters are defined to be state vector, i.e., $x = [X, Y, Z, \dot{X}, \dot{Y}, \dot{Z}, \alpha, \beta, \gamma, \dot{\alpha}, \dot{\beta}, \dot{\gamma}]^T$. The pose estimation system model is given by

$$x_k = Ax_{k-1} + w_k \tag{1}$$

$$z_k = G(x_k) + v_k \tag{2}$$

where k is the sample step, w_k and v_k are bounded noises, i.e.,

$$w_k^T w_k \leq \delta_w, \ v_k^T v_k \leq \delta_v \tag{3}$$

where δ_w and δ_v are unknown.

It is a reasonable assumption that the relative target velocity is usually to be constant during each sample period, thus the state transition matrix is given by

$$A = \mathrm{mdiag}\left\{F_A, F_A\right\}, F_A = \begin{bmatrix} I_3 & tI_3 \\ 0 & I_3 \end{bmatrix} \tag{4}$$

where t is the sample period. The measurement $z_k \triangleq [x_{1,k}^I, y_{1,k}^I, ..., x_{p,k}^I, y_{p,k}^I]^T$ is a nonlinear function of state x_k, where p is the number of feature points and $[x_{i,k}^I, y_{i,k}^I]^T$ represents the coordinate of feature point in image frame at time k. To describe the relationship between z_k and x_k, the following coordinate transformation [12] and pin-hole camera model [7] will be introduced by

$$P_i^C = T + R(\Theta)P_i^O \tag{5}$$

$$[x_{i,k}^I, y_{i,k}^I]^T = \frac{F}{Z_i^C}\left[\frac{X_i^C}{P_X} \ \frac{Y_i^C}{P_Y}\right]^T \tag{6}$$

where $P_i^O \triangleq [X_i^O, Y_i^O, Z_i^O]^T$ and $P_i^C \triangleq [X_i^C, Y_i^C, Z_i^C]^T$ are the coordinate vectors of the i-th feature point in object frame and camera frame, respectively. P_i^O is modeled or measured in advance. The rotation matrix $R(\Theta)$ is given by

$$
R(\Theta) = \begin{bmatrix} \cos\beta\cos\gamma & \cos\beta\sin\gamma & -\sin\beta \\ \sin\alpha\sin\beta\cos\gamma & \sin\alpha\sin\beta\sin\gamma & \sin\alpha\cos\beta \\ \cos\alpha\sin\beta\cos\gamma & \cos\alpha\sin\beta\sin\gamma & \cos\alpha\cos\beta \end{bmatrix} \tag{7}
$$

P_X and P_Y are interpixel spacing in X^I-axes and Y^I-axes of the image plane, respectively. The parameters (P_X, P_Y, F) of pin-hole camera model are all determined from camera-calibration tests [7].

Consequently, based on nonlinear measurement z_k, the aim of this paper is to design a BRO approach for pose estimation such that the statistical information of noise are not required.

Remark 1. In terms of pose estimation problem, the noise statistics for EKF [6] is not possible to be known in practice since the exact statistical information of noises will vary with time. In this sense, the proposed BRO approach, which does not require any noise statistics or bounds of noises, is more reasonable in practical applications.

3   Main Results

The estimation of pose at time k is calculated by the following recursive form:

$$
\hat{x}_k^- = A\hat{x}_{k-1} \tag{8}
$$
$$
\hat{x}_k = \hat{x}_k^- + K_k(z_k - G(\hat{x}_k^-)) \tag{9}
$$

where an optimal time-varying estimator gain K_k will be presented in Theorem 1 by minimizing an upper bound of estimation error square.

Theorem 1. For a given $\eta > 0$, an optimal estimator gain K_k for pose estimation can be obtained by solving the following convex optimization problem:

$$
\min_{\vartheta_k > 0, \Phi_k > 0, P_k > 0} \mathrm{Tr}\{P_k + \Phi_k\}
$$
$$
\text{s.t.} : \begin{cases} \begin{bmatrix} -I & G_{L,k}A & B_{L,k} \\ * & -P_k & 0 \\ * & * & -\Phi_k \end{bmatrix} < 0 \\ P_k - \vartheta_k I < 0 \\ \vartheta_k < \eta \end{cases} \tag{10}
$$

where $G_{L,k} \triangleq I - K_k H_k$, $B_{L,k} \triangleq [G_{L,k} \ - K_k]$ and the Jacobian matrix H_k is given by

$$
H_k \triangleq \frac{\partial G(x)}{\partial x}\Big|_{x=\hat{x}_k^-} \tag{11}
$$

Proof. Define $\tilde{x}_k \overset{\Delta}{=} x_k - \hat{x}_k$ and $\tilde{x}_k^- \overset{\Delta}{=} x_k - \hat{x}_k^-$, one has that

$$\tilde{x}_k = \tilde{x}_k^- - K_k[G(x_k) - G(\hat{x}_k^-) + v_k] \tag{12}$$

Notice that $G(x_k)$ can be represented as $G(x_k) = G(\hat{x}_k^-) + H_k\tilde{x}_k^- + \Delta([\tilde{x}_k^-]^2)$ by Taylor series expanding about "$\hat{x}_k^-$", where $\Delta([\tilde{x}_k^-]^2)$ represents the high-order terms of the Taylor series expansion. $\Delta([\tilde{x}_k^-]^2)$ is an unknown noise, and the term $\tilde{v}_k$ is introduced to model the affection factors caused by this unknown noise [10,11]. Thus, by defining $\xi_k \overset{\Delta}{=} \mathrm{col}\{w_{k-1}, \tilde{v}_k\}$, the nonlinear error system is equivalent to:

$$\tilde{x}_k = G_{L,k}A\tilde{x}_{k-1} + B_{L,k}\xi_k \tag{13}$$

To construct an upper bound of estimation error square, the following performance index is introduced:

$$J_k \overset{\Delta}{=} \tilde{x}_k^T\tilde{x}_k - \tilde{x}_{k-1}^T P_k\tilde{x}_{k-1} - \xi_k^T \Phi_k\xi_k \tag{14}$$

where $P_k > 0$ and $\Phi_k > 0$, then it follows from (13) that

$$J_k = \begin{bmatrix} \tilde{x}_{k-1} \\ \xi_k \end{bmatrix}^T \begin{bmatrix} A^T G_{L,k}^T G_{L,k} A - P_k & A^T G_{L,k}^T B_{L,k} \\ * & B_{L,k}^T B_{L,k} - \Phi_k\xi_k \end{bmatrix} \begin{bmatrix} \tilde{x}_{k-1} \\ \xi_k \end{bmatrix} \tag{15}$$

The condition $J_k < 0$ must be satisfied to make the term $\tilde{x}_{k-1}^T P_k\tilde{x}_{k-1} + \xi_k^T \Phi_k\xi_k$ an upper bound of estimation error square. According to Schur complement lemma, $J_k < 0$ is equivalent to the first inequality in (10). Moreover, the optimization objective "$\mathrm{Tr}\{P_k + \Phi_k\}$" is selected when minimizing this upper bound at time k.

Based on Theorem 1, the computation procedure of BRO approach for pose estimation is summarized as Algorithm 1.

Algorithm 1

1: Initialization: $\hat{x}_0$;
2: **for** $k := 1, 2, \dots$ **do**
3:     Calculate state estimation time update $\hat{x}_k^-$ by eq. (8);
4:     Determine the Jacobian matrix "H_k" by eq. (11);
5:     Calculate the optimal gain K_k by solving the optimization problem (10);
6:     Determine $\hat{x}_k$ by eq. (9);
7: **end for**

Remark 2. The convex optimization problem (10) is established in terms of linear matrix inequalities (LMIs), and thus it can be directly solved by the function "*mincx*" of MATLAB LMI Toolbox [13]. On the other hand, the proposed BRO approach does not need the initial estimation error covariance matrix, and only depends on the initial estimated value.

4   Simulation Results

In this section, the simulation is conducted to study the performance of proposed BRO approach for pose estimation and the results are compared with EKF. The camera parameters are given by $\frac{F}{P_X} = 816.96$ and $\frac{F}{P_Y} = 811.69$, and the sample time is taken as $t = 0.05$ s. There are four feature points used for pose estimation, and their coordinates in object frame are $(-12.5; -46; 0)$, $(12.5; -46; 0)$, $(12.5; -21; 0)$ and $(-12.5; -21; 0)$.

The moving object is assumed to travel through a predefined trajectory, thus the relative target velocity is changed once in a while. When the object in a relative slow motion, a well tuned EKF has shown good estimation performance [12]. In this case, the results of EKF in pose estimation is used for comparison.

Case 1: The dynamic and measurement noises are set as zero-mean Gaussian white noises with their covariance $Q_w = \text{diag}[0, q_1, 0, q_1, 0, q_1, 0, q_2, 0, q_2, 0, q_2]$ and $Q_v = \text{diag}[r_1, r_1, r_1, r_1, r_1, r_1, r_1, r_1, r_1, r_1, r_1, r_1, r_1, r_1, r_1, r_1]$, where $q_1 = 0.01$, $q_2 = 0.0001$, $r_1 = 0.01$. The purpose of the simulation in Case 1 is to show that the BRO approach can achieve good estimation performance without any statistical information of noises. It is assumed that EKF knows the covariance of noises and the well tuned results are plotted in Fig. 2, while the BRO approach does not use any statistical information of noises and the pose estimation results are shown in Fig. 3. Compared with EKF, the estimated position and orientation by BRO can better track the object as far as the relative velocity changed. The absolute value of estimation error by EKF and BRO under Gaussian noises is plotted in Fig. 4, which shows the effectiveness of BRO approach without any statistical information of noises. Moreover, it is seen from Fig. 4 that the pose estimation performance of BRO approach is better than that of EKF method in most cases.

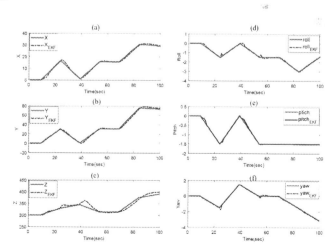

Fig. 2. Dynamic performance of pose estimation by EKF with Gaussian noises.

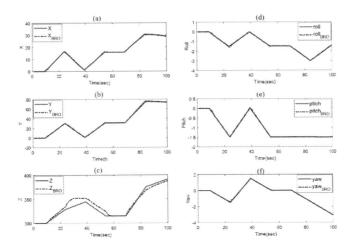

Fig. 3. Dynamic performance of pose estimation by BRO with Gaussian noises.

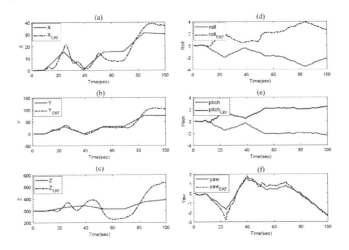

Fig. 4. Absolute value of estimation error under Gaussian noises.

Case 2: The dynamic and measurement noises are set as bounded noises, i.e., $w(t) = 0.2\phi_w(t) - 0.1$ and $v(t) = 0.2\phi_v(t) - 0.1$, where $\phi_w(t)$ and $\phi_v(t)$ are random variables that can be generated by the function "rand" of MATLAB. It is obvious that $\phi_w(t)$ and $\phi_v(t)$ are not Gaussian white noises. The pose estimation results of EKF and BRO under bounded noises are plotted in Figs. 5 and 6, respectively. It is seen from Fig. 5 that EKF suffers from significant pose estimation performance degradation under bounded noises, while the estimation

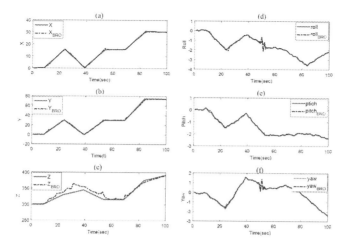

Fig. 5. Dynamic performance of pose estimation by EKF with bounded noises.

results by BRO approach is within a tolerable range, this is as expected for the bounded noises based methods. The absolute value of estimation errors by EKF and BRO under bounded noises are plotted in Fig. 7, which shows the superiority of the proposed BRO approach under bounded noises as compared with the EKF.

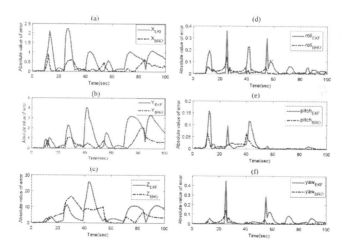

Fig. 6. Dynamic performance of pose estimation by BRO with bounded noises.

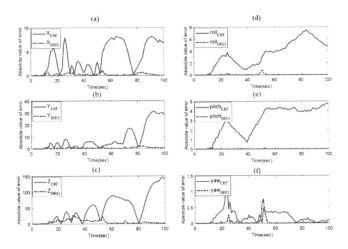

Fig. 7. Absolute value of estimation error under bounded noises.

5   Conclusion

In this paper, a BRO approach is developed for pose estimation in RVS, where the pose estimation problem was converted into a convex optimization problem that can be directly solved by the LMI Toolbox in MATLAB. Notice that the BRO approach does not require any statistical information of measurement and dynamic noises. Finally, a pose estimation simulation was exploited to show the advantages and effectiveness of the proposed methods.

References

1. Janabi-Sharifi, F., Wilson, W.J.: Automatic selection of image features for visual servoing. IEEE Transact. Robot. Autom. **13**(6), 890–903 (1997)
2. Haralick, B.M., Lee, C.N., Ottenberg, K., Nölle, M.: Review and analysis of solutions of the three point perspective pose estimation problem. Int. J. Comput. Vis. **13**(3), 331–356 (1994)
3. Faugeras, O., Faugeras, O.A.: Three-dimensional Computer Vision: A Geometric Viewpoint. MIT press, Cambridge (1993)
4. Lowe, D.G.: Three-dimensional object recognition from single two-dimensional images. Artif. Intell. **31**(3), 355–395 (1987)
5. Lu, C.P., Hager, G.D., Mjolsness, E.: Fast and globally convergent pose estimation from video images. IEEE Transact. Pattern Anal. Mach. Intell. **22**(6), 610–622 (2000)
6. Wilson, W.J., Hulls, C.W., Janabi-Sharifi, F.: Robust Image Processing and Position-Based Visual Servoing, pp. 163–201. IEEE Press, New York (2000)
7. Ficocelli, M., Janabi-Sharifi, F.: Adaptive filtering for pose estimation in visual servoing. In: Proceedings 2001 IEEE/RSJ International Conference on Intelligent Robots and Systems. Expanding the Societal Role of Robotics in the the Next Millennium (Cat. No. 01CH37180), vol. 1, pp. 19–24. IEEE (2001)

8. Janabi-Sharifi, F., Marey, M.: A kalman-filter-based method for pose estimation in visual servoing. IEEE Transact. Rob. **26**(5), 939–947 (2010)
9. Chen, B., Hu, G., Ho, D.W., Zhang, W.A., Yu, L.: Distributed robust fusion estimation with application to state monitoring systems. IEEE Transact. Syst. Man Cybern. Syst. **47**(11), 2994–3005 (2017)
10. Chen, B., Hu, G., Ho, D.W., Yu, L.: A new approach to linear/nonlinear distributed fusion estimation problem. IEEE Transact. Autom. Control **64**(3), 1301–1308 (2019)
11. Chen, B., Hu, G.: Nonlinear state estimation under bounded noises. Automatica **98**, 159–168 (2018)
12. Wilson, W.J., Hulls, C.W., Bell, G.S.: Relative end-effector control using cartesian position based visual servoing. IEEE Transact. Robot. Autom. **12**(5), 684–696 (1996)
13. Boyd, S., El Ghaoui, L., Feron, E., Balakrishnan, V.: Studies in applied mathematics: Vol. 15. Linear matrix inequalities in system and control theory. Philadelphia, PA: SIAM (1994)

The Energy Management
for the Impact/Vibration Control
in the Non-cooperative Space Target Capture

Li-sheng Deng[1], Qun Fang[1(✉)], Cheng-xi Wang[1], Hao Shi[2],
and Ming-Xiao Wang[3]

[1] National Key Laboratory of Aerospace of Flight Dynamics,
Northwestern Polytechnical University, Xi'an 710072, China
qfang@nwpu.edu.cn
[2] Aerospace System Engineering Shanghai, Shanghai 201109, China
[3] North Automatic Control Technology Institute, Taiyuan, Shanxi, China

Abstract. On orbit capture is an essential technical for space debris removal,
refueling or malfunction satellite repairing. While due to the uncertainty of non-
cooperative targets, the impact between the manipulator and the space non-
cooperative target is inevitable. It may alter the position and the attitude of the
spacecraft's base, and cause the on-orbit tasks fail, and the energy of the
impact/vibration is dissipated. In this paper, a novel approach is proposed for
impact/vibration control and energy management in the process of non-
cooperative space target capture. In which, a passive energy harvesting device,
which is installed between the satellite and the capture device, is design to
harvest the energy of the impact/vibration in the space target capture. In the
capture process, the impact/vibration perturbation is reduced by nonlinear
damping and friction of the isolation device, and the energy of which is harvested. The dynamic equation of the energy harvesting system is provided, and a
sliding control approach is developed to stable the impact/vibration perturbation.
Then a novel energy management for the impact perturbation control of the
capture process is proposed, in which the total energy consumption is defined as
the control energy consumption minus the harvested energy. The control time is
regarded as a free variable to optimize and minimized the total energy consumption is the optimization target. This work provides a useful method for the
passive suppression system design and optimization for the perturbation control
of the non-cooperative spacecraft capture.

Keywords: Energy management · Energy harvest ·
Impact/vibration perturbation control · Nonlinear damping ·
System optimization

Q. Fang—The National Nature Science Foundation of China: 11802238.

H. Yu et al. (Eds.): ICIRA 2019, LNAI 11740, pp. 498–512, 2019.
https://doi.org/10.1007/978-3-030-27526-6_44

1   Introduction

As a kind of environmental friendly green renewable energy, vibration energy has a broad application prospect. Suspension vibration of vehicles traveling on uneven roads [1, 2], the movement of a person in motion [3, 4], tidal movement [5, 6] can be recycled as vibration energy. For this reason, a large number of scholars have studied the method of converting vibration energy into electrical energy. Among them, a typical linear method is the electromagnetic generator [7], which can generate electric energy through the vibration of magnet. The typical nonlinear energy collector structure is a bistable or tristable piezoelectric energy collector, which consists of a ferromagnetic cantilever beam and two permanent magnets placed symmetrically near the free end of the cantilever beam [8–10].

In the process of capturing non-cooperative targets in space, shock/vibration will inevitably occur due to the unpredictability of non-cooperative targets in space. Therefore, in the process of space non-cooperative target capture, the recovery and reuse of energy is also a problem that needs to be studied. To solve this problem, in order to improve the efficiency of energy recovery, this paper proposes an energy recovery system with nonlinear scissor structure, through which the vibration energy generated in the process of capture is recovered to reduce the energy consumption of capture. In order to study the energy recovery efficiency of the system in the process of space non-cooperative target capture, we optimized and analyzed the energy recovery efficiency of the system under the fixed-time synovial capture control [11] through the simulated annealing particle swarm optimization algorithm [12] under constraints, so as to minimize the energy consumption in the capture process.

2   Dynamic Modeling of the Energy Harvesting

2.1   Geometric Relationship

For the non-cooperative spacecraft capture, the motion parameters of the space target cannot be obtained accurately. Thus, the perturbation between the manipulator and the space target is inevitable. The impact perturbation caused by the spacecraft capture can affect the stability and security of the base of the spacecraft, which may result the failure of the on-orbit task. In this paper, an X-shaped perturbation isolation structure is applied to reduce the impact/vibration perturbation impact. As is shown in Fig. 1, the perturbation isolation structure is installed between the robot arm and the manipulator, in order to weaken the impact perturbation caused by the space non-cooperative target capture.

The schematic diagram of two-degree X-shaped perturbation isolation structure is shown in Fig. 2, and $F(t)$ is the perturbation force, m_1 is the mass of the target spacecraft, m_2 is the mass of the base. Same as the 6DOFs passive Stewart platform in Ref. [16], there are n layers of the X shape structure in the perturbation suppression system, and y_1, y_2 represent the displacements of m_1 and m_2. The constrained coordinates x, ϕ are employed in the dynamical modeling as shown in Fig. 4, where x is the vertical displacement of the connecting joint A, and θ_2 is the angle of the rotation of the

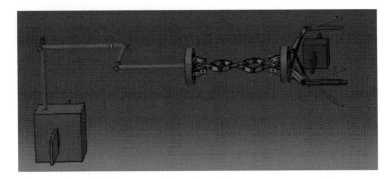

Fig. 1. The non-cooperative spacecraft capture using perturbation suppression system

rod A. $h = (y_2 - y_1)/2n$ is the horizontal displacement of point A, which is used in the constructing the geometric relations, l, θ_1, θ_2 are the length of the rods and the initial assembly angle. In the proposed of the isolation structure, two springs in the vertical direction and horizon direction are installed in order to increase the structure's stiffness for the space application.

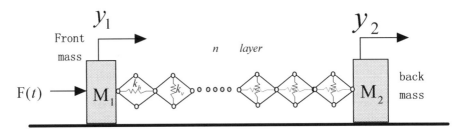

Fig. 2. Two-degree impact perturbation suppression system

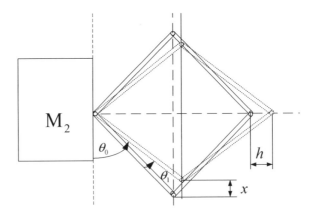

Fig. 3. The geometric relationship of the perturbation suppression system

From Fig. 3, the geometrical relation of variables $l, x, h, \theta_0, \theta_1$ can be obtained as,

$$\begin{cases} h = (y_1 - y_2)/n \\ l \sin \theta_0 - h = l \sin(\theta_0 - \theta_1) \\ l \cos \theta_0 + x = l \cos(\theta_0 - \theta_1) \end{cases} \tag{1}$$

Then it has,

$$\begin{cases} x = \sqrt{l^2 - [l \sin \theta_0 - (y_1 - y_2)/n]^2} - l \cos \theta_0 \\ h = (y_1 - y_2)/n \end{cases} \tag{2}$$

2.2 Dynamic Model of X-Shaped Structure

The Lagrange's equations are used to formulate the nonlinear dynamical system. The kinetic energy of the impact suppression system is,

$$T = \frac{1}{2}m_1 \dot{y}_1^2 + \frac{1}{2}m_2 \dot{y}_2^2 \tag{3}$$

And the potential energy of the whole system can be written as,

$$V = \frac{1}{2}k_1(x_0 + 2x)^2 + \frac{1}{2}k_2\left(y_0 - \frac{y_1 - y_2}{n}\right)^2 + \frac{1}{2}k_b(x_b + y_2)^2 \tag{4}$$

Then the whole energy is

$$L = T - V = \frac{1}{2}m_1 \dot{y}_1^2 + \frac{1}{2}m_2 \dot{y}_2^2 - \frac{1}{2}k_1(x_0 + 2x)^2 - \frac{1}{2}k_2\left(y_0 - \frac{y_1 - y_2}{n}\right)^2 - \frac{1}{2}k_b(x_b + y_2)^2 \tag{5}$$

where x_0, x_b are the elongation of spring k and compression of spring k_b in the initial state respectively. It is assumed that the two springs are untensioned, then $x_0 = 0, x_b = 0$. The virtual work done by the non-conservative force can be written as,

$$\begin{aligned} \delta W &= -2n_x c \dot{\theta}_2 \delta\theta_2 + C_d(y_2 - y_1)(\delta y_1 - \delta y_2) + F(t)\delta y_1 \\ &= Q_1 \delta y_1 + Q_2 \delta y_2 \\ &= \left[-2n_x c \dot{\theta}_2 \frac{\partial \theta_2}{\partial y_1} + C_d(y_2 - y_1) + F(t)\right]\delta y_1 + \left[-2n_x c \dot{\theta}_2 \frac{\partial \theta_2}{\partial y_1} + C_d(\dot{y}_1 - \dot{y}_2)\right]\delta y_2 \end{aligned} \tag{6}$$

The equations of motion of the present system under the external forces can be established by Lagrange's equations:

$$\frac{d}{dt}\left(\frac{\partial L}{\partial \dot{y}_i}\right) - \left(\frac{\partial L}{\partial y_i}\right) = Q_i \tag{7}$$

Then the dynamic equation can be obtained as,

$$\begin{cases} m_1\ddot{y}_1 + 2k_1(x_0 + 2x)\dfrac{l\sin\theta_0 - \frac{y_1-y_2}{2n}}{2n\sqrt{l^2 - (l\sin\theta_0 - \frac{y_1-y_2}{2n})^2}} - \dfrac{k_2}{n}\left(y_0 - \dfrac{y_1-y_2}{n}\right) + 2n_x c\dot{\theta}_2 \dfrac{l\sin\theta_0 - \frac{y_1-y_2}{2n}}{2n\sqrt{l^2 - (l\sin\theta_0 - \frac{y_1-y_2}{2n})^2}} = F(t) \\ m_2\ddot{y}_2 + 2k_1(x_0 + 2x)\dfrac{-(l\sin\theta_0 - \frac{y_1-y_2}{2n})}{2n\sqrt{l^2 - (l\sin\theta_0 - \frac{y_1-y_2}{2n})^2}} + k_b(x_b + y_2) + \dfrac{k_2}{n}\left(y_0 - \dfrac{y_1-y_2}{n}\right) - n_x c\dot{\theta}_2 \dfrac{1}{n\sqrt{l^2 - (l\sin\theta_0 - \frac{y_1-y_2}{2n})^2}} = 0 \end{cases} \tag{8}$$

Then it has,

$$\begin{cases} m_1\ddot{y}_1 + \dfrac{2k_1 l\cos\theta_0(l\sin\theta_0 - \frac{y_1-y_2}{2n})}{n\sqrt{l^2 - (l\sin\theta_0 - \frac{y_1-y_2}{2n})^2}} - \dfrac{2k_1 l\cos\theta_0}{n}\dfrac{(l\sin\theta_0 - \frac{y_1-y_2}{2n})}{\sqrt{l^2 - (l\sin\theta_0 - \frac{y_1-y_2}{2n})^2}} + \left\{\dfrac{n_x c}{2n^2[l^2 - (l\sin\theta_0 - \frac{y_1-y_2}{2n})^2]} + C_d\right\}(\dot{y}_1 - \dot{y}_2) \\ \quad - \dfrac{k_1}{n^2}(y_1 - y_2) + \dfrac{2k_1 l\sin\theta_0}{n} + \dfrac{k_2}{n^2}(y_1 - y_2) = F(t) \\ m_2\ddot{y}_2 - \dfrac{2k_1 l\cos\theta_0(l\sin\theta_0 - \frac{y_1-y_2}{2n})}{n\sqrt{l^2 - (l\sin\theta_0 - \frac{y_1-y_2}{2n})^2}} + \dfrac{2k_1 l\cos\theta_0}{n}\dfrac{(l\sin\theta_0 - \frac{y_1-y_2}{2n})}{\sqrt{l^2 - (l\sin\theta_0 - \frac{y_1-y_2}{2n})^2}} - \left\{\dfrac{n_x c}{2n^2[l^2 - (l\sin\theta_0 - \frac{y_1-y_2}{2n})^2]} + C_d\right\}(\dot{y}_1 - \dot{y}_2) \\ \quad + \dfrac{k_1}{n^2}(y_1 - y_2) - \dfrac{2k_1 l\sin\theta_0}{n} - \dfrac{k_2}{n^2}(y_1 - y_2) = 0 \end{cases} \tag{9}$$

Using Taylor expansion series, this equation can be transformed as,

$$\begin{cases} m_1\ddot{y}_1 + [\lambda_0 + \lambda_1(y_1 - y_2) + \lambda_2(y_1 - y_2)^2 + \lambda_3(y_1 - y_2)^3](\dot{y}_1 - \dot{y}_2) + \eta_1(y_1 - y_2) \\ \quad + \eta_2(y_1 - y_2)^2 + \eta_3(y_1 - y_2)^3 + \eta_4(y_1 - y_2)^4 = F(t) \\ m_2\ddot{y}_2 + [\lambda_0 + \lambda_1(y_1 - y_2) + \lambda_2(y_1 - y_2)^2 + \lambda_3(y_1 - y_2)^3](\dot{y}_1 - \dot{y}_2) - \eta_1(y_1 - y_2) \\ \quad - \eta_2(y_1 - y_2)^2 - \eta_3(y_1 - y_2)^3 - \eta_4(y_1 - y_2)^4 = 0 \end{cases} \tag{10}$$

Where

$$\begin{cases} \lambda_0 = \dfrac{n_x c}{2n^2 l^2}\sec^2\theta_0 + C_d \\ \lambda_1 = -\dfrac{n_x c}{2n^3 l^3}\tan\theta_0\sec^3\theta_0 \\ \lambda_2 = \dfrac{n_x c}{8n^4 l^4}\left(\sec^4\theta_0 + 3\tan^2\theta_0\sec^4\theta_0\right) \\ \lambda_3 = \dfrac{n_x c}{4n^5 l^5}\left(\tan\theta_0\sec^7\theta_0 + \tan^3\theta_0\sec^5\theta_0\right) \end{cases}$$

$$\begin{cases} \eta_1 = \dfrac{k_1}{n^2}\left(\sec^2\theta - 1\right) + \dfrac{k_2}{n^2}(y_2 - y_1) \\ \eta_2 = -\dfrac{3k_1}{4n^3 l}\sec^3\theta_0\tan\theta_0 \\ \eta_3 = \dfrac{k_1}{8n^4 l^2}\sec^6\theta_0(2\cos 2\theta_0 - 3) \\ \eta_4 = -\dfrac{k_1}{32n^5 l^3}\sec^6\theta_0(9\sin\theta_0 - \sin 3\theta_0) \end{cases}$$

The model shows the motion law of the passive bionic structure under the action of damping, which lays a foundation for the energy collection system.

2.3   Dynamic Model of Energy Harvesting

Assume that k_2 is the damping coefficients of the energy harvesting system. The instantaneous power of the energy harvesting can be expressed as the product of damping and the square of motion velocity at corresponding time $k_2\dot{h}^2$. Thus, we can express the instantaneous power of the energy collection system as follows

$$p_t = \frac{k_2(\dot{y}_1 - \dot{y}_2)^2}{n^2} \tag{11}$$

And the total energy recovered by the energy collection system is

$$E_h = \int_0^t |p_t| dt \tag{12}$$

3   Fixed Time Synovial Control Based on ESO

Considering the time-limited mission of satellite capture, we propose a fixed time synovial control method based on ESO. We design sliding mode surface and the reaching law based on fixed time, the system not only has faster convergence speed, but in the case of don't know state of initial value can also estimate the time of the system state to reach the sliding surface and sliding on the sliding mode, it can effectively suppress external interference, and it has strong robustness to the initial value.

3.1   Design of Tracking Differentiator

Given a reference signal, the TD is designed to track the reference signal, and provide the tracked signal and its differential signal for the controller. The form of the TD is given as,

$$\begin{cases} \dot{V}_1 = V_2 \\ \dot{V}_2 = fhan(V_1 - V_0, V_2, r_0, h_0) \end{cases} \tag{13}$$

where V_0 is the given input, and V_1 is the output tracking V_0, and V_2 is the differential signal of V_1. Both of V_1 and V_2 are regarded as parts of control inputs based on the control theory, and $fhan(x_{tr} - x_{ref}, v, r_0, h_0)$ is shown in following,

$$\begin{cases} d = r_0 h_0^2 \\ A_0 = h_0 V_2 \\ y = V_1 - V_0 + A_0 \\ s_y = [sign(y+d) - sign(y-d)]/2 \\ A_1 = d(d+8|y|) \\ A_2 = A_0 + sign(y)(A_1 - d)/2 \\ A = (A_0 + y - A_2)s_y + A_2 \\ s_A = [sign(A+d) - sign(A-d)]/2 \\ fhan(V_1 - V_0, V_2, r_0, h_0) = -r_0[A/d - sign(A)]s_A - r_0 sign(A) \end{cases} \tag{14}$$

3.2   Design of Extended State Observer

Here, the extended-state observer is introduced to deal with the strong non-linearity of the system. The unknown nonlinear term $f(x, \dot{x}, t)$ is continuously differentiate and bonded, and it is treated as an extended state x_3, and it has $f(x, \dot{x}, t) = x_3$, thus the system can be expressed as follows,

$$\begin{cases} \dot{x}_1 = x_2 \\ x_2 = x_3 + b_0 u \\ \dot{x}_3 = \omega(t) \end{cases} \tag{15}$$

Here $\omega(t)$ is the derivative of x_3, and it is bounded in practice. Here define $E_1 = z_1 - y$, then the extended-state observe of the system is represented as follows,

$$\begin{cases} \dot{z}_1 = z_2 - \beta_1 E_1 \\ \dot{z}_2 = z_3 - \beta_2 fal(E_1, \sigma_1, \delta) + b_0 u \\ \dot{z}_3 = -\beta_3 fal(E_1, \sigma_2, \delta) \end{cases} \tag{16}$$

where z_1, z_2, z_3 are observations of x_1, x_2, x_3, and $\beta_1, \beta_2, \beta_3$ are observer gains. The detail of function $fal(e, \sigma, \delta)$ is,

$$fal(e, \sigma, \delta) = \begin{cases} \frac{e}{\delta^{1-\sigma}}, |e| \le \delta \\ sign(e)|e|^\sigma, |e| > \delta \end{cases} \tag{17}$$

For simplicity $fal(E_1, \sigma_1, \delta)$ is denoted as $f_1(E_1)$, and $fal(E_1, \sigma_2, \delta)$ is denoted as $f_2(E_1)$. We get the error system:

$$\begin{cases} \dot{E}_1 = E_2 - \beta_1 E_1 \\ \dot{E}_2 = E_3 - \beta_2 f_1(E_1) + b_0 u \\ \dot{E}_3 = -\omega(t) - \beta_3 f_2(E_1) \end{cases} \tag{18}$$

3.3 Fixed-Time Sliding Controller and Energy Consumption Optimization Theorems and Lemmas

Definition 1 [13]. Consider the following nonlinear systems:

$$\dot{x} = f(x(t)), x(0) = 0, f(0) = 0 \tag{19}$$

Where $x \in R^n$ is the system state variable, and $f(x(t))$ is a nonlinear continuous function. If the system is Lyapunov stable, and existence time function $T(x)$ that for all $t \geq T(x)$, we have $x(t) = 0$, the system is said to be time-limited and stable.

Definition 2 [14]. If the system described in Definition 1 is stable in finite time, and the convergence time of the system has an upper bound, and if the bounds are independent of x, the system is said to be stable at a fixed time.

Lemma 1 [14]. For the nonlinear system described in Definition 1, a continuous differentiable positive definite function $V(x)$ is assumed: $R^n \to R$, $\alpha, \beta, p, g, k \in R^+$, $pk < 1, gk < 1$, and a neighborhood $D \in R^n$ that includes the equilibrium point, let $V(x)$ satisfy: $D^*V(x) \leq - (\alpha V(x)^p + \beta V(x)^g)^k$ or $\dot{V}(x) \leq - (\alpha V(x)^p + \beta V(x)^g)^k$, any function $V(x)$ which from the $D \in R^n$ can be reached $V(x) \equiv 0$ at a fixed time T, that is, the system is stable at a fixed time, and its convergence time is:

$$T \leq \frac{1}{\alpha^k(1 - pk)} + \frac{1}{\beta^k(gk - 1)} \tag{20}$$

Where $D^*V(x)$ is $\dot{V}(x)$.

Lemma 2 [15]. For all $x \in R^n$, $a \in R$, we have,

$$\frac{d|x|^{a+1}}{dt} = (a+1)diag(sig(x)^a)\dot{x}$$

$$\frac{dsig(x)^{a+1}}{dt} = (a+1)diag(|x|^a)\dot{x}$$

Where $sig(x)^a = |x|^a \mathrm{sgn}(x)$.

Fixed-Time Based SM
According to the dynamic model of passive bionic structure, We Choose y_2 as state variable. So, the Fixed-time based SM can be designed as follow:

$$s = \dot{y}_2 + sig\left(sig(\dot{y}_2)^2 + a_1 y_2 + b_1 y_2^3\right)^{0.5} \tag{21}$$

Theorem 1. For the nonlinear system described in Definition 1, such as selecting the fixed time sliding surface above to design the controller, When the system state is stable on the sliding surface, it will converge to $x \equiv 0$ at a fixed time T_x. T_x can be express as,

$$T_x \leq \frac{2\sqrt{2}}{\sqrt{a_1}} + \frac{2\sqrt{2}}{\sqrt{b_1}} \tag{22}$$

Proof. When $s = 0$, the sliding mode surface is transformed into:

$$\dot{y}_2 = -sign(y_2)\left(0.5a_1|y_2| + 0.5b_1|y_2|^3\right)^{0.5} \tag{23}$$

Select the Lyapunov function $V_{y_2} = |y_2|$, take the derivative and substitute it into the above equation to get:

$$\dot{V}_{y_2} = sign(y_2)\dot{y}_2 = -\left(0.5a_1|y_2| + 0.5b_1|y_2|^3\right)^{0.5} = -\left(0.5a_1 V_{y_2} + 0.5b_1 V_{y_2}^3\right)^{0.5} \tag{24}$$

Therefore, we can conclude from Lemma 1 that the time when the system converges to $x = 0$ after reaching the sliding surface should be $T_x \leq \frac{2\sqrt{2}}{\sqrt{a_1}} + \frac{2\sqrt{2}}{\sqrt{b_1}}$.

Fixed Time Controller

The dynamic model of passive bionic structure is written as,

$$\ddot{y}_2 = f(y_1, y_2, \dot{y}_1, \dot{y}_2, d) + u \tag{25}$$

Where $f(y_1, y_2, \dot{y}_1, \dot{y}_2, d)$ is an unknown function, It includes the unpredictability of system modeling and the unpredictability of external disturbances.

Assumption 1. $f(y_1, y_2, \dot{y}_1, \dot{y}_2, d)$ is bounded.

Then the problem of fixed time attitude stability can be described as follows: aiming at the motion model of passive bionic structure described in this paper, a kind of controller is designed to make the system state converge to the equilibrium point in a fixed time, it means $y_2 \to 0, \dot{y}_2 \to 0$, and the fixed time is independent of the initial state of the system.

Therefore, according to the above sliding surface, we construct the fixed time control law as follows:

$$u = -\hat{f}sign(s) - \frac{1}{2}\left[a_1 y_2 + 3b_1 y_2^3\right]sign(s) - sig\left(a_2 s + b_2 sig(s)^3\right)^{0.5} \tag{26}$$

Where $\hat{f}$ is the real-time observation value of the extended state observer for $f(y_1, y_2, \dot{y}_1, \dot{y}_2, d)$, and a_2, b_2 is the designable controller parameters.

Thus, the following fixed time theorem is given:

Theorem 2. For the motion model of the passive bionic structure described in Theorem 1, the fixed time sliding mode and control law described above are designed.

Then, after the system state reaches the sliding surface from any initial value at a fixed time T_s, it will slide to the equilibrium point at a fixed time T_q, that is, the state variable will be stable within $T = T_s + T_q$, and T is independent of the initial value and T can be expressed as follow,

$$T = T_s + T_q \leq \frac{2}{\sqrt{a_2}} + \frac{2}{\sqrt{b_2}} + \frac{2\sqrt{2}}{\sqrt{a_1}} + \frac{2\sqrt{2}}{\sqrt{b_1}} \tag{27}$$

Proof: the arrival stage of the system state and the taxi stage are separately proved.

(1) the arrival stage. Select the Lyapunov function $V_s = |s|$, and take the derivative as follow,

$$D^*|s| = sign(s)\left\{\ddot{y}_2 + 0.5\left|y_2^2 + a_1 y_2 + b_1 y_2^3\right|^{-0.5}\left(2|\dot{y}_2|\ddot{y}_2 + a_2\dot{y}_2 + 3b_1 y_2^2\dot{y}_2\right)\right\}$$

$$= sign(s)\ddot{y}_2 + 0.5sign(s)\left(\left|y_2^2 + a_1 y_2 + b_1 y_2^3\right|^{-0.5}\right)\left[2\ddot{y}_2 + \left(a_1 + 3b_1 y_2^2\right)sign(\dot{y}_2)\right]|\dot{y}_2| \tag{28}$$

By substituting the control law into the kinetic equation, we can obtain:

$$\ddot{y}_2 = -\hat{f}sign(s) + f - \frac{1}{2}\left[a_1 + 3b_1 y_2^2\right]sign(s) - sig\left(a_2 s + b_2 sig(s)^3\right)^{0.5} \tag{29}$$

Substitute the above equation into $\dot{V}_s$, and we get:

$$\dot{V}_s = -(\hat{f} - f) - \frac{1}{2}\left[a_1 + 3b_1 y_2^3\right] - \left(a_2|s| + b_2|s|^3\right)^{0.5} + \left|y_2^2 + a_1 y_2 + b_1 y_2^3\right|^{-0.5}$$

$$\left[-(\hat{f} - f) - \frac{1}{2}\left(a_1 + 3b_1 y_2^3\right) - \left(a_2|s| + b_2|s|^3\right)^{0.5} + \frac{1}{2}\left(a_1 + 3b_1 y_2^3\right)sign(s)sign(\dot{y}_2)\right]|\dot{y}_2| \tag{30}$$

If we can make $\hat{f}$ track the unknown function f in real time, we can get:

$$\dot{V}_s \leq -\left(a_2 V_s + b_2 V_s^3\right)^{0.5} \tag{31}$$

According to Lemma 1, the system state will reach the sliding surface at a fixed time T_s, and T_s can be expressed as follow,

$$T_s \leq \frac{2}{\sqrt{a_2}} + \frac{2}{\sqrt{b_2}} \tag{32}$$

(2) the taxi stage. Select the Lyapunov function $V_{y_2} = |y_2|$.

When the state of the system remains on the sliding surface, $s = 0$ is always maintained, then it can be obtained from the sliding surface at a fixed time:

$$\dot{y}_2 = -sign(y_2)\left(\frac{1}{2}a_1|y_2| + \frac{1}{2}b_1|y_2|^3\right)^{0.5} \tag{33}$$

Take the derivative of V_{y_2}, And substitute the above equation to get:

$$\dot{V}_{y_2} = sign(y_2)\dot{y}_2 = -\left(\frac{1}{2}a_1 V_q + \frac{1}{2}b_1 V_q^3\right)^{0.5} \tag{34}$$

According to Lemma 1, the system state will reach the sliding surface at a fixed time T_q, and T_q can be expressed as follow,

$$T_q \le \frac{2\sqrt{2}}{\sqrt{a_1}} + \frac{2\sqrt{2}}{\sqrt{b_1}} \tag{35}$$

Therefore, we can prove that the fixed time when the system state converges from any initial value to the equilibrium point is,

$$T = T_s + T_q \le \frac{2}{\sqrt{a_2}} + \frac{2}{\sqrt{b_2}} + \frac{2\sqrt{2}}{\sqrt{a_1}} + \frac{2\sqrt{2}}{\sqrt{b_1}} \tag{36}$$

4 Fixed-Time Control Energy Management and Optimization

Under the fixed-time control, the total energy consumption of the energy harvesting system is related to the control time. Therefore, to solve the problem of energy management under fixed-time control in the capture of space non-cooperative targets, we take fixed control time as constraint $g(x)$ and the total energy consumption of the biomimetic passive structure as optimization objective $f(x)$, and use the improved simulated annealing particle swarm optimization algorithm with constraints to carry out intelligent optimization of this problem.

We can describe the optimization problem with inequality constraints as follows:

$$\begin{cases} \min_{x \in s} f(x) \\ g(x) \le 0 \end{cases} \tag{37}$$

Where $x \in s$ is the decision variable, $s \in R^n$ is the decision space, $f(x)$ is the objective function, and $g(x) \le 0$ is the inequality constraint condition.

In solving constrained function optimization problem by evolutionary algorithm, the key of the research is to deal with the infeasible solution and compare the feasible individual with the infeasible individual. Because the evolutionary algorithm itself lacks a clear constraint processing mechanism, it is a kind of unconstrained search technology. When dealing with constrained function optimization problems, a certain constraint processing technology must be combined to get a better result. Therefore, we adopted simulated annealing punishment method and unified all the individuals. In other words, the evaluation function of feasible individuals and infeasible individuals is not designed separately, but the violation degree of penalty function is taken as the mark to evaluate its performance. The specific evaluation function is as follows:

$$eval(x) = f(x) + \frac{1}{2\tau}G^2(x) \tag{38}$$

Where $G(x) = \max(0, g(x))$.

Therefore, the specific process of simulated annealing particle swarm optimization algorithm is shown as follows.

Step 1: Particle population $P(t)$ is initialized. At this stage, a certain number of particles are randomly generated.

Step 2: The individual adaptive value and the constraint violation value were evaluated. Each individual was judged by fitness function $f(x)$ and constraint condition $g(x) \leq 0$.

Step 3: The termination condition is satisfied. Query to see if any individuals meet the termination criteria. If so, the optimization terminates; If not, proceed to the next step.

Step 4: Update individual location and speed. The updating formula of particle swarm optimization's position and speed is as follows:

$$
\begin{aligned}
v_{ij}^{k+1} &= w_k v_{ij}^k + c_1 r_1 \left(p_{bestij}^k - x_{ij}^k \right) + c_2 r_2 \left(g_{bestij}^k - x_{ij}^k \right) \\
x_{ij}^{k+1} &= x_{ij}^k + v_{ij}^{k+1} \\
w_k &= \left(1 - t^2 \right) \times \left(w_{max} - w_{min} \right) + w_{min} \\
t &= \frac{j}{j_{max}}
\end{aligned}
\tag{39}
$$

Where, subscript i represents the ith particle, subscript j represents the evolutionary algebra, c_1, c_2 is the learning factor, r_1, r_2 is the random number between $[0, 1]$, p_{bestij}^k is the contemporary optimal value, g_{bestij}^k is the current global optimal value, and w_k is the weight

Step 5: The individuals were ranked according to the evaluation function $eval(x)$.

Step 6: Determine the annealing coefficient.

Step 7: Determine the current contemporary optimal and global optimal.

Step 8: Keep the global optimal value.

Step 9: Repeat step 3.

By using of the improved simulated annealing particle swarm optimization algorithm with constraints, the total energy consumption in the control process is optimized, which can minimize the total energy consumption of the capture system under the requirement of fixed control time, so as to reduce energy consumption and extend the life of the spacecraft.

5   Optimization, Simulation and Result Analysis

5.1   Optimal Energy Management

In this paper, the parameters of the energy collection system are selected as: $m_1 = 2, m_2 = 100, k_1 = 1500, k_2 = 200, n = 2, \theta_0 = \frac{\pi}{6}, l = 0.2, c = 0.2, C_d = 0.1$, the parameters of the simulated annealing particle swarm optimization algorithm with constraints are selected as: $c_1 = 1.8, c_2 = 1.8, \tau = 0.2$, and the constraint conditions are: $T \leq 15$, the fitness function: $E = E_c - E_h$. The corresponding Simulink simulation module runs on the GCAir simulation platform developed by Global Crown Technology Co. Limited, and the final simulation results are shown in Fig. 4.

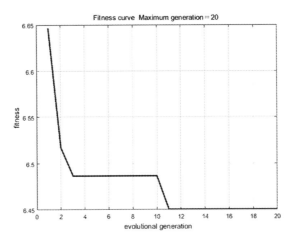

Fig. 4. Optimization results of energy management

Figure 4 shows the optimization results of simulated annealing particle swarm optimization algorithm with constraints. We can see from this that the fitness function has been convergent in the 11th generation with the minimum value of 6.54 s. At this time, the control parameter is $a = 8.8137, b = 11.9804, a_2 = 0.2169, b_2 = 0.7895$ and the convergence time $T = 8.3152 \leq 15$, which indicates that we have obtained an effective optimization result satisfying the constraint conditions.

5.2   Fixed-Time Control

Figure 5 shows the real-time trend of y_2. We can see that in the control process, the maximum deviation is 11.9×10^{-6} m and the stabilization time is $T_1 = 1.565$ s $\leq T = 8.3152$ s. This indicates that the system satisfies the fixed time stability principle.

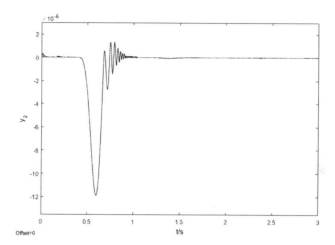

Fig. 5. The control result diagram of y_2

We can know from the simulation results, the energy management method of the fixed-time control designed to solve non-cooperative space target capture tasks, can make the spacecraft quickly converge to the expected value with high accuracy, and through the energy harvesting system and the intelligent algorithm, we can design the control parameters which can meet control time, make the minimum total energy consumption in the process of capture.

6   Conclusions

In this paper, the stability control problem in the capture process of space non-cooperative targets is studied. In order to deal with the shock/vibration disturbance in the capture process, we design an adaptive controller by using the fixed-time sliding mode method to make the system stable in a fixed time. In order to reduce the energy consumption in the control process, we design an energy recovery device based on the bionic passive structure, which can recover energy and extend the life of spacecraft. Finally, the control system is optimized by simulated annealing particle swarm optimization with constraints, and the appropriate controller parameters are selected to minimize the total energy consumption under the control time constraint. Simulation results show that this method can effectively make the spacecraft quickly converge to the expected value with high precision, and through the energy harvesting system and intelligent algorithm, design the control parameters to meet the control time, and minimize the total energy consumption in the capture process.

References

1. Li, Z., et al.: Electromagnetic energy-harvesting shock absorbers: design, modeling, and road tests. IEEE Trans. Veh. Technol. **62**(3), 1065–1074 (2013)
2. Wei, C., Taghavifar, H.: A novel approach to energy harvesting from vehicle suspension system: half-vehicle model. Energy **134**, 279–288 (2017)
3. Berdy, D.F., Valentino, D.J., Peroulis, D.: Kinetic energy harvesting from human walking and running using a magnetic levitation energy harvester. Sens. Actuators A **222**, 262–271 (2015)
4. Cao, J., et al.: Nonlinear time-varying potential bistable energy harvesting from human motion. Appl. Phys. Lett. **107**(14), 143904 (2015)
5. Wu, N., Wang, Q., Xie, X.: Ocean wave energy harvesting with a piezoelectric coupled buoy structure. Appl. Ocean Res. **50**, 110–118 (2015)
6. Xie, X.D., Wang, Q., Wu, N.: Energy harvesting from transverse ocean waves by a piezoelectric plate. Int. J. Eng. Sci. **81**, 41–48 (2014)
7. Joon Kim, K., et al.: Energy scavenging for energy efficiency in networks and applications. Bell Labs. Tech. J. **15**(2), 7–29 (2010)
8. Erturk, A., Inman, D.J.: Broadband piezoelectric power generation on high-energy orbits of the bistable Duffing oscillator with electromechanical coupling. J. Sound Vib. **330**(10), 2339–2353 (2011)
9. Erturk, A., Hoffmann, J., Inman, D.J.: A piezomagnetoelastic structure for broadband vibration energy harvesting. Appl. Phys. Lett. **94**(25), 254102 (2009)
10. Cao, J., et al.: Nonlinear dynamic characteristics of variable inclination magnetically coupled piezoelectric energy harvesters. J. Vibrat. Acoust. **137**(2), 021015 (2015)
11. Jiang, B., Chen, Z., Hu, Q., et al.: Fixed time control method for spacecraft attitude in the case of disturbance (2014). (in Chinese)
12. Si, C.: Application of an improved simulated annealing particle swarm optimization algorithm in constrained function optimization. Intelligent automation professional committee of Chinese association of automation. In: Proceedings of 2011 Chinese Academic Conference on Intelligent Automation, vol. 1 (2011). (in Chinese)
13. Bhat, S., Bernstein, D.: Finite-time stability of continuous autonomous systems. SIAM J. Control Optim. **38**(3), 751–766 (2000)
14. Polyakov, A.: Nonlinear feedback design for fixed-time stabilization of linear control systems. IEEE Trans. Autom. Control **57**(8), 2106–2110 (2012)
15. Yu, S., Yu, X., Shirinzadeh, B., Man, Z.: Continuous finite-time control for robotic manipulators with terminal sliding mode. Automatica **41**(11), 1957–1964 (2005)
16. Wu, Z., Jing, X., Sun, B., et al.: A 6DOF passive vibration isolator using X-shape supporting structures. J. Sound Vib. **380**, 90–111 (2016). S0022460X16302255

Force Analysis and Experiment
of Variable Stiffness Soft Actuator
Based on Particle Jamming

Fengyou Jiang[1,2] , Fengyu Xu[1,2(✉)] , Hongliang Yu[1,2] ,
Yurong Song[1,2] , and Xudong Cao[1,2]

[1] College of Automation & College of Artificial Intelligence, Nanjing University
of Posts and Telecommunications, Nanjing 210023, China
xufengyu598@163.com
[2] Jiangsu Engineering Laboratory for IOT Intelligent Robots (IOTRobot),
Nanjing 210023, China

Abstract. At present, the jamming mechanism has some problems such as particles rearrangement and elastoplastic deformation. Therefore, this paper proposes a variable stiffness soft actuator based on the combination of large and small particles. According to the Hertz contact model, we analyzed the interaction force between the membrane and jamming particles. Then We regard the filling particles as rigid body. Based on this assumption and PASCAL's law application, we establish the mechanical model of the mechanism. The stiffness is analyzed by using the locking torque and we put derived result to simulated. Through analysis and experiment, the soft actuator made in this paper has been improved in the aspects of variable stiffness, repetitive positioning accuracy and stability.

Keywords: Particle jamming · Variable stiffness · Soft actuator

1 Introduction

In recent years, the field of soft robot has become a hotspot of international research. Not only will the variable stiffness robot have the stability, strength, and manipulation performance of a rigid system but also the maneuver ability and access benefits of a soft system [1]. Although the soft robot has obvious advantages, its stiffness is not easy to control and its structure is not stable.

Compared with small animals, large animals usually have a rigid skeleton supporting their own weight [2]. Most soft robots are inspired by the soft structure of small molluscs whose stiffness is difficult to control. Among the suitable strategies for changing the stiffness of a soft robot, the jamming-based systems are becoming a new set of possibilities [3, 4]. Soft robot structure such as the caterpillar soft robot developed by Barry laboratory of Tufts university; A typical example of muscle-hydrostatic skeleton [5, 6] is the bionic octopus (Europe); Therefore, it is of great academic significance and application value to design a flexible robot with variable stiffness [7].

© Springer Nature Switzerland AG 2019
H. Yu et al. (Eds.): ICIRA 2019, LNAI 11740, pp. 513–525, 2019.
https://doi.org/10.1007/978-3-030-27526-6_45

There are two kinds of flexible robot based on jamming principle: One is to add particles in the film which can grasp the object, but problems still exist in controllability and control accuracy of variable stiffness. Professor Brown used the jamming principle to design a universal gripper [8] and VERSABALL is one of the few commercial universal grippers [9] which are based on the principle of jamming; The other is to add thin film inside the film. Although this soft robot is not easy to be heterotopic, its deformation control has some problems. In addition, the jamming mechanism can be combined with a special mechanical structure to form a variable stiffness mechanism. The jamming mechanism can be integrated with the rope actuator. Kim integrated the NiTi rope actuator technology with the layered jamming technology to designed the snake-like robot [10] and a robot integrated with minimally invasive surgery (MIS) was obtained. Cheng [11] combined the rope actuator with the particle jamming principle to design a modular mechanical arm and realized the control of local stiffness. Li designed a soft gripper, which consists of a jamming mechanism, a strain limiting leather cover and a gas elastic actuator [12]. Wei integrated a number of spherical joints in series with particle jamming mechanism and proposed a spherical joint mechanical arm with adjustable stiffness [13], whose end position and variable stiffness are well controllable. The stiffness of the integrated arm is 13 times higher than that of the mechanical arm without particle jamming.

Most of the jamming mechanisms mentioned above are filled with small particle materials. However, the fact that small particles are prone to deformation and rearrangement of particles. The mechanism may lead to different motion patterns and reduce the repetitive positioning accuracy of the mechanism or even cause positioning errors of the mechanism.

Based on the above analysis, this paper proposes a jamming mechanism based on the size of particles and combined with the rhomboid mechanism to establish the corresponding mathematical model for further analysis of the jamming mechanism. After the static model's end of the jamming mechanism is established, the variable stiffness principle is analyzed and simulated that the stiffness of the jamming mechanism and the stability of repetitive positioning accuracy can be studied by experiment.

2 Structure of the Variable Stiffness Soft Actuator

The soft actuator proposed in this paper includes the following parts: film, filling particle, large ball particle, elastic rope and trachea. The model diagram of the soft actuator is shown in Fig. 1(a) below.

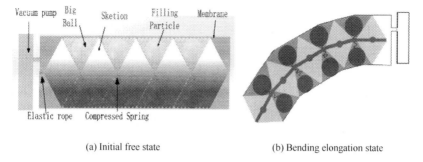

(a) Initial free state   (b) Bending elongation state

Fig. 1. Large and small particles coupled with jamming mechanism profile

The working principle of the jamming mechanism: Under the applied vacuum pressure, the small particles in the membrane change from fluid state to solid state and the actuator stiffness is adjusted by controlling the vacuum degree in the membrane. As shown in Fig. 1(b), when the mechanism moves, the large ball particles are always embedded in the joint skeleton and will not randomly scatter. The jamming mechanism not only limits particle recombination but also realizes variable stiffness and overcomes the disadvantage that particle recombination may lead to uncertain position or even wrong positioning in the process of movement of small particle jamming mechanism.

3   Analysis of Variable Stiffness Characteristics

3.1   Analysis of Locking Force

We analyzed the influence of jamming particles on the stiffness of the proposed mechanism. Under the action of vacuum pressure, it is assumed that all particles in the membrane are rigid and restricted to a whole. Then all particles and films in the membrane are regarded as a particle block. The actual load distribution may be seen in Figs. 2 and 3. According to the static equilibrium equation of particles, the locking force can be described as:

$$F_L = 2f_U + f_p + f_L \qquad (1)$$

f_L is the friction force of particles in the contact area A_1 with Fig. 2. f_P is the static force of the particle block on the locking area Fig. 2. f_U is the horizontal friction between the lower particles and the larger ball. The static force of the granular layer on the locking region f_P which can be estimated by the fluid pressure model [14]. According to Fig. 4 and PASCAL's law, we can get:

$$P_1 = P_2 = P_3 = P_4 = \frac{F_{ext}}{A_2} \qquad (2)$$

Therefore, the force F_{A1} exerted on the region A_1 (Fig. 4):

$$F_{A1} = \frac{F_{ext}}{A_2} \cdot A_1 \tag{3}$$

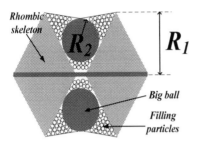

Fig. 2. End module with parameters

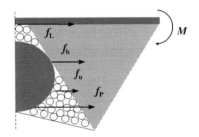

Fig. 3. Load analysis of the lower end module

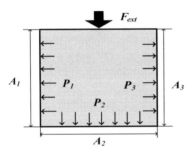

Fig. 4. Pressurized fluid model

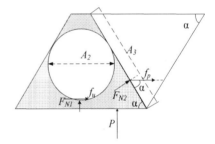

Fig. 5. Particle jamming model

The small particles are equivalent to fluid, forming a static fluid model as shown in Fig. 5. The static force fp of the particle block acting on the horizontal direction of the locking zone A_3 is:

$$f_P = F_{N2} \sin \alpha = P'A_3 \sin \alpha = \pi R_1^2 P' \sin \alpha \tag{4}$$

F_{N2} is the positive pressure of granular blocks on the rhomboid skeleton, R_1 is the radius of the thin film tube, α is the top Angle of the diamond skeleton (Fig. 5), P' is the equivalent pressure exerted by the particle block on the diamond skeleton and the large ball. Then the friction force f_L of the particle block in the contact area A_1 with the rhomboid skeleton is:

$$F_L = \pi P' \left(R_1^2 \sin \alpha + 2R_2^2 \mu_2 + R_1^2 \mu_1 \right) \tag{5}$$

Where f_L is the friction coefficient between the particles and the skeleton, A_1 is the equivalent area of the contact area between the particle block and the rhomboid skeleton. The horizontal friction between the large ball and the particle block is f_U:

$$f_U = \mu_2 F_{N1} = \mu_2 P' A_2 = \pi R_2^2 P' \mu_2 \tag{6}$$

F_{N1} is the positive pressure of the particle block on the large ball, R_2 is the large ball radius, μ_2 is the friction coefficient between the particle and the large ball and A_2 is the equivalent area of the contact between the particle block and the large ball. Formula (4), (5) and (6) are substituted into formula (1), then the locking force F_L is:

$$\begin{aligned} F_L &= \pi R_1^2 P' \sin \alpha + 2\pi R_2^2 P' \mu_2 + \pi R_1^2 P' \mu_1 \\ &= \pi P' \left(R_1^2 \sin \alpha + 2R_2^2 \mu_2 + R_1^2 \mu_1 \right) \end{aligned} \tag{7}$$

Where R_1 is the radius of the thin film tube, R_2 is the radius of the big ball, μ_1 is The friction coefficient between the particles and the skeleton, μ_2 is Coefficient of friction between a particle and a large ball, P' is equivalent pressure in the thin-film tube.

3.2 Hertz Contact Model

According to the Hertz contact theory and the Hertz contact model of the two spheres as shown in Fig. 6, the relative deformation displacement and stress at the center of the two spheres after contact are as follows:

$$\delta^3 = \frac{9}{16} \cdot \frac{R_a + R_b}{R_a R_b} \left(\frac{1 - v_a^2}{E_a} + \frac{1 - v_b^2}{E_b} \right)^2 \cdot P \tag{8}$$

$$P''^3 = \frac{6}{\pi^3} \left(\frac{R_a + R_b}{R_a R_b} \right)^2 \left(\frac{1 - v_b^2}{E_b} + \frac{1 - v_a^2}{E_a} \right)^{-2} \cdot P \tag{9}$$

R_a is ball radius a, R_b is ball radius b, V_a is ball poisson's ratio a, V_b is ball poisson's ratio b, E_a is ball young's modulus a, E_b is ball young's modulus b. In the natural state, the radius of small particles R_3 is much smaller than the radius of thin film tube R_1. So in formula (8) and (9), the parameters of thin film tube and small particles are substituted into the formula which is related to (8) and (9).

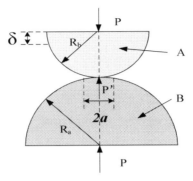

Fig. 6. The Hertz model of two spheres contact

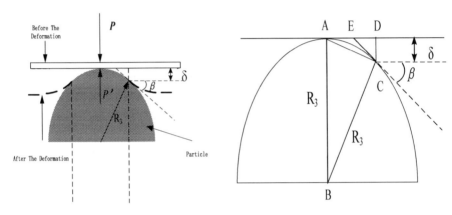

Fig. 7. Particle Hertz contact model with planar

Fig. 8. Particle - plane contact Hertz simplified model

In Fig. 6 of the Hertz simplified model of particle contact with plane, the following relation can be obtained from the properties of the isosceles $\angle ABC$, $\angle AEC$ and right $\angle ADC$ and $\angle EDC$ (Figs. 7 and 8):

$$AC = \sqrt{2R_3^2 - 2R_3^2 \cos \angle ABC} \tag{12}$$

$$AC = \frac{\delta}{\sin \angle DAC} \tag{13}$$

$$\angle ABC = 2\angle DAC = \angle \beta \tag{14}$$

Combined with the formula (12), (13), (14), the deformation Angle of the film after contact deformation with the pellet particles is:

$$\cos \beta = \frac{2R_3 - \sqrt{2}\delta}{2R_3} = 1 - \left[\frac{9}{32\sqrt{2}R_3^4} \left(\frac{1-\mu_1^2}{E_1} + \frac{1-\mu_2^2}{E_2} \right)^2 \cdot P \right]^{\frac{1}{3}} \quad (15)$$

Then the locking force F_L at the end of the mechanism is:

$$F_L = \left[\frac{6}{\pi^3 R_3^2} \left(\frac{1-\nu_1^2}{E_1} + \frac{1-\nu_2^2}{E_2} \right)^{-2} \right]^{\frac{1}{3}} \left(R_1^2 \mu_1 + R_1^2 \sin \alpha + 2R_2^2 \mu_2 \right) P^{\frac{1}{3}} \quad (16)$$

The radius of the thin-film tube is d, so the locking torque M_L of the mechanism is:

$$M_L = F_L \cdot d = \left[\frac{6}{\pi^3 R_3^2} \left(\frac{1-\nu_1^2}{E_1} + \frac{1-\nu_2^2}{E_2} \right)^{-2} \right]^{\frac{1}{3}} \left(R_1^2 \mu_1 + R_1^2 \sin \alpha + 2R_2^2 \mu_2 \right) P^{\frac{1}{3}} d \quad (17)$$

Where D is the radius of the thin film tube. Take the ultimate vacuum degree $Pm = 101$ kPa and substitute the value into formula (17) to obtain the maximum locking torque $M_{LM} = 304.5$ N mm. Based on the classical linear elasticity theory, Gent proposed the relation between young's modulus value E and shore's hardness value S [15] as:

$$E = \frac{0.0981(56 + 7.62336S)}{0.137505(254 - 2.54S)} \quad (18)$$

Where E is young's modulus in MPa and S is indicated by ASTM D2240 standard hardness tester. Based on Eqs. (17) and (18), it can be concluded that the relationship between the hardness of small particles and the locking torque is:

$$M_L = \left[\frac{6}{\pi^3} \left(\frac{0.137505(254 - 2.54S_1)(1 - \nu_1^2)}{0.0981(56 + 7.62336S_1)} + \frac{1-\nu_2^2}{E_2} \right)^{-2} \right]^{\frac{1}{3}} \cdot \left(R_1^2 \mu_1 + R_1^2 \sin \alpha + 2R_2^2 \mu_2 \right) P^{\frac{1}{3}} d$$

$$(19)$$

4   Simulation

In formula (15), the parameter of the mechanism: Diamond skeleton radius $R_1 = 14$ mm, Large ball particle radius $R_2 = 6.5$ mm, filling Particle radius $R_3 = 3$ mm. The relationship between the film deformation Angle and the vacuum pressure P is obtained as shown in Fig. 9. As can be seen from the figure, the larger the vacuum pressure P is, the larger the deformation Angle of the film will be. At the same time, as the pressure increases gradually, the increment of the deformation Angle of the thin film decreases with the same pressure increment.

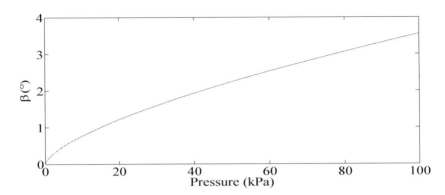

Fig. 9 The deformation angle of the film at the different vacuum

According to formula (16), set the parameter: $R_1 = 14$ mm, $R_2 = 6.5$ mm, $R_3 = 3$ mm, $P = 80$ kPa, Thin-film tube radius d = 16 mm. The relationship between moment M and vacuum pressure P is obtained as shown in Fig. 10. As can be seen from the figure, the higher the vacuum pressure P is, the higher the torque M is. Therefore, the stiffness of the mechanism can be controlled by adjusting the vacuum pressure.

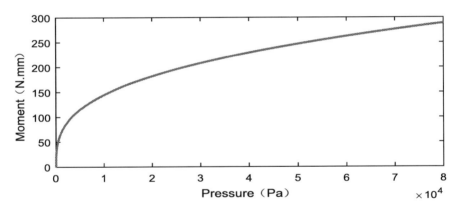

Fig. 10. The corresponding relationship between terminal moment M and vacuum pressure P

In formula (17), the parameter of the mechanism: $R_1 = 14$ mm, $R_2 = 6.5$ mm, $P = 80$ kPa, d = 16 mm and R_3 set the range between 2 mm and 6 mm. The relationship between the external torque M and the radius of small particles is obtained as shown in Fig. 11. It can be seen from the figure that the larger the radius of small particles R_3 is, the smaller the end torque M is. With the decrease of particle size, the reduction of end torque becomes smaller and smaller.

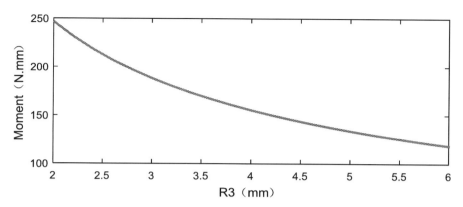

Fig. 11. The relationship between the terminal moment M and the radius R_3 of small particles

5 Experiment Platform and Experiment

5.1 Experimental Platform and Environment

The actual figure of the stiffness test platform is shown in Fig. 12. One end of the test prototype is fixed on the support by a double clamping device, and the other end is suspended vertically. The height and angle of the prototype can be adjusted by the clamping device. The measuring end of the digital pressure sensor is fixed on the sliding block of the linear guide which is actuated by a stepping motor. During the horizontal movement test, the end of the mechanism is contacted with the sensor. The moving distance of the sensor is controlled by the stepping motor, the range is 0–20 mm and each movement is 2 mm. For each movement of the sensor, the reading on the digital display panel of the sensor is recorded, namely the terminal force F_C.

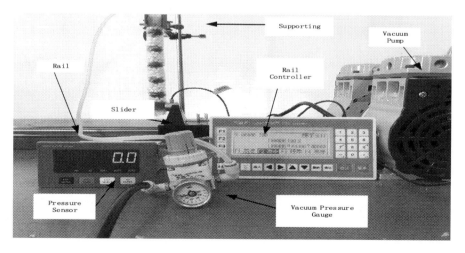

Fig. 12. Performance test platform of variable stiffness mechanism

5.2   Analysis of the Factors Affecting the Stiffness of the Mechanism

From the perspective of particle size, the filling mechanism with particle radius of 4 mm, 3 mm and 2 mm was tested at 80 kPa and 0 kPa, as shown in Fig. 13.

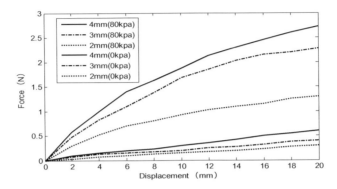

Fig. 13. Relationship between end force and displacement of different particle size mechanism

Linear fitting was performed on the experimental data to obtain the stiffness of the particles' different sizes, as shown in Table 1. The stiffness ratio of the mechanism with a filling particle radius of 2 mm under pressure of 80 kPa and 0 kPa is 5.10; The stiffness ratio of a mechanism with a radius of 3 mm under pressure of 80 kPa and 0 kPa is 6.57; The stiffness ratio of a mechanism with a radius of 4 mm under pressure of 80 kPa and 0 kPa is 4.53. Therefore, the change rate of the stiffness of the mechanism with a radius of 3 mm is the highest which provides an important reference for the optimal design of the mechanism.

Table 1. Stiffness performance of mechanism with different particle size

Particle radius	Stiffness at 80 kPa (N/mm)	Stiffness at 0 kPa (N/mm)	Ratio of stiffness change
2 mm	0.07605	0.0149	5.10
3 mm	0.1355	0.0206	6.57
4 mm	0.1581	0.0349	4.53

In Fig. 14, the theoretical analysis and simulation values's stiffness of variable stiffness structure are compared with the actual measured values based on Fig. 10 in the third section of this paper. We found that when the pressure is 60 kPa, the structure of the mechanism changes greatly; When the vacuum pressure is greater than 60 kPa, the increase of vacuum pressure can no longer make the mechanism hard. Therefore, the theoretical model cannot properly describe the behavior of variable stiffness.

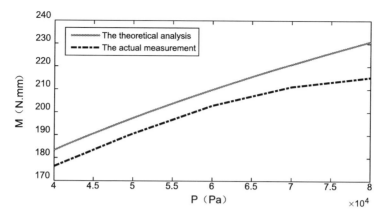

Fig. 14. Theoretical analysis of the relationship between end torque and vacuum pressure and comparison of actual measurement results

5.3 Stiffness Repeatability Accuracy and Stability Test Experiments

The platform and method for repeated positioning accuracy stability test are the same as the platform and method for stiffness test. In the experiment, the size particle mechanism and the small particle mechanism were compared and tested respectively. The sensor actuator by the stepping motor moves a fixed distance of 20 mm each time. After recording the force sensor data, the initial position is restored and each mechanism is tested for 100 times. The stability and accuracy of the mechanism are measured by the standard deviation, coefficient of variation and maximum absolute deviation calculated from 100 sets of data.

The standard deviation of the data is used to describe the deviation (discrete) degree between the data and the average value, that is, the overall stability of the data. Coefficient of variation is a normalized measure used to evaluate the dispersion degree's multiple sets of data in the probability distribution. The maximum absolute deviation is the maximum value of the absolute value of the difference between the measured value and the average value of the data, which is used to describe the repeated accuracy under repeated tests.

As shown in Table 2, the stiffness, stability and repeated positioning accuracy of the mechanism in this paper have been improved.

Table 2. Comparison of stiffness test data of mechanism with variable stiffness

Serial number	The standard deviation (N/mm)	Coefficient of variation	Maximum absolute deviation (N/mm)
Mechanism of this paper	0.0021	1.5427%	0.00625
Small particle mechanism	0.0029	2.1837%	0.0078
Percentage reduction	27.59%	29.3550%	19.871795%

6 Conclusion

It can be obtained from the experimental data that the standard deviation and coefficient of variation of the experimental stiffness data of the mechanism with variable stiffness of large particles proposed in this paper are 0.0021 N/mm and 1.5427% respectively under the same experimental conditions; the standard deviation and coefficient of variation of the experimental stiffness data of the mechanism with variable stiffness of small particles proposed in this paper are 0.0029 N/mm and 2.1837% respectively. In the stiffness test experiment, compared with the variable stiffness mechanism based on small particles, the variable stiffness structure based on large particles in this paper reduced the standard deviation of experimental data by 27.59%, reduced the coefficient of variation by 29.3550% and improved the stability. The maximum absolute deviation (repeat precision) of the stiffness of the mechanism in this paper is 0.00625 N/mm, which is 19.871795% lower than the 0.0078 N/mm of the small-particle mechanism and the repeat precision is improved. The data show that the performance of the variable stiffness mechanism based on large particles is better than that of the variable stiffness mechanism based on small particles in terms of stiffness repetition accuracy and stability. In addition, it is found from the data that when the radius of the filling particles is 3 mm, the obtained stiffness change rate is the highest.

The next step is to combine the active pneu-actuator structure with the passive jamming mechanism to study the dynamic modeling and control methods of variable stiffness soft actuator.

References

1. Cianchetti, M., et al.: Soft robotics technologies to address shortcomings in today's minimally invasive surgery: the stiff-flop approach. Soft Robotics. https://doi.org/10.1089/soro.2014.0001
2. Rus, D., Tolley, M.T.: Design, fabrication and control of soft robots. Nature **521**(7553), 467–475 (2016)
3. Ilievski, F., Mazzeo, A.D., Shepherd, R.E., Chen, X., Whitesides, G.M.: Soft robotics for chemists. Angew Chem. Int. Ed. Engl. **50**, 1890–1895 (2011)
4. Kim, S., Laschi, C., Trimmer, B.: Soft robotics: a bioinspired evolution in robotic. Trends Biotechnol. **31**, 287–294 (2013)
5. Cao, Y., Shang, J., Liang, K.: A review of soft robot research. J. Mech. Eng. **48**(3), 25–33 (2012)
6. Zhang, R., Wang, H., Chen, W.: The shape control of the fish-like soft robots. Robotics **38** (6), 754–759 (2016)
7. Rus, D., Tolley, M.T.: Design, fabrication and control of soft robots. Nature **521**(7553), 467–475 (2015)
8. Amend Jr., J.R., Brown, E., Rodenberg, N., et al.: A positive pressure universal gripper based on the jamming of granular material, IEEE Trans. Robotics **28**(2), 341–350 (2012)
9. Amend, J., Cheng, N., Fakhouri, S., et al.: Soft robotics commercialization: Jamming grippers from research to product. Soft Robot. **3**(4), 213–222 (2016)

10. Kim, Y.J., Cheng, S., Kim, S., et al.: A novel layer jamming mechanism with tunable stiffness capability for minimally invasive surgery. IEEE Trans. Robot. **29**(4), 1031–1042 (2013)
11. Cheng, N.G., Lobovsky, M.B., Keating, S.J., et al.: Design and analysis of a robust, low-cost, highly articulated manipulator enabled by jamming of granular media. In: IEEE International Conference on Robotics and Automation, pp. 4328–4333 (2012)
12. Li, Y., Chen, Y., Yang, Y., et al.: Passive particle jamming and its stiffening of soft robotic grippers. IEEE Trans. Robot. **33**(2), 446–455 (2017)
13. Wei, Y., Chen, Y., Yang, Y., Li, Y.: A soft robotic spine with tunable stiffness based on integrated ball joint and particle jamming. Mechatronics **33**, 84–92 (2016)
14. Hongliang, Y., Fengyu, X., Yudong, Y., et al.: Design and analysis of variable stiffness soft manipulator based on jamming structure. In: IEEE International Conference on Robotics and Biomimetics, pp. 657–662 (2017). (EI: 2018290556084)
15. Gent, A.N.: On the relation between indentation hardness and Young's modulus. Rubber Chem. Technol. **31**(4), 896–906 (2008)

Close-Range Angles-Only Relative Navigation of Multi-agent Cluster for On-Orbit Servicing Mission

Baichun Gong[1(✉)], Sha Wang[1], Shuang Li[1], and Lili Zheng[2]

[1] Nanjing University of Aeronautics and Astronautics, Nanjing 210016, China
baichun.gong@nuaa.edu.cn
[2] Beijing Institute of Aerospace System Engineering, Beijing 100076, China

Abstract. This research studies the close-range angles-only relative navigation problem for multi-agent cluster for on-orbit servicing mission when the camera offset from the vehicle center-of-mass allows for range observability. Emphasis is placed on developing navigation algorithm based on consensus Unscented Kalman Filter within the context of the second-order nonlinear dynamics and evaluate the performance of the navigation algorithm in two-body dynamics environment. Further, the geometric topology information of multi-agent is utilized to construct the consensus constraint.

Keywords: On-orbit servicing · Spacecraft cluster · Relative navigation · Consensus Kalman Filter

1 Introduction

Angles-only relative navigation using line-of-sight (LOS) observations to the space object, i.e. pairs of azimuth and elevation angles, is well known. It is clear that angles only relative navigation is simple, robust, and well proven in many applications [1]. Unfortunately, Woffinden elegantly shows that angles-only relative navigation problem during space proximity operations suffers from a range observability problem [2].

Many works have been done to overcome the range observability problem. Woffinden and Geller [3] proposed the orbital maneuver method to improve observability. Grzymisch and Ficher [4] analyzed the observability from a novel perspective and provided observable/unobservable maneuver sets. Jagat and Sinclair [5] researched on this problem in the view of relative motion control based on LQG algorithm. Gaias et al. [6] investigated on this topic from the view point of the relative orbit elements.

The objectives of this paper are to study the close-range angles-only relative navigation problem for multi-agent cluster for on-orbit servicing mission when the camera offset from the vehicle center-of-mass allows for range observability, establish the consensus constraint model based on geometric topology information, develop relative navigation filtering algorithm based on an Consensus Unscented Kalman Filter, validate and evaluate the performance of the proposed algorithm in a standard non-linear two-body environment. Although contributions due to oblateness of earth,

© Springer Nature Switzerland AG 2019
H. Yu et al. (Eds.): ICIRA 2019, LNAI 11740, pp. 526–532, 2019.
https://doi.org/10.1007/978-3-030-27526-6_46

atmospheric drag, solar radiation pressure are important, these effects are specific to spacecraft orbit selection, geometry, mass which are beyond the scope of this paper.

The relative motion equations are reviewed and measurement model are set up in Sect. 2. The relative Orbit Estimation algorithm included consensus constraint is developed in Sect. 3. The nonlinear simulation and results are presented in Sect. 4. Conclusions are presented in Sect. 5.

2 Relative Motion Dynamics and Measurement Model

2.1 Relative Motion Dynamics

Under the assumption of the two body problem and the distance between the chaser and target is small compared to the distance of the target to the center of the Earth, the relative motion dynamics during coasting flight that is applicable to eccentric orbit can be given in the chaser-orbital Local Vertical Local Horizontal (LVLH) frame as the following [7]

$$
\begin{aligned}
\ddot{x} - 2\omega\dot{z} - \omega^2 x - \dot{\omega}z + \frac{\mu}{R_C^3}x &= f_x \\
\ddot{y} + \frac{\mu}{R_C^3}y &= f_y \\
\ddot{z} + 2\omega\dot{x} - \omega^2 z + \dot{\omega}x - \frac{2\mu}{R_C^3}z &= f_z
\end{aligned}
\tag{1}
$$

where z-axis points to the nadir direction, y-axis is normal to the orbital plane and opposite the angular momentum vector, while x-axis completes the right-hand orthogonal set that points to the along-track direction, ω is the angular rate of the chaser orbit. Moreover, μ is the gravitational parameter and R_C is the radius of the chaser orbit. In the rest of this manuscript, it is assumed that the vectors without a superscript are coordinatized in LVLH frame.

Then, the state to be estimated can be expressed by the relative position and velocity between the chaser and targets' center-of-mass in LVLH coordinates, i.e. $X = [x, y, z, \dot{x}, \dot{y}, \dot{z}]^T$. Thus, the relative motion dynamics shown in Eq. (1) can be re-organized into vector form as follows

$$
\dot{X} = AX + BU
\tag{2}
$$

Where

$$
A = \begin{bmatrix}
 & 0_{3\times3} & & & I_{3\times3} & \\
\omega^2 - \frac{\mu}{R_C^3} & 0 & \dot{\omega} & 0 & 0 & 2\omega \\
0 & -\frac{\mu}{R_C^3} & 0 & 0 & 0 & 0 \\
-\dot{\omega} & 0 & \omega^2 + \frac{2\mu}{R_C^3} & -2\omega & 0 & 0
\end{bmatrix}
\tag{3}
$$

$$
B = [0_{3\times3}, \quad I_{3\times3}], \quad U = [f_x, \quad f_y, \quad f_z]^T
\tag{4}
$$

2.2   Measurement Model

Figure 1 illustrates the observation geometry associated with the camera offset angles-only navigation problem. It is assumed that the origin of the chaser body-fixed reference frame is co-located with the chaser center-of-mass. Without loss of generality it is also assumed that a camera is mounted on the body at a distance d from the chaser center-of mass. The camera measurement frame is assumed to be aligned with the focal-plane of the camera, and its orientation with respect to the chaser body frame is supposed to be known and constant.

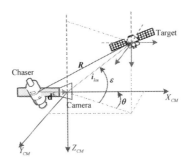

Fig. 1. Measurement frame and geometry.

Then, the measurement in the chaser LVLH frame, i.e. elevation ε' and azimuth θ', can be easily transited to the counterpart in target LVLH frame, ε and θ [8]. In the rest of the manuscript, $\varepsilon \in [-\pi/2, \pi/2]$ and $\theta \in [0, 2\pi]$ will be used directly. Secondly, suppose the camera measurement frame is coincident with the chaser's LVLH frame. This assumption could be realized by attitude control which has been demonstrated in PRISMA [9]. This assumption is not necessary for the navigation problem, but simplifies the development of the observability derivation.

Then, approximate observation equations in the target LVLH frame can be obtained as a function of the camera offset location dc = $[d_x; d_y; d_z]$

$$\mathbf{Z} = \begin{bmatrix} \varepsilon \\ \theta \end{bmatrix} = \begin{bmatrix} \arctan \dfrac{z+d_z}{\sqrt{(x+d_x)^2 + (y+d_y)^2}} + \upsilon_\varepsilon \\ \arctan \dfrac{y+d_y}{x+d_x} + \upsilon_\theta \end{bmatrix} \tag{5}$$

3   Relative Orbit Estimation Included Consensus Constraint

3.1   Consensus Constraint for Geometric Topology

Figure 2 illustrates an example of the geometric topology of spacecraft formation. It is obvious that the topology should satisfy the vector loop constraint as follows [10]

$$r_{12} + C_3^2 r_{23} + C_1^2 r_{31} = 0 \tag{6}$$

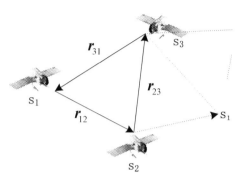

Fig. 2. Geometric topology of the formation

where r_{ij} denotes the relative position of spacecraft i with respect to spacecraft j in the LVLH frame of j, C_i^j presents the direction cosine matrix from l_i to l_j. Getting the derivative of Eq. (6) yields

$$v_{12} + C_3^2 v_{23} + C_3^2 \times \left(C_3^2 \omega_3 - \omega_2\right) r_{23} + C_1^2 v_{31} - C_1^2 \times \left(C_1^2 \omega_1 - \omega_3\right) r_{23} = 0 \tag{7}$$

where ω_i is the orbital rate of spacecraft i, v_{12} denotes the corresponding relative velocity. Denote $x_{ij} = \left[r_{ij}^T, v_{ij}^T\right]^T$, then combining Eqs. (6)–(7) produces

$$x_{12} + \begin{bmatrix} C_3^2 & 0_{3\times3} \\ C_3^2 \times \left(C_3^2 \omega_3 - \omega_2\right) & C_3^2 \end{bmatrix} x_{23} + \begin{bmatrix} C_1^2 & 0_{3\times3} \\ C_1^2 \times \left(C_1^2 \omega_1 - \omega_2\right) & C_1^2 \end{bmatrix} x_{31} = 0 \tag{8}$$

Till now, the constraint model of the geometric topology has been constructed.

3.2 Consensus Unscented Kalman Filter for Distributed Estimation

Unscented Kalman Filter (UKF), introduced by Julier and Uhlmann [11], does not have the linearization process for any nonlinear systems. Stastny [12] has studied the difference between EKF (Extended Kalman Filter) and UKF for angles-only relative navigation and concluded that UKF generally leads to better estimation than EKF and the improvement will be bigger when the relative range is larger or the filtering period is longer. But the increasing burden of computation is not as significant as expected. Thus, UKF is chosen to conduct the consensus filtering in this research.

Under the assumption of that the process and measurement noises are purely additive, the standard addictive form of UKF algorithm can be referred to [11]. The consensus UKF shares the same algorithm with UKF but includes a consensus term for the measurement update as follows:

$$\hat{X}_k = \hat{X}_k^- + K_k\left(\mathbf{Z}_k - \hat{\mathbf{Z}}_k^-\right) - \lambda\frac{P_k^-}{1 + \left\|P_k^-\right\|_F}\left(\hat{X}_k^- - \tilde{X}_k^-\right) \tag{9}$$

Where $\lambda(>0)$ is the scalar consensus feedback gain, P_k^- is the estimation error covariance matrix, $\|\ \|_F$ is the operator of Frobenius norm, and $\tilde{X}_k^-$ is calculated from the consensus constraint of geometric topology shown in Eq. (8).

4   Numerical Simulations

The initial inertial orbit parameters for the three spacecraft are presented in Table 1. The camera is 5 m offset from the mass-of-center of spacecraft in the cross-track direction. The line-of-sight angles measurement is polluted by white noise with 10–3 rad density. Moreover, the guess errors for the initial relative position and velocity are 1 km and 5 m/s per axis. The consensus feedback gain is chosen to be 0.3.

Table 1. Initial orbit of three spacecraft.

Spacecraft	Inertial orbit
1	[7600.0 km, 13.3 km, 0.3 km, 0.0126 km/s, 7.2406 km/s, 0.1466 km/s]
2	[7592.4 km, 26.5 km, 0.6 km, −0.0253 km/s, 7.2476 km/s, 0.1569 km/s]
3	[7569.5 km, 39.6 km, 0.9 km, −0.0379 km/s, 7.2691 km/s, 0.1650 km/s]

The estimation results for three spacecraft are shown in Figs. 3, 4 and 5.

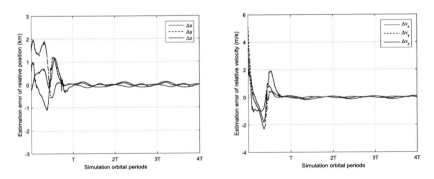

Fig. 3. Estimation error for spacecraft 1

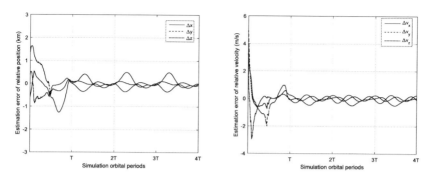

Fig. 4. Estimation error for spacecraft 2

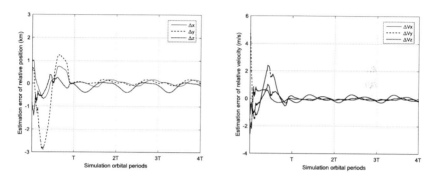

Fig. 5. Estimation error for spacecraft 3

5   Conclusions

This paper studied the close-range angles-only relative navigation problem for multi-agent cluster for on-orbit servicing mission when the camera offset from the vehicle center-of-mass allows for range observability. Navigation algorithm based on consensus Unscented Kalman Filter within the context of the second-order nonlinear dynamics is developed and the performance of the proposed algorithm is evaluated in two-body dynamics environment. The simulation results show that the utilizing of the geometric topology as the consensus constraint and the introduction of the camera offset does provide state observability.

Acknowledgements. This work is partially supported by the National Natural Science Foundation of China (11802119), National Postdoctoral Program for Innovative Talents (BX201700304), and Fundamental Research Funds for Central Universities (NT2019023).

References

1. Geller, D., Schmidt, J., Chavez, F.: Viability of angles-only navigation for orbital rendezvous operation. In: AIAA 2010, Toronto, Ontario Canada, p. 7755, August 2010
2. Woffinden, D.C., Geller, D.K.: Observability criteria for angles-only navigation. IEEE Trans. Aerosp. Electron. Syst. **45**(3), 1194–1208 (2009)
3. Woffinden, D.C., Geller, D.K.: Optimal orbital rendezvous maneuvering for angles-only navigation. J. Guid. Control Dyn. **32**(4), 1382–1387 (2009)
4. Grzymisch, J., Ficher, W.: Observability criteria and unobservable maneuvers for in-orbit bearings-only navigation. J. Guid. Control Dyn. **37**(4), 1250–1259 (2014)
5. Jagat, A., Sinclair, A.J.: Control of spacecraft relative motion using angles-only navigation. In: AAS/AIAA Astrodynamics Specialist Conference, AAS 15-444, Vail, Colorado, USA, August 2015 (2015)
6. Gaias, G., D'Amico, S., Ardaens, J.-S.: Angles-only navigation to a non-cooperative satellite using relative orbital elements. J. Guid. Control Dyn. **37**(3), 439–451 (2014)
7. Tschauner, J., Hempel, P.: Rendezvous zu einem in elliptischer bahn umlaufenden ziel. Acta Astronaut. **11**(2), 104–109 (1965)
8. Luo, J., Gong, B., Yuan, J., Zhang, Z.: Angles-only relative navigation and closed-loop guidance for spacecraft proximity operations. Acta Astronaut. **128**, 91–106 (2016)
9. D'Amico, S., Ardaens, J.-S., Gaias, G., Benninghoff, H., Schlepp, B.: Noncooperative rendezvous using angles-only optical navigation: System design and flight results. J. Guid. Control Dyn. **36**(6), 1576–1595 (2013)
10. Wang, J., Butcher, E.: Decentralized estimation of spacecraft relative motion using consensus extended Kalman filter. In: AAS Space Flight Mechanics Meeting, Kissimmee, USA, January 2018
11. Julier, S.J., Uhlmann, J.K.: A new extension of the Kalman filter to nonlinear systems. In: The 11th International Symposium on Aerospace/Defence Sensing, Simulation and Controls (1997)
12. Stastny, N., Bettinger, R., Chavez, F.: Comparison of the extended and unscented Kalman filters for angles based relative navigation. In: AIAA/AAS Astrodynamics Specialist Conference and Exhibit, AIAA 2008, Honolulu, Hawaii, USA, p. 7083, August 2008 (2008)

Human Centered Robotics

Deep Learning Based Noise Level Classification of Medical Images

Yifei Zhang[1], Chengdong Wu[2(✉)], Jianning Chi[2], and Xiaosheng Yu[2]

[1] College of Information Science and Engineering,
Northeastern University, Shenyang 110819, China
1770731@stu.neu.edu.cn
[2] Faculty of Robot Science and Engineering,
Northeastern University, Shenyang 110819, China
wuchengdong@mail.neu.edu.cn

Abstract. In recent years, medical image technology is widely used in medical field. However, the process of imaging, storage and transmission often make the image quality reduced and affect the visual and post-processing effect, and the degradation of medical image often leads to the interference of noise. Therefore, obtaining the level of noise in medical images is an important part in image quality improvement. In order to obtain the noise level in medical image, a novel image noise level classification network based on deep learning is designed, which incorporates inception structure and dense blocks to make full use of their advantages to extract the features of noise. The inception structure is used to extract the features of noise under different resolutions to get the features of different receptive fields. Meanwhile, the dense block structure is used to take advantage of feature reuse to ensure noise features transfer across the network. Experiments on lung CT images show that the classification accuracy of the proposed method is 99.5%. The method proposed has a good effect in the application of noise level classification and provides a reliable noise prior for the image enhancement using SRMD (super-resolution of MAP and dimensionality stretching) method.

Keywords: Noise level classification · Deep-learning · Medical images · Inception · Dense block

1 Introduction

With the development of modern medical technology, more and more attention has been paid to medical image. However, the process of imaging, storage and transmission often suffer from image noise. Thus, to obtain the level of noise in medical images is an important part in image quality improvement, which is helpful for image enhancement, feature extraction and segmentation.

There are many traditional image noise estimation methods which can be mainly categorized into image block-based methods [1], filter-based methods [2] and transform-based methods [3]. The image block based methods mainly included the following methods: using local statistical models to estimate noise [4]; using the distribution of local statistics to select uniform blocks from a single noise image [1]; using

H. Yu et al. (Eds.): ICIRA 2019, LNAI 11740, pp. 535–546, 2019.
https://doi.org/10.1007/978-3-030-27526-6_47

intensity variance homogeneity classification technique to find planar image blocks [5]. The image block based method was simple, but it was difficult to find uniform image block in high frequency image with more details and edges. Because there are many high frequency details in medical image, this methods were not suitable for noise level estimation. The filter-based methods were aimed to calculate the noise level of the residual diagram. However, the residual diagram obtained by this method may contain a large amount of high-frequency information such as edges. The transform based methods transformed the original image into wavelet domain or decomposed the original image into singular value decomposition (SVD) [6]. The noise level estimated by this method was always higher than the real situation.

Although the traditional method has a good effect in processing some natural images, the performance will decline sharply when there are a lot of high-frequency details in the images. Traditional methods mostly estimated the noise level as the statistical variance of the noise extracted from the image, so they had a strong dependence on the distribution of noise and details in the image, and they were not suitable for noise estimation in the medical image where there were many high-frequency details and relatively less noise. The methods based on deep learning learn from the labeled data set, so that it can accurately acquire related image features and make prediction according to the extracted features. Deep learning based methods are used to predict and classify the noise level in the image, which do not depend on the noise statistics distribution, but extract the global noise features in the image, thus reducing the interference of high-frequency details in the image.

Convolutional neural network (CNNs) [7] is the basis of most image classification methods based on deep learning. Experiments show that with the increase of network depth, the expression ability of network will be greatly improved. The VGGNet [8] proposed by Karen et al. proved that the increasing of network layer was conducive to improving the accuracy of image classification. At the same time, the larger the network width was, the higher the classification accuracy of the network would be. In addition, the size of different convolution kernels was also an important factor affecting the classification effect. GoogLeNet [9] adopted inception structure to fuse features extracted from convolution kernels of different receptive fields and increased the depth and width of the network. DenseNet [10] fused the features extracted from the previous layers as the input of the next layer. In this way, the features can be reused, avoiding the problem that the useful features disappear with the increase of the network. Compared with traditional methods, deep leaning based methods are more adaptable to medical images with more edges and textures, and its prediction accuracy is greatly improved.

The noise feature is a shallow global feature, if the network is too deep, the features will easily disappear in the process of network transmission, and overfitting is likely to happen. This paper make use of the advantages of inception structure and dense blocks and fuses them together to classify the noise levels in medical images. This paper focus on the network structure of inception and dense blocks, rather than on simply deepening the depth of the network. The advantages of Inception structure that different convolution kernels can extract the features of different receptive fields are used to extract the noise features of medical images at different resolutions, so as to obtain accurate global noise features. The advantage of feature reuse in dense blocks can avoid the problem of disappearing in the process of noise feature disappearing in the process of transmission, and can speed up the training of the network. Experimental results on CT images of the lungs show that the classification accuracy of the proposed method is quite high, and this method provides a reliable noise prior for the image enhancement in a blind manner using the SRMD method.

2 Method

2.1 Overall Network Structure

Because there are a lot of edges and details in medical images, and noise features are relatively shallow, it is hoped that the risk of network overfitting can be reduced in the process of noise features extraction in images, so as to reduce the number of parameters in the network as much as possible. The overall network structure is shown in the Fig. 1:

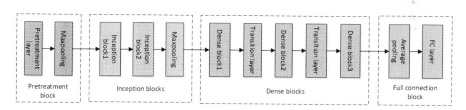

Fig. 1. Overall network structure

Pre-processing Network: The pre-processing layer of the network is mainly used to extract image features and provide appropriate feature maps for next layer. When extracting feature, the pre-processing layer maps the input image from the image space to the feature space, and extracts the 96-dimensional feature graph through convolution kernels. The convolution kernel of 3 * 3 is adopted, and a batch normalization (BN) and a Rectified Linear Units (ReLU) are added to extract image features. Then, a max-pooling layer is used to reduce the size of the feature maps and the amount of calculation.

Inception Module: Feature maps processed by pre-processing layer are further extracted through inception module. As the inception structure is composed of 1 * 1 convolution, 7 * 7 convolution, and 3 * 3 convolution layer in parallel, the features extracted from each branch are fused as the input of the next layer, so the network can judge which resolution features are more representative in the training. Two inception modules are designed in the network, which can make full use of different receptive fields to extract noise information in the image. Finally, a max-pooling layer is added to reduce the size of the feature diagram so as to reduce the amount of calculation.

Dense Block: The features extracted from two inception modules serve as the input of the dense layer. Since the dense layer supports the reuse of features, it can reduce the disappearance of image noise features in the process of feature transmission and fusion. In this paper, the dense block adopts bottle neck, which can reduce the parameters and thus alleviate overfitting. In this paper, three dense blocks are adopted to extract features, and there is a transition layer between each dense block, which has the effect of reducing the dimension and size of feature maps, so as to reduce parameters and the amount of calculation. Transition layer reduces the dimension of feature map by 1 * 1 convolution, and reduces the size of feature map by max-pooling.

Global Average-Pooling and Fully Connected Layer: After inception module and dense blocks, the size of the feature map is 6 * 6. Kernel size of global average-pooling is the size of feature graphs. Average the sum of each feature maps, and the size of feature maps become 1 * 1 and the dimension of the feature maps remains the same. This operation is equivalent to making a full connection inside each feature graph to prepare for the next full connection layer, which reduces the number of parameters in the whole connection layer and is conducive to easing overfitting. Finally, a full connection layer follows, whose outputs are the probability of the image noise level classification through softmax layer, and the type with the largest probability is the classification result of the noise level.

In the entire network, the inception structure and the dense block structure are the main parts, so the emphasis is on the inception structure and the development block structure.

2.2   Inception Structure

Since noise in the image is a global feature, we hope to extract its features with convolution kernels of different receptive fields, so as to improve the accuracy of noise feature extraction. At the same time, the larger the receptive field is, the closer the extracted noise features are to the global noise features. Therefore, we hope to adopt a larger convolution kernel. Because noise level features in medical images are not deep features, we do not want too many network parameters to lead to overfitting. In order to reduce network parameters and speed up training while taking advantage of inception structure, the inception-ResNet structure is adopted as shown in the Fig. 2. Each convolution module includes a convolution layer, a batch normalization (BN) layer to normalize data, and a ReLu activation function. The structure of the inception convolution module is shown in the Fig. 3:

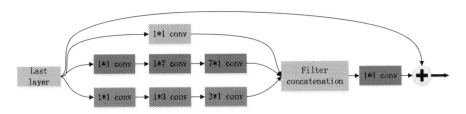

Fig. 2. Inception-ResNet structure

Fig. 3. Convolution module of inception-ResNet

Since the dimension of the feature maps is relatively high in the original inception structure, 1 * 1 convolution is adopted to reduce the dimension of the feature maps to reduce the number of parameters and increase the number of layers of the network to improve the network expression ability.

The large convolution kernel of 7 * 7 is adopted to obtain a larger receptive field, and the convolution kernel can be decomposed into the stack of 1 * 7 and 7 * 1 convolution kernels, and the convolution kernel of 3 * 3 can be decomposed into the stack of 1 * 3 and 3 * 1 convolution kernel. The size of the receptive field is guaranteed while the number of parameters is reduced. The ResNet structure in the structure can accelerate the training and avoid gradient disappearance or gradient explosion. This structure can effectively avoid overfitting in the process of extracting noise level features of medical images, and can extract features with different resolution by using different receptive fields, which can improve the accuracy of classification and accelerate training at the same time. Some of the features extracted through inception blocks are shown in the Fig. 4. It can be seen from the figure that inception blocks can extract a large number of noise features.

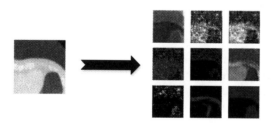

Fig. 4. Some of the features extracted through inception blocks

2.3 Dense Structure

DenseNet connects each layer to all the others in a feedforward manner, which means that the feature maps for all the previous layers are used as input to the next layer. Similarly, the feature map of this layer will serve as the input of all the subsequent layers.

Assuming the image input is X_0, the network has l layers, and each layer contains a nonlinear transformation $H_l(.)$, which can be BN, ReLU, Pooling or convolution layers. Assuming the output of layer l is X_l, the relationship between them can be represented by the formula (1):

$$X_l = H_l(X_0, X_1, \ldots, X_{l-1}) \tag{1}$$

Where X_l is the feature graph of the output of the lth layer, and $H_l(.)$ represents the convolution operation of the lth layer, that is, the input of the X_l layer is the feature fusion of the output feature graph of the previous $l - 1$ layer.

The connection of DenseNet is equivalent to that each layer is directly connected to input and loss, so the gradient can be transmitted between each layer, avoiding the problem of gradient disappearing. DenseNet with bottleneck layers tend to lower the dimensionality of input by 1 * 1 convolution, reducing the number of parameters and alleviating overfitting.

In medical images, because the noise features in the image is shallow, in the process of feature extraction, noise features may disappear along with the deepening of network. Fortunately, the dense structure supports the reuse of features, and the required features will always appear in the input features of the next layer, thus avoiding the problem of the disappearance of shallow features with convolution. To reduce the number of parameters and avoid overfitting, this article adopts the dense structure with bottleneck layer. The dense structure adopted in this paper is shown in the Fig. 5. The convolution module adopted is slightly different from what is used in inception structure. The sequence of the convolution module is changed into the BN layer, a ReLu activation function and finally a convolution layer. The convolution module is shown in the Fig. 6:

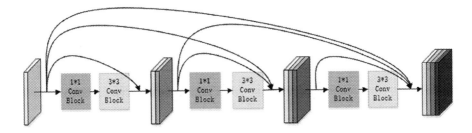

Fig. 5. Dense block adopted

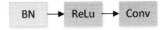

Fig. 6. Convolution module of dense block

3   Experiment

3.1   Experimental Materials

In the experiment, there were 40,000 noisy lung CT images with noise level labels for training, which came from the online public CT image data set TCIA. The size of each image was 100 * 100, and the noise level was a randomly generated integer with a variation range of 0 to 18, so the noise level was divided into 10 categories. The test set contains 2000 CT images of noisy lungs with a size of 100 * 100. The images also came from TCIA. The sampled images of 10 types of lung CT images with different noise levels are shown in the Fig. 7.

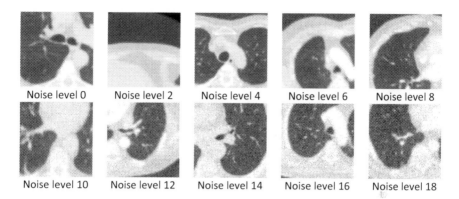

Fig. 7. The sampled images of different noise levels

As can be seen from the figure, the difference between adjacent noise levels in the image is very small, which is difficult to be distinguished by the human eye, and the error of traditional method estimation is large, so the true level of noise in the image cannot be well obtained. The noise classification method proposed in this paper can accurately obtain the noise level information in the image, and provide reliable noise level information for further image de-noising processing or image quality enhancement by using SRMD [11] method.

The evaluation index of the noise level classification method proposed in this paper is confusion matrix, precision, recall and f-measure. Since there is no previous method for image noise classification estimation based on deep learning, the method proposed in this paper can only be compared with traditional methods. The classical methods used to compare with the methods in this paper mainly include filtering based methods, automatic noise parameter estimation (ANPE) [12], structure-oriented-based approach (SOBA) [13], principal component analysis based approach (PCA) [14, 15]. Their parameters are the optimal parameters in the original paper.

3.2 Network Training

In the experiment, the cross entropy loss was adopted as loss function. Regularization coefficient was set to 10 ^ 4. Network was trained by Adam optimizer, and the initial learning rate was set to 0.001, β1 was set to 0.9, β2 was set to 0.999. During training, the batch size was set to 40, and total epoch was 40. All the training and testing were carried out under the Pytorch framework with the following hardware parameters: Intel Core i7-4790 K 4.0 GHz, NVIDIA TITAN Xp GPU.

This experiment was carried out under the Pytorch framework, and the changes of loss in the training process were visualized with Visdom visualization tool to generate loss curve diagram in the training process. The loss curve is shown in the Fig. 8. The training set accuracy curve and test set accuracy curve were generated in the same coordinate system, as shown in the Fig. 9.

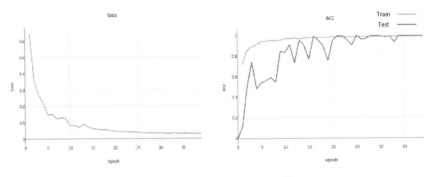

Fig. 8. Loss curve   Fig. 9. Accuracy curve

It can be seen from the Fig. 8 that the loss decreases rapidly in the early stage of training. From 1 to 10 epoch, the loss decreases by 0.56. After 10 epoch, the loss decreases to a smaller extent and the learning rate decreases. After 20 epoch, the loss basically tend to be stable. The method proposed in this paper has fast convergence speed and can speed up network training. It can be seen from the Fig. 9 that the accuracy of training classification increases with the increase of training epoch, while the test accuracy varies greatly, which is caused by the large learning rate. Therefore, after the 10th epoch, the learning rate was reduced to one tenth of the original learning rate, and the test accuracy gradually tend to the training accuracy, and the test accuracy increase slowly and finally level off. In this paper, the accuracy of the testing set for noise level classification in the image can reach 0.995, and the minimum loss is 0.0027.

3.3   Results Analysis

Performance: In the experiment, the trained model is verified by testing set, which contains 2000 noisy images, and 200 for each category. The confusion matrix is obtained by statistical analysis of the classification results of noise level in the image, and the confusion matrix, precision, recall and f-measure of the 10 classes are given in the Table 1. In the confusion matrix, the row corresponds to the label and the column to the predicted class. Precision (P) is a measure of the correlation of the results, while recall (R) is a measure of how many truly relevant results are returned. The two evaluation indexes are calculated by the formulas (2) and (3):

$$P = \frac{TP}{TP + FP} \tag{2}$$

$$R = \frac{TP}{TP + FN} \tag{3}$$

Where TP, FP and FN are the number of true positive, false positive and false negative respectively. F-measure is defined as the harmonic mean of precision and recall, which can be represented by the formula (4):

$$\text{F-measure} = \frac{2 * P * R}{P + R} \tag{4}$$

Table 1. The confusion matrix, precision, recall and f-measure of the 10 classes

		Predicted									
		0	2	4	6	8	10	12	14	16	18
Actual	0	192	8	0	0	0	0	0	0	0	0
	2	31	169	0	0	0	0	0	0	0	0
	4	0	0	200	0	0	0	0	0	0	0
	6	0	0	0	200	0	0	0	0	0	0
	8	0	0	0	3	196	1	0	0	0	0
	10	0	0	0	0	0	198	2	0	0	0
	12	0	0	0	0	0	0	200	0	0	0
	14	0	0	0	0	0	0	0	200	0	0
	16	0	0	0	0	0	0	0	1	199	0
	18	0	0	0	0	0	0	0	0	0	200
P		0.86	0.955	1.00	0.985	1.00	0.995	0.99	0.995	1.00	1.00
R		0.96	0.84	1.00	1.00	0.98	0.99	1.00	1.00	0.995	1.00
F		0.91	0.89	1.00	0.992	0.99	0.992	0.99	0.997	0.997	1.00

It can be seen from the table that the method proposed in this paper has relatively high P, R and F values for the classification of noise levels in images. Except the P, R and F values of category 1 and category 2 are relatively low, the P and R values of other categories are almost all above 0.99, and the P, R and F values of category 3 and category 10 are as high as 1.00. The reason why the P and R of category 1 and category 2 are relatively low is that the noise level in the image is low and the noise feature is not obvious enough, and it is easy to confuse the noise level of category 1 and category 2. However, with the increase of noise level, the P and R values of the classification can maintain a high value. It can be seen from the confusion matrix table that the correct classification results are located on the diagonal of the matrix, and the samples misclassified are mainly concentrated around the diagonal, that means the error between the noise level and the real label in the image is at most one level. Therefore, it can be considered that the method proposed in this paper is reliable, and it is accurate in the application of noise level prediction in images.

Compared to Traditional Methods: The proposed method is mainly compared with filtering based methods, ANPE, SOBA and PCA. The data used in the experiment were CT images of the lungs with added noise, whose noise levels are 0, 6, 10 and 18, and the average value of the noise estimation results was obtained. The prediction results of noise level are shown in the Table 2.

Table 2. The prediction results of different methods

Noise level	0	6	10	18
Filter based	0.68	1.73	6.19	19.44
ANPE	1.03	6.95	10.82	19.11
SOBA	0.62	6.73	10.93	19.09
PCA	1.17	6.38	10.29	18.51
Ours	**0.18**	**6.00**	**10.01**	**18.00**

As can be seen from the table, these methods are able to estimate the noise level in the image, but their performance is different. It can be seen from the results of noise estimation that, in most cases, the method proposed in this paper has the best performance. The method based on filter is simple in principle and method, but its applicability is poor. Compared with the filter based method, the ANPE and SOBA methods have improved the noise estimation accuracy, but the error is still large. With the increase of noise level, the estimation error will gradually increase and show an unstable trend. PCA is an image block-based method, which selects some pixels from the overall noise to estimate the noise intensity. PCA method is better than the previous methods in noise estimation. However, in the case of low noise level, the noise level in the image is much lower than the level of texture edge in the image, so the estimation error of low noise level is large. The deep learning method adopted in this paper can extract noise information on the basis of the whole image, and the prediction and estimation of noise level is more accurate. In the experiment, except that there is a little error in the estimation of 0 noise level, there is almost no deviation in the estimation of other noise levels. Although there are small errors in the estimation of 0-level noise, compared with the traditional methods, the error of the proposed method is much smaller than that of other methods. In terms of 0-level noise estimation, the proposed method reduces the error by 0.5, 0.85, 0.44 and 0.99 respectively compared with the filter based method, ANPE, SOBA and PCA methods. In terms of 6-level noise estimation, the proposed method reduces the error by 4.27, 0.95, 0.73 and 0.38 respectively compared with the filter based method, ANPE, SOBA and PCA methods. In terms of 10-level noise estimation, the proposed method reduces the error by 3.81, 0.82, 0.93 and 0.29 respectively compared with the filter based method, ANPE, SOBA and PCA methods. In terms of 18-level noise estimation, the proposed method reduces the error by 1.44, 1.11, 1.09 and 0.51 respectively compared with the filter based method, ANPE, SOBA and PCA methods. Therefore, the proposed method has a good effect in the application of noise level classification and estimation.

Application: The method proposed in this paper can predict and classify the noise level in the image, so as to make up the disadvantage of the need for noise prior in SRMD method. By combining the method proposed in this paper with SRMD method, image de-noising and super-resolution enhancement can be dealt with in blind way, so as to avoid the disadvantages of human intervention and the need for prior knowledge and improve the convenience of image quality enhancement. For comparison purposes, the experiments that the true value of noise and the predicted value of PCA are used as SRDM priors are done. The effect is shown in the Fig. 10, and PSNR is used as the evaluation index of image quality enhancement:

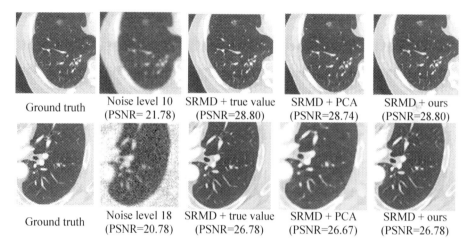

| Ground truth | Noise level 10 (PSNR= 21.78) | SRMD + true value (PSNR=28.80) | SRMD + PCA (PSNR=28.74) | SRMD + ours (PSNR=28.80) |

| Ground truth | Noise level 18 (PSNR=20.78) | SRMD + true value (PSNR=26.78) | SRMD + PCA (PSNR=26.67) | SRMD + ours (PSNR=26.78) |

Fig. 10. Image quality enhancement effect

It can be seen from the figure that SRMD method has a good effect in processing both super-resolution and de-noising. The experimental results of the proposed method are consistent with the truth value, while the effect of PCA method is slightly worse due to the prediction error.

4   Conclusion

A method of noise level estimation and classification in images based on deep learning is proposed, which fuses inception structure and dense block structure into a deep learning network. The method considers that the noise features are shallow features, so it is necessary to use inception structure to extract the features of image features under different resolutions, and extract the noise features in the image. Meanwhile, the dense block structure is used to avoid the problem of the reduction or disappearance of the noise features with the increase of the depth of the network because of the characteristic of its feature reuse. At the same time, many 1 * 1 convolutions are adopted to reduce network parameters to reduce the risk of overfitting. Experimental results on CT images of the lungs show that the classification accuracy of the proposed method is 99.5%, and it also provides a reliable noise prior for the image enhancement in a blind manner using the SRMD method.

Acknowledgement. This work is supported by National Robotic Major Project of the Ministry of Science and Technology of China (No. 2017YFB1300900); National Natural Science Foundation of China (No. U1713216, No. 61701101); Research Fund of Shenyang (No. 17-500-8-0); Intelligent Robot Laboratory of Shenyang (No. 18-007-0-06); Fundamental Research Funds for the Central Universities (N172603001).

References

1. Jiang, P., Zhang, J.: Fast and reliable noise level estimation based on local statistic. Pattern Recogn. Lett. **78**, 8–13 (2016)
2. Rank, K., Lendl, M., Unbehauen, R.: Estimation of image noise variance. IEE Proc.-Vis. Image Sig. Process. **146**(2), 80–84 (1999)
3. Hashemi, M., Beheshti, S.: Adaptive noise variance estimation in BayesShrink. IEEE Sig. Process. Lett. **17**(1), 12–15 (2010)
4. Tian, J., Chen, L.: Image noise estimation using a variation-adaptive evolutionary approach. IEEE Sig. Process. Lett. **19**(7), 395–398 (2012)
5. Rakhshanfar, M., Amer, M.A.: Estimation of Gaussian, Poissonian-Gaussian, and processed visual noise and its level function. IEEE Trans. Image Process. **25**(9), 4172–4185 (2016)
6. Liu, W., Lin, W.: Additive white Gaussian noise level estimation in SVD domain for images. IEEE Trans. Image Process. **22**(3), 872–883 (2013)
7. Krizhevsky, A., Sutskever, I., Hinton, G.E.: ImageNet classification with deep convolutional neural networks. In: Advances in Neural Information Processing Systems, pp. 1097–1105 (2012)
8. Simonyan, K., Zisserman, A.: Very deep convolutional networks for large-scale image recognition. arXiv preprint arXiv:1409.1556 (2014)
9. Szegedy, C., Ioffe, S., Vanhoucke, V., et al.: Inception-v4, inception-resnet and the impact of residual connections on learning. In: Thirty-First AAAI Conference on Artificial Intelligence (2017)
10. Huang, G., Liu, Z., Van Der Maaten, L., et al.: Densely connected convolutional networks. In: Proceedings of the IEEE Conference on Computer Vision and Pattern Recognition, pp. 4700–4708 (2017)
11. Zhang, K., Zuo, W., Zhang, L.: Learning a single convolutional super-resolution network for multiple degradations. In: Proceedings of the IEEE Conference on Computer Vision and Pattern Recognition, pp. 3262–3271 (2018)
12. Aja-Fernández, S., Vegas-Sánchez-Ferrero, G., Martín-Fernández, M., et al.: Automatic noise estimation in images using local statistics. Additive and multiplicative cases. Image Vis. Comput. **27**(6), 756–770 (2009)
13. Amer, A., Dubois, E.: Fast and reliable structure-oriented video noise estimation. IEEE Trans. Circ. Syst. Video Technol. **15**(1), 113–118 (2005)
14. Pyatykh, S., Hesser, J., Zheng, L.: Image noise level estimation by principal component analysis. IEEE Trans. Image Process. **22**(2), 687–699 (2013)
15. Chi, J., Yu, X., Zhang, Y., et al.: A novel local human visual perceptual texture description with key feature selection for texture classification. Math. Probl. Eng. **2019** (2019)

Deep Learning Based Gesture Recognition and Its Application in Interactive Control of Intelligent Wheelchair

Xingqun Zhou[1], Fei Wang[2(✉)], Jianhui Wang[1], Yufan Wang[3],
Junlang Yan[2], and Guilin Zhou[2]

[1] College of Information Science and Engineering, Northeastern University,
Shenyang 110819, China
[2] Faculty of Robot Science and Engineering,
Northeastern University, Shenyang 110819, China
wangfei@mail.neu.edu.cn
[3] Sino-Dutch Biomedical and Information Engineering School,
Northeastern University, Shenyang 110819, China

Abstract. With the development of robotics technology, new human-robot interaction technology has gradually received more and more attention. Bioelectric-based gesture recognition, which is to be studied in this article, has become a frontier subject of new human-robot interaction because of its natural and intuitive information representation function and it is not restricted from complex background conditions. A deep neural network model based on the Alexnet-based network structure is used for gesture recognition based on sEMG (surface electromyography) and inertial information. The data is collected by the sliding window method, the recognition thread loads the trained model and performs online recognition in real time. Moreover, in order to improve the robustness of the algorithm to the input data, a verification model based on the twin neural network is used to verify whether the input data belongs to the identification type. And the human-robot interaction method proposed is verified on the omnidirectional intelligent wheelchair, and the obvious control effect is obtained.

Keywords: Human-robot interaction · Deep learning · Gesture recognition

1 Introduction

With the development of artificial intelligence and robotics, it has become a research hotspot that human and robots give play to their own advantages and cooperate to complete the target task. The intelligent control method studied in this article is a new type of human-robot interaction system based on multi-sensor fusion information based on surface EMG signals and inertial signals. In the field of home service, the new method of human-robot interaction accurately identifies the wearer's action state, and naturally controls the smart hardware of the home.

With the development of bioelectrical signal sensing technology, there are many works on the use of sEMG for HCI (Human-Computer Interaction), especially hand

H. Yu et al. (Eds.): ICIRA 2019, LNAI 11740, pp. 547–557, 2019.
https://doi.org/10.1007/978-3-030-27526-6_48

and finger movement for recognizing gesture input and control. Some researchers have explored a fusion method that uses sEMG and other types of signals to achieve high-precision gesture recognition. Saponas et al. [1] studied the real-time gesture recognition method based on sEMG. Through the demonstration results, the universality of this method in different arm postures was demonstrated and the trade-offs of providing real-time visual feedback were discussed. Zhang et al. [2] proposed a gesture recognition framework based on multi-channel sEMG signals and three-axis accelerometer fusion information to identify sign language through hidden Markov models and decision trees. Matsubara et al. [3] used a bilinear model to construct a multi-user electromyography interface and applied the proposed method to the recognition task of five gestures controlled by a robot. The method obtained 73% accuracy. Khushaba et al. [4] proposed a framework for multi-user Myoelectric interface by using typical correlation analysis. The method proposed can overcome individual differences, and the accuracy rate of multiple users was 83%. David [5] designed a PC mouse, an electromyographic signal command obtained from two muscles of the forearm palmar muscle and extensor tendon. Amma et al. [6] analyzed the effects of electrode size used and proposed two methods for estimating inter-session electrode offset based on a small amount of calibration data. McIntosh et al. [7] achieved a high-precision gesture recognition system EMPress by obtaining a four-channel sEMG signal and a four-channel force-sensitive resistor signal through a wearable device placed on the wrist. Geng et al. [8] proposed that the mode within the instantaneous value of the high-density sEMG enabled gesture recognition to be performed using the sEMG signal only at specific times. Lu et al. [9] proposed an algorithm framework for processing gesture recognition acceleration and surface EMG signals. By wearing the device on the forearm, the user was able to manipulate the mobile phone using 19 predefined gestures or even personalized gestures. Côté-Allard et al. [10] presented a novel CNN architecture that can control the 6 DoF robotic arm with the same speed and precision as the joystick. Huang et al. [11] identified the movement of the human arm based on sEMG. Correlation analysis and improved LDA were integrated to reduce the size of the sEMG features and enabled motion recognition of the human arm.

According to the characteristics of human factors uncertainty and individual differences in the process of human-robot interaction, the control intention extraction of multi-source information based on sEMG and inertial information is studied. During the experiment, the experimenters need to wear the wearable sensor device myoelectric collection device. The extraction method of control intent in the process of human-robot cooperation based on multi-source information is studied in the article. The acquired sEMG and inertial information are preprocessed and input into the deep neural network based on Alexnet. Moreover, in order to improve the robustness of online recognition of algorithms, a verification model based on twin neural network is adopted to further distinguish different gestures. Finally, the algorithm is verified on the omnidirectional intelligent wheelchair and a good control effect is obtained.

The rest of this paper is structured as follows: in Sect. 2, gesture classifier model proposed in this paper is introduced in detail. Online gesture recognition process and interference analysis are illustrated in Sect. 3. Experiments and results are shown in Sect. 4. In Sect. 5, present the conclusions.

2 Gesture Classifier Model Based on Deep Neural Network

2.1 Data Collection

A single sEMG message may not be sufficient to characterize the entire arm and hand gestures, resulting in a low recognition rate. To solve the problem, the obtained forearm sEMG and inertial information are combined and pre-processed. The sEMG signal of the forearm is related to the movement of the wrist. Because the joint movements of the fingers and wrists need to be completed by the contraction and stretching movements of the related muscle groups of the forearm, the acquired inertial data can reflect the spatial position and specific posture of the end of the arm when the demonstrator performs the action.

The demo multi-source information experimental collection device is the MYO bracelet. The MYO armband is made up of an eight-channel sEMG sensor, a three-axis gyro inertial sensor, and a three-axis acceleration inertial sensor on a flexible arm ring which is easy to wear on the forearm. The maximum sampling frequency of the device is 200 Hz. In the gesture movement collection experiment, seven healthy lab members acted as the demonstrators to collect multi-source gesture data.

Table 1. The information of volunteers

Serial Number	Age	Height (cm)	Body weight (kg)
1	23	174	65
2	22	169	62
3	22	173	72
4	21	180	70
5	25	171	76
6	24	163	51
7	24	183	90

Each presenter performs 5 different gesture actions (as shown in Fig. 1), and each gesture motion data is divided into three groups according to the wearing positions of different devices. The experimental object data is shown in Table 1. Each group of actions is about 200 times, and a total of about 42,000 gesture data are collected. According to the common type design, 5 kinds of gestures as shown in Fig. 1 are collected.

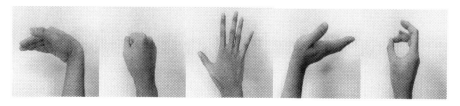

Fig. 1. Five human-robot interaction gestures selected

2.2   Gesture Classifier Model Based on Alexnet Deep Neural Network

The collected demo gesture data is about 42,000, which is 14 channels of data. The data size of each channel is 64, 8 channels are sEMG data, 6 channels are inertial data, and the input size is 14×64. The deep learning network model designed based on Alexnet's network structure is shown in Fig. 2.

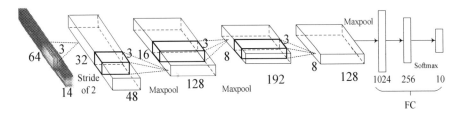

Fig. 2. Alexnet-based gesture recognition network structure

The network has been improved from the Alexnet network [12] and has four layers of convolutional layers. The convolution kernels of the first layer to the fourth layer have a size of 3, and the number of convolution kernels is 48, 128, 192, 128, respectively. The first layer of convolution has a step size of 2, and the remaining convolutional layers have a step size of 1 [13]. The first layer, the second layer and the fourth layer are followed by the largest pooling layer (Maxpool) [14]. The third largest pooling layer is followed by two layers of fully connected layers and one layer of output layers, and the number of neurons is 1024, 256, and 10, respectively.

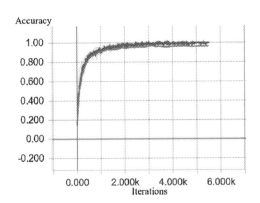

Fig. 3. Accuracy curve of gesture recognition based on Alexnet.

Cross entropy

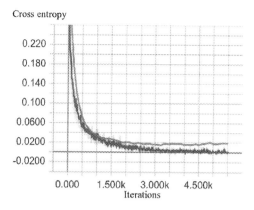

Fig. 4. Cross entropy curve of gesture recognition based on Alexnet.

The training and test results of the classifier model based on Alexnet's deep neural network are shown in Figs. 3 and 4. As can be seen from the average accuracy curve in Fig. 3, the final recognition accuracy rate is about 95%. And compared with the SVM algorithm in the machine learning algorithm. Due to the non-stationary randomness of the sEMG signal, it cannot be directly used as the input of the classifier. Therefore, the hidden feature information is extracted from the EMG signal. The main extracted features include: RMS in the time domain, average absolute value MAV, and zero crossing point ZC, 3rd order autoregressive coefficient ARC, power spectral density in the frequency domain and short time Fourier transform in the time-frequency domain. The radial basis kernel function is selected, and the formula is as shown in Eq. (1).

$$K(u, v) = \exp\left(-g \cdot |u - v|^2\right) \tag{1}$$

The accuracy of gesture recognition of the two algorithms is shown in Table 2. As can be seen from the table, the deep neural network based on Alexnet is more than 3% higher than the recognition rate based on SVM.

Table 2. Gesture recognition effect of each CNN network

	Algorithm	Test accuracy (%)
sEMG	Alexnet	90.2
sEMG + inertia	Alexnet	95.2
sEMG	SVM	89.12
sEMG + inertia	SVM	89.96

3 Online Gesture Recognition Process and Interference Analysis

According to the designed collection experiment, the multi-source information collection of the experimenter process is performed, the sEMG information and the inertia information are collected and the gesture recognition deep learning network is trained through the pre-processing and segmentation process [15], and the trained model is saved. During online recognition, the data acquisition and recognition process is performed by multiple threads. The data acquisition thread collects the data and uses the sliding window method [16] to collect the data. The recognition thread loads the trained model and performs online recognition in real time. The gesture recognition process is shown in Fig. 5.

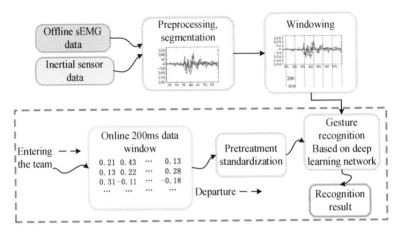

Fig. 5. Gesture online recognition process

In the online recognition process, the sliding window inevitably introduces incomplete and erroneous data into the gesture recognition model. Therefore, it is considered to use the verification model to verify whether the input data belongs to the recognition type. A twin neural network as verification model is used to feed the twin neural networks through randomly generated data of the same category and different categories and gives similar and dissimilar labels. Through the loss function, the degree of discrimination of similar data is continuously reduced and the degree of discrimination of different categories of data is increasing. The specific structure of the Siamese Network is shown in Fig. 6. After the training is completed, a reference vector set is generated by synthesizing all the coding vectors for each assembly gesture.

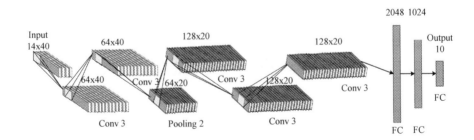

Fig. 6. Twin neural network validates model structure

The implementation process of the demonstrator's gesture online identification verification process is shown in Fig. 7. First, the gesture data collected by the sliding window is input into the trained verification model and the classification model. The output of the verification model is the coding vector output by the motion process via the neural network [17]. The classification model output is an assembly gesture classification result with which the category reference vector is indexed. The similarity evaluation function is used to evaluate the similarity of the two model output vectors, and the similarity results are output. Only the recognition results with high output similarity are retained.

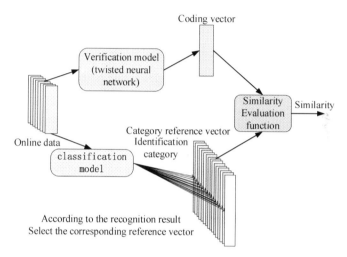

Fig. 7. Demonstrate the process of online recognition and verification of human assembly gestures

4   Intelligent Wheelchair Gesture Control Experiment

4.1   Data Preprocessing

The preprocessing process of the sEMG signal first removes the bias of the original sEMG and filters out the power frequency interference using a Butterwort low-pass filter with a cutoff frequency of 500 Hz and a 50 Hz notch filter. Equation 2 is the calculation formula of the preprocessing process, in which, L the filter function; $e(t)$ the original sEMG signal; $\bar{e}(t)$ the average value in the selected time window; $u(t)$ the preprocessed sEMG signal; u_0 and the offset.

$$u(t) = L(|e(t) - \bar{e}(t)|) - u_0 \tag{2}$$

For the EMG signals with regular continuous motion, there are resting state and active state in each cycle. The detection of the active segment as basic unit is to determine the starting and ending point of the action, and effectively segment the different gesture data, and use this as the classification and recognition. Commonly activity detection techniques used include moving average method, short-time Fourier transform, base entropy theory, Sobel operator based on edge maximum a posteriori probability estimation, and the multi-threshold detection method used [18]. Considering the real-time control, the entropy-based or model-based active segment extraction method is accurate, but the calculation is complicated and the versatility is poor. Therefore, based on the consideration of computational complexity and precision, a multi-threshold threshold detection based on moving average method and root mean square method is proposed based on the single threshold multi-threshold. The instantaneous average energy formula of sEMG is:

$$E(t) = [\frac{1}{N} \sum_{i}^{N} S_i(t)]^2 \tag{3}$$

The formula for RMS:

$$RMS = \sqrt{\frac{\int_{t}^{t+T} S_i^2(t)dt}{T}} \tag{4}$$

Where N is the number of channels, i is the channel number, and T is the window time, $S_i(t)$ is the myoelectric signal after denoising. Select the rectangular active window on the moving window. The window width is 40 sampling points (the window time is 200 ms at the sampling frequency of 200 Hz), and the moving window is 10 sampling points (the window time is 50 ms), so there is half of the time window. It is overlapping, as much as possible to ensure the integrity of the data representation information.

In the selection of the threshold, the threshold TH1 is set according to the magnitude of the energy value, and the threshold TH2 is set according to the observation value of the root mean square. The value of TH2 is greater than TH1, when the average energy is greater than TH1, and the values of three consecutive time windows are greater than TH1. It is considered that it is possible to enter the active section area or enter the area where the fluctuation of the noise is large. When the time window is moved three times in succession to make the energy value larger than H2, it is considered to be the starting position start marker of the active section. The determination of the cutoff position of the active segment is reversed.

4.2   Intelligent Wheelchair Control Experiment

In order to verify the effectiveness of the sEMG-based gesture recognition control method, the omnidirectional intelligent wheelchair independent construction is used as the experimental object. The platform object supports the ROS operating system, and the platform is naturally used by sEMG and inertial information as control information. The gesture control experiment process of the intelligent wheelchair is divided into offline training and online recognition. The PC is used as the server and the omnidirectional intelligent wheelchair experimental object is used as the client. The two communicate through the ROS node. The specific process diagram is shown in Fig. 8.

The sliding window method is used to collect data and the Alexnet-based gesture recognition network is used, which has better versatility. And the online recognition method based on twin neural network has better recognition robustness, so it is used as the core algorithm of robot gesture control experiment for omnidirectional intelligent wheelchair.

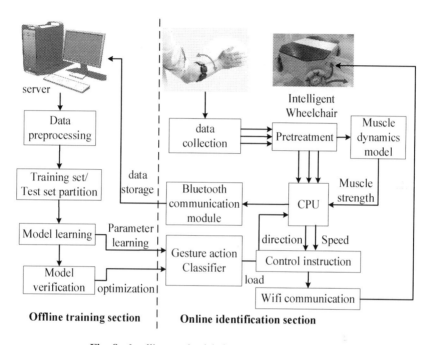

Fig. 8. Intelligent wheelchair gesture control system

5 kinds of assembly gestures are selected as control commands, click the switching gesture to control the robot switch mode, the gesture refers to the gesture to control the robot to advance, the fist gesture to control the robot to retreat [19], and the left-hand gesture to control the robot to rotate left and right. The gesture controls the robot to rotate right. The moving linear velocity and angular velocity of the omnidirectional intelligent wheelchair are determined by the manipulator's manipulation gesture strength. The specific estimation method is the method of the Hill muscle model and the specific manipulation effect is shown in Fig. 9.

When the intelligent wheelchair is controlled by the gesture action, the greater the intensity of the gesture action, the higher the degree of muscle activation and thus the speed of the control robot is accelerated. On the other hand, when the "forward" control gesture and the "reverse" control gesture are performed, the arm rotation angle is obtained from the arm acceleration and the gyro inertia data, and the rotation direction of the robot during the forward or reverse travel is controlled by the continuous amount, And realize the steering control of the robot in all directions, making the platform more flexible.

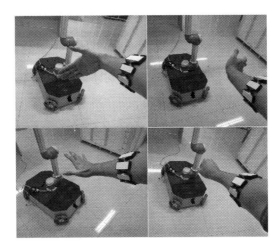

Fig. 9. Omnidirectional intelligent wheelchair manipulation experiment based on gesture recognition

5   Conclusion

The collection of multi-source data such as sEMG information and inertial information in human-robot interaction process and the recognition method of gesture action based on multi-source information are studied in the article. The physiological characteristics of muscle electrical signals are analyzed, and then the natural control process extraction method based on MYO bracelet is presented. The natural assembly process extraction of the presenter is realized. The sEMG is used as an input signal for the classification of gesture recognition, and the original sEMG signal is subjected to pre-processing such as denoising and active segment detection to facilitate the recognition process using the deep learning network model. In addition, a comparison experiment is conducted between the deep neural network algorithm based on Alexnet and the SVM algorithm, and the former achieved higher accuracy. In view of the possible errors in data acquisition, the verification model (twisting neural network) is added in the online recognition process of human-robot interaction gestures, which makes the online recognition result more accurate and reliable, and the test accuracy and online recognition effect are greatly improved.

Acknowledgments. This research was funded by Fundamental Research Funds for the Central Universities of China, grant number N172608005, N182612002, N182608003 and Liaoning Provincial Natural Science Foundation of China, grant number 20180520007.

References

1. Saponas, T.S., Tan, D.S., Dan, M., et al.: Enabling always-available input with muscle-computer interfaces. In: ACM Symposium on User Interface Software and Technology, Victoria, BC, Canada, October 2009, pp. 167–176. DBLP (2009)
2. Zhang, X., Chen, X., Li, Y., et al.: A framework for hand gesture recognition based on accelerometer and EMG sensors. IEEE Trans. Syst. Man Cybern. Part A Syst. Hum. **41**(6), 1064–1076 (2011)
3. Matsubara, T., Morimoto, J.: Bilinear modeling of EMG signals to extract user-independent features for multiuser myoelectric interface. IEEE Trans. Biomed. Eng. **60**(8), 2205–2213 (2013)
4. Khushaba, R.N.: Correlation analysis of electromyogram signals for multiuser myoelectric interfaces. IEEE Trans. Neural Syst. Rehabil. Eng. **22**(4), 745–755 (2014)
5. David, R.L., Cristian, C.L., Humberto, L.C.: Design of an electromyographic mouse. In: Signal Processing, Images and Computer Vision, pp. 1–8. IEEE (2015)
6. Amma, C., Krings, T., Böer, J., et al.: Advancing muscle-computer interfaces with high-density electromyography, pp. 929–938 (2015)
7. Mcintosh, J., Mcneill, C., Fraser, M., et al.: EMPress: practical hand gesture classification with wrist-mounted EMG and pressure sensing. In: CHI Conference on Human Factors in Computing Systems, pp. 2332–2342. ACM (2016)
8. Geng, W., Du, Y., Jin, W., et al.: Gesture recognition by instantaneous surface EMG images. Sci. Rep. **6**, 36571 (2016)
9. Lu, Z., Chen, X., Li, Q., et al.: A hand gesture recognition framework and wearable gesture-based interaction prototype for mobile devices. IEEE Trans. Hum.-Mach. Syst. **44**(2), 293–299 (2017)
10. Côté-Allard, U., Fall, C.L., Campeau-Lecours, A., Gosselin, C., Laviolette, F., Gosselin, B.: Transfer learning for sEMG hand gestures recognition using convolutional neural networks. In: 2017 IEEE International Conference on Systems, Man, and Cybernetics (SMC), Banff, AB, pp. 1663–1668 (2017)
11. Huang, Y., Chen, K., Wang, K., Chen, Y., Zhang, X.: Estimation of human arm motion based on sEMG in human-robot cooperative manipulation. In: 2018 IEEE International Conference on Robotics and Biomimetics (ROBIO), Kuala Lumpur, Malaysia, pp. 1771–1776 (2018)
12. Lecun, Y., Bengio, Y., Hinton, G.: Deep learning. Nature **521**(7553), 436–444 (2015)
13. Luo, S.: Study on sampling technologies based on deep learning for protein structure prediction. Soochow University (2016)
14. Ou, X.-F., Xiang, C.-Q., Guo, L.-Y.: Research of recognition of digital characters on vehicle license based on caffe deep learning framework. J. Sichuan Univ. (Nat. Sci. Ed.) **54**(05), 971–977 (2017)
15. Yu, X., Liu, Z., Geng, Z., Chen, S.: A UAV target recognition method for no flying zone based on deep learning. J. Changchun Univ. Sci. Technol. **41**(03), 95–101 (2018)
16. Zhang, S., Liu, Y.: Prediction of moving target trajectory with sliding window polynomial fitting. Opto-Electron. Eng. **2003**(04), 24–27 (2003)
17. Shen, Y., Wang, H., Dai, Y.: Deep siamese network-based classifier and its application. Comput. Eng. Appl. **54**(10), 19–25 (2018)
18. Ma, Z.: Epilepsy analysis and control based on neural mass model. Shangdong University (2016)
19. Qi, J., Xu, K., Ding, X.: Vision-based hand gesture recognition for human-robot interaction: a review. Robot **39**(4), 565–584 (2017)

Cross-Subject EEG-Based Emotion Recognition with Deep Domain Confusion

Weiwei Zhang[1], Fei Wang[1(✉)], Yang Jiang[1], Zongfeng Xu[2], Shichao Wu[1], and Yahui Zhang[2]

[1] Faculty of Robot Science and Engineering, Northeastern University, Shenyang, Liaoning, China
18840630892@163.com,
{wangfei,jiangyang}@mail.neu.edu.cn
[2] College of Information Science and Engineering, Northeastern University, Shenyang, Liaoning, China

Abstract. At present, the method of emotion recognition based on Electroencephalogram (EEG) signals has received extensive attention. EEG signals have the characteristics of non-linear, non-stationary and low spatial resolution. There are great differences between EEG signals collected from different subjects as well as the same subjects from different experimental sessions. Therefore, it's difficult for traditional emotion recognition methods to achieve high recognition accuracy. To tackle this problem, this paper proposes a cross-subject emotion recognition method based on convolutional neural network (CNN) and deep domain confusion (DDC). Firstly, the Electrodes-frequency Distribution Maps (EFDMs) is constructed from EEG signals, and the residual blocks based deep CNN is used to automatically extract the features related emotion recognition from the EFDMs. Then, the difference of the feature distribution between source and target domain are narrowed by the DDC. Finally, the EEG emotion recognition task is realized with EFDMs and CNN. On SEED, we set up two experiments, the proposed method achieved an average accuracy of 90.59% and 82.16%/4.43% for mean accuracy and standard deviation under conventional and cross-subject experimental protocols, respectively. Finally, this paper uses the gradient-weighted class activation mapping (Grad-CAM) to get a glimpse of what features the CNN has learned during the training from EFDMs, and obtained the conclusion that the high frequency EEG signals are more favorable for emotion recognition.

Keywords: Emotion recognition · Electroencephalogram ·
Deep domain confusion · Cross-subject · Convolutional neural network

1 Introduction

Human emotions play an important role in communication with others in daily decision-making, which can be detected by emotion recognition to produce user-friendly products [1]. In medical applications, emotion recognition can be used to detect the emotional state of patients with dyslexia and some mental disorders, such as severe depression [2]. Compared with emotion recognition based on non-physiological

© Springer Nature Switzerland AG 2019
H. Yu et al. (Eds.): ICIRA 2019, LNAI 11740, pp. 558–570, 2019.
https://doi.org/10.1007/978-3-030-27526-6_49

signals, such as facial expression and voice intonation [3, 4], emotion recognition based on brain electrophysiological signals has attracted much attention because of its objective evaluation and immediate response to emotion stimuli.

A variety of machine learning methods are widely used in Electroencephalogram (EEG)-based emotion recognition. Many of scholars have made breakthroughs in this field, such as support vector machine (SVM) [5], KNN [6], RF [7]. In addition, DBN network is used to detect important channels and bands of emotion recognition, and recognizes three kinds of emotions: positive, neutral, and negative, which show excellent performance [8, 9]. Using the bimodal deep auto-encoder (BDAE) model based on DBN, Emotion Meter is a multi-modal emotion recognition system which combines EEG signals and eye movement data, and the accuracy rate is 85.11% [10]. However, EEG signals have the characteristics of non-linear, non-stationary and low spatial resolution, which makes it difficult to classify EEG signals. The conditional distribution and edge distribution of training data and test data may not match, which makes it difficult to satisfy the assumption of independent and identical distribution of traditional classification methods. In order to solve this problem, more and more attention has been paid to adaptive methods in the field of transfer learning.

Domain adaptive method aims at finding common invariant features of source data and target data, and reducing distribution differences. This method has a lot of research on emotion recognition. The classical domain adaptive method TCA [11] assumes that there exists a feature mapping source domain data and target domain data to Reproducing Kernel Hilbert Space (RKHS) to make their distribution closer. Maximum Mean Discrepancy (MMD) [12] is used to learn the transfer component of subspace. Utilize the new representation of subspace, machine learning can be applied to train classifiers or regression models based on source domain for use in target domain. Subspace Alignment (SA) method employs a mapping function to find feature space and align different data [13]. SDA adds probability distribution adaptive transformation based on SA method to compensate for performance degradation by transferring and adapting the source domain to the target domain [14].

The research on cross-subject and cross-session is relatively novel, Yin *et al.* [15] developed a new EEG feature selection approach, Transfer Recursive Feature Elimination (T-RFE). The algorithm is valid for cross-subject emotion classification paradigm on DEAP datasets. Yin *et al.* [16] proposes an adaptive Stacked Denoising Auto-Encoder (SDAE), which uses electroencephalogram (EEG) to process cross-session mental classification tasks. The adaptive SDAE algorithm consists of two steps: initializing the deep model; adaptive classification by iteratively adjusting the weights between the adaptive layer and the former layer. The results show that the adaptive SDAE has high performance in across-session EEG characteristics. Zheng *et al.* [17] discusses two types of subject-to-subject migration methods. One is to use shared infrastructure between source data and target data. The other is to train multiple classifiers for source objects, transfer the knowledge of classifier parameters to target objects. The experimental results demonstrate that subject transfer framework achieves the mean accuracy of 76.31% in comparison with a conventional generic classifier with 56.73% in average. For the research of cross-subject and domain adaptive emotion recognition, Chai *et al.* [18] proposes a Subspace Alignment Auto-Encoder (SAAE) method based on subspace alignment method, which combines self-coding network and subspace alignment solution in a unified framework by using non-linear transformation and consistency constraint. However, this method uses domain-invariant subspace twice, which will lead to a large loss of source domain and target domain information. For any new example from the test session, the domain invariant feature must be relearned. Chai *et al.* [19] proposes Adaptive Subspace Feature Matching (ASFM) strategy, which combines edge distribution and conditional distribution in a unified framework (without any marker samples from the target object) and develops a linear transformation function.

Domain adaptation strategy is actually a trade-off between invariant features of learning domain and information preserved in both source and target domains. Converting data into an intermediate common subspace may result in loss of information in both source and target domains. DDC method based on CNN architecture uses an adaptive layer and domain confusion loss based on Maximum Mean Discrepancy (MMD) to automatically learn a representation jointly trained to optimize classification and domain invariance [20]. Compared with subspace alignment method, one advantage of this method is that it can classify data while adapting to the domain and retain original distribution information. The other advantage of DDC method is that the labeled source domain data can be used for unsupervised adaptive training of unlabeled target domain data. EEG analysis methods are mainly divided into frequency domain, time domain and time-frequency domain [21]. The frequency domain analysis is to transform the EEG signal in time domain into the frequency domain signal, which has obvious characteristics and high resolution.

This paper proposes an EEG emotion recognition method based on deep residual convolutional neural network and DDC method with EFDMs as input data. Based on the publicly available EEG dataset SEED, we firstly valid the effectiveness of our method on EEG emotion recognition task with EFDMs and CNN under conventional experimental settings. Then, combined with CNN and DDC, we set up another experiment for cross-subject emotion recognition task. Finally, we analyze the focus of the network in specific emotional classification tasks through the Grad-CAM.

2 Methods

2.1 Short-Time Fourier Transform

Fourier transform (FT) can transform complex time and space signals into frequency domain, and then use relatively simple spectrum characteristics to find the dynamic characteristics of the original signal. However, FT assumes that the signal is stationary and that the spectrum description is global, it can't reflect the local information of time dimension. Because of the high nonstationary of EEG signals, it is not suitable for the hypothesis of FT signals. In this paper, the method of Short-Time Fourier Transform (STFT) is used. STFT method regards long nonstationary EEG signal as a series of short-time random stationary EEG signal superposition, which is realized by adding time window. The calculation formula of STFT is as follows:

$$STFT_x(t,f) = \int_{-\infty}^{+\infty} [x(t')r^*(t'-t)]e^{-j2\pi ft'}\,dt' \tag{1}$$

$$w[n] = \frac{1}{2}\left[1 + \cos(2pi * \frac{n}{N-1})\right] n \in \left[-\frac{N-1}{2}, \frac{N-1}{2}\right] \tag{2}$$

Where, $x(t')$ is the original signal, f represents the sampling frequency, $r * (t - t')$ is Hanning window, (which shown in (2), a discrete version) is a linear combination of modulated rectangular windows, and it usually emerges in applications that require low aliasing and less spectrum leakage. n is the window length and N is the sampling number.

2.2 Emotion Recognition Model Based on CNN and DDC

In domain adaptation, because there is little or no labeled data in the target domain, the tagging cost is usually reduced by establishing effective algorithms. One of the typical methods is to predict the labels of the target domain using the labeled source domain data, the other is to train the available source and target data jointly so as to minimize the loss of accuracy. Use source data directly to train classifiers often leads to over-fitting of source distribution, which results in performance degradation in target domain recognition. DDC method can not only learn a representation of minimizing the distance between two domains (maximizing the domain confusion), but also has superior classifier which trained in the source domain is directly applied to the target domain to reduce the loss of accuracy. To minimize the distance, the method uses the standard distributed distance metric (MMD):

$$MMD(X_S, X_T) = \left\| \frac{1}{|X_S|} \sum_{x_s \in X_S} \Phi(x_s) - \frac{1}{|X_T|} \sum_{x_t \in X_T} \Phi(x_t) \right\| \tag{3}$$

Where, x_s represent data points in source domain, represent data points in target domain, $\Phi(\cdot)$ is mapping, used to map variables to Reproducing Kernel Hilbert Space (RKHS). DDC uses an assessment method to minimize losses:

$$L = L_C(X_L, y) + \lambda MMD^2(X_S, X_T) \tag{4}$$

Where, $L_C(X_L, y)$ denotes classification on tagged source domain data, and ground truth labels y, $MMD(X_S, X_T)$ denotes the distance between the source data, X_S, and the target data, X_T. Super parameters λ represent the strength of domain confusion.

This paper introduces a new convolutional neural network structure based on three-layer residual blocks. The gradient disappearance of the neural network is effectively alleviated by jumping connections between the residual blocks, as shown in the Fig. 2 (b). After each residual layer, the maximum pooling layer is employed to down sample the data. In the design of residual blocks, the convolution kernel of 3 * 3 size can reduce memory consumption [22] while ensuring recognition accuracy, and solve the internal covariate shift problem [23] by standardizing each level of data batch after convolution. We design a set of controlled trials. A method is designed to verify the feasibility of emotion recognition on SEED datasets by using traditional machine learning methods. The traditional machine learning method model uses a CNN architecture introduced above, as shown in the Fig. 1. Another method is deep domain adaptive experiment across subjects, as shown in the Fig. 2(a). A low-dimensional bottleneck layer is added to the convolutional neural network structure as an adaptive layer to standardize the training of classifier and prevent over-fitting of the special nuances of source distribution. The loss of domain distance is placed at the top of the bottleneck layer to normalize the invariant features of source and target domains. The structure includes two CNN architectures, source and target CNN, which share weights between the two architectures. After the adaptive layer, a fork is used. One branch is used to train the classifier with labeled data, and the other branch is used to calculate the distance between source and target domains for all data.

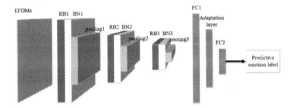

Fig. 1. Experimental CNN architecture

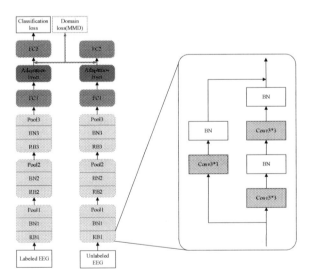

Fig. 2. (a) Deep CNN model based on DDC (b) Residual block structure

3   Dataset Description and Analysis

3.1   SEED Dataset Introduction and Preprocessing

SEED Dataset (SJTU Emotion EEG Dataset) is an electroencephalogram dataset which is publicly provided by Zheng et al. for emotional recognition research [24]. The dataset consisted of 15 Chinese movie clips with specific emotions (positive, neutral and negative) and was tested in 15 subjects (7 males and 8 females). Each participant participated in the experiment three times, with an interval of about 7 days. According to the international 10–20 system, EEG signals of subjects watching movie clips were recorded at a sampling rate of 1 kHz from 62 channel electrode caps using ESI NeuroScan device. A single experiment consisted of 15 movie segments, with 5 s of prompting time before the beginning of each segment, 45 s of information feedback time after the end of each segment (participants were self-assessed according to the degree of specific emotion), and 15 s of rest before the next segment was tested. In the process of data preprocessing, the original EEG signal is down sampled to 200 Hz and filtered by 0–75 Hz band pass filter.

The length of EEG signals collected under different stimulation fragments is not the same. In the design of this experiment, we first count the length of all EEG signal fragments, and then cut them (take the first 37000 sample points for subsequent analysis) to ensure that the final number of emotional samples is the same. Finally, EEG data in each channel is divided into 1 s data fragments in a non-overlapping way. A total of 185 samples were obtained in each film segment of the single experiment, so 41625 samples were obtained in all kinds of emotional states.

3.2   Data Distribution Analysis

In order to illustrate the difference between the EEG signals collected in different subjects, 50 samples of each of the three emotions were randomly selected from a single experiment of one subject for feature distribution analysis. Firstly, the Differential Entropy (DE) features of five sub-bands of EEG signals in all channels of each sample are extracted, and form the feature vectors. Then the dimensionality of the feature data is reduced by Principal Component Analysis (PCA), and two components with the largest eigenvalues are retained to analyze the data distribution.

As shown in the Fig. 3. The data distribution among different subjects is quite different, which does not satisfy the assumption of independent and identical distribution between training data and test data in traditional machine learning. In addition, the difference between the three emotional characteristics of the same subject is not obvious. Therefore, in this case, conventional machine learning methods often fail to achieve good recognition results. The recently proposed transfer learning method is specifically designed to solve this problem.

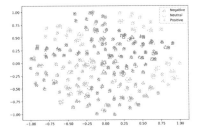

Fig. 3. Data distribution of different subjects in SEED dataset

3.3   Electrode-Frequency Distribution Map

Firstly, the SFFT is utilized to each channel of EEG signals of all the data samples obtained above, and then normalized transformation results to obtain the data form suitable for the input of convolutional neural network. In this paper, they are called Electrode-frequency Distribution Maps (EFDMs). EFDMs of EEG signal can be regarded as an RGB image, and its transformation results can be compared with the pixel value after normalization. Therefore, EFDMs as input of CNN achieve the goal of constructing emotion recognition model. The Fig. 4 shows the EFDMs under three emotions.

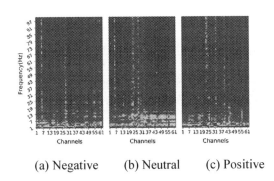

(a) Negative   (b) Neutral   (c) Positive

Fig. 4. EFDMs under three emotions

4   Experiments and Results Analysis

In this section, two experiments are designed as Fig. 5. Firstly, according to the traditional machine learning method, the feasibility of the EFDMs combined with convolutional neural network for emotion recognition is verified on SEED dataset. Then, a cross-subject deep domain adaptive experiment is designed. Finally, the focus of the network in the input data is analyzed through the Grad-CAM.

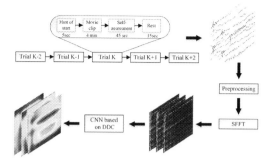

Fig. 5. Flow chart of experiment

4.1 Conventional (Subject-Dependent) EEG Emotion Recognition

In this experiment, a CNN architecture is used in the traditional machine learning model. A total of 2775 samples were taken as test sets in three experiments, and the remaining 14 samples were taken as training sets. The conventional (subject-dependent) EEG emotion recognition method achieved an average accuracy of 90.59%, which validated excellent effectiveness of our method on EEG emotion recognition task with EFDMs and CNN. The SGD algorithm was used as the optimization method in the training process. The learning rate was 0.0001, and the loss function was the cross-entropy loss function. The Pytorch deep learning framework was used to realize the network training curve as shown in the Fig. 6.

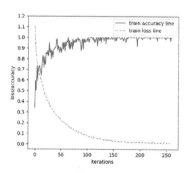

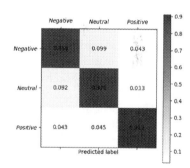

Fig. 6. Training process of CNN   **Fig. 7.** Confusion matrix

Here we compare our method with Canonical Correlation Analysis (CCA) [25], Group Sparse Canonical Correlation Analysis (GSCCA) [26], and Deep Believe Network (DBN) [27], GraphSLDA [28], DANN [29] in Table 1.

Table 1. The mean accuracies (ACC) and standard deviations (STD) on SEED dataset for conventional EEG emotional recognition experiment.

Method	ACC (%)	STD (%)
CCA [25]	77.63	13.21
GSCCA [26]	82.96	09.95
DBN [27]	86.08	08.34
GraphSLDA [28]	87.39	08.64
DANN [29]	91.36	08.30
EFDMs, CNN [our method]	90.59	08.49

To see the results of recognizing each emotion, we depict the confusion matrix corresponding to the experiments on SEED, as shown in Fig. 7. Each row of the confusion matrix represents the target class and each column represents the predicted class that a classifier outputs. The element (i, j) is the percentage of samples in class i that was classified as class j. From the results, we can see that in general, positive emotion can be recognized with high accuracies, while negative emotion is most difficult to recognize. They confuse negative emotion with neutral and positive emotion, and cannot classify negative emotion very well.

4.2   Cross-Subject EEG Emotion Recognition

In this experiment, we use a leave-one-subject-out (LOSO) cross-validation strategy to evaluate the performance of our model, which is the same as Zheng et al. [17]. Specifically, in the LOSO cross-validation experiment, 14 subjects were trained with EEG data, and the remaining 1 subjects were tested with EEG data. The experiment was repeated in three experiments. Each subject's EEG data was used as test data, and the average classification accuracy and standard deviation corresponding to each experiment were calculated separately. Using cross-subject emotion recognition method based on CNN and deep domain confusion DDC, the SEED data set was compared to the three experiments, the number of samples in the single experiment was 925 and 2775 samples of three emotions were collected from each participant in each experiment. The cross-validation method was used to test the data. There were 38850 training samples and 2775 test samples.

The model-based transfer method is adopted in the experiment, which helps to improve the accuracy of training and the generalization ability of the model. The weights of the model trained in experiment 4.1 are loaded into the CNN-DDC model to find the shared parameter information from the source domain and the target do-main, so that the model parameters can be shared between the two domains. As expected, the experiment achieved much better performance at 82.16%/4.43% for mean accuracy and standard deviation. In the training process, Adam algorithm is used as the optimization method. The learning rate is 0.00001 and the loss function are the cross-entropy loss function. The Pytorch deep learning framework is used to realize the training process. This comparative experiment is based on literature [30] in Table 2.

Table 2. Leave-one-subject-out cross validation accuracy, mean% (STD %)

Method	Session1	Session2	Session3	Average
MIDA [31]	72.31(10.86)	69.45(15.18)	75.64(11.37)	72.47(12.47)
TCA [11]	75.91(11.52)	74.19(12.26)	75.87(06.87)	75.32(11.07)
TSC [32]	73.33(07.61)	72.61(09.08)	67.03(09.79)	70.84(06.44)
TJM [33]	77.62(10.90)	74.30(12.06)	76.79(05.69)	76.24(10.38)
SAAE [18]	80.22(08.00)	74.68(12.76)	78.73(12.96)	77.88(07.33)
ASFM [19]	83.51(07.40)	76.68(12.16)	81.20(10.68)	80.46(06.84)
EFDMs, CNN, DDC	78.40(06.76)	83.30(02.09)	85.69(04.14)	82.16(04.43)

4.3 Deep Neural Network Attention Analysis

For the trained network, we use the Gradient-weighted Class Activation Mapping (Grad-CAM) [34] to explore the feature information learned by the deep network. Grad-CAM aims to obtain the input part of the network's attention by calculating the derivative of the output characteristic map of the network, as shown in Eqs. (5) and (6).

$$\alpha_k^c = \frac{1}{Z} \sum_i \sum_j \frac{\partial y^c}{\partial A_{ij}^k} \tag{5}$$

$$L_{Grad-CAM}^c = RELU\left(\sum_k \alpha_k^c A^k\right) \tag{6}$$

Where, A^k is the feature map of the kth layer of the convolutional neural network, and α_k^c is the weight corresponding to the kth layer feature map. The idea of Grad-CAM is to calculate the derivative of the output to the feature graph to get the importance of each feature graph for recognition effect, and use the weight obtained to average each feature graph to get the area that the network pays attention to when recognizing this kind of target. It has been proved that Grad-CAM can effectively capture the object to be processed in image processing.

In this paper, Grad-CAM is obtained by deriving the output of the last layer of network convolution using the above method. The Fig. 8 is a Grad-CAM based on the network trained by SEED dataset. As can be seen from the figure, the trained network pays more attention to the high frequency part (beta and gamma band) of EEG signal, which is consistent with the conclusion in literature [8, 24], that is, the high frequency characteristic component contains more important distinguishing information.

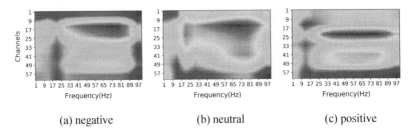

(a) negative   (b) neutral   (c) positive

Fig. 8. Grad-CAM based on SEED dataset training

5 Conclusion

Due to the complexity of EEG signals and the limitation of traditional machine learning methods, in this paper, we present a comparative study on domain adaption method, and a preliminary study utilize EFDMs on across-subject emotion recognition with the combination of CNN and DDC. The effectiveness of the proposed methods was verified on SEED, a popular dataset in the field. The proposed method achieved an average accuracy of 90.59% in conventional (subject-dependent) EEG emotion recognition and 82.16% (04.43%) in across-subject emotion recognition. Finally, Grad-CAM of computational network is used to verify the feasibility of emotion recognition based on CNN. The experimental results show that high frequency (beta and gamma band) EEG signals are more conducive to emotion recognition. The emotion recognition model based on CNN and DDC strategy proposed in this paper can well realize the emotion recognition task, and contribute to the promotion of EEG emotion recognition system in engineering field. At present, our work is focused on DDC method to make the data of source domain and target domain share parameters, which can match the distribution of source data and target data. In the future, we will continue to explore the application of transfer learning in emotion recognition, in order to achieve the recognition with different marginal and conditional distributions of small samples.

References

1. Mühl, C., Jeunet, C., Lotte, F.: EEG-based workload estimation across affective contexts. Front. Neurosci. **8**, 114 (2014)
2. Al-Kaysi, A.M., Al-Ani, A., Loo, C.K., et al.: Predicting tDCS treatment outcomes of patients with major depressive disorder using automated EEG classification. J. Affect. Disord. **208**, 597–603 (2017)
3. Fan, Y., Lu, X., Li, D., et al.: Video-based emotion recognition using CNN-RNN and C3D hybrid networks. In: Proceedings of the 18th ACM International Conference on Multimodal Interaction, pp. 445–450. ACM (2016)
4. Yan, J., Zheng, W., Cui, Z., et al.: Multi-cue fusion for emotion recognition in the wild. Neurocomputing **309**, 27–35 (2018)

5. Zhang, J., Chen, M., Zhao, S., et al.: ReliefF-based EEG sensor selection methods for emotion recognition. Sensors **16**(10), 1558 (2016)
6. Chen, J., Hu, B., Wang, Y., et al.: A three-stage decision framework for multi-subject emotion recognition using physiological signals. In: 2016 IEEE International Conference on Bioinformatics and Biomedicine (BIBM), pp. 470–474. IEEE (2016)
7. Kollia, V., Elibol, O.H.: Distributed processing of biosignal-database for emotion recognition with mahout. arXiv preprint arXiv:1609.02631 (2016)
8. Zheng, W.L., Guo, H.T., Lu, B.L.: Revealing critical channels and frequency bands for emotion recognition from EEG with deep belief network. In: 2015 7th International IEEE/EMBS Conference on Neural Engineering (NER), pp. 154–157. IEEE (2015)
9. Zheng, W.L., Zhu, J.Y., Peng, Y., et al.: EEG-based emotion classification using deep belief networks. In: 2014 IEEE International Conference on Multimedia and Expo (ICME), pp. 1–6. IEEE (2014)
10. Zheng, W.L., Liu, W., Lu, Y., et al.: EmotionMeter: a multimodal framework for recognizing human emotions. IEEE Trans. Cybern. **99**, 1–13 (2018)
11. Pan, S.J., Tsang, I.W., Kwok, J.T., et al.: Domain adaptation via transfer component analysis. IEEE Trans. Neural Netw. **22**(2), 199–210 (2011)
12. Borgwardt, K.M., Gretton, A., Rasch, M.J., et al.: Integrating structured biological data by kernel maximum mean discrepancy. Bioinformatics **22**(14), e49–e57 (2006)
13. Fernando, B., Habrard, A., Sebban, M., et al.: Subspace alignment for domain adaptation. arXiv preprint arXiv:1409.5241 (2014)
14. Sun, B., Saenko, K.: Subspace distribution alignment for unsupervised domain adaptation. In: BMVC, vol. 4, pp. 24.1–24.10 (2015)
15. Yin, Z., Wang, Y., Liu, L., et al.: Cross-subject EEG feature selection for emotion recognition using transfer recursive feature elimination. Front. Neurorobotics **11**, 19 (2017)
16. Yin, Z., Zhang, J.: Cross-session classification of mental workload levels using EEG and an adaptive deep learning model. Biomed. Signal Process. Control **33**, 30–47 (2017)
17. Zheng, W.L., Lu, B.L.: Personalizing EEG-based affective models with transfer learning. In: Proceedings of the Twenty-Fifth International Joint Conference on Artificial Intelligence, pp. 2732–2738. AAAI Press (2016)
18. Chai, X., Wang, Q., Zhao, Y., et al.: Unsupervised domain adaptation techniques based on auto-encoder for non-stationary EEG-based emotion recognition. Comput. Biol. Med. **79**, 205–214 (2016)
19. Chai, X., Wang, Q., Zhao, Y., et al.: A fast, efficient domain adaptation technique for cross-domain electroencephalography (EEG)-based emotion recognition. Sensors **17**(5), 1014 (2017)
20. Tzeng, E., Hoffman, J., Zhang, N., et al.: Deep domain confusion: maximizing for domain invariance. arXiv preprint arXiv:1412.3474 (2014)
21. Li, M., Chen, W., Zhang, T.: Classification of epilepsy EEG signals using DWT-based envelope analysis and neural network ensemble. Biomed. Signal Process. Control **31**, 357–365 (2017)
22. He, K., Zhang, X., Ren, S., et al.: Deep residual learning for image recognition. In: Proceedings of the IEEE Conference on Computer Vision and Pattern Recognition, pp. 770–778 (2016)
23. Ioffe, S., Szegedy, C.: Batch normalization: accelerating deep network training by reducing internal covariate shift. arXiv preprint arXiv:1502.03167 (2015)
24. Zheng, W.L., Lu, B.L.: Investigating critical frequency bands and channels for EEG-based emotion recognition with deep neural networks. IEEE Trans. Auton. Ment. Dev. **7**(3), 162–175 (2015)

25. Thompson, B.: Canonical correlation analysis. In: Encyclopedia of Statistics in Behavioral Science (2005)
26. Zheng, W.: Multichannel EEG-based emotion recognition via group sparse canonical correlation analysis. IEEE Trans. Cogn. Dev. Syst. **9**(3), 281–290 (2017)
27. Liu, W, Zheng, W.L., Lu, B.L.: Multimodal emotion recognition using multimodal deep learning. arXiv preprint arXiv:1602.08225 (2016)
28. Li, Y., Zheng, W., Cui, Z., Zhou, X.: A novel graph regularized sparse linear discriminant analysis model for EEG emotion recognition. In: Hirose, A., Ozawa, S., Doya, K., Ikeda, K., Lee, M., Liu, D. (eds.) ICONIP 2016. LNCS, vol. 9950, pp. 175–182. Springer, Cham (2016). https://doi.org/10.1007/978-3-319-46681-1_21
29. Ganin, Y., Ustinova, E., Ajakan, H., et al.: Domain-adversarial training of neural networks. J. Mach. Learn. Res. **17**(1), 2096–2130 (2016)
30. Lan, Z., Sourina, O., Wang, L., et al.: Domain adaptation techniques for EEG-based emotion recognition: a comparative study on two public datasets. IEEE Trans. Cogn. Dev. Syst. **11**(1), 85–94 (2019)
31. Yan, K., Kou, L., Zhang, D.: Learning domain-invariant subspace using domain features and independence maximization. IEEE Trans. Cybern. **48**(1), 288–299 (2018)
32. Long, M., Ding, G., Wang, J., et al.: Transfer sparse coding for robust image representation. In: Proceedings of the IEEE Conference on Computer Vision and Pattern Recognition, pp. 407–414 (2013)
33. Long, M., Wang, J., Ding, G., et al.: Transfer joint matching for unsupervised domain adaptation. In: Proceedings of the IEEE Conference on Computer Vision and Pattern Recognition, pp. 1410–1417 (2014)
34. Selvaraju, R.R, Cogswell, M., Das, A., et al.: Grad-CAM: visual explanations from deep networks via gradient-based localization. In: Proceedings of the IEEE International Conference on Computer Vision, pp. 618–626 (2017)

Development of Mixed Reality Robot Control System Based on HoloLens

Xuanmeng Sha, Zixi Jia$^{(\boxtimes)}$, Weidong Sun, Yida Hao, Xingang Xiao,
and Hanlu Hu

Faculty of Robot Science and Engineering,
Northeastern University, Shenyang 110169, Liaoning, China
1069760532@qq.com, jiazixi@mail.neu.edu.cn

Abstract. By using HoloLens, a wearable mixed reality device, and Unity3D, a 3D real-time driving engine, to simulate the robot kinematics and dynamics control in a mixed reality environment, we can test the performance of the control algorithm in virtual space before the physical simulation of the robot control algorithm. This paper first introduces the method of constructing a parameter-adjustable manipulator model with arbitrary degrees of freedom using Unity3D, and then introduces the method of using C# programming to implement the inverse kinematics simulation of the manipulator, and establishes a six-degree-of-freedom manipulator inverse kinematics control model to verify the feasibility of this method. Finally, we use the classic one-stage inverted pendulum model to verify the feasibility of robot dynamics control in Unity3D. This method changes the situation that the existing simulation method is difficult to interact with the real environment. Users can use the virtual robot model to verify the feasibility of the control scheme in complex environments.

Keywords: HoloLens · Six-degree-of-freedom manipulator ·
Inverse kinematics · Inverted pendulum · Robotic dynamics ·
Double closed-loop control · Mixed reality

1 Introduction

1.1 Mixed Reality Technology

Mixed reality (MR) technology is a new technology that attaches the virtual objects to the real world and combines the virtual world with the real one. Through spatial mapping, holographic projection technology, human-computer interaction technology and sensor technology, MR technology can provide users with a semi-immersive environment, users can not only perceive the real objects in the real world but also perceive the virtual objects. An information loop of interactive feedback is established between the real world, the virtual world, and the users, which enhances the reality of the user experience [1].

The hardware support of this system is HoloLens, which is a Windows 10-based head-mounted mixed display device released by Microsoft. It has an independent computing unit and can be used without cables. HoloLens can overlay virtual objects

H. Yu et al. (Eds.): ICIRA 2019, LNAI 11740, pp. 571–581, 2019.
https://doi.org/10.1007/978-3-030-27526-6_50

into the real world, allowing users to interact with digital content and holographic images in the surrounding environment [2].

1.2   3D Real-Time Drive Engine

The software support of this system is Unity 3D, which is a game development tool that supports cross-platform release. It provides users with a powerful physics engine system, including a variety of physical simulation components, such as the Rigid body, Character Controller, Collision body, Joints, etc. Developers can build complex virtual scenes easily using the encapsulated API functions in the engine. The script can be used to set the parameters to make the object showing physical behavior similar to reality. The combination of multiple components can show the most realistic physics for users [3].

1.3   The Six-Degree-of-Freedom Manipulator Inverse Kinematics Control Model and One-Stage Inverted Pendulum

The Six-Degree-of-Freedom Manipulator. This manipulator consists of six one-degree-of-freedom joints in series with each other. The model of the manipulator is modeled by DH parameters. The system can get each joint angle by inverse kinematics arithmetic for a given end pose of the manipulator.

One-Stage Inverted Pendulum. The inverted pendulum control system is a typical multivariable, high order, nonlinear, strong coupling, natural unstable system, which can intuitively display many classic abstract concepts in control theory, such as the system's rapidity, stability, Anti-interference capacity [4], etc. Its applications have been widely distributed in the fields of robot control, industrial automation control, artificial intelligence and so on. This system can achieve the function of stabilizing the inverted pendulum in the equilibrium position by adjusting the PID parameters of the inner loop and the outer loop.

2   Related Works

There are several studies, the simulation of virtual reality robot control systems, in the research of universities. Peng Zhang's team, a university scientific research team from the China University of Petroleum, used MATLAB V-Realm Builder to model and used Simulink to build a simulation model of virtual reality 3-DOF manipulator [5]. Jianbo Xiao's team, a university scientific research team from the Wuhan University of Technology, established a double closed-loop one-stage inverted pendulum simulation model using a similar method [6]. Linyi Cai's team, a university scientific research team from Chongqing University of Posts and Telecommunications, used 3DMAX to model and used Unity3D to build the inverted pendulum controller simulation model [7]. Lei Lei's team, a university scientific research team from Dalian Jiaotong University used SolidWorks to model and used Unity3D to build a simulation model of virtual manipulator [8]. The above-mentioned systems are all simulated in PC. We can clearly test the feasibility of tasks that performed in a simple environment by using the above-mentioned systems before the robot is manufactured. However, these above-mentioned systems all require an additional environment model that complicates the simulation, when the environment for performing tasks becomes complicated.

This paper presents a method for building a mixed reality robot control system, a system suitable for operation in HoloLens, using Unity3D. We can directly combine the virtual robot model with a realistic environment by using this method and easily test the feasibility of tasks that performed in a complex environment. The inverse kinematics control model of the six-degree-of-freedom manipulator and the dynamic control model of the inverted pendulum are designed in this paper, and the feasibility of the scheme in robot kinematics and dynamics is demonstrated.

3   Development of Robot Control System in Mixed Reality

3.1   Virtual 3D Models with Adjustable Physical Parameters in Unity3D

Inverted Pendulum Model. We build a simple model of a one-stage inverted pendulum in Unity 3D based on the required components. The inverted pendulum model, including the track, car, and pendulum, consists of several cubes and cylinders which can be customized shapes and sizes. They are all rigid bodies to be in accord with reality. The mass of the car and pendulum is 0.5 kg and 0.2 kg, the length of the pendulum and track is 2 m and 20 m, the left-most and the right-most coordinate is −10 and 10.

Besides, we use UI components in Unity3D to build three interfaces. The first interface is the PID parameter adjustment interface controlled by the slider, which is used to adjust the PID parameters and observe the control effect in real time. The second interface is two coordinate planes that can display the relationship images between the position and time of the car and the relationship between the angle of pendulum and time. The third interface has a size adjustment slider and the system reset button (Fig. 1).

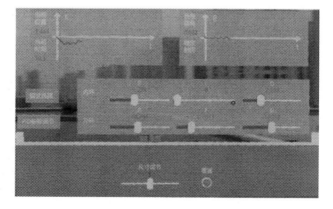

Fig. 1. One-stage inverted pendulum mixed reality system

Six-Degree-of-Freedom Manipulator Model. In order to reduce the rendering pressure of HoloLens on virtual scenes, we used the basic model in Unity3D to build the scene that performing a six-degree-of-freedom manipulator. In the actual design, the Cube model is used instead of the link in the six-degree-of-freedom manipulator, and the Cylinder model is used instead of the joint in the six-degree-of-freedom manipulator. The small ball with an arrow indicates the target that the six-degree-of-freedom manipulator grabs. The collision model and the relative position of each component of the six-degree-of-freedom manipulator can be adjusted in the Transform module, a panel of the Inspector component in Unity3D, according to the actual requirements.

For the user interface of the six-degree-of-freedom manipulator, we use one slider to control the size of the model, and three sliders to control the attitude of the ball. The position of the six-degree-of-freedom manipulator and the ball can be directly changed by dragging-gesture (Fig. 2).

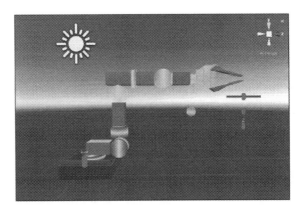

Fig. 2. Six-degree-of-freedom manipulator model and operator interface (to make the model scalability, add a redundant degree of freedom)

3.2   Virtual 3D Models with Adjustable Physical Parameters in Unity3D

The One-Stage Inverted Pendulum Control Model. According to the analysis of the one-stage inverted pendulum structure, the physical model is as shown in Fig. 3.

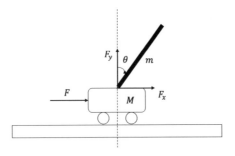

Fig. 3. Physical model of one-stage inverted pendulum

Where M is the quality of the car, m is the quality of pendulum, l is the length of the pendulum, θ is the angle of the pendulum, F_x is the horizontal force of pendulum, F_y is the vertically upward direction force of pendulum. According to Newton's laws of motion, then we can get [9]:

$$J\ddot{\theta} = F_y l \sin\theta - F_x l \cos\theta \tag{1}$$

$$\begin{cases} F_x = m\frac{d^2}{dt^2}(x + l\sin\theta) \\ F_y = mg - m\frac{d^2}{dt^2}(l\cos\theta) \end{cases} \tag{2}$$

Analyze the horizontal force of pendulum, then we can get:

$$F - F_x = M\frac{d^2x}{d^2t} \tag{3}$$

According to the above equations, we can get the specific model of the one-stage inverted pendulum:

$$\begin{cases} \ddot{x} = \frac{(J+ml^2)F + ml(J+ml^2)\sin\theta\cdot\dot{\theta}^2 - m^2l^2g\sin\theta\cos\theta}{(J+ml^2)(M+m) - m^2l^2\cos^2\theta} \\ \ddot{\theta} = \frac{ml^2\cos\theta\cdot F + m^2l^2\sin\theta\cos\theta\cdot\dot{\theta}^2 - (M+m)mlg\sin\theta}{m^2l^2\cos^2\theta - (J+ml^2)(M+m)} \end{cases} \tag{4}$$

In these two equations, J is the pendulum's moment of inertia:

$$J = \frac{ml^2}{3} \tag{5}$$

Since there is little amplitude, we can assume that $\dot{\theta} \approx 0$, $\sin\theta \approx 0$, $\cos\theta \approx 1$. We can get:

$$\begin{cases} \ddot{x} = \frac{(J+ml^2)F - m^2l^2g\theta}{J(M+m) - Mml^2} \\ \ddot{\theta} = \frac{(M+m)mlg\theta - mlF}{J(M+m) + Mml^2} \end{cases} \tag{6}$$

The inverted pendulum is a single-input and multi-output system. the control goal is to stabilize the car near the equilibrium position and keep the pendulum in an upright position at the same time. So a double closed-loop control system is designed. The inner loop controls the angle of the inverted pendulum, and the outer loop controls the car displacement. In that case, the angle of the pendulum is a perturbation to the outer loop, which makes the position of the car a controllable factor under the condition of keeping the pendulum from falling down [10].

Above all, we can get our one-stage inverted pendulum double closed loop control system [11] (Fig. 4):

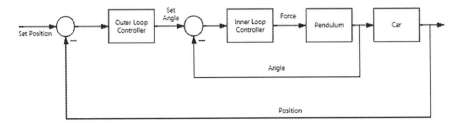

Fig. 4. One-stage inverted pendulum model implementation flow chart

The Six-Degree-of-Freedom Manipulator Inverse Kinematics Control Model

For solving the six-degree-of-freedom manipulator inverse kinematics, we use the geometric solution to obtain the solution of the six-degree-of-freedom manipulator. The geometric solution has the advantages of fast calculation speed and less singular solution, which can greatly reduce the CPU operation overhead of HoloLens (Fig. 5 and Table 1).

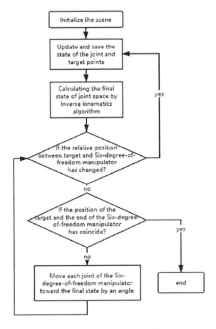

Fig. 5. The Six-degree-of-freedom manipulator inverse kinematics control model implementation flow chart

Table 1. Robot D-H parameter table

Joint i	α_{i-1}	a_{i-1}/mm	d_i/mm	θ_i
1	0°	0	1.5	0°
2	−90°	1.25	0	−90°
3	0°	1.75	0	60°
4	90°	0.5	2	−90°
5	90°	0	0	0°
6	−90°	0	1.75	0°

According to the rotation mode and the positional relationship of the six-degree-of-freedom manipulator link, we can infer that the centers of the joints 1, 2, 3, 4, 5 are in the same plane. Set the current positions of joints 1, 2, 3, 4, 5, 6 to $\{P_1, P_2, P_3, P_4, P_t, P_6\}$, set the target positions to $\{P_{t1}, P_{t2}, P_{t3}, P_{t4}, P_{t5}, P_{t6}\}$, set the target angle to $\{\theta_{t1}, \theta_{t2}, \theta_{t3}, \theta_{t4}, \theta_{t5}, \theta_{t6}\}$, set the position of the target to P_T. Taking P_1 as the coordinate origin, it is easy to get $P_{t1} = P_1$. By solving these two equations:

$$\begin{cases} P_{t6} = P_T \\ P_{t6} - P_{t5} = \frac{P_T}{|P_T|}|P_6 - P_5| \end{cases} \tag{7}$$

to get P_{t5}, because the centers of joints 1, 2, 3, 4, 5 are in the same plane, by solving these two equations:

$$\begin{cases} (P_{t2})_z = (P_{t1})_z \\ \frac{[(P_{t5}-P_{t1})_x, (P_{t5}-P_{t1})_y]}{\sqrt{(P_{t5}-P_{t1})_x^2 + (P_{t5}-P_{t1})_y^2}} = \frac{[(P_{t2})_x, (P_{t2})_y]}{|P_2-P_1|} \end{cases} \tag{8}$$

to get P_{t2}, by solving these three equations:

$$\begin{cases} |P_5 - P_3| = |P_{t5} - P_{t3}| \\ |P_3 - P_2| = |P_{t3} - P_{t2}| \\ [(P_{t5} - P_{t3}) \times (P_{t3} - P_{t2})] \times [(P_{t5} - P_{t2}) \times (P_{t2} - P_{t1})] = 0 \end{cases} \tag{9}$$

to get P_{t3}, by solving these three equations:

$$\begin{cases} |P_5 - P_4| = |P_{t5} - P_{t4}| \\ |P_4 - P_3| = |P_{t4} - P_{t3}| \\ [(P_{t5} - P_{t4}) \times (P_{t4} - P_{t3})] \times [(P_{t5} - P_{t2}) \times (P_{t2} - P_{t1})] = 0 \end{cases} \tag{10}$$

to get P_{t4}.

Till then we can obtain the solutions of the final positions $\{P_{t1}, P_{t2}, P_{t3}, P_{t4}, P_{t5}, P_{t6}\}$ that indicating the six joints of the manipulator. After that, it is easy to get the final state $\{\theta_{t1}, \theta_{t2}, \theta_{t3}, \theta_{t4}, \theta_{t5}, \theta_{t6}\}$ indicating the six joints of the manipulator by geometric relation. In the actual algorithm implementation process, considering the moving speed of the mechanical, we rotate the joint $\Delta\theta$ in the direction to target angle each frame.

Considering the actual manipulator Operational situation, we set the maximum error angle θ_e for all joints. When $|\theta_t - \theta| \leq \theta_e$, the manipulator will stop running. So far, the six-degree-of-freedom manipulator control model has been completed.

4   Simulation

4.1   Constructing a One-Stage Inverted Pendulum Mixed Reality Simulation Scene

We export the inverted pendulum system scene to the visual studio and compile it, then connect the HoloLens to the computer. Export the scene to the HoloLens and conduct the experiment in the mixed reality environment. Observe the control effect of the inverted pendulum under circumstances of several PID parameters, then record the control precision and stability time. Evaluate the applicability and control effect of the inverted pendulum system in the mixed reality environment. The experiment process as shown in Fig. 6.

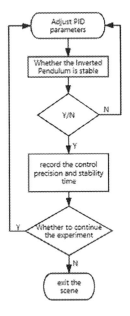

Fig. 6. Inverted pendulum experiment process

4.2   Constructing a Six-Degree-of-Freedom Manipulator Mixed Reality Simulation Scene

After building the simulation model with Unity3D, write C# code in Visual Studio to implement the six-degree-of-freedom manipulator inverse kinematics control model. Then debug in Unity3D and publish the model to HoloLens. Start the scene in

HoloLens, drag the manipulator base to the test position, and drag the slider to scale the manipulator to the test size. When the preparation is completed, drag the ball to the specified position and adjust the attitude of the ball to the specified posture. When the manipulator is running, observe whether the manipulator collides with the surrounding environment. When the manipulator stops, observe whether the manipulator reaches the specified position accurately (Fig. 7).

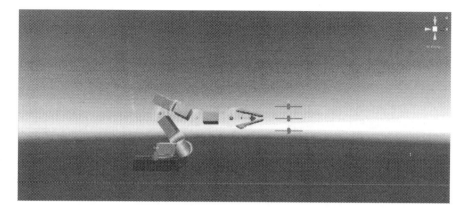

Fig. 7. Six-degree-of-freedom manipulator capture test chart

Test multiple sets of positions in different environments, observe the operation of the virtual manipulator, and observe the impact of the realistic environment on the operation of the manipulator.

4.3 One-Stage Inverted Pendulum Mixed Reality Simulation Results

After multiple sets of experiments, we get the optimal PID parameter combination of the inverted pendulum by trial and error (Table 2):

Table 2. PID parameters of one-stage inverted pendulum

	Proportion coefficient	Integral coefficient	Differential coefficient
Outer loop PID parameters	19	0.0012	12
Inner loop PID parameters	1.2	0	3

In this case, the stabilization time of the system is 25.7 s.

Through the above experiments, we can conduct the double-closed-loop PID control experiment on the inverted pendulum in a mixed reality environment, so the dynamic control model can be applied to the virtual environment, which can also be applied to control the manipulator.

4.4 Six-Degree-of-Freedom Manipulator Mixed Reality Simulation Results

The simulation results show that the virtual Six-degree-of-freedom manipulator performs well in different scenarios. During the simulation process, the interaction between the surrounding environment and the manipulator can be clearly observed. The collision model of the manipulator is clearly visible to the surrounding environment, and each grabbing of the manipulator can reach a preset error range, $|\theta_t - \theta| \leq \theta_e$, $\theta_e = 0.01$ (Fig. 8).

Fig. 8. The Six-degree-of-freedom manipulator grabbing test

Through the above experiments, we can achieve the purpose of accurately implementing the inverse of the six-degree-of-freedom manipulator in a mixed reality environment. And in this process, the moving trajectory of the manipulator, the size of the manipulator, and the running speed of the manipulator are all controllable. We can achieve the goals that the operator can real-time adjust the size and position of the manipulator to prevent the simulated arm from colliding with the surrounding environment. So that we can achieve the purpose of assisting the design of the manipulator in a complex environment.

5   Conclusion

The six-degree-of-freedom manipulator mixed reality simulation system and double closed loop one-stage inverted pendulum mixed reality simulation control system, which combines the Unity3D engine with the mixed reality device HoloLens, can make good use of the mixed reality characteristics of HoloLens and the simulation performance of the 3D real-time driving engine Unity3D to achieve the purpose of simulating the virtual robot dynamics and kinematics control system with certain complexity. And achieving the expected performance in actual performance. The system can simulate the situation that the robot control system interacting with the actual environment, and it can quickly and effectively verify the influence of a certain parameter on the application of the robot control system in the actual environment. It provides an effective parameter basis for the design of the robot control system, which greatly reduces the manufacturing cost of the robot control system and improves the design efficiency of the robot control system.

Acknowledgment. Liaoning Provincial Natural Science Foundation Project (20180520013); Liaoning Provincial Doctoral Research Fund (20170520211); National Natural Science Foundation of China (U1713216, 61872073); National Robot Key Project (2017YFB1300900).

References

1. Gong, C.: Application research of HoloLens mixed reality technology in construction industry. Mod. Inf. Technol. **3**(04), 147–149 (2019)
2. Gao, Y.: Development and enlightenment of virtual reality technology—taking Microsoft HOLOLENS as an example. Internet Econ. (12), 50–55 (2017)
3. You, W.: Design of virtual teaching system for robot noumenon based on Unity3D. Mech. Res. Appl. **31**(04), 230–234 (2018)
4. Zhang, X., Ma, J., Zhang, C.: Visualized modeling and simulation of inverted pendulum control based on MATLAB. Comput. Eng. Des. **39**(10), 3214–3219 (2018)
5. Zhang, P., Wang, X., Chen, J.: Virtual reality simulation of multi-degrees of freedom mechanical arm. Mach. Des. Manuf. (01), 128–130 (2015)
6. Xiao, J., Zheng, W.: Virtual reality technology—modeling and simulation of double closed loop one-stage inverted pendulum system. Intell. Robot. (10), 40–42 (2016)
7. Chen, S.: Research and implementation on virtual experiment environment oriented to automatic control. Chongqing University of Posts and Telecommunications (2017)
8. Wang, S.: Development of virtual interaction platform system for industrial robot based on Unity3D. Dalian Jiaotong University (2018)
9. Lu, Y., Guo, W.: Robot double-loop PID control system design inverted pendulum. In: Sun, W. (ed.) Industrial Design and Collaborative Innovation Conference and the 20th National Industrial Design Conference 2015, Proceedings of the Industrial Design and Collaborative Innovation Conference and the 20th National Industrial Design Academic Conference, Tian Jin, China, pp. 151–152 (2015)
10. Fei, F., Ru, L., Zhang, L.: Design and research of double closed-loop control strategy for inverted pendulum system. In: 2013 Third International Conference. IEEE, Hong Kong (2013)
11. Guo, B.: Design of cascade control system for inverted pendulum. Sci. Technol. Vis. (19), 151–152 (2016)

Improvement of Mask-RCNN Object Segmentation Algorithm

Xin Wu[1], Shiguang Wen[1(✉)], and Yuan-ai Xie[2]

[1] Northeastern University, Shenyang 110004, China
wenshiguang@mail.neu.edu.cn
[2] Yanshan University, Qinhuangdao 066004, China

Abstract. Semantic maps play a key role in tasks such as navigation of mobile robots. However, the visual SLAM algorithm based on multi-objective geometry does not make full use of the rich semantic information in space. The map point information retained in the map is just a spatial geometric point without semantics. Since the algorithm based on convolutional neural network has achieved breakthroughs in the field of target detection, the target segmentation algorithm MASK-RCNN is combined with the SLAM algorithm to construct the semantic map. However, the MASK-RCNN algorithm easily treats part of the background in the image as foreground, which results in inaccuracy of target segmentation. Moreover, Grubcut segmentation algorithm is time-consuming, but it's easy to take foreground as background, which leads to the excessive edge segmentation. Based on these, our paper proposes a novel algorithm which combines MASK-RCNN and Grubcut segmentation. By comparing the experimental results of MASK-Rcnn, Grubcut and the improved algorithm on the data set, it is obvious that the improved algorithm has the best segmentation effect and the accuracy of image target segmentation is significantly improved. These phenomenons demonstrate the effectiveness our proposed algorithm.

Keywords: Semantic map · Robot positioning and navigation · Scene segmentation · Deep learning

1 Introduction

In the mainstream SLAM algorithm, the position of the robot and the map point information are only geometric points which are located densely or sparsely in the space. Estimating the position of these spatial points provides us with a relatively accurate location information, but doesn't provide a higher level of semantic information. Moreover, although robots can use the SLAM algorithm to accurately estimate their position, they can't identify and model objects which exist in space. As a result, the robot is unable to take advantage of the rich environmental semantic information in subsequent tasks.

Current advances in deep learning provide a direction for solving this problem. The powerful feature learning ability of deep neural network [1] has made

© Springer Nature Switzerland AG 2019
H. Yu et al. (Eds.): ICIRA 2019, LNAI 11740, pp. 582–591, 2019.
https://doi.org/10.1007/978-3-030-27526-6_51

significant progress in the field of target detection and scene segmentation. In the aspect of target detection, the faster-RCNN -based deep learning method has greatly improved the accuracy of target detection [2]. In the aspect of scene segmentation, the MASK-RCNN-based neural network has detected and segmented the target well in the image [3]. However, the MASK-Rcnn segmentation algorithm has a high time overhead and a poor accuracy of image segmentation edge. Motivated by these limitations, our paper improves the scene segmentation algorithm in the semantic map construction project. As a result, the improved algorithm increases the accuracy of target segmentation in the process of dynamically building the semantic map [4]. By using the algorithm of this paper, the robot will identify the target more accurately in the scene and accomplish the purpose of positioning and navigation better.

2   Related Work

In recent years, many kinds Semantic Neural Networks have been proposed to segment target. To illustrate these better, the development of scene segmentation is given as follows:

(a) The introduction of Fully Convolution Networks [5] in 2015 opened a new chapter of semantic segmentation. The current classification network (AlexNet, VGG Net, and GoogLeNet) is modified as a full convolution network to generate accurate and detailed segmentation by combining the semantic information of the deep, rough network layer with the superficial information of the shallow, fine network layer. The network architecture is shown in Fig. 1.

(b) SegNet [6], the novelty lies in the way in which the decoder up-samples its lower resolution input feature map. The network architecture is shown in Fig. 2.

(c) U-Net [7], the feature map of the encoder is concisely spliced to the up-sampling feature map of the decoder at each stage, thus a trapezoidal structure is formed.

(d) DeepLab V1 [8] proposed atrous convolution which is also known as dilated convolution. The resolution of the feature graph is not reduced in the last two maximum pooling operations, and empty convolution is used in convolution after the penultimate maximum pool. After that, the conditional stochastic field (CRF) is used as post-processing, restore boundary details to achieve accurate positioning effect;

(e) DeepLab V2 [9] proposed a multi-scale robust segmentation method for hollow spatial pyramid Pooling (ASPP), and the location of target boundary is improved by combining DCNNs method and probabilistic graph model.

(f) DeepLab V3 [10], the Multi-Grid method is used to introduce different cavitation rates in the residual block. The image-level features are added to the hollow Space Pyramid pooling module, and Batch Normalization techniques are used.

(g) Based on Generating Against Networks (GANs), a semi-supervised framework is proposed. This semi-supervised framework includes a generator network to provide additional training samples for multi-class classifiers as discriminators in the GAN framework, from K possible The class assigns a label y to the sample or marks it as a fake sample (extra class). To ensure that the images produced by GANs are of higher quality, with improved pixel categorization, we extend the above framework by adding weak annotation data, which means we provide class-level information to the generator.

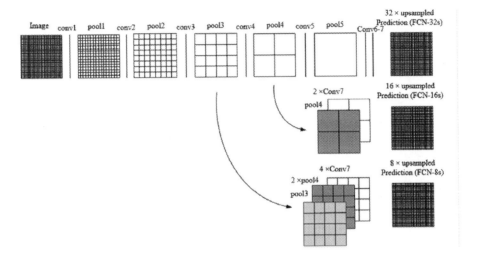

Fig. 1. FCN network architecture

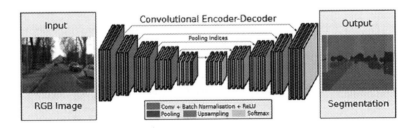

Fig. 2. SegNet network architecture

3   MASK-RCNN Target Segmentation Algorithm

3.1   Introduction to the Principle of MASK-RCNN

Instance segmentation should not only correctly find the objects in the image, but also accurately segment it. So Instance Segmentation [11] can be seen as a combination of object detection and semantic segmentation. Mask RCNN is an extension of Faster RCNN, for each faster Box of RCNN proposal to use FCN semantic segmentation [12], segmentation tasks and positioning, classification tasks are carried out at the same time. ROI Align [13] is introduced instead of RoI Pooling in Faster RCNN. Because the RoI Pooling is not aligned according to pixel one by one (Pixel-to-pixel alignment) [14], perhaps this has not a significant impact on bbox [15], but it has a significant impact on the accuracy of mask. The accuracy of mask after using RoI Align increased significantly from 10% to 50%. The semantic Segmentation branch is introduced to realize the decoupling of the relationship between mask and class prediction, and the Mask branch only does semantic segmentation [16], and the task of type prediction is given to another branch. This is different from the original FCN network, where the original FCN also predicts the types to which mask belongs when predicting mask [17]. The network structure of MASK R-CNN is shown in Fig. 3.

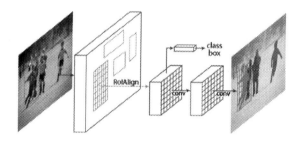

Fig. 3. The MASK R-CNN framework for instance segmentation

3.2 MASK-RCNN Test Results

By shooting in school to get the dataset, and then through the Mask-RCNN detection, the effect is shown in the following figure, found that the target detection effect is still very good, but in the contour edge of the task found there is still a certain error, in the edge part of the foreground is regarded as the background, there is a part of the background as the foreground, This results in the inaccuracy of the image segmentation effect. The original image is shown in Fig. 4, The image segmented by Mask-RCNN is shown in Fig. 5.

4 Grabcut Image Segmentation

Grabcut an interactive image segmentation technique using Graph cut graph segmentation and maximum flow technology. Grab cut replaces the model of the target and background of Graph with the hybrid Gaussian model GMM of the RGB three-channel, and divides the image by continuously dividing the segmentation estimation and the interactive iteration of the Model parameter learning.

Fig. 4. Original Image

Fig. 5. Image after segmentation by Mask-RCNN

4.1   Color Models

We use RGB color space to model the target and background with a K Gaussian component ($K = 5$) full covariance mixed Gaussian model (GMM). Thus there is an additional vector, which is the Gaussian component corresponding to the nth pixel. For each pixel, either from a Gaussian component of the target GMM, or from a Gaussian component of the background GMM. So the Gibbs energy used for the entire image is (Formula 1):

$$\mathbf{E}(\alpha, \mathbf{k}, \theta, \mathbf{z}) = U(\alpha, \mathbf{k}, \theta, \mathbf{z}) + V(\alpha, \mathbf{z}), \tag{1}$$

$$U(\alpha, \mathbf{k}, \theta, \mathbf{z}) = \sum_n D(\alpha_n, k_n, \theta, z_n), \tag{2}$$

$$D(\alpha_n, k_n, \theta, z_n) = -\log \pi(\alpha_n, k_n) + \frac{1}{2} \log \det \Sigma(\alpha_n, k_n)$$

$$+\frac{1}{2} \left[z_n - \mu(\alpha_n, k_n) \right]^T \Sigma(\alpha_n, k_n)^{-1} \left[z_n - \mu(\alpha_n, k_n) \right]. \tag{3}$$

$$\theta = \{ \pi(\alpha, k), \mu(\alpha, k), \Sigma(\alpha, k), \alpha = 0, 1, k = 1 \dots K \}, \tag{4}$$

where U is a regional item that represents a penalty for a pixel to be classified as a target or background, that is, a negative logarithm of the probability that a pixel belongs to the target or background. The mixed Gaussian density model is shown in the following formula:

$$\begin{cases} D(x) = \sum_{i=1}^{k} \pi_i g_i(x; \mu_i, \Sigma_i), \\ \sum_{i=1}^{k} \pi_i \leq 1, \\ 0 \leq \pi_i \leq 1. \end{cases} \tag{5}$$

$$g(x; \mu, \Sigma) = \frac{1}{\sqrt{(2\pi)^d |\Sigma|}} \exp \left[-\frac{1}{2}(x - \mu)^T \Sigma^{-1}(x - \mu) \right]. \tag{6}$$

So after taking the negative logarithm, it becomes the form of formula (3), in which there are three parameters: the weight π of each Gaussian component, the mean vector μ of each Gaussian component (because there are RGB three channels, so three element vectors) and the covariance matrix Σ (because there are RGB three channels, so the 3×3 matrix), formula (4). That is, these three parameters, which describe the GMM of the target and the GMM describing the background, need to be determined by learning. Once these three parameters have been determined, then when we know the RGB color value of a pixel, we can substitute the GMM of the target and the GMM of the background to get the probability that the pixel belongs to the target and background respectively, that is, the regional energy item of the Gibbs energy can be determined, That is, we can find out the weights of the t-link of the graph.

$$V(\alpha, z) = \gamma \sum_{(m,n) \in C} [\alpha_n \neq \alpha_m] \exp \left[-\beta \| z_m \neq z_n \|^2 \right], \tag{7}$$

Boundary items reflect discontinuous penalties between neighborhood pixels m and N, and if the two neighborhood pixels differ very little, then it is highly likely that they belong to the same target or the same background, and if they are very different, it means that the two pixels are likely to be at the edge of the target and background, and are more likely to be split open. So the greater the difference between the two neighborhood pixels, the smaller the energy. In RGB space, the similarity of two pixels is measured, and we use the European distance (two norm). The parameters of this beta are determined by the contrast of the image, and it can be imagined that if the contrast of the images is low, for pixels m and N, their difference is lower, we need to multiply this difference by multiplying a larger one, while for high contrast images, the difference between the pixels m and N for the same target is higher, It needs to be multiplied by a smaller one to narrow the difference so that the V can work properly with high or low contrast. At this point, the weight of the n-link can be determined by formula (7), when the diagram we want can be obtained, we can split it.

4.2   Iterative Energy Minimization Segmentation Algorithm

Initialization

- Step 1: The user gets an initial trimap T through a direct box selection target, which is all pixels outside the box as the background pixel, and the pixels in the box are all pixels that are "probably targets".
- Step 2: Each pixel n on the inside, initializes the label of the Pixel N, that is, the background pixel, and each pixel n on the inside, initializes the label of the Pixel N, which is the pixel as "may be the target".
- Step 3: After the above two steps, you can get some pixels that belong to the target ($\alpha_n = 1$), and the rest are pixels that belong to the background ($\alpha_n = 0$), and you can use this pixel to estimate the GMM of the target and background. By using the K-mean algorithm, the pixel clustering belonging to the target and background is the K class, that is, the K Gaussian model in the GMM, and each Gaussian model in the GMM has some pixel sample set, at which point its parameter mean and covariance can be estimated by their RGB value. The weight value of the Gaussian component can be determined by the ratio of the number of pixels belonging to the Gaussian component to the total number of pixels.

Iteration Minimization

- Step 1: Assign the Gaussian component in the GMM to each pixel:

$$k_n : \arg\min_{k_n} = D_n(\alpha_n, k_n, \theta, z_n) \tag{8}$$

- Step 2: For a given image data Z, learn to optimize the parameters of the GMM:

$$\theta : \arg\min_{\theta} = U(\alpha, k, \theta, z) \tag{9}$$

- Step 3: Split estimation (through the Gibbs Energy terms analyzed in 1, a graph is established and the weights T-link and N-link are obtained, and then segmented by the Max Flow/min cut algorithm):

$$\min_{\{\alpha_n : n \in T_u\}} \min_{k} = \mathbf{E}(\alpha, k, \theta, z) \tag{10}$$

- Step 4: Repeat steps (1) to (3) until convergent. After the segmentation of (3), each pixel belongs to the target GMM or the background GMM changes, so each pixel changes, so the GMM also changed, so each iteration will interactively optimize the GMM model and segmentation results. In addition, because the process of step (1) to (3) is the process of decreasing energy, it can be guaranteed that the iterative process will converge.
- Step 5: Use border matting to smooth the partitioned boundary and other post-processing.

(a) Original image

(b) Effect diagram after Mask-RCNN segmentation

(c) Image Effect diagram after Grabcut segmentation

(d) The effect diagram of the Mask-RCNN after the split image is then split grabcut

Fig. 6. Comparison diagram of the effect of Mask-RCNN, grabcut and improved algorithm under the original diagram

5   Experimental Results

It can be clearly seen from Fig. 6(b) that the edge contour of the Mask is beyond the edge of the target object, resulting in inaccuracy of the segmentation. It is obvious from Fig. 6(c) that the edge of the object is excessively segmented after the grabcut segmentation. Figure 6(d) It can be seen that the target object is well segmented. Therefore, it can be seen from the above experimental results that after the Mask-RCNN detection and segmentation, the image segmentation can significantly improve the accuracy of image segmentation.

6   Conclusion

In this work, Mask-RCNN is easy to use the background as the foreground at the edge, so that the edge exceeds the outline of the object itself, and Grabcut splits the edge of the foreground pixel as a background pixel, causing excessive segmentation and object edge contouring. Inaccurate, therefore, this paper combines Mask-RCNN and Grabcut algorithms to first pass the image through the Mask-RCNN algorithm and then Grabcut, and finds that the edge accuracy of the segmented object is greatly increased. Moreover, the effect of Grabcut segmentation only needs to be iterated several times, and the time consumed is far from the Mask-RCNN algorithm. In the real-time scene segmentation, the time of segmentation can be greatly reduced by combining Grabcut.

Acknowledgment. This work was supported by National Key R&D Program of China Number 2017YFB1301103, and the Fundamental Research Fund for the Central Universities of China N172604003, N172603001, and supported by Doctoral Foundation of Liaoning Science and Technology Department Number 20170520244, and the National Natural Science Foundation of China under Grant nos. 61701101, U1713216, 61803077, 61603080.

References

1. Tang, P., Wang, C., Wang, X., Liu, W., Zeng, W., Wang, J.: Object detection in videos by high quality object linking. arXiv preprint arXiv:1801.09823 (2018)
2. Neumann, L., Zisserman, A., Vedaldi, A.: Relaxed softmax: efficient confidence auto-calibration for safe pedestrian detection (2018)
3. Chen, L.C., Papandreou, G., Kokkinos, I., Murphy, K., Yuille, A.L.: DeepLab: semantic image segmentation with deep convolutional nets, atrous convolution, and fully connected CRFs. IEEE Trans. Pattern Anal. Mach. Intell. **40**(4), 834–848 (2018)
4. Fathi, A., et al.: Semantic instance segmentation via deep metric learning. arXiv preprint arXiv:1703.10277 (2017)
5. Arnab, A., Torr, P.H.: Pixelwise instance segmentation with a dynamically instantiated network. In: Proceedings of the IEEE Conference on Computer Vision and Pattern Recognition, pp. 441–450 (2017)

6. Bell, S., Lawrence Zitnick, C., Bala, K., Girshick, R.: Inside-outside net: Detecting objects in context with skip pooling and recurrent neural networks. In: Proceedings of the IEEE Conference on Computer Vision and Pattern Recognition, pp. 2874–2883 (2016)
7. Cao, Z., Simon, T., Wei, S.E., Sheikh, Y.: Realtime multi-person 2D pose estimation using part affinity fields. In: Proceedings of the IEEE Conference on Computer Vision and Pattern Recognition, pp. 7291–7299 (2017)
8. Girshick, R., Iandola, F., Darrell, T., Malik, J.: Deformable part models are convolutional neural networks. In: Proceedings of the IEEE Conference on Computer Vision and Pattern Recognition, pp. 437–446 (2015)
9. Hayder, Z., He, X., Salzmann, M.: Shape-aware instance segmentation (2016)
10. Kirillov, A., Levinkov, E., Andres, B., Savchynskyy, B., Rother, C.: InstanceCut: from edges to instances with MultiCut. In: Proceedings of the IEEE Conference on Computer Vision and Pattern Recognition. pp, 5008–5017 (2017)
11. Li, Y., Qi, H., Dai, J., Ji, X., Wei, Y.: Fully convolutional instance-aware semantic segmentation. In: Proceedings of the IEEE Conference on Computer Vision and Pattern Recognition, pp. 2359–2367 (2017)
12. Lin, T.Y., Dollár, P., Girshick, R., He, K., Hariharan, B., Belongie, S.: Feature pyramid networks for object detection. In: Proceedings of the IEEE Conference on Computer Vision and Pattern Recognition, pp. 2117–2125 (2017)
13. Long, J., Shelhamer, E., Darrell, T.: Fully convolutional networks for semantic segmentation. In: Proceedings of the IEEE Conference on Computer Vision and Pattern Recognition, pp. 3431–3440 (2015)
14. Sun, C., Shrivastava, A., Singh, S., Gupta, A.: Revisiting unreasonable effectiveness of data in deep learning era. In: Proceedings of the IEEE International Conference on Computer Vision, pp. 843–852 (2017)
15. Andriluka, M., Pishchulin, L., Gehler, P., Schiele, B.: 2D human pose estimation: new benchmark and state of the art analysis. In: Proceedings of the IEEE Conference on Computer Vision and Pattern Recognition, pp. 3686–3693 (2014)
16. Arbeláez, P., Pont-Tuset, J., Barron, J.T., Marques, F., Malik, J.: Multiscale combinatorial grouping. In: Proceedings of the IEEE Conference on Computer Vision and Pattern Recognition, pp. 328–335 (2014)
17. He, K., Zhang, X., Ren, S., Sun, J.: Spatial pyramid pooling in deep convolutional networks for visual recognition. IEEE Trans. Pattern Anal. Mach. Intell. **37**(9), 1904–1916 (2015)

Development of High-Performance Joint Drive for Robots

The Multi-section Design of a Novel Soft Pneumatic Robot Arm with Variable Stiffness

Yao Ligang$^{(\boxtimes)}$, Jingyi Li, Xiaodong Liu, and Hui Dong

Fuzhou University, Fuzhou 350116, China
ylgyao@fzu.edu.cn

Abstract. By using flexible material, there are lots of researches on soft robot arm for taking its advantages. Compare with conventional rigid manipulator, soft robot arm can provide dexterity, safety and light weight. Besides upon unique characteristics, researchers also focused on solving its disadvantages like weak stiffness. This paper introduces a novel soft pneumatic robot arm with multi-section serially connection and variable stiffness by coupling structure. One-section arm consists of two connecting plates on the upper and bottom, three motion air chambers between in the plates and variable stiffness air chamber in the middle. There are three fields: static mechanical modeling, kinematic tests and variable stiffness analysis in this paper to demonstrate the design can be a solution to overcome current limitation of soft robot arms. Also, this paper evaluates the kinematic and mechanical characteristics through experiments and finally the validity of this multi-section and variable stiffness design in couple approach is proved.

Keywords: Soft robot arm · Static mechanism · Variable stiffness · Multi-section design

1 Introduction

1.1 Soft Pneumatic Robot Arm and Related Research

Inspired by the biomimetics from octopus tentacles and elephant trunks, researchers can obtain a good way to achieve higher flexibility and DOFs in manipulator fields by paying attention to develop soft robot arm [1, 2]. Compare with other soft robot arm drive by cables, electro active polymers (EAP) or shape memory alloys (SMA) [3–5], pneumatic is an efficient path for reducing weight and human-machine safety [6]. Besides, soft pneumatic robot arm with multi-section design, can be seen as a hyper-redundant manipulator in serial continuum assembly or a hyper-elastic rigid segment in each modules [7], which respectively has to improve the structure stiffness for higher payload and the positional movement accuracy.

In historically, researchers define the air chamber outputting the motion torques for arm structure as pneumatic artificial muscles (PAM) [8]. Through contraction and expansion of the muscles, Robot arms, like Octarm VI and Bionic Handing Assistant (BHA) [9, 10], are both has accurate movement in task space. But the disadvantages of them are disable to keep constant bending attitude and handle external loads [11, 12].

© Springer Nature Switzerland AG 2019
H. Yu et al. (Eds.): ICIRA 2019, LNAI 11740, pp. 595–607, 2019.
https://doi.org/10.1007/978-3-030-27526-6_52

In the aspect of soft robotic kinematics, Walker [13] suggested piece-wise constant curvature (PCC) method to analyze the motion of soft robotic arms. For soft pneumatic robot arm, it is a necessary part for researchers to decouple bending of the arm from every chambers' infusion pressure so that analyze the motion. As a pneumatic couple structure, many researchers tried to achieve variable stiffness based on this kind of structure [14, 15]. The main ideal is adjust the stiffness by applying redundant torques to increase the resistance of the structure [16]. However, there are lack of detailed experimental data to evaluate the degree of variable stiffness.

1.2   Contribution of This Paper

In this paper, a soft pneumatic robot arm with variable stiffness is designed, which is based on a simple multi-section module to achieve continuum assembly and variable stiffness. As most kind of flexible, the main usage of soft pneumatic robot arm is medical industry as assistant equipment. Following the design, characteristics of the arm can be analyzed by establishing mechanical model and movement test. All of these works in the paper are effective for simplifying and optimizing the design of soft biomimetic manipulators.

In order to present the soft pneumatic robot arm in this paper, organization is followed as:

Section 2: describes the design on how to set the air chambers in the arm and accomplish its basic function;

Section 3: establishes mathematical model especially in static mechanism for analyzing the strain by deriving the stiffness matrix. Besides, we describe the relation between infusion pressure and expansion of the chambers by deriving the compliance matrix. The matrix is from the inverse operation on the stiffness matrix and both of them will be considered in local and global coordinate frames. Finally, the model will be showed in the mapping from infusion pressure to the kinematic model;

Section 4: provides analysis through FEM and simulation on the structure of arm, which illustrates the effect of loads from different direction on the section and the degree of variable stiffness on the arm. And finally this paper designs a experiment for evaluating task space on the multi-section arm;

Section 5: gives conclusions and future works at the same time.

2   Design Conception of the Arm

2.1   Multi-section Design

Figure 1 describes the consists of one-section soft pneumatic arm:

(1) Two connecting plates: *1, 2,* on the upper and bottom of a section, each of their diameter is 135 mm wide;

(2) Three motion air chambers: *a, b* and *c* between in the connecting plates *1, 2* and variable stiffness air chamber d in the middle. All of these chambers are 195 mm long;

(3) In a connecting plate, *see* Fig. 1(b), setting three fillisters around three motion air chambers, *a*, *b* and *c* for bolting together a serial of the section to make up a continuum arm and passing the air tube which diameter is 6 mm.

Through the serial Assembly of one section, this kind of multi-section design shows advantages in dexterity because each section can provide at least 3DOF like redundant manipulator [17]. And more stable task space features due to the radial expansion of continuum arm is divided into every section. Generally, the meaning of multi-section design is helpful for analyzing the mechanical and kinematic characteristics from local segment which designers are able to control the optimal features of segments and put them into the continuum robot arm.

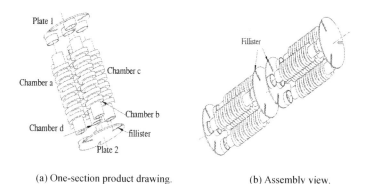

(a) One-section product drawing.   (b) Assembly view.

Fig. 1. Design of the arm.

2.2   Variable Stiffness Function

This paper makes assumption on bending torques from per chambers at one-section of the arm are conservative. So based on hyper-elasticity theory, these torques can be described as:

$$M_a + M_b + M_c = 0 \tag{1}$$

Where, M_a, M_b and M_c respectively is the torques from chamber *a*, *b* and *c*. Actually, existing M_d from variable stiffness air chamber *d*, so the torques balance equation of the arm is:

$$M_a + M_b + M_c + M_d = 0 \tag{2}$$

In the arm's bending, M_d can be defined as a redundant torques. While in the arm's static structure, M_d could change the parameters of the other three motion air chambers. For most designers, it is a kind of coupling variable stiffness. They generally set the chamber which provide redundant torque in the middle of soft manipulator [19]. In the design of the arm, variable stiffness air chamber is precisely set in every sections.

598 Y. Ligang et al.

3 Static Mechanical Model

3.1 Displacement of Air Chamber

Firstly, this paper establishes local coordinate frames to assume one-section arm as a silicon hyper-elastic module so we can derive the local stiffness matrix [20] and transfer these features into every chambers. In local coordinate frames, its deformation in space can be denoted by:

$$d = \begin{bmatrix} \delta_x & \delta_y & \delta_z & \theta_x & \theta_y & \theta_z \end{bmatrix}^T \tag{3}$$

Where $\delta_x, \delta_y, \delta_z$ represents the translational deflections in the vector δ and $\theta_x, \theta_y, \theta_z$ represents the rotational deflections in the vector θ. Correspondingly, as a piece-wise strain beam, there is loading force should be considered in the coordinates:

$$F = \begin{bmatrix} f_x & f_y & f_z & m_x & m_y & m_z \end{bmatrix}^T \tag{4}$$

Where divide F into two vectors: $f = \begin{bmatrix} f_x, f_y, f_z \end{bmatrix}^T$ is the local force from the direction of axis and $m = \begin{bmatrix} m_x, m_y, m_z \end{bmatrix}^T$ is the local wrench from the force around the axis. For considering the Young's modulus of silicon, the stiffness matrix of one-section arm can be expressed:

$$k = diag \begin{bmatrix} \frac{12EI}{L^3} & \frac{12EI}{L^3} & \frac{EA}{L} & \frac{4EI}{L} & \frac{4EI}{L} & \frac{GJ}{L} \end{bmatrix}^T \tag{5}$$

Where E is the Young's modulus of silicon, L is the length of one-section arm, A is the area of a connecting plate, G is the shear module, I is the inertia moment, exists:

$$I = \frac{\pi D^4}{64} \tag{6}$$

In which D is diameter of the plate. Besides, see (5), J is the torsional moment. To consider there are force and twist on the axis z, setting the one-section arm as a leg element in the direction z. This paper considers the vectors f and m, setting the arm as a beam element in the direction x and y, which loading the bending force and wrench because of the vectors f and m. So we can derive the relation between loading force and deformation for analyzing the effect of load on one section:

$$kd = F \tag{7}$$

For considering the inverse operation of stiffness matrix, we can summarize the compliance matrix of the arm:

$$k^{-1}F = cF = d \qquad c = k^{-1} \tag{8}$$

Introducing the compliance matrix to derive the relation between displacement and infusion pressure of the air chambers. Where considering the expansion only occur on the direction of axis z, so the relation can be described as:

$$c'p = d'$$
(9)

Where c' is the local compliance matrix of air chambers:

$$c' = diag\left[\frac{E}{L'} \quad \frac{E}{L'} \quad \frac{E}{L'} \quad \frac{E}{L'}\right]$$
(10)

In which, L' is the length of chambers. Besides, see (6), p is the pressure vector and d' is the displacement vector. Both of they can be denoted as:

$$p = [p_a \quad p_b \quad p_c \quad p_d]^T d' = [d_a \quad d_b \quad d_c \quad d_d]^T$$
(11)

Where all the vectors contain four elements from motion air chamber a, b, c and variable stiffness air chamber d.

3.2 Global Stiffness Matrix and Loads in Robot Arm

Introducing the stiffness matrix of one-section arm, see*(5), we can establish global stiffness matrix for analyzing the effect of loads in soft pneumatic robot arm. This paper assumes the multi-section structure as a kind of piece-wise strain beams see Fig. 2. So the end of beam only loading the bending force from the direction of axis, which can be expressed:

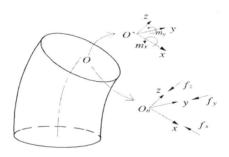

Fig. 2. Different kinds of payload in different sections.

In the ending section, upper connecting plate loading forces like O_n; In the other section, the connecting plate loading wrenches from the upper section like O'.

$$k_n = \begin{bmatrix} \frac{12EI}{L^3} & -\frac{12EI}{L^3} & 0 \\ -\frac{12EI}{L^3} & \frac{12EI}{L^3} & 0 \\ 0 & 0 & \frac{EA}{L} \end{bmatrix}$$
(12)

Where exists the relation, *see* (3) and (4), can be derived as: $k_n\delta = f$. And in the other part of beam, this relation can be derived as:

$$\begin{bmatrix} \frac{4EI}{L} & \frac{2EI}{L} \\ \frac{2EI}{L} & \frac{4EI}{L} \end{bmatrix}\begin{bmatrix} \theta_x \\ \theta_y \end{bmatrix} = \begin{bmatrix} m_x \\ m_y \end{bmatrix} \tag{13}$$

Where only considers the wrench from the force around the axis x and y, which is caused by payload from the end of beam and passed to the next sections. So followed the relation, *see* (13), the derivation can be simplified as: $k_n m = 0$. In which $n \in [1 \quad n-1]$. While the stiffness matrix should consider the position in global coordinates as a piece of constant beam. So the actual local stiffness matrix is:

$$K_n = [T][k_n][T]^T \tag{14}$$

Where:

$$T = \begin{bmatrix} \cos\theta_n & \sin\theta_n & 0 \\ -\sin\theta_n & \cos\theta_n & 0 \\ 0 & 0 & 1 \end{bmatrix} \text{ while } n \in [1 \quad n-1], \text{ it could be:}$$

$$T = \begin{bmatrix} \cos\theta_n & \sin\theta_n \\ -\sin\theta_n & \cos\theta_n \end{bmatrix} \tag{15}$$

Totally, the global stiffness matrix can be expressed:

$$K = K_n \oplus K_{n-1} \oplus \cdots \oplus K_1 \tag{16}$$

Where $\oplus$ is the operation of superposition which is similar to the continuum beams. For the relation between loading force and deformation, *see* (7), exists $d = \begin{bmatrix} \delta_n^x & \delta_n^y & \delta_n^z & \theta_{n-1}^x & \theta_{n-1}^y & \cdots & \theta_1^x & \theta_1^y \end{bmatrix}^T$ and $F = \begin{bmatrix} f_n^x & f_n^y & f_n^z & m_{n-1}^x & m_{n-1}^y & \cdots & m_1^x & m_1^y \end{bmatrix}^T$. Similarly, in global coordinates frame, exists the compliance matrix of chambers in multi section, *see* (11), which deriving from inverse operation of global stiffness matrix and the relation between displacement and infusion pressure can be denoted as:

$$CP = d \tag{17}$$

Where $C = c_n \oplus c_{n-1} \oplus \cdots \oplus c_1$, and it is the global compliance of chambers, in which $\oplus$ is the operation of superposition at the chambers from per section. Besides, $P = \begin{bmatrix} p_n^a & p_n^b & p_n^c & p_n^d & \cdots & p_1^a & p_1^b & p_1^c & p_1^d \end{bmatrix}^T$ and $D = \begin{bmatrix} d_n^a & d_n^b & d_n^c & d_n^d & \cdots & d_1^a & d_1^b & d_1^c & d_1^d \end{bmatrix}^T$.

3.3 Kinematic and Mechanical Model

In order to analyze the map between kinematics and mechanism, this paper divides the motion of soft pneumatic robot arm into three kinematic spaces: actuation space, configuration space and task space. The relation among the spaces can be drew as Fig. 3:

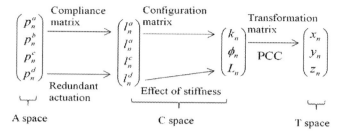

Fig. 3. The map and relation among kinematic spaces.

From actuation space to configuration space in one-section arm, infusion pressure vectors p are transferred into the actual chambers length l' vectors through the compliance matrix as:

$$\begin{bmatrix} \frac{E}{L'} & & \\ & \frac{E}{L'} & \\ & & \frac{E}{L'} \end{bmatrix} \begin{bmatrix} p_a \\ p_b \\ p_c \end{bmatrix} = \begin{bmatrix} d_a \\ d_b \\ d_c \end{bmatrix} \tag{18}$$

Where based on the geometrical theory, *see* Fig. 4, this paper derives the relation between the actual lengths and the kinematic parameters from the formula $Hl' = \omega$, it is also the map in configuration space which used to decouple the arm movement to per chambers' expansion and it include three factors for task space as:

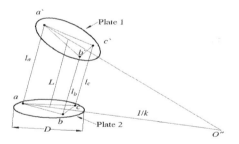

Fig. 4. The geometric relation in a section between motion chambers.

$$\begin{bmatrix} \frac{r}{2\tau} & \frac{r}{2\tau} & \frac{r}{2\tau} \\ -\frac{2\sqrt{3}}{3\eta} & \frac{\sqrt{3}}{3\eta} & \frac{\sqrt{3}}{3\eta} \\ \frac{1}{3} & \frac{1}{3} & \frac{1}{3} \end{bmatrix} \begin{bmatrix} l+d_a \\ l+d_b \\ l+d_c \end{bmatrix} = \begin{bmatrix} \rho \\ \tan\phi \\ L \end{bmatrix} \tag{19}$$

Where l is the original length of chambers, r is the radius of connecting plate, H is the configuration matrix, its parameters from the derivation in geometry [21], ω is the parameters from configuration space and the parameters:

$$\tau = \sqrt{l_a'^2 + l_b'^2 + l_c'^2 - l_a'l_b' - l_a'l_c' - l_b'l_c'} \quad \eta = l_2' - l_3' \tag{20}$$

In order to describe the relation between construction space and task space, this paper introduces the piece-wise constant curvature (PCC) to form the transformation matrix in one-section arm [22]:

$$A_n = \begin{bmatrix} R_n & \alpha_n \\ 0 & 1 \end{bmatrix} \tag{21}$$

Where R is the rotation matrix which consists by three rotation vectors in space coordinate frame and α is the positional translation vectors. In detail, they are:

$$R_n = \begin{bmatrix} \cos^2\phi_n(\cos k_n L_n - 1) & \sin\phi_n\cos\phi_n(\cos k_n L_n - 1) & -\cos\phi_n\sin k_n L_n \\ \sin\phi_n\cos\phi_n(\cos k_n L_n - 1) & \cos^2\phi_n(\cos k_n L_n - 1) + \cos k_n L_n & -\sin\phi_n\sin k_n L_n \\ \cos\phi_n\sin k_n L_n & \sin\phi_n\sin k_n L_n & \cos k_n L_n \end{bmatrix}$$

$$\alpha_n = \begin{bmatrix} \frac{\cos\phi_n(\cos k_n s_n - 1)}{k_n} & \frac{\sin\phi_n(\cos k_n s_n - 1)}{k_n} & \frac{\sin k_n s_n}{k_n} \end{bmatrix}^T \tag{22}$$

To summarize, $n \in [1 \quad n]$, it means each section from the base to the ending section, k is the curvature of the arm, in which $k = \frac{1}{\rho}$. And φ is the orientation angle, L is the length of the arc. For all section of the soft pneumatic robot arm in global task space, the ending position of the arm can be described as:

$$A = A_1 A_2 \cdots A_n \tag{23}$$

Through the verified the relation between three kinematic spaces, we can see transfer the infusion pressures into the position of the arm in task space at coordinate frame by compliance matrix, configuration matrix and transformation matrix.

4   Simulation and Experiment

Firstly, this paper based on the static mode to analyze the effect of loads on the arm. Then, we use virtual work principle to operate the torques from the chambers so we can test the degree of variable stiffness [23]. These works can be succeed by using the FEM software. Finally, according to the model and the simulation results, the experiment evaluated the kinematic features by observing the movement of the arm which we assembled two sections and using mathematics toolbox to explain them.

4.1   Loads Effect and Variable Stiffness on the Arm

In Fig. 5(a), this paper uses planar axisymmetric element in FEM simulation software for analyzing the loads more efficiently. In one-section arm, this paper sets two types of loads in different parameters from axial and radial direction respectively. The result of the simulation see in Fig. 5(b), where theoretical values are from the model, it makes sure there are different effect between axial and radial loads to the arm and the theoretical stiffness through the simulation. Secondly, this paper assumes the infusion pressures of motion chambers are constant and we can get the constant displacements. Through changes the redundant torque M_d and extended it from one-section to multi-section arm, we can analyze the ability of variable stiffness in Fig. 6.

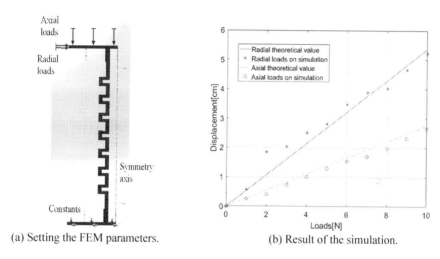

(a) Setting the FEM parameters.   (b) Result of the simulation.

Fig. 5. The effect of loads.

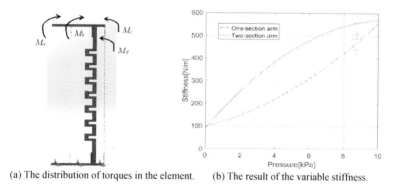

(a) The distribution of torques in the element.   (b) The result of the variable stiffness.

Fig. 6. Simulation on the Stiffness.

In summary, Based on the FEM, we can illustrate the effect of load on the soft pneumatic robot arm and the level of variable stiffness, which can indirectly demonstrates mechanical model in previous section of this paper and tests preliminarily for movement feature of the arm. Through the infusion pressure of variable stiffness chambers, the bending torques are changed in the condition of displacements are constant. So we operate it in matrix (14) and finally verified in multi-section structure of the arm, the effect of variable stiffness will be more obvious in the pressure range from 3 kPa to 7 kPa than one section of the arm.

4.2   Evaluation of Multi-section Design

Based on the test platform, this paper experimented the bending movement in two-section arm in order to evaluate the movement of performance especially in variable stiffness to the arm. Inflating the motion chambers to pursue the planning attitude in task space, using the variable stiffness chambers to control the deformation and recording the parameters. In Fig. 7, we set the below section arm is Sect. 1 and the upper is Sect. 2, both of sections we collect three pressure parameters from three motion chambers: p_1^a, p_1^b, p_1^c and p_2^a, p_2^b, p_2^c. And the pressure parameters: p_1^d, p_2^d from variable stiffness chambers in two sections.

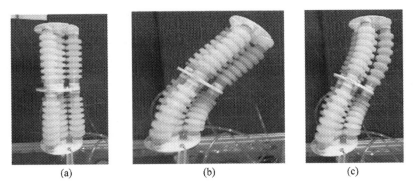

|(a)|(b)|(c)|

Fig. 7. Result of the experiment:

(a) Initial status (t = 0 s), where all the pressure of chambers are 0 kPa, t is the running time; (b) Bending status (t = 3 s, k = 6.5 m^{-1}), where p_1^a = 5.1 kPa, p_1^b = 5.06 kPa, the other chambers are 0 kPa, we set p_2^d = 0.73 kPa due to the need of keeping the bending attitude toward aside; (c) Achieving the planning attitude status (t = 6 s, k1 = 6.5 m^{-1}, k2 = 5.5 m^{-1}), where p_1^a = 5.1 kPa, p_1^b = 5.06 kPa, p_2^c = 5.14 kPa, the other chambers are 0 kPa, we set p_1^d = 1.07 kPa in order to keep the accuracy of arm attitude.

According to the transformation matrix, this paper gains the kinematic parameters through the operation of transferring maximum pressure of motion chambers into configuration space like Eqs. (18) and (19). Using the Matlab robotic toolbox, *see* Fig. 8, we can see the task space of one-section it can work well in. In the toolbox, this paper considers the arm bending toward 36 directions in task space and sets five degrees in the range of bending arc. In Table 1, this paper evaluates the difference of task space among the counts of section in a soft pneumatic robot arm.

Table 1. Result of the evaluation.

Counts of section	Maximum curvature	Range of arc	Volume in task space
1	8.15 m^{-1}	195–330 mm	20.6 dm^3
2	7.82 m^{-1}	385–505 mm	39.7 dm^3
3	7.48 m^{-1}	570–680 mm	58.5 dm^3

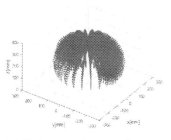

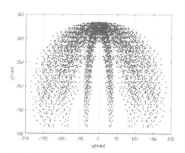

(a) Task space of one-section arm.   (b) Task space on the view of y-z axial plane.

Fig. 8. Evaluation of multi section.

5 Conclusion

(1) This paper presented a novel design in continuum soft pneumatic robot arm which can achieve multi-section assembly and variable stiffness. In this paper, we start the design project from reviewed the related research on pneumatic couple structures. Based on existing pneumatic soft manipulators, we achieved the multi-section design which is useful for the application of the arm.

(2) This paper paid attention to derive stiffness matrix of the arm and introduce it into load analysis of the multi-section arm. Besides, with the inverse operation of stiffness matrix, we derived the compliance matrix of the arm, which simplified the decoupling process for analyzing the effect of every chambers' contraction and expansion to the bending motion of the arm. So we can clarify the relation between kinematic parameters of the arm and the infusion pressure of the chambers.

(3) FEM and the principle of virtual work are effective tools to analyze the effect of load to the arm and the level of variable stiffness. The simulation results showed that the effect of radial loads are bigger than axial loads. In the same loads, for two kinds of direction, radial displacement is bigger as twice as radial displacement, but in one-section arm, the experiment showed the coupling variable stiffness can counteract it efficiently.

(4) Following the map between actuation space, construction space and task space. This paper evaluated the working performance in task space. We summarized task spaces in different section of the arm through the software toolbox. More section means more task space but less dexterity in local attitude. Through the experiment, we also find variable stiffness is useful for keeping the movement accuracy, so the design of the arm is feasible.

Future work including a wide range investigation on the optimization of mechanical modeling and experimental platform. Through the design of more accurate soft manipulator motion and stiffness control experiments, decoupling the various factors of arm driving and stiffness change will be analyzed more clearly. Which will help to make progress in the theory of the arm design and it is finally becoming a successful manipulator design in medical industry or other special fields.

References

1. Rus, D., Tolley, M.T.: Design, fabrication and control of soft robots. Nature **521**(7553), 467 (2015)
2. Renda, F., Cianchetti, M., Giorelli, M.: A 3D steady-state model of a tendon-driven continuum soft manipulator inspired by the octopus arm. Bioinspiration Biomim. **7**(2), 025006 (2012)
3. Wang, H., Chen, J., Henry, L.: Motion planning based on learning from demonstration for multiple segment flexible soft robots actuated by electroactive polymers. IEEE Robot. Autom. Lett. **1**(1), 391–398 (2016)
4. Wang, H., Wang, C., Chen, W., et al.: Three-dimensional dynamics for cable-driven soft manipulator. IEEE/ASME Trans. Mechatron. **22**(1), 18–28 (2017)
5. Cianchetti, M., Calisti, M., Margheri, L., et al.: Bioinspired locomotion and grasping in water: the soft eight-arm OCTOPUS robot. Bioinspiration Biomim. **10**(3), 035003 (2015)
6. Mahl, T., Hildebrandt, A., Sawodny, O.: A variable curvature continuum kinematics for kinematic control of the bionic handling assistant. IEEE Trans. Robot. **30**(4), 935–949 (2014)
7. Deashapriya, K.P., Sampath, P.A., Wijekoon, W.M.S.B., et al.: Biomimetic flexible robot arm: design and kinematic analysis of a novel flexible robot arm. In: 2016 IEEE Conference on MERCon, pp. 385–390 (2016)
8. Trivedi, D., Lotfi, A., Rahn, C.D.: Geometrically exact models for soft robotic manipulators. IEEE Trans. Robot. **114**(24), 773–780 (2018)
9. Laschi, C., Mazzolai, B., Mattoli, V., Etrla, L.: The bionic handling assistant: a success story of additive manufacturing. Assem. Autom. **31**, 329–333 (2011)
10. Chawla, A., Frazelle, C., Walker, I.D.: A comparison of constant curvature forward kinematics for multisection continuum manipulators. In: 2018 IEEE IRC Conference, pp. 217–223 (2018)
11. Lakhal, O., Melingui, A., Merzouki, R.: Hybrid approach for modeling and solving of kinematics of a compact bionic handling assistant manipulator. IEEE/ASME Trans. Mechatron. **6**, 1326–1335 (2016)
12. Mustaza, S.M., Mahdi, D., Chakravarthini, S., et al.: Tuneable stiffness design of soft continuum manipulator. In: 2015 IR&A Conference, pp. 152–163 (2015)
13. Walker, I.D.: Continuous backbone "continuum" robot manipulators. ISRN Robot. 726506 (2013)

14. De Falco, I., Cianchetti, M., Menciassi, A.: A soft multi-module manipulator with variable stiffness for minimally invasive surgery. Bioinspiration Biomim. **12**(5), 1–16 (2017)
15. Mazzolai, B., Margheri, L., Dario, P.: Measurements of octopus arm elongation: evidence of differences by body size and gender. J. Exp. Mar. Biol. Ecol. **447**(3), 160–164 (2013)
16. Manti, M., Pratesi, A., Falotico, E., et al.: Soft assistive robot for personal care of elderly people. In: 2016 6th IEEE RAS/EMBS Conference on BioRob, pp. 833–838 (2016)
17. Gong, Z., Xie, Z., Yang, X., et al.: Design, fabrication and kinematic modeling of a 3D-motion soft robotic arm. In: 2016 R&BIO Conference, pp. 509–514 (2016)
18. Bosman, J., Bieze, T.M., Lakhal, O., et al.: Domain decomposition approach for FEM quasistatic modeling and control of continuum robots with rigid vertebras. In: 2015 ICRA Conference, pp. 4373–4378 (2015)
19. Lindenroth, L., Junghwan, B., Schoisengeier, A., et al.: Stiffness-based modelling of a hydraulically-actuated soft robotics manipulator. In: 2016 IEEE/RSJ Conference on IROS, pp. 2458–2463 (2016)
20. Peng, Q., Chen, Q., Liu, H.: A novel continuum manipulator design using serially connected double-layer planar springs. IEEE/ASME Trans. Mechatron. **21**(3), 1281–1292 (2016)
21. Singh, I., Amara, Y., Melingui, A., et al.: Modeling of continuum manipulators using pythagorean hodograph curves. Soft Robot. **5**, 425–442 (2017)
22. Renda, F., Cacucciolo, V., Dias, J., et al.: Discrete Cosserat approach for soft robot dynamics: a new piece-wise constant strain model with torsion and shears. In: 2016 IROS Conference, pp. 5495–5502 (2016)
23. Renda, F., Giorelli, M., Calisti, M.: Dynamic model of a multibending soft robot arm driven by cables. IEEE Trans. Robot. **30**(5), 1109–1122 (2014)

Nonlinear Finite Element Simulation and Analysis of Double Circular Arc Spiral Bevel Gear Nutation Drive

Yu-jing Su, Li-gang Yao[✉], and Jun Zhang

School of Mechanical Engineering and Automation, Fuzhou University,
Fujian 350108, China
yjs_su@163.com, {ylgyao,zhang_jun}@fzu.edu.cn

Abstract. This paper describes the nonlinear finite element analysis model of double circular helical bevel gear nutation drive, the model considering the changes of elastic contact deformation, friction force and the number of meshing tooth of gear, reflecting the actual driving situation of the gear in nutation transmission and dynamic loading. The dynamic meshing of double circular arc spiral bevel gears at different rotate speeds is simulated by nonlinear finite element analysis software,and vibration displacement, dynamic meshing stress and contact force of nutation gear and output gear are analyzed. In order to improve the stability of nutation drive and reduce the vibration and noise, the nonlinear dynamic meshing analysis of nutation drive cannot be ignored.

Keywords: Nutation drive · Double circular arc · Dynamic meshing · Nonlinear finite element

1 Introduction

Nutation drive is a new type of motion in machinery. Compared with traditional gear transmission, Nutation gear drive has the characteristics of high transfer efficiency, large reduction ratio and steady transmission,it is usually used in robot joint reducer [1–4]. In nutation system, rotors and wobbling bodies [5] rotate about a point and are characterized by a kinematical constraint that prevents them from rotating around the axis. In the pericyclic mechanical transmission system [6], the nutation gear provides high reduction rate and large load bearing capacity. The multi-body model and dynamic balance conditions of nutation system was discussed in paper [7]. A new type of motor [8–10] which with high torque was developed based on the principle of nutation. Nutation drive with rolling tooth [11, 12] was described, it also has a large deceleration ratio. Finally, the development of nutation coordinate system, meshing equation and 3D tooth surface model of double circular spiral bevel gears [13–18] optimizes the performance of nutation drive.

Concerning gear simulation research, multi-body dynamic [19] or static method [20] are often used. These methods can obtain the meshing stiffness or load stress, etc.

© Springer Nature Switzerland AG 2019
H. Yu et al. (Eds.): ICIRA 2019, LNAI 11740, pp. 608–615, 2019.
https://doi.org/10.1007/978-3-030-27526-6_53

However, the elastic gear and continuous transmission process are not considered, so these methods cannot accurately calculate the dynamic response of the whole meshing process. Finite element method is used for analysis and calculation the contact stress of spiral bevel gears [21, 22], and dynamic finite element simulation method is usually used for dynamic meshing analysis of gears [23, 24], and carrying out the dynamic transmission error, tooth surface meshing force, vibration acceleration and other dynamic responses. These studies attach great importance on gear transmission, but there is still not specific research on dynamic nonlinear finite element of nutation gear yet.

In this paper, a dynamic model of double circular spiral bevel gear nutation drive is depicted, gear are set as elastic bodies, and the continuous meshing contact deformation is nonlinear. The model considers the friction, elastic contact deformation and the change of the number of teeth. Dynamic meshing simulation of two-stage spiral bevel gear nutation reducer is carried out. The relative vibration displacement of input external bevel gear and output internal bevel gear, the equivalent stress of dynamic meshing between tooth root and addendum, the position distribution of contact stress on tooth surface during dynamic loading, and the changing rule of dynamic meshing force with time were obtained. It has great significance for improving transmission precision, tooth load capacity and transmission stability of gear nutation.

2   Finite Element Dynamic Analysis Model

In this paper, nonlinear finite element analysis of the two-stage double arc spiral bevel gear nutation reducer is shown in Fig. 1. Main parameters of input external bevel gear 1 and output internal bevel gear 3 in the secondary nutation drive are presented in Table 1. We built a dynamic analysis model in finite element analysis software Ansys/LS-Dyna. In order to obtain high quality mesh and save computing time, element solid164 and shell163 are adopted for mesh division in finite element analysis model. The solid164 is a hexahedron element with six tetrahedrons and the element shell163 has 12 degrees of freedom. Using solid164 elements to divide elastic gear, and shell163 elements are used to divide the internal ring surface of gear, and set it as rigid body,and elastic gears are driven by rigid body. We use the explicit dynamics algorithm, and tooth surface of the input nutation gear and output gear are defined as surface to surface automatic contact. The torque was added to the internal bevel gear, and the rotate speed was set on the input external bevel gear. Elastic modulus was set as 2.06 Gpa, Poisson's ratio 0.269, density 7850 kg/m^3, and friction coefficient was set as 0.02. Adjusting element size and mesh density, the appropriate mesh was obtained, and final dynamic model is illustrated in Fig. 2. A total of solid analysis model has 116704 elements with 140126 nodes.

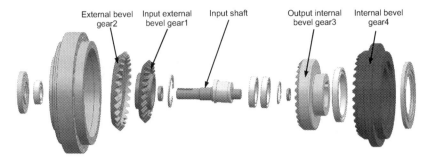

External bevel
gear2   Input external
bevel gear1   Input shaft   Output internal
bevel gear3   Internal bevel
gear4

Fig. 1. Assembly model of two-stage double arc nutation reducer

Table 1. Main design parameters of gear

Parameter	Nutation gear	Output gear
Spiral angle β	25°	25°
Nutation angle ϕ	5°	5°
Number of teeth	26	28
Pitch cone angle δ	47.19°	127.8°
Normal module m_n	2	2
Cone distance R	50 mm	50 mm

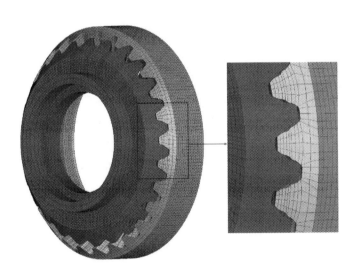

Fig. 2. Finite element dynamic analysis model

3 Simulation Experiment Analysis

In order to verify the accuracy of the model, we set simulation time as 3 ms to solve the dynamic model, the change of the relative circumferential vibration displacement of the nutation input gear 1 and output external bevel gear 3 with time are shown as Fig. 3. In 0–1 ms, with the improving of rotation speed, vibration amplitude and the offset of relative displacement average value increases dramatically, and nutation gear is in a bilateral impact state. At various rotating speeds, the vibration displacement amplitude of nutation drive is small, in the order of 10^{-3}, this indicates that the double circular spiral bevel gear nutation drive has higher transmission accuracy and the precision of the model is proved.

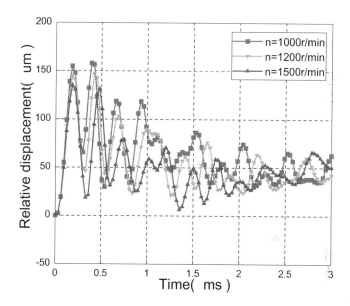

Fig. 3. Relative displacement time domain with time

Nutation output bevel gear with oscillates is up and down, it is subjected to impact stress during meshing. Contact stress distribution during the steady-meshing process of nutation gear and output gear are depicted as Fig. 4 with range level. The input speed was set as 1500 r/min and simulation time as 0.05 s. At different rotating time, the performance of contact stress is diverse. Contact stress position of nutation input external bevel gear and output internal bevel gear from single meshing to triple meshing are shown as Fig. 4(a)–(b). In Fig. 4(c)–(d), stress distribution of single tooth and triple tooth of nutation input gear were shown. The contact stress distribution position of output internal bevel gear meshing is shown as Fig. 4(e)–(f).

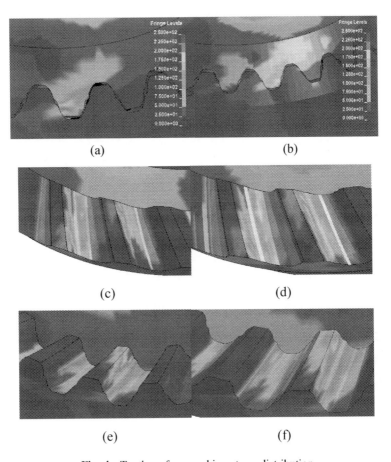

Fig. 4. Tooth surface meshing stress distribution

For contact stress patterns of dedendum and addendum, elements at crown and root of nutation gear and output gear are selected respectively. The location and number of the element are shown in Fig. 5. The variation of meshing equivalent stress of the elements with time is indicated in Fig. 6. Since the gear is a continuous elastomer, the gear tooth may still be subjected to equivalent stress within non-meshing time.

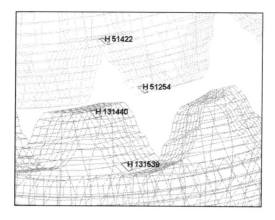

Fig. 5. Element location and number

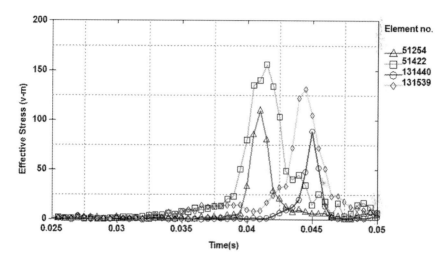

Fig. 6. Element equivalent stress

In nutation drive, meshing points changes with time and the meshing force changes periodically, it can be seen from Fig. 7 that the respective influence on the dynamic meshing force of the gear caused by the different input speed, the input speed was set to 1000 r/min, 1200 r/min, 1500 r/min and 2000 r/min. According to the results, with the increase of input speed, the vibration frequency of contact force gose up.

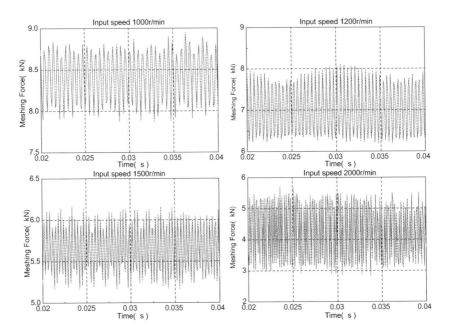

Fig. 7. Dynamic meshing force at different input speeds

4 Discussion and Summary

A 3D dynamic finite element analysis model of double circular spiral bevel gear nutation drive is established,and the dynamic analysis model was solved by finite element analysis software. The basic dynamic meshing rules at different input speeds are obtained. Through the analysis of contact stress and contact force of nutation input external bevel gear and output internal bevel gear, the result proves that the nutation gear meshing transmission is stable and has high load bearing capacity.

Acknowledgment. This paper is supported by National Science Foundation of China, No. 51775114, No. 51875105, and Science and Technology Project 2014H2004 of Fujian Province, China.

References

1. Hsieh, S.P., Hwang, T.S., Ni, C.W.: Twin-VCM controller design for the nutator system with evolutionary algorithms. IETE Tech. Rev. **26**, 290–302 (2009)
2. Uzuka, K., Enomoto, I., Suzumori, K.: Comparative assessment of several nutation motor types. IEEE/ASME Trans. Mechatron. **14**, 82–92 (2009)
3. He, S.-J.: Theory research on output mechanism of conical roller in nutation gear. Coal Mine Machinery (2007)
4. Kemper, Y.: The nutating traction drive. J. Eng. Power **103**, 154–157 (1981)

5. Green, I.: On the kinematics and kinetics of mechanical seals, rotors, and wobbling bodies. Mech. Mach. Theory **43**, 909–917 (2008)
6. Saribay, Z.B., Bill, R.C.: Design analysis of pericyclic mechanical transmission system. Mech. Mach. Theory **61**, 102–122 (2013)
7. Fanghella, P., Bruzzone, L., Ellero, S.: Dynamic balancing of a nutating planetary bevel gear train. In: Ceccarelli, M., Hernández Martinez, E.E. (eds.) Multibody Mechatronic Systems. MMS, vol. 25, pp. 23–33. Springer, Cham (2015). https://doi.org/10.1007/978-3-319-09858-6_3
8. Uzuka, K.: Development of nutation motors, (1st report: driving principle and basic characteristics of pneumatic nutation motor). Nihon Kikai Gakkai Ronbunshu, C (Trans. Jpn. Soc. Mech. Eng. Ser. C) **72**, 180–185 (2006)
9. Uzuka, K., Enomoto, I., Suzumori, K.: Development of nutation motors (4th report, development of small-sized and high torque pneumatic nutation motor by the OFW type bevel gears and principle of lever). Nippon Kikai Gakkai Ronbunshu C Hen (Trans. Jpn. Soc. Mech. Eng. Part C) (Jpn.) **19**, 1731–1737 (2007)
10. Oda, S., Suzumori, K., Uzuka, K., Enomoto, I.: Development of nutation motors (improvement of pneumatic nutation motor by optimizing diaphragm design). J. Mech. Sci. Technol. **24**, 25–28 (2010)
11. Wang, G.X., Guan, T.M.: Modeling of nutation drive with rolling teeth. Appl. Mech. Mater. **16–19**, 708–712 (2009)
12. Wang, G.X., Li, L.J., Guan, H., Guan, T.M.: Modeling and simulation for nutation drive with rolling teeth. Adv. Mater. Res. **538–541**, 470–473 (2012)
13. Yao, L., Gu, B., Haung, S., Wei, G., Dai, J.S.: Mathematical modeling and simulation of the external and internal double circular-arc spiral bevel gears for the nutation drive. J. Mech. Des. **132**, 021008–021010 (2010)
14. Zhang, J., Yao, L., Huang, S., Bing, G.: Tooth profile accurate modeling of internal and external double circular-arc spiral bevel gears. Modern Manufacturing Engineering (2015)
15. Ji, W., Yao, L., Zhang, J.: Mathematical modeling and characteristics analysis for the nutation gear drive based on error parameters. J. Chongqing Univ. **15**, 149–158 (2016)
16. Huang, D.-J., Yao, L.-G., Li, W.-J., Zhang, J.: Geometric modeling and torque analysis of the magnetic nutation gear drive. Forsch. Ingenieurwes. **81**, 101–108 (2017)
17. Hong, J., Yao, L., Ji, W., Huang, Z.: Kinematic modeling for the nutation drive based on screw theory. Procedia CIRP **36**, 123–128 (2015)
18. Lin, Z., Yao, L.G., Huang, S.J.: Transmission ratio analysis and controllable tooth profile modeling for the nutation drive with double circular-arc external and internal spiral bevel gears. Adv. Mater. Res. **97–101**, 3128–3134 (2010)
19. Han, X., Hua, L., Deng, S., Luo, Q.: Influence of alignment errors on contact pressure during straight bevel gear meshing process. Chin. J. Mech. Eng. **28**, 1089–1099 (2015)
20. Doğan, O., Karpat, F.: Crack detection for spur gears with asymmetric teeth based on the dynamic transmission error. Mech. Mach. Theory **133**, 417–431 (2019)
21. Simon, V.: Load distribution in spiral bevel gears. J. Mech. Des. **129**, 201–209 (2007)
22. Litvin, F.L., Fuentes, A., Hayasaka, K.: Design, manufacture, stress analysis, and experimental tests of low-noise high endurance spiral bevel gears. Mech. Mach. Theory **41**, 83–118 (2006)
23. Chen, S., Tang, J., Liu, X.: The dynamic transmission error and the tooth meshing force based on ANSYS/LS-DYNA, pp. 547–552 (2007)
24. Wang, P.-Y., Fan, S.-C., Huang, Z.-G.: Spiral bevel gear dynamic contact and tooth impact analysis. J. Mech. Des. **133**, 084501 (2011)

Design and Analysis of Gear Profile of Two-Tooth Difference Swing-Rod Movable Teeth Transmission System

Rui Wei[1], Herong Jin[1,2(✉)], and Yali Yi[1,2]

[1] School of Mechanical Engineering, Yanshan University,
Qinhuangdao 066004, China
ysujhr@ysu.edu.cn
[2] Jiangsu Tailong Decelerator Machinery Co., Ltd., Taixing 225400, China

Abstract. The transmission performance of two-tooth difference swing-rod movable teeth transmission system depends on the gear profile design. Based on the transmission principle of forward and inverse cam mechanism, tooth profile equations of wave generator and ring gear are deduced by setting the motion law of swing rod to realize the normalized design of tooth profile. Curvature radius of the ring gear tooth profile is derived. On this basis, by analyzing the relationship between amplitude coefficient and the curvature radius, the non-interference conditions of ring gear profile is obtained. And then the influence of amplitude coefficient on the transmission angle is analyzed. Thus, the amplitude coefficient range of the transmission system with good power transmission performance is obtained on the premise that the ring gear profile is free from interference under the given tooth profile parameters. This study provides a reference for the tooth profile design and parameter selection of the two-tooth difference swing-rod movable teeth transmission system.

Keywords: Swing rod movable teeth transmission · Tooth profile design · Curvature radius · Transmission angle

1 Introduction

The movable teeth reducer is a transmission device evolved from the planetary transmission device with small tooth difference, which has the advantages of a large transmission ratio range, compact structure and strong bearing capacity [1]. In recent years, researchers have done a series of research on the movable teeth reducer, such as tooth profile design [2, 3], transmission error analysis [4–6], force analysis [7–9], tooth surface flash temperature [10, 11] and so on. Two-tooth difference swing-rod movable teeth transmission system as a type of movable teeth reducer, because of the central symmetry of its wave generator, it is easy to balance the static and dynamic forces of the whole machine during the transmission process [12]. It has broad application prospects in heavy load, high speed and other occasions where the dynamic characteristics of mechanical equipment are demanding. However, the transmission performance of the drive designed at present cannot meet the requirements of practical application, so the design and analysis of the drive need further research.

© Springer Nature Switzerland AG 2019
H. Yu et al. (Eds.): ICIRA 2019, LNAI 11740, pp. 616–628, 2019.
https://doi.org/10.1007/978-3-030-27526-6_54

Tooth profile parameters affect the performance of the movable teeth transmission system. Reasonable tooth profile design is the key to determine the transmission performance of the drive. In this paper, on the basis of the structural characteristics and transmission principle of the two-tooth difference swing-rod movable teeth transmission system, given the motion law of swing rod, the tooth profile equations of wave generator and ring gear are constructed by the mechanism inversion method. Then, the ring gear curvature radius and the transmission angle are deduced, and the influence of amplitude coefficient on them is discussed. Thus, the amplitude coefficient range of the transmission system with good power transmission performance is obtained on the premise that the ring gear profile is free from interference under the given tooth profile parameters. This study provides a theoretical reference for the tooth profile design of the two-tooth difference swing-rod movable teeth transmission system with active controllable motion.

2   Structure of Two-Tooth Difference Swing-Rod Movable Teeth Transmission System

The two-tooth difference swing-rod movable teeth transmission system is composed of 5 basic components: a ring gear, a wave generator, a separator, several movable teeth and swing-rods. Figure 1 shows the schematic diagram of the drive.

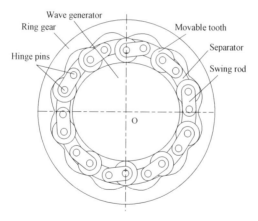

Fig. 1. Diagram of two-tooth difference swing-rod movable teeth transmission

When the two-tooth difference swing-rod movable teeth transmission system works, the input torque drives the wave generator to rotate counterclockwise, and the wave generator drives swing-rod movable tooth to reciprocate. Because the swing rod is restrained by the pin, the swing rod can only swing around the rotation center O_1. Because of the constraint of the meshing pair between the ring gear and the movable tooth, the movable tooth drives the ring gear to rotate around the rotating center O, so as to realize the speed conversion and power transfer of the drive under a given transmission ratio. In the process of rotation, under the geometric constraint of the tooth profile of the wave generator and the ring gear, the swing-rod movable tooth in the non-working state return to the initial position successively, thereby completing a cycle of movement.

3   Tooth Profile Design

3.1   Derivation of the Wave Generator Tooth Profile

The transmission mode is studied with the separator fixed, the wave generator as input part and the ring gear as output part. The simple harmonic motion of the swing rod is made to realize its controllable motion, so as to ensure that there is no impact when the swing rod moves. According to the motion law of the swing rod, the tooth profile equations of the wave generator and the ring gear are derived by using the mechanism inversion method.

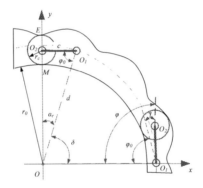

Fig. 2. Tooth profile design schematic diagram of the drive

Figure 2 shows the tooth profile design schematic diagram of the drive. Under the action of driving torque, when the wave generator rotates an angle δ counterclockwise around its rotation center O at the angular velocity ω, the swing rod swings according to the set motion law under the push of the wave generator. The swing-rod swing angle $\gamma = A \cdot (1 - \cos (Z_H \cdot \delta))$, where A is the amplitude coefficient, Z_H is the wave number of the wave generator and $Z_H = 2$. Add an angular velocity $-\omega$ to the drive. At this time, the relative motion between the wave generator and the swing-rod movable tooth does not change, but the angular velocity of the wave generator is 0. The swing-rod movable tooth rotates around the center O with the separator on the one hand, and rotates around O_1 with the set motion law on the other hand. After the wave generator rotates an angle δ counterclockwise, the coordinate of the movable tooth center O_2 can be expressed as

$$\begin{cases} x_{O_2} = d \cdot \sin(\delta + \alpha_r) - c \cdot \sin(\delta + \alpha_r + \varphi) \\ y_{O_2} = d \cdot \cos(\delta + \alpha_r) - c \cdot \cos(\delta + \alpha_r + \varphi) \end{cases} \tag{1}$$

where $\varphi = \varphi_0 + \gamma$, φ_0 is the initial angle between OO_1 and O_1O_2. d is the distance from the swing-rod rotation center O_1 to the center O of the system. c is the length of the swing rod O_1O_2. α_r is the initial angle between OO_2 and OO_1.

The value of φ_0 and α_r can be obtained by the cosine theorem, and the formula is as follows:

$$\alpha_r = arccos\left(\frac{d^2 + (r_0 + r_c)^2 - c^2}{2 \cdot d \cdot (r_0 + r_c)}\right) \tag{2}$$

$$\varphi_0 = arccos\left(\frac{d^2 + c^2 - (r_0 + r_c)^2}{2 \cdot d \cdot c}\right) \tag{3}$$

where r_0 is the base radius of the wave generator. r_C is the radius of the movable tooth.

The actual tooth profile of the wave generator is the inner equidistance line of the theoretical tooth profile of the wave generator with the movable tooth radius r_c as the offset. When the coordinate of the point $O_2(x_{O_2}, y_{O_2})$ on the theoretical tooth profile of the wave generator is obtained, a point $M(x_M, y_M)$ is taken along the normal direction of the point O_2, and the distance from the point M to the point O_2 is r_c. Point M is the corresponding point on the actual tooth profile of the wave generator. The slope of normal line at the point O_2 of the wave generator theoretical tooth profile (the negative inverse of the tangent slope at the point O_2) is

$$tan\theta = \frac{dx}{-dy} = \frac{dx/d\delta}{-dy/d\delta} = \frac{sin\theta}{cos\theta} \tag{4}$$

where θ is the inclination angle of the normal line of the wave generator theoretical tooth profile at O_2.

According to Eqs. (1) and (4)

$$\begin{cases} sin\theta = \dfrac{dx/d\delta}{\sqrt{(dx/d\delta)^2 + (dy/d\delta)^2}} \\ cos\theta = \dfrac{-(dy/d\delta)}{\sqrt{(dx/d\delta)^2 + (dy/d\delta)^2}} \end{cases} \tag{5}$$

The coordinate of the corresponding point $M(x_M, y_M)$ on the actual tooth profile of the wave generator is

$$\begin{cases} x_M = x_{O_2} - r_C cos\theta \\ y_M = y_{O_2} - r_C sin\theta \end{cases} \tag{6}$$

Parameters were selected as follows: c = 12 mm, d = 45 mm, r_0 = 40 mm, r_C = 5 mm, and the tooth profile of the wave generator was shown in Fig. 3 when A = 0.2,

0.4 and 0.6, respectively. It can be seen from the figure that the long axis of the wave generator increases with the increase of the amplitude coefficient.

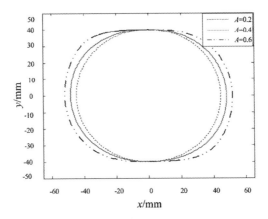

Fig. 3. The tooth profile of the wave generator

3.2   Derivation of the Ring Gear Tooth Profile

The transmission ratio of the drive is the ratio of the angular velocity between the active part and the driven part. According to the movable tooth transmission theory, the transmission ratio i_{HK}^G of the drive can be expressed as

$$i_{HK}^G = \frac{Z_K}{Z_K - Z_G} \tag{7}$$

where Z_K is the tooth number of the ring gear. Z_G is the number of the movable tooth.

$Z_K > Z_G$ is set. According to the movable tooth transmission theory, the relationship between the ring gear tooth number and the movable tooth number can be expressed as

$$Z_K = Z_G + 2 \tag{8}$$

When the separator is fixed, the ring gear rotates in the same direction as the wave generator. When the wave generator rotates an angle δ around the rotation center O, the swing rod will rotate an angle γ around its rotational center under the action of the wave generator. At this time, the ring gear rotates an angle η around its own rotation center O. According to the transmission principle, it can be known that $\eta = \delta/i_{HK}^G$. The ring gear is regarded as an inverse cam, and the derivation of the ring gear tooth profile can be analogous to the derivation of the wave generator tooth profile. By using the mechanism inversion method, after the ring gear rotates an angle η counterclockwise, the coordinate of point O_2 on the theoretical tooth profile of the ring gear can be expressed as

$$\begin{cases} x_2 = d \cdot \sin(\eta + \alpha_r) - c \cdot \sin(\eta + \alpha_r + \varphi) \\ y_2 = d \cdot \cos(\eta + \alpha_r) - c \cdot \cos(\eta + \alpha_r + \varphi) \end{cases} \quad (9)$$

The slope of normal line at the point O_2 of the ring gear theoretical tooth profile is

$$tan\vartheta = \frac{dx}{-dy} = \frac{dx/d\eta}{-dy/d\eta} = \frac{sin\vartheta}{cos\vartheta} \quad (10)$$

where ϑ is the inclination angle of the normal line of the ring gear theoretical tooth profile at O_2.

According to Eqs. (9) and (10)

$$\begin{cases} sin\vartheta = \dfrac{dx/d\eta}{\sqrt{(dx/d\eta)^2 + (dy/d\eta)^2}} \\ cos\vartheta = \dfrac{-(dy/d\eta)}{\sqrt{(dx/d\eta)^2 + (dy/d\eta)^2}} \end{cases} \quad (11)$$

The coordinate of the corresponding point $E(x_E, y_E)$ on the actual tooth profile of the ring gear is

$$\begin{cases} x_E = x_{O_2} + r_C cos\vartheta \\ y_E = y_{O_2} + r_C sin\vartheta \end{cases} \quad (12)$$

According to the previously selected tooth profile parameters. The tooth profile of the ring gear was shown in Fig. 4 when A = 0.2, 0.4 and 0.6, respectively. As can be seen from the figure, with the increase of the amplitude coefficient, the ring gear tooth profile will interfere, and the cusp at the root and top of the ring gear tooth becomes more and more obvious.

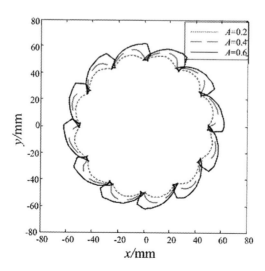

Fig. 4. The tooth profile of the ring gear

Based on the tooth profile parameters given previously, and set the tooth number of ring gear $Z_K = 12$, take the amplitude coefficient $A = 0.28$. The tooth profiles of the wave generator and the ring gear of the drive are calculated by MATLAB programming. Figure 5 shows the tooth profile diagram of the two-tooth difference swing-rod movable teeth transmission system generated by MATLAB.

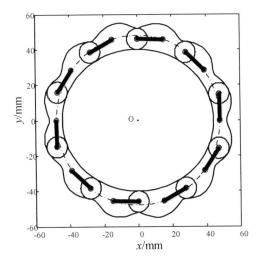

Fig. 5. Tooth profile of the drive

4   Profile Analysis

4.1   Analysis of the Curvature Radius of the Ring Gear Tooth Profile

According to the knowledge of differential geometry, curvature radius of the ring gear actual tooth profile is

$$\rho = \frac{\left[x_E'^2 + y_E'^2\right]^{3/2}}{x_E' y_E'' - x_E'' y_E'} \tag{13}$$

The formula for calculating the curvature radius of the ring gear theoretical tooth profile is

$$\rho_0 = \frac{\left[x_{O_2}'^2 + y_{O_2}'^2\right]^{3/2}}{x_{O_2}'' y_{O_2}' - x_{O_2}' y_{O_2}''} \tag{14}$$

where $x_{O_2}' = \frac{dx_{O_2}}{d\eta}$, $y_{O_2}' = \frac{dy_{O_2}}{d\eta}$, $x_{O_2}'' = \frac{dx_{O_2}'}{d\eta}$, $y_{O_2}'' = \frac{dy_{O_2}'}{d\eta}$.

The actual tooth profile of the ring gear is the outer equidistant line of the theoretical tooth profile, so the curvature radius of the ring gear actual tooth profile is

$$\rho = \rho_0 \pm r_C \qquad (15)$$

The tooth profile of the ring gear is composed of concave and convex, where the curvature radius of the concave part at the root of the tooth is $\rho = \rho_0 + r_C$, and the curvature radius of the convex part at the top of the tooth is $\rho = \rho_0 - r_C$. In order to avoid the interference of the ring gear actual tooth profile, the curvature radius should meet the requirement of $\rho > 0$, otherwise the tooth profile of the ring gear will interfere, resulting in the undercut of the ring gear.

According to the formula for calculating the curvature radius, the curvature radius ρ is a function of time and amplitude coefficient. Therefore, the amplitude coefficient has an effect on the curvature radius. Using the tooth profile parameters given previously, a three-dimensional diagram of the curvature radius ρ varying with time and amplitude coefficient can be calculated by MATLAB programming, as shown in Fig. 6.

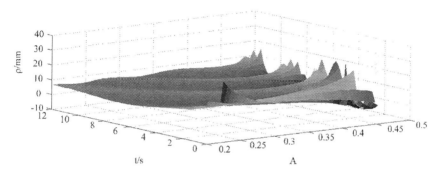

Fig. 6. 3D diagram of the curvature radius ρ varying with time and amplitude coefficient

In the running process of swing rod movable teeth transmission system, as long as there is a little interference in a cycle, then the tooth profile will be interfered. Figure 7 shows the relationship between the curvature radius and the amplitude coefficient. If the amplitude coefficient $A > 0.428$, then the curvature radius ρ will be less than 0, and the tooth profile of the ring gear will interfere. Therefore, the value of the amplitude coefficient should be less than 0.428.

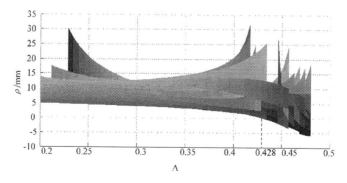

Fig. 7. Relation diagram of the amplitude coefficient and the curvature radius

4.2   Transmission Angle Analysis

In the design of the transmission device, in order to ensure the transmission device has good transmission performance, the minimum value of transmission angle is usually controlled between 40° and 50°.

Figure 8 shows transmission angle diagram of the transmission system, in which F_{KY} is the force exerted by the swing-rod movable tooth on the ring gear, and F_{HY} is the force exerted by the wave generator on the swing-rod movable tooth. According to the definition of transmission angle, angle γ_K is the transmission angle when the ring gear meshes with the swing-rod movable tooth, and angle γ_H is the transmission angle when the wave generator meshes with the swing-rod movable tooth.

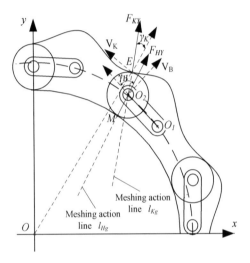

Fig. 8. Transmission angle diagram of the transmission system

According to the definition of the transmission angle, it can be known that the transmission angle is an acute angle, when the ring gear meshes with the swing-rod movable tooth, the calculation formula of transmission angle γ_K is

$$\gamma_K = \angle O_2EO = arccos\frac{\left|\overrightarrow{OE} \cdot \overrightarrow{O_2E}\right|}{OE \cdot O_2E} \tag{16}$$

When the wave generator meshes with the swing-rod movable tooth, the calculation formula of transmission angle γ_H is

$$\gamma_H = \angle O_1O_2M = arccos\frac{\left|\overrightarrow{MO_2} \cdot \overrightarrow{O_1O_2}\right|}{MO_2 \cdot O_1O_2} \tag{17}$$

According to the parameters given previously, and set the amplitude coefficient A = 0.28. When the ring gear meshes with the swing-rod movable tooth, the curve of the transmission angle γ_K in one cycle is obtained by MATLAB programming, as shown in Fig. 9.

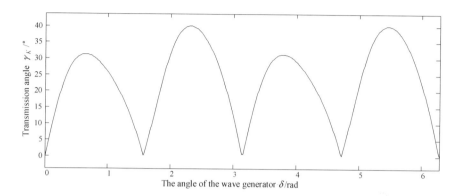

Fig. 9. The curve of the transmission angle γ_K in one cycle

The curve of the transmission angle γ_H in one cycle when the wave generator meshes with the swing-rod movable tooth is shown in Fig. 10.

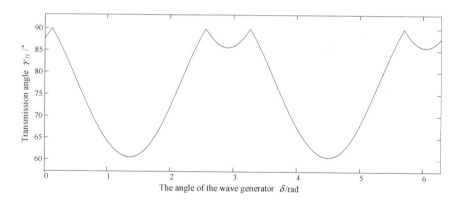

Fig. 10. The curve of the transmission angle γ_H in one cycle

When the wave generator rotates counterclockwise, the ring gear meshes with the swing-rod movable tooth in an area where the angle of the wave generator is 0 to 1.57 and π to 4.71. When the wave generator rotates clockwise, the ring gear meshes with the swing-rod movable tooth in an area where the angle of the wave generator is 1.57 to π and 4.71 to 2π. It can be seen from Fig. 9 that the transmission angle of clockwise rotation is larger than that of counter-clockwise rotation. Therefore, when the critical transmission angle is larger than the transmission angle when rotating counterclockwise and less than the transmission angle when rotating clockwise, the system can rotate forward but cannot reverse. Comparing the transmission angle γ_K in Fig. 9 with the transmission angle γ_H in Fig. 10. The transmission angle when the wave generator meshes with the swing-rod movable tooth is larger than that when the swing-rod movable tooth meshes with the ring gear, so the transmission performance between the wave generator and the swing-rod movable tooth is better. In Fig. 9, a convex peak appears in a meshing area, which is the result of the tooth profile changes from convex to concave. In Fig. 10, a small wave trough appears at the crest of the wave, because the given initial value d is greater than the value of $r_0 + r_C$.

According to the formula of the transmission angle, the transmission angle is a function of amplitude coefficient and rotation angle. Because the two-tooth difference swing-rod movable teeth transmission is a kind of multi-tooth meshing transmission, it is only necessary to ensure that the maximum transmission angle of the movable tooth participating in the meshing meets the transmission requirement. Based on the parameters given previously, three-dimensional diagrams of the transmission angle γ_K and γ_H varying with the amplitude coefficient and the wave generator angle are respectively calculated, as shown in Fig. 11.

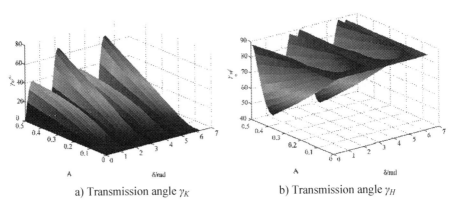

a) Transmission angle γ_K b) Transmission angle γ_H

Fig. 11. 3D diagrams of the transmission angle varying with angle and amplitude coefficient

Only the influence of amplitude coefficient on the transmission angle is considered, and the relationship between the maximum transmission angle and the amplitude coefficient is shown in Fig. 12. Figure 12(a) shows the relationship between the transmission angle γ_K and the amplitude coefficient, and Fig. 12(b) shows the relationship between the transmission angle γ_H and the amplitude coefficient.

As shown in the figure, the transmission angle γ_K increases with the increase of the amplitude coefficient, while the transmission angle γ_H decreases with the increase of the amplitude coefficient. To ensure good mechanical transmission performance, the transmission angle should be between 40°–50°. Combined with the condition that the ring gear tooth profile does not interfere, the amplitude coefficient should be between 0.28–0.428 on the premise of the design parameters in this study.

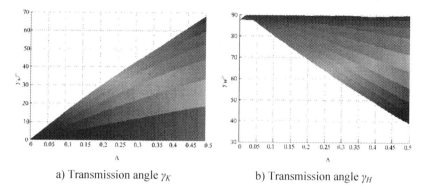

a) Transmission angle γ_K b) Transmission angle γ_H

Fig. 12. Relation diagrams of the amplitude coefficient and the transmission angle

5 Conclusion

In this paper, a method for deriving the tooth profile equations of the wave generator and the ring gear by using the mechanism inversion method is presented. The curvature radius of the ring gear and the transmission angle of the drive are deduced and analyzed. The results of the study are as follows:

(1) The cosine function without rigid impact is selected as the movement law of the swing rod to make the swing rod movement controllable. The theoretical tooth profile equations of the wave generator and the ring gear are derived by using the mechanism inversion method. And the actual tooth profile equations of the wave generator and the ring gear are obtained according to the envelope principle.

(2) The equation of the curvature radius of the ring gear is derived, and the relationship between the amplitude coefficient and the curvature radius of the ring gear is calculated according to the selected design parameters. The condition that the ring gear tooth profile does not interfere is obtained.

(3) Based on the meshing principle of movable tooth transmission, the transmission angle curve of the transmission system is calculated, and the influence of the amplitude coefficient on the transmission angle is analyzed. It provides a theoretical basis for the optimization of amplitude coefficient.

Acknowledgment. This project is supported by the National Natural Science Foundation of China (No. 51605416), Colleges and Universities in Hebei Province Science and Technology Research Youth Fund (No. QN2016095), and Independent Research Program of the Young Teachers of Yanshan University (No.15LGA004).

References

1. Qu, J.F.: Theory of Movable Teeth Drive, 1st edn. China Machine Press, Beijing (1993). (In Chinese)
2. Yi, Y.L., Liu, P.P., An, Z.J., et al.: Tooth profile design and meshing characteristics analysis of any tooth-difference pure rolling movable tooth transmission. J. Mech. Eng. 52(11), 50–62 (2016)
3. Li, J.F., Zhao, H.W., Zhang, L.Y., et al.: Transmission and tooth profile equation of swing output movable teeth cam mechanism. J. Mech. Eng. 54(23), 23–31 (2018)
4. Han, L.S., Guo, F.: Global sensitivity analysis of transmission accuracy for RV-type cycloid-pin drive. J. Mech. Sci. Technol. 30(3), 1225–1231 (2016)
5. Li, X., Li, C.Y., Wang, Y.W., et al.: Analysis of a cycloid speed reducer considering tooth profile modification and clearance-fit output mechanism. J. Mech. Des. 138(3), 1–12 (2017)
6. Xun, C., Long, X.H., Hua, H.X.: Effects of random tooth profile errors on the dynamic behaviors of planetary gears. J. Sound Vib. 415, 91–110 (2018)
7. Tran, T.L., Pham, A.D., Ahn, H.J.: Lost motion analysis of one stage cycloid reducer considering tolerances. Int. J. Precis. Eng. Manuf. 17(8), 1009–1016 (2016)
8. Xu, L.X., Yang, Y.H.: Dynamic modeling and contact analysis of a cycloid-pin gear mechanism with a turning arm cylindrical roller bearing. Mech. Mach. Theory 104, 327–349 (2016)
9. Sheu, K.B., Chien, C.W., Chiou, S.T., et al.: Kinetostatic analysis of a roller drive. Mech. Mach. Theory 39(8), 819–837 (2004)
10. Liang, S.M., Zhou, J., Li, H.: Study on modal of two-tooth difference swing-rod movable teeth transmission based on thermal analysis. J. Sichuan Univ. (Eng. Sci. Ed.) 48(06), 99–104 (2016). (In Chinese)
11. Liang, S.M., Zhang, J., He, F.F.: Study on flash temperature of swing movable teeth transmission. J. Sichuan Univ. (Eng. Sci. Ed.) 45(02), 176–181 (2013). (In Chinese)
12. Zhao, C.K., Liang, S.M., Zhang, J.: Tooth profile analysis and simulation of the tow-tooth difference swing-rod movable teeth transmission. J. Sichuan Univ. (Eng. Sci. Ed.) 47, 151–157 (2015). (In Chinese)

Transmission Error Simulation Analysis for RV Reducer with Orthogonal Experiment Method

Zhang Yinghui[1]([✉]), He Weidong[1], Wang Xiaoyu[2],
and Luo Yuechong[3]

[1] School of Mechanical Engineering, Dalian Jiaotong University Dalian,
Liaoning, China
roscoezhang@126.com
[2] CRRC Qishuyan Locomotive and Rolling Stock Technology Research
Institute Co., Ltd., Changzhou, Jiangsu, China
[3] Ningbo Zhongda Leader Intelligent Transmission Co., Ltd., Cixi City,
Zhejiang, China

Abstract. For the RV (rotate vector) reducer, taking the rule between the assembly clearance and transmission error of RV reducer as the research object. Based on the multi-body system dynamics theory and virtual prototype technology, the mixed contact test algorithm within relative coordinate system shape space method and boundary box method, and the Lankarani contact force model based on Hertz contact theory to define the contact pair, which including the contact between cycloid gear and pin wheels, the contact between pin wheels and pin wheel housing, and the mating involutes gear pair, define the rotate pair between the crank shaft and cycloid gear connection as bushing to eliminate the over constrained condition in the parallel double crank kinematic mechanism, define the clearance of arm bearings, supporting bearings and main bearings as 0 μm, a virtual prototype model of RV reducer is established. On the basis of this virtual prototype model, define the clearances of the main bearings, arm bearings and the supporting bearings as factors, a orthogonal simulation experiment with three factors and four levels is designed (the level of all factors are four), which used for studying the rule between the different clearance with the angular transmission error and no-load hysteresis error. Through orthogonal simulation results, the conspicuousness of each bearing clearance on angular transmission error and no-load hysteresis error is obtained: the Significant order from large to small are supporting bearing clearance larger than main bearing clearance and larger than arm bearing clearance.

Keywords: RV reducer · Orthogonal method · Transmission error ·
Virtual prototype

© Springer Nature Switzerland AG 2019
H. Yu et al. (Eds.): ICIRA 2019, LNAI 11740, pp. 629–640, 2019.
https://doi.org/10.1007/978-3-030-27526-6_55

1   Introduction

As shown in Fig. 1, RV (Rotary-Vector) reducer is composed by cycloid gear and planetary gear with advantages as large transmission ratio, high precision [1], high carrying capacity, high transmission efficiency and stable working performance with small volume.

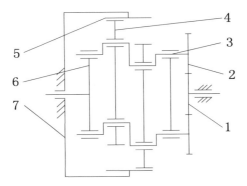

Fig. 1. Working principle of RV reducer 1. Sun gear 2. Planet wheel 3. Crankshaft 4. Cycloid wheel 5. Needle wheel 6. Planet carrier 7. Pin wheel housing

For improving the load carrying ability of RV reducer, based on the forming principle of cycloid tooth profile, a universal cycloid profile equation contains general kinds of profile modification was put forward [2, 3]. Based on the general equation, optimal design of the cycloid gear, accurate force analysis and accurate measurement of the cycloid tooth profile are also proposed [4]. According to the characteristics of RV reducer requires a small hysteresis, the cycloid tooth profile with negative isometric and negative shift combination modification method was developed [5], through isometric and shift modification method, the "against the bow tooth profile modification methods" have been applied in engineering [6]. In addition to the combination of equidistant and shift modification method of modification, new type of cycloid section modification method appeared in recent years, this modification methods of composite tooth profile in the work period of guarantee for the conjugate tooth profile, non-working period by curve fitting the right within the scope of the tooth profile [7]. Specific means is, at the period of cycloid tooth profile that bear force, take additional trace drum transition modification method, and at the non-working period of the dedendum and the addendum, take the circular arc fixed subsection composite modified method [8]. Blanche and others adopt the pure geometry method to study the single cycloid gear planetary reducer angle transmission accuracy, backstroke error and speed ratio fluctuation and torsion vibration are discussed. The study defined the model with only the single stage, single cycloid gear of cycloid pinwheel reducer transmission precision, ignore the double-stage and cycloid gear and the crank of the RV reducer, only consider the radius change of pin tooth in a relation of the influence of the error and the torsion vibration, did not involve the two-stage and cycloid gear and the crank and the components of the processing, the assemble error [9, 10]. Japanese scholars, Rio and others studied the transmission accuracy of the RV reducer, established the mathematics model of cycloid-pin gear planetary gear reducer transmission error, discusses the single processing error and assembly error influence on the transmission accuracy, and also discussed the error synthesis of some effects on the transmission accuracy. WU established a RV reducer dynamic transmission accuracy analysis model which consider the machining errors of components, assembly error and elastic deformation, and transfer matrix method is adopted to establish the dynamic high precision RV transmission analysis model, programming to solve the RV transmission reducer system dynamic accuracy, and get the system transmission error value [10].

Considering cycloid wheel, needle teeth, clearance between the planet carrier deformation and parts that affect the transmission precision, a coupled rigid and flexible model of RV reducer was set up, analyses the typical errors which affect the transmission error in the system, each type of error is not a simple superposition, but the conclusion of mutual coupling effect [11–13].

Yun-wen Shen, Haijun Dong and Linshan Han considering various parts processing error factors, such as the assembly error and bearing clearance error etc., built and analysis a mathematical model for dynamic transmission accuracy of the RV reducer, render research from linear to nonlinear field [14–19].

In the study of the RV reducer backstroke error, Mr. Zhang, Jianrun Zhang put forward a kind of optimization design method as the upper limit of RV reducer geometric backlash for the constraints of system parameters, established a optimization design model which configure geometric difference as objective function, system parameters as variables, and the system parameter sensitivity analysis was done [20]. Haiming Zhao, analyzed the factors influence the backstroke error of RV reducer. Established the mathematical model for the analysis on backstroke error, and deduced the mathematical model of central circle radius error and other 16 errors [21]. Zhang Jin summarizes the factors influencing the backstroke error of RV system, established the mathematical model of factors which influence with the backstroke error, analyze the distribution of these factors, and apply statistical method to calculate the backstroke of RV reducer system [20].

2 CAD Model Establishment for RV Reducer

As shown in Fig. 2, according to the design dimension of the RV80E-81 type reducer, using top-down assembly modeling method in 3D modeling software, and establish the 1:1 ratio geometry CAD model of the RV reducer without interference, the establishment of a geometric model as shown in Fig. 1. The key design parameters related to the gear parts in the 3D geometric model of the RV80E-81 type reducer are shown in Table 1. The simplified RV reducer CAD model is shown in Fig. 3 (the planetary frame is hidden).

Fig. 2. RV reducer with three parallel double crankshaft mechanism

Fig. 3. Three parallel double crank mechanisms

Table 1. The main parameters of gear parts

Part name	Number	Remarks
Input gear shaft	1	Tooth number 16, module 1.75, the coefficient of variation +0.5
Planetary gear	3	Tooth number 32, module 1.75, the coefficient of variation −0.5
Cycloidalal gear	2	Standard tooth profile, three section profile modification
Pin gear	40	Tooth number 40, the standard tooth shape, with the shape (diameter of non-standard circle)
Pin gear housing	1	Standard size of the Pin gear, the shaped pin gear socket

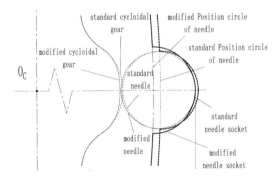

Fig. 4. Comparison of the standard tooth profile and the modified profile of cycloidalal gear-needle gear

As shown in Fig. 4, in order to facilitate comparison, in the same coordinate the addendum of cycloid gear with standard profile, the standard needle tooth, the standard needle tooth socket and the addendum of cycloid gear with modified profile, the modified needle tooth, the modified needle socket are drawn.

3   Definition of Multi-body Dynamics Simulation Model of RV Reducer

3.1   Multi Body Dynamic Contact Algorithm and Gear Contact Modeling

Before the dynamic simulation of RV reducer, define gear contact between gears, and establish the bearing clearance model. In the established simulation model of the RV reducer with bearing clearance, all contact theory algorithms used for involutes gear in first stage, cycloid gear and needle wheel in second stage) are based on the Lankarni variable type vary from Hertz contact theory:

$$f_n = k\delta^{m_1} + c\frac{\dot{\delta}}{|\dot{\delta}|}\left|\dot{\delta}\right|^{m_2}\delta^{m_3}$$

f_n : Contact force
k : Contact stiffness
δ : Penetration   (1)
c : Damping
m_1 : Nonlinear exponent
m_2 : Damping index
m_3 : indentation index

Figure 5 shows the Contact force diagram of Hertz contact theory model and Lankarni contact theory model. As shown in Figs. 6, 7 and 8, establish contact pair in sun gear and planetary gear, cycloid gear and needle wheel, needle and needle socket by using the method of shape space and bounding box.

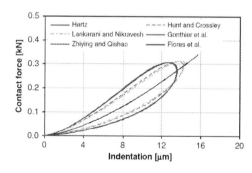

Fig. 5. Contact force model

Fig. 6. Contact pair of involute gears

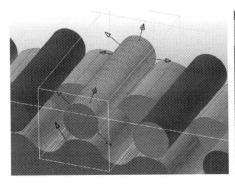
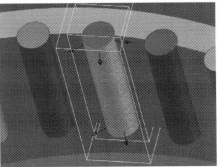

Fig. 7. Contact pair of cycloidalal gear and needle gear   **Fig. 8.** Contact of pin gear and needle socket

3.2 Removal of Redundant Constraints and the Establishment of Clearance Bearing Model

Virtual constraint: As shown in Fig. 9, the eccentric motion of the second grade cycloid gear is performed by three parallel double crank mechanisms, these redundant constraints must be removed. To remove redundant constraints, we introduce spring force to replace the hinge kinematic pair between components, as shown in Fig. 10.

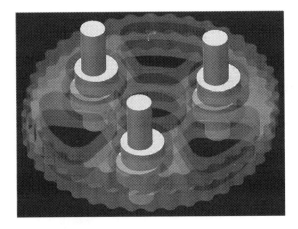

Fig. 9. Three parallel double crank mechanism

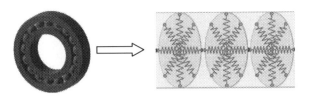

Fig. 10. Spring bearing instead of solid bearing

Bearing clearance: Research shows that the three bearing clearance are important factors affecting the transmission accuracy of the reducer, The dynamic simulation model must contain the bearing clearance.

Mechanism with spring force instead of bearings is shown in Fig. 11, spring force replaces the support bearings between the flange and the crankshaft, arm bearing between cycloid gear and crankshaft. The multi-body dynamics simulation model with bearing clearance of RV reducer based on spring force and dynamic multi contact is shown in Fig. 12.

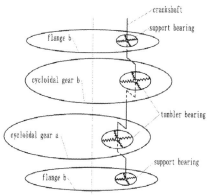

Fig. 11. Spring force mechanism

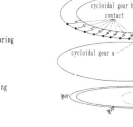

Fig. 12. Multi-body dynamics simulation model

3.3   Simulation and Verification of Dynamic Transmission Error of RV Reducer

According to Table 2, the relative error of the theoretical calculation value and the simulation value of the angular velocity of the parts of RV80E-81 virtual prototype reducer is Far less than 1% and can be ignored. The simulation results show that the transmission ratio is quite close to the calculated value. It is proved that the kinematics simulation results of the virtual prototype are correct and meet the kinematic requirements of the transmission ratio.

Under the condition that the clearance of all bearings is 0, adjust two dynamic simulation models of RV reducer A and B, and the A model of the reducer is assembled with the standard tooth profile cycloid gear, and the B model is assembled with the modified tooth profile cycloid gear, and perform dynamics simulation to model A and B respectively. As can be seen from Figs. 13 and 14, under the condition that the bearing clearance is 0, The simulation value of the angle.

Transmission error of the RV reducer fitted with the standard tooth cycloid gear is 0.043′; the simulation value of the angle transmission error of the RV reducer fitted with cycloid wheel with modified tooth profile is 0.089′. Comparison of the two curves shows that the amplification effect is not obvious. The simulation value of the backstroke error of the RV reducer fitted with cycloid wheel with modified tooth profile is 0.147′.

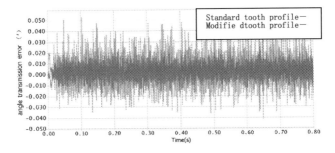

Fig. 13. Comparison of angle transmission error of RV reducer fitted cycloidal gear with standard tooth profile and modified tooth profile

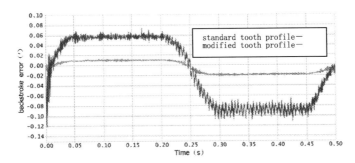

Fig. 14. Comparison of back stroke error of RV reducer fitted cycloidal gear with standard tooth profile and modified tooth profile

3.4   Orthogonal Experimental of Transmission Error Simulation Data Consider Bearing Clearance

As shown in Fig. 15, the bearing structure used in RV reducer is special, the causes of main bearing clearance, support bearing clearance and tumbler bearing clearance of RV reducer is the main factor affecting the dynamic transmission accuracy of RV reducer. The experimental factors and levels are shown in Table 3.

Table 2. Theoretical values and simulation values of angular velocity

Project	Symbol	Theoretical angular velocity (degree/s)	Simulated angular velocity (degree/s)	Relative error (%)
Solar gear angular velocity	n_1	7290	7290	0
Planet gear angular velocity	n_2	−3510	3516.426	0.183.
Planetary carrier angular velocity	n_H	90	89.843	0.174
Transmission ratio	n_1/n_H	81	81.141	0.175

Table 3. The experimental factors and levels

Levels factors	Main bearing clearance (μm)	Support bearings clearance (μm)	Arm bearing clearance (μm)
1	0	0	0
2	3	10	5
3	6	20	10
4	10	30	15

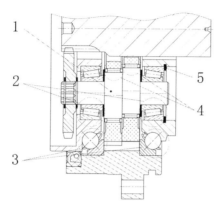

Fig. 15. Main bearings, crank shaft bearing, crank shaft bearing installation diagram 1. Crank shaft, 2. Support bearing, 3. Main bearing, 4. Crank shaft tumbler bearing 5. Adjusting spring for hole

4   Orthogonal Experiment Simulation and Data Analysis

Through the simulation of the 16 groups' dynamic model and analysis of the experimental results, the variance analysis and significance analysis of the orthogonal experiment data of angle transmission error of RV reducer are shown in Tables 4 and 5. By the analysis of variance and F significance test, it can be seen that the support bearing clearance and the main bearing clearance of the RV reducer in the angle transmission error simulation is a key significant factor. Based on the contribution rate, the main factors can be judged.

From the calculation of contribution rate data, when the simulation angle transmission error of RV reducer difference in the range of 0.4708′–5.265′, 59.283% of the reason is due to the varying of the crank shaft bearing clearance from the 0–30 μm range, 9.745% of the reason is due to the change of the crank shaft bearing clearance from the 0–10 μm range and tumbler bearing clearance from the 0–30 μm range has little influence.

Table 4. Orthogonal test analyses of angle transmission error.

Factor	Main bearing clearance (μm)	Support bearing clearance (μm)	Tumbler bearing clearance (μm)	Dynamic transmission error x_i (')
Experiment 1	0	0	0	0.196
Experiment 2	0	10	5	0.602
Experiment 3	0	20	10	1.916
Experiment 4	0	30	15	1.386
Experiment 5	3	0	5	0.223
Experiment 6	3	10	0	1.661
Experiment 7	3	20	15	2.794
Experiment 8	3	30	10	4.186
Experiment 9	6	0	10	0.471
Experiment 10	6	10	15	2.019
Experiment 11	6	20	0	3.419
Experiment 12	6	30	5	5.265
Experiment 13	10	0	15	0.603
Experiment 14	10	10	10	1.317
Experiment 15	10	20	5	2.388
Experiment 16	10	30	0	5.169
K1	3.376	1.492	10.444	$\bar{x} = 2.055$
K2	8.864	5.600	8.480	T = 32.893
K3	11.172	9.952	7.164	
K4	9.476	16.004	6.800	
k1	0.844	0.373	2.611	
k2	2.216	1.400	2.120	
k3	2.793	2.488	1.791	
k4	2.369	4.001	1.700	
Variance S	0.844	0.373	2.611	
Significant sequence	Support bearing clearance > Main bearing clearance > Tumbler bearing clearance			

Table 5. Significance test of angular transmission error

Variance sources	SS	Degree of freedom	Variance estimation	F	Saliency
Main bearing clearance	8.523	3	2.841	5.834	**
Support bearing clearance	29.568	3	9.856	20.238	***
Tumbler bearing clearance	2.017	3	0.672		
Experimental error	2.374 + 2.017	6 + 3	0.487		
Total variation	42.482				

5   Conclusions

(1) Base on the dynamics and virtual prototyping theory, we set up a virtual dynamic simulation prototype model of RV reducer with bearing clearance in main bearing, support bearing and arm bearing, and this dynamic simulation prototype model could be used to test the influence of cycloidal gear with modified gear profile on the angular transmission error and backlash of RV reducer.

(2) Define the bearing clearances of nonlinear mechanism of RV reducer as variable, set up the orthogonal test as three factors and four levels with clearance volume of main bearings, support bearings and arm bearings. By simulation and apply variance analysis and sensitivity analysis to find out the sensitivity of different bearing clearances of RV reducer, the analysis result find that the clearance of support bearings plays significant effects on transmission error, provide a reference for the tolerance design and manufacturing of the transmission accuracy of the RV reducer.

Acknowledgments. This work is supported by The National Key Research and Development Program of China (2017YFB1300700) and The Key Research and Development Program of Jiangsu Providence (BE2015006-4). The author would also like to acknowledge the anonymous reviewers for their insightful comments and suggestions on an earlier draft of this paper references.

References

1. Nabtesco: Technical data set of high speed reducer for precision control (2014)
2. Li, L.X.: Tooth profile modification and force analysis of cycloidal pin gear planetary transmission. Chin. J. Dalian Railway Inst. (4), 29–40 (1984)
3. He, W.D., Li, L.X.: Optimal profile modification of cycloidal gear in high precision RV reducer. J. Dalian Railw. Inst. **20**(2), 54–58 (1999)
4. Zhang, S.A.: The analysis and calculation of the optimum profile of cycloidal gear in cycloidal drive. Mech. Sci. Technol. **6**(21), 906–908 (2002)
5. Guan, T.M., Zhang, D.S.: Study and optimization design of reverse arch profile in cycloidal planetary transmission. J. Mech. Eng. **3**, 151–156 (2005)
6. Liu, M.X.: The research of cycloidal pin gear and small RV two stage reducer. Beijing Jiaotong University, Beijing (2008)
7. Yan, Y., Tang, L.: Method for determining optimum compound modification and correction of cycloid gear. J. Chongqing Univ. **16**(5), 137–140 (1993)
8. Blanche, J.G.: Design and application guidelines for cycloidal drives with machining tolerances. Mech. Mach. Theory **25**(5), 487–501 (1990)
9. Wu, X.H.: A new method of gear profile optimization for RV reducer and research on transmission precision used in robot. Dalian Jiaotong University, Dalian (2015)
10. He, W.D.: Research on high precision RV drive for robot. Harbin Institute of Technology, Harbin (1999)
11. Shan, L.J., Fan, T., He, W.D.: Analysis of nonlinear dynamic accuracy on RV transmission. Adv. Mater. Res. **5**(10), 529–535 (2012)

12. Zhu, Z.X., Dong, H.J., Han, L.S.: Sensitivity analysis of the error combination method for the transmission accuracy of RV reducer. Mech. Des. **25**(10), 69–73 (2008)
13. Yuan, X., Wu, L.Y., Han, L.S.: Study on the sensitivity of the error to the transmission accuracy of RV reducer. Dev. Innov. Mech. Electr. Prod. **22**(2), 38–46 (2009)
14. Han, L.S., Shen, Y.W.: Theoretical study on dynamic transmission accuracy of 2 K-V transmission. Chin. J. Mech. Eng. **6**, 81–86 (2007)
15. San, L.S., Shen, Y.W., Dong, H.J.: Research on transmission accuracy of cycloidal pin gear system based on nonlinear analysis. China Mech. Eng. **9**, 1039–1043 (2007)
16. San, L.S., Shen, Y.W., Dong, H.J.: Influence of manufacturing error of 2 K-V transmission device to transmission precision. Mech. Sci. Technol. **9**, 1135–1140 (2007)
17. Han, L.S., Shen, Y.W., Tan, Q.Y.: Influence of clearance and torque on transmission accuracy of transmission. Mech. Sci. Technol. **8**, 1011–1014 (2007)
18. Wu, Y.K., Zheng, J.Y.: Analysis and calculation of geometric difference of cycloidal pin gear planetary transmission. J. Dalian Railw. Instit. **20**(2), 28–32 (1999)
19. Zhao, H.M., Wang, M.: Study on static difference analysis and error distribution of RV reducer. J. Tianjin Univ. **49**(2), 164–169 (2016)
20. Zhang, J.: Research on transmission accuracy of RV reducer. Harbin University of Science and Technology, Harbin (2013)
21. Shen, B.X.: Experimental design and engineering application, China Metrology Publishing House (2005)

Design and Finite Element Analysis of Fiber-Reinforced Soft Pneumatic Actuator

Xianqi Xue, Ziheng Zhan, Yongwu Cai, Ligang Yao[(✉)],
and Zongxing Lu[(✉)]

School of Mechanical Engineering and Automation, Fuzhou University,
No. 2, Xueyuan Road, Fuzhou 350116, Fujian, China
{ylgyao,luzongxing}@fzu.edu.cn

Abstract. Soft fluid actuators consisting of the flexible materials are of particular interest to the robotics field because of the low cost and the potential applications, which can be easily customized to a given devices. However, the great potential of such actuators is currently limited due to that their designs are mostly based on experience. In this paper, we designed and manufactured a fiber-reinforced soft pneumatic actuator. Through ingenious design, the actuator can produce bending movement under low pressure, which has simple structure, convenient fabrication and low cost. This paper provides a finite-element method (FEM) model for the bending of the fiber-reinforced soft pneumatic actuator in the free space, which can present a more realistic description of the nonlinear response of the system. With the FEM model, the deformation and stress of the soft actuators can be visualized readily, leading to a better understanding about the influence of geometric parameters, input air pressure and material selection on bending angel performance. Finally, corresponding experiments have also been taken, successfully demonstrating the validity of the FEM model.

Keywords: Soft robot · Fiber-reinforced · Simulation · Finite element model

1 Introduction

Soft robotics is a fast-growing emerging research direction, which involved robotics, materials science, and electronics, etc. The complex locomotion would be realized by researching and designing of soft material with certain flexible elastomeric materials (Young's modulus of 102-106 Pa) [1, 2]. Soft robots are very suitable for grabbing and operating vulnerable objects by their adaptive abilities in response to environmental changes. Scholars pay more and more attention to the research on the soft robotics due to its advantages of the low production cost and adaptive ability [3, 4].

As a kind of soft robots, soft actuators are usually made of flexible material (silicon rubber, dielectric elastomer (DE) [5], electro active polymer (EAP) [6], shape memory alloy (SMA) [7] and shape memory polymer (SMP) [8]). And they can be driven by a number of stimuli, such as electrical charges [7, 9–11], chemical reactions [12, 13] and pressurized fluids [2, 12–19]. At present, soft actuators are constructed by hyperelastic materials, which are driven by the pneumatic and hydraulic combined, become research

© Springer Nature Switzerland AG 2019
H. Yu et al. (Eds.): ICIRA 2019, LNAI 11740, pp. 641–651, 2019.
https://doi.org/10.1007/978-3-030-27526-6_56

hotspots, because of the characteristic of lightweight, low cost of materials, and easiness to fabricate and control. According to the different design, the elastomer expands in the directions associated with low stiffness after pressing to the inner cavity of elastomers, resulting in the motion of bending, twisting, and extending or contracting. In addition, the soft actuators can be integrated in the soft system of the robot by being used as an actuator or components.

Although soft robots have many advantages and potentials, their potentials are limited by the fact that there is less analytical solution to the model of soft robot but only numerical solution, due to the characteristics of the material itself. Because of the nonlinear response and complex geometry of the soft actuator, it is not easy to predict its performance (such as deformation and force output with a pressurized fluid) before manufacturing. Soft actuators have been widely concerned in recent years, but their modeling work is limited. In order to make these actuators widely used, it is necessary to systematically understand the relationship between the geometry of the actuator and its performance.

In this paper, we have successfully designed and manufactured a kind of actuator, which is made of a hyperelastic silicone rubber and inextensible materials (fabrics and fibers) and driven by pressurized air, namely, the fiber-reinforced soft pneumatic actuator. The structure of soft actuator is simple that offers ease of manufacture. It is able to bend in the specified direction. In order to realize that the movement behavior of pressurized condition was analyzed intuitively, the FEM model of the soft actuator is established in this paper. Comparison of the trajectory and the deformation angel of the FEM with that of the actual prototype in response to a pressurized air is given to verify the correction of the FEM model, and modeling with FEM lays the foundation for follow-up study.

2   Design of the Soft Actuator

2.1   Working Principle of the Soft Actuator

When an elastomer with a cavity is inflated, the cavity expands under pressure. (like a balloon). While the cavity is elongated, the expansion of actuator is reflected in axial elongation and radial expansion. The axial and radial motion of the elastomer can be limited by the using of attaching an object with inextensible property to the elastomer surface. Bending occurs when the axial motion of one side of the elastomer is limited and that of the other side is not. By wrapping the winding around the surface of the elastomer, the radial expansion of the elastomer is restricted, so that the actuator can have a greater bending angle at the same pressure. (as shown in Fig. 1). At the same time, according to different winding patterns, the cavity will have different axial motion patterns.

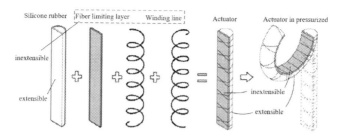

Fig. 1. Diagram of the soft actuator bending

2.2   Design of the Soft Actuator

In this paper, an actuator, which made of hyperelastic silicone rubber, with a semi-cylindrical cavity is designed. The plane side of the actuator chamber is attached with an axial fiber limiting layer. The outer side of the actuator chamber and the axial fiber limiting layer are wound with a fiber winding at an angle of 0 degree, which can limit the radial expansion of the actuator and fix the axial fiber limiting layer and the chamber. After the inner chamber is attached with gauze and winding line, the same hyperelastic silicone rubber is used to make an outer wrapping wall, whose function is to fix and protect the fiber winding and the axial fiber limiting layer, so that the actuator is integrated. A flange is designed around the upper end of the outer wrapping layer to make a coordinate with the groove of the connector and to ensure the air impermeability.

The fiber winding with high strength coefficient is used to be a fiber reinforcement layer. The fiber winding has the characteristics of small tensile deformation which means almost no elastic deformation under great stress. The axial fiber limiting layer is made up of non-malleable materials (e.g., glass fiber, high-density polyethylene fiber), which leads to the better movement characteristic. The fiber winding cooperate with the axial fiber limiting layer when the cavity expands due to air pressure. The axial fiber limiting layer limits the stretch of the plane side of the actuator, and the other side of the actuator expands, so as to realize the bending movement of the actuator in the specified direction. The pneumatic soft actuator designed in this paper is shown in Fig. 2 and the geometric parameters of actuator is shown in Table 1.

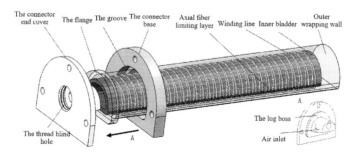

Fig. 2. Actuator overall design

The actuator is installed in the groove of the connector base that fits the flange on the upper end of its outer wrapping wall. The middle part of the side of the end cover is provided with a thread blind hole. The bottom of the thread blind hole is connected with an air inlet. The air source is matched with the threaded blind hole through the quick plug. The connector end cover, base and actuator are bolted together.

In order to ensure the air impermeability, the air inlet is designed to cone-shape. The maximum size of the air inlet is larger than the cavity size, and the minimum size is smaller than the actuator cavity size. Interference fit will be formed when the air inlet is inserted into the upper end of the cavity. At the same time, the groove on the connector base, the lug boss on the end cover and the flange on the actuator are designed to fit with interference to ensure the air impermeability by compressing the silicone rubber. Sufficient raw material tape is wound on the thread of the quick plug to match the internal thread on the end cover to ensure air impermeability.

Table 1. Geometric parameters of actuator.

Geometric parameters	Value
Length of actuator	140 mm
Length of chamber	130 mm
Wall thickness of actuator	4 mm
Turning numbers of winding	35

3   Finite Element Method Modeling of the Soft Actuator

FEM models provide a more realistic description of the nonlinear response of the system, although at a higher computational cost. An additional advantage of FEM is that the deformation and stress in soft actuators can be readily visualized, leading to a better understanding of the influence about local strain on global actuator performance.

3.1   Material Model of the Soft Actuator

The soft actuator body is made of silicon rubber, a hyperelastic material. Since the material property of the hyperelastic material is non-linear under external forces, the strain energy density function is usually used to describe the mechanical properties of silicon rubber material. Assuming that the rubber material is isotropic and incompressible, the constitutive relationship of the rubber material is established based on the stress-strain relationship and the phenomenological theory. The strain energy density function is expressed as follows:

$$W = W(I_1, I_2, I_3) \tag{1}$$

where

$$I_1 = \lambda_1^2 + \lambda_2^2 + \lambda_3^2 \tag{2}$$

$$I_2 = \lambda_1^2 \lambda_2^2 + \lambda_2^2 \lambda_3^2 + \lambda_1^2 \lambda_3^2 \tag{3}$$

$$I_3 = \lambda_1^2 \lambda_2^2 \lambda_3^2 = 1 \tag{4}$$

$$\lambda_i = 1 + \gamma_i \tag{5}$$

where, I_1, I_2, I_3 are strain tensor invariants, λ_1, λ_2, λ_3 is the principal stretch ratios, γ_i is the axial strain and $I_3 = 1$ for incompressible materials.

Common functions include Neo-Hookean model, Yeoh model, Mooney-Rivlin model, etc. Specially, according to the data of uniaxial tensile strength test, the Yeoh model can fit the mechanical behavior of other different deformation modes, such as uniaxial compression and shear. And Yeoh model is suitable for simulating large deformation. Therefore, the Yeoh model is adopted in this paper to establish the nonlinear relationship between stress and strain of materials. Yeoh believed that the strain tensor invariants I_2 have little influence on the strain energy and could be completely ignored. The strain energy density function is simplified as

$$W = \sum_{i=1}^{N} C_{i0}(I_1 - 3)^i + \sum_{k=1}^{N} \frac{1}{d_k}(J - 1)^{2k} \tag{6}$$

where N, C_{i0} and d_k are material constants, which are determined by the material experiment, and $J = 1$ for incompressible materials. The typical two-parameter form is

$$W = C_{10}(I_1 - 3)^1 + C_{20}(I_1 - 3)^2 \tag{7}$$

For 0-degree silicone rubber, two-parameter model can be used to fit its stress-strain characteristics in a certain range.

3.2   Finite Element Method Model of the Soft Actuator

For the actual soft actuator, the FEM model can directly reflect the nonlinear response of the actuator. The deformable displacement, internal stress and strain of the actuator can be visualized, which make a better understanding of the soft actuator.

Before the simulation, accurate material properties should be tested. According to standard ASTM D638 (Type IV), accurate material samples are subjected to a tensile test at a rate of 500 mm/min to obtain the stress-strain data curve, which was fitted by the least square method to obtain the unknown parameters (C_{10} and C_{20}) in the model.

For the silicone material used in this paper, the material parameters are $C_{10} = 0.11$ MPa, $C_{20} = 0.016$ MPa. Actuator surface fiber winding and the axial fiber limiting layer is defined as linear elastic material, where young's modulus E = 32 000 MPa, Poisson's ratio $v = 0.36$ for the fiber winding, and the young's modulus E = 6 000 MPa, Poisson's ratio $v = 0.2$ for the axial fiber limiting layer.

To simulate the property of actuator, according to the size of actual, the FEM models of the soft actuator were established by ABAQUS/Standard (Simulia, Dassault Systemes), as is shown in Fig. 3. In order to improve the computation efficiency and convergence of the FEM model, the air inlet was not modeled in the FEM. All the parts of the actuator were modeled using solid tetrahedral quadratic hybrid elements (Abaqus element type C3D10H) and the fiber windings around the surface were modeled using quadratic beam elements (Abaqus element type B32). And the fiber windings and the axial fiber limiting layer were connected to the actuator by the tie constraints. To decrease the stiffness of the beam elements and increase the computation speed and convergence, the radius of the beam elements was set at a value of half the actual value. This reduction of radius resulted little influence to the model, while fiber winding remained meaningfully stiffer than elastomer. Ignoring the effects of gravity and friction, the internal pressure was acted on the entire chamber which will be filled with air actually. The actuator deformation results of every angle are shown in Fig. 4.

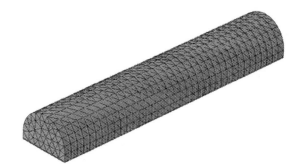

Fig. 3. Finite element model of the sofe actuator

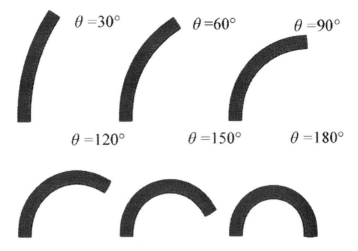

Fig. 4. Finite element model of the sofe actuator in different wending angle

4 Experimental

4.1 Actuator Fabrication

Based on the size of the design, the soft actuators were manufactured. First, the hyperelastic silicone rubber A and B glue were mixed at 1:1 and then mixing liquid silicone rubber was taken to the vacuum machine for removing the air bubbles. Second, mixing liquid silicone rubber were poured into the mould 1 (as shown in Fig. 5(a)) evenly and stand about 6 h to the formation of the chamber. An axial fiber limiting layer was added to the side of the chamber plane (the glass fiber was used in this article) and the winding line (the kevlar wire was used in this article) twined the axial fiber limiting layer and the chamber at an Angle of 0 degrees and fixed them together. Third, put the inner chamber into mould 2 (as shown in Fig. 5(b)) after winding, then poured the same mixing liquid silicone rubber into the mould 2 evenly, and removed the inner-core after stand about 6 h, actuator main body was completed. The mould designed in this paper is made by 3D printing (as shown in Fig. 6), so the liquid silicone rubber needs to be set at room temperature. When the mould is made of other materials, liquid silicone rubber can also accelerate the curing speed and reduce the production time at a high temperature. The finished soft actuator is shown in Fig. 7.

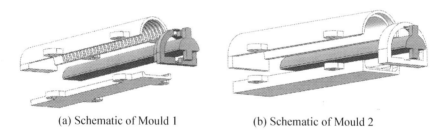

(a) Schematic of Mould 1   (b) Schematic of Mould 2

Fig. 5. Schematic of mould

Fig. 6. The 3D printing mould

Fig. 7. Actuator

4.2 Experimental Platform

In this section, we mainly conduct experiments on the soft actuator. The experimental platform is shown in Fig. 8. The upper computer sends signals, and under the condition of maintaining the continuous pumping of the air pump, the Pulse Width Modulation (PWM) wave is used to control the on/off switch of the solenoid valve, so as to realize the filling and exhausting of the actuator. The pressure gage is connected to the branch between the actuator and the solenoid valve, which lead to the pressure inside the cavity is reflected in numerical signal with the pressure gage. The air is output from the air pump, and fed into the five-way solenoid valve after decompressing by the pressure-reducing valve. The solenoid valve selected in this paper is a c-type enclosed five-way solenoid valve. When the solenoid valve is not energized, the five-hole solenoid valve is closed to stabilize the pressure. The solenoid valve fills and releases the gas to the soft actuator by receiving the PWM signal to control the on and off status. The adjustment of the pressure inside the actuator is realized by observing the pressure information of the pressure gage and adjusting the duty ratio of PWM signal to control the on and off status of the solenoid valve.

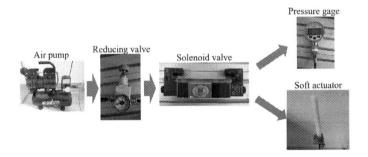

Fig. 8. Experimental testing equipment

4.3 Experimental Results

Bending experiments were carried out on the actuator prototype, bending angle and end trajectory were obtained in response to pressure. The data are compared with the FEM model simulation results. As presented in Fig. 9, which shows the end trajectory of the central axis of the actuator in the FEM model and experimental data at different bending angles.

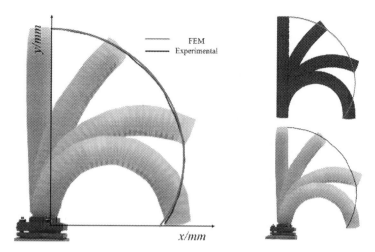

Fig. 9. Compare of End trajectory with actuator prototype and the finite element simulation result

Displacement error e_i (as shown in Fig. 10) and displacement root-mean square error e_s between the FEM model and the actual prototype are calculated to verify the correctness of the FEM model.

$$e_i = \sqrt{(x_i - x'_i)^2 + (y_i - y'_i)^2} \tag{8}$$

$$e_s = \sqrt{\frac{\sum_{i=1}^{N}(x_i - x'_i)^2 + (y_i - y'_i)^2}{s}} \tag{9}$$

where x_i and y_i are the position coordinates of the actuator end center point in the FEM model; x'_i and y'_i are the position coordinates of the actuator end center point in the experimental data at the same bending angle. s is the number of tests. In this paper, the terminal center position at 12 different bending angles was tested, so $s = 12$.

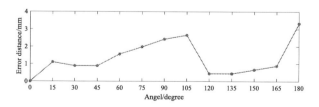

Fig. 10. Displacement error of the finite element simulation result

The displacement root-mean square error $e_s = 1.326$ mm according to the formula (9) is obtained, thus proving that the FEM model proposed in this paper can better simulate the actual actuator. The main reason for the above errors may be that there are some errors in the selection of material parameters in the axial fiber limiting layer model and manufacture.

5   Conclusions

Soft actuators can produce complex three-dimensional motion outputs at a very low mechanical cost through simple control inputs. Up to now, the development of such actuators was basically an empirical process. In order to enable the soft robot to be designed deterministically and have a determinate performance before manufacture, an accurate and experimentally validated FEM model was developed for a specific soft actuator, a flexible fiber-reinforced soft pneumatic actuators.

In this paper, a fiber-reinforced soft actuator is designed and manufactured. The actuator has simple structure, convenient fabrication, low cost and able to produce complex motion.

The FEM model for the designed actuator can better simulate the function of the actual actuator, and highlight the local stress/strain concentration, such as the interaction between fiber and elastomer. In addition, a simplified analysis method can provide a method of predicting the performance of actuator in the later study. The clear associations between input pressure, geometrical parameter and actuator bending angle, output force, which can understand the influence of the individual parameters on the performance of actuators better through the simulations. Last, the results of modeling are evaluated by experimental verifications.

In the future, the influence of geometrical parameters of the fiber-reinforced bending actuator will be further studied, such as the influence of wall thickness, length and winding number on the performance of the actuator will be analyzed through the FEM model established in this paper.

Acknowledgements. The authors would like to thank the financial support from the National Natural Science Foundation of China (Grant No. 61801122), the Natural Science Foundation of Fujian Province (Grant No. 2018J01762) and the Science Project of Fujian Education Department (Grant No. JK2017002).

References

1. Ilievski, F., Mazzeo, A.D., Shepherd, R.F., Chen, X., Whitesides, G.M.: Soft robotics for chemists. Angew. Chem. Int. Ed. Engl. **50**(8), 1890–1895 (2011). https://doi.org/10.1002/anie.201006464
2. Shepherd, R.F., et al.: Multigait soft robot. Proc. Natl. Acad. Sci. U.S.A. **108**(51), 20400–20403 (2011). https://doi.org/10.1073/pnas.1116564108
3. Seok, S., Onal, C.D., Wood, R., Rus, D., Kim, S.: Peristaltic locomotion with antagonistic actuators in soft robotics, pp. 1228–1233. IEEE (2010)

4. Suzumori, K., Endo, S., Kanda, T., Kato, N., Suzuki, H.: A bending pneumatic rubber actuator realizing soft-bodied manta swimming robot, pp. 4975–4980. IEEE (2007)
5. Shintake, J., Rosset, S., Schubert, B., Floreano, D., Shea, H.: Versatile soft grippers with intrinsic electroadhesion based on multifunctional polymer actuators. Adv. Mater. **28**(2), 231–238 (2016). https://doi.org/10.1002/adma.201504264
6. Shen, Q., Trabia, S., Stalbaum, T., Palmre, V., Kim, K., Oh, I.: A multiple-shape memory polymer-metal composite actuator capable of programmable control, creating complex 3D motion of bending, twisting, and oscillation. Sci. Rep.-U.K. **6**(1), 24462 (2016). https://doi.org/10.1038/srep24462
7. Laschi, C., Cianchetti, M., Mazzolai, B., Margheri, L., Follador, M., Dario, P.: Soft robot arm inspired by the octopus. Adv. Robot. **26**(7), 709–727 (2012). https://doi.org/10.1163/156855312X626343
8. Firouzeh, A., Salerno, M., Paik, J.: Soft pneumatic actuator with adjustable stiffness layers for Multi-DoF actuation, pp. 1117–1124. IEEE (2015)
9. Carpi, F., Bauer, S., De Rossi, D.: Materials science. Stretching dielectric elastomer performance. Science **330**(6012), 1759–1761 (2010). https://doi.org/10.1126/science.1194773
10. Keplinger, C., Kaltenbrunner, M., Arnold, N., Bauer, S.: Rontgen's electrode-free elastomer actuators without electromechanical pull-in instability. Proc. Natl. Acad. Sci. U.S.A **107**(10), 4505–4510 (2010). https://doi.org/10.1073/pnas.0913461107
11. Lin, H.T., Leisk, G.G., Trimmer, B.: GoQBot: a caterpillar-inspired soft-bodied rolling robot. Bioinspir. Biomim. **6**(2), 26007 (2011). https://doi.org/10.1088/1748-3182/6/2/026007
12. Onal, C.D., Rus, D.: A modular approach to soft robots, pp. 1038–1045. IEEE (2012)
13. Shepherd, R.F., et al.: Using explosions to power a soft robot. Angew. Chem. Int. Ed. Engl. **52**(10), 2892–2896 (2013). https://doi.org/10.1002/anie.201209540
14. Brown, E., et al.: Universal robotic gripper based on the jamming of granular material. Proc. Natl. Acad. Sci. U.S.A **107**(44), 18809–18814 (2010). https://doi.org/10.1073/pnas.1003250107
15. Martinez, R.V., et al.: Robotic tentacles with three-dimensional mobility based on flexible elastomers. Adv. Mater. **25**(2), 205–212 (2013). https://doi.org/10.1002/adma.201203002
16. Chou, C., Hannaford, B.: Measurement and modeling of McKibben pneumatic artificial muscles. IEEE Trans. Robot. Autom. **12**(1), 90–102 (1996). https://doi.org/10.1109/70.481753
17. Kang, B., Kothera, C.S., Woods, B.K.S., Wereley, N.M.: Dynamic modeling of Mckibben pneumatic artificial muscles for antagonistic actuation, pp. 182–187. IEEE (2009)
18. Bishop-Moser, J., Krishnan, G., Kim, C., Kota, S.: Design of soft robotic actuators using fluid-filled fiber-reinforced elastomeric enclosures in parallel combinations, pp. 4264–4269. IEEE (2012)
19. Roche, E.T., et al.: A bioinspired soft actuated material. Adv. Mater. **26**(8), 1200–1206 (2014). https://doi.org/10.1002/adma.201304018

Configuration Design and Simulation of Novel Petal Tooth Nutation Joint Drive for Robot

Linjie Li[1,2], Guangxin Wang[1(✉)], Lili Zhu[1], and Weidong He[1]

[1] School of Mechanical Engineering, Dalian Jiaotong University,
Dalian 116028, Liaoning, People's Republic of China
gx_wang@126.com
[2] CRRC Qiqihar Rolling Stock Co., Ltd., Qiqihar 161002, Heilongjiang,
People's Republic of China

Abstract. As the core component of the robot, the transmission performance of the precision joint drive directly affects the efficiency of the whole system. The purpose of this paper is to propose and analyze a new joint drive for robot about a novel nutation drive with petal teeth. Configuration design are developed and the models are then verified by kinematics simulation and interference detection by virtual prototype technology. Further, the digital design and motion simulation of the nutation gear drive and CNC machining of the key parts are accomplished. The verification of the working process of the nutation joint drive can show the validity of the desired value on the designed joint drive for robot.

Keywords: Robot · Nutation drive · Simulation · Petal tooth

1 Introduction

Reducers for manipulator joints need some characteristics such as large transmission ratio, large torque, high torque stiffness, small backlash, easy assembly, small size and light weight. At present, harmonic reducer, RV reducer, cycloid planet-based reducer and multi-stage precision gear reducer are generally available [1–3]. However, many problems including the difficulty to process the key parts and more complex structures have not been solved yet, which restricted the development of them. The nutation drive is being extensively interested due to its ability to achieve a high reduction ratio with a compact structure and the potential for low vibration, high efficiency and design flexibility.

The typical systems of nutation drive consist of bevel gears [4, 5]. Trying to improve their design, researchers have done a lot, focusing on the geometric properties and manufacturing approaches of the involute profile, cycloid profile and spiral bevel gears. Kedrowski and Slimak [6] has presented a nutation drive for cordless screw-driver reducer using the involute bevel gears. Meng [7] has finished the theoretical and experimental research on the nutation involute bevel gear drives. Litvin *et al.* [8, 9] proposed an efficient way of design to do the tooth contact analysis (TCA) and stress analysis for spiral bevel gears by overcoming the difficulties of surface conjugation caused by Formate-generation. Nelson and Cipra [10, 11] tried to classify all the nutating mechanisms and find the similarity of them, also modeled and analyzed the

© Springer Nature Switzerland AG 2019
H. Yu et al. (Eds.): ICIRA 2019, LNAI 11740, pp. 652–663, 2019.
https://doi.org/10.1007/978-3-030-27526-6_57

bevel epicyclic gear trains. He [12, 13] has done a lot of studies on analyzing the profile and proposing the manufacture approaches of the involute nutation gears, then focused on the research of addendum, radial and overlapping interference to find the condition of noninterference of that. Yao *et al.* [14–16] proposed the double circular-arc as the basic profile of the spiral bevel gears and studied that in order to solve the problems of the nutation drive, where pitch cone angle of the internal bevel gear is larger than 90° and the involute spiral profile is difficult to process. Fanghella [17, 18] presented a dynamic model of a planetary gear train based on nutating bevel gears and determined the conditions under which the mechanism do not transmit shaking inertial forces and moments to its frame. Saribay *et al.* [19, 20] put forward the pericyclic drive and applied it into the main reducer of helicopter. Wang *et al.* [21, 22] proposed the nutation drive combined with movable teeth, that is rolling substituting tooth meshing, the bevel gear processing difficulties and other issues can be avoided while the nutation tooth drive also can be realized.

In summary, different from the transmission principles of RV and harmonic reducers of existing robot joint drive, it is an effective way for joint reducers to make great progress to study the new transmission principles and structures of reducers for robots to meet the requirements of large reduction ratio, high precision, high stiffness, high efficiency and high reliability of robotic joints. So, this paper will aim to propose a novel nutation drive with petal teeth. Gear configuration is inspired by ancient lotus in nature. Nelumbo nucifera gaertn is a kind of lotus, which belongs to large plant type and few petals, which petals are shield-shaped and circular, and each layer of petals is interlaced. Combining nelumbo nucifera gaertn petal structure with nutation transmission principle can greatly improve the motion accuracy and power density of transmission, which can be verified by kinematics simulation and interference detection by virtual prototype technology. Further, the digital design and motion simulation of the nutation gear drive and CNC machining of the key parts are accomplished. The verification of the working process of the nutation joint drive can show the validity of the desired value on the designed joint drive for robot.

2 Generation of Petal Tooth Nutation Joint Drive

2.1 Gear Configuration

In the forming process of internal-external face gears, the external face gears will produce the phenomenon of tooth tip sharpening and tooth root undercutting, while the internal face gears will produce the phenomenon of tooth root sharpening and tooth top undercutting, so the tooth width of meshing face gears is often limited. Although the structure size of gears can be raised by increasing the tool modulus, the size of box body will be increased and the structure will not be compact. The profile of petal gear structure can improve the bearing capacity of the tooth surface without increasing the volume. According to the principle of bionics, the layout of lotus petals in nature is conducive to the growth of plant petals in a compact space. For nutation gear drive, the

654   L.J. Li et al.

combination of lotus petal layout and nutation drive can produce compact structure, high load-carrying capacity, and the effect of improving transmission accuracy. The forming principle of petal tooth is shown in Fig. 1, when the tool modulus is changed, at the same time, the bevel angle of the gear pitch, the angle between axles and the bevel angle of the tool pitch remain unchanged, and the center distance will be changed. The numbers of teeth of cutter a and b are the same but the modulus are different. When the modulus of cutter a and b are changed, the meshing position of forming cutter and meshing gear pair will also be changed, which forms multi-layer "petal" gear. The components are the same for another side of cutter c and d.

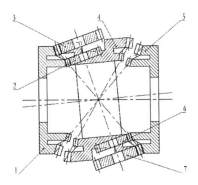

1 external "petal" teeth on stator 2 cutter a 3 cutter b 4 internal "petal" teeth

5 external "petal" teeth on rotor 6 cutter c 7 cutter d

Fig. 1. Forming principle for nutation drive with petal face-gears

A lotus and a spatial "petal" nutation gear model are also shown in Figs. 2 and 3, respectively.

Fig. 2. Lotus flower in water

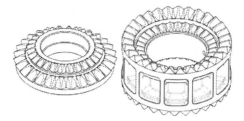

Fig. 3. Model of nutation petal teeth gears

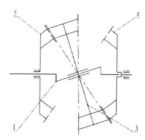

1 input shaft 2 stator 3 planetary disk 4 rotor

Fig. 4. Nutation drive with petal teeth face-gears diagram

In a "petal" nutation transmission with face gear (shown in Fig. 4), the power is input from the input shaft 1, the motion and torsion are transmitted to the "petal" planetary face gear 3 through the fixed "petal" face gear 2, and then from 3 to the rotary face gear 4 for output.

The structure of "petal" nutation face gear makes use of the end space of the gear, increases the number of meshing teeth, has greater load-carrying capacity, lower noise, higher accuracy and smaller volume under the same working conditions. The number of layers can be 2 or more, and there can be angle difference between each layer, so as to avoid the phenomenon of "same in and out" in meshing and make the transmission more stable and accurate.

3   Modeling and Simulation

"Petal" nutation transmission with face gear can not only improve the overall performance of reducer device, but also design a new type of transmission mechanism. In order to further study the correctness of its theory, a 30-speed-ratio machine is designed. The specific design parameters are as follows in Table 1.

Table 1. Basic parameters of petal teeth nutation joint drive

Parameter	Value
Shaft angle (β)	5°
Teeth number (N_1)	29
Teeth number (N_2)	31
Teeth number (N_3)	31
Teeth number (N_4)	30
Teeth number of shaper (N_{s1})	10
Teeth number of shaper (N_{s2})	10
Module of shaper (m_1)	1.7 mm
Module of shaper (m_2)	2 mm
Pressure angle of shaper (α_1)	20°
Pressure angle of shaper (α_2)	20°

3.1 Model Design

Calculating point data from Mathematica can not be directly designed in CATIA in the form of "point cloud", and need to be fitted to re-pavement. The error analysis of tooth profile surface and "point cloud" data are shown in Fig. 5. The analysis shows that about 90% of tooth surface error is controlled within the order of magnitude 10^{-5} mm and the overall error is controlled within 2×10^{-4} mm.

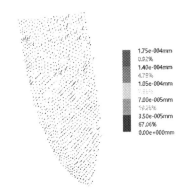

Fig. 5. Error analysis of tooth surface and point cloud

In addition to fitting accuracy, surface smoothness is also very important. The evaluation method of class A surface can be used in automobile industry for reference, and the quality of surface are analyzed by means of parallel light illumination and curvature analysis. The results of parallel illumination are shown in Fig. 6(a). It can be seen that the "zebra line" generated by the tooth surface under strong parallel illumi-nation is smooth and continuous. Figure 6(b) analyses the curvature radius comb of the surface. It can be seen that the lines show uniform changes, indicating that the curve is fairer and the surface quality is higher. This method can generate high quality and high precision surface in CATIA software. Its quality and precision are enough to meet the actual production needs, and the number of point coordinates is almost unlimited.

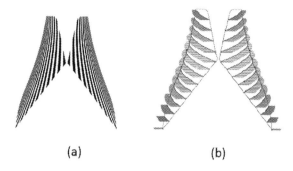

(a)   (b)

Fig. 6. Analysis of gear surface quality

3.2 Multi-body Kinematics Simulation

The parts are imported into ADAMS to create a multi-body dynamic simulation model, as shown in Fig. 7.

Fig. 7. Multibody simulation model

The main settings are as follows: fixed face gear is fixed with the earth; input shaft and earth are fixed with rotary motion pairs; planetary wheel and input shaft are inclined with rotary motion pairs; rotary face gear and earth are set with rotary motion pairs. Gear meshing adopts 3D solid contact algorithm.

The input shaft speed is set to 9000°/s. The simulation time is 0.1 s and after 5000 analysis steps, the calculation is submitted. The output shaft speed is shown in Fig. 8. The output results are consistent with the design objectives.

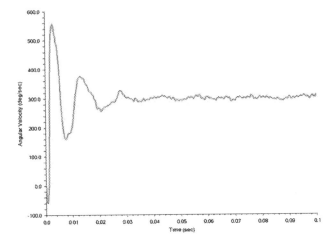

Fig. 8. Multi-body simulation results

4 Manufacturing and Verification

The structure inspiration of "petal" gear comes from nature. From the bionics point of view, the arrangement of lotus petals is used for reference, and the space on the face gear end surface is skillfully utilized. In theory, it has better bearing capacity, lower noise, higher transmission accuracy and smaller volume under the same power. In order to accumulate more experience, a small physical model machine is manufactured. On the one hand, it is to verify the theoretical design and check the meshing condition of the tooth surface. On the other hand, it is to accumulate experience for subsequent test machine manufacturing.

4.1 Structure Design of Model Machine

In order to observe the meshing of the tooth surface of the model machine more intuitively, the transmission ratio of the model machine i = 30 is selected, and the design parameters are arranged as shown in Table 2. In order to take into account the size matching of the two ends of the intermediate planetary wheel, different modulus are selected. Figure 9 shows the detailed structure of the model tester of the "petal" nutation joint drive with face gear.

Table 2. Parameters to nutation petal teeth joint drive with face-gears

Parameter	Value
Transmission ratio	30
Pitch cone angle (β_1)	50.140°
Pitch cone angle (β_2)	124.860°
Pitch cone angle (β_3)	108.080°

(continued)

Table 2. (*continued*)

Parameter	Value
Pitch cone angle (β_4)	66.920°
Pitch cone angle (γ_1)	65.489°
Pitch cone angle (γ_2)	109.512°
Pitch cone angle (γ_3)	90.222°
Pitch cone angle (γ_4)	84.778°
Pitch cone angle (γ_{s1})	15.349°
Pitch cone angle (γ_{s2})	17.858°

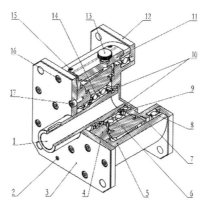

1 input shaft, 2 positioning pins, 3 end cap 1, 4 fixed face gears, 5 boxes, 6 planetary face gears, 7 rotary face gears, 8 bearing 1, 9 baffle ring, 10 bearing 2, 11 observation cover, 12 end cap 2, 13 rolling high head bolt, 14 bearing 3, 15 bolt 1, 16 bolt 2, 17 bolt 3

Fig. 9. Structure of nutation petal teeth joint drive with face-gears

In the transmission system, all the gears involved in meshing are "petal" nutation face gears, and all the input shafts are in series. Fixed face gears, planetary face gears and rotary face gears are respectively sleeved on the input shaft through bearings. Fixed face gear and end cap 1 are fastened by bolts. Rotary face gear is connected with the box body through bearings to form a rotary pair. In order to observe the meshing of gears conveniently, an observation window is opened on the box. There are positioning pin holes on the end cover and the corresponding box body to facilitate the final assembly and positioning of the reducer. Four spare bolt holes are designed at the four corner positions of the end cap for easy fixing when connecting the motor drive. A spring retaining ring is used to fix the bearing on the inclined shaft.

In addition to the input shaft and standard parts, 6061 aluminum alloy is selected as the material of gear parts, box parts and end caps. Grease lubrication is mainly used for internal tooth surface lubrication, or a small amount of lubricating oil is evenly applied on the tooth surface through the observation window.

4.2 Manufacturing of Model Machine

The parts to be processed by the model machine include: input shaft, fixed disk, planetary disk, rotary disk, end cover 1, box body, end cover 2, observation cover, a total of 8 pieces. The manufacturing methods of main parts are introduced as follows.

The input shaft is an important component of nutation face gear reducer. Its structure is shown in Fig. 10. Because of the inclined part of the shaft section, it is difficult to process. The processed method [21] has been used for reference in this processing. The main idea is to calculate the apex position by the nutation angle. The machining process requires two apexes. One pair of apex center lines coincides with the rotation center line of the axis, the other pair coincides with the rotation center line of the inclined axis, and then turning. Therefore, the precise apex position and shape are very important to the whole machining accuracy.

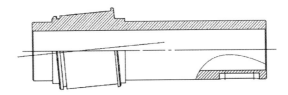

Fig. 10. Structure of input shaft

The processing methods of stator, planetary gear and rotor are similar, which are to use lathe to process the outline firstly, then finish the matching part, use five-axis high-speed machining center to set the table and correct, and process "petal" tooth surface lastly. The difference is that the planetary disk is treated by weight reduction and is processed by milling on turning-milling compound machining center.

Figure 11 shows the structures of planetary disk and rotor. Figure 12 shows the finished product drawings of several main parts, of which Fig. 12(a) is external fixed face gear, Fig. 12(b) is internal planetary face gear, Fig. 12(c) is external rotary face gear, and Fig. 12(d) is other parts drawings. The surface quality of finished parts is good, and the measured surface roughness is about Ra0.8.

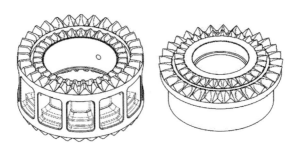

Fig. 11. Structures of planetary disk and rotor

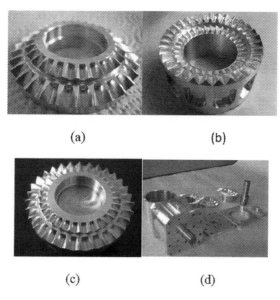

(a)   (b)

(c)   (d)

Fig. 12. Finished parts

After assembling and debugging the above parts, the final machine of the "petal" nutation joint drive with face gear is shown in Fig. 13. The maximum shape size of the model machine is 102 mm × 100 mm × 92 mm, the weight is about 1.05 kg, and the transmission ratio is 30. When manually twist the input shaft, the internal-external face gears mesh well, the transmission ratio is consistent with the initial design. In the process of manual driving, it is effortless and has a uniform force sense, and hardly feels the existence of back-haul clearance. The successful trial production of the model machine of the "petal" nutation face gear reducer verifies the correctness of the theory of nutation face gear transmission, and accumulates valuable experience for the manufacture and research of the test prototype.

Fig. 13. Test prototype

5   Conclusions

Based on the principles of bionics and mechanism innovation, the structure of petal-shaped face gear is proposed from the basic principle of nutation drive. The correctness of the meshing theory of petal-shaped tooth nutation drive is verified by using three-dimensional design software and multi-body dynamics software. On this basis, a prototype of petal nutation reducer for new robot joints is designed and manufactured, which verifies the correctness of the proposed theory and provides support for the expansion and application of nutation drive theory.

Acknowledgements. This work was supported by the Foundation of the Youth Science and Technology of Dalian, China [grant number 2015R072]; the Research Foundation for Doctor of Liaoning Province, China [grant number 201601263] and the Natural Fund Guidance Scheme of Liaoning Province, China [grant number 20180551106].

References

1. He, W.D., Li, L.X., Li, X.: New optimized tooth-profile of cycloidal gear of high precision RV reducer used in robot. Chin. J. Mech. Eng. **36**(3), 51–55 (2000)
2. Zhao, J.: Development and challenge of Chinese industrial robot. Aeronaut. Manuf. Technol. **55**(12), 26–29 (2012). (in Chinese)
3. Zhang, J.F., Yu, M.J., Zhou, J.J.: New cycloid drives technology for robot transmissions. J. Hangzhou Inst. Electron. Eng. **22**(3), 67–72 (2002)
4. Yu, Y.B., Zhang, J.M., Yu, W.B.: Analysis and optimization of gyro moment in nutation drive of bevel differential. Mach. Tool Hydraul. **29**(6), 32–33+110 (2001)
5. Huang, W.: Design and simulation of nutation gear transmission deceleration mechanism. Master Dissertation, Kunming University of Science and Technology, Yunnan, P. R. China (2007)
6. Kedrowski, D.K., Slimak, S.P.: Nutating gear drivetrain for a cordless screwdriver. Mech. Eng. ASME **116**(1), 70–74 (1994)
7. Meng, X.Z.: Theoretical and experimental study on nutation gear drive. Master Dissertation, Northeastern University, P. R. China (1998)
8. Litvin, F.L., Fuentes, A., Fan, Q., et al.: Computerized design, simulation of meshing, and contact and stress analysis of face-milled formate generated spiral bevel gears. Mech. Mach. Theory **37**(5), 441–459 (2002)
9. Litvin, F.L., Fuentes, A., Hayasaka, K.: Design, manufacture, stress analysis, and experimental tests of low-noise high endurance helical bevel gears. Mech. Mach. Theory **41**(1), 83–118 (2006)
10. Nelson, C.A., Cipra, R.J.: Similarity and equivalence of nutating mechanisms to bevel epicyclic gear trains for modeling and analysis. J. Mech. Des. **127**(2), 1305–1311 (2015)
11. Nelson, C.A., Cipra, R.J.: Simplified kinematic analysis of bevel epicyclic gear trains with application to power-flow and efficiency analyses. J. Mech. Des. **127**(2), 278–286 (2015)
12. He, S.J.: Strength study on output mechanism of zero tooth difference type in nutation gearing. Mach. Des. Manuf. **198**(8), 23–24 (2007)
13. He, S.J., Liu, X.D.: Problema and solution in involute nutation gearing. J. Dalian Natl. Univ. **36**(1), 56–58 (2007)

14. Yao, L.G., Gu, B., Haung, S.J., et al.: Mathematical modeling and simulation of the external and internal double circular-arc spiral bevel gears for the nutation drive. J. Mech. Des. T ASME **132**, 1–10 (2010)
15. Gu, B., Yao, L., Wei, G., et al.: The analysis and modeling for nutation drives with double circular-arc helical bevel gears. In: International Conference on Advanced Manufacture, pp. 949–954. Materials Science Forum, Taipei, P. R. China (2006)
16. Cai, Y.W., Yao, L.G., Xie, Z.Y., Zhang, J.: Influence analysis of system parameters on characteristics of the nutation drive with double circular arc spiral bevel gears. Forschung Im Ingenieurwesen **81**(2–3), 125–133 (2017)
17. Fanghella, P., Bruzzone, L., Ellero, S.: Dynamic balancing of a nutating planetary bevel gear train. In: Ceccarelli, M., Hernández Martinez, E. (eds.) Multibody Mechatronic Systems. Mechanisms and Machine Science, vol. 25, pp. 23–33. Springer, Cham (2015). https://doi.org/10.1007/978-3-319-09858-6_3
18. Fanghella, P., Bruzzone, L., Ellero, S., Lando, R.: Kinematics, efficiency and dynamic balancing of a planetary gear train based on nutating bevel gears. Mech. Based Des. Struct. Mach. **44**(1–2), 72–85 (2016)
19. Saribay, Z.B.: Analytical investigation of the pericyclic variable-speed transmission system for helicopter main-gearbox (2009)
20. Saribay, Z.B., Bill, R.C.: Design analysis of pericyclic mechanical transmission system. Mech. Mach. Theory **61**, 102–122 (2013)
21. Wang, G.X., Jin, Z.Z., Li, L.J., Zhu, L.L., He, W.J.: Machining method for tilting shaft and shaft parts by common CNC machine tools. CN201410299555.0 (2016)
22. Zhu, L.L., Wang, G.X., Fan, W.Z.: Modeling and simulation of the nutation drive with movable taper teeth. Recent Pat. Mech. Eng. **12**(1), 72–82 (2019)

Modular Robots and Other Mechatronic Systems

A Bio-inspired Self-reparation Approach for Lattice Self-reconfigurable Modular Robots

Dongyang Bie[1,3], Yu Zhang[2], Xingang Zhao[3], and Yanhe Zhu[2(✉)]

[1] The Institute of Robotics and Automatic Information Systems,
College of Artificial Intelligence, and the Tianjin Key Laboratory of Intelligent
Robotics, Nankai University, Tianjin, China
bdy@nankai.edu.cn
[2] State Key Laboratory of Robotics and System (HIT),
Harbin Institute of Technology, Harbin, China
yhzhu@hit.edu.cn
[3] State Key Laboratory of Robotics, Shenyang Institute of Automation,
Chinese Academy of Sciences, Shenyang, China

Abstract. The self-reparation of modular self-reconfigurable robots is a fundamental primitive that can be used as part of higher-lever functionality. A bio-inspired approach is proposed for distributed self-reparation, which can lead the robot recover from module fails to the initial configuration. This approach is inspired by the natural growth of plant. The L-systems for describing natural growth is translated to construct robotic structures. Robots reconstruct lost parts by leading other modules to needed positions through the symbol rewriting strategy in L-systems. Simulations and experiments on Seremo robots are provided to verify this method with successful reparation of module fails or removed from the global structure.

Keywords: Self-reparation · Modular robots · Decentralized control · L-systems

1 Introduction

Modular self-reconfigurable (MSR) robotic systems [1,2] are consist of multi homogeneous modules. Fail modules can be replaced with normal working ones in the system. This is also the self-reparation of modular robots. The physical possibility calls for the same function of control method. Because if the probability of fails for independent modules is 0.01. A system may have module fails with the possibility $1-(0.99^{1}00) = 0.63$ with 100 modules, 0.87 with 200 modules and 0.95 with 300 modules. This means a higher possibility for fails in robotic systems with more modules. So it is so necessary to design the self-reparation method for MSR robots.

© Springer Nature Switzerland AG 2019
H. Yu et al. (Eds.): ICIRA 2019, LNAI 11740, pp. 667–671, 2019.
https://doi.org/10.1007/978-3-030-27526-6_58

Both centralized control and decentralized control methods collect catch attentions of researcher around the word. The centralized mechanism for optimal control is proven to be NP problem [3,4]. And the decentralized approach has been studied from different points of view [5] for the scalability to module numbers, robustness to module fails.

Each module is a complete robot with onboard battery, sensing, computing and moving ability [6].

From the decentralized nature by multi independent agents point of view, the self-reconfiguration process of MSR robots is a complex and collective decision making system. The behavior of the individual modules formulates the overall state of the global robotic system. Decentralized modular self-reconfigurable robotic systems are generally analyzed by studying the transition of relative positions of inner modules and their states, referred to local surroundings including the neighboring modules environments. All the local condition of multi independent modules contribute to the robotic system's global states.

An excellent feature of a modular robotic system is its ability of self-healing and self-improving. Advanced MSRs can also possibly perform mutual healing. A robot system capable of self-repairing must be equipped with necessary hardware and algorithms for detecting module damage and performing self-healing of the system. In this paper, our focus will be on the algorithm design, especially ,,,, to perform self-healing.

2   Methods

In this section, we will consider the case when the Hamiltonian $H(x)$ is autonomous. For the sake of simplicity, we shall also assume that it is C^1.

We shall first consider the question of nontriviality, within the general framework of (A_∞, B_∞)-subquadratic Hamiltonians. In the second subsection, we shall look into the special case when H is $(0, b_\infty)$-subquadratic, and we shall try to derive additional information.

3   Simulations

Simulations are did on Microsoft Robotics Developer Studio 4 (MRDS) with C# simulation languages. We illustrate the proposed method through simulation using different module sources. As shown in Figs. 1 and 2, two simulations for different target configurations are did with different module numbers. Robots in those two simulation repair the global structure by using modules in reverse and external modules.

As shown in Fig. 2, when working modules destroy the connection relationship with failed modules, a part of structure get off from the global configuration. External modules can move and joint the current group of modules and repair the lost parts. During this process, the reconnection of two groups of modules takes hybrid control method, which will be explained in another paper.

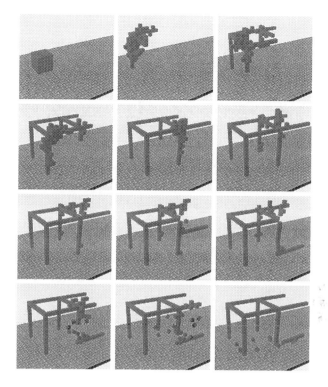

Fig. 1. The self-reparation by using reverse modules in the system

4   Experiments

The proposed approach is verified on Seremo robots. As shown in Fig. 3, a system with 9 modules reconfigure continually to cross-shape and T-shape configuration. Then one module is removed to simulate the module fails. For the lost of connecting neighbor, the left neighboring module will attract new modules to the neighboring position. During the locomotion of reserve modules, the global structure recovers to predefined configurations.

Notes and Comments. The first results on subharmonics were obtained by Rabinowitz in [?], who showed the existence of infinitely many subharmonics both in the subquadratic and superquadratic case, with suitable growth conditions on H'. Again the duality approach enabled Clarke and Ekeland in [?] to treat the same problem in the convex-subquadratic case, with growth conditions on H only.

Recently, Michalek and Tarantello (see [?] and [?]) have obtained lower bound on the number of subharmonics of period kT, based on symmetry considerations and on pinching estimates, as in Sect. 5.2 of this article.

670   D. Bie et al.

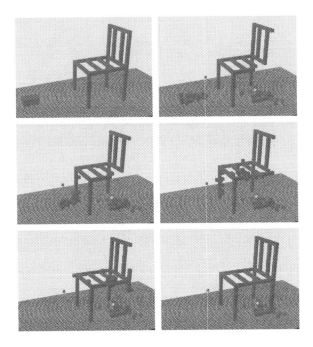

Fig. 2. The self-reparation using external modules

Fig. 3. The self-reparation using external modules

Acknowledgement. The work reported in this paper is supported by the Joint Research Fund (U1713201) between the National Natural Science Foundation of China (NSFC) and Shen Zhen. The work is also supported by the State Key Laboratory of Robotics (2018-O10).

References

1. Chennareddy, S.S.R., Agrawal, A., Karuppiah, A.: Modular self-reconfigurable robotic systems: a survey on hardware architectures. J. Robot. **2017**, 19 (2017). https://doi.org/10.1155/2017/5013532
2. Gilpin, K., Rus, D.: Modular robot systems. IEEE Robot. Autom. Mag. **17**(3), 38–55 (2010). https://doi.org/10.1109/MRA.2010.937859
3. Hou, F., Shen, W.M.: On the complexity of optimal reconfiguration planning for modular reconfigurable robots. In: 2010 IEEE International Conference on Robotics and Automation, pp. 2791–2796 (2010). https://doi.org/10.1109/ROBOT.2010.5509642
4. Hou, F., Shen, W.M.: Graph-based optimal reconfiguration planning for self-reconfigurable robots. Robot. Auton. Syst. **62**(7), 1047–1059 (2014). https://doi.org/10.1016/j.robot.2013.06.014. Reconfigurable Modular Robotics
5. Stoy, K.: Lattice automata for control of self-reconfigurable robots. In: Sirakoulis, G., Adamatzky, A. (eds.) Robots and Lattice Automata. Emergence, Complexity and Computation, vol. 13, pp. 33–45. Springer, Cham (2015). https://doi.org/10.1007/978-3-319-10924-4_2
6. Vergara, A., Lau, Y.S., Mendoza-Garcia, R.F., Zagal, J.C.: Soft modular robotic cubes: toward replicating morphogenetic movements of the embryo. PLOS ONE **12**(1), 1–17 (2017)

Reconfigurable Design and Structure Optimization of SCARA

Chun Zhao[1,2(✉)], Yanjie Wang[1,2], Muyu Hao[1,2], and Minzhou Luo[1,2]

[1] College of Mechanical and Electrical Engineering, Hohai University,
Changzhou 213022, Jiangsu, China
861398949@qq.com
[2] Jiangsu Key Laboratory of Special Robot Technology, Hohai University,
Changzhou 213022, Jiangsu, China

Abstract. Selective compliance assembly robot arm (SCARA) has several unique characteristics with high speed, accuracy and stability in horizontal motion and so on. In order to make SCARA to have variable working radius, the big arm was designed into modular combination in this paper. The SCARA can change the length of the robot arm and further meet more industrial needs by adjusting the number of modules in the big arm. A topology optimization method based on inherent frequency and maximum stress is used to improve its strength and stiffness to reduce the weight of SCARA. The optimization model is established to optimize the topology of each module, and the optimal size is selected to increase inherent frequency and reduce maximum stress. The mass of the forepart module, the middle part module and the rear-end module of the big arm has been reduced by 13.85%, 15.3% and 13.18% respectively, which basically reach the goal of 15% optimization with significant weight loss.

Keywords: SCARA · Reconfigurable design · Optimization

1 Introduction

According to different needs of biological tissues, biological cells can transfer and repair, which makes biological tissues have diversified characteristics. Inspired by this phenomenon, a reconfigurable robot consisting of a series of modules is proposed. The robot can change its structure to fulfill specific task requirements in unknown environments according to different needs, so that a single robot can accomplish a variety of tasks with a very high cost performance ratio.

Most reconfigurable robot systems adopt active modular design, which encapsulates actuators, connection systems, sensor systems and controllers into individual modules, enabling the robot to reconstruct each module according to different task requirements, so as to meet specific work needs [1–5]. In contrast, there are few studies on passive reconfigurable robots. ICubes reconfigurable robot [6] is composed of active joints and rigid links, which drive cube movement by controlling the active mechanism. Reconfigurable robots are also called modular robots. Modules and modules are connected by connectors. Therefore, efficient and stable connectors are essential. The common connection modes are mechanical connection and magnetic connection [7–9].

© Springer Nature Switzerland AG 2019
H. Yu et al. (Eds.): ICIRA 2019, LNAI 11740, pp. 672–679, 2019.
https://doi.org/10.1007/978-3-030-27526-6_59

Compared with magnetic connection, mechanical connection is more stable. PolyBot reconfigurable robot [1] and CONRO reconfigurable robot [10] adopt pin connection, that is, two modules are connected by pins, and then locked by latches. Unsal reconfigurable robot [11] uses rack and gear to drive the loosening and clamping of the connecting mechanism, so that each module can be assembled and disassembled quickly. ICubes Reconfigurable Robot [12] uses locking keys to connect modules. The connector rotates the keys into the hole and locks the modules in a fixed position. In contrast, the ATRON Reconfigurable robot [13] uses magnetic connection between the module and the module through the magnet attraction of two connecting planes, while the M-TRAN reconfigurable robot [14] uses SMA coil to realize the magnetic connection between the modules. Although magnetic connection is simple and convenient, it lacks stability seriously and is not suitable in conventional environment. In the meantime, robots used in industrial production require higher stability and accuracy of the whole system. Pin connection, rack-and-pin connection and lock-key connection are convenient and fast, but the rigidity is poor, which brings greater error to robots.

This paper designs the reconfigurable big arm for SCARA to meet the need of multi-purpose production in enterprises. The big arm will be divided into three different specifications of modules. By adjusting the number of modules, the SCARA has variable working radius. In order to meet the requirements of high precision and high stability of industrial robots, bolt connection structure is adopted between modules to improve the rigidity and stability of SCARA. In the meantime, a topology optimization method based on inherent frequency and maximum stress is proposed to improve the inherent frequency and reduce the angle of maximum stress, and to make the optimal size selection.

The rest of this paper is organized as follows. In the second chapter, the design scheme of SCARA is described in detail, and the mechanical analysis of the big arm module with maximum force is carried out. In the third section, a topology optimization method based on inherent frequency and maximum stress is proposed. The optimization model is established to optimize the topology of each module, and the optimum size is selected to increase the inherent frequency and reduce maximum stress. In the fourth section, some conclusions are drawn.

2   Reconfigurable Design and Mechanical Analysis of SCARA

2.1   Reconfigurable Design of the Big Arm of SCARA

The overall structure of SCARA is shown in Fig. 1. Because this paper mainly studies the stability of the big arm, SCARA is reconstructed and the fourth joint is omitted. The big arm of SCARA is divided into the forepart module, the middle part module and the rear-end module. The forepart module and the rear-end module are respectively connected with the first joint reducer and the second joint reducer of SCARA, while the middle part module is composed of two identical modules. Users can choose the number of the middle part module from the requirements of different working radius, so that the length of the big arm has a variety of specifications to meet the needs of different working radius. Bolts are used to connect the modules to facilitate the free disassembly and installation of the modules, which makes the reconfigurable big arm of

SCARA have the disadvantages of poor rigidity and high jitter compared with the traditional SCARA. Therefore, it is very important to increase the stiffness of each module and reduce the jitter, and this important work will be completed at a later stage.

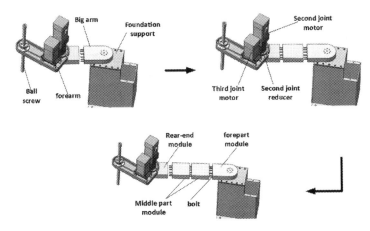

Fig. 1. Overall structure of reconfigurable SCARA

2.2 Mechanical Analysis of SCARA

After determining the design size and structure of the SCARA, the structure parameters and quality parameters of each module are determined by adding material to Solid-works and consulting the manual of motor and reducer. As shown in Fig. 2, the big arm of the SCARA is subjected to downward gravity and clockwise bending moments in the vertical direction under the action of load and body gravity, and shear force and torque opposite to motor acceleration in the horizontal direction under the action of acceleration and deceleration of the motor. The force values of the forepart module are obtained by consulting and calculating the speed reducer manual, as shown in Table 1.

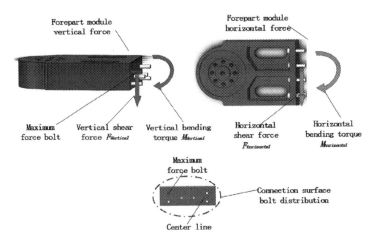

Fig. 2. Force analysis diagram of the forepart module

Table 1. Force values of the forepart module

Force	Shear force N	Torque	Torque N · m
Vertical shear force $F_{vertical}$	61.2N	Vertical bending torque $M_{vertical}$	29.25N · m
Horizontal shear force $F_{horizontal}$	120N	Horizontal bending torque $M_{horizontal}$	23.25N · m

3   Modal Analysis and Topology Optimization of SCARA

3.1   Static Analysis Based on ANSYS

The two ends of the big arm of SCARA and the modules are connected by bolts, so the force of each module is different. As shown in Figs. 3(a), (c), (e), the free mesh method is adopted to obtain accurate solutions at important locations, simplify the analysis model and reduce the calculation time. Hexahedral elements are used to mesh the important locations with bolt holes at the front and back ends, while tetrahedral elements are used to mesh the non-dangerous locations in the middle. According to the mechanics analysis of Chapter 1.2, the forepart module, the middle part module and the rear-end module can be regarded as cantilever beams, one end is fixed by bolts, the other end is applied vertical shear force $F_{vertical}$, vertical bending moment $M_{vertical}$, horizontal shear force $F_{horizontal}$ and horizontal torsion $M_{horizontal}$ through bolt holes.

The defined constraints and response loads are applied to the corresponding positions of each module, and the internal stress distribution diagrams of each module are obtained. It can be seen that the stress variation of each module is very small, and the maximum stress is 3.79×10^7 Pa in the bolt installation hole, which is far less than the yield limit, so each module has a very large optimization space. The inherent frequencies and modes of each module can be obtained by modal analysis. Because the low-order modes have great influence on the vibration of each module, the first second-order of modal analysis are taken as the basis of inherent frequency analysis. It can be seen from the table that the first-order inherent frequencies of the forepart module (Table 2), the middle part and the rear-end module are greater than 1100 Hz, while the rated speed of the motor used in the SCARA is 3500 r/min, and its rotation frequency is 58 Hz, which is far less than the first-order inherent frequencies, and the safety factor is higher, so it has a larger optimization space.

Table 2. First fourth-order natural frequencies of each module

Orders n	Inherent frequency of Front Arm Module ω_1/Hz	Inherent frequency of Middle Arm Module ω_2/Hz	Inherent frequency of End Arm Module ω_3/Hz
1	1160.5	1180.2	1410.9
2	4386.8	1632.8	6946

3.2   Topology Optimization Analysis Based on ANSYS

There is a lot of room for structural optimization of each module based on the previous
static and modal analysis, and the topology optimization function of ANSYS Workbench is used to reduce the weight of the big arm and the influence of self-weight on
the strength and stiffness of SCARA. The evolutionary structural optimization of each
module is carried out based on the grid partition in static analysis and the boundary
conditions in modal analysis. Fifteen percent weight loss is set for the forepart module,
the middle arm module and the rear-end module respectively. The optimization results
are shown in Fig. 3(a), (b), (c). The orange part is the removal part recommended, and
the gray part is the retention part recommended. It can be seen that the proposed
removal parts of the forepart module and the rear-end module mainly concentrate on
the edge of the bolt hole used to install reducer and both sides, while the proposed
removal parts of the middle part module mainly concentrate on both sides of module.
These suggested removal parts are non-uniform distribution, and long grooves are set
up in the middle part with dense orange distribution for processing convenience. The
edge of the bolt hole used to install reducer of the forepart module and the rear-end
module is arc-cut.

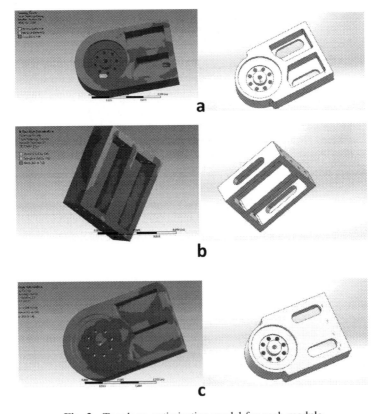

Fig. 3. Topology optimization model for each module

The removal of materials with high stress or high strain energy density will affect the inherent frequencies and stresses of components due to the irregular distribution of orange in the middle part of each module, thus reducing the mechanical properties of each module. The long slot in the middle part of the preliminary optimization model was accurately optimized to further avoid unreasonable optimization size and improve the optimization accuracy of each module. According to the topology optimization model, it can be determined that the length range of the long groove of the forepart module, the middle part module and the rear-end module is 20 mm–50 mm, 22 mm–70 mm and 20 mm–50 mm respectively, and the width range of the long groove has little change. The corresponding change curve is drawn by using MATLAB to show the change rule of inherent frequency, maximum stress and length of long groove. As shown in Fig. 4, the first longitudinal coordinate is inherent frequency, the second longitudinal coordinate is maximum stress value, and the horizontal ordinate is the length of long groove. From the corresponding curves of the forepart module, the middle part module and the rear-end module, it can be seen that the natural frequencies of the first two orders change very little with the change of the length of the long groove, so it can be neglected, but the maximum stress value has a great change, and there is an obvious depression, which makes the maximum stress at the minimum value. Therefore, it can be judged from the figure that when $L_1 = 30$ mm, $L_2 = 46$ mm, $L_3 = 30$ mm, the forepart module, the middle part module and the rear-end module are optimized.

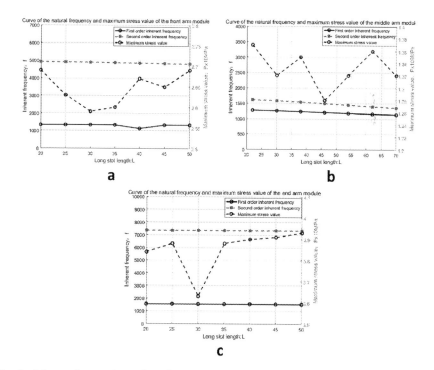

Fig. 4. Inherent frequencies and maximum stress curves varying with the length of long grooves

The optimization models of each module are established (L1 = 30 mm, L2 = 46 mm, L3 = 30 mm) to further show the effect of topological optimization. Static analysis and modal analysis are carried out in turn. The first-order inherent frequencies, the maximum stress and overall weight are compared with the models before optimization respectively. As shown in Table 3, it can be seen that first-order natural frequency of forepart module and rear-end module are increased by 10.53%, 14.78% respectively, which can effectively improve vibration resistance, but the first-order natural frequency of middle part module slightly lower, but it has small influence on the vibration resistance; In the meantime, the maximum stress of the forepart module, the middle part module and the rear-end module were reduced by 1.15%, 3.76% and 4.73% respectively, which effectively improved the strength of each module and achieved good optimization effect. The mass of the forepart module, the middle part module and the rear-end module have been reduced by 13.85%, 15.3% and 13.18% respectively, and the optimal weight loss target of 15% was achieved basically.

Table 3. Comparison of parameters before and after topology optimization

	Optimization parameters	Pre-optimization structure	Optimized structure	Change rate/%
The forepart module	First-order inherent frequency/Hz	1411.2	1559.9	Raise 10.53%
	Overall weight/kg	0.693	0.597	Reduce 13.85%
	Maximum stress/MPa	26.2	25.9	Reduce 1.15%
The middle part module	First-order inherent frequency/Hz	1280.2	1255.3	Reduce 1.95%
	Overall weight/kg	0.366	0.31	Reduce 15.3%
	Maximum stress/MPa	133	128	Reduce 3.76%
The rear-end module	First-order inherent frequency/Hz	1160.5	1332	Raise 14.78%
	Overall weight/kg	0.599	0.52	Reduce 13.18%
	Maximum stress/MPa	38.1	36.3	Reduce 4.73%

4 Conclusion

Reconfigurable design of traditional SCARA is carried out to satisfy different industrial needs. Different working radius is realized by changing the number of big arm modules. In the meantime, modal analysis and topology optimization of each module are carried out, and the lightweight design is realized by evolutionary structural optimization to achieve the high-strength and lightweight design of SCARA. Aiming at the problem of strength reduction caused by material removal optimization, the size of material removal is carefully selected to increase inherent frequency and reduce maximum deformation. The overall weight of each module is effectively reduced through the topology optimization, while the strength and first-order inherent frequency of each module are effectively improved.

Acknowledgements. This research is supported by the Fundamental Research Funds for the Central Universities (2019B21514), the National Natural Science Foundation of China (91748124 and 51875171), the Foundation (2017B21114) of Jiangsu Key Laboratory of Special Robot Technology, the Foundation (BFM1707) of Jiangsu Provincial Key Laboratory of Bionic Functional Materials, and the Research Foundation of Changzhou College of Information Technology (KYPT201801G), P.R. China. The authors gratefully acknowledge the supports.

References

1. Yim, M., Zhang, Y., Roufas, K., Duff, D., Eldershaw, C.: Connecting and disconnecting for chain self-reconfiguration with PolyBot. IEEE/ASME Trans. Mechatron. **7**(4), 442–451 (2002)
2. Castano, A., Shen, W.M., Will, P.: CONRO: towards deployable robots with inter-robots metamorphic capabilities. Auton. Robots **8**(3), 309–324 (2000)
3. Kurokawa, H., Tomita, K., Kamimura, A., Kokaji, S., Hasuo, T., Murata, S.: Distributed self-reconfiguration of M-TRAN III modular robotic system. Int. J. Robot. Res. **27**(3–4), 373–386 (2008)
4. Zykov, V., Mytilinaios, E., Adams, B., Lipson, H.: Self-reproducing machines. Nature **435**, 163–164 (2005)
5. Suh, J.W., Homans, S.B., Yim, M.: Telecubes: mechanical design of a module for self-reconfigurable robotics. In: Proceedings of the IEEE International Conference on Robotics and Automation, Washington, USA, pp. 4095–4101 (2002)
6. Garcia, R., Stoy, K.: The odin modular robot: electronics and communication. M.Sc. thesis, the Maersk Mc-Kinney Moller Institute, University of Southern Denmark, Odense, Denmark (2008)
7. Dai, J.S., Zoppi, M., Kong, X.W.: Advances in Reconfigurable Mechanisms and Robots I (ReMAR 2012). Springer, Heidelberg (2012). https://doi.org/10.1007/978-1-4471-4141-9. ISBN 978-1-4471-4140-2
8. Dai, J.S., Zoppi, M., Kong, X.W.: Reconfigurable Mechanisms and Robots (ReMAR 2009). KC Edizioni (2009). ISBN 978-88-89007-37-2
9. Song, C.Y., Feng, H., Chen, Y.: Reconfigurable mechanism generated from the network of Bennett linkages. Mech. Mach. Theory **88**, 49–62 (2015)
10. Shen, W.M., Will, P.: Docking in self-reconfigurable robots. In: Proceedings of the IEEE/RSJ International Conference on Intelligent Robots and Systems, Maui, USA, pp. 1049–1054 (2001)
11. Rus, D., Vona, M.: Crystalline robots: self-reconfiguration with compressible unit modules. Auton. Robots **10**(1), 107–124 (2001)
12. Unsal, C., Khosla, P.: Mechatronic design of a modular self-reconfiguring robotic system. In: Proceedings of the IEEE International Conference on Robotics and Automation, San Francisco, USA, pp. 1742–1747 (2000)
13. Ostergaard, E.H., Kassow, K., Beck, R., Lund, H.H.: Design of the ATRON lattice-based self-reconfigurable robot. Auton. Robots **21**(2), 165–183 (2006)
14. Murata, S., Yoshida, E., Kamimura, A., Kurokawa, H., Tomita, K., Kokaji, S.: M-TRAN: self-reconfigurable modular robotic system. IEEE/ASME Trans. Mechatron. **7**(4), 431–441 (2002)

Modular Design of 7-DOF Cable-Driven Humanoid Arms

Hao Jiang, Tao Zhang, Cai Xiao, Jian Li, and Yisheng Guan$^{(\boxtimes)}$

Biomimetic and Intelligent Robotics Lab (BIRL),
School of Electro-Mechanical Engineering,
Guangdong University of Technology, Guangzhou 510006, China
ysguan@gdut.edu.cn

Abstract. With the rapid development of AI, it is prospective for humanoid robots to be applied for various social and home services. And humanoid robots for services demand excellent performance with anthropomorphic bodies besides AI. Take the dual arms for example, they are desired to be dexterous and light-weighted for mimicking human arm motion, which is hard to be satisfied by traditional design. To this end, we have designed novel humanoid arms with unconventional design method in this paper. With seven degrees of freedom (DOFs) according to human arm anatomy, each of our humanoid arm is composed of three parts, which are the shoulder with three DOFs, the elbow with one DOF, the wrist with three DOFs, and the hand. Each part is designed as one module. Since the shoulder and the wrist have the same configuration and DOFs, they are actually of the same type of module but with different size and power. They are implemented with parallel mechanisms, and most of the joints are driven with cables for light weight. In this way, one arm is composed of four modules of three types, which are the shoulder, the elbow, the wrist and the hand. With the modularity design, it is trivially to compose the right and left arms with the same modules, and may be with different lengths of the arms mimicking different persons, which would be largely beneficial for mass production with relatively low costs. The design method, the structure design of the modules are presented in this paper. Kinematic simulation of the arm is carried out to simple show its kinematic performance.

Keywords: Modular design · Humanoid arm · Parallel mechanism · Cable-driven robot

---

The work in this paper is supported in part by the Program for Guangdong Yang-fan Introducing Innovative and Entrepreneurial Teams (Grant No. 2017YT05G026), the Natural Science Foundation of Guangdong (Grant No. 2015A030308011), the Frontier and Key Technology Innovation Special Funds of Guangdong (Grant No. 2017B090910002, 2017B050506008), and the Key Research and Development Program of Guangdong Province (Grant No. 2019B090915001).

H. Yu et al. (Eds.): ICIRA 2019, LNAI 11740, pp. 680–691, 2019.
https://doi.org/10.1007/978-3-030-27526-6_60

1   Introduction

As a highly anthropomorphic robot, humanoid robot has been widely used in many scenarios, such as family, hospital, airport, shopping mall and so on. Robotic arm, one of the most functional and flexible components, was attracted significant attention by most researches in various fields [3,4,8,11]. Then, a series of humanoid arms have been designed for different application scenarios in recent years. Among them, Handy 1 [10], MANUS [7], and ARMAR anthropomorphic arm [1,2] are more representative. Take the ARMAR's arm for example,it is a 7-DOF cable-driven arm applied modular design method. Although these existing robotic arms possess several features similar to the human (i.e., the number of DOFs, types of joints, link lengths and scales, and motion characteristics), their mechanism designs and driving schemes are still quite different from a real human arm. There are many factors limit the design of this arm, such as functionality, performance and intelligence, among which the complexity and high costs of building robotic systems are important factors.

Modularization is an effective methodology in system development to solve aforementioned problems caused using traditional method and bring the following benefits: easily and quickly built this simple configurations, increase or decrease the freedom, reduce the design and manufacture costs. Then, a variety of modules have been developed and constructed with them for security and inspection tasks [6,14]. These modules usually have two joints whose axes are parallel or perpendicular to each other. Modularization design is also applied in the development of multi-fingered hand or a multi-legged robot, the fingers or legs are usually identical, therefore can be considered as module units [5,9].

To construct humanoid robotic arm flexibly and quickly with lower costs, we have developed two types of joint modules for general purpose, which are called 3-DOF joint module with parallel mechanism (3DPM) and 1-DOF joint module with tension-amplification (1DTAM). Using these joints and connector modules, a 7-DOF cable-driven humanoid arm is designed and analysis in this paper. The organization of this paper is as follows: Sect. 2 present the human arms anatomical structure and its geometric model. Based on them, Sect. 3 describes the basic mechanics and the detailed joint design under modularization of a humanoid robotic arm. Section 4 illustrates the kinematic animation of imitating human hugging and analyzed the workspace of this right arm. The conclusion of this paper is in Sect. 5.

2   Anatomy of a Human Arm and Its Geometric Model

A human arm is an combination of the scapula, humerous, ulna & radius, and carpus (as shown in Fig. 1), the relative displacement of them determine the movement of an arm. The connections and relative motions of these bones form three joints, namely: wrist, elbow, and shoulder joints. Although these joints are different, they all provide similar motion performance to traditional mechanical joints. The joint between the head of the humerus and the concave part of the scapula forms the shoulder joint, which can be regarded as a mechanical spherical joint. Thus, the spherical shoulder joint enables the movement of the humerus with respect to the scapula in three mutually perpendicular axes. The linkage between the post-arm and forearm (the humerous bone) form the elbow joint, which realized the flexion and extension of the forearm.

The movement of the human wrist is more complex due to it's capability of motions (flexion and extension) around the radiocarpal and midcarpal joint axis. It is also capable of rotating about an axis that passed through the capitate bone. In addition, the whole wrist has a rotary movement about the axis of the forearm due to the relative movement between the ulna & radius bones. Hence the human wrist is normally considered as a universal joint, whose movement is analogous to that a spherical. In brief, the human arm can be represented by a 7-DOF configuration, i.e., a 3-DOF (spherical) wrist portion, a 1-DOF (revolute) elbow portion, and a 3-DOF (spherical) shoulder portion.

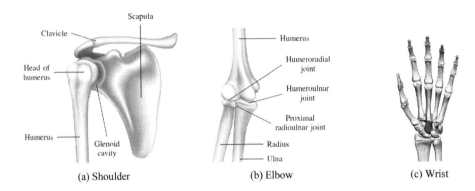

(a) Shoulder   (b) Elbow   (c) Wrist

Fig. 1. Human arm anatomical structure

Inspired by the human arms anatomical structure, it can be concluded that that regardless of the left and right arms is difference in the human body, the structure of the joints in the same module of two arm is identical. Therefore, the geometric design of a 7-DOF robotic arm is proposed is this paper, as shown in Fig. 2. Similar to the human arm, this robotic arm is formed by three serially connected modules, i.e., the 3-DOF shoulder module, the 1-DOF elbow module, and the 3-DOF wrist module. Because wrist module and shoulder module have the same basic structure except for different size and driving power, so they can be divided into 3-DOF parallel mechanism joint module (3DPM). Then, the elbow module is divided into another type called 1-DOF joint module (1DTAM).

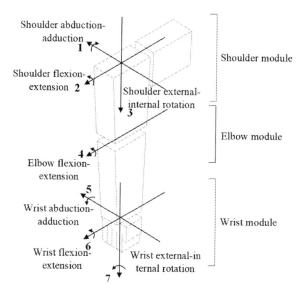

Fig. 2. Arm freedom

3 Joint Configuration of Modular Anthropomorphic Arm

The joint types of modular anthropomorphic arm can be classified into the 3-DOF joint module and the 1-DOF joint module. In this section, design principle and mechanism of this two kind of joints will be described.

3.1 3-DOF Module with Parallel Mechanism

Several robot wrists have been proposed in academic and industry, such as the CDSLRA robot [15]. In general, they consist of plates, backbones, joints and cables. Based on the backbone, robot wrists can be classified into two categories: one utilizes a rigid backbone connected by universal or spherical joints [13], while the others employ flexible material as the backbone [12].

For a rigid backbone wrist, the flexibility is determined by the universal or spherical joints range which limit the flexibility and the capability of obstacle avoidance. Regarding the flexible backbone, due to its elasticity, the whole backbone performs as a universal joint, resulting in a great bending angle of the wrist. Nevertheless, the drawback caused by this design is lack of the backbone stiffness, which significantly limits the load capability.

In terms of actuation, there are two different methods: one employs three independent cables/actuators to drive the wrist mechanism, and the other utilizes two actuators/cables. The former is applied to most existing wrist mechanisms because of its simple control, while the latter is limited because the driving force cannot maintain tension. However, if this problem is solved, the latter method can minimize weight and size.

In order to overcome the conflict of wrist flexibility and stiffness caused by rigid backbone or flexible rod. A new wrist structure which improves the flexibility and stiffness of the wrist is proposed, and two driving actuators can be used.

Design Principle. As anti-parallelogram mechanism can be used to produce a pure rolling along two ellipses. In this section, a conventional anti-parallelogram mechanism approximating a 1-DOF rolling motion is described, Fig. 3(a) illustrates the anti-parallelogram and the corresponding ellipse, which are represented by the red line. By naming the lengths of the short and long links as s_e and l_e, and the height between the two plates in a straight pose as h_e, then the ellipse equation is as follows:

$$\frac{x^2}{(s_e/2)^2} + \frac{y^2}{(h_e/2)^2} = 1 \tag{1}$$

$$l_e^2 = s_e^2 + h_e^2 \tag{2}$$

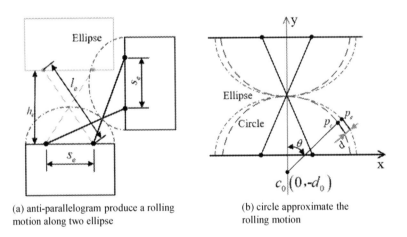

(a) anti-parallelogram produce a rolling motion along two ellipse

(b) circle approximate the rolling motion

Fig. 3. Wrist actuation theory

In order to keep a constant cable length when the wrist moves, assuming that there exists a circle to approximate the ellipse, and the center c_0 is located along y axis with an offset d_0 from the origin, as shown in Fig. 3(b). Considering a line from c_0 to a point on the ellipse p_e, while this line intersects the equivalent circle on point p_c. Then the equation of this line and the circle can be expressed as:

$$x - tan\theta \cdot y - tan\theta \cdot d_0 = 0 \tag{3}$$

$$x^2 + (y + d_0)^2 = r^2 \tag{4}$$

where θ denotes the angle between the line and y axis. By solving Eqs. (1) and (3), we get the intersection point p_e (x_e, y_e) between this line and the ellipse. By solving Eqs. (3) and (4), we can obtain the intersection point p_c (x_c, y_c) between this line and the circle. Let $d(\theta)$ be the distance between p_e and p_c:

$$d(\theta) = \sqrt{(x_c - x_e)^2 + (y_c - y_e)^2} \tag{5}$$

If the value $d(\theta)$ is near zero, it can be considered that this anti-parallelogram mechanism can be viewed approximate a pure rolling motion along two circles.

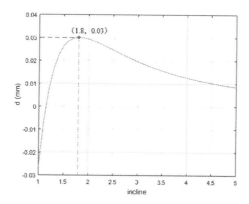

Fig. 4. Position error between ellipse and equivalent circle

Whether in terms of freedom, driving actuator or scale, we would like to propose a wrist to imitate human beings. Owing to the maximum length of human's wrist is approximately 60 mm, we set s_e, l_e and d_0 to 20, 60, 3.05 mm, respectively. By using conjugate gradient method to optimize $d(\theta)$, it reaches an almost value with the maximum error 0.03 mm, as shown in Fig. 4. It can be validated that proper geometric parameters help anti-parallelogram mechanism to accomplish a circular pure rolling motion with a reasonable accuracy.

Wrist Configuration. By extending the above principle to 3-dimensional space, a novel parallel mechanism approximating 2-DOF spherical rolling motion is proposed. For accomplishing the goal 3-DOF wrist, a shaft is added to transfer the rotation motion. As can be seen from Fig. 5, the proposed design consists of a base plate, a moving plate and four linkages which pass through the mechanism to restrict and define the bending motion. This mechanism is driven by two pairs of cables. Owing to the intrinsic characteristic to move as a pure rolling, this wrist can avoid the tension problem when the moving plate moves. The actuator can be installed at a relatively far location from the mechanism, and this makes the wrist lightweight and can be remotely actuated.

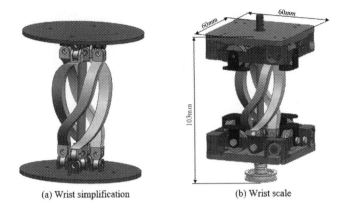

(a) Wrist simplification   (b) Wrist scale

Fig. 5. Wrist scale

3.2   1-DOF Elbow Module with Tension-Amplification

Design Principle. Figure 6 shows the basic concept of the tension-amplification mechanism. An actuator on the left side is connected by a cable with a reduction mechanism, which is composed of fixed and movable pulleys. If the wire tension exerted by the actuator is T_{in}, and the number of wires turning around the pulleys is n (in Fig. 6, n = 6), the resultant tension T_{out} by the tension-amplification mechanism is simply

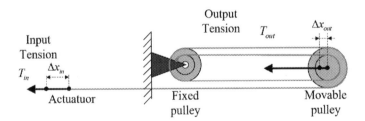

Fig. 6. Concept of tension amplification

$$T_{out} = nT_{in} \qquad (6)$$

Where it is assumed that this friction in this mechanism is negligible. If we consider the reduction of motion, the output motion x_{out} is n times smaller than actuation motion x_{in}, i.e., $x_{out} = x_{in}/n$. Therefore, the result stiffness of the tension-amplification mechanism is

$$K_{out} = \frac{T_{out}}{\Delta x_{out}} = \frac{nT_{in}}{\Delta x_{in}/n} = n^2 \frac{T_{in}}{\Delta x_{in}} = n^2 K \qquad (7)$$

where K denotes the spring coefficient of the whole wire and it satisfies $K = T_{in}/\Delta x_{in}$. This shows that the mechanism amplifies the tension in the quadratic order.

For the rotational motion of this elbow module, a pair of the tension-amplification mechanism are needed to form antagonistic wire motion, as shown in Fig. 7. The motions of the wire pair are symmetrical, and the ROM can be larger. Two rolling surfaces are circular, and rectangle slot are designed to prevent slipping and allow pure rolling with these two parts. In order to keep the distance along the center unchanged during the operation process, a connecting rod is added to limit this center distance.

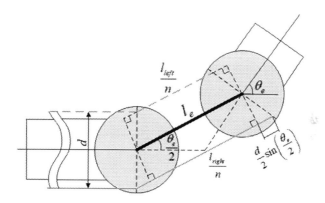

Fig. 7. Elbow actuation theory

Elbow Configuration. Inspired by the tension-amplification characteristic, elbow mechanism is appeared, as shown in Fig. 8. Two sets of fixed pulleys are placed at points equidistant from the center of the rolling surface of the proximal link, while the set of movable pulleys are placed at points equidistant from that of the distal link. This arrangement of pulleys keep the length of the wire unchanged which are droved by the agonistic and antagonistic wire actuation.

The main body of the elbow movement is the forearm turning frame and upper turning frame, and other components in this system are connected by some connectors. During the movement of the elbow, the rope pull the pulleys on the upper and lower sides of the arm (the pulleys pointed at 1, 2, 3, and 4 in the figure) to make the forearm turning frame rotates along the upper turning frame. In the beginning of movement, the 2nd and 3rd pulleys are gradually approached by the ropes due to the agonistic and antagonistic traction, and the 1st and 4th pulleys are passively moved away, thus realizing the rotation of the forearm along the upper arm.

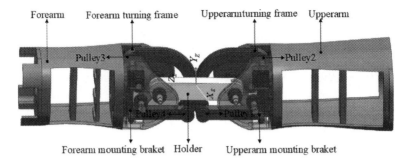

Fig. 8. Elbow configuration

3.3 Overall Configuration

Figure 9 shows the combination of two types of joint modules (3DPM and 1DTAM) for the anthropomorphic arm manipulator. It is well known that the joint structure of two arms in the same module is identical. Thus, combining the module element of 3DPM and 1DTAM proposed by some connectors before, the overall configuration of the humanoid 7-DOF arm can be obtained conveniently and quickly (as shown in Fig. 10), the length of forearm, upperarm and overall is 213, 285 and 701 mm, respectively, which is same to the real human.

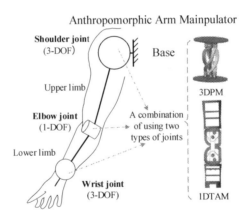

Fig. 9. Combination of this anthropomorphic arm

As is known to all, the difference between human arms is the proportion. Thus, changing the proportion of joint modules (3DPM and 1DTAM), the configuration (mechanical structure) of humanoid arm can be easily modified to adapt to different persons.

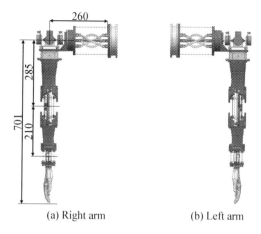

(a) Right arm   (b) Left arm

Fig. 10. Overall configuration of this dual arm

4   Kinematic Analysis and Workspace of Right Arm

To verify the feasibility and effectiveness of the presented modular design methodology, we carried out simulation and workspace analysis. In the simulation, the right arm presented before imitate human to perform hug action. Figure 11 show the entire process of this right arm hugging from initial state to end.

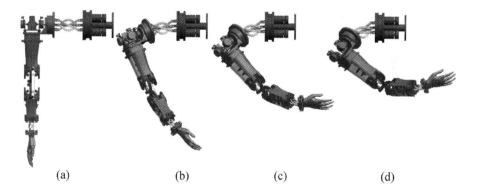

(a)   (b)   (c)   (d)

Fig. 11. Imitating the human's hugging

As is known to all, to design an anthropomorphic robotic arm, it is expected that the workspace of the arm should closely match to that of a human arm. However, it is a complicated issue to analyze the operational workspace of a redundant 7-DOF arm, because it involves the analysis of both position workspace and orientation workspace that are often coupled with each other. To simplify the analysis, this paper only computes the position workspace of this humanoid arm.

Since this arm is a combination of wrist, elbow and shoulder module, and every freedom of each module is independent each other. Therefore, this humanoid arm can be equivalent to the serial link mechanism in workspace analysis, and the equivalent model is shown as Fig. 12(a). Then, this paper sets the rotation range of each link in Matlab, and applies the Monte Carlo method to analyze the workspace, and finally obtains the workspace result of the anthropomorphic arm, as shown in Fig. 12(b). As can be seen form this result, the proposed humanoid arm has a larger workspace, which will make it as flexible as the human arm.

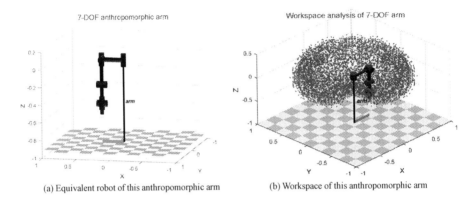

(a) Equivalent robot of this anthropomorphic arm   (b) Workspace of this anthropomorphic arm

Fig. 12. Workspace analysis

5   Conclusion

Aiming at social and home services with humanoid robots, novel humanoid arms have been designed in this paper by modularity approach. Being anthropomorphic and with the same degrees of freedom (seven DOFs) as human arms, each arm consists of four parts, which are the shoulder, the elbow, the wrist and the hand, and each part is suggested to be designed as a module. Specifically, two kinds of joint modules, namely the 3-DOF joint module for the shoulder and wrist, and the 1-DOF joint module for the elbow, have been proposed. In this way, the right and left arms may be easily obtained with the same modules by connecting them one by one, and various arms with different lengths may be also made through the connecting links with different lengths to mimic different persons (the male or female, the adults or children), which would be greatly beneficial for mass production in terms of high scalability, high flexibility and low costs.

What is more, the 3-DOF joint module has been implemented with a parrel mechanism, and most of the joint DOFs are driven through cables. Employing parallel mechanisms and cables for transmission made it possible to remotely install the actuating motors of the modules at one end and hence decease the weight of the moving part of each joint module, which is beneficial to improve the dynamic performance of the arms.

The joint modules are being manufactured. They will be soon mounted together as an arm for physical tests and experiments. The layout and installation of driving motors, the structure, the mechanical and electrical interfaces of the modules will be improved or optimized.

References

1. Albers, A., Brudniok, S., Ottnad, J., Sauter, C., Sedchaicharn, K.: Upper body of a new humanoid robot-the design of ARMAR III. In: 2006 6th IEEE-RAS International Conference on Humanoid Robots, pp. 308–313. IEEE (2006)
2. Asfour, T., Berns, K., Dillmann, R.: The humanoid robot ARMAR: design and control. In: The 1st IEEE-RAS International Conference on Humanoid Robots (Humanoids 2000), pp. 7–8. Citeseer (2000)
3. Beattie, W.: Orthotics and prosthetics in rehabilitation (2001)
4. Graf, B., Reiser, U., Hägele, M., Mauz, K., Klein, P.: Robotic home assistant Care-O-bot® 3-product vision and innovation platform. In: 2009 IEEE Workshop on Advanced Robotics and its Social Impacts, pp. 139–144. IEEE (2009)
5. Kajikawa, S.: Development of a robot finger module with multi-directional passive compliance. In: 2006 IEEE/RSJ International Conference on Intelligent Robots and Systems, pp. 4024–4029 (2006)
6. Kamimura, A., Murata, S., Yoshida, E., Kurokawa, H., Tomita, K., Kokaji, S.: Self-reconfigurable modular robot - experiments on reconfiguration and locomotion. In: Proceedings 2001 IEEE/RSJ International Conference on Intelligent Robots and Systems. Expanding the Societal Role of Robotics in the the Next Millennium (Cat. No. 01CH37180), vol. 1, pp. 606–612 (2001)
7. Kwee, H., Quaedackers, J., van de Bool, E., Theeuwen, L., Speth, L.: Adapting the control of the MANUS manipulator for persons with cerebral palsy: an exploratory study. Technol. Disabil. **14**(1), 31–42 (2002)
8. Pineau, J., Montemerlo, M., Pollack, M., Roy, N., Thrun, S.: Towards robotic assistants in nursing homes: challenges and results. Robot. Autonom. Syst. **42**(3–4), 271–281 (2003)
9. Sun, Y., Chen, X., Yan, T., Jia, W.: Modules design of a reconfigurable multi-legged walking robot. In: 2006 IEEE International Conference on Robotics and Biomimetics, pp. 1444–1449 (2006)
10. Topping, M., Smith, J.: The development of handy 1, a rehabilitation robotic system to assist the severely disabled. Ind. Robot: Int. J. **25**(5), 316–320 (1998)
11. Tsagarakis, N.G., Caldwell, D.G.: Development and control of a 'soft-actuated' exoskeleton for use in physiotherapy and training. Autonom. Robot. **15**(1), 21–33 (2003)
12. Xu, K., Simaan, N.: Actuation compensation for flexible surgical snake-like robots with redundant remote actuation. In: Proceedings 2006 IEEE International Conference on Robotics and Automation, ICRA 2006, pp. 4148–4154. IEEE (2006)
13. Yigit, C.B., Boyraz, P.: Design and modelling of a cable-driven parallel-series hybrid variable stiffness joint mechanism for robotics. Mech. Sci. **8**(1), 65–77 (2017)
14. Yim, M., Duff, D.G., Roufas, K.D.: Polybot: a modular reconfigurable robot. In: IEEE International Conference on Robotics & Automation (2002)
15. Zhang, Z.: Design optimization of a cable-driven two-DOF flexible joint module. Int. J. Adv. Robot. Syst. **9**(5), 213 (2012)

Design and Locomotion Analysis
of a Retractable Snake-like Robot
Based on 2-RRU/URR Parallel Module

Hui Bian[1,2(✉)], Lanlan Sun[1,2], and Yunfei Lei[1,2]

[1] Parallel Robot and Mechatronic System Laboratory of Hebei Province,
Yanshan University, Qinhuangdao 066004, China
ysubh@ysu.edu.cn
[2] Key Laboratory of Advanced Forging and Stamping Technology and Science,
Yanshan University, Ministry of Education, Qinhuangdao 066004, China

Abstract. Snake-like robots have always been the research focus for the unique hyper-redundant structure. The existing snake-like robots can move on complex surfaces, swim in the water, and even climb a tree. However, they cannot pass through a long, narrow hole whose diameter is similar to their own. Even the snakes in nature also face the same problem because of their series physical structure. Inspired by the annelid earthworms and leeches, a new type of retractable snake-like robot based on 2-RRU/URR parallel module is proposed. And its length can be adjusted between 850 mm to 1500 mm because of the translational degree of freedom (DOF) of 2-RRU/URR. Further, typical movement such as serpentine locomotion, traveling wave locomotion and rectilinear locomotion are analyzed and verified by experiments.

Keywords: Bionic robot · Snake-like robot · Modular design ·
Locomotion analysis

1 Introduction

In nature, snake can perform many kinds of motions to adapt to complex environment of soft or rugged ground surfaces because of its 200–400 vertebrae [1]. Similarly, snake-like robots usually consist of 8–16 joint modules and their motions are mainly depended on the DOFs and their arrangement of the joint modules [2]. The simplest kind of snake-like robots are composed of several 1-DOF rotating modules whose axes are parallel to each other, such as ACM [3] which can only move on a planar surface. In order to fit different environment, snake-like robots based on two-axis rotating modules are proposed. The two axes are orthogonal and they could be intersectant or skew. The axes could be actuated directly or with gears such as Uncle SAM [4], CSR [5], Kullo [6], ACM-R7 [7] and ACM-R8 [8], and they could also be actuated by spatial linkages such as the robots based on 2-RSS/U [9] or 2-UPS/U [10] which would be regarded as parallel mechanism. Further, snake-like robots based on three-axis rotating modules are proposed to improve the flexibility and adaptability, such as GMD-Snake 2 [11] and

© Springer Nature Switzerland AG 2019
H. Yu et al. (Eds.): ICIRA 2019, LNAI 11740, pp. 692–700, 2019.
https://doi.org/10.1007/978-3-030-27526-6_61

Inspector 2 [12]. They all have difficulties when passing through a long narrow hole whose diameter is similar to that of the robot.

In nature, Annelida such as earthworms and leeches could change the length of their bodies dramatically which are different from the biological snakes. So they can easily pass through the long narrow hole. Inspired by that, a new retractable snake-like robot with excellent flexibility and adaptability in moving ability is proposed. The proposed snake-like robot is based on a parallel mechanism which has two rotational DOFs and one translational DOF. Considering the elongation and contraction function along the longitudinal axis of the robot, the typical movement such as serpentine locomotion, traveling wave locomotion and emerging rectilinear locomotion and retractable serpentine locomotion are analyzed and verified.

2 Design of the Snake-like Robot

As shown in Fig. 1, the snake-like robot is composed of a head, a tail, 9 connecting plates and 24 linkages.

Fig. 1. Appearance of the snake-like robot

In the head, there is a microcontroller based on ARM Cortex-M, several sensors perceiving the surroundings, a communication module based on Bluetooth, a buzzer and several LEDs, and the battery is assembled on the tail to decrease the weight of the head. It could move based on the sensing information and also be controlled by a remote controller. Table 1 shows some physical parameters of the proposed snake-like robot.

In the snake-like robot, each of the 24 linkages mainly consists a steering servo, a driving arm, a slave arm, a universal joint, a connecting pin. The driving arm is fixed with the output shaft of the steering servo, the driving arm and the slave arm are connected by the connecting pin, the universal joint is fixed with the slave arm and one of its axes is parallel to that of the connecting pin. For the sake of description, the linkage can be represented by RRU, where R and U denote revolute pair and universal pair respectively. Any two adjacent connecting plates and three linkages between them compose a parallel mechanism which has the advantages of compact structure, flexible movement and accumulation of small error, high precision, small movement quality.

Table 1. Parameters of the snake-like robot

Physical parameters	Values of the snake-like robot
Power	DC 7.4 V 6000 mA
Weight	5.0 kg
Maximum width	200 mm
Maximum height	170 mm
Length	850 mm–1500 mm
DOF	3×8
Wheels	Passive ratchet wheel $\times$ 18
Camera	Pixel: 2048H $\times$ 1563 V
Infrared sensor	Measuring range: 200–1500 mm Size: 29.5 $\times$ 13 $\times$ 21.6 mm
Ultrasonic sensor	Measuring range: 20–4500 mm Size: 45 $\times$ 20 $\times$ 15 mm

As shown in Fig. 2, two of the three linkages are of symmetric arrangement and the axes of the steering servos are parallel to each other, and the third linkage is installed in the opposite way and the axis of the steering servo is perpendicular to that of the other two steering servos. Therefore, the parallel mechanism can be represented by 2-RRU/URR which has two rotational DOFs and one translational DOF. As shown in Fig. 2, the two rotating axes of 2-RRU/URR are orthogonal to each other without a point of intersection and the distance between them is adjustable.

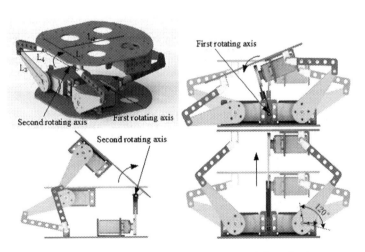

Fig. 2. Freedom display of 2-RRU/URR parallel mechanism

Since a snake-like robot is normally composed of 8–10 modules, the workspace of the module plays an important role in its flexibility. The main structural dimension parameters of the 2-RRU/URR parallel mechanism are as follows: $L_1 = 84$ mm,

$L_2 = 90$ mm, $L_3 = 60$ mm, $L_4 = 60$ mm and the rotation angle of the driving arm is set between $-10°$ to $100°$. Applying the search-based approach, the theoretical workspace of the 2-RRU/URR is calculated. As shown in Fig. 3, the range of three DOF of the moving platform can be obtained, which are $-24° \leq \alpha \leq 35°$, $-30 \leq \beta \leq 30°$,30mm $\leq h \leq 100$mm.

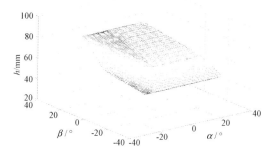

Fig. 3. Workspace of 2-RRU/URR parallel mechanism

3 Realization of Different Locomotion

3.1 Typical Locomotion of Snake-like Robot

Serpentine Locomotion. The serpentine locomotion which is similar to the sine wave is the most common form of locomotion realized by snake-like robots. The oscillations of different modules produce propulsive forces to propel the robot forward along a straight line. By optimizing the serpenoid curve presented in Hirose [1] the curve in two planes is obtained:

$$\begin{cases} \theta_i(s) = -2\alpha_0\sin\left(\frac{k_n\pi}{n_\theta}\right)\sin\left(\frac{2k_n\pi}{L}s + \frac{k_n\pi}{n_\theta}i + \frac{k_n\pi}{n_\theta}\right) + k_1 l_n \\ \varphi_i(s) = -2\alpha_\varphi\sin\left(\frac{k_n\pi}{n_\varphi}\right)\sin\left(\frac{2k_n\pi}{L}s + \frac{k_n\pi}{n_\varphi}i + \frac{k_n\pi}{n_\varphi} + \delta_\varphi\right) + k_2 l_n \end{cases} \quad (1)$$

Where i denotes the number of joint modules, α_θ and α_φ denote the initial bend angle in two planes, n_θ and n_φ denote the number of joints in the locomotion plane, δ_φ denotes the phase shift between the joints, k_1 and k_2 denote the curvature deviation, k_n denotes the number to form a propagation wave, s denotes arc length. The locomotion speed and the direction of the snake-like robot can be changed by modifying the arc length s and turning locomotion can be achieved by changing k_1 and k_2. The curve is continuous, so it can't be applied to the locomotion control of snake-like robot. The main parameters are set as follow: $\alpha_\theta = 30°$, $k_n = 2$, $k_1 = 0$, the serpenoid curve and its discrete approximation can be obtained. In the process of serpentine locomotion, the whole snake-like robot forms a complete wave shape. And all 8 joint modules move along the wave shape until the robot changes to the initial position, as shown in Fig. 4(a).

During the serpentine locomotion which is mainly depends on one of the two rotating DOFs, all joint modules have the same length and the length remain unchanged. The angle of the joint module around the first rotating axis perpendicular to the ground keeps changing. In this process, the parallel modules are partly actuated. Only the first two linkages need to be actuated and the input of the third linkage remains unchanged.

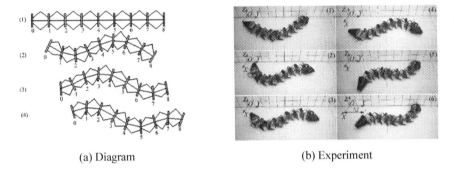

(a) Diagram   (b) Experiment

Fig. 4. Serpentine locomotion

For the convenience of analysis, a scale wallpaper is set on the wall and the side length of the square is 70 cm. Due to the influence of the robot's position error in the process of wave transmission, there is a slight difference from the initial position. As shown in Fig. 5(b), the amount of forward movement of the bionic robot is about 150 mm in a cycle.

Traveling Wave Locomotion. Similar to the serpentine locomotion, the traveling wave locomotion is in the plane perpendicular to the supporting surface. With the rotating DOF around the second rotating axis parallel to the ground, the traveling wave locomotion can be achieved. The formula of traveling wave locomotion in a cycle can be described as follows:

$$L_c = \sum_{i=1}^{n-1} l \times (1 - \cos\theta_i) \tag{2}$$

Where θ_i is the rotating angle of the ith module, and it is only related to the input of the third linkage. n is the number of modules required to form a wave. The main parameters are set as follow: $n = 4$, $l = 80$ mm, $\theta_i = 20°$. The traveling wave is transmitted from the tail to the head gradually to realize forward movement, as shown in Fig. 5 and the snake-like robot moves about 40 mm in a cycle.

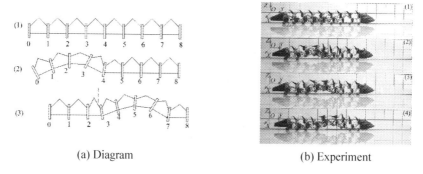

(a) Diagram   (b) Experiment

Fig. 5. Traveling wave locomotion

Limited to the range of the rotating angle around the second rotating axis, the traveling wave locomotion is not a highly efficient locomotion compared with the serpentine locomotion. But it is meaningful to make the snake-like robot adapt to narrow channels or obstacles.

3.2 Rectilinear Locomotion of the Snake-like Robot

Complete Rectilinear Locomotion and Its Improvement. The snake-like robot use passive ratchet wheels fixed to each connecting plate to provide forward friction to realize the complete rectilinear locomotion. The formula of the rectilinear locomotion in a cycle can be described as follows:

$$L = N \times \sum_{i=1}^{n} (L_{ei} - L_{si}) \qquad (3)$$

Where N is the period number of the rectilinear locomotion, n is the number of modules whose length changes in the moving, L_{ei} and L_{si} denote the final and the initial lengths of the module respectively. Set the initial and final lengths of each module as follows: $L_{si} = 60$ mm, $L_{ei} = 110$ mm, and the motion process is shown in Fig. 6.

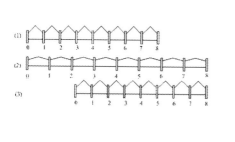

(a) Diagram   (b) Experiment

Fig. 6. Complete rectilinear locomotion

Ideally, the forward distance of the snake-like robot is 400 mm in one cycle. But the actual value is about 210 mm mainly because the wheels near the head can't provide enough friction to pull the whole robot. As a result, the snake-like robot have a large backward movement.

In order to avoid this problem, the partial rectilinear locomotion shown in Fig. 7 is obtained based on the complete rectilinear locomotion. The lengths of the front and the rear two modules of the robot remain unchanged and only the middle 4 modules change their lengths during the movement. Although the snake-like robot has a relatively smaller forward distance in a cycle, the actual value meets the theoretical value.

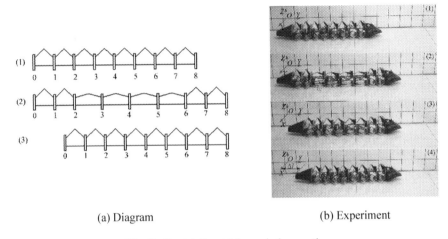

(a) Diagram   (b) Experiment

Fig. 7. Partial direct telescopic locomotion

Recursive Locomotion. Keeping the length of the first and the last module unchanged, the middle six joint modules are divide into two groups intermittently and the two groups shortening and lengthening in turn. The forward distance is about 150 mm in a cycle, as shown in Fig. 8.

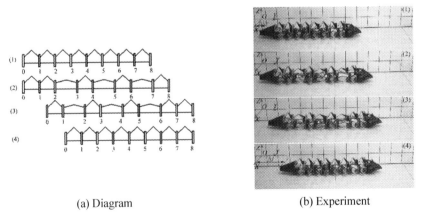

(a) Diagram   (b) Experiment

Fig. 8. Recursive locomotion

The experimental results show that the partial rectilinear locomotion has the highest efficiency in the above three rectilinear locomotion.

Retractable Serpentine Locomotion. Compared with the typical serpentine locomotion, the lengths of different joint modules could be adjusted based on their locations and phases in the curve in the process of the retractable serpentine locomotion. As shown in Fig. 9, the lengths of some joint modules change to fit the theoretical curve. And the forward distance is 160 mm in a cycle, which is improved compared to that of the typical serpentine locomotion.

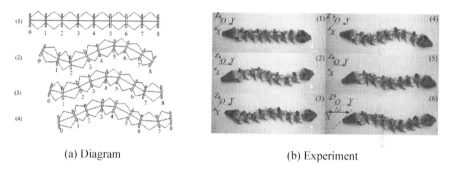

(a) Diagram   (b) Experiment

Fig. 9. Retractable serpentine locomotion

4 Conclusion

In this paper, a snake-like robot based on 2-RRU/URR parallel mechanism is presented. The structure and the composition of the joint module are described in detail. The experimental results show that the serpentine locomotion, the traveling wave locomotion, the rectilinear locomotion and the retractable serpentine locomotion can be well realized. The robot can pass through long, narrow hole efficiently and easily adapt itself to the environment because of the ability of the rectilinear locomotion.

Acknowledgments. This research was financially supported by Natural Science Foundation of China (Grant No. 51305380) and Natural Science Foundation of Hebei Province (Grant No. E2015203144).

References

1. Gray, J.: The mechanism of locomotion in snakes. J. Exp. Biol. **23**, 101–120 (1946)
2. Liljebäck, P., Pettersen, K.Y., Stavdah, Ø., Gravdahl, J.T.: A review on modelling, implementation, and control of snake robots. Robot. Auton. Syst. **60**, 29–40 (2012)
3. Hirose, B.S.: Biologically Inspired Robots: Snake-Like Locomotors and Manipulators. Oxford University Press, Oxford (1993)
4. Wright, C., et al.: Design of a modular snake robot. In: IEEE/RSJ International Conference on Intelligent Robots and Systems, pp. 2609–2614 (2007)

5. Sun, H., Liu, L., Ma, P.: A new type climbing snake robot. Drive Syst. Tech. **22**, 34–37 (2009)
6. Liljebäck, P., Pettersen, K.Y., Stavdahl, Ø.: A snake robot with a contact force measurement system for obstacle-aided locomotion. In: IEEE International Conference on Robotics and Automation, pp. 683–690 (2010)
7. Ohashi, T., Yamada, H., Hirose, S.: Loop forming snake-like robot ACM-R7 and its serpenoid oval control. In: IEEE/RSJ International Conference on Intelligent Robots and Systems, pp. 413–418. IEEE (2010)
8. Komura, H., Yamada, H., Hirose, S.: Development of snake-like robot ACM-R8 with large and mono-tread wheel. Adv. Robot. **29**, 1081–1094 (2015)
9. Zhao, T., Lin, G., Liao, L., Wang, C.: A snake-like robot based on spatial linkage mechanism. Robot **28**, 629–635 (2006)
10. Wu, C., Cao, Z., Xiao, Q., Fu, Y.: Dynamics analysis of bionic parallel joint mechanism for the snake robot. In: Control Conference, pp. 6301–6306 (2016)
11. Klaassen, B., Paap, K.L.: GMD-SNAKE2: a snake-like robot driven by wheels and a method for motion control. In: Proceedings of IEEE International Conference on Robotics and Automation, vol. 3014, pp. 3014–3019 (1999)
12. Ye, C., Ma, S., Li, B., Wang, Y.: Development of a three dimensional snake-like robot perambulator II. J. Mech. Eng. **45**, 128–133 (2009)

Compliant Manipulation Learning and Control for Lightweight Robot

A Nonsqueezing Torque Distribution Method for an Omnidirectional Mobile Robot with Powered Castor Wheels

Wenji Jia[1,2], Guilin Yang[1,2(✉)], Chongchong Wang[2], Qiang Liu[2],
Zaojun Fang[2], and Chinyin Chen[2]

[1] University of Chinese Academy of Sciences, Beijing 100049, China
[2] Zhejiang Key Laboratory of Robotics and Intelligent Manufacturing
Equipment Technology, Ningbo Institute of Materials Technology
and Engineering, CAS, Ningbo 315201, China
glyang@nimte.ac.cn

Abstract. This paper presents a novel dynamic modelling approach for omnidirectional mobile robots (OMRs) with powered caster wheels (PCWs). For the conventional dynamic modeling, the internal forces induced by the redundant actuation of the OMR are not analyzed, which will affect the dynamic performance and result in unstable robot motions. To eliminate the internal forces, a general nonsqueezing load distribution model is proposed and integrated with the dynamic model of the OMR. By the nonsqueezing dynamic model, the driving torques applied by the PCWs all contribute to the motion of the OMR. Consequently, the required driving torques are reduced compared to the conventional torque distribution method, which will improve the dynamic performance and energy efficiency for the OMR. To illustrate the effectiveness of the nonsqueezing dynamic model, simulation examples are provided.

Keywords: Omnidirectional mobile robot · Torque distribution ·
Dynamic model

1 Introduction

Omnidirectional mobile robots have the ability to move in any directions regardless of the current poses, so that they are widely employed to perform tasks in narrow and congested environment. Compared to the conventional mobile robots, the OMRs have higher maneuverability and agility. Among various types of the OMRs, the mobile robots with PCWs is a simple and efficient wheel design to achieve omnidirectional motions [1]. It can carry heavy payload and is less sensitive to the road conditions due to the continues contact between the wheels and the ground.

The OMRs often need to fulfill missions that require high compatibility with human involved environment. Therefore, the dynamic behavior of the OMRs must be considered in motion planning and control. Many research works have been conducted pertaining to the dynamics of the OMRs. As the OMRs with PCWs are always redundantly actuated [2], the distribution of joint torques is nonunique. To obtain the torque distribution, the pseudoinverse of the robot Jacobian is widely employed.

© Springer Nature Switzerland AG 2019
H. Yu et al. (Eds.): ICIRA 2019, LNAI 11740, pp. 703–714, 2019.
https://doi.org/10.1007/978-3-030-27526-6_62

Different methods for computing the pseudoinverses are investigated to achieve better dynamic performance. Holmberg [3] and Li [4] both adopt the augmented object model (AOM) to obtain the operational space dynamics. Holmberg employs a pseudoinverse Jacobian matrix to minimizing the total perceived slip, while Li uses another to minimizing the joint velocity differences. Chung et al. [5] derive a singularity-free, exact dynamic model for an OMR with PCWs by using Lagrangian formulation and virtual work principle. Yong et al. [6] design a controller for torque distribution of 4-PCWs OMR by identification of the status of the vehicle and the wheel slip ratio. Zhao et al. [7] present an integrated scheme for motion control and internal force control for an OMR with PCWs. The motion controller guarantees the robotic motion while the internal force controller minimizes the internal force occurring during robot motion. For the redundantly actuated OMR, the driving forces applied by the PCWs may result in internal forces that will not contribute to the motion of the robot, and will induce counteractive forces among the PCWs. This will consequently cause some defects in the dynamic performance of the robot, such as vibration, unexpected internal stresses, and slippages of the wheels. However, the analysis of the internal forces in the dynamic model and torque distribution method of the OMRs are not well investigated.

This paper proposes a dynamic model of the OMR with PCWs integrated with nonsqueezing torque distribution model which eliminates the internal forces, inspired by the motion and load distribution analysis proposed for multiple cooperating manipulators [8–10]. An OMR with PCWs can be treated as a moving platform supported by multiple 3-DOF articulated legs. The interactive forces between the moving platform and the PCWs are determined by the joint torques of each PCW, and they can be decomposed into two parts: motion-induced forces and internal forces. The relationship between the interactive forces and the joint torques is based on the PCW configuration. The interactive forces are analyzed for nonsqueezing load distribution and then mapped into joint space dynamics of the PCW. By eliminating the internal forces, the OMR can be more energy efficient, the stability and accuracy of the robot motion can also be improved.

2 Dynamic Model of a Single PCW and the Platform

In the OMR, PCWs are designed as modular driving units. They are installed in the chassis of the platform and controlled by the devices inside the platform. Figure 1 shows the simplified structure of OMR equipped with 4 PCWs. There two actuators in each PCW, the PCW can produce actuating forces $F_i^w = \left(f_{x_i}, f_{y_i}, m_{z_i}\right)^T (i = 1, 2, 3, 4)$ to the platform and the resultant forces by all PCWs will make the OMR perform the desired trajectory. Each PCW has two active actuated joints accounting for rolling and steering motions respectively (and one passive joint). The points $A_i(i = 1, 2, 3, 4)$ are the install positions for the PCWs, which are called support points. The support points can also be regarded as the distal ends of the PCWs. The kinematic constraints of each PCWs at the distal ends can be expressed by

$$\ddot{p}_i = \ddot{p}_o + \dot{\omega}_o \times r_i + \omega_o \times (\omega_o \times r_i) \tag{1}$$

$$\dot{\omega}_o = \dot{\omega}_i \tag{2}$$

where p_i and ω_i are the position and angular velocity of the distal end of the ith PCW expressed in world frame, p_o and ω_o are the position and angular velocity of the platform expressed in the same frame respectively, r_i is the vector from the origin of the platform frame to the distal end of ith PCW.

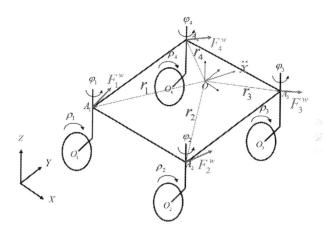

Fig. 1. Simplified model of the mobile plat

2.1   Dynamic Model of a Single PCW

The equations of motion of a single PCWs is derived at first. Figure 2 shows the simplified structure of a single PCW. It contains three parts: the wheel, the bracket and a "virtual" link from the castor to the center of the mobile platform. Here the link is called "virtual" because physically it doesn't exist. The PCWs are rigidly installed into the chassis of the platform, the link just describes the position information from the support points to the center of the platform.

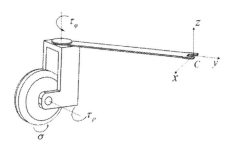

Fig. 2. Simplified PCW model subjected to driving torques

The dynamic model of a single PCW is derived by Lagrangian method. Since the platform moves on a plane, there is only kinetic energy in the system. The rolling motion ρ is always orthogonal to the steering motion φ thus they can be decoupled and calculated by

$$K_i = \frac{I_r \dot{\rho}_i^2}{2} + \frac{I_s \dot{\varphi}_i^2}{2} + \frac{m_w (\dot{\rho}_i r)^2}{2} \tag{3}$$

where I_r is the inertial moment of the wheel about its rolling axis, I_s is the inertial moment of the PCW about the steering axis, and m_w is the mass of the PCW. The dynamic model of a PCW in the joint space can be derived as

$$\frac{d}{dt}\frac{\partial K_i}{\partial \dot{q}_i} - \frac{\partial K_i}{\partial q_i} = \begin{bmatrix} \tau_{\rho_i} \\ \tau_{\varphi_i} \end{bmatrix} \tag{4}$$

Because K is only in regard to $\dot{q}_i$, $\partial K_i / \partial q_i = 0$ holds. Then the equations of motion of a PCW can be written as

$$M_i \ddot{q}_i = \tau_i - \tau_{f_i} + P_i^T (-F_i^w) \tag{5}$$

where

$$M_i = \begin{bmatrix} I_r + mr^2 & 0 \\ 0 & I_s \end{bmatrix}, \ddot{q}_i = \begin{bmatrix} \ddot{\rho}_i \\ \ddot{\varphi}_i \end{bmatrix}, \text{ and } P_i^T = \begin{bmatrix} -r\cos\varphi_i & b\sin\varphi_i & 0 \\ 0 & 0 & 1 \end{bmatrix}.$$

In (5), τ_i is the driving torques and τ_{f_i} is the friction torques, P_i is the matrix which maps the ith joint velocity to the support point velocity, and $-F_i$ is the external wrench applied by the platform. The compact form of all PCWs dynamics can be written as

$$M\ddot{q} = \tau - \tau_f + P^T (-F^w) \tag{6}$$

2.2   Dynamic Model of the Platform Without PCWs

The platform excluding all the PCWs can be considered as a manipulated object. The wrench applied by the end effector of ith PCW is denoted by F_i^w. The motion equations of the platform can be written as

$$M_o \ddot{x} + D_o(x,\dot{x}) = F_o^w \tag{7}$$

where $M_o = diag[m_o \quad m_o \quad I_o]$ is the inertial term of the platform, $D_o(x,\dot{x})$ is the Coriolis and centrifugal term which is zero here, F_o^w is the resultant wrench applied by all the PCWs.

3 Nonsqueezing Torque Distribution Analysis and Closed-Form Dynamic Model

Based on the equations of motion expressed in (8), the desired wrench F_o^w applied on the origin of the mobile platform frame can be computed by the given desired motion of the platform. The desired PCW wrenches acting on the platform are denoted by F_i^w. The position vector from the origin of the platform frame to the ith PCW distal end is denoted by r_i. F_o^w is unambiguous determined by the PCW wrenched F_i^w with a grasp matrix G

$$F_o^w = G \begin{bmatrix} F_1^w \\ F_2^w \\ \vdots \\ F_n^w \end{bmatrix} \tag{8}$$

where

$$G = \begin{bmatrix} I_3 & 0_3 & \cdots & I_3 & 0_3 \\ S(r_1) & I_3 & \cdots & S(r_n) & I_3 \end{bmatrix}$$

with the skew symmetric matrix $S(r_i)$.

3.1 Nonsqueezing Load Distribution Analysis

For the desired wrench F_o^w, the set of potential desired PCW wrenches F^w realizing F_o^w is not unique. The wrench of each PCW F_i^w can be decomposed into two parts, the external wrench component and the internal wrench component, as

$$F = F^{ext} + F^{int} \tag{9}$$

With the internal wrenches inside the OMR, the PCWs will be counteractant to each other and this may cause unexpected internal stress and vibration. Therefore, the internal wrench free model is benefit to the smooth and stable motion of the OMR. The internal wrench free model is also called the nonsqueezing distribution model by Walker [8]. In the study of Udwadia [11], for a constrained discrete dynamical system, the internal wrenches h^c result from the projection of the desired acceleration $\ddot{x}^d$ onto the kinematic constraints $A\ddot{x} = b$, written as

$$h^c = M_a^{1/2} \left(A M_a^{-1/2} \right)^\dagger \left(b - A\ddot{x}^d \right) \tag{10}$$

where the matrix M_a incorporates inertial of the system. From (10), it is straightforward to know that the internal wrenches h^c will vanish if the motion of the PCWs' end-effectors are compatible to their kinematic constraints.

The general load distribution model can be derived based on a particular parameterization of the generalized inverse of the grasp matrix [10]. The dynamics of a virtual end-effector system subjected to the kinematic constraints is considered and this gives the parameters the meaning of virtue masses and inertias. Given the desired wrench F_o^w to be applied on the platform, the virtual acceleration $\ddot{x}_o^*$ which the platform will experience can be computed as

$$\begin{bmatrix} m_o^* I_3 & 0_3 \\ 0_3 & J_o^* \end{bmatrix} \ddot{x}_o^* = F_o^w \tag{11}$$

where m_o^* and J_o^* are the assumed mass and inertia of the platform. By assigning virtual masses m_i^* and inertias J_i^* to the ith PCW distal end, the required wrench F_i^w can be computed as

$$F_i^w = \begin{bmatrix} m_i^* I_3 & 0_3 \\ 0_3 & J_i^* \end{bmatrix} \ddot{x}_i^* \tag{12}$$

where x_i^* is the virtual acceleration of the distal end of the ith PCW. In order to vanish the internal force, x_i^* can be deduced from $\ddot{x}_o^*$ by the use of the kinematic constraints in (1) and (2). This leads to

$$m_o^* \ddot{p}_o^* = \sum_i m_i^* \left[\ddot{p}_o^* + \dot{\omega}_o^* \times r_i + \omega_o^* \times (\omega_o^* \times r_i) \right] \tag{13}$$

By comparing the coefficients of $\ddot{p}_o^*$, we can conclude on $m_o^* = \sum_i m_i^*$ immediately. Since ω_o^* and $\dot{\omega}_o^*$ can take arbitrary values, the virtual mass needs to satisfy $\sum_i r_i m_i^* = 0$ for cancelling the terms involving them. Then, the inertia terms in (13) and (14) can be written as

$$J_o^* \dot{\omega}_o^* = \sum_i J_i^* \dot{\omega}_o^* + \sum_i r_i \times m_i^* \left[\ddot{p}_o^* + \dot{\omega}_o^* \times r_i + \omega_o^* \times (\omega_o^* \times r_i) \right] \tag{14}$$

Comparing coefficients of $\dot{\omega}_o^*$ yields $J_o^* = \sum_i J_i^* + \sum_i S(r_i) m_i^* S(r_i)^T$, wherein the cross product is expressed in skew-symmetric matrices form. The general non-squeezing load distribution then can be obtained:

$$G^+ = \begin{bmatrix} m_1^* [m_o^*]^{-1} I_3 & m_1^* [J_o^*]^{-1} S(r_1)^T \\ 0_3 & J_1^* [J_o^*]^{-1} \\ \vdots & \vdots \\ m_n^* [m_o^*]^{-1} I_3 & m_n^* [J_o^*]^{-1} S(r_n)^T \\ 0_3 & J_n^* [J_o^*]^{-1} \end{bmatrix} \tag{15}$$

With

$$m_o^* = \sum_i m_i^* \qquad (16)$$

$$J_o^* = \sum_i J_i^* + \sum_i S(r_i) m_i^* S(r_i)^T \qquad (17)$$

$$\sum_i r_i m_i^* = 0 \qquad (18)$$

It should be noticed that the wrenches F_o^w and F_i^w is analyzed in 3-D space with all 6 components. The mobile platform moves in 2-D plane and only three components (f_x, f_y, m_z) will be engaged. Hence the columns and rows corresponding to f_z, m_x, m_y in G^+ are eliminated and the load distribution for the OMR is rewritten as

$$\bar{F}^w = \bar{G}^+ \bar{F}_o^w \qquad (19)$$

where $\bar{F}^w = \left(f_{x_1}^d, f_{y_1}^d, m_{z_1}^d, \cdots, f_{x_n}^d, f_{y_n}^d, m_{z_n}^d \right)^T$ and $\bar{F}_o^w = \left(f_{x_o}^d, f_{y_o}^d, m_{z_o}^d \right)^T$ are relative to the planar motions only.

3.2 Closed-Form Dynamic Model of the OMR

The dynamic model of the platform excluding all the PCWs is derived in the previous section and expressed in task space. Recall the kinematics of the OMR [12], it can be transformed into joint space by

$$\dot{x} = J\dot{q} \qquad (20)$$

where J is the Jacobian matrix of the OMR. Differentiate both sides of (20) and substitute it into (7):

$$M_o J\ddot{q} + M_o \dot{J}\dot{q} = \bar{F}_o^w \qquad (21)$$

The wrench to be applied on the platform can be written as

$$\bar{F}_o^w = M_o J\ddot{q} + M_o \dot{J}\dot{q} \qquad (22)$$

Combine (22) with (6) and (7), one has

$$\left(M + P^T \bar{G}^+ M_o J \right)\ddot{q} + \left(P^T \bar{G}^+ M_o \dot{J} \right)\dot{q} + \tau_f = \tau \qquad (23)$$

where $M = (M_1, \cdots, M_n)$ denotes the inertias of the PCWs, $\tau_f = (f_x, f_y, m_z)$ denotes the friction torques, $\tau = \left(\tau_{\rho_1}, \tau_{\varphi_1}, \cdots, \tau_{\rho_n}, \tau_{\varphi_n} \right)^T$ denotes the joint torques of the PCWs. Equation (23) is the closed form dynamics of the mobile platform system. In this model, by giving the trajectory of the OMR, the required joint torques of each PCW can be calculated, and the nonsqueezing torque distribution guarantees that all these torques contributes to the motion of the OMR.

4 Simulation Examples

In this section, two simulation examples are provided to validate the proposed dynamic model with nonsqueezing torque distribution. The OMR is designed as shown in Fig. 1 with 4 identical PCWs assigned at 4 corners of a square. The parameters of the OMR are given as follows: the mass of the platform without PCWs is 60 kg, the side length L of the platform is 0.5 m, the radius of each wheel is 0.05 m, the offset of the castor wheel is 0.03 m, and the mass of each PCW is 2 kg.

4.1   Case 1: Task Space Motion Without Rotation

The OMR is commanded to track a cosine-function trajectory without rotation on the ground, which is expressed as:

$$
\begin{aligned}
x &= 4 - 4\cos(t/20)\,; \\
y &= 3 - 3\cos(t/10)\,; \\
\theta &= 0
\end{aligned}
\tag{24}
$$

In (24), the unit for position parameters is meter, while the unit for angular parameters is radian. In this case, the mass center is assumed to locate at the centroid of the OMR, by setting $m_i^* = 1$ and $J_i^* = I$ in the nonsqueezing load distribution matrix $\bar{G}^+$.

To track such a trajectory, the required driving torques of the PCWs are showed in Fig. 3. The OMR moves in the X-Y plane without rotating about the Z axis, hence the driving torques of each PCW are the same theoretically. Though this situation may change in practice, due to external disturbances and differences between each PCW, it is sufficient to illustrate the set of joint torques of only one PCW in the simulation results. In contrast, the torque distribution method by the Jacobian pseudoinverse is also presented. By this method, the joint torque differences are minimized in a least-squares manner [4]. The following can be observed from Fig. 4:

- The required rolling torques by the nonsqueezing dynamic model is reduced obviously compared to the ones by the pseudoinverse method, which means the nonsqueezing dynamic model is more energy-efficient for the OMR. It is also illustrated that the acceleration performance of the rolling motion can be improved if the nonsqueezing dynamic model is adopted.
- The required steering torques calculated by the two methods are nearly the same. Which means the nonsqueezing dynamic model mainly affects the rolling motion of the PCW compared to the pseudoinverse method.

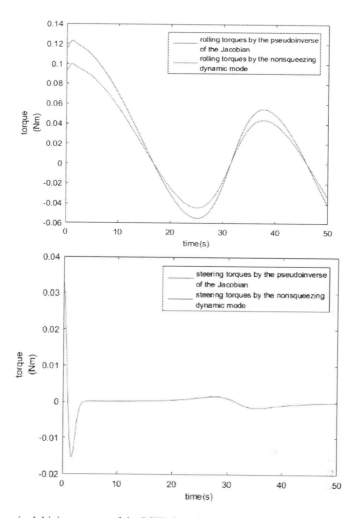

Fig. 3. Required driving torques of the PCWs based on two distribution methods in trajectory 1

4.2   Case 2: Task Space Motion with Rotation

The OMR is commanded to track the same cosine-function trajectory with self-rotation on the ground, which is expressed as:

$$x = 4 - 4\cos(t/20);$$
$$y = 3 - 3\cos(t/10);$$
$$\theta = 3 - 3\cos(t/30)$$
(25)

Furthermore, the mass center no longer locates at the centroid of the OMR, but at the point $(0.125,0,0)$, with respect to the frame C showed in Fig. 1. The load distribution matrix also changes due to the different position of the mass center.

712   W. Jia et al.

In the second trajectory, the OMR moves with both translational and rotational motions, therefore, the joint torques of each PCW are different. For representativeness, we choose the required joint torques of the PCW which has maximum peak (wheel 3) to illustrate in Fig. 4.

- For the second planned motion, the required rolling torques by the nonsqueezing dynamic model is still smaller than which by the pseudoinverse method, means the nonsqueezing dynamic model is still more energy-efficient for the OMR in a more complicated motion.
- The required steering torques obtained by the two methods are significantly different for the second motion. With the OMR rotating about the vertical axis, the nonsqueezing dynamic model shows its superiority in steering actuation. Except for the first few seconds, the required steering torques by the nonsqueezing model is much smaller than which by the pseudoinverse Jacobian method.

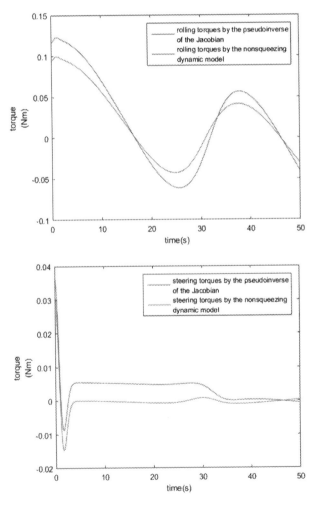

Fig. 4. Required driving torques of the PCWs based on two distribution methods in trajectory 2

5   Conclusion

In the conventional dynamic modeling of an OMR with PCWs, the driving torques are computed by employing the pseudoinverse of the Jacobian matrix of the OMR, which will result in internal forces, as the pseudoinverse cannot be directly used for internal force analysis. In this paper, a new dynamic modeling method is presented by introducing a nonsqueezing load distribution model. The nonsqueezing dynamic model guarantees that the driving torques of the PCWs totally contribute to the platform motions without inducing any internal forces. As a result, the internal stresses in the OMR are reduced, and the stability and running accuracy of the OMR are improved. Moreover, the required driving torques of each PCW are reduced for a given trajectory, which will improve the dynamic performance and energy-efficiency of the OMR. The effectiveness of the proposed nonsqueezing dynamic model are validated through the simulation examples.

Acknowledgement. This research is supported by National Key R&D Program of China (2017YFB1300400), NSFC-Zhejiang Joint Fund (U1509202), Equipment Pre-research fund Project (6140923010102), and Innovation Team of Key Components and Technology for the New Generation Robot (2016B10016).

References

1. Yang, G., Li, Y., Lim, T.M., Lim, C.W.: Decoupled powered caster wheel for omnidirectional mobile platforms. In: 2014 IEEE 9th Conference on Industrial Electronics and Applications (ICIEA), pp. 954–959. IEEE (2014)
2. Campion, G., Bastin, G., Dandrea-Novel, B.: Structural properties and classification of kinematic and dynamic models of wheeled mobile robots. IEEE Trans. Robot. Autom. **12**(1), 47–62 (1996)
3. Holmberg, R., Khatib, O.: Development and control of a holonomic mobile robot for mobile manipulation tasks. Int. J. Robot. Res. **19**(11), 1066–1074 (2000)
4. Li, Y.P., Oetomo, D., Ang, M.H., Lim, C.W.: Torque distribution and slip minimization in an omnidirectional mobile base. In: International Conference on Advanced Robotics (2005)
5. Chung, J.H., Yi, B.J., Kim, W.K., Lee, H.: The dynamic modeling and analysis for an omnidirectional mobile robot with three caster wheels. In: IEEE International Conference on Robotics & Automation (2003)
6. Yong, L., Jia, Y., Ning, X.: Dynamic model and adaptive tracking controller for 4-powered caster vehicle. In: IEEE International Conference on Robotics & Automation (2010)
7. Zhao, D., Deng, X., Yi, J.: Motion and internal force control for omnidirectional wheeled mobile robots. IEEE/ASME Trans. Mechatron. **14**(3), 382–387 (2009)
8. Walker, I.D., Freeman, R.A., Marcus, S.I.: Analysis of motion and internal loading of objects grasped by multiple cooperating manipulators. Int. J. Robot. Res. **10**(4), 396–409 (1991)
9. Chung, J.H., Yi, B.J., Kim, W.K.: Analysis of internal loading at multiple robotic systems. J. Mech. Sci. Technol. **19**(8), 1554–1567 (2005)
10. Erhart, S., Hirche, S.: Internal force analysis and load distribution for cooperative multi-robot manipulation. IEEE Trans. Rob. **31**(5), 1238–1243 (2017)

11. Udwadia, F.E., Kalaba, R.E.: A new perspective on constrained motion. Proc. Math. Phys. Sci. **439**(1906), 407–410 (1992)
12. Jia, W., Yang, G., Gu, L., Zheng, T.: Dynamics modelling of a mobile manipulator with powered castor wheels. In: IEEE International Conference on Cybernetics and Intelligent Systems, pp. 730–735 (2017)

A Two-Step Self-calibration Method with Portable Measurement Devices for Industrial Robots Based on POE Formula

Lefeng Gu[1,2], Guilin Yang[1,2(✉)], Zaojun Fang[1(✉)], Wenjun Shen[1,2], Tianjiang Zheng[1], Chinyin Chen[1], and Chi Zhang[1]

[1] Zhejiang Key Laboratory of Robotics and Intelligent Manufacturing Equipment Technology, Ningbo Institute of Materials Technology and Engineering, CAS, Ningbo 315201, China
{glyang, fangzaojun}@nimte.ac.cn
[2] University of Chinese Academy of Sciences, Beijing 100049, China

Abstract. A two-step self-calibration method based on portable calibration devices is proposed in this paper. In the first step, the distance errors in a large-range workspace is utilized to calibrate the manipulator. In the second step, the position errors is utilized to calibrate an external world frame to describe all the coordinate systems in a robot cell and further enhance the calibration results in the first step. For each step, a linear and simplified calibration model is then formulated by employing the local POE formula and introducing the *position adjoint conversion matrix*. Based on the calibration model, portable and cost-effective self-calibration devices are designed, which consist of a spherical center measuring device, a movable ball bar and Tri-ball plate. The calibration devices presented can obtain distance errors in a large-range workspace and position errors in a local workspace of a manipulator, which enhance the reliability of the calibration results and set an external reference frame. Finally, an accurate kinematic model with respect to the external user-defined frame is given, which enables the off-line programming to be more accurate and effective. The simulation results demonstrate that the proposed two-step self-calibration algorithm is effective and robust.

Keywords: Self-calibration · POE formula · Kinematic calibration

1 Introduction

There is an increasing demand for applications where the robot should be programmed through off-line programming in modern intelligent manufacturing. However, industrial robots normally have high repeatability but low positioning accuracy, which limits the application of industrial robots in cases requiring off-line programming. Kinematic calibration serves as an effective solution to improve the positioning accuracy of an industrial robot.

From the measurement viewpoint, kinematic calibration can be classified into two categories [1]: external calibration and self-calibration. External calibration methods usually make use of expensive external metrology equipments to measure the robot pose,

© Springer Nature Switzerland AG 2019
H. Yu et al. (Eds.): ICIRA 2019, LNAI 11740, pp. 715–727, 2019.
https://doi.org/10.1007/978-3-030-27526-6_63

such as laser trackers [2, 3] and CMMs [4]. Self-calibration methods utilize geometric constraints and sensors to obtain the robot pose, which not only reduce the cost but also normally have good portability and adaptability to working condition. Generally, an ideal self-calibration method should have a complete and parametrically continuous calibration model as well as a low-cost and large-workspace calibration device [5].

Therefore, cost-effective self-calibration methods have been widely investigated. Hage et al. [6] proposed a self-calibration device composed of an in-contact probe and a fixed precision cube. An absolute coordinate system to locate the robot base and working object was set on this device and a constraint equation with position errors was formulated. The calibration model was then derived by using the Denavit-Hartenberg (D-H) model. Gaudreault et al. [7] proposed a novel self-calibration method by utilizing a new 3D position measuring device with setting an external world frame, in which the high repeatability of a fixed kinematic coupling was fully used to achieve precise position measurements. And the self-calibration model was formulated by adopting the Modified Denavit-Hartenberg (M D-H) model. Zhuang et al. [8] developed a self-calibration method utilizing a camera mounted on the wrist of a manipulator to implement pose measurements. With the pose errors obtained, a calibration model based on the Complete and Parametrically Continuous (CPC) model was then derived. Hu et al. [9] presented a calibration method based on a new distance error detecting device which can measure the distance error within the entire robot workspace. A relative calibration model is then obtained by using the Product of Exponentials (POE) formula. Du et al. [10] also developed a relative self-calibration approach using distance error. With the PSD and laser beam utilized, distance measurements could implement in a large space.

Most of the existing self-calibration methods have the advantage of low cost, but there are still some problems in the calibration models and devices. Calibration models based on the D-H model [6] and CPC model [8] either fail to meet the requirement of parametric continuity when the two consecutive axes of a robot are parallel or introduce redundant parameters which make the model complicated. Calibration models based on POE formula are complete and can avoid the problem of parametric continuity. However, the conventional POE based models [9] require unitization to joint twists in each parameter updating step, which makes the calibration process complex. As for the calibration devices, most of the calibration devices [5] utilizing position errors measurement can merely obtain error information in a local robot workspace. Calibration devices utilizing [9] relative position errors usually have a large measurement workspace but cannot be used to locate the robot base and working objects, which is critical to the accuracy of off-line programming.

In order to solve the problems mentioned above, we propose a novel self-calibration method with two-step calibration process in this paper. The self calibration devices designed can obtain distance errors in a large-range workspace and position errors in a local workspace of a manipulator respectively, which enhances the reliability of the calibration results and sets an external coordinate system to describe all the frames in a robot cell. Two linear calibration models with distance and position errors respectively are then formulated by utilizing the local POE formula [11] and introducing the *position adjoint conversion matrix*, which not only meets the requirements mentioned but also further simplify the conventional POE based calibration models due to avoiding the unitization to joint twists. With the proposed approach, we finally obtain an accurate kinematic model with respect to an external user-defined frame.

2 New Self-calibration Devices

2.1 Design of the Self-calibration Devices

The portable self-calibration devices proposed in this paper includes a spherical center measuring device mounted on the flange of the robot, a movable ball bar and an assembly of three steel balls denoted by Tri-ball plate. When the measuring device touches the ball of ball bar or Tri-ball plate, it is convenient to compute the coordinate of the spherical center with respect to the flange frame $\{f\}$. In the measuring experiments with the calibration devices, the TCP (Tool Center Point) of the robot is extended to the spherical centers of the ball bar and Tri-ball plate. Therefore, we can constraint the TCP in a fixed distance i.e. the center distance of the ball bar and in three fixed points i.e. the spherical centers of Tri-ball plate. The distance errors and position errors of a robot are then obtained with the calibration devices.

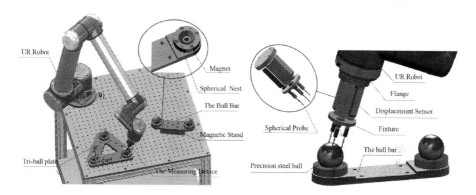

Fig. 1. Schematic diagram of the self-calibration device.

As shown in Fig. 1, the measuring part of the devices consists of three uniformly distributed displacement sensors and spherical probes. When the probes touch the surface of the steel ball of ball bar and Tri-ball plate, we can obtain the center coordinate of the ball by utilizing the sphere surface constraint and the measurement information of the three displacement sensors. The movable ball bar installed on a magnetic stand is composed of two precision steel balls, spherical nests and magnets, which can be conveniently placed at different locations within a large-range robot workspace. Thus, the calibration results based on measurements with the ball bar is more reliable. The fixed Tri-ball plate consists of a base and three identical modules to the ball bar. With the three precision steel balls, we can set an external user-defined world frame $\{w\}$ to describe all the coordinate systems in a robot cell, which enables the off-line programming to be more accurate and effective.

2.2   Measuring Principle of the Calibration Devices

Assuming the initial center coordinates of the three spherical probes with respect to $\{f\}$ are $\boldsymbol{p}_{0i} = [a_i, b_i, c_i]$ ($i = 1, 2, 3$). Denoting the variables of the displacement sensors by l_i, the center coordinates of the spherical probes in touching measurements can be rewritten as $\boldsymbol{p}_i = [a_i, b_i, c_i - l_i]$. The coordinate of the spherical center of the ball bar or Tri-ball plate, $\boldsymbol{p}_T = [x, y, z]$ relative to $\{f\}$ can be obtained by solving the following equations:

$$(a_i - x)^2 + (b_i - y)^2 + (c_i - l_i - z)^2 = (r + R)^2, \quad i = 1, 2, 3 \tag{1}$$

where r and R represent the radii of the spherical probes and the steel balls respectively, a_i, b_i, c_i are constant coefficients depending on the physical design of the measuring devices.

3   Local POE Formula for Robot Forward Kinematics

In this section, the rigid body transformation based on local POE formula is briefly introduced and the POE representation of a serial robot forward kinematics is given accordingly.

In the local POE model [11], the transformation matrix between the two adjacent frames, $\{i\}$ and $\{i - 1\}$, is defined as follows:

$$\boldsymbol{T}_{i-1,i}(q_i) = e^{\hat{s}_i q_i} \boldsymbol{T}_{i-1,i}(0) \tag{2}$$

where $\boldsymbol{T}_{i-1,i}(0) \in SE(3)$ ($i = 1, 2 \cdots n, n+1$) is the initial pose of $\{i\}$ relative to $\{i - 1\}$, q_i is the displacement of joint i, $\hat{s}_i \in se(3)$ is the ith screw axis expressed in $\{i - 1\}$ and its twist coordinate is given by $s_i = [v_i, w_i]^T$, in which v_i is the position of the screw axis relative to the origin of $\{i - 1\}$ and w_i is the unit direction vector of the screw axis [12].

According to the mapping from $se(3)$ to $SE(3)$, $\boldsymbol{T}_{i-1,i}(0) = e^{\hat{t}_i}$, and $\hat{t}_i \in se(3)$ is the corresponding Lie Algebra element of $\boldsymbol{T}_{i-1,i}(0)$. Hence, Eq. (1) can be rewritten as:

$$\boldsymbol{T}_{i-1,i}(q_i) = e^{\hat{s}_i q_i} e^{\hat{t}_i} \tag{3}$$

For a n-dof serial robot, the forward kinematics can be formulated as:

$$\boldsymbol{T}_{0,n+1}(\boldsymbol{q}) = e^{\hat{s}_1 q_1} \boldsymbol{T}_{0,1}(0) e^{\hat{s}_2 q_2} \boldsymbol{T}_{1,2}(0) \cdots e^{\hat{s}_n q_n} \boldsymbol{T}_{n-1,n}(0) \boldsymbol{T}_{n,n+1} \tag{4}$$

where $\boldsymbol{T}_{n,n+1}$ is a fixed transformation representing the tool frame $\{n + 1\}$ with respect to the last link frame $\{n\}$.

4   The Two-Step Self-calibration

This section presents a two-step calibration method with two different error models based on the self-calibration devices designed. In the first step, the proposed method utilizes a distance error model to identify the kinematic errors and minimize the position errors. Subsequently, a position error model is presented to calibrate an external world frame and further compensate the residual position error of a fixed deflection.

4.1   Error Model with TCP Position

Since the error model with TCP position is the basis of our two-step self-calibration model, we derive a concise and linear position error model by employing the local POE formula and introducing the *position adjoint conversion matrix* at the first part.

Based on Eq. (4), the position coordinate of the TCP with respect to the base frame, $^0\boldsymbol{p} = [^0p_z, {}^0p_y, {}^0p_z]^\mathrm{T}$, is given by:

$$\begin{bmatrix} ^0\boldsymbol{p} \\ 0 \end{bmatrix} = e^{\hat{s}_1 q_1} e^{\hat{t}_1} e^{\hat{s}_2 q_2} e^{\hat{t}_2} \cdots e^{\hat{s}_n q_n} e^{\hat{t}_n} e^{\hat{t}_{n+1}} \begin{bmatrix} ^T\boldsymbol{p} \\ 1 \end{bmatrix} \tag{5}$$

where $^T\boldsymbol{p} = [^Tp_z, {}^Tp_y, {}^Tp_z]^\mathrm{T}$ is the coordinate of the TCP relative to the tool frame. According to [11], we can assume the kinematic errors occur only in $\boldsymbol{T}_{i-1,i}(0)$ and $\boldsymbol{T}_{n,n+1}$. In this way, the calibration model is highly simplified. Through linearizing Eq. (5) with respect to $\hat{t}_i$, we have:

$$\begin{bmatrix} \delta^0\boldsymbol{p} \\ 0 \end{bmatrix} = e^{\hat{s}_1 q_1} e^{\hat{t}_1} \delta\hat{t}_1 e^{\hat{s}_2 q_2} e^{\hat{t}_2} \cdots e^{\hat{s}_n q_n} e^{\hat{t}_n} e^{\hat{t}_{n-1}} \begin{bmatrix} ^T\boldsymbol{p} \\ 1 \end{bmatrix} + e^{\hat{s}_1 q_1} e^{\hat{t}_1} e^{\hat{s}_2 q_2} e^{\hat{t}_2} \delta\hat{t}_2 \cdots e^{\hat{s}_n q_n} e^{\hat{t}_n} e^{\hat{t}_{n-1}} \begin{bmatrix} ^T\boldsymbol{p} \\ 1 \end{bmatrix}$$
$$+ \cdots + e^{\hat{s}_1 q_1} e^{\hat{t}_1} e^{\hat{s}_2 q_2} \cdots e^{\hat{s}_n q_n} e^{\hat{t}_n} \delta\hat{t}_n e^{\hat{t}_{n-1}} \begin{bmatrix} ^T\boldsymbol{p} \\ 1 \end{bmatrix} + e^{\hat{s}_1 q_1} e^{\hat{t}_1} e^{\hat{s}_2 q_2} e^{\hat{t}_2} \cdots e^{\hat{s}_n q_n} e^{\hat{t}_n} e^{\hat{t}_{n-1}} \delta\hat{t}_{n+1} \begin{bmatrix} ^T\boldsymbol{p} \\ 1 \end{bmatrix} \tag{6}$$

Based on the forward kinematic model, Eq. (6) can be rewritten as:

$$\begin{bmatrix} \delta^0\boldsymbol{p} \\ 0 \end{bmatrix} = \boldsymbol{T}_{0,1}\delta\hat{t}_1 \begin{bmatrix} ^1\boldsymbol{p} \\ 1 \end{bmatrix} + \boldsymbol{T}_{0,2}\delta\hat{t}_2 \begin{bmatrix} ^2\boldsymbol{p} \\ 1 \end{bmatrix} + \cdots + \boldsymbol{T}_{0,n}\delta\hat{t}_n \begin{bmatrix} ^n\boldsymbol{p} \\ 1 \end{bmatrix} + \boldsymbol{T}_{0,n+1}\delta\hat{t}_{n+1} \begin{bmatrix} ^T\boldsymbol{p} \\ 1 \end{bmatrix}$$
$$= \sum_{i=1}^{n+1} \boldsymbol{T}_{0,i}\delta\hat{t}_i \begin{bmatrix} ^i\boldsymbol{p} \\ 1 \end{bmatrix} \tag{7}$$

in which $\boldsymbol{T}_{0,i}$ represents the transformation matrix from the base frame $\{0\}$ to the link frame $\{i\}$.

Obviously, Eq. (7) is a nonlinear differential equation. In order to obtain a linear error model, we can introduce a special matrix $\boldsymbol{T}_{p_i} = \begin{bmatrix} \boldsymbol{I}_{3\times3} & -{}^i\hat{\boldsymbol{p}} \end{bmatrix} \in \Re^{3\times6}$, which satisfies the equation:

$$\delta \hat{t}_i \begin{bmatrix} {}^i p \\ 1 \end{bmatrix} = \begin{bmatrix} T_{p_i} \\ 0 \end{bmatrix} \delta t_i \tag{8}$$

where ${}^i p$ represents the position coordinate of TCP relative to link frame $\{i\}$. We term such a matrix, T_{p_i}, as *position adjoint conversion matrix*. As $T_{0,i} = \begin{bmatrix} R_{0,i} & p_{0,i} \\ 0 & 1 \end{bmatrix}$, where $R_{0,i}$ and $p_{0,i}$ are the orientation and position of $\{i\}$ relative to $\{0\}$ respectively. Thus, Eq. (7) can be further simplified as:

$$\delta^0 p = R_{0,1} T_{p_1} \delta t_1 + R_{0,2} T_{p_2} \delta t_2 + \cdots + R_{0,n} T_{p_n} \delta t_n + R_{0,n+1} T_{p_{n+1}} \delta t_{n+1}$$
$$= \sum_{i=1}^{n+1} R_{0,i} T_{p_i} \delta t_i \tag{9}$$

Equation (9) can also be expressed in a linear and concise form: $y = Ax$, where

$$y = \delta^0 P \in \Re^{3 \times 1}, \; x = [\delta t_1, \delta t_2, \cdots, \delta t_n, \delta t_{n+1}]^T \in \Re^{6(n+1) \times 1}$$
$$A = [R_{0,1} T_{p_1}, R_{0,2} T_{p_2}, \cdots, R_{0,n} T_{p_n}, R_{0,n+1} T_{p_{n+1}}] \in \Re^{3 \times 6(n+1)} \tag{10}$$

In Eq. (10), y is the position error of TCP, x is the kinematic error to be identified and A is the position error Jacobian matrix which can be computed with measuring configuration.

4.2   Step 1: Self-calibration with Distance Error Model

With the ball bar in the proposed calibration devices, the two extended TCPs in the two ends are constrained in a fixed distance, i.e. the center distance of ball bar. Based on the error information, the actual center distance is identical to the center distance of the ball bar but different from the nominal center distance computed with kinematic model and the measuring information of the calibration devices, we can formulate the self-calibration model utilizing the distance constrain.

Denoting the center distance of a ball bar by l and the spherical centres in the two ends by $P_1 = [p_{1x}, p_{1y}, p_{1z}]^T$ and $P_2 = [p_{2x}, p_{2y}, p_{2z}]^T$ respectively, the distance between the spherical centres can be expressed as:

$$(P_2 - P_1)^T (P_2 - P_1) = l^2 \tag{11}$$

Differentiating both sides of Eq. (10), we have:

$$(\delta P_2 - \delta P_1)^T (P_2 - P_1) + (P_2 - P_1)^T (\delta P_2 - \delta P_1) = 2l \cdot \delta l \tag{12}$$

Since

$$(\delta P_2 - \delta P_1)^{\mathrm{T}}(P_2 - P_1) = \left[(\delta P_2 - \delta P_1)^{\mathrm{T}}(P_2 - P_1)\right]^{\mathrm{T}} = (P_2 - P_1)^{\mathrm{T}}(\delta P_2 - \delta P_1) \in \Re^{1 \times 1} \quad (13)$$

we have the self-calibration model with the distance error:

$$\delta l = l_a - l_n = \frac{(P_2 - P_1)^{\mathrm{T}}}{l}(\delta P_2 - \delta P_1) \quad (14)$$

where l_a and l_n represent the actual center distance and the nominal center distance respectively, $l = l_n = \|P_1 - P_2\|$, and δl is the difference between the actual center distance and nominal center distance.

With Eq. (10), Eq. (13) can be expressed in a concise and linear form: $y = Jx$, where

$$y = \delta l \in \Re^{1 \times 1}, x = [\delta t_1, \delta t_2, \cdots, \delta t_n, \delta t_{n+1}]^T \in \Re^{6(n+1) \times 1},$$

$$J = \frac{(P_2 - P_1)^{\mathrm{T}}}{\|P_1 - P_2\|}(A_2 - A_1) \in \Re^{1 \times 6(n+1)}, \quad (15)$$

$$A_i = [R_{0,1}T_{p_1}, R_{0,2}T_{p_2}, \cdots, R_{0,n}T_{p_n}, R_{0,n+1}T_{p_{n+1}}] \subset \Re^{3 \times 6(n+1)}$$

In order to obtain reliable calibration results, we can place the ball bar at different locations within the whole robot workspace and implement calibration measurement. With m sets of measurements, we have: $\tilde{Y} = \tilde{J}x$, where

$$\tilde{Y} = [\delta l_1, \delta l_2, \cdots, \delta l_m]^{\mathrm{T}} \in \Re^{m \times 1}, m \ge 6(n+1)$$
$$x = [\delta t_1, \delta t_2, \cdots, \delta t_n, \delta t_{n+1}]^{\mathrm{T}} \in \Re^{6(n+1) \times 1}, \tilde{J} = [J_1, J_2, \cdots, J_m]^{\mathrm{T}} \in \Re^{m \times 6(n+1)} \quad (16)$$

With the formulated self-calibration model utilizing distance error, the calibration process in Step 1 is conducted by updating the kinematic model iteratively. Given $\tilde{J}^* = (\tilde{J}^{\mathrm{T}}\tilde{J})^{-1}\tilde{J}^{\mathrm{T}}$ as the pseudoinverse matrix of $\tilde{J}$, then the error parameters can be computed by $x = \tilde{J}^*\tilde{Y}$. The kinematic parameter to be updated is computed by $T_{i-1,i}^{new}(0) = T_{i-1,i}^{old}(0)e^{\delta \hat{t}_i}$. The kinematic parameter is then iteratively updated until the errors $\tilde{Y}$ converge.

4.3   Step 2: Self-calibration with Position Error Model

After the self-calibration with distance error in the first step, it is verified that the kinematic model features with high distance accuracy. However, we find out that there is still a residual error of a deflection, which results in a fixed transformation on the TCP position. We denote the fixed transformation by $T_b = e^{\hat{t}_b}$. Furthermore, it is of great significance to define and calibrate an absolute reference frame to locate the robot base and working objects for off-line programming, which can not be obtained by the relative calibration in Step 1.

In order to compensate the residual transformation error, we set an external world coordinate system denoted by $\{w\}$, which is attached to Tri-ball plate designed. According to the arrangement of Tri-ball plate with respect to the robot, the initial transformation $T_{w,0}$ between the world frame $\{w\}$ and the robot base frame $\{0\}$ can be obtained in advance. Subsequently, with Eqs. (2) to (5), the position coordinate of TCP with respect to $\{w\}$ can be described as:

$$\begin{bmatrix} {}^w p \\ 0 \end{bmatrix} = e^{\hat{t}_w} e^{\hat{s}_1 q_1} e^{\hat{t}_1} e^{\hat{t}_2} e^{\hat{s}_2 q_2} \cdots e^{\hat{s}_n q_n} e^{\hat{t}_n} e^{\hat{t}_{n+1}} \begin{bmatrix} {}^T p \\ 1 \end{bmatrix} \quad (17)$$

where ${}^w P = [{}^w p_z, {}^w p_y, {}^w p_z, 1]^{\mathrm{T}}$, t_i, s_i, q_i are the kinematic parameters updated after the self-calibration process in step 1, $e^{\hat{t}_w} = T_{w,0} \in SE(3)$ is the pose of $\{w\}$ relative to $\{0\}$, and $\hat{t}_w \in se(3)$ is the corresponding Lie Algebra element of $T_{0,w}$.

Therefore, the fixed deflection error T_b can be lumped into the external kinematic parameter $T_{0,w}$. Linearizing Eq. (17) with respect to $\hat{t}_w$, we have a special self-calibration model utilizing position errors as follows:

$$\begin{bmatrix} \delta^w p \\ 0 \end{bmatrix} = e^{\hat{t}_w} \delta\hat{t}_w e^{\hat{s}_1 q_1} e^{\hat{t}_1} e^{\hat{t}_2} e^{\hat{s}_2 q_2} \cdots e^{\hat{s}_n q_n} e^{\hat{t}_n} e^{\hat{t}_{n+1}} \begin{bmatrix} {}^T p \\ 1 \end{bmatrix} \quad (18)$$

where $\delta^w p = [\delta^w p_z, \delta^w p_y, \delta^w p_z]^{\mathrm{T}}$. Based on Eqs. (6) to (9), Eq. (18) can be rewritten as:

$$\delta^w p = R_{w,0} T_{p_0} \delta t_w \quad (19)$$

A linear and concise self-calibration model based on position error is formulated as: $y = Kx$, where

$$y = \delta^w P \in \Re^{3\times1}, \quad x = \delta t_w \in \Re^{6\times1}, \quad K = R_{w,0} T_{p_0} \in \Re^{3\times6} \quad (20)$$

As there are 6 independent variables in the fixed deflection T_b, it is required to implement at least 6 sets of measurements to sufficiently identify and compensate the residual error $\hat{t}_b$. With m sets of measurements, we have: $\tilde{y} = \tilde{K}x$, where

$$\tilde{Y} = [\delta^w P_1, \delta^w P_2, \cdots, \delta^w P_m]^{\mathrm{T}} \in \Re^{3m\times1}, m \geq 6$$
$$x = \delta t_w \in \Re^{6\times1}, \tilde{K} = [K_1, K_2, \cdots, K_m]^{\mathrm{T}} \in \Re^{3m\times6} \quad (21)$$

With the self-calibration model formulated in this step, the residual deflection T_b can be identified and compensated by updating the external kinematic parameter $T_{0,w}$ iteratively. Given $\tilde{K}^* = (\tilde{K}^{\mathrm{T}}\tilde{K})^{-1}\tilde{K}^{\mathrm{T}}$ as the pseudoinverse matrix of $\tilde{K}$, then the error parameters can be computed by $x = \tilde{K}^*\tilde{Y}$. The external kinematic parameter $T_{0,w}$ is computed by $T_{w,0}^{new} = T_{w,0}^{old} e^{\delta t_w}$ and it is iteratively updated until the errors $\tilde{Y}$ converge.

Finally, we obtain an accurate kinematic model with respect to the world frame $\{w\}$ based on Tri-ball plate. Furthermore, the calibrated frame $\{w\}$ is set as an absolute reference frame to describe all the coordinate system such as objects frames and the robot base frame in a robot cell, with which we can conveniently locate the actual position of the robot base and different working objects. Therefore, off-line programming with the proposed self-calibration method can be more accurate and effective.

5 Simulation Experiments and Results

In this section, simulation experiments of calibrating a 6-DOF serial manipulator (ABB IRB 140) are conducted to demonstrate the effectiveness of the two-step self-calibration algorithm (Fig. 2).

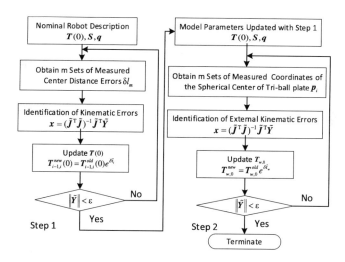

Fig. 2. Flow chart of the two-step calibration algorithm.

The initial configuration of ABB IRB 140 is shown in Fig. 3 and the corresponding kinematic parameters are given as follows:

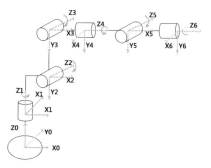

Fig. 3. Schematic diagram of link coordinates of ABB IRB140.

$$T_{0,1}(0) = \begin{bmatrix} 1 & 0 & 0 & 0 \\ 0 & 1 & 0 & 0 \\ 0 & 0 & 1 & 100 \\ 0 & 0 & 0 & 1 \end{bmatrix}, T_{1,2}(0) = \begin{bmatrix} 1 & 0 & 0 & 70 \\ 0 & 0 & 1 & 0 \\ 0 & -1 & 0 & 252 \\ 0 & 0 & 0 & 1 \end{bmatrix},$$

$$T_{2,3}(0) = \begin{bmatrix} 1 & 0 & 0 & 0 \\ 0 & 1 & 0 & -360 \\ 0 & 0 & 1 & 0 \\ 0 & 0 & 0 & 1 \end{bmatrix},$$

$$T_{3,4}(0) = \begin{bmatrix} 0 & 0 & 1 & 239 \\ 0 & 1 & 0 & 0 \\ -1 & 0 & 0 & 0 \\ 0 & 0 & 0 & 1 \end{bmatrix}, T_{4,5}(0) = \begin{bmatrix} 0 & 0 & -1 & 0 \\ 0 & 1 & 0 & 0 \\ 1 & 0 & 0 & 141 \\ 0 & 0 & 0 & 1 \end{bmatrix},$$

$$T_{5,6}(0) = \begin{bmatrix} 0 & 0 & 1 & 65 \\ 0 & 1 & 0 & 0 \\ -1 & 0 & 0 & 0 \\ 0 & 0 & 0 & 1 \end{bmatrix},$$

$s_1 = [0 \ 0 \ 0 \ 0 \ 0 \ 1]^T$, $s_2 = [-252 \ 0 \ 70 \ 0 \ 1 \ 0]^T$, $s_3 = [-360 \ 0 \ 0 \ 0 \ 0 \ 1]^T$,
$s_4 = [0 \ 0 \ 0 \ 1 \ 0 \ 0]^T$, $s_5 = [0 \ -141 \ 0 \ -1 \ 0 \ 0]^T$, $s_6 = [0 \ 0 \ 0 \ 1 \ 0 \ 0]^T$

The units employed for the kinematic parameters are radians for angular (orientational) parameters and millimeters for linear (positional) parameters. To simulate the actual condition of the robot, we assign the kinematic errors in each dyad, which is listed in Table 1.

Finally, through the two-step calibration algorithm proposed, we can solve δt with q and s retaining their nominal values and then update the nominal kinematic model. Since it's not required to update the joint twist s in the calibration process, the unitization to s in each updating step can be avoided. Therefore, the calibration process is further simplified compared with the conventional POE based calibration method.

Table 1. Preset kinematic errors.

Dyad	δt	δs	δq/rad
0–1	$[1 \ 2 \ 2 \ -0.02 \ 0.02 \ 0.1]^T$	$[0 \ 2 \ 2 \ -0.02 \ 0 \ 0]^T$	0.001
1–2	$[0 \ 2 \ 2 \ 0.02 \ 0.2 \ 0.01]^T$	$[0 \ 2 \ 2 \ 0.02 \ 0 \ 0]^T$	0.02
2–3	$[2 \ 2 \ 2 \ 0.02 \ 0.02 \ 0.02]^T$	$[2 \ 2 \ 2 \ 0.02 \ 0.02 \ 0.02]^T$	0.02
3–4	$[2 \ 2 \ 2 \ 0.02 \ 0.02 \ 0.02]^T$	$[2 \ 2 \ 2 \ 0.02 \ 0.02 \ 0.02]^T$	0.002
4–5	$[2 \ 2 \ 2 \ 0.02 \ 0.02 \ 0.02]^T$	$[2 \ 2 \ 2 \ 0.02 \ 0.02 \ 0.02]^T$	0.001
5–6	$[2 \ 2 \ 2 \ 0.02 \ 0.02 \ 0.02]^T$	$[0 \ 0 \ 0 \ 0 \ 0 \ 0]^T$	0.002

In order to better assess the proposed self-calibration algorithm, a uniformly distributed noise added to the measured information p_i from the self-calibration devices is considered: $n_1 \in [0, 0.1]$ mm representing the measuring error of the self-calibration devices, the repeatability of the robot calibrated and other environment interference.

In the simulation experiments, there are 36 kinematic parameters to be identified in Step 1 and 6 external kinematic parameters to be identified in Step 2. Thus, we generate 38 measuring configurations for Step 1 and 8 measuring configurations for Step 2 respectively.

Figure 4(a) shows the convergence of the distance error during the calibration process in Step 1. After 7 iterations, the initial error of 15.22 mm reduced to nearly zero. Figure 5(b) shows the convergence of the residual position error during the calibration process in Step 2. After 4 iterations, the initial error of 177.98 mm reduced to the magnitude of the added noise. After the two-step calibration, we obtain an accurate kinematic model with respect to the external user-defined frame $\{w\}$.

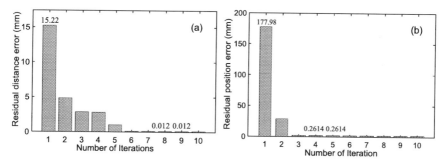

Fig. 4. Calibration convergence in step 1 (a) and step 2 (b)

To verify the effectiveness of the self-calibration algorithm, we picked 20 sets of configurations other than the configurations used to calibrate the robot. Subsequently, the position errors before and after compensation with the algorithm can be computed by substituting the joints of these configurations into the actual kinematic model T^a, the nominal kinematic model T^n and the calibrated kinematic T^c (obtained through 10 iterations with the added noise).

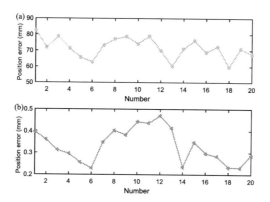

Fig. 5. Position errors before (a) and after (b) calibration.

As shown in Fig. 5, the position errors of each configuration drop dramatically to nearly the magnitude of the added noise after calibration, which demonstrates that our two-step self-calibration algorithm is effective and robust.

6 Conclusion

In this paper, a two-step self-calibration method based on portable calibration devices and two different error models have been presented. With the proposed self-calibration approach, we obtain an accurate kinematic model with respect to an external user-defined frame $\{w\}$ through a two-step calibration process, which enables the off-line programming to be more accurate and effective. Simulation experiments on a 6-dof serial robot are conducted. The simulation results have shown the position errors after calibration are nearly reduced to the magnitude of the added noise, which proves that the proposed self-calibration algorithm is effective and robust.

Acknowledgements. This work was supported by the National Key R & D Program of China (Grant No. 2017YFB1300400), the National-Zhejiang Joint Natural Science Foundation of China (Grant No. U1509202), Equipment Advanced Research Fund of China (Grant No. 6140923010102), the Key R & D Program of Zhejiang Province (Grant No. 2018C01086), NSFC-Shenzhen Robotic Fundamental Research Center Project (Grant No. U1813223).

References

1. Siciliano, B., Khatib, O.: Springer Handbook of Robotics. Springer, New York (2016). https://doi.org/10.1007/978-3-319-32552-1
2. He, R., et al.: A kinematic calibration method based on the product of exponentials formula for serial robot using position measurements. Robotica **33**(6), 1295–1313 (2015)
3. Nubiola, A., Bonev, I.A.: Absolute calibration of an ABB IRB 1600 robot using a laser tracker. Robot. Comput.-Integr. Manufact. **29**(1), 236–245 (2013)
4. Borm, J.H., Menq, C.H.: Determination of optimal measurement configurations for robot calibration based on observability measure. Int. J. Robot. Res. **10**(1), 51–63 (1991)
5. Gaudreault, M., Joubair, A., Bonev, I.A.: Local and closed-loop calibration of an industrial serial robot using a new low-cost 3D measuring device. In: IEEE International Conference on Robotics and Automation, Shanghai, pp. 4312–4319 (2016)
6. Hage, H., Bidaud, P., Jardin, N.: Practical consideration on the identification of the kinematic parameters of the Stäubli TX90 robot. In: Proceedings of the 13th World Congress in Mechanism and Machine Science, Guanajuato, p. 43 (2011)
7. Gaudreault, M., Joubair, A., Bonev, I.: Self-calibration of an industrial robot using a novel affordable 3D measuring device. Sensors **18**(10), 3380 (2018)
8. Meng, Y., Zhuang, H.Q.: Self-calibration of camera-equipped robot manipulators. Int. J. Robot. Res. **20**(11), 909–921 (2001)
9. Hu, S., Zhang, M., Zhou, C., Tian, F.: A novel self-calibration method with POE-based model and distance error measurement for serial manipulators. J. Mech. Sci. Technol. **31**(10), 4911–4923 (2017)

10. Du, S., Ding, J., Liu, Y.: Industrial robot kinematic calibration using virtual line-based sphere surface constraint approach. In: IEEE International Conference on Cyber Technology in Automation, Control, and Intelligent Systems, Shenyang, pp. 48–53 (2015)
11. Chen, I.M., Yang, G.L., Tan, C.T., Yeo, S.H.: Local POE model for robot kinematic calibration. Mech. Mach. Theory **36**(11–12), 1215–1239 (2001)
12. Lynch, K.M., Park, F.C.: Modern Robotics. Cambridge University Press, Cambridge (2017)

Obstacle Avoidance of a Redundant Robot Using Virtual Force Field and Null Space Projection

Yiming Jiang[1], Chenguang Yang[1(✉)], Zhaojie Ju[2], and Jinguo Liu[3]

[1] College of Automation Science and Engineering,
South China University of Technology, Guangzhou 510640, China
cyang@ieee.org
[2] School of Computing, University of Portsmouth, Portsmouth PO1 3HE, UK
[3] Institutes for Robotics and Intelligent Manufacturing,
Chinese Academy of Sciences, Shenyang 110016, China

Abstract. This paper presents a novel algorithm for redundant robot control when obstacles are approaching to the robot. The proposed controller is constructed by a multi-hierarchy control framework where a main task controller is designed to track a given Cartesian space trajectory and an extra impedance controller is developed in the null space to guarantee compliant joint motion. A virtual force field is designed and applied on the robot body to achieve the goal of the avoidance of the obstacle. Simulation studies illustrated the proposed controller is not only to guarantee the task space control, but also able to avoid the obstacle by joint movements.

1 Introduction

In recent years, the potential of physical interactions in human robot co-existent scenarios has elicited large interests in industry and academia and leads to the recent growth of research in physical human-robot interactions (pHRI) [1–6]. Redundant robots are well known for their abundant joint actuators which are useful to enhance the dexterous of the robot motion. This is based on the fact that the redundant robot has more degree of freedom (DOF) than required to complete a given task. However, the increased DOFs generate complexity of the controller design, which is regarded as a challenge problem as the inverse kinematic solution of the robot is not unique. In order to address the control problem of the redundant robot system, many works have been presented in the past researches.

To solve kinematic control of a redundant manipulator, the pseudo-inverse of the Jacobian was used to calculate the minimum-morn joint velocity for the desired end-effector velocity [7]. But repetitive joint motion is not guaranteed from the repetitive end-effector motion. In [8], a dual neural network is proposed

© Springer Nature Switzerland AG 2019
H. Yu et al. (Eds.): ICIRA 2019, LNAI 11740, pp. 728–739, 2019.
https://doi.org/10.1007/978-3-030-27526-6_64

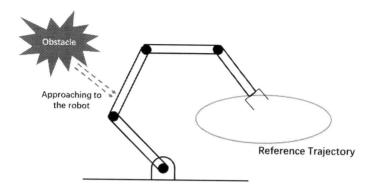

Fig. 1. An overview of the 4 DOF planar robot

to solve the inverse kinematics problem of redundant robots. In this kinematics control scheme, the kinematic equation is described as a bi-criteria of the infinity and Euclidean norms, in which the constraints of the robot joint position and velocity are incorporated. In [9], a trajectory planning method is proposed for redundant robots by combining a closed-loop pseudoinverse and the genetic algorithm, and in this way the trajectory planning problem can be reformulated as an optimization problem. In this work, the inverse solution of the kinematics is derived such that proper joint angles can be generated.

For the design of kinematic control of redundant robots, the null space of Jacobian matrix is extensively investigated to maintain manipulability or avoid obstacles while finish the required end-effector tasks. In [10], a dynamic feedback control law was presented by providing redundancy resolution with null-space joint velocity tracking. In [11], a velocity control algorithm was proposed in an extended operational space to guarantee stable operations based on a minimal null-space projection. In these studies, the robot dynamics is decomposed into two parts, the task space dynamics and the null space dynamics. In this way specific self motion of the joint can be designed by optimizing a certain function. But how to select a proper optimize function is still an open problem.

The obstacle avoidance is an important issue and therefore has been widely investigated during the past decades. In [12], by dividing the required task into subtasks, a task-priority based redundancy control is proposed, in which the low priority subtask can be performed on joint motion so that the obstacle avoidance can be accomplished in the low priority task. In [13], the optimization strategy is generated for a redundant manipulator subject to the constraints of a mobile object. In [14], an extended Jacobian method was proposed for the obstacle avoidance by using an optimization of a criterion function. However, algorithm singularities may arise due to the restriction of the motion. It should be emphasized that the design of the kinematic control could be much difficult if there are obstacles existed in the workspace of the robot. Hence, it is necessary to design an appropriate null motion to enhance the control performance of obstacle avoidance.

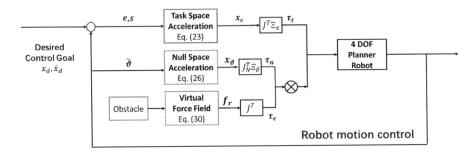

Fig. 2. Control block of our proposed motion controller

Note that artificial potential field method has been widely applied to deal with the obstacle avoidance problem for mobile robot or manipulator. The basic idea is to design the control of robot movement due to a virtual potential field where the target point generates "gravitational force" to the mobile robot, and the obstacle generates a "repulsive force" to the mobile robot [15]. A potential field representation is proposed to deal with the path planning problem of a three dimensional mover [16].

Inspired by the works mentioned above, in this paper, we introduce a concept of virtual force field where the obstacle can generates a repulsive force field and apply on the robot. Additionally, an impedance control law is integrated into the null space control, such that self motion of robot can been performed according to the resulted virtual force applied on robot.

2   System Description and Control Objective

The system we studied in this paper is a redundant robot as shown in Fig. 1, where the robot could be a 4-DOF planer redundant robot while an obstacle is approaching to the robot during the movement. The control objective of the robot is to track a desired trajectory in the Cartesian space while to avoid the possible collision to the obstacle. The control framework is depicted as shown in Fig. 2.

2.1   Kinematics of a Redundant

Consider a redundant robot which has n revolute joints and operates in an m dimensional Cartesian space with $m < n$, the differential kinematic equation can be described as follows,

$$\dot{x} = J(q)\dot{q} \tag{1}$$

where $\dot{x}$ is the Cartesian space velocity, q and $\dot{q}$ are the position and velocity of the robot joints, respectively, and $J(q)$ is the Jacobian matrix from the robot end-effector to the joints.

The inverse kinematics of a redundant robot (1) can be generally formulated as

$$\dot{q} = J^{\#}(q)\dot{x} + N\zeta \tag{2}$$

where $J^{\#}(q)$ satisfies $J = JJ^{\#}J$, denoting the generalized inverse of $J(q)$, $N = I - J^{\#}J$ is the null space of the Jacobian Matrix $J(q)$, while ζ an arbitrarily selected vector.

2.2 Robot Dynamics

The robot dynamic system is formulated by using the Lagrange formulation as below,

$$M(q)\ddot{q} + C(q,\dot{q})\dot{q} + G(q) = \tau' + J^T(q)f(t) \tag{3}$$

where $M(q)$, $C(q,\dot{q})$ and $G(q)$ are the inertia/mass matrix, Coriolis/centrifugal matrix and gravity vector, respectively, $f(t)$ is the external force applied on the robot end-effector by the human arm, and τ' is the actuated torque of the joint.

To facilitate the formulation, let us introduce the control signal as follows

$$\tau' = C(q,\dot{q})\dot{q} + G(q) + \tau \tag{4}$$

Then the system dynamics can be rewritten as

$$M(q)\ddot{q} = \tau + J^T(q)f(t) \tag{5}$$

2.3 Extended Jacobian Formulation

For a redundant robot described in (2), there are m DOFs in task space and n DOFs in joint space with $n > m$. Thus we have $r = n - m$ redundant DOFs. Then we can rewrite the velocity in null space as

$$\dot{q}_n = J_N(q)\vartheta = N\zeta \tag{6}$$

with $\dot{q}_n$ being the redundancy solution, $J_N(q)$ is a selected $n \times r$ full column rank matrix to satisfy $J(q)J_N(q) = \mathbf{0}$, and ϑ is a vector of the null space velocity and defined as

$$\vartheta = J_N^{\#}(q)\dot{q}_n \tag{7}$$

with $J_N^{\#}$ being the generalized inverse of $J_N(q)$ and defined as

$$J_N^{\#} = (J_N^T W_{J_N} J_N)^{-1} J_N^T J_N \tag{8}$$

where W_{J_N} is a weight matrix. In this way, ϑ can be designed to realized the null space motion without affecting the motion in Cartesian space.

By combining (1) and (7), an extended velocity vector $\dot{x}_e$ is constructed as

$$\dot{x}_e = \begin{bmatrix} \dot{x} \\ \vartheta \end{bmatrix} = \begin{bmatrix} J(q) \\ J_N^{\#}(q) \end{bmatrix} \dot{q} \tag{9}$$

Let $J_e = \begin{bmatrix} J(q) \\ J_N^{\#}(q) \end{bmatrix}$, and taking the time derivative of (9), we have

$$\ddot{x}_e = \begin{bmatrix} \ddot{x} \\ \dot{\vartheta} \end{bmatrix} = \begin{bmatrix} J(q)\ddot{q} + \dot{J}(q)\dot{q} \\ J_N^{\#}(q)\ddot{q} + \dot{J}_N^{\#}\dot{q} \end{bmatrix} \tag{10}$$

According to the definition of J_e, (10) can be rewritten as

$$\ddot{x}_e = J_e \ddot{q} + \dot{J}_e \dot{q} \tag{11}$$

As the properties $J_e^\#(q)J_e = I$ and $J_e J_e^\#(q)J_e = J_e$ holds for $J_e^\#(q)$, we can define the generalized inverse of $J_e(q)$ as $J_e^\#(q) = [J^\#(q) \ J_N(q)]$. Then premultiplying $J_e^\#$ on both sides of (11), we can obtain

$$\ddot{q} = J_e^\#(\ddot{x}_e - \dot{J}_e \dot{q}) \tag{12}$$

From the above theorem, the convergence of the interaction force is achieved.

3   Control Design for the Redundant Robot

3.1   Decoupled System Dynamics

Substituting (12) into (5), and considering $\dot{q} = J^\# \dot{x} + J_N(q)\vartheta$, then the system dynamics can be rewritten as

$$J_e^{\#T} \tau = \Xi_e(q)\ddot{x}_e + \eta_e \dot{x}_e + J_e^{\#T} J^T f(t) \tag{13}$$

where

$$\Xi_e = J_e^{\#T} M J_e^\# = \begin{bmatrix} J^{\#T} M J^\# & J^{\#T} M J_N \\ J_N^T M J^\# & J_N^T M J_N \end{bmatrix} \tag{14}$$

$$\eta_e = J_e^{\#T} \dot{J}_e J_e^\#$$

Note that the matrix Ξ_e in (14) is not diagonal. The off-diagonal terms lead to the coupled dynamics between the task space and null space. In order to control the task space motion while achieve specified null space motion, these coupled terms should be appropriately cancelled. Motivated by the work in [17], we introduce an inertia-weighted generalized inverse by choosing $W_J = W_{J_N} = M$, such that

$$\begin{cases} J^\# = M^{-1} J^T (J M^{-1} J^T)^{-1} \\ J_N^\# = (J_N^T M J_N)^{-1} J_N^T M \end{cases} \tag{15}$$

Since we have $J(q)J_N(q) = 0$, the equality $J^{\#T} M J_N = J_N M J^\# = 0$ holds. Then, Ξ_e becomes

$$\Xi_e = \begin{bmatrix} J^{\#T} M J^\# & 0 \\ 0 & J_N^T M J_N \end{bmatrix} \tag{16}$$

From (16) we can see that Ξ_e is a diagonal matrix. Hence, we can design the controller for the two subsystems respectively.

$$\begin{cases} J^{\#T} \tau_x = J^{\#T} M J^\# \ddot{x} + \eta_x \dot{x} + J^{\#T} J^T(q) f(t) \\ J_N^T \tau_n = J_N^T M J_N \dot{\vartheta} + \eta_\vartheta \vartheta + J_N^T \tau_e \end{cases} \tag{17}$$

where $\eta_x = \begin{bmatrix} J^{\#T}\dot{J}(q)J^{\#}(q) \\ J^{\#T}\dot{j}^{\#}_N(q)J_N(q) \end{bmatrix}$, $\eta_\vartheta = \begin{bmatrix} J^T_N\dot{j}^{\#}_N(q)J^{\#}(q) \\ J^T_N\dot{J}(q)J_N(q) \end{bmatrix}$, and τ_e is external torque applied on the robot. Note that the property $J(q)J_N(q) = \mathbf{0}$ holds, therefore the two subsystems in the above formulation are orthogonal to each other. Also, τ_e is in the null space of the main task. We rewritten (17) compactly as

$$\begin{cases} J^{\#T}\tau_x = \Xi_x\ddot{x} + \eta_x\dot{x} + f(t) \\ J^T_N\tau_n = \Xi_\vartheta\dot{\vartheta} + \eta_\vartheta\vartheta + J^T_N\tau_e \end{cases} \tag{18}$$

where $\Xi_x = J^{\#T}MJ^{\#}$, $\Xi_\vartheta = J^T_NMJ_N$.

3.2   Design of the Controller

Error Signal. Remind that the objective of the robot inter-loop controller is to track the given trajectory, the tracking error is defined as

$$e = x - x_r \tag{19}$$
$$s = \dot{x} - \dot{x}_s \tag{20}$$

where $\dot{x}_s = \dot{x}_r + K_s e$ with K_s being a positive definite matrix. Note x and x_r are uniformly continuous and bounded, thus the convergence of the signal s could lead to the convergence of $\dot{e}$ and e.

Task Space Control. To track a given trajectory x_r, the acceleration control command x_c is designed as follows,

$$\ddot{x}_c = \ddot{x}_s - \Xi_x^{-1}(K_p + \eta_x)s + \Xi_x^{-1}\eta_x\dot{x} + \Xi_x^{-1}J^T\hat{f}(t) \tag{21}$$

where K_p is a positive definite matrix. Combining (21) and (17), we can design the control law in task space as,

$$\tau_{xd} = J^T\Xi_x\left(\ddot{x}_s - \Xi_x^{-1}(K_p + \eta_x)s + \Xi_x^{-1}\eta_x\dot{x}\right) + J^T\hat{f}(t) \tag{22}$$

where $\hat{f}(t)$ is the measurement of $f(t)$. Then, substituting (22) into the first equation of (17), the error dynamics of the system can be obtained as,

$$\Xi_x\dot{s} = -(K_p + \eta_x)s + J^T(q)\tilde{f}(t) \tag{23}$$

with $\tilde{f}(t) = f(t) - \hat{f}(t)$.

Null Space Control. In order to control the motion of the null space, we select the null space control law as

$$\dot{\vartheta}_c = \dot{\vartheta}_d + \Xi_\vartheta^{-1}((K_\vartheta + \eta_\vartheta\vartheta) + \eta_\vartheta\vartheta + J^T_NK_v\tilde{q}) \tag{24}$$

where ϑ_d is the desired null space command, $\tilde{\vartheta} = \vartheta - \vartheta_d$, K_ϑ and K_v are positive-definite symmetric matrices selected by the designer, respectively. Thus, the null space control law can be described as follows,

$$\tau_{nd} = J_N^{\#T}(\Xi_\vartheta \dot{\vartheta}_d + (K_\vartheta + \eta_\vartheta)\vartheta + \eta_\vartheta \vartheta + J_N^T K_v \tilde{q}) \tag{25}$$

Substitute (24) into (17), we can obtain the closed-loop dynamics of the null motion as below,

$$\Xi_\vartheta \dot{\tilde{\vartheta}} + (K_\vartheta + \eta_\vartheta)\tilde{\vartheta} + J_N^T K_v \tilde{q} = J_N^T \tau_e \tag{26}$$

with τ_e being the external torque applied on the robot.

3.3   Virtual Force Field

In this part, a virtual force field is designed to achieve the obstacle avoidance through null motion. To drive the robot body move away from the obstacle, path planning methods such as configuration space, probabilistic road maps [18], randomly exploring randomized trees [19] and potential field method have been widely investigated. Herein, we employ a force vector field on obstacle to generate external repulsive forces on robot manipulator. Then self motion of the robot can be then performed by the impedance property of the null motion control.

For each link of the robot, a potential energy U_{ir} is designed as,

$$U_{ir}(\boldsymbol{p_i}) = \begin{cases} 0 & \eta_i > \eta_{0i} \\ \frac{1}{2}\gamma_i(\frac{1}{\eta_i(\boldsymbol{p_i})} - \frac{1}{\eta_{0i}})^2 & \eta_{\min} < \eta_i(\boldsymbol{p_i}) \le \eta_{0i} \\ \nu_{\max} & \eta_i(\boldsymbol{p_i}) \le \eta_{\min} \end{cases} \tag{27}$$

where γ_i is the scaling factor represented the intensity of the repulsive force, $\boldsymbol{p_i}$ is a control point on the ith robot link, $\eta_i(\boldsymbol{p_i})$ denotes the distance between the ith link and the obstacle, η_{0i} is the effective range of the force field, $\nu_{\max}$ denotes the maximum repulsive force and $\eta_{\min}$ is the threshold to avoid very large force.

Then we can calculate the resulted repulsive force f_{ir} applied on ith robot link as

$$f_{ir} = -\nabla U_{ir} = \begin{cases} 0 & \eta_i > \eta_{0i} \\ \gamma_i(\frac{1}{\eta_i(\boldsymbol{p_i})} - \frac{1}{\eta_{0i}})\nabla \eta_i(\boldsymbol{p_i}) & \eta_{\min} < \eta_i \le \eta_{0i} \\ f_{\max} & \eta_i \le \eta_{\min} \end{cases} \tag{28}$$

where $f_{\max}$ denote the maximum repulsive force, and $\nabla \eta_i = \frac{\partial \eta_i}{\partial \boldsymbol{p}}$ is the gradient vector. Then, the joint torque can be obtained through the Jacobian matrix of the ith control point as,

$$\tau_e = -\sum_{i=1}^{n} J_i^T f_{ir} \tag{29}$$

where J_i is Jacobian matrix with respect to the control point $\boldsymbol{p_i}$.

Noted that the impedance model regulates the system dynamics concerning the interaction force and motion error. Here, we employ the impedance controller to regulate the null space motion of the robot under the virtual repulsive force produced from the obstacle.

4   Simulation Studies

In this section, a group of simulation studies is performed to verify the effectiveness of our proposed controller. The robot is a 4-DOF planar robot as shown in Fig. 1. Each link is weighted with 1 kg and the center of mass (COM) is assumed to locate at the centre of the link. The length of each link is chosen the same as 1 m. The robot has 4-DOF while the required task is 2 DOF tracking.

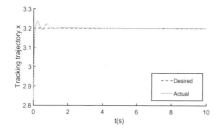

Fig. 3. Tracking trajectory of the proposed controller x direction

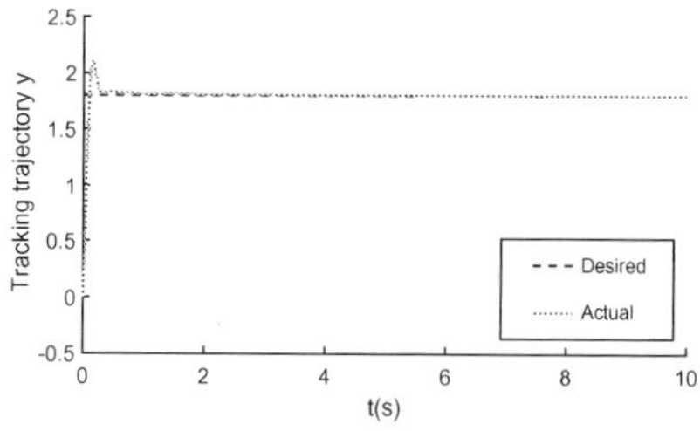

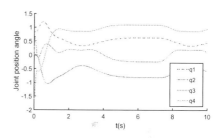

Fig. 4. Tracking trajectory of the proposed controller y direction

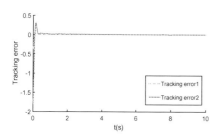

Fig. 5. Tracking error of the proposed controller

Fig. 6. The joint angles of the robot during tracking

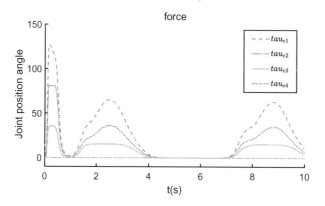

Fig. 7. The applied repulsive force τ_e on each joint

In the simulation study, totally 2 cases are performed. In this first simulation case, the robot tracks a desired point in the workspace. While a planer circle disk is slowly approaching to the robot. The virtual force filed is generated in term of the position of the disk center.

The robot initial configuration is chosen to be $q = [pi/4, 0, -pi/2, 0]^T$, and the initial position of the obstacle centre is chosen to be $[1.8, 2.1]^T$. The robot is controlled to track a set position at $x_d = [3.2, 1.8]^T$. The obstacle is movable and follows a sinusoidal trajectory $y(t) = 2.1 - sin(t - 1)$ in y direction.

The simulation results are performed in Figs. 3, 4, 5, 6 and 7. Figures 3 and 4 depict the tracking performance of the given point tacking task. Also in Fig. 5, we can see that the robot end-effector well follows the reference trajectory, and the tracking errors converge to zero. The applied virtual repulsive force from the obstacle on each joint is performed in Fig. 7. We can see that the applied force increased when the obstacle approaches the robot and reduced when obstacle away from the robot.

The trajectory of all joints angle is depicted shown in Fig. 6. We can see the movement of all joint angles according to the change of force field. Also, we can see that in the same period, the end-effector is able to hold on at the fix position. This is because that the effect of virtual forces mainly adds on the null motion of the robot, and the resulted self motion of joints doesn't disturb the end-effector motion. Thus the control goal of the avoidance of a mobile robot is achieved.

In this second simulation case, the robot track a desired trajectory while an obstacle is set on the path of robot movement. The initial configuration of the robot is chosen as the same as the first simulation case, and the initial position of the centre of the obstacle is chosen to be $[1.6, 2.1]^T$. The robot is controlled to track a trajectory as $x_d = [2.5, 0.5 - 0.04t^3 + 0.06t^2]$.

The simulation results can be illustrated in Figs. 8, 9, 10, 11 and 12. Figures 8 and 9 show the trajectory tracking performance, where robot end-effector follows the reference trajectory very well. Note the tracking errors could converge to zero in a short period of time as shown in Fig. 10. The trajectory of all joints angle is depicted in Fig. 11. The applied virtual repulsive force from the obstacle on each joint is performed in Fig. 12. We can see that the applied forces maintain small value at first and then increase as the obstacle closing to the robot. Here, the effective of our proposed controller is verified.

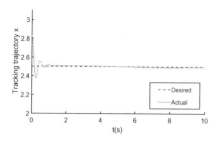

Fig. 8. Tracking trajectory of the proposed controller x direction

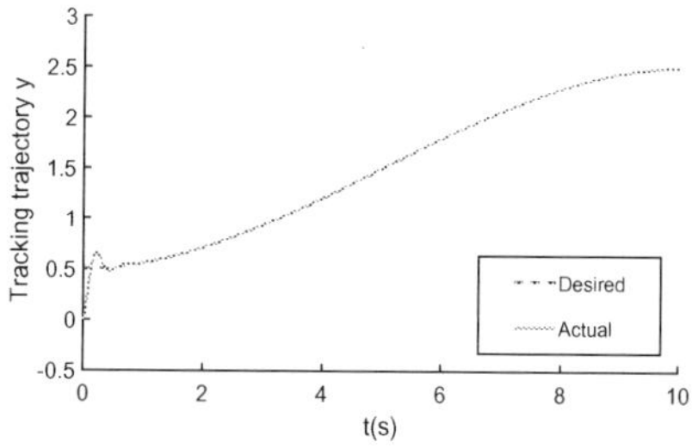

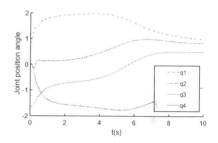

Fig. 9. Tracking trajectory of the proposed controller y direction

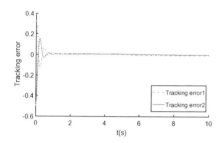

Fig. 10. Tracking error of the proposed controller

Fig. 11. The joint angles of the robot during tracking

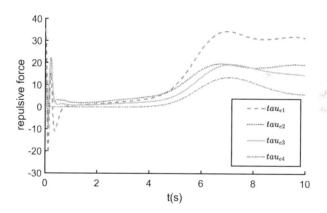

Fig. 12. The applied repulsive force τ_e on each joint

5   Conclusion

This paper develops a novel algorithm for redundant robot control by using virtual fore field and null space projection. Two sub-controllers are designed to realized the control goal based on the decomposition of the system dynamics, namely the task space controller and the null space controller. Moreover, a minimum null space projection is employed to describe the null space motion, such that the virtual forces are projected to the null space and will not affect the task space motion. An extra impedance controller is developed in the null space of the main task to guarantee compliant joint motion. A virtual force field is introduced and applied on the robot body to achieve the goal of the avoidance of the obstacle. Based on a 4 DOF planner robot, the simulation studies demonstrate that the proposed controller is not only to guarantee the task space control, but also able to avoid the obstacle by joint movements.

Acknowledgement. This work was partially supported by National Nature Science Foundation (NSFC) under Grants 61861136009 and 61811530281.

References

1. Yang, C., Ganesh, G., Haddadin, S., Parusel, S., Albu-Schaeffer, A., Burdet, E.: Human-like adaptation of force and impedance in stable and unstable interactions. IEEE Trans. Robot. **27**(5), 918–930 (2011)
2. Li, Y., Ge, S.S., Yang, C., Li, X., Tee, K.P.: Model-free impedance control for safe human-robot interaction. In: 2011 IEEE International Conference on Robotics and Automation (ICRA), pp. 6021–6026. IEEE (2011)
3. Yang, C., Huang, K., Cheng, H., Li, Y., Su, C.-Y.: Haptic identification by ELM-controlled uncertain manipulator. IEEE Trans. Syst. Man Cybern.: Syst. **47**(8), 2398–2409 (2017)
4. Tonietti, G., Schiavi, R., Bicchi, A.: Design and control of a variable stiffness actuator for safe and fast physical human/robot interaction. In: Proceedings of the 2005 IEEE International Conference on Robotics and Automation, ICRA 2005, pp. 526–531. IEEE (2005)
5. Kong, K., Bae, J., Tomizuka, M.: Control of rotary series elastic actuator for ideal force-mode actuation in human–robot interaction applications. IEEE/ASME Trans. Mechatron. **14**(1), 105–118 (2009)
6. Edsinger, A., Kemp, C.C.: Human-robot interaction for cooperative manipulation: handing objects to one another. In: The 16th IEEE International Symposium on Robot and Human Interactive Communication, RO-MAN 2007, pp. 1167–1172. IEEE (2007)
7. Doty, K.L., Melchiorri, C., Bonivento, C.: A theory of generalized inverses applied to robotics. Int. J. Robot. Res. **12**(1), 1–19 (1993)
8. Zhang, Y., Wang, J., Xu, Y.: A dual neural network for bi-criteria kinematic control of redundant manipulators. IEEE Trans. Robot. Autom. **18**(6), 923–931 (2002)
9. da Graça Marcos, M., Machado, J.T., Azevedo-Perdicoúlis, T.-P.: Trajectory planning of redundant manipulators using genetic algorithms. Commun. Nonlinear Sci. Numer. Simul. **14**(7), 2858–2869 (2009)
10. Hsu, P., Mauser, J., Sastry, S.: Dynamic control of redundant manipulators. J. Robot. Syst. **6**(2), 133–148 (1989)
11. Nemec, B., Žlajpah, L., Omrčen, D.: Comparison of null-space and minimal null-space control algorithms. Robotica **25**(5), 511–520 (2007)
12. Nakamura, Y., Hanafusa, H., Yoshikawa, T.: Task-priority based redundancy control of robot manipulators. Int. J. Robot. Res. **6**(2), 3–15 (1987)

13. Daachi, B., Madani, T., Benallegue, A.: Adaptive neural controller for redundant robot manipulators and collision avoidance with mobile obstacles. Neurocomputing **79**, 50–60 (2012)
14. Baillieul, J.: Avoiding obstacles and resolving kinematic redundancy. In: Proceedings of the 1986 IEEE International Conference on Robotics and Automation, vol. 3, pp. 1698–1704. IEEE (1986)
15. Khatib, O.: Real-time obstacle avoidance for manipulators and mobile robots. In: Cox, I.J., Wilfong, G.T. (eds.) Autonomous Robot Vehicles, pp. 396–404. Springer, New York (1986). https://doi.org/10.1007/978-1-4613-8997-2_29
16. Hwang, Y.K., Ahuja, N.: A potential field approach to path planning. IEEE Trans. Robot. Autom. **8**(1), 23–32 (1992)
17. Nemec, B., Zlajpah, L.: Force control of redundant robots in unstructured environment. IEEE Trans. Ind. Electron. **49**(1), 233–240 (2002)
18. Kavraki, L.E., Svestka, P., Latombe, J., Overmars, M.H.: Probabilistic roadmaps for path planning in high-dimensional configuration spaces. IEEE Trans. Robot. Autom. **12**(4), 566–580 (1996)
19. LaValle, S.M., Kuffner Jr., J.J.: Rapidly-exploring random trees: progress and prospects (2000)

Modeling of Torque Ripple for Integrated Robotic Joint

Yusheng Liao[1,2,3], Chi Zhang[1,2,3(✉)], Chongchong Wang[1,2,3],
Chin-Yin Chen[1,3], Qiang Xin[1,2,3], and Si-Lu Chen[1,3]

[1] Ningbo Institute of Materials Technology and Engineering, CAS,
Ningbo 315201, Zhejiang, China
zhangchi@nimte.ac.cn
[2] University of Chinese Academy of Sciences, Beijing 100049, China
[3] Zhejiang Key Laboratory of Robotics and Intelligent Manufacturing
Equipment Technology, Ningbo 315201, Zhejiang, China

Abstract. The torque ripple that leads to vibration greatly affects the performance of robotic joint like motion accuracy. However, the torque ripple models currently used in feedforward control are incomprehensive because only motor or harmonic drive torque ripple of the joint is considered. In this paper, a new torque ripple model based on experimental data and the spectrum of the whole transmission chain are proposed and analyzed. In the model, the torque ripple includes the fluctuation caused by transmission error of the harmonic drive and cogging torque of the motor. The transmission error is modeled with the comparison of position signals of two encoders which are installed at motor and load sides respectively. In order to study the torque ripple produced by the motor and the load variation in transmission chain, experimental tests with different motor velocity and varying load inertia are conducted. The robotic joint torque ripple is accurately modeled through analyzing dynamic characteristic of position difference between the motor side and load side.

Keywords: Robotic joint · Transmission chain · Harmonic drive ·
Transmission error · Torque ripple

1 Introduction

Integrated robotic joint mainly consists of motor, load and Harmonic Drive (HD). In the transmission chain of the joint, permanent magnet synchronous motor provides high torque and strong power, HD is frequently used for zero-backlashed and high reliability motion system, and load simulates the next joint inertia of the manipulator. However, the torque ripple of transmission chain normally caused by the transmission error of HD, cogging torque of motor and the variation of load inertia may lead to poor accuracy of position tracking even give rise to vibration.

Transmission error of HD is a periodical error, whose primary frequency is the main reason of the load vibration [1]. So far, the vibration due to transmission error on HD is normally suppressed by feedforward filters such as notch filter in [2] or peak filter in [3]. Due to the strongly repeating characteristic of transmission error in HD, feedforward

© Springer Nature Switzerland AG 2019
H. Yu et al. (Eds.): ICIRA 2019, LNAI 11740, pp. 740–750, 2019.
https://doi.org/10.1007/978-3-030-27526-6_65

compensator based on transmission error model is also used in [4] and 2-DOF feed-forward compensator is applied in [5]. The fast response and simple control structure of feedforward compensation lead to wide application of model-based approaches in vibration suppression. Therefore, the model accuracy determines the motion perfor-mance and is intensively studied. Literature [2] analyzes static transmission error in multi-axis robot but do not discuss the origins of the harmonic components. In order to obtain the accurate transmission error of HD, the synchronous component and hysteresis component of transmission error are decomposed and analyzed in [4, 5] with special experimental setup. While they lose sight of the characteristics of other components of the transmission chain such as motor and the load of the joint.

Besides transmission error of HD, the cogging torque of motor caused by the interaction of the rotor permanent magnets and the stator teeth-slots is another important component of torque ripple in robotic joint. Some scholars compensate cogging ripple based on the model of current and flux linkage in [6]. The waveform of cogging torque is discussed and the model of cogging ripple is proposed in [7, 8] by using different methods. However, they still neglect the motor torque ripple when the load varies in transmission chain. From the above, study on torque ripple analysis considering load variation is necessary [9].

In this paper, the influence of transmission error of HD on robotic joint is discussed and parameters of the transmission error model are identified in Sect. 2. The motor cogging and load inertia in the torque ripple are experimentally measured based on varying motor velocity and load inertia in Sect. 3. The spectrum components are also analyzed and modeled. Conclusions and future work are discussed in Sect. 4.

2 Modeling of Transmission Error for Harmonic Drive

2.1 The Necessity of Transmission Error Modeling

The experimental setup in this paper is shown as Fig. 1, where robotic joint is inte-grated with permanent magnet synchronous motor, harmonic drive, incremental encoder at motor side and absolute encoder at link side etc. Relevant parameters of the experimental setup are listed in Table 1.

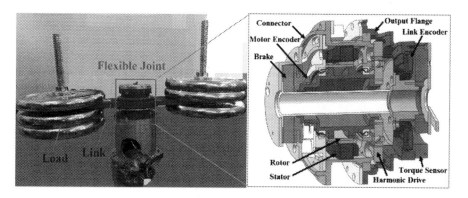

Fig. 1. Experimental setup.

Table 1. Experimental setup components' parameters.

Components	Parameter names	Parameters
Harmonic drive	Reduction ratio N	160
	Number of teeth Z	322(CS), 320(FS)
	Stiffness K (N m/rad)	32500
Motor	Stator slot number	18
	Rotor pole number (pair)	10
Encoders	Motor encoder resolution (turn)	2^{-18}
	Link encoder resolution (bit)	19
Link and load	Link and load inertia J_l (kg m^2)	4.1454/2.2598/0.21

High precision HD gear component sets with only three precision components, i.e. Wave Generator (WG), Flex spline (FS) and Circular Spline (CS). In robotic joint, WG is the transmitting input element connected to the motor output shaft, and FS is the output of the transmitting fitted together with link and load. Transmission error is defined as the desire output minus the actual output, which is expressed as followed

$$\theta_{err} = \frac{\theta_{wgi}}{N} - \theta_{fso}$$
$$= \frac{\theta_m}{N} - \theta_l \tag{1}$$

Where N is gear ratio, θ_{wgi} is the input of WG which can be measured by motor encoder and is equal to motor position θ_m. θ_{fso} is the output of FS which can be measured by link encoder and is equal to load position θ_l.

According to [4], the hysteresis phenomenon is included into the transmission error. While in this study, the hysteresis is neglected but consider the angular transmission error not only in the harmonic drive, but also in the whole transmission chain. The former named periodic synchronous component θ_{sync}, which is caused by manufacturing error, assembly error and kinematic error of FS and CS. It's synchronized with the motor rotation. The expression of transmission error can be in motor position domain:

$$\theta_{TE} = \sum_{i=1}^{n} A_i \sin(i\theta_m + \varphi_i)$$
$$= A_1 \sin(\theta_m + \varphi_1) + A_2 \sin(2\theta_m + \varphi_2) + \ldots + A_n \sin(n\theta_m + \varphi_n) \tag{2}$$

Where i called harmonic order, is the frequency ratio of transmission error and motor angular velocity, it can be regard as the frequency of transmission error in motor position domain. A_i and φ_i are corresponding amplitude and phase of each frequency.

The existence of transmission error degrades the position tracking precision and vibration of the motion like Fig. 2. Where, A_i is set to 2.9e−4 rad as manual [10], i is set to 2 as traditional study, And the encoder can measure 2.4e−5 rad as minimum since the resolution listed in Table 1. Therefore Fig. 2(d) shows that it's very important for transmission error to be eliminated.

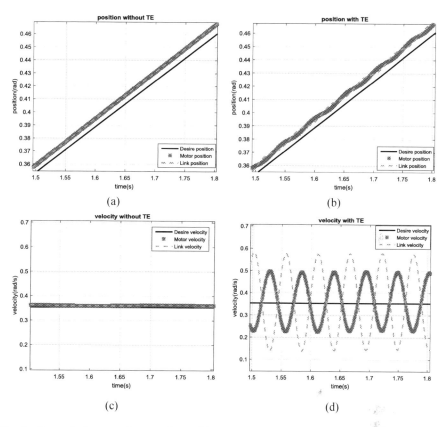

Fig. 2. Transmission error impacts the position tracking precision and vibration of the velocity. (a) Position without TE. (b) Position with TE. (c) Velocity without TE. (d) Velocity with TE.

2.2 Modeling of Transmission Error

In order to obtain a high resolution model of transmission error, 5000 points for one turn on link position is record, where 400 points (29.25°) is revealed in Fig. 3. Figure 3(a) is transmission error in the motor position domain, Fig. 3(b) is the fast Fourier transform of the waveform in Fig. 3(a). It can be seen that the frequency ratio i of HD in Fig. 3 is not always an integer while there are other disturbance imposed on the system like assembly error, friction, etc. For example, $i = 0.4$ is a manufacturing error of every 5 gear on harmonic gear. It happens 64 times every N turns on motor. The frequency ratio of $i = 1.6$ is the Fourfold Frequency of 0.4. The frequency ratio of 2 is due to the gear tooth number difference of FS and CS. Note that the numbers marked in the Figs. 3, 6 and 8 present the value on x-axis.

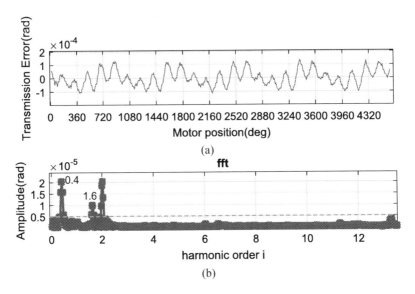

Fig. 3. The waveform and spectrum of transmission error.

According to the model of transmission error in (2) and taking amplitude upper dash line, the model of transmission error including relevant parameters of amplitude, frequency and phase are listed in Table 2. The curve fitting result based on the model (2) and parameters in Table 2 is shown in Fig. 4(a).

Table 2. Transmission error model parameters.

Frequency ratio i	Amplitude A_i (rad)	Phase Φ_i (rad)
0.4	5.1671e−5	2.2445
1.6	2.0432e−5	0.4251
2.0	5.8857e−5	2.1543

In order to make sure the transmission error model (2) with parameters listed in Table 2 is correct, repeat the experiment in the same position again, and do in the opposite direction, respectively. The accuracy of the transmission error model is validated. The standard deviation (3) is given below to show the error between the model and actual data is 2.5548e−5 in the same direction (Fig. 4(b)) and 3.93e−05 in the opposite direction.

$$\text{RMS} = \sqrt{\frac{1}{N}\sum_{i=1}^{N}\left(y_{fit} - y_{measure}\right)^2} \tag{3}$$

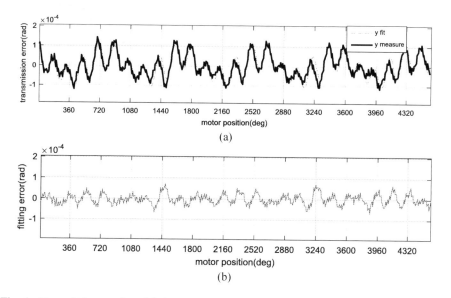

Fig. 4. Curve fitting result and fitting error. (a) The actual transmission error in motor position domain and the curve fitting result with frequency ratio of 0.4, 1.6 and 2. (b) The error between curve fitting and actual transmission error.

3   Modeling of Torque Ripple for Transmission Chain

3.1   Torque Ripple in Different Motor Velocity

The torque ripple in this study is modeled based on the transmission error of HD in time domain (4) and motor and link of transmission chain.

$$\theta_{TE} = \theta_{sync} = \sum_{i=1}^{n} A_i \sin(i\omega_m t + \varphi_i) \tag{4}$$

In order to study the impact of motor characteristics on torque ripple, different motor velocities are given as the experimental condition as Fig. 5. Three continuous linear trajectories travel the same link distance of 360° from the same start position, which present the constant motor angular velocity of 100 rpm, 300 rpm and 500 rpm. Figure 6 shows the spectrum of torque ripple with the same load inertia while motor velocity is respectively in 100 rpm, 300 rpm and 500 rpm, and load angle displacement is as in Fig. 5.

It is found from Fig. 6 that the waveform frequency component of the torque ripple is mainly at 0.4, 1.6 and 2, which is as the same as those of the transmission error in Fig. 3. Meanwhile, a low frequency ratio about 0.00625 is due to the misalignment installation of link side and motor side. The suppose can be verified by driving load angle moving in a small range angle such as under 30 deg that it's eliminated as transmission error shown in Fig. 3.

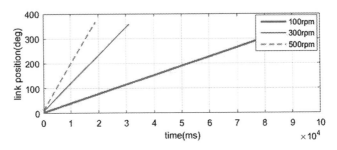

Fig. 5. Continuous linear trajectories in constant motor angular velocity (CW).

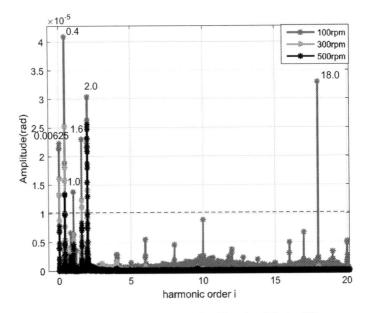

Fig. 6. Spectrum of torque ripple with the same load inertia while in different motor velocity (CW).

The frequency ratio of 18 is higher than other frequencies. It can be explained that in low motor velocity it is the slot number of motor (Table 1) that has impact on the HD, while the noise of high motor velocity drowns the influence of motor slot. It happens one time every 20° of motor, which is coincide with the measured motor cogging torque shown in Fig. 7.

3.2   Torque Ripple with Different Load Inertia

Besides motor, the load is also contained in transmission chain. In order to study the effect of different load inertia on transmission error, different load inertias are given as the experimental condition. Figure 8 shows the spectrum of torque ripple with different load inertia of 0.21 kg m^2 (link and no-load), 2.2598 kg m^2 (link and 30 kg),

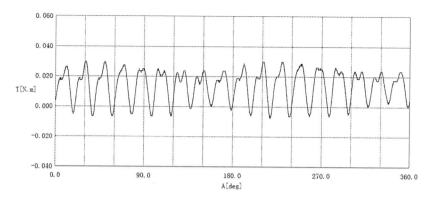

Fig. 7. Cogging torque of motor in velocity of 1 rpm.

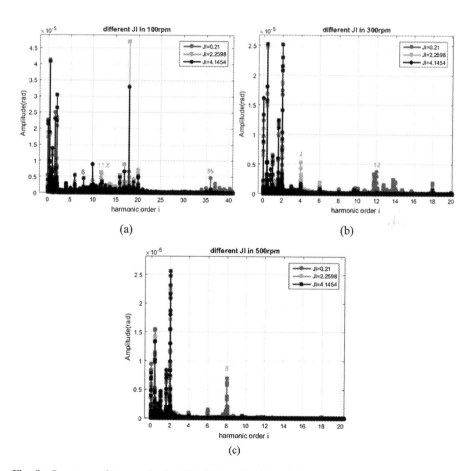

Fig. 8. Spectrum of torque ripple with different load inertia in the same velocity respectively. (a) 100 rpm. (b) 300 rpm. (c) 500 rpm.

4.1454 kg m^2 (link and 60 kg) respectively in different motor velocity of 100 rpm, 300 rpm, 500 rpm. Meanwhile, the transmission error amplitude over 1e−05 rad is illustrated in Table 3.

Table 3. Torque ripple model parameters.

Motor velocity (rpm)	Frequency ratio	$J_l = 4.1454$ (kg m^2)	$J_l = 2.2598$ (kg m^2)	$J_l = 0.21$ (kg m^2)
100	0.4	4.09E−05	4.07E−05	4.13E−05
	1.6	2.30E−05	2.32E−05	2.50E−05
	2	3.03E−05	2.31E−05	2.33E−05
	8	4.49E−06	-	-
	11.8	-	6.36E−06	-
	18	3.292E−05	4.70E−05	6.651E−06
	36	-	-	4.72E−06
300	0.4	2.53E−05	2.48E−05	2.63E−05
	1.6	1.24E−05	1.23E−05	1.23E−05
	2	2.52E−05	1.88E−05	1.74E−05
	3	1.28E−06	-	-
	4	-	5.23E−06	-
	12	-	-	7.26E−06
500	0.4	1.34E−05	1.42E−05	1.54E−05
	1.6	8.35E−06	7.67E−06	7.50E−06
	2	2.56E−05	2.25E−05	1.18E−05
	8	-	-	6.99E−06

It could be also found that the frequency ratio of 11.8 with 2.2598 kg m^2 load inertia and 36 with 0.21 kg m^2 load inertia in 100 rpm in Fig. 8(a), 4 with 2.2598 kg m^2 and 12 with 0.21 kg m^2 in 300 rpm in Fig. 8(b), 8 with 0.21 kg m^2 in 500 rpm in Fig. 8(c), are standing out compared to other frequencies, which can be explained by that – the resonance frequency of equivalent inertia is coupling with the motor frequency by the following formula:

$$\omega = \sqrt{\frac{K}{J_l}} = 2\pi f \tag{5}$$

Where, f is resonance frequency, K is system stiffness, J_l is load inertia.

According to (5), the resonance frequency with 0.21 kg m^2 is 62.6 Hz, 2.2598 kg m^2 is 19.1 Hz and 4.1454 kg m^2 is 14 Hz. (due to compliance of HD is much larger than any other components in the joint, K can be taken as stiffness of HD as Table 1). In the motor velocity of 100 rpm, the resonance is coming while it happens to 36, 11.8 and 8 times of the motor frequency. For the same reason in 300 rpm and 500 rpm, which are shown in Fig. 8(b), (c) and Table 3. The x-label of Fig. 8(b) and

(c) is short cut to 20 because of the amplitude of i from 20 to 40 can be neglected (below 1e−7 rad).

On the base of above analysis, without thinking of the hysteresis phenomenon, the torque ripple of robotic joint can be revised as below:

$$\theta_{ripple} = \theta_{TE} + \Delta\theta_{chain} \qquad (6)$$

Where, the $\Delta\theta_{chain}$ includes the component of motor slot number in low velocity and the component of different load inertia. Thus, we can have (7)

$$\theta_{ripple} = \sum_{i=1}^{n} A_i \sin(i\omega_m t + \varphi_i) + \sum_{m=1}^{2} A_m \sin(i_m\omega_m t + \varphi_m) + A_l \sin(i_l\omega_m t + \varphi_l) \quad (7)$$

Where, motor cogging ripple is presented by the second term with two frequency ratios i_m. One (i_1) is the slot number and another (i_2) is the least common multiple of slot number and pair of pole number of the motor, which can be found above; A_m and φ_m is the amplitude and phase of frequency ratio i_m component, the empirical value is shown in Table 3; ω_m in the second term is the motor angle velocity under 100 rpm i.e. 10.47 rad/s; in particular, i_l in the third term is relative to the different load inertia and the motor velocity as (8) and A_l in Table 3 is as reference.

$$i_l = \frac{1}{\omega_m}\sqrt{\frac{K}{J_l}} \qquad (8)$$

4   Conclusion

Form the experiments above, a comprehensive torque ripple model of robotic joint which includes the terms of motor cogging, HD and the varying load inertia is proposed. It is shown that the frequency ratio of HD is not always integer because of some disturbance such as friction, manufacturing and assembly error. Every main frequency component is analyzed and it is found that besides the transmission error of HD, motor slot number and load inertia contribute to the torque ripple of transmission chain. As to HD, the amplitude of the transmission error is related to the position tracking error between motor side and load side. That is, with the higher motor angular velocity and the larger load side inertia, the position tracking error between motor side and load side are larger and model of torque ripple is changing with these factors.

The torque ripple model with the three terms corresponding to three components of transmission chain makes it more accurate and effective to be applied in the feedforward compensation and control for further vibration suppression.

Acknowledgement. This paper is supported by the National Key R & D Program of China (Grant No. 2017YFB1300400); NSFC-Fund (Grant No. 51805523); NSFC-Shenzhen Robotic Fundamental Research Center Project (Grant No. U1813223); Equipment Advanced Research Fund of China (Grant No. 6140923010102); The Innovation Team of Key Components and Technology for the New Generation Robot under Grant No. 2016B10016.

References

1. Musser, C.W.: CSG-CSF_Component (1955)
2. Iwasaki, M., Nakamura, H.: Vibration suppression for angular transmission errors in HDG and application to industrial robots. In: Proceedings of the 19th World Congress the International Federation of Automatic Control, Cape Town, South Africa (2014)
3. Han, C.H., Wang, C.C., Tomizuka, M.: Suppression of vibration due to transmission error of harmonic drives using peak filter with acceleration feedback, pp. 182–187 (2008)
4. Iwasaki, M., et al.: Modeling and compensation for angular transmission error of HDG in high precision positioning. In: IEEE/ASME International Conference on Advanced Intelligent Mechatronics (2009)
5. Sasaki, K., et al.: Method for compensating for angular transmission error of wave gear device. US8296089 (2012)
6. Qian, W., Nondhal, T.A.: Mutual torque ripple suppression of surface-mounted permanent magnet synchronous motor. In: 8th International Conference on Electrical Machines & Systems (2005)
7. Islam, R., et al.: Permanent-magnet synchronous motor magnet designs with skewing for torque ripple and cogging torque reduction. IEEE Trans. Ind. Appl. **45**(1), 152–160 (2009)
8. Kim, K.-C.: A novel method for minimization of cogging torque and torque ripple for interior permanent magnet synchronous motor. IEEE Trans. Magn. **50**(2), 793–796 (2014)
9. Pham, A.D., Ahn, H.J.: High precision reducers for industrial robots driving 4th industrial revolution: state of arts, analysis, design, performance evaluation and perspective. Int. J. Precis. Eng. Manuf.-Green Technol. **5**(4), 519–533 (2018)
10. csd-shd-catalog. http://www.datasheetarchive.com/whats_new/e9c18edf952ac23e50c67970 42cc670b.html
11. Hirano, Y., et al.: Vibration suppression control method for trochoidal reduction gears under load conditions. IEEJ J. Ind. Appl. **5**(3), 267–275 (2015)
12. Tuttle, T.D., Seering, W.: Modeling a harmonic drive gear transmission. In: IEEE International Conference on Robotics and Automation. IEEE, Atlanta (1993)

Author Index